JavaServer Faces 2.0: The Complete Reference

About the Authors

Ed Burns is a senior staff engineer at Sun Microsystems. Ed has worked on a wide variety of client- and server-side Web technologies since 1994, including NCSA Mosaic, Mozilla, the Sun Java Plugin, Jakarta Tomcat, and most recently, JavaServer Faces. Ed is currently the co-spec lead for JavaServer Faces. Find Ed's blog and other goodies at **http://purl.oclc.org/NET/edburns/**.

Chris Schalk is a Developer Advocate and works to promote Google's APIs and technologies. He is currently engaging the international Web development community with the new Google App Engine and OpenSocial APIs. Before joining Google, Chris was a Principal Product Manager and technology evangelist at Oracle in the Java development tools group.

About the Contributing Author

Neil Griffin represents Liferay on the JSR 314 (JSF 2.0) expert group and has 15 years of professional experience in software engineering. As a Liferay project committer, Neil is responsible for interfacing with ICEsoft in order to ensure that ICEfaces integrates properly within Liferay Portal. Neil is the cofounder of the PortletFaces project, which makes JSF portlet development easier. He has authored training classes for Liferay and ICEsoft and has served as a consultant for clients implementing JSF and ICEfaces portlets.

JavaServer Faces 2.0: The Complete Reference

Ed Burns
Chris Schalk
with Neil Griffin

New York Chicago San Francisco
Lisbon London Madrid Mexico City
Milan New Delhi San Juan
Seoul Singapore Sydney Toronto

The McGraw·Hill Companies

Cataloging-in-Publication Data is on file with the Library of Congress

JavaServer Faces 2.0: The Complete Reference

1 2 3 4 5 6 7 8 9 0 WFR WFR 0 1 9

ISBN 978-0-07-162509-8
MHID 0-07-162509-7

Sponsoring Editor
Wendy Rinaldi

Editorial Supervisor
Patty Mon

Project Manager
Smita Rajan,
Glyph International

Acquisitions Coordinator
Joya Anthony

Copy Editor
Bob Campbell

Proofreader
Mike Read

Indexer
Jack Lewis

Production Supervisor
George Anderson

Composition
Glyph International

Illustration
Glyph International

Art Director, Cover
Jeff Weeks

To Amy, my best friend, partner, and wife.
Thank you for helping me
achieve my dreams.

—Ed Burns

For my dad, Frank, the coolest
engineer/rocket scientist/cold warrior
there ever was!
As you used to say,
"If you're going to do something,
do it with Audace!*"*

—Chris Schalk

To my beloved wife Liz,
and to my dear children, Pauly and Anna.

—Neil Griffin

Contents at a Glance

Contents

Part III JavaServer Faces Tools and Libraries

Acknowledgments

JavaServer Faces is a foundation technology that builds on top of many other layers of software technology. Like any foundation software product, it is the result of the hard work and dedication of many individuals and organizations over many years of time. It is the same way with books that document such technologies, and I'd like to take the opportunity to thank some of the people who helped make this book, and JavaServer Faces itself, possible.

In a world where more and more information is available only online, and much of that information is coming from self-published individuals, I want to say that the publishing system is still the best way to deliver high-quality useful information in a portable and easily digestible way. A Web reference is no substitute for a dog-eared, marked-up, and well-worn book. After working with the publishing team at McGraw-Hill, I know why this is so. Our editor, Herb Schildt, has been my mentor as well as providing sure guidance as I made my way through this large book. Thanks, Herb, for your veteran insights. Acquisitions coordinator Joya Anthony did a great job keeping together all the disparate parts of the book. McGraw-Hill editorial director Wendy Rinaldi went through plenty of ups and downs on this project but never lost confidence; I am proud to deliver this book for her. Thanks to copy editor Robert Campbell and project manager Smita Rajan.

To my wonderful wife, Amy. Thank you for your understanding and patience as I spent all this time on this book; you picked up the slack in our family big-time. I could not have done it without your help and commitment. Thanks also to my sons, Owen and Logan, for understanding why Daddy was away all that time.

I need to thank those who brought me to, worked on, and helped complete JSF. Naturally, JSF is a JCP project, so the expert group deserves prominent mention. Key members of the JSF 2.0 expert group, in alphabetical order, include Dan Allen, Keith Donald, Mike Freedman, David Geary, Ted Goddard, Jeremy Grelle, Roger Keays, Gavin King, Jason Lee, Ryan Lubke, Craig McClanahan, Kito Mann, Martin Marinschek, Pete Muir, Joseph Ottinger, Ken Paulsen, Andy Schwartz, Alexandr Smirnov, and Adam Winer. Not only is JSF a JCP project, it is also a community-driven project, and there are many people to thank who have helped JSF succeed in the developer community. Some of these people include Lincoln Baxter III, Dennis Byrne, Çağatay Çivici, Hanspeter Dünnenberger, Alexander Jesse, Max Katz, Alberto Lemos (Dr. Spock), Imre Oßwald, Hazem Saleh, Stan Silvert, Yara and Vinicius Senger, and Matthias Weßendorf. George Drapeau recommended I interview for the job of leading the implementation team back in 2001. Thanks, George! Amy Fowler, the original spec lead, profoundly influenced the success of JSF and was a joy to work with.

Jim Driscoll, Mimi Hills, Tony Ng, Sridatta Viswanath, and Barbara Louis have been supportive managers throughout the development of JSF. To my original core JSF team of Jayashri Visvanathan and Roger Kitain, I give deepest thanks. You are the soul of this project and I have never worked with a better team. Ryan Lubke, Justyna Horwat, and Jennifer Ball deserve thanks as the extended JSF implementation team. Ryan, you also deserve special thanks for your unswerving commitment to quality and innovation in continuing to lead Sun's JSF implementation. I want to thank Jacob Hookom for his contribution to the JSF ecosystem in the form of Facelets, and his continuing creativity in establishing JSF as the best way to do AJAX.

I want to extend a special thank you to Neil Griffin for his writing Chapters 15, 16, and the Appendix.

Of course, I have to thank Chris Schalk for bringing me in to this project and for being a great collaborator. I know I am not the easiest person to work with at such close proximity, and I thank you for your patience and continued advocacy of the novice user and reader. Without you, there would be no book.

Finally, I want to thank the unswerving support team of Mom, Dad, Brendan Burns, Lisa Lane, Diana Dean, Jeff Beckberger, Joe McCabe, and Vern Singleton.

—Ed Burns
Altamonte Springs, FL

Introduction

What's new in JSF 2.0?

The number and scope of the changes between versions 1.2 and 2.0 of the JavaServer Faces specification is quite significant, arguably larger than any other two adjacent versions of any specification in the Java EE platform. With so many changes, it is important to have a handy reference to what is new. This section provides a categorized and complete breakdown of new features with references to the chapters in the book where the feature is described. A graphical index of all the JSF subsystems is shown in Figure 1.

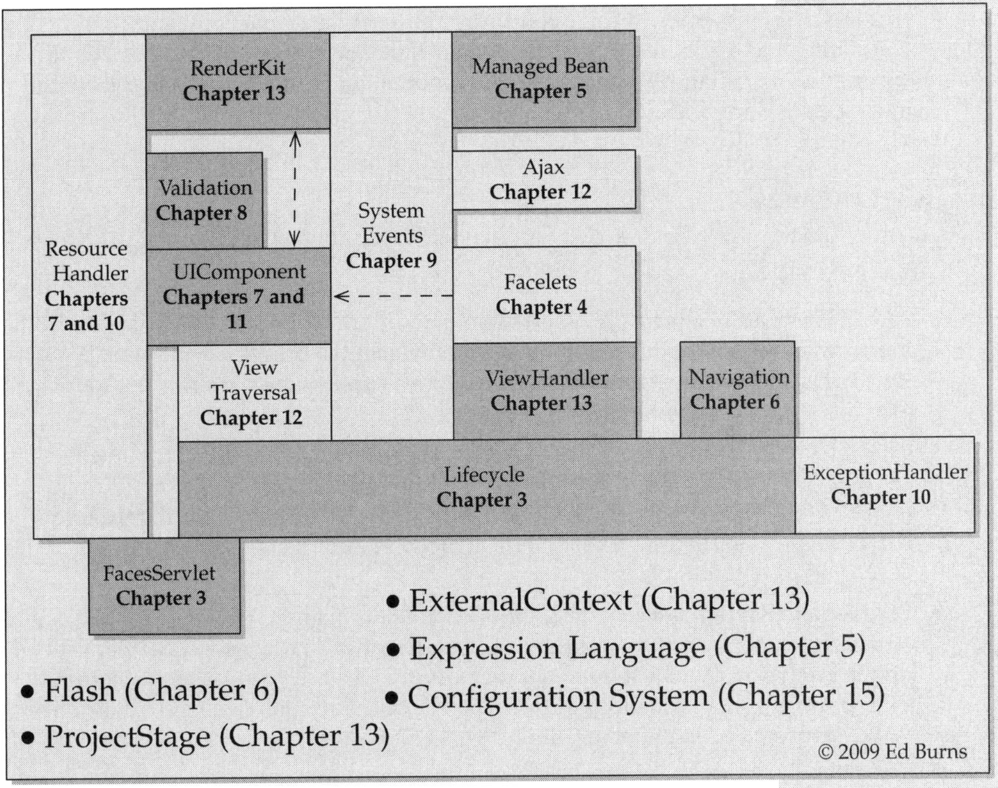

Figure 1 Graphical Index of JSF Subsystems

Lighter shaded boxes indicate features that are entirely new in JSF 2.0. Darker shaded boxes are existing features of JSF that have had changes and enhancements in JSF 2.0. The arrangement of the boxes indicates dependencies between features. In cases where the features have dependencies, but the boxes cannot be adjacent, arrows indicate the dependencies.

In the following text, the features are grouped by a subjective measure of "size" where bigger features were more difficult to design and are more important to understand than smaller ones. The categories used in the breakdown follow.

Foundational Features

These features were developed by the expert group specifically to enable other features in JSF 2.0; however, they are useful as features in their own right and are thus exposed in the public API.

- **System Events** This feature provides a very fined-grained level of detail to observe and act upon the JSF runtime as it processes requests. It is described in detail in Chapter 9.
- **Resources** This feature allows the JSF runtime to serve up static resources, such as style sheets, scripts, and images, in addition to the previously available capability to serve up JSF pages. It is introduced in Chapter 7 and described in detail in Chapter 10.
- **Facelets** Facelets began as an open-source JSF extension that provided first-class templating and easy integration between markup and the JSF API. This made the experience of writing JSF pages easier and more maintainable. Facelets is included in the core JSF specification in version 2.0 and is described in detail in Chapter 4.

Big Ticket Features

These features are the main "release drivers" that add new value over the previous release of the specification.

- **Ajax** This feature enables JSF views to communicate with the server directly from the browser without requiring a full-page refresh of the browser window. Ajax is an essential element of most production-quality Web applications currently in production. This feature is described in detail in Chapter 12.
- **Composite Components** This feature enables creating true JSF components as aggregations of other JSF components. With this feature, it is easy to build your own custom JSF components and to refactor your existing views into reusable components, complete with listeners, attributes, and events. The feature is described in detail in Chapter 11.
- **Partial State Saving** One of the biggest complaints against JSF has been the amount of memory it consumes to maintain view state between requests. This feature dramatically reduces the amount of memory for this purpose, as well as greatly simplifying the API for handling state when developing custom components. This feature is described in detail in Chapter 11.

- **View Parameters** Another big complaint against JSF is its insistence on using POST for all inter-page navigations. This feature is described in detail in Chapter 6.

Medium-Sized Features

These features are of interest to advanced JSF developers and also add value over the previous release, but are not as large in scope as the Big Ticket Features.

- **Navigation Enhancements** JSF 2.0 bring several enhancements to navigation, including bookmarkability, navigation without XML navigation rules, conditional navigation, support for the POST-REDIRECT-GET pattern, the flash, and runtime inspection of navigation rules. These features are described in Chapter 6.
- **Exception Handling** JSF 2.0 now has a central **ExceptionHandler** through which all exceptions are funneled. This enables easily constructing an error page that uses JSF components. This feature is described in detail in Chapter 10.
- **Expression Language Enhancements** Several new implicit objects have been introduced, and the EL now supports method invocation on arbitrary Java methods, including parameter passing. This feature is described in detail in Chapter 5.
- **Validation** An entirely new Java specification has been developed to address validation, JSR-303 Bean Validation. This specification integrates well with JSF 2.0 and is described completely in Chapter 8.
- **New Scopes** In addition to the flash scope described in Chapter 5, JSF 2.0 also provides a mechanism for defining custom scopes. This is described in Chapter 13.

Small New Features

These features are mainly bug fixes that were too big to do in a minor revision of the specification.

- Access to the FacesContext is now available during application startup and shutdown. This feature is used in Chapter 10.
- The **UISelectItems** child of components that extend from **UISelectOne** and **UISelectMany** can now refer to arbitrary collections of Objects.
- JSF now allows the developer to tell the runtime in what phase of the software development lifecycle the runtime is executing. This "ProjectStage" feature enables the runtime to output more informative error messages and hints as the project is being iteratively developed. This feature is used in Chapter 13.
- Annotations may obviate the need for XML. For nearly every XML element that can reside in a **faces-config.xml** file, there is now a Java language annotation that can be used in its place. This annotation feature, combined with the "navigation without XML navigation rules" feature, makes it possible to build JSF applications entirely without a **faces-config.xml** file. These annotations are described in Chapter 15.

Petite New Features

These features round out the list of new features and include things that are simply small bug fixes that have been rolled into the JSF 2.0 spec release.

- New methods on **ExternalContext** and **FacesContext** are described in Chapter 13.
- Wrappers to aid in extending JSF via the decorator design pattern are described in Chapter 13.
- The new **DataModel.iterator** feature is shown in Chapter 10.
- There are several new **context-param** settings, described in detail in Chapter 15.

If you are an experienced JSF user, you can use the preceding index of new features to skip straight to the new stuff. If you're just coming to JSF for the first time, you needn't know that the features are new in JSF 2.0, or how to migrate from previous versions. All of the new features will be presented naturally in context. Indeed, the entire book is written from the perspective that JSF 2.0 is the way that JSF was always meant to be.

This book provides in-depth content on the following topics:

- Tutorial content for using every aspect of JavaServer Faces technology
- Complete coverage of all new features in JSF 2.0, not added as an afterthought, but written from scratch to show how to do things "the JSF 2.0 way"
- A graphical index that quickly shows where to find information on all of the subsystems in JSF
- JSF 2.0 tips outlining the differences in the latest version of JSF and how best to use them
- Expert Group Insights that offer the rationale behind the design of the technology, giving readers a better understanding of how to use JSF in their own work
- Detailed coverage on custom UI component development with numerous examples, including JSF 2.0 composite components
- Complete coverage of the standard Ajax support in JSF 2.0
- Real-world influenced examples, including support for POST, REDIRECT, GET, Implicit Navigation, and bookmarkable JSF pages
- A complete guide to extending the entire JSF framework in areas such as security, mobile rendering, localization, and Expression Language enhancements
- A complete guide to the JSF config file by Neil Griffin, JSF 2.0 Expert Group member and Liferay Portal JSF Team leader
- Complete reference and tutorial information for the specification's Standard components

Your Development Environment

While offering substantial coverage on a variety of Java- and JSF-enabled IDEs, this book does not require the reader to use any IDE at all. A simple base environment consisting of

- Java SE 6
- A Servlet 2.5 container such as Apache Tomcat 5.x
- Apache Maven

is all that a reader will need to try out the code samples from the book. The easiest environment in which to try JSF 2.0 is Sun's Glassfish Application Server, **www.glassfish.org**.

Online Example Code Resources

Throughout the book there are references to online code, sometimes with a URL or simply referred to as the "online extension." All of the code examples in the book are available for download at McGraw-Hill's Web site: **www.mhprofessional.com/computingdownload**. In addition, the book's own Web site, **www.jsfcompref.com**, offers downloadable source code.

PART I

The JavaServer Faces Framework

CHAPTER 1

Introduction to JavaServer Faces

JavaServer Faces (JSF) has changed the way that Java-based Web applications are written. Designed to streamline the creation of user interfaces (UIs) for high-performance Java Web applications, JSF also simplifies the development process. JavaServer Faces offers an elegant solution to the key problems often associated with commercial-quality Web application development.

Before beginning an in-depth examination of JSF, it is important to understand in a general way what JavaServer Faces is and why it is important. Therefore, this chapter begins our discussion of JSF by describing its history, design goals, and lifecycle. It also explains how JavaServer Faces fits into the overall Web application development process.

What Is JavaServer Faces?

At its core, JavaServer Faces is a standard Java framework for building user interfaces for Web applications. Most important, it simplifies the development of the user interface, which is often one of the more difficult and tedious parts of Web application development. Although it is possible to build user interfaces by using foundational Java Web technologies (such as Java servlets and JavaServer Pages) without a comprehensive framework designed for enterprise Web application development, these core technologies can often lead to a variety of development and maintenance problems. More important, by the time the developers achieve a production-quality solution, the same set of problems solved by JSF will have been solved in a nonstandard manner. This approach is known as "building an in-house framework." JavaServer Faces avoids these problems by offering a robust, "best of breed" framework with well-established development patterns, built upon the experience of many preexisting Java Web development frameworks.

JavaServer Faces was created through the Java Community Process (JCP) by a group of technology leaders, including Sun Microsystems, Oracle, Borland, BEA, and IBM, along with a collection of Java and Web experts well known in the industry. The original Java specification request for JavaServer Faces (JSR 127) was initiated in mid-2001 and reached its 1.0 milestone along with J2EE 1.4 in March 2004.

JavaServer Faces is designed to simplify the development of user interfaces for Java Web applications in the following ways:

- It provides a component-centric, client-independent development approach to building Web user interfaces, thus improving developer productivity and ease of use.
- It simplifies the access and management of application data from the Web user interface.
- It automatically manages the user interface state between multiple requests and multiple clients in a simple and unobtrusive manner.
- It supplies a development framework that is friendly to a diverse developer audience with different skill sets.
- It describes a standard set of architectural patterns for a web application.

Beyond these specifics, JSF offers another important benefit. It takes the best elements found through years of experience in Web application development and combines them into a single, comprehensive, and standard API for building Java Web application user interfaces. Furthermore, it brings unprecedented ease and productivity to Java EE Web application development without sacrificing power and flexibility.

The History of JavaServer Faces

Like most other important programming technologies, the creation of JSF was the result of an evolutionary process of refinement and adaptation in which new and better techniques replaced older ones. In the case of JavaServer Faces, the force that drove this evolution was the need for a simpler, more effective, and more efficient way to build dynamic Web user interfaces that are based on a well-designed and maintainable architecture. The story begins with CGI.

The Common Gateway Interface

In the mid-1990s, Web application development was still relatively new, and the predominant technology for assembling Web applications used a simple method known as the Common Gateway Interface (CGI) for producing dynamic content. CGI was introduced by Rob and Mike McCool, who were originally from the HTTP server development team at the National Center for Supercomputing Applications (NCSA). Incidentally, NCSA was also responsible for the world's first graphical Web browser, Mosaic.

CGI is a technique that allows a Web page to invoke a server-side process to generate output dynamically, such as for a stock quote or reporting the number of Web site hits. The program that produced the dynamic output was usually an operating system (OS) shell script, a natively compiled program, or an interpreted language such as Perl. A CGI-enabled Web server allowed a new CGI process to be invoked from an HTML page. Unfortunately, this architecture doesn't scale to high performance due to the resource consumption of processes.

One early remedy to this problem was to create APIs that allowed developers to write dynamic modules that operated within the same memory space as the Web server. Each request would simply invoke a new thread as opposed to a new independent process, which was a lot less taxing on the server. The only downside to this approach was that it then required the developer to code Web applications to a specific Web server's API, such as

Microsoft's Internet Server Application Programming Interface (ISAPI) or the Netscape Server Application Programming Interface (NSAPI). This is the historical origin of the choice faced by present-day Web application developers: .NET, Java, or other (usually PHP or Ruby on Rails).

The Servlet API

The next step forward in the evolution of Web application development was the introduction of the Java Servlet API in March 1998. Prior to servlets, Java was not widely utilized as a server-side technology for Web applications. Instead Java was mainly used in Web pages in the form of Java Applets that would run on browser clients. Although Java Applets were relatively good at providing dynamic or animated content on Web pages, they were never really suited for broad Web application development. It wasn't until the Servlet API was created that Java became a valid server-side technology for Web development.

The Java Servlet API enabled Java developers to write server-side code for delivering dynamic Web content. Like other proprietary Web server APIs, the Java Servlet API offered improved performance over CGI; however, it had some key additional advantages. Because servlets were coded in Java, they provided an object-oriented (OO) design approach and, more important, were able to run on any platform. Thus, the same code was portable to any host that supported Java. Servlets greatly contributed to the popularity of Java, as it became a widely used technology for server-side Web application development.

Although an improvement, the Java Servlet API still had a problem: it only provided a low-level way to generate HTML, and it was often a tedious and error-prone experience. Consider this awkward syntax of a servlet statement to print out an HTML table tag:

```
out.println("<table width=\"75%\"
                                    border=\"0\"align=\"center\">");
```

Notice how the quote symbols (") have to be individually escaped using the backslash. Obviously, a better alternative for generating dynamic markup was needed, and thus began a development approach that continues to this day: providing a simpler programming model built on top of servlets.

JavaServer Pages

The next evolution in Java Web development came with the introduction of JavaServer Pages (JSP). JSP was built on top of servlets and provided a simpler, page-based solution to generating large amounts of dynamic HTML content for Web user interfaces. JavaServer Pages enabled Web developers and designers to simply edit HTML pages with special tags for the dynamic, Java portions. JavaServer Pages works by having a special servlet known as a *JSP container*, which is installed on a Web server and handles all JSP page view requests. The JSP container translates a requested JSP into servlet code that is then compiled and immediately executed. Subsequent requests to the same page simply invoke the runtime servlet for the page. If a change is made to the JSP on the server, a request to view it triggers another translation, compilation, and restart of the runtime servlet.

JSP provided an improvement but was not a complete solution. As Web applications became more complex, JSP pages often tended to get cluttered with Java code, making them harder to manage and more error prone. What was needed was a better separation of Java application code from the presentation markup. What was needed was MVC.

Apache Struts

One of the most dominant server-side Java frameworks to emerge in the last few years was the Jakarta Struts Web application development framework. Struts was created by Craig McClanahan and was offered to the open source community through Apache's Jakarta project. Struts proved to be a success because of its cost (gratis) and sufficiently intelligent architecture.

Struts' popularity is largely due to its implementation of the Model-View-Controller (MVC) design paradigm described by Trygve Reenskaug in Smalltalk in 1979. One of the problems of using JSPs and servlets without a framework was the tendency for developers to fall into the bad habit of mixing UI and server-side code in one place (the JSP page), which led to predictable problems. Struts solved this problem by strictly following the MVC architecture design, where the View is the user-interface code and the Model is the server-side code for processing application data. As you'll see shortly, JavaServer Faces also embraces the MVC approach and is similar to Struts in this regard.

In Struts, the Controller is simply a servlet that handles all incoming Web requests and dispatches them to the appropriate View components or pages. For accessing the Model or application data, Struts provides *Actions* that are Web-accessible execution points for Java. For the View, Struts provides a modest set of JSP tag libraries that are fairly low level. These tag libraries provide rendering for the common HTML elements, display messages, and support logic operations.

Although architecturally sound, Struts still often required a substantial amount of custom development for building user interfaces. Even when coupled with the usage of JSTL tags, user interface development with Struts could still be fairly complicated and was really not on a par with what was available with other proprietary technologies such as Microsoft's ASP.NET, where the user interface development experience is more component-based and usually less complex.

The Spring Framework and Spring MVC

Shortly after Struts had become the de facto standard web framework, but during the development of JSF 1.0, Rod Johnson invented the Spring Framework as an alternative programming model to J2EE. The most important innovations delivered by Spring were "Inversion of Control" and the accompanying concept of informal contract programming. These innovations became popular because they allow a very clean separation of business logic from application logic without imposing any compile-time constraints on the business logic code. With Spring, business logic code resides in Plain Old Java Objects (POJOs). A POJO is a Java Object that need not implement any particular Java interface, nor extend any particular Java class; therefore, the software contract to which it adheres is informal. The configuration of the POJOs in an application was declared in a configuration file external to the POJOs. This architecture fits the needs of enterprise application development by allowing a smooth evolution of software as requirements change.

In practice, Spring is often used with Struts, though Spring includes its own simply MVC framework called Spring MVC.

The Birth of JavaServer Faces

As Struts gained in popularity, the Java Community Process saw the benefits that Struts offered by explicitly following an MVC approach. However, Struts still lacked a robust user-interface-oriented framework similar to what is possible in other technologies, including traditional Java client technologies such as Swing. In short, a better way to handle the View tier was needed.

To address this need, several leading software vendors, including Sun, Oracle, IBM, and BEA, met through the Java Community Process in May 2001 and voted to proceed with a comprehensive and detailed specification for building Java EE thin-client Web applications whose primary goal was to provide a standard and much simpler way to build user interfaces for Java Web applications. This resulted in Java Specification Request (JSR) #127, and JavaServer Faces was born.

JSF combines an MVC design approach with a powerful, component-based UI development framework that greatly simplifies Java EE Web development while using existing markup and servlet technologies. The way this was accomplished is spelled out in the original design goals specified by JSR #127.

The JavaServer Faces Design Goals

JSR #127 specified eight design requirements for JSF. These goals continue to describe the design focus for JSF, up to and including JSF 2.0.

1. Create a standard UI component framework that can be leveraged by development tools to make it easier for tool users to both create high-quality UIs and manage the UI's connections to application behavior.
2. Define a set of simple, lightweight Java base classes for UI components, component state, and input events. These classes will address UI lifecycle issues, notably managing a component's persistent state for the lifetime of its page.
3. Provide a set of common UI components, including the standard HTML form input elements. These components will be derived from the simple set of base classes (outlined in #1) that can be used to define new components.
4. Provide a JavaBeans model for dispatching events from client-side UI controls to server-side application behavior.
5. Define APIs for input validation, including support for client-side validation.
6. Specify a model for internationalization and localization of the UI.
7. Provide for automatic generation of appropriate output for the target client, taking into account all available client configuration data, such as the browser version.
8. Provide for automatic generation of output containing required hooks for supporting accessibility, as defined by the Web Accessibility Initiative (WAI).

To accomplish goals 1–3, JavaServer Faces provides a component-centric API from which Web application user interfaces can easily be assembled. The JSF specification defines a set of base user interface components (referred to in the JSF specification as *UI components*) that can be used as is, or extended to achieve more specialized behaviors.

We'll cover the entire Faces UI component model in much greater detail in Chapter 7, but for now it is important to understand the key concepts of UI components.

The initial or "standard" UI components provided in the specification are accompanied with a set of "Core" and "HTML" tag libraries. The Core component tag library enables common Web application operations such as assigning validations, converting input values, and loading resource bundles. The HTML component tag library creates and renders HTML components. These include components for displaying simple text labels, input fields, links, and buttons, as well as more complex container components for displaying tabular data or panels of child components.

To accomplish goal 4, which is to provide an event-based, JavaBean model way of interacting with application data, JavaServer Faces provides an easy-to-use mechanism by which Web-accessible user interface components loosely coupled to server-side Java POJOs that are declared as *managed beans.* Managed beans may be declared in an XML file (**faces-config.xml**) or via annotations. Beans are loosely coupled to a user interface with a simple-to-use Expression Language, which is almost identical to JSTL's Expression Language syntax. Once bound, updating bean properties or invoking bean methods from a Web interface is handled automatically by the *JSF request processing lifecycle.*

The JSF request processing lifecycle also accomplishes goal 5 for handling input validation. In addition to providing a means to update server-side application data, the JSF request processing lifecycle and event model allows for the validation and/or data type conversion of data depending on certain events in the application, such as when a form is submitted or when UI components are accessed or manipulated. JSF provides built-in validation capabilities as well as the option to create custom validation. For data type conversion, such as when a date needs to be converted from a **String** data type supplied by an HTML input field to a **Date** type on the server, JSF has a set of prebuilt converters that can convert **String** values to various data types. Both JSF validators and converters can be extended and customized in many ways. In Chapter 7 we'll step through how to use the built-in validators and converters as well as review the different ways of building custom validation and conversion.

JSF accomplishes goal 6, which is to allow for easy internationalization, by providing a simple way to handle multilingual message bundles and locales. Once a message bundle has been configured for a predefined set of supported locales, the JSF UI components can then automatically render themselves in the appropriate language based on the incoming request's locale setting. In Chapter 14 we'll review all the steps required for internationalizing a JSF application.

The seventh and eighth goals of the original JSF specification request, which are to have the ability to automatically generate the appropriate output (including output supporting accessibility) depending on the target client, are achieved by the JSF API's extremely flexible, *pluggable* rendering technology. This makes it possible to associate multiple renderers with a single UI component and have the appropriate renderer respond with the appropriate markup for the client. For example, it is possible to create a JSF UI component that can render itself in HTML when a browser makes a request or WML when a PDA or another WAP-enabled browser makes a request, or iPhone-specific HTML when serving content to an iPhone.

JSF has had two major revisions since the original 1.0 release. JSF 1.2 (JSR 252) featured the following themes:

- Along with JSP 2.1 (JSR 245), JSF 1.2 introduces the Unified Expression Language as a separate specification, common to JSF and JSP.
- Fix integration with JSP and JSTL.

JSF 2.0 (JSR 314) featured the following themes:

- Built-in Facelets support for advanced templating
- First-class support for Ajax
- Composite components
- Improved validation by integrating Beans Validation (JSR 303)
- First-class support for resources
- Greater ease of development

JSF 2.0 offers many other improvements, and all of them will be discussed in context, and in detail, throughout the rest of this book.

JSF Application Architecture

One of the most elegant design aspects of the JavaServer Faces specification is that it completely relies on existing Java EE Web technology at its foundation. This means that a JSF application is really just a standard Java EE Web application with a few specific configurations:

- An entry in the Web application's **web.xml** file enables the Faces Controller servlet when a certain URL pattern is specified, such as **/faces/***. When running JSF 2.0 on a Servlet 3.0 container, such as Sun's Glassfish v3, the web.xml is optional. If no **web.xml** is found, the Faces Controller servlet is automatically mapped to the most popular URL patterns: **/faces/***, ***.jsf**, and ***.faces**.
- An optional JSF configuration file, **faces-config.xml**, allows for configuration of all elements of a JSF application. JSF has Java annotations for nearly everything that can be put in to the **faces-config.xml**, obviating the need for the file in most cases. This file is treated as a peer of the **web.xml** file and is usually located in the Web application's **WEB-INF/** directory. The exact structure of this file and the elements contained within are detailed in later chapters.
- When running an application in a container that does not provide built-in support for JSF, the libraries composing the JSF implementation must be included in **WEB-INF/lib**.

Once a Java EE Web application is properly configured for JSF, you can construct the View using Facelets XHTML pages. (Versions of JSF prior to 2.0 emphasized JSP as the page declaration language. JSPs are indeed still supported in JSF 2.0, but few of the features unique to 2.0 are available to pages built with JSP. Therefore, this book will use Facelets for all examples. An online Appendix, at **http://jsfcompref.com/**, gives detailed instructions for migrating from JSP to Facelets.) Building JSF applications with XHTML is done by using JSF-enabled Facelets tag libraries. For an XHTML page to be JSF-enabled, it must first contain JSF XML namespace directives provided by a JSF implementation. The following namespace directives are for the Core and HTML libraries available from all JSF implementations:

```
<html xmlns=http://www.w3.org/1999/xhtml
      xmlns:h=http://java.sun.com/jsf/html
      xmlns:f="http://java.sun.com/jsf/core">
```

Because this is XHTML, the HTML elements must be in all lowercase and must always be balanced. If the page processes form input, as opposed to just displaying output, you'll need to add a **<h:form>** tag as a child of the **<body>** or **<h:body>** tag. Subsequent child tags of the **<h:form>** tag will become the form elements such as **<h:inputText>**, which renders an input field, and **<h:commandButton>**, which renders a form submission button.

To understand how JavaServer Faces creates and manages a server-side tree of components in memory, that directly corresponds to the components included in a page, consider the following JSF-enabled XHTML page:

```
<html xmlns=http://www.w3.org/1999/xhtml
      xmlns:h=http://java.sun.com/jsf/html
      xmlns:f="http://java.sun.com/jsf/core">
  <body>
   <h:form>
     <h2>A Simple JSF Page</h2>
     <h:inputText value="#{modelBean.username}"/>
     <h:commandButton value="Click Here"/>
   </h:form>
 </body>
</html>
```

As you can see in Figure 1-1, the JSF UI component tree instantiated on the server exactly matches the UI components in the page (except for the automatically created **UIViewRoot**). Once the UI component tree is instantiated and in memory, it is possible to interact with the server-side UI components, and manipulate and change properties of these components on the server.

As you'll see in later chapters, knowing how to interact with the server-side UI component tree is often needed for more advanced JSF development. For basic JSF applications, one simply has to drop some UI components onto a page, set some attributes, and rely on the JSF built-in "plumbing" to take care of the job of processing input. Let's take a closer look at JSF's "plumbing," otherwise known as the JSF request processing lifecycle.

The JSF Request Processing Lifecycle

When a JSF-enabled XHTML page is requested or when the user invokes an action on a UI component in a JSF-enabled XHTML page, it is important to understand the exact sequence of events that occur on the server in order to fulfill the request to view or submit a JSF page.

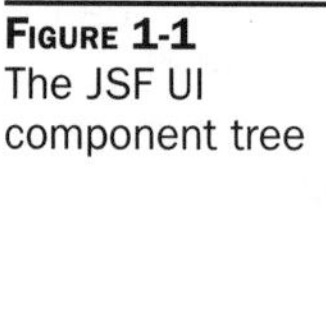

FIGURE 1-1 The JSF UI component tree

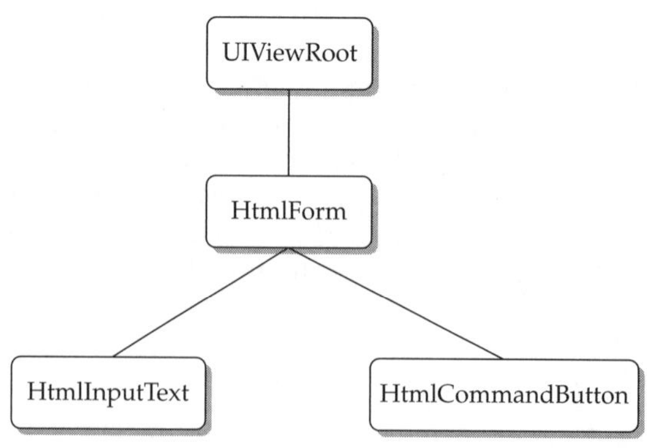

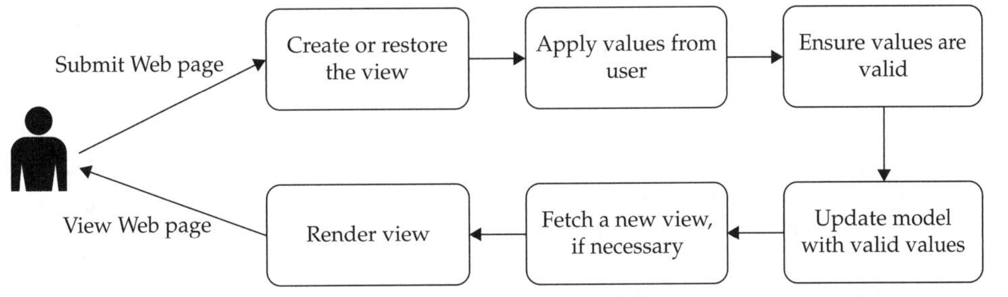

Figure 1-2 The JSF request processing lifecycle

The sequence of events that are triggered during requests to JSF pages is known as the *JSF request processing lifecycle* or sometimes simply as the *JSF lifecycle*. This is shown in Figure 1-2.

We've already touched on what happens when a JSF page is requested for the first time, when the JSF runtime creates a component tree in memory. In between requests, when nothing is happening in the application, the component tree is often cached. Upon a subsequent request, the tree is quickly reconstituted, and if form input values are sent in the request, they are processed and validations are executed. Upon successful validation, the server-side model values of the input fields are updated. What follows is continued event processing, and any errors are reported. Once all event processing and model updates (if needed) have finished, a completed response is finally rendered back to the client.

A more detailed review of the JSF request processing lifecycle is presented in Chapter 3, but for now it is sufficient to know that the JSF lifecycle is simply the sequence of back-end "plumbing" events that automatically manage input data so that the Web developer does not need to write code to process the request manually. This differs to a certain degree from most other Web technologies, including CGI, PHP, and Struts, where the developer specifically writes code to handle the incoming requests and process the results. This is one of the advantages that JSF brings to Web application development. It removes the whole notion of having to manually process incoming Web requests. Instead, the Web developer can rely on the JSF lifecycle to handle back-end plumbing automatically and can use the JSF event model to jump in and do custom processing only when needed.

It is important to recognize that the work done by the JSF request processing lifecycle: applying request values, performing validation, interacting with the business logic and application model, performing navigation, and rendering a response, is a fact of life for all Web applications, JSF or not. A Web application must deal with at least these concerns in order to be considered production quality. A Web application can choose to let a framework, such as JSF, handle these concerns, or it can handle them explicitly. The point is, in either case, they *must* be addressed.

As a simple example where no custom events are handled, one simply has to bind a UI component such as an input field to a managed bean's property and the lifecycle will automatically update the value of the managed bean's property with the value of the UI component. Recall the JSF XHTML example shown earlier where an **inputText** component is bound to the "username" property of the managed bean "modelBean" using the JSF Expression Language (EL).

```
<h:inputText value="#{modelBean.username}" />
```

To allow the user to *submit* the form and initiate the JSF lifecycle, a **command Button** UI component is added to the page using

```
<h:commandButton value="Click Here"/>
```

Since the JSF lifecycle utilizes the JavaBeans event model, the user simply clicks the rendered command button at runtime and the JSF lifecycle automatically updates the JavaBean's "username" property with the value provided in the input field!

More in-depth coverage of the JSF request processing lifecycle as well as JSF's Expression Language is detailed in later chapters.

The JSF Navigation Model

Like Struts, JSF follows a Model-View-Controller design paradigm. Recall that an MVC application is segmented into three distinct application components:

- The Model, which contains the business logic or non-UI code
- The View, which is all the code necessary to present a UI to the user
- The Controller, which is a front-end agent that directly handles the user's requests and dispatches the appropriate view

These three elements, also depicted in Figure 1-3, combine to produce an architecture that yields distinct, separately maintainable code.

JavaServer Faces from the start was created to adhere precisely to the MVC design methodology. It does so by providing a clean way to separate presentation (View) code from the back-end business logic (Model) code. It also provides a front-end (Controller) servlet that handles all Faces requests and dispatches them, along with the necessary application

Figure 1-3 The Model-View-Controller design paradigm

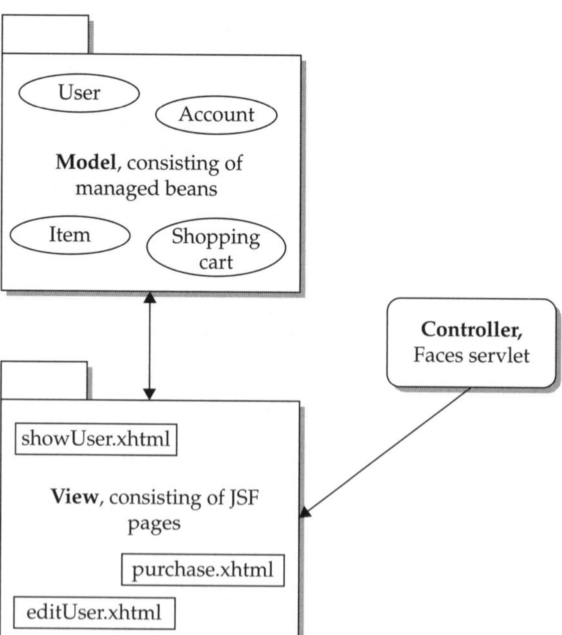

data, to the appropriate View component (page). As you have seen, the View segment of a JSF application is created using JSF-enabled JSP pages with UI components. The Model is bound to methods and properties in managed beans specified in the **faces-config.xml** file or in annotations on the managed bean classes. Now, let's take a look at how the Faces Controller works in a JSF application.

As mentioned before, the Faces Controller is implemented as a servlet that responds to all requests conforming to a certain URL pattern, such as **/faces/***, as defined in the **web.xml** file. The **FacesServlet** is provided by the implementation, you don't have to write it yourself. A request that uses the appropriate Faces URL pattern can be considered a "Faces request," and when received by the Faces Controller, it processes the request by preparing an object known as the JSF context, which contains all accessible application data and routes the client to the appropriate View component (page). The rules that the controller uses for routing these requests are centrally managed in the **faces-config.xml** file and are known as the *JSF Navigation Model.*

The JSF Navigation Model is an elegant solution for keeping track of all navigation in the entire JSF application. This greatly improves the manageability of the application because it is easier to maintain a central navigation model than to update multiple page links in multiple pages. The central location of the navigation model in an XML file is also very "tool friendly" in that vendor tools now offer visual ways to easily define JSF navigation models.

***JSF 2.0* TIP** *If you really want to put the navigation information directly in the pages, JSF 2.0 allows you to do so. In this case, no external navigation rules are required.*

The navigation model is based on a set of "navigation rules," which define a "from" page (from-view-id) and one or many "to" navigation cases. Each navigation case has an associated "outcome" and "to" page (to-view-id). For example, to navigate from **page1** to **page2** when the outcome "success" is encountered, the following rule is specified in **faces-config.xml**:

```
<navigation-rule>
  <from-view-id>/page1.xhtml</from-view-id>
  <navigation-case>
    <from-outcome>success</from-outcome>
    <to-view-id>/page2.xhtml</to-view-id>
  </navigation-case>
</navigation-rule>
```

As you can guess, a second navigation case can be defined for a "failure" outcome that will route the viewer to **page3.xhtml**.

```
<navigation-rule>
  <from-view-id>/page1.xhtml</from-view-id>
  <navigation-case>
    <from-outcome>success</from-outcome>
    <to-view-id>/page2.xhtml</to-view-id>
  </navigation-case>
  <navigation-case>
    <from-outcome>failure</from-outcome>
    <to-view-id>/page3.xhtml</to-view-id>
  </navigation-case>
</navigation-rule>
```

Your next question may be, How is an "outcome" determined? This can either be hard-coded or derived dynamically from the return value of a method that is triggered when a button is clicked. As you recall, UI components can be bound to both properties and methods, so it is possible to associate a button click with a specific method in a managed bean, which can then return an "outcome" as a **String** value. The JSF event model then processes this "outcome" **String** value and follows any navigation case defined in the navigation model that corresponds to the outcome of the method.

Now that you know the history and theory behind JSF and have seen a very simple example of a working JSF page, it's time to review a more detailed JSF example application. Chapter 2 develops a short, yet practical registration form example that exercises many of the key features of JavaServer Faces. It will also serve as one of several modules of a more intricate "Virtual Trainer" example application, which will be introduced in Part II of this book.

CHAPTER 2

Building a Simple JavaServer Faces Application

One of the best ways to learn a new technology is to work through a simple, yet practical example. Toward this end, this chapter develops a typical Web registration application using JavaServer Faces (JSF) technology. A Web registration application provides just enough functionality to show how to use the core JSF technologies, such as User Interface (UI) components, managed beans, the navigation model, and basic data validation and conversion. In later chapters this registration application will be incorporated into a larger, more comprehensive "Virtual Trainer" example application that will be referenced throughout the book. For now, working through this registration example gives you an understanding of the key elements and architecture of a JSF application. It also provides an overview of the JSF development process.

In addition to showing how to build a simple JSF registration application, this chapter also explains how to set up your own JSF development environment, which will allow you to compile, package, and run the application. In the interest of ensuring a firm understanding of the core technology requirements of a JSF application, the application in this chapter will be built from the command line using an open source technology called Maven 2. In later chapters, you will see how to rapidly build JSF applications using several of the leading integrated visual development environments for JavaServer Faces.

Application Overview

This sample application is called JSFReg and is a simple Web registration application similar to the ones that you've no doubt encountered many times while registering for numerous services on the Web today. The application consists of several XHTML pages, each containing JSF UI components, a Java class to temporarily store user information, and a set of configuration files and required runtime libraries.

The application's opening page is the registration form. The registration form allows users to enter their name, sex, and other basic personal information. A **Register** button is also included on the form. Clicking the button invokes a validation on the data entered. If any validation errors occur, error messages are displayed next to the invalid input fields.

The user can then revise the incorrect fields in order to pass validation. After the input data passes validation, the user can still revise any input data or proceed to confirm the registration. When the confirmation button is clicked, a final page is displayed showing the actual "registered" data for the user. A registration Java method is also invoked at the same time. This Java method could actually be linked to a database or any service to perform an actual data record insertion. In this simple example, the Java registration method simply prints the message "Adding new user" to the standard output (or console) of the application server.

Figure 2-1 depicts all of the pages in the JSFReg application.

The somewhat detailed registration process with various options to go back and revise or proceed on to a confirmation page may seem a little excessive, but this was done intentionally to show how to handle different page navigation options depending on different cases. The registration page illustrates how to build a form using a collection of the various UI components provided in the JSF specification's standard HTML component library. These include input text fields, radio buttons, and a select menu, along with form submission buttons. The application's fairly robust validation requirements highlight both JSF's built-in validation and data type conversion technology as well as how to implement (very simple) custom validation logic. More thorough coverage of JSF validation and conversion is provided in Chapter 8.

Since JSF provides both a set of usable UI components along with a modest amount of built-in validation and data conversion capabilities, you'll see that a large portion of JSF application development is simply a matter of assembling user interfaces using ready-to-use UI components. As also highlighted in the example, these components can be configured with certain validations and then bound to existing Java bean properties and methods. The same components can also be bound to a set of page flow navigation rules known as the JSF *Navigation Model,* which provides navigation rules for the entire application. That in a nutshell is what JSF application development entails. Now let's take a closer look at how the example application is built.

The JSFReg Application Files

All JSF applications consist of a specific set of required configuration files and Web content files. The key configuration files required are **faces-config.xml**, and a standard Java EE Web application's configuration/deployment descriptor, **web.xml.** Web content files can be composed of Facelet and/or general HTML content such as HTML pages, images, and cascading style sheets (CSS).

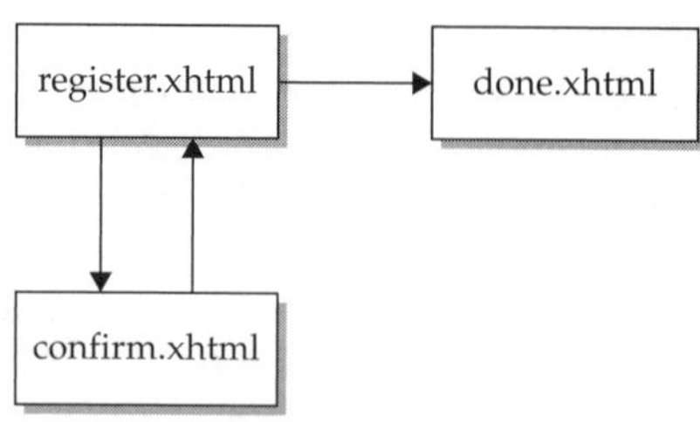

FIGURE 2-1 Diagram of JSFReg application

The following table lists each file used in the JSFReg application and its purpose.

File	Description
web.xml	The Java EE Web deployment descriptor and master configuration file required by any Java EE Web application. A JSF application's **web.xml** file also has specific settings for JSF, such as the servlet mapping "/faces", which allows the JSF controller servlet to process this request separately from any other request.
register.xhtml	The application's Facelets page that contains the registration form for the application. The registration form is composed of the different JSF UI components that render the input fields, menus, and buttons.
confirm.xhtml	A Facelets page that displays the validated user-entered data with two buttons providing the options **Edit** or **Confirm**. Clicking the **Edit** button will send the user back to the registration form, whereas clicking the **Confirm** button confirms the input and redirects to the final "done" page.
done.xhtml	A Facelets page that indicates that the user information was successfully submitted along with a final display of the confirmed user information.
UserBean.java	A Java class that is used as a "managed bean" by JSF to temporarily store the registration information supplied by the user. It contains the fields for the user's name, gender, e-mail, birth date, etc. It also contains a simple validation method for the e-mail address.

In addition to these core application files, several Java libraries are also needed to compile and create a deployable packaged application. These details will be covered at the end of the chapter.

The JSF Software Stack

The term "software stack" is loosely used to mean a collection of software packages from possibly different vendors that are used to build a complete solution for the user. The basic software stack for the examples in this book and how to install each element of the stack are described in this section. All of the source code for the examples, and download links for all the elements of the software stack can be found at http://jsfcompref.com/.

Development Environment

Unless otherwise stated, all of the examples in the book were developed using Sun Microsystems Java SE 6, Version 1.6.0_07. This software may be downloaded from **http://java.sun.com/javase/downloads/**.

On top of Java SE 6, the examples in this book will use Apache Maven 2 software, version 2.0.9, to direct the compilation and assembly of the source files into a deployable web application. Maven 2 may be downloaded from **http://maven.apache.org/download.html**. The core strengths of Maven 2 are its dependency management feature and its strict project structure. The dependency management feature is explicitly designed for projects using extremely heterogeneous software stacks. In Maven 2, Java code and related resources are grouped into a "project." Each project has exactly one "project object model" file that describes everything Maven 2 needs to know, including dependencies on all manner of external jar files to compile and build the project into some kind of target artifact.

The project object model is described in a file called **pom.xml**. When Maven 2 is requested to build a project, it looks at the **pom.xml**, downloads any dependencies not already found on local disk, and performs the build, generating the target artifact. Most of the examples in this book will build into a Java EE Web Application WAR file.

Please see the Web site for this book, **http://jsfcompref.com/**, for instructions on how to set up your Maven 2 environment to easily build the examples in the book.

Runtime Environment

All the examples in this book were designed for JSF 2.0 and therefore require a runtime capable of running JSF 2.0. Such environments include, but are not limited to, Sun Glassfish versions 2.1 or 3.0 and Jakarta Tomcat Version 6. The Web site for the book has instructions for downloading and installing a suitable JSF 2.0 runtime environment. For each such environment, instructions are provided for starting and stopping the environment, and for deploying and undeploying an application.

Assembling the JSFReg Application

If you are already familiar with basic Java EE Web applications, you will notice that all JSF applications are simply standard Java EE applications, but with a few distinctions. At a minimum, this includes a JSF setting in the Web application's **web.xml** file. Let's see how to build the JSFReg application from the command line with Maven 2.

To start building JSFReg, you'll need to create a development directory on your file system that will serve as the root directory for your Java EE Web application. This directory can reside anywhere on your file system, and we will call the directory **jsfreg**. This directory will contain all of the necessary elements for building the JSFReg Web application. The subdirectories and their contents will follow the structure of a Maven 2 WAR project. This will include a Java source directory, **src/main/java**, as well as a Java EE Web module root directory, **src/main/webapp**, which will contain the Facelets Views and application deployment descriptors. The **src/main/java** directory will contain the full path of the Java source files needed for this application. All of the Java source files in this book will be in packages that are subpackages of **com.jsfcompref**. Therefore, the Java source files will be in subdirectories of the **src/main/java/com/jsfcompref** directory. Java EE Web developers will recognize the **src/main/webapp** subdirectory as a standard Java EE Web module directory. It will contain the required **WEB-INF** subdirectory tree, which contains the Web module deployment descriptor, **web.xml**, along with the application's Web content, including Facelets XHTML pages, images, scripts, CSS files, and so on. Your empty directory structure will look like what is shown in Figure 2-2.

Your complete directory structure will eventually contain the following files:

- **jsfreg/src/main/webapp/WEB-INF/web.xml**
- **jsfreg/src/main/webapp/confirm.xhtml**
- **jsfreg/src/main/webapp/done.xhtml**
- **jsfreg/src/main/webapp/register.xhtml**
- **jsfreg/src/main/java/com/jsfcompref/model/UserBean.java**
- **jsfreg/pom.xml**

The remainder of the chapter will describe each of these files, how to use Maven 2 to deploy the application to the two most popular servers for running JSF: Sun's Glassfish,

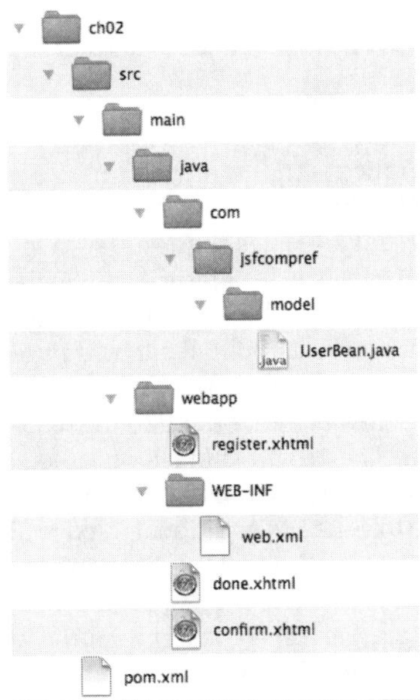

FIGURE 2-2 JSFReg application directory structure

and Apache Tomcat. Once finished, the WAR file built from this directory structure will be universally deployable to any standard Java EE Web container/application server.

The Configuration File

To begin building the application, first create a new Web module deployment descriptor (**web.xml**), which must reside in the **src/main/webapp/WEB-INF** directory. Note that when running in a Servlet 3.0 container, such as Sun's Glassfish v3, the **web.xml** is optional. In this case, the **FacesServlet** is automatically mapped to the ***.faces**, ***.jsf**, and **/faces/*** url-patterns.

Here is the initial **web.xml** file:

```
<web-app version="2.5"
  xmlns="http://java.sun.com/xml/ns/javaee"
  xmlns:xsi="http://www.w3.org/2001/XMLSchema-instance"
  xsi:schemaLocation="http://java.sun.com/xml/ns/javaee
http://java.sun.com/xml/ns/javaee/web-app_2_5.xsd">
  <display-name>JSFReg</display-name>
  <description>Simple Registration Application</description>
<context-param>
  <param-name>javax.faces.PROJECT_STAGE</param-name>
  <param-value>Development</param-value>
</context-param>
  <servlet>
    <servlet-name>Faces Servlet</servlet-name>
    <servlet-class>javax.faces.webapp.FacesServlet</servlet-class>
    <load-on-startup>1</load-on-startup>
  </servlet>
  <servlet-mapping>
    <servlet-name>Faces Servlet</servlet-name>
    <url-pattern>/faces/*</url-pattern>
  </servlet-mapping>
```

```
    <welcome-file-list>
      <welcome-file>faces/register.xhtml</welcome-file>
    </welcome-file-list>
</web-app>
```

The key thing to notice is that the **web.xml** file has a **Faces Servlet** entry, **javax.faces .webapp.FacesServlet**, which serves as the Faces Controller servlet. The Faces Controller servlet is able to intercept all **Faces** requests, provided they have the **/faces/*** pattern that matches the servlet mapping's **url-pattern**. Actually the **url-pattern** can be set to anything, such as ***.faces** or ***.jsf**. It simply has to be a pattern that allows the application to distinguish Faces requests from non-Faces requests. All JSF-enabled pages must be accessed via a Faces request (using a suitable mapping pattern) so as to first invoke the Faces servlet Controller whose job is to prepare the JSF Context before routing to the requested page. More coverage on the JSF lifecycle and Context will be provided in later chapters. Notice the <context-param> whose name is **javax.faces.PROJECT_STAGE**. The value shown here is **Development**. This setting causes the JSF runtime to generate additional in page aids when common developer mistakes are detected. Other values are **Production**, **SystemTest**, and **UnitTest**.

Another important element is the **<welcome-file-list>**. The **<welcome-file>** element within that list directs the Servlet container to automatically direct the flow of control to the specified page within the application. Because the content of the **<welcome-file>** element includes the value given in the **url-pattern** for the Faces Servlet, any request to the root of the application, such as **http://localhost:8080/jsfreg/** will automatically take the user to the front page of the application, which is **http://localhost:8080/jsfreg/faces/register.xhtml**.

Versions of JSF prior to 2.0 required another file in the **WEB-INF** subdirectory: **faces-config.xml**. This file is unnecessary in many cases with JSF 2.0 due to the addition of Java language annotations that convey information formerly only specified in **faces-config.xml**.

The Facelets Pages

Let's start with the page listed as the **<welcome-file>** in **web.xml**: **register.xhtml**. The rendered appearance of this page is shown in Figure 2-3.

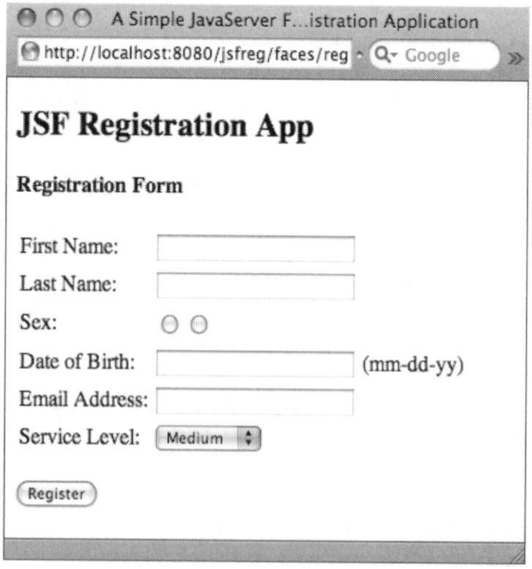

FIGURE 2-3 The JSFReg welcome page

A Simple JavaServer F...istration Application
http://localhost:8080/jsfreg/faces/reg
Google

JSF Registration App

Registration Form

First Name:
Last Name:
Sex:
Date of Birth: (mm-dd-yy)
Email Address:
Service Level: Medium

Register

```
<!DOCTYPE html PUBLIC "-//W3C//DTD XHTML 1.0 Transitional//EN"
"http://www.w3.org/TR/xhtml1/DTD/xhtml1-transitional.dtd">
<html xmlns="http://www.w3.org/1999/xhtml"
      xmlns:h="http://java.sun.com/jsf/html"
      xmlns:f="http://java.sun.com/jsf/core">
<h:head>
  <title>A Simple JavaServer Faces Registration Application</title>
</h:head>
<h:body>
  <h:form>
    <h2>JSF Registration App</h2>
    <h4>Registration Form</h4>
    <table>
      <tr>
        <td>First Name:</td>
        <td>
          <h:inputText label="First Name"
                       id="fname" value="#{userBean.firstName}"
                       required="true"/>
          <h:message for="fname" />
        </td>
      </tr>
      <tr>
        <td>Last Name:</td>
        <td>
          <h:inputText label="Last Name"
                       id="lname" value="#{userBean.lastName}"
                       required="true"/>
          <h:message for="lname" />
        </td>
      </tr>
      <tr>
        <td>Sex:</td>
        <td>
          <h:selectOneRadio label="Sex"
                            id="sex" value="#{userBean.sex}"
                            required="true">
            <f:selectItem itemLable="Male" itemValue="male" />
            <f:selectItem itemLable="Female" itemValue="female" />
          </h:selectOneRadio>
          <h:message for="sex" />
        </td>
      </tr>
      <tr>
        <td>Date of Birth:</td>
        <td>
          <h:inputText label="Date of Birth"
                       id="dob" value="#{userBean.dob}" required="true">
            <f:convertDateTime pattern="MM-dd-yy" />
          </h:inputText> (mm-dd-yy)
          <h:message for="dob" />
        </td>
      </tr>
```

```
        <tr>
          <td>Email Address:</td>
          <td>
            <h:inputText label="Email Address"
                         id="email" value="#{userBean.email}"
                         required="true"
                         validator="#{userBean.validateEmail}"/>
            <h:message for="email" />
          </td>
        </tr>
        <tr>
          <td>Service Level:</td>
          <td>
            <h:selectOneMenu label="Service Level"
                             value="#{userBean.serviceLevel}">
              <f:selectItem itemLabel="Medium" itemValue="medium" />
              <f:selectItem itemLabel="Basic" itemValue="basic" />
              <f:selectItem itemLabel="Premium" itemValue="premium" />
            </h:selectOneMenu>
          </td>
        </tr>
      </table>
      <p><h:messages /></p>
      <p><h:commandButton value="Register" action="confirm" /></p>
    </h:form>
  </h:body>
</html>
```

The first thing to notice are the three XML namespace directives at the top of the page, within the **<html>** element:

```
<html xmlns="http://www.w3.org/1999/xhtml"
    xmlns:h="http://java.sun.com/jsf/html"
    xmlns:f="http://java.sun.com/jsf/core">
```

The first is standard practice for XHTML pages. The second two directives allow the Facelets page to use the JSF Core and HTML tag libraries that are provided in the JSF specification, which in turn allows the Facelets page to use the underlying JSF UI components in the page. Keep in mind that JSF UI components are client-independent and can be used in different clients as long as there are corresponding renderers. The specifics on UI component rendering will be covered in later chapters, but for now, the main thing to know is that JSF is designed to work not only with traditional HTML browsers as the client, but with other types of clients as well, such as PDAs and other devices.

After the namespace directives, the next thing you'll notice are the **<h:head>** and **<h:body>** elements. These are new with JSF 2.0 and cause the **<head>** and **<body>** markup required of all XHTML pages to be rendered. Note that you could just as easily use the regular XHTML markup instead of the JSF components, but it is good practice to use the JSF components wherever possible. These components are useful when pages need to include JavaScript or CSS, as will be described in Chapter 12.

Next is the **<h:form>** tag. This tag is required to be the parent tag for all JSF UI components that can participate in an HTML form submission, such as buttons and text fields. We'll cover this in more detail in later chapters, but just remember that a JSF page is rendered for a client (such as a browser), and an identical component tree is instantiated into memory on the server with the View component at its root. You'll also notice that an HTML table is used to provide the layout structure of the form. As we'll cover later on, JSF also has components that provide layout structure as well, such as **<h:panelGrid>**, which provides a similar layout to an HTML table but without requiring row and cell tags. There is no requirement, however, to use one approach or the other.

Moving on to the first real, usable UI components, you see:

```
<h:inputText label="First Name"
  id="fname" value="#{userBean.firstName}"
  required="true"/>
<h:message for="fname" />
```

In order to require the user to enter a value, you'll notice the **required** attribute is set to "true." If the user attempts to leave the field blank while submitting the form, a built-in validation error message will appear exactly in the same location as the **<h:message>** tag. Notice that the message tag can actually reside anywhere in the page because it is linked to the **inputText** field by its ID "fname." This is an example of some of the built-in validation mechanisms provided by JSF. Notice the **label** attribute. The value of this attribute will be shown as the label next to the message telling the user that a value is required for this field. The next and most important thing to notice is the **value** attribute of the **inputText** tag: **#{userBean.firstName}**. This is known as a JSF *value expression* and provides direct linkage to the **firstName** property of the managed bean **userBean**.

So what is a *managed bean*? You may have heard the terms "inversion of control" or "dependency injection." These are simply fancy terms for a way to hook together different parts of your application without introducing too much interdependence ("tight coupling"). Managed beans do just that. Basically, a managed bean is an officially registered Java class for a JSF application. It is a POJO (Plain Old Java Object) that conforms to JavaBeans naming conventions. In order for a JSF application to refer to Java classes, and their methods and properties, it has to be available in the Java classpath and registered in **faces-config.xml** or with the appropriate annotation. Here are the Java language annotations that declare the class **UserBean** should be exposed as a managed bean in the application.

```
@ManagedBean
@SessionScoped
public class UserBean {...
```

The **@ManagedBean** annotation may have a **name** attribute, but if this is omitted, the system will take the unqualified Java classname, lowercase the first letter, and use the result as the name. In this case, the result is **userBean**. The equivalent **faces-config.xml** syntax for managed beans will be described in Chapter 5. Once registered, a managed bean can be referred to in any UI component attribute using JSF value expressions. Finally, notice the **@SessionScoped** annotation; this is similar but not exactly identical to the scope setting of a standard JSP **<jsp:useBean>** directive that allows the developer to control the lifespan of the Java class by designating it with one of the following settings: *request, view, session, application,* or *none.*

NOTE *Further coverage of managed beans and scope settings is provided in Chapter 5.*

Now that we've shown how to register a Java class as a managed bean, let's take a look at the actual managed bean, **UserBean.java**, which is used in this example application:

```
package com.jsfcompref.model;

import java.util.Date;
import javax.faces.application.FacesMessage;
import javax.faces.component.UIComponent;
import javax.faces.context.FacesContext;
import javax.faces.bean.ManagedBean;
import javax.faces.bean.SessionScoped;
import javax.faces.validator.ValidatorException;

@ManagedBean
@SessionScoped
public class UserBean {

    protected String firstName;
    protected String lastName;
    protected Date dob;
    protected String sex;
    protected String email;
    protected String serviceLevel = "medium";

    public String getFirstName() {
        return firstName;
    }

    public void setFirstName(String firstName) {
        this.firstName = firstName;
    }

    public String getLastName() {
        return lastName;
    }

    public void setLastName(String lastName) {
        this.lastName = lastName;
    }

    public Date getDob() {
        return dob;
    }

    public void setDob(Date dob) {
        this.dob = dob;
    }

    public String getSex() {
        return sex;
    }

    public void setSex(String sex) {
        this.sex = sex;
    }
```

```
    public String getEmail() {
        return email;
    }

    public void setEmail(String email) {
        this.email = email;
    }

    public String getServiceLevel() {
        return serviceLevel;
    }

    public void setServiceLevel(String serviceLevel) {
        this.serviceLevel = serviceLevel;
    }

    public void validateEmail(FacesContext context,
                              UIComponent toValidate,
            Object value) throws ValidatorException {
        String emailStr = (String) value;
        if (-1 == emailStr.indexOf("@")) {
            FacesMessage message = new FacesMessage("Invalid email
            address");
            throw new ValidatorException(message);
        }
  }

  public String addConfirmedUser() {
      boolean added = true; // actual application may fail to add user
      FacesMessage doneMessage = null;
      String outcome = null;
      if (added) {
        doneMessage = new FacesMessage("Successfully added new user");
        outcome = "done";
      } else {
        doneMessage = new FacesMessage("Failed to add new user");
        outcome = "register";
      }
      FacesContext.getCurrentInstance().addMessage(null, doneMessage);
      return outcome;
    }
}
```

As you can see, the **UserBean** Java class is a straightforward Java bean with various fields—**firstName, lastName, sex, dob** (Date of Birth), and **serviceLevel**—all of which are of type **String** except **dob**, which is of type **Date**. Notice also the getters and setters for each field as well. Each of these fields is represented in the **register.xhtml** registration form with corresponding JSF UI components, which are value bound to the bean properties. You'll also notice the extra methods: **validateEmail( )** and **addConfirmedUser( )**. These are custom methods that essentially do exactly what their name indicates. These methods are also bound to the UI components in the page. You will see how shortly.

Now that we've reviewed what managed beans are, as well as how to configure them and access their properties, let's get back to the **register.xhtml** page. As you continue browsing the rest of the page, you see a radio button **UI component** that is actually made from a combination of tags:

```
<h:selectOneRadio id="sex" value="#{userBean.sex}" required="true"/>
 <f:selectItem itemLabel="Male" itemValue="male"/>
 <f:selectItem itemLabel="Female" itemValue="female"/>
</h:selectOneRadio>
<h:message for="sex"/>
```

The main parent tag, **<h:selectOneRadio>**, is the one that is value-bound to the **userBean**'s gender property via the JavaBeans getter and setter. This means that whatever value is selected in the radio button control, it will be updated in the gender property of the managed bean when the form is submitted. For the individual select choices, the child tags **<f:selectItem>** provide both a displayed value or *itemLabel* along with an actual *itemValue*, which is the actual value used when a selection occurs. As before, a selection is required and if left blank, an error message will appear via the **<h:message>** tag.

Moving on to the next input field, you see the following code:

```
<h:inputText value="#{userBean.dob}" id="dob" required="true" >
 <f:convertDateTime pattern="MM-dd-yy"/>
</h:inputText> (mm-dd-yy)
<h:message for="dob"/>
```

As before, this input field is required, but this time instead of being bound to a bean property that is a **String**, this **inputText** component is bound to the **userBean.dob** property that is of type **java.util.Date**. In order to translate the incoming string value into the server-side **Date** type, a JSF converter is used with the tag **<f:convertDateTime>**. Notice the **pattern** attribute of the Converter tag also defines the expected date format pattern of "MM-dd-yy".

NOTE *To JSF, the uppercase "MM" actually means month and "mm" means minutes. However, most end users wouldn't necessarily know this, so the date pattern prompt is left intentionally in lowercase (mm-dd-yy).*

When the user enters a date string following the specified format, the Converter will convert it to a **Date** object and assign it to the **userBean.dob** property. However, if an incorrect date format pattern is used, a conversion error will be displayed.

To see what occurs when improper information is entered and submitted in the registration form, Figure 2-4 contains a screenshot of the registration page with various validation and converter error messages shown.

Notice the *Email Address* error message is shown when "foo" is entered? This is because the associated validation method **validateEmail( )** in the **UserBean** managed bean is not accepting the "foo" string as a valid e-mail address:

```
<h:inputText id="email" value="#{UserBean.email}" required="true"
 validator="#{UserBean.validateEmail}"/>
<h:message for="email"/>
```

This is actually the simplest form of custom validation in JavaServer Faces. Another method for creating custom validation can be achieved by creating a separate **Validator**

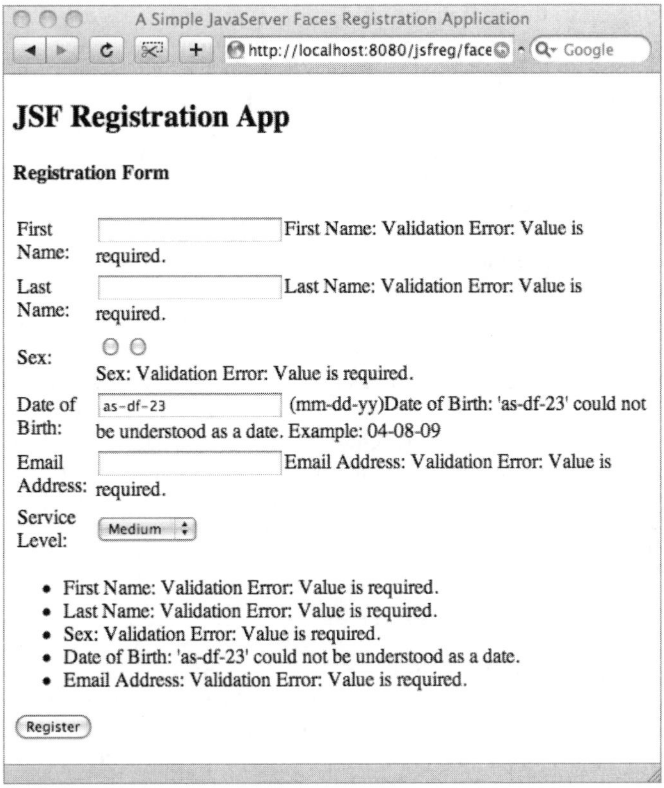

Figure 2-4 JSFReg with validation errors

class and then registering it with an annotation or an element in **faces-config.xml**. Also, an even more robust custom validation procedure involves using JSR-303 Bean Validation, a standard part of the Java EE 6 platform.

Later chapters will examine many more validation examples. To understand how the simple e-mail validation works, let's examine the **validateEmail( )** code again:

```
public void validateEmail(FacesContext context, UIComponent toValidate,
             Object value) throws ValidatorException {
 String eMail = (String) value;
 if(eMail.indexOf("@")<0) {
  FacesMessage message = new FacesMessage("Invalid email address");
  throw new ValidatorException(message);
 }
}
```

The key thing to notice in the custom validation method is that the **value** of the field is checked to see if it contains an @ symbol and if it's not found, an appropriate "Invalid e-mail . . ." **FacesMessage** is created. A **ValidatorException** is then thrown, which halts further processing and causes the error message to appear next to the e-mail input field.

Moving on to the next input field in the **register.jsp** page, you see another input select menu. This time it is created with the **<h:selectOneMenu>** tag.

```
<h:selectOneMenu value="#{userBean.serviceLevel}">
 <f:selectItem itemLabel="Basic" itemValue="basic"/>
 <f:selectItem itemLabel="Medium" itemValue="medium"/>
 <f:selectItem itemLabel="Premium" itemValue="premium"/>
</h:selectOneMenu>
```

This tag's usage is basically identical to the previous radio-button tag except that it renders a drop-down menu as opposed to a radio button. It has the same type of child **<f:selectItem>** tags as drop-down menu choices, but it renders the different select choices.

Finally, at the bottom of the page is an **<h:messages />** element and the **Register** button. It is good practice to put an **<h:messages>** element on every page to show any messages not otherwise accounted for. In this case, such a message is shown when the act of adding the validated user fails. When the **Register** button is clicked, it causes a form submission that triggers the JSF event model to perform a validation and update the Model or managed bean properties with the new input field values. To navigate to the confirmation page upon a successful validation of input data, the button has its **action** attribute set to the literal value "register."

```
<h:commandButton value="Register" action="confirm" />
```

The **h:commandButton** uses the JSF **action** "confirm" to navigate to the **confirm.xhtml** page by using a new feature in JSF 2.0 known as "implicit navigation." If there is no **faces-config.xml** file (or no navigation rules within that file), the value of the **action** attribute is inspected. If an XHTML page can be located with the same base name, it is used as the page that will be loaded when the button is pressed. In this case, the **confirm.xhtml** page will be shown.

Upon a successful navigation to the **confirm.xhtml** page, shown in Figure 2-5, the user sees the entered data along with buttons at the bottom of the page that provide the choice of either

FIGURE 2-5 The JSFReg confirmation page

returning to the registration form (**register.xhtml**) to revise any data entry, or proceeding on to the final **done.xhtml** page to complete the registration process.

The values for the registration data displayed in the confirmation page use the standard **<h:outputText>** tags such as:

```
<h:outputText value="#{userBean.firstName}"/>
...
<h:outputText value="#{userBean.lastName}"/>
```

The two buttons at the bottom of the page are coded as

```
<h:commandButton value="Edit" action="register" />
<h:commandButton value="Confirm" action="#{userBean.addConfirmedUser}" />
```

The **Edit** button returns the user to the **register.xhtml** page. The **Confirm** button specifies an *action method,* **addConfirmedUser( )**, that determines the outcome programmatically in the logic of the method. For this simple case, the action method causes a message stating **"Successfully added new user"** to the page and returns **"done"** as the outcome. This will cause the implicit navigation to take the user to the **done.xhtml** page.

```
public String addConfirmedUser() {
  boolean added = true; // actual application may fail to add user
  FacesMessage doneMessage = null;
  String outcome = null;
  if (added) {
    doneMessage = new FacesMessage("Successfully added new user");
    outcome = "done";
  } else {
    doneMessage = new FacesMessage("Failed to add new user");
    outcome = "register";
  }
  FacesContext.getCurrentInstance().addMessage(null, doneMessage);
  return outcome;
}
```

NOTE *In a real-world application, the method **addConfirmedUser( )** would typically call an external data management method that could interface with a database or other type of data service.*

The **addConfirmedUser( )** method takes care to consider both possible outcomes in attempting to add a new user, adding an appropriate descriptive message that will be displayed at the location of the **<h:messages/>** element in the page.

After clicking Confirm, the user is navigated to the final page of the application, **done.jsp**. This is shown in Figure 2-6.

The source code for this final page is similar to previous confirmation pages where the **outputText** UI components render the current values of the **UserBean** fields. However, this final page no longer needs the two Edit and Confirm buttons at the bottom of the page.

FIGURE 2-6 JSFReg's confirmation complete page

Building and Running the Application

Now that you have set up your JSF development environment and have reviewed the JSF application in detail, it's time to build and package the application for deployment.

The JSFReg application is composed of several files; however, only the Java source code files need to be compiled before you package and run the application. Our choice of Maven 2 as the technology for building and packaging the application makes this process very simple.

JSF Runtime Dependencies and Maven

When using Tomcat as the container, developers have the choice of including the JSF runtime libraries within each individual application or including them in the Tomcat container's **lib** directory. In the former case, the **pom.xml** file must be modified to direct Maven 2 to include the JSF runtime libraries. Edit the **pom.xml** file and replace

```
<dependency>
 <groupId>javax.faces</groupId>
 <artifactId>jsf-api</artifactId>
 <version>2.0 </version>
 <scope>provided</scope>
</dependency>
```

with

```
<dependency>
 <groupId>javax.faces</groupId>
 <artifactId>jsf-api</artifactId>
 <version>2.0 </version>
</dependency>
```

```
<dependency>
 <groupId>com.sun.faces</groupId>
 <artifactId>jsf-impl</artifactId>
 <version>2.0.0-SNAPSHOT</version>
</dependency>
```

Note that the **<scope>provided</scope>** has been removed and an additional dependency with the **<artifactId>jsf-impl</artifactId>** has been added. These actions cause Maven 2 to bundle the JSF runtime libraries into the completed product. It is easier to simply copy the runtime libraries into the Tomcat Container's **lib** directory, and this technique will be assumed for the rest of the book. Note that proper Java EE containers such as Sun's Glassfish already have the JSF libraries in the proper place.

At the command line, change to the directory containing the file **pom.xml** and type

```
mvn install
```

The **pom.xml** file for this example directs Maven 2 to traverse the source files found in subdirectories of the directory in which the **pom.xml** file is found and build a standard Java EE Web Application Archive, which is also packaged as a Java JAR file named **jsfreg.war** and located in the **target** subdirectory. This table describes the process by which this building and packaging occurs.

Source File Type	Source File Location Relative to pom.xml	Action Performed	Final Location Relative to pom.xml
Java source code	**src/main/java/** and its subdirectories, corresponding to the package name of each class	Compile with Java compiler	**target/jsfreg/WEB-INF/classes/** and its subdirectories, corresponding to the Java package name of each class
.xhtml files	**src/main/webapp/** and its subdirectories	Copied	**target/jsfreg/** and any subdirectories corresponding to **src/main/webapp/**
web.xml	**src/main/webapp/WEB-INF/**	Copied	**target/jsfreg/WEB-INF/**

After the **mvn** build completes successfully, a new directory, **target**, has been created, which contains **jsfreg** and **classes** subdirectories as well as a **jsfreg.war** file. The **jsfreg.war** file is the Web Application Archive file. The **jsfreg** directory is the root web application directory from which the **jsfreg.war** file was created. Such a directory is known as an "exploded war" because if one were to expand the **jsfreg.war** file into a directory, one would end up with the same arrangement of files and directories as is present in the **jsfreg** directory. The **classes** directory is an intermediate directory created by Maven 2 and is of no interest here. To clean up the compiled files, run the command

```
mvn clean
```

at the command line.

Deploying and Running the Application

Once you have packaged your application as a **.war** or exploded war, follow the steps for deploying it in the container of your choice. Web Application runtimes, such as Tomcat and Glassfish support the deployment of **.war** files and exploded war directories. If you choose to deploy an exploded war, you will have the added benefit of being able to edit your **.xhtml** files while the application is deployed and see the result of your changes simply by reloading the page in the browser. When using this development style, take care to ensure that any changes you make to the source files are preserved outside of the exploded war directory.

The default network port for most containers is **8080**; therefore, we will use that port in all the example URLs in this book. Furthermore, we will assume that the server is running on the same computer on which the example is developed. The TCP network stack ensures the hostname **localhost** refers to this computer. To access the JSFReg application, point your browser to **http://localhost:8080/jsfreg/**. You'll notice that the name of your **.war** file or exploded war directory name is used for the URL of your application. Because you packaged the application in a file called **jsfreg.war**, **/jsfreg/** is used in the application's URL.

When you first access the **http://localhost:8080/jsfreg/** URL, the **<welcome-file>faces/register.xhtml</welcome-file>** statement in **web.xml** will redirect the browser to the URL **http://localhost:8080/jsfreg/faces/register.xhtml**.

Reviewing the Key Portions of the Application

Before moving on to the more advanced features of JavaServer Faces technology, let's quickly review the core areas of JavaServer Faces discussed in the process of building the JSFReg application.

A JSF application is essentially a standard Java EE Web application but with the following specific aspects:

- A specific configuration in the **web.xml** file that specifies the Faces Controller servlet and its url-pattern.
- A collection of Facelets **.xhtml** files.
- One or more managed Java Objects. These can be simple JSF Managed Beans, annotated with the **@ManagedBean** annotation or declared with the **<managed-bean>** element in a **faces-config.xml** file. They can also be Spring Beans, Enterprise JavaBeans, or several other kinds of managed Java Objects.

In building this example application, you have seen that basic JSF development is a straightforward process, which typically involves:

- Building Java classes and adding them as JSF managed beans
- Creating Facelets pages to contain JSF UI component tags that are bound to the managed bean's properties and methods
- Defining how the user will traverse from page to page within the application

The JSFReg example used the Standard HTML UI components provided in the JSF Reference Implementation to build a registration form with different types of input fields, menus, and buttons that were bound to a managed bean's properties and methods. For JSFReg we specified both built-in validation and data conversion for the input fields. A custom validation method was also built and associated with an e-mail input field to validate an e-mail address. Finally, we devised a basic navigation model and bound the command buttons and links to these navigation cases.

Now that you have seen a complete, working example, you should have a solid understanding of the basic structure of a JSF application. It's now time to move on to more advanced aspects of JavaServer Faces.

CHAPTER 3

The JavaServer Faces Request Processing Lifecycle

The preceding chapter presented a simple example of a JavaServer Faces application and introduced many of the practical aspects of JSF. There is, however, another important part of JSF that must be discussed before we can begin an in-depth examination of each JSF feature. This is the *request processing lifecycle.* The request processing lifecycle serves as the "behind-the-scenes" engine that makes JavaServer Faces possible. This chapter examines the key concepts behind the JavaServer Faces request processing lifecycle and explains how it processes Web requests in a well-defined, event-based manner. A thorough understanding of the request processing lifecycle is important because its various phases will be referred to numerous times in later chapters where more advanced JSF development topics are covered.

A High-Level Overview of the JSF Request Processing Lifecycle

Historically, the bulk of the development required for a Web application has been devoted to processing HTTP requests from Web clients. As the Web transformed from a traditional, static document delivery model (in which static Web pages were simply requested without parameters) to a dynamic environment (with Web applications processing numerous incoming parameters), the need to process increasingly complex requests has grown substantially. This has resulted in Web application development becoming rather tedious. For example, consider the following code used in either a Java servlet or a JSP scriptlet to process the incoming request parameters **firstname** and **lastname**:

```
String firstname = request.getParameter("firstname");
String lastname = request.getParameter("lastname");
// Do something with firstname and lastname
```

Now, consider that most advanced Web applications today process hundreds if not thousands of parameters and you'll see how this approach to processing parameters can easily become quite cumbersome.

As any experienced Web developer knows, writing code to process incoming request parameters usually involves the following tasks:

- Providing a context for this request, including any state that may be left over from previous requests.
- Performing validation and conversion to server-side data types on the incoming data as well as initiating error messages when validation/conversion fails.
- Updating server-side data objects with the new data.
- Invoking any server-side applications that perform tasks such as issuing queries on a database.
- Accounting for any state that needs to be present on the next request.
- Rendering a response back to the client, including the "follow-up" requests made by the browser for images, scripts, and style sheets.

Any application with a Web-based user interface must account for these tasks, regardless of the use of JavaScript or Ajax and regardless of the kind of framework or programming language(s) used. The necessity for handling these tasks follows as a side effect of using a Web browser to display a user interface while connecting to a standard Web server using the HTTP network protocol as the only transport between the browser and the server. Fortunately, these tasks are what the request processing lifecycle performs automatically in a consistent, event-based manner.

EXPERT GROUP INSIGHT *Of all the elements of JavaServer Faces that the Expert Group debated, the request processing lifecycle was the one that had the most input from the widest range of members and evolved the most over the development of the specification. For example, initially, the view description was required to be in a separate XML file, in addition to the JSP page. This requirement was lifted with the invention of the* ***ViewHandler*** *class, which came about during discussions of the lifecycle.*

What Exactly Does the Request Processing Lifecycle Do?

In short, the request processing lifecycle performs all of the necessary back-end processing for which one would otherwise have to write his or her own code. The lifecycle directs the processing of incoming request parameters, and it manages a server-side set of UI components and synchronizes them to what the user sees in a client browser. It also satisfies follow-up requests for images, style sheets, scripts, and other kinds of resources required to complete the rendering of the UI.

How Does It Differ from Other Web Technologies?

In contrast to other more traditional Web technologies, ranging from CGI and Java servlets to frameworks like Struts, the request processing lifecycle performs a majority of the common server-side Web development tasks automatically in a well-defined, event-based way.

With frameworks such as Struts, where some of the request processing is more formalized in code with Form Beans and Struts Actions, the actual processing of the data is still done at a lower level compared to JSF. The Struts programming model provides less of an abstraction from the servlet API than that provided by JSF. For example, in Struts, you can define a Form Bean that represents the properties of your submitted form:

```
<form-bean name="loginbean" type="org.apache.struts.action.DynaActionForm">
  <form-property name="userid" type="java.lang.String"/>
  <form-property name="password" type="java.lang.String"/> </form-bean>
```

Once it is defined, you can access the field values in your application, as shown here:

```
String userid = (string)((DynaActionForm)form).get("userid");
```

This is very similar to what you can do with JSF; however, with Struts you don't have the ability to *bind* the field properties directly to properties of Java classes and have their values synchronized automatically upon form submissions.

Automatic Server-Side View Management and Synchronization

As shown in Figure 3-1, the JSF request processing lifecycle's ability to automatically synchronize server-side Java Bean properties to a hierarchical set of components that are based on the UI presented to the client user is a major advantage over other Web technologies. This capability is known as "state management" and is a cornerstone of the value provided by JSF.

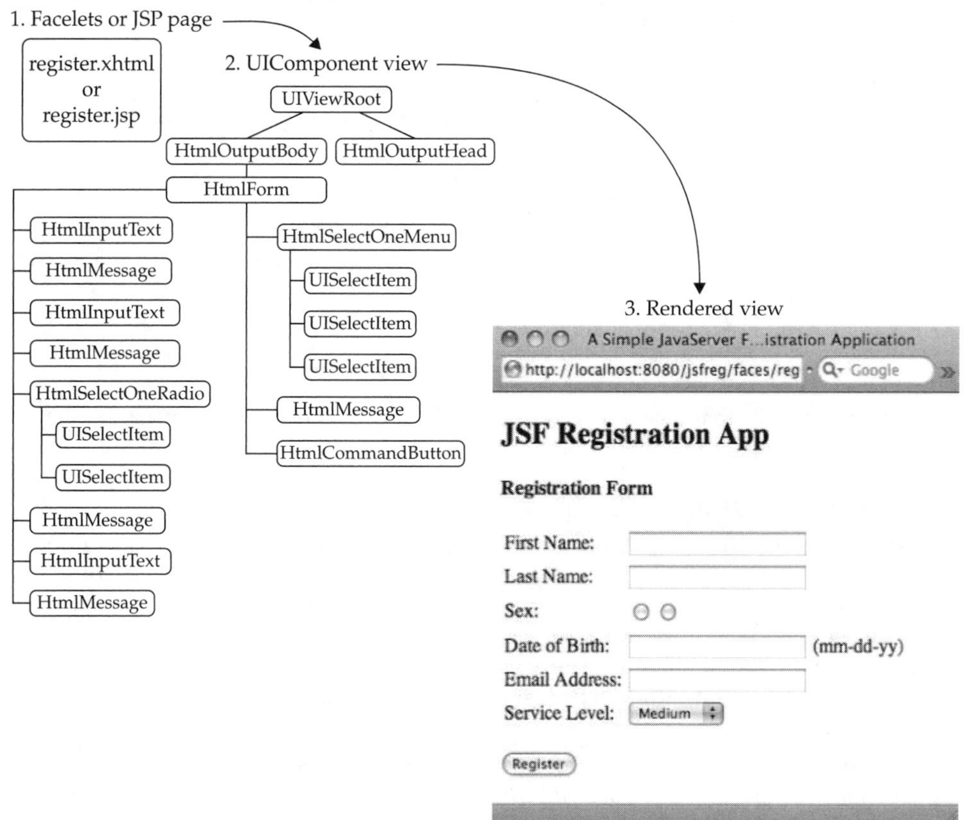

FIGURE 3-1 A server-side representation of the client's UI

A brief aside about the evolution of Web applications will set the stage for a better understanding of state management in JSF.

The success of the Web as a platform for software is due mainly to its simplicity and versatility. The user sits in front of a piece of software that understands a standard, lightweight syntax for describing a user interface (HTML). Information encoded with this syntax is delivered to the user-agent with a standard lightweight network protocol (HTTP). The user-agent responds to user actions and initiates further HTTP requests to the server as necessary, and the cycle continues. For the Web to reach as wide an audience as possible, both HTML and HTTP needed to be as simple as possible, but no simpler, and certainly needed to be open standards.

One key ingredient in this successful recipe is the "statelessness" of HTTP. Stateless means that one transaction between a client and server has no memory of the previous transaction. Unfortunately, this can be a problem for sophisticated Web applications that require a persistent state. JavaServer Faces solves this problem by automatically maintaining a server-side *View* that represents the important parts of the current state of the client. This allows the JSF developer to focus on the server-side components, letting the request processing lifecycle, or "plumbing," take care of the synchronization of the server-side View and what is presented in the client browser. The often-tedious job of writing code to handle each individual request value or change in state of the UI is handled automatically by the JavaServer Faces request processing lifecycle through a set of *phases* during which specific tasks are performed to process the data in a consistent manner.

JSF 2.0 Tip *JSF 2.0 has optimized state management to greatly reduce the cost of maintaining state while also simplifying the task of writing UI Components that maintain state.*

During the execution of the lifecycle, the JSF runtime will

1. Determine if this is a page request or a resource request. If this is a resource request, it will serve the bytes of the resource to the user-agent. Otherwise, it will load the Facelets or JSP page.
2. Create a server-side representation of the UI.
3. Produce markup suitable for rendering in the browser.

The JSF lifecycle automatically keeps track of the changed portions of the state, so the client-side view is always in step with the server-side view.

The Request Processing Lifecycle Phases

The processing of incoming request data often requires different types of jobs, including: checking if the incoming data is valid, triggering server-side application logic to fulfill the request, and finally rendering the response to the client. The JSF request processing lifecycle performs these tasks in a consistent order and is governed by a set of well-defined phases. This approach allows each phase to clearly state the preconditions that exist before executing the phase, and the post conditions that exist after it is executed.

JSF 2.0 Tip *Follow-up requests for resources referenced in the page markup, such as images, scripts, and style sheets, can be handled by JSF. While this behavior does indeed happen as a part of the JSF lifecycle, it is not a part of the core page processing lifecycle and is best described in the context of the* ***UIComponent*** *system, in Chapter 7.*

Here are the lifecycle phases:

- **Restore View** Restores or creates a server-side component tree (View) in memory to represent the UI information from a client.
- **Apply Request Values** Updates the server-side components with fresh data from the client.
- **Process Validations** Performs validation and data type conversion on the new data.
- **Update Model Values** Updates any server-side Model objects with new data.
- **Invoke Application** Invokes any application logic needed to fulfill the request and navigate to a new page if needed.
- **Render Response** Saves state and renders a response to the requesting client.

Figure 3-2 shows a high-level view of how these phases work together to form the request processing lifecycle. As you can see, it performs all the tasks for processing incoming data in a Web application. We'll be referring to the different events and phases in this figure throughout the rest of this chapter, and throughout the book.

Now, let's drill down and examine exactly what happens during the processing of each lifecycle phase.

Restore View

As previously mentioned, the Faces View is a server-side tree of UI components that provides a mirror representation of the user interface presented in a client (see Figure 3-3). It is the job of the *Restore View* phase to either restore an existing View from a previous transaction or create a fresh View based on a new request. If the request is a new one ("nonpostback"), a new View is created and will be stored in a parent container object known as the **FacesContext**. The **FacesContext** serves as storage for all of the data pertinent to the current request's run through the request processing lifecycle.

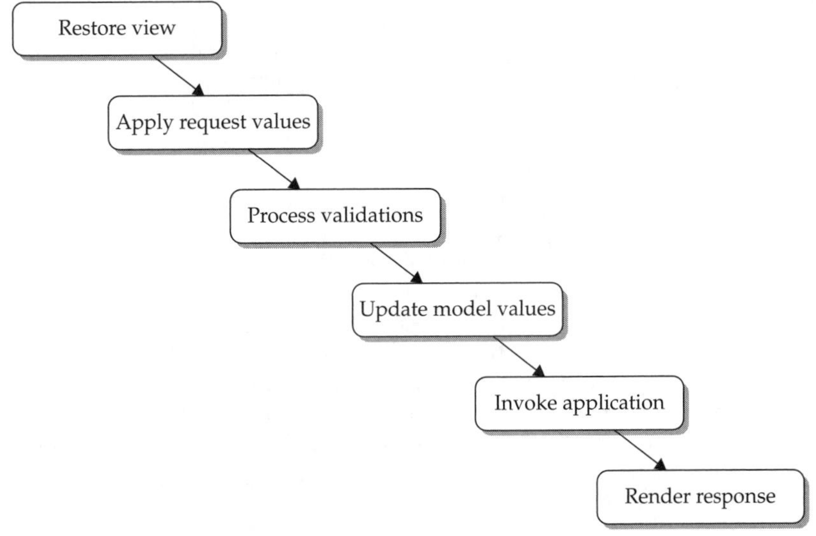

Figure 3-2 The JavaServer Faces request processing lifecycle

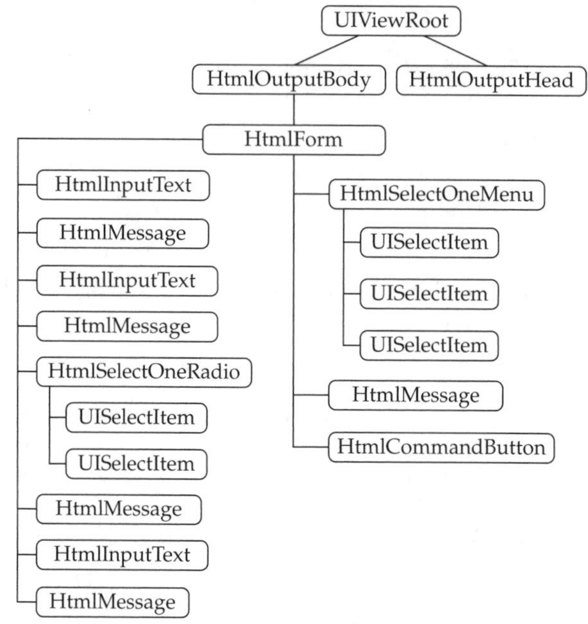

FIGURE 3-3 The server-side UI component tree, also known as the "View"

Web developers needn't worry about application data in the **FacesContext** being accidentally mixed from multiple user requests because the servlet API guarantees that operations on a request are thread-safe—that is, all operations on the **FacesContext** are guaranteed to occur on a single thread, per user request.

JSF 2.0 TIP *"Page Parameters," a popular feature from the JBoss Seam Framework, have been introduced to JSF under the name of "View Parameters." This feature will be fully covered in Chapter 6. However, it must be mentioned here that View Parameters are full JSF* ***UIComponents*** *and thus are a part of the normal request processing lifecycle. View Parameters allow JSF to handle incoming request parameters even on a "nonpostback" request.*

Apply Request Values

After the View has been restored, the next phase, known as the *Apply Request Values* phase, performs the job of processing the incoming request values or name-value pairs of information. Each UI component node in the View hierarchy is now able to take on the updated values sent by the client as shown in Figure 3-4.

Behind the scenes, the JSF runtime applies request values to UI components by calling a high-level method (**processDecodes( )**) on the View (or **UIViewRoot**) of the UI component tree. This causes all of the child components to call their **processDecodes( )** methods recursively. As you will see in Chapter 11, the **processDecodes( )** method, or more specifically the **decode( )** method of UI components, is the method that allows the component to "decode" the incoming request name-value pairs and apply a matching new incoming value to the **value** attribute of the UI component.

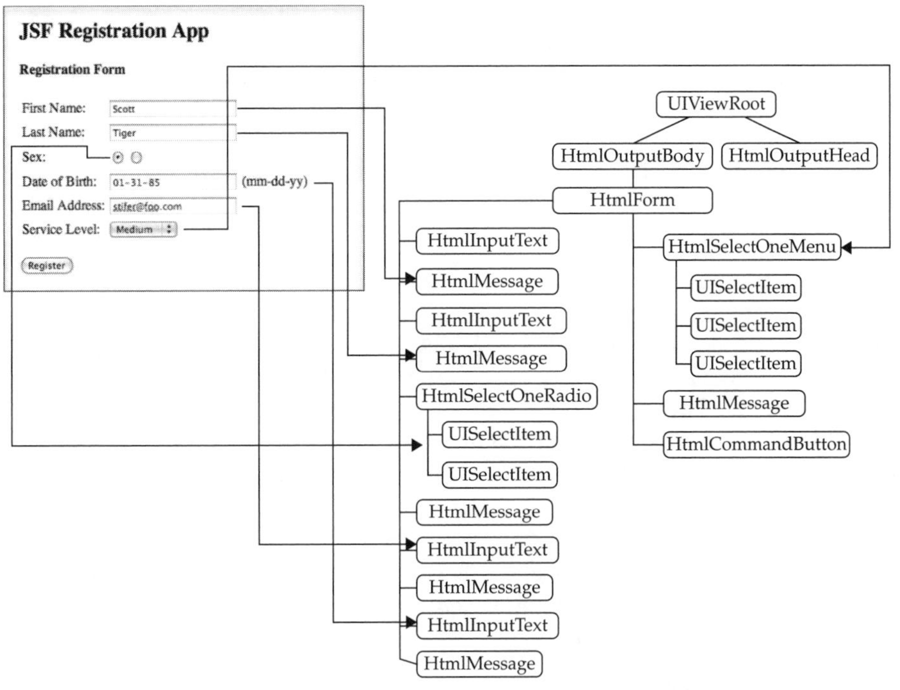

FIGURE 3-4 Applying the request values

It should be pointed out that only UI components that are capable of holding a value (such as an input field) can have new values applied to them. In general, there are two types of components: those that have values, such as text fields, check boxes, and labels; and those that cause actions, such as buttons and links. All components that have a **value** attribute implement the **ValueHolder** interface. All form element–type components that have values that are editable by the user implement the **EditableValueHolder** interface. All components that cause actions (buttons or links) implement the **ActionSource** interface.

***JSF 1.2* TIP** *For JSF 1.2, action components implement the ActionSource2 interface instead of ActionSource. ActionSource2 extends from JSF 1.1's ActionSource and allows for usage of 1.2's new Unified EL. Details on 1.2's Unified EL is provided in Chapter 5.*

For example, a button (**UICommand** or any component that implements **ActionSource**) doesn't get updated with a new value during form submission; it just needs to record whether or not it was clicked on. If clicked, this results in an event, called an action event (**ActionEvent**), being queued. Later you'll see exactly what an action event is and how it allows for execution of custom code that corresponds to a button or link click.

***JSF 2.0* TIP** *JSF 2.0 introduced a new class of events, called System Events, that will be covered in Chapter 9. Briefly, System Events provide a very precise way to observe the state of the JSF lifecycle and are used by JSF to enable many of the new features in JSF 2.0, such as Ajax and enhanced state saving.*

Although the request processing lifecycle processes the different phases in a consistent manner, the execution order of the phases can be altered for special cases. For example, you may want to add a Cancel button to a form. When clicked, it will skip all validation and simply navigate to another page without processing the values in a form. To alter the processing order of the request processing lifecycle, simply set the **immediate** attribute on a component. As described later in this chapter, setting the **immediate** attribute causes a different effect on different components.

Process Validations

Once the Apply Request Values phase is completed, the *Process Validations* phase, where conversion and validation of the incoming data occurs, is performed. (Data type conversion and validation is explained in detail in Chapter 8.) The JSF runtime initiates this phase by calling a master **processValidators( )** method (on the **UIViewRoot** instance), which is similar to the **processDecodes( )** method in that it recursively propagates down the component tree calling each component's **processValidators( )** method. When each component's **processValidators( )** method is called, any converter or validator associated with the component will be invoked.

NOTE *Data type conversion actually occurs before validation but is still initiated in the same Process Validations phase. This is needed because in order to perform a validation, the data must first be converted to its server-side data type.*

As you saw in the JSFReg example in Chapter 2, UI components can have validators and converters associated with them in several ways. In the example, a validation requirement was associated with some of the components either by setting an attribute of the component itself (such as setting the **required** attribute to "true" for an **inputText** component) or by registering custom validation code (such as when the e-mail validation method was attached to the component by setting its **validator** attribute). The example in Chapter 2 also had a converter associated with the "date of birth" (dob) **inputText (UIInput)** component by inserting a **convertDateTime** converter tag as a child of the input component.

Any component failing validation (or conversion) will have its **valid** property set to "false" and a **FacesMessage** will be queued onto the **FacesContext** as shown in Figure 3-5. Later, when the response is rendered back to the user (in the *Render Response* phase), the messages can be displayed using the Faces **Message** or **Messages** component so the user can correct and re-submit.

Update Model Values

Assuming the incoming data has passed validation and conversion, it is now time for the data to be promoted and assigned to any Model objects that have been *value bound* to the UI component. Again, recall the example in Chapter 2. In it, we created a Java class, **UserBean**, which was registered as a managed bean, and bound its properties to the different UI components on the page using JSF Expression Language. It is during the *Update Model Values* phase that the actual managed bean or Model object's properties are updated with the new values of the UI components to which they were bound.

The actual mechanism behind this is similar to the other phases. A master **processUpdates( )** method is called on the **UIViewRoot** instance, which initiates a cascading set of **processUpdates( )** method calls. The **UIInput** class overrides the **processUpdates( )**

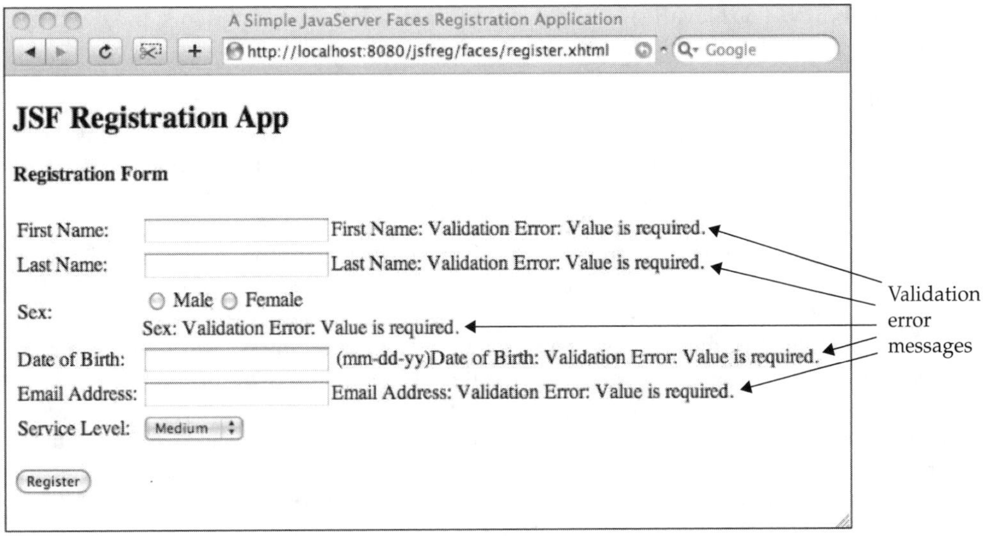

FIGURE 3-5 Encountering validation and conversion errors in the Process Validations phase

method to take the additional action of calling **updateModel( )**. This is logical since **UIInput**-type components (that is, input fields, select menus) are the only type of components that can pass user input value on to a model property. As shown in Figure 3-6, at the end of this phase, any value-bound properties of any Model objects (managed beans) are updated with the new values from the components. This phase accounts for part of the magic of JavaServer Faces.

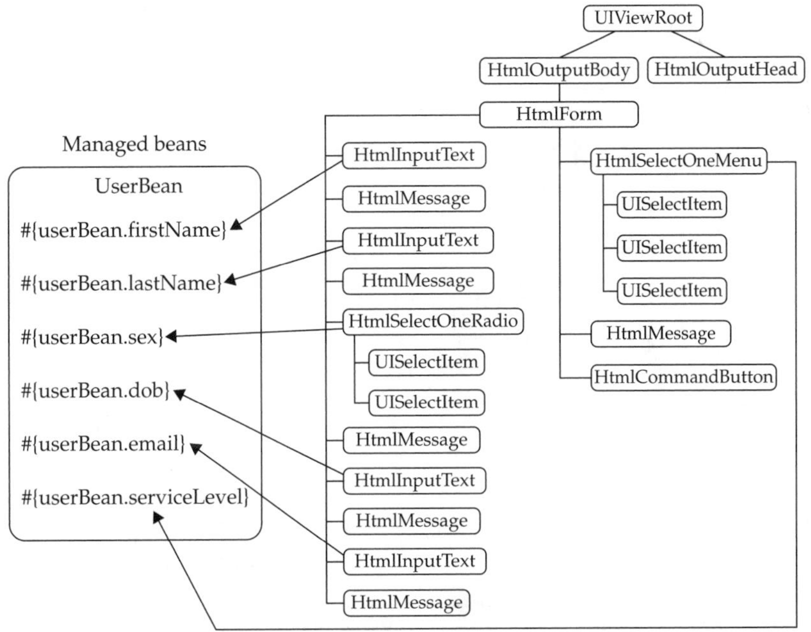

FIGURE 3-6 Updating Model object properties in the Update Model Values phase

Once you've bound your JavaBeans properties to a set of JSF UI components, they will be updated automatically without requiring any manual coding.

Invoke Application

So far you've seen how the JSF request processing lifecycle performs the job of taking incoming data from a Web request, validates and/or converts it to the appropriate server-side data type, and then assigns it to a model object. For Web developers this is only half of the job of writing Web applications. The other half consists of taking the incoming data and actually doing something with it, such as invoking an external method to process the data. This is where the *Invoke Application* phase comes in.

As explained earlier in this chapter, UI components can either hold values (implement **EditableValueHolder**) or they can be a source of an **ActionEvent** (implement **ActionSource**), such as when a button (**UICommand**) is clicked. It is during the Invoke Application phase that any custom action code, also known as an *action method* or *action listener method,* is invoked.

Behind the scenes, it is in the Invoke Application phase that the **processApplication( )** method of the **UIViewRoot** is called, and it broadcasts any queued events for this phase to each **UIComponent** that implements **ActionSource** (or **ActionSource2** for JSF 1.2). This is achieved by calling each **UIComponent**'s **broadcast( )** method, which essentially "fires" *action events,* and subsequently any action listeners will process these action events. Custom action methods or action listener methods can be written and bound to **UIComponent**s (which implement **ActionSource**) to process action events using a *default action listener.* Writing custom action methods or action listener methods and binding them to **ActionSource UIComponent**s provides the developer with a hook into the request processing lifecycle where a developer can then call any custom logic. This is illustrated in Figure 3-7.

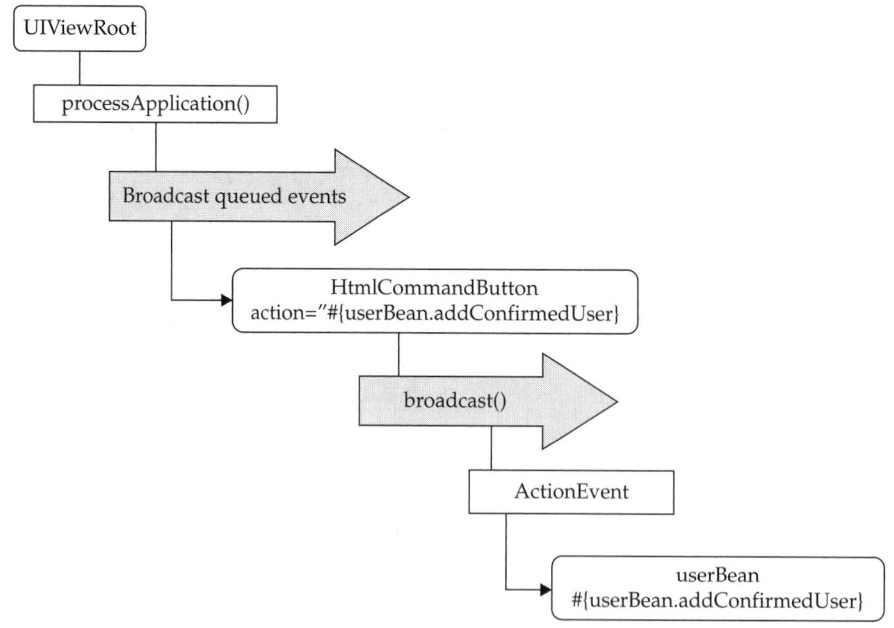

FIGURE 3-7 Invoking custom application logic in the Invoke Application phase

Chapter 9 will revisit exactly how the JSF event model works and will provide more detail on the exact sequence of how Faces events are processed.

It should be noted that navigations to different pages also occur in the Invoke Application phase. Chapter 6 will review exactly how this occurs by describing a basic *login* application that uses a simple action method that is bound to a *login* (**UICommand**) button. When a user clicks the button, it fires an action event, which in turn calls the custom action method during the Invoke Application phase to process the login credentials. Remember that this code will only execute if the incoming data has passed the earlier phases where conversion and validation was performed. When login is successful, a navigation to a new page occurs.

Render Response

Now we come to the final phase of the JSF request processing lifecycle, where the response is rendered. To render the entire response back to the client, once again a cascading set of **encodeXX( )** methods are called on each component. Encode methods are how UI components (or more specifically, their renderers) render the component to the client. The rendered markup language can be anything, such as HTML, WML, XML, and so on.

In addition to rendering the response to the client, the *Render Response* phase also saves the current state of the View in order to make it accessible and restorable upon subsequent Web requests. Figure 3-8 illustrates how the response has been rendered in a client markup. At this point the current state of the View is saved for future requests.

One other point: There are actually some more intricate, behind-the-scenes details associated with the Render Response phase that go beyond the scope of this chapter. These include: handling situations where static content, also referred to as "template" source, is interleaved with dynamic content from the components; dealing with a variety of dynamic output sources; and collating them together in a single viewable response while preserving the correct ordering. Normally, you won't need to deal with these details when using JSF.

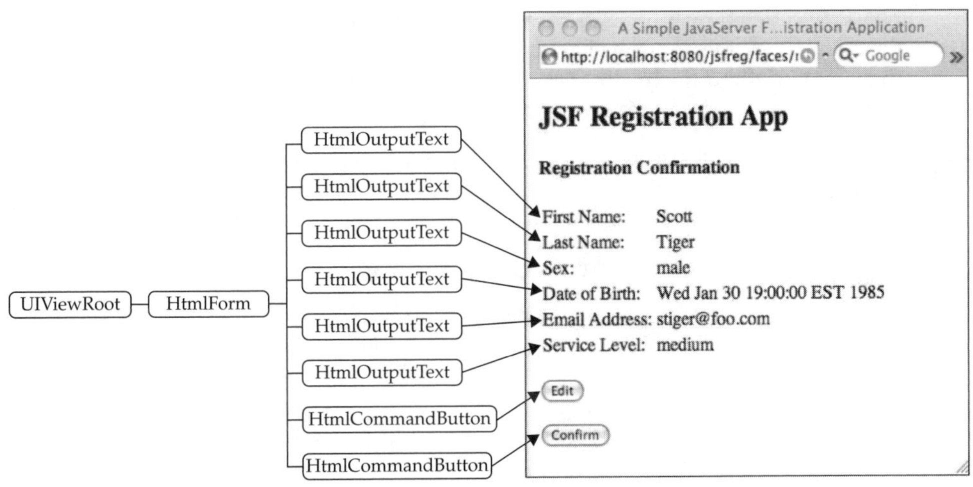

FIGURE 3-8 Rendering the response and saving state in the Render Response phase

Observing the Request Processing Lifecycle in Action

Now that you have seen the theory behind each request processing lifecycle phase, it's time to see the lifecycle in action. Recall the JSF Registration (JSFReg) application shown in Chapter 2 and again here in Figure 3-9. We will step through the lifecycle phases as a user interacts with the application and submits the registration form (**register.xhtml**).

1. **Initial request to view the register.xhtml page** In order to view the registration form page in the first place, a user submits a request to the URL of the register page, which triggers a run through the request processing lifecycle in an abbreviated fashion. The request is processed first by the Faces Controller servlet, which creates a **FacesContext** instance for this request and initiates a call to the lifecycle. Since this is an initial request (also referred to as a "non-postback" request) to view the registration page, the Restore View phase creates an empty View (**UIViewRoot**) component tree and stores it in the **FacesContext** instance.

   After the View is created, the lifecycle immediately proceeds directly to the Render Response phase, since there was no incoming field data in the request to validate or process (also referred to as a "non-postback" request). It is during this phase that the empty View component tree is populated with the components that are referenced in the source of the registration page and represent the input fields and submit button. Once the tree is populated, the components then render themselves to the client. At the same time, the state of the View component tree is saved for future requests. The user now sees the registration page rendered in a browser.

2. **User enters invalid data in the registration page** Let's say the user forgets to enter his last name and also enters the wrong format for the date, and then clicks Register (as illustrated in Figure 3-10).

   As the JSF runtime receives the request, it enters the initial Restore/Create View phase, and this time it restores the earlier View component tree that was saved after the user's previous request. This is commonly referred to as a "postback" because the HTTP method for this request is POST, since it is "posting" new form data. The Apply Request Values phase is then entered, and the components are updated

Figure 3-9 **register.xhtml**: the registration page of the JSFReg application

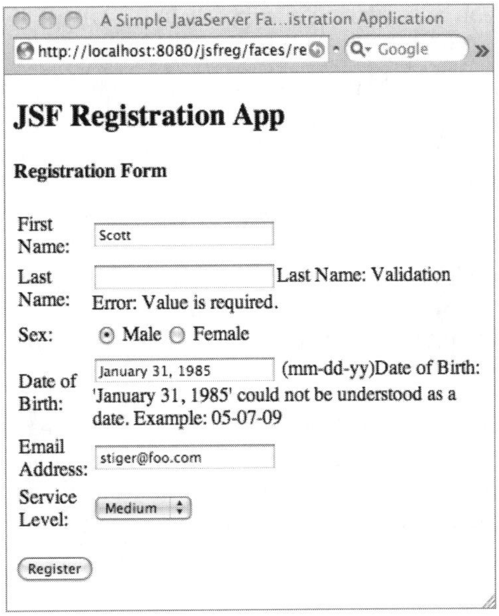

Figure 3-10 Entering invalid data in the registration page

with the incoming values from the request, even though they may not be fully valid yet. No errors occur here because each UI component simply stores the *submitted values* as **String** values of the request parameter, not the actual converted (server-side data type) or validated value. The UI component stores this in a special preconverted/validated **submittedValue** JavaBean property, which literally stores the **String** value of a request parameter.

As the Apply Request Values phase completes, the Process Validations phase is initiated. At this point a conversion error occurs when the incoming date value cannot be converted to a **java.util.Date** data type, which corresponds to the managed bean **UserBean**'s "dob" property, because of its invalid format. A message is queued, the component is marked invalid, and the processing continues. The remaining valid field values are applied to their respective UI components.

As each UI component has its validate method called, the component that is supposed to be holding the **lastName** value encounters a validation error because no value was supplied in the postback request. Recall that we set the "required" attribute of the Last Name input field to "true." As a result of the validation error, the lifecycle sets the state of the **lname** (last name) **UIInput** component to invalid and queues the appropriate Faces message indicating that the field requires a value. At this point the Process Validations phase is complete.

Because there were validation and conversion errors, the lifecycle jumps directly to the Render Response phase, which then renders the same registration page (**register.xhtml**) with the appropriate error messages next to the last name field and the date field. Recall that individual Message components were assigned to each input field component by assigning their IDs, as shown here:

```
<h:inputText value="#{UserBean.lastName}" required="true" id="lname"/>
<h:message for="lname"/>
```

In addition to rendering a response to the client, the Render Response phase also saves the View component tree for future requests.

3. **User corrects validation errors and resubmits the form** Upon seeing the error messages in the response, the user corrects the form by supplying a last name and entering a properly formatted date value and resubmits. This time, as the request is processed, the Restore View phase restores the saved View tree and proceeds to the Apply Request Values phase, where the new values are applied to the View component tree. The phase transitions to the Process Validations phase, where this time no validation or conversion errors are encountered. The Update Model Values phase is then triggered. At this point, the managed bean's (**UserBean**) properties are now updated with the new values that were submitted in the form, as illustrated in Figure 3-11.

Once the Update Model Values phase completes, the next phase that is triggered is the Invoke Application phase. Recall that the Invoke Application phase provides a way for JSF developers to invoke any custom logic. For example, the application may need to execute code to query a database. The way this is performed is through action methods, which are invoked during the Invoke Application phase, but only if any action events are in the queue,

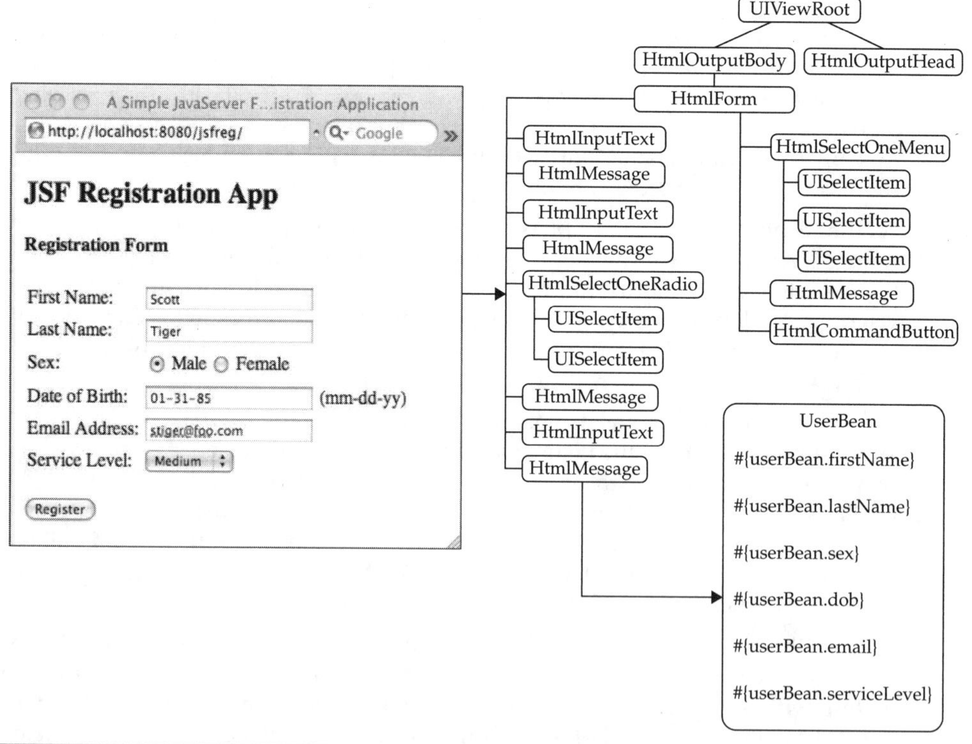

FIGURE 3-11 Updating the **UserBean** Model object with the validated values

such as when a button or link is clicked. With the JSFReg example, an action event is queued when the Register button is clicked, but since the **action** attribute of the Register button (**UICommand** component) is hard-coded to the literal value "register," no custom action method will be invoked and the Invoke Application phase completes. At this point the navigation handler processes the action event, and a navigation will occur. The result of the navigation event will then be displayed in the final Render Response phase.

Let's review that again. Once the registration page has successfully passed validation and the **UserBean** managed bean has been updated with the values submitted in the form, the lifecycle comes to the Render Response phase, where a formatted response needs to be sent back to the user. At this point, the response to be sent back to the client has to be determined. The navigation handler is responsible for determining whether to simply respond with the same page, or to *navigate* to a new page. Recall that the JSFReg example has an **action** attribute hard-coded to "register," and since this corresponds to a navigation rule (case) defined in the **faces-config.xml** file, a response will be rendered of the new page being navigated to (**confirm.xhtml**). Remember that if either the registration button did not have its **action** attribute set or there was no corresponding navigation rule, the response rendered would simply be the same page and no navigation would occur. Figure 3-12 illustrates how the **NavigationHandler** uses the rules defined in the **faces-config.xml** to determine if a navigation is needed.

NOTE *A detailed description of the Faces Navigation Model is provided in Chapter 6.*

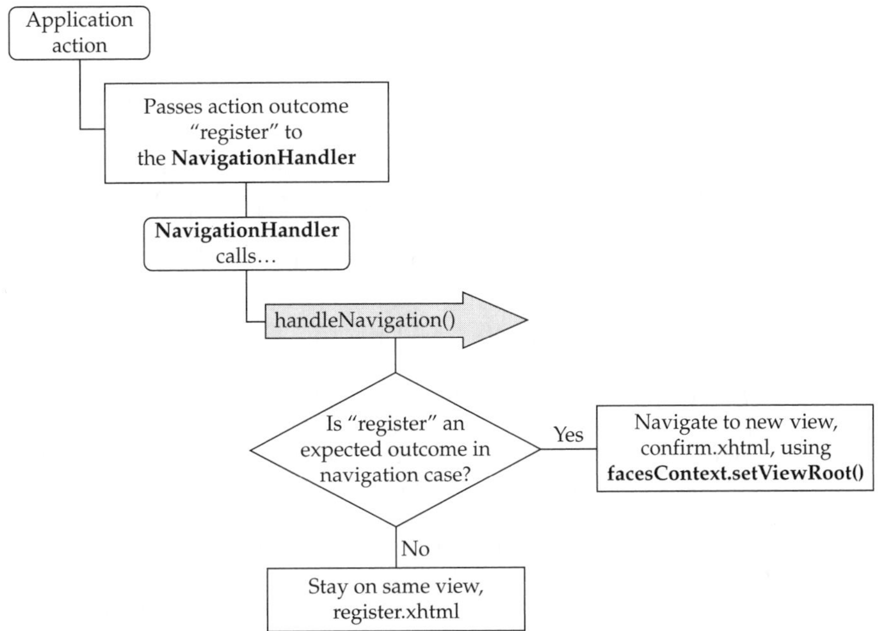

FIGURE 3-12 Rendering a response based on the outcome of an action in the Invoke Application phase

Advanced Topics Related to the Request Processing Lifecycle

Now that you've seen how the JSF request processing lifecycle works under default circumstances for a basic form, let's look at some of the slightly more complex examples.

Using the immediate Attribute

An extremely important feature of Faces is the **immediate** attribute. It allows more flexibility in how the lifecycle executes. The following sections present an overview.

Processing Action Events Immediately

Suppose you want to add a Cancel button to the registration page so that clicking on the button would immediately route users back to a **main.xhtml** page regardless of what was entered in the form. First, we'll need to add the **main.xhtml** page.

```
<!DOCTYPE html PUBLIC "-//W3C//DTD XHTML 1.0 Transitional//EN" "http://www
.w3.org/TR/xhtml1/DTD/xhtml1-transitional.dtd">
<html xmlns="http://www.w3.org/1999/xhtml"
      xmlns:h="http://java.sun.com/jsf/html"
      xmlns:f="http://java.sun.com/jsf/core">
<h:head>
  <title>Please Register</title>
</h:head>
<h:body>
    <p><h:link outcome="register">Click here to register</h:link></p>
</h:body>
</html>
```

Note that this page uses the new **<h:link>** component. This element renders a regular HTML link that does not cause a JSF postback when clicked. Therefore it can be used outside of an **<h:form>** element.

Now that you have added a **main.xhtml** page, you have to add an implicit navigation that returns back to the main page by putting a button or link component onto the page with an **action** set to **main**.

Here is the new Cancel button added to the Register page with the hard-coded **action** set to "cancel":

```
<h:commandButton value="Cancel" action="main" />
```

However, if we stop here, we'll quickly run into a problem! As shown in Figure 3-13, if you tried running the application again but immediately clicked the Cancel button, you would get stuck. This happens because even though you are just clicking the Cancel button with an empty form, it is still handled as a "postback" request, meaning that the JSF lifecycle commences to process an assumed incoming set of name-value pairs from the form. But since the form is empty, validation errors are encountered before the navigation handler can process the "cancel" action event and a response of the same page is rendered back to the client. Obviously, a solution is needed that allows for exceptions to the normal flow of the lifecycle processing. This is exactly what JSF provides in its **immediate** attribute.

If an **immediate** attribute is added to the Cancel button (or any **UICommand** component) and its value is set to "true," it will allow the lifecycle to immediately bypass any validation and navigate back to the **main.xhtml** page. In general, setting the **immediate** attribute to

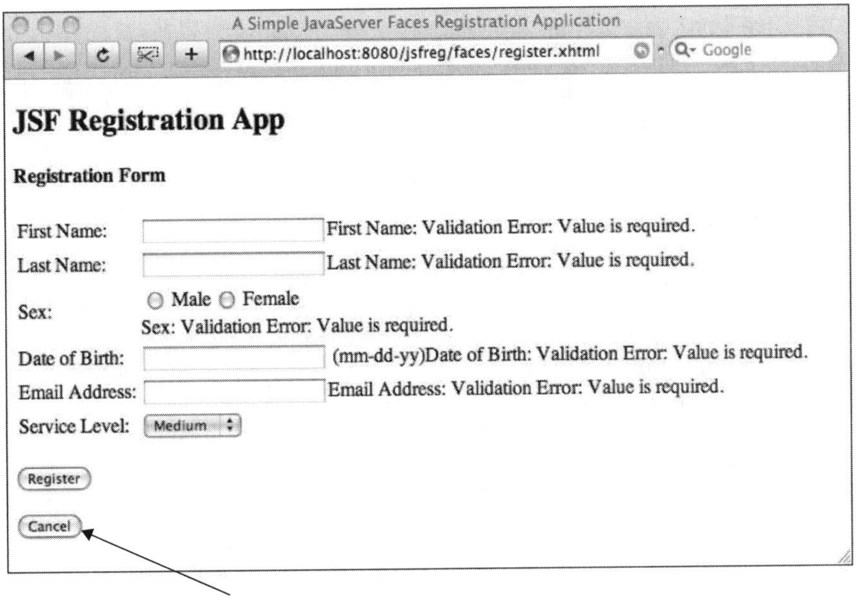

Clicking **cancel** without **immediate=true** can cause validation errors

FIGURE 3-13 Getting stuck on a page because of validation errors

"true" on a **UICommand** component triggers an action event to be fired immediately during the Apply Request Values phase before the Process Validations phase, so no validation errors are encountered. This has the effect of "short-circuiting" the lifecycle to avoid validation and cancel updating any values to the model.

```
<h:commandButton value="Cancel" action="main" immediate="true" />
```

Note that with JSF 2.0, the **<h:link>** and **<h:button>** elements have the same effect as placing an **immediate** attribute on a **<h:commandLink>** or **<h:commandButton>**.

Processing Validations and Conversions Immediately

Components that implement the **EditableValueHolder** interface (like an input field) have the option of having their validations and conversions performed immediately during the Apply Request Values phase or during the usual Process Validations phase, depending on the value of the **immediate** attribute supplied. If the value is "true," then validation and conversion occur immediately for that component. More important, having the **immediate** attribute set to "true" allows the component to be updated with a new validated value before entering the Process Validations phase, where the rest of the validations will occur for non-**immediate** components. This is useful when performing UI-only modifications, such as enabling an input field to be editable without submitting and validating the entire data in a form.

In Chapter 9, you'll find more detailed coverage of how to modify UI properties without validating the contents in a form using the **immediate** property and *value change listeners*.

EXPERT GROUP INSIGHT *The* ***immediate*** *attribute was initially present only on the* ***ActionSource*** *interface, but it was added to the* ***EditableValueHolder*** *interface to enable the scenario where an input component is intended strictly to cause a change to happen in the UI, such as when a check box causes the UI to render differently if checked.*

Phase Listeners

There are times when you need code to execute at exact times within the request processing lifecycle. For example, you may want to double-check something within your View component tree before continuing on to the next phase. JavaServer Faces provides an easy way to do this by allowing for the development of custom Faces components known as phase listeners. In short, phase listeners provide a simple way to execute custom Java code at distinct points within the different phases of the lifecycle. For example, you may want to customize an error message based on a value supplied dynamically at runtime, or you may want to verify that a database connection has been established for this session ahead of processing the postback lifecycle.

JSF 2.0 TIP *The JSF System Event feature provides a very precise way to observe the activity of the JSF lifecycle.*

Building a phase listener is simply a matter of writing a Java class that implements the **PhaseListener** interface. In the class, you specify in which phase you want the code to execute along with the actual code you want to execute at this point in time. To add the phase listener to the JSF application, it must be registered in **faces-config.xml** or programmatically registered on the lifecycle instance.

An example of building a phase listener is provided in Chapter 10.

Exception Handler

JSF 2.0 provides a new feature called the **ExceptionHandler**. This provides a central point of control for handling all unexpected exceptions thrown during the execution of the JSF lifecycle.

JSF 2.0 TIP *With the introduction of the* ***ExceptionHandler****, the JSF Expert Group chose to also introduce an incompatibility. Prior to JSF 2.0, any exceptions that happened during the processing of* ***PhaseListeners*** *were caught, logged, and swallowed. Now such exceptions are caught, processed by the* ***ExceptionHandler****, and re-thrown. This allows the Servlet* ***<error-page>*** *to handle the* ***Exception****, which is more consistent with the rest of the Web platform. Applications desiring the old behavior may have it by adding this text in the* ***<factory>*** *section of the* ***faces-config.xml****:*

```
<exception-handlerfactory>
 javax.faces.webapp.PreJsf2ExceptionHandlerFactory
</exception-handlerfactory>
```

The ***<exception-handler>*** *element may be used to install a custom* ***ExceptionHandler****, which will be covered in Chapter 9.*

Lifecycle Concepts to Remember

This chapter has briefly touched on a lot of areas, but you needn't worry about having to understand every single item before you begin building JSF applications. Instead, if you are a new JSF developer, it is sufficient to appreciate the JSF request processing lifecycle at a high level, knowing that it does most of the typically tedious (form processing) work for you. More advanced JSF developers and aspiring JSF component developers will find that the concepts covered in this chapter provide a solid foundation for moving on to the more advanced topics, including custom component development.

Before concluding this chapter, here are some key request processing lifecycle concepts to take into the rest of the book:

1. *The Faces request processing lifecycle does the "busy work" for you.* In fact, that is why it was implemented—to take the tedious work of processing request parameter values out of Web application development and let the developer focus more on the application logic.
2. *New JSF developers needn't know every single detail of the lifecycle to build simple JSF applications.* Thinking that you have to understand all of the details of the JSF lifecycle is kind of like thinking that in order to drive a car you must understand exactly how an engine works. For most drivers, simply knowing that your car occasionally needs gasoline is sufficient. However, having some understanding of how an engine works can often come in handy if a breakdown occurs or if you want to make modifications to improve engine performance.
3. *However, having a firm understanding of the request processing lifecycle provides a great foundation for advanced JSF development.* As you progress from building JSF applications to building custom JSF components, you'll find that having a complete understanding of the entire request processing lifecycle is extremely helpful so that you will have a complete understanding of what is occurring behind the scenes at all times.

4

CHAPTER

The Facelets View Declaration Language

This chapter presents a brief but complete guide to using the Facelets View Declaration Language technology, invented as a JSF extension by Expert Group member Jacob Hookom, and now incorporated into the core JSF specification in JSF 2.0. Facelets was created to replace the use of JSP as a View Declaration Language for JSF, with the following goals in mind:

- Provide a server-side templating facility that allows composing the actual view from several separate physical pages in a way that maximizes markup code reuse and eliminates redundancy among views.
- Designed entirely with JSF in mind.
- Provide a way to declare a JSF View using standard XHTML syntax.
- Provide an extensible "tag library" feature.
- Enforce clean Model-View-Controller separation by disallowing the inclusion of Java code in markup pages.

Templating is the feature of greatest interest to the general JSF developer. Most of this chapter is devoted to explaining how to use this feature. The more advanced features such as custom tags and tag libraries will be covered in Chapter 11.

JSF 2.0 Tip *Nearly all of the new features in JSF 2.0 are enabled by the inclusion of Facelets in the core specification. The Expert Group decided to move forward with Facelets as the basis for new features while letting JSP remain as a backward compatibility layer. The online Appendix provides complete coverage for how to migrate a JSP-based application to use Facelets.*

The Power of Templating in Faces

The terms "templating" and "composition" are used interchangeably to describe building a single logical page view for the user out of several separate files. Consider the following pseudocode in a fictional markup language:

```
<!-- This is the main page for the application –>
<f:view>
<include name="menubar" file="menubar.xml" user="#{currentUser}"/>
<include name="sidebar" file="sidebar.xml" user="#{currentUser}"/>
<include name="summary" file="summary.xml" user="#{currentUser}"/>
</f:view>
```

This shows the power of using a composition mechanism. The constituent parts—**menubar**, **sidebar**, and **summary**—can be reused in multiple pages, and their display can be customized by "passing in" parameters, optionally leveraging the EL. Naturally, we expect that any Faces components contained within the included files will be added to the **UIViewRoot** and function as expected.

JSF 2.0 Tip *This chapter explains the basics of composition using Facelets. A closely related concept is that of "composite components", a powerful new feature in JSF 2.0. With composite components, the facelet compositions you build become actual JSF UI components, complete with listeners, events, and attributes. This new feature is covered in detail in Chapter 11.*

While it is possible to use JSP's **jsp:include** and **<%@ include %>**, and JSTL's **c:import** to do templating, these approaches have some drawbacks. For example, it is impossible to pass parameters from the host file to the included file. The **<jsp:param>** feature doesn't work for JSF because it stores its content in page scope, which is not supported in JSF. Furthermore, the current implementations of the containers can cause unexpected replication of the included content. These drawbacks go beyond being mere bugs in a particular container's implementation.

Facelets addresses these problems by providing a simple, EL-aware, parameter passing, templating mechanism with full support for the JSF component model. Let's recast the previous pseudocode using Facelets.

```
<!DOCTYPE html PUBLIC "-//W3C//DTD XHTML 1.0 Transitional//EN"
"http://www.w3.org/TR/xhtml1/DTD/xhtml1-transitional.dtd"> <html
xmlns="http://www.w3.org/1999/xhtml"
       xmlns:ui="http://java.sun.com/jsf/facelets"
       xmlns:h="http://java.sun.com/jsf/html">
<!-- This is the main page for the application -->
<ui:include src="menubar.xml">
  <ui:param name="user" value="#{currentUser}"/> </ui:include>
<ui:include src="sidebar.xml">
  <ui:param name="user" value="#{currentUser}"/> </ui:include>
<ui:include src="summary.xml">
  <ui:param name="user" value="#{currentUser}"/> </ui:include>
```

This example is a template that can be used by any page in the application. It provides for a menu bar, a sidebar, and a summary. It shows that included documents are passed a **user** parameter to customize their display. This EL-aware parameter passing mechanism is a powerful feature of Facelets and will be fully explained in the reference section on **ui:include**, later in this chapter. Now let's examine some similarities and differences between JSP and Facelets to build a conceptual understanding of the technology.

Similarities and Differences Between JSP and Facelets

From a high level, Facelets and JSP are very similar. As far as core JSF is concerned, they are both just view description technologies. In fact, you can use both JSP and Facelets in a single application because the Facelets **ViewHandler** will delegate any requests it doesn't understand to the default **ViewHandler**, which uses JSP. As you'd expect, there are significant similarities between the two, as shown in Table 4-1, but the differences, displayed in Table 4-2, are more telling.

The two most important differences between Facelets and JSP are Facelets' ability to author JSF pages in plain HTML and to do first-class templating. In fact, Facelets was created in response to user demand for these two features. The remaining differences reflect how Facelets was designed with JSF in mind, in contrast to JSP, which was designed well before JSF was invented. The remainder of this chapter covers the details of Facelets from a perspective of how it differs from JSP.

JSF 2.0 Tip *Because JSF 2.0 includes Facelets, the Facelets jar file* must *no longer be included in the application's* `WEB-INF/lib` *directory, nor in the container's classpath, with one exception: Facelets for JSF 2.0 is* not *compatible with any application that has Java code that has a compile-time dependency on any class in the package* `com.sun.facelets` *or its subpackages. Such an application must* continue *to include the Facelets jar file* and *must set the **web.xml** **<context-param>** named* `javax.faces.DISABLE_FACELET_JSF_VIEWHANDLER` *to* `true`*. This action will disable the built-in Facelets for JSF 2.0, allowing time to migrate the code containing the dependency on* `com.sun.facelets` *classes to the new classes in package* `javax.faces.view.facelets`*. This process is explained in the online Appendix.*

View Description Concept	Facelets	JSP
Pages authored in XML	Yes, or XHTML	Yes, the JSP XML syntax
Leverages a page compiler concept	XML is parsed into a **TagHandler** object tree, which is executed. There is no bytecode generation	XML is translated into Java, then compiled into a **.class** file and executed
Uses the unified EL	Yes	Yes (JSP 2.1)
Supports the concept of tag libraries (taglibs)	Yes	Yes
Supports the concept of tag files	Yes	Yes
Dynamic tag attributes	Required	Optional

Table 4-1 Some Similarities Between Facelets and JSP

View Description Concept	Facelets	JSP
Authors pages using raw HTML	Yes, with **jsfc** attribute or **TagDecorators**	No
Supports Faces-aware parameter passing to templated content	Yes	No
Expressions that reference other expressions work appropriately	Yes, built in to the **FaceletContext**	Yes, but only in JSP 2.1 and must be specified explicitly or set twice
Tag lifecycle	All tag instances are stateless, only one instance of each tag per application	Stateful tags are pooled
Built-in templating engine	Yes	No (only has simple include capabilities)
Tags perform rendering and other display-related tasks	No, tags just help to build the **UIComponent** tree	Yes, and there is a wide variety of third-party taglibs available to help in rendering the view

TABLE 4-2 Differences Between Facelets and JSP

Templating with Facelets

There are two main perspectives in templating with Facelets: the *template file* and the *template client* file. These are shown in Figure 4-1.

The *template client* is the file whose name actually corresponds to a **viewId**, such as **greeting.xhtml**. The template client employs one or more *template files* to achieve reuse of page content. A useful analogy is to consider building a stack of papers on a table. Lay the first sheet of paper down on the table. This sheet contains the real content that you want to convey to the user. This first sheet corresponds to the template client. Now imagine another sheet, this one with holes cut into it. This second sheet contains content that embellishes the content from the first sheet. The second sheet corresponds to the template file. When we lay the second sheet on top of the first, you can see the core content from the first sheet through the holes cut into the second. Still more sheets, with more holes cut in them, can be laid on the stack. When viewed from above, the stack shows one logical page, and the exact same thing happens in Facelets.

Let's illustrate templating with Facelets by rewriting the **register.xhtml** page from the JSFReg application in Chapter 2 using Facelets templates. As indicated at the beginning of this section, one of the main values of templating is the reuse of page designs in multiple pages of your application. Let's define a simple template that could be used in every page in the Virtual Trainer application: **lnf-template.xhtml** (which stands for "look and feel" template).

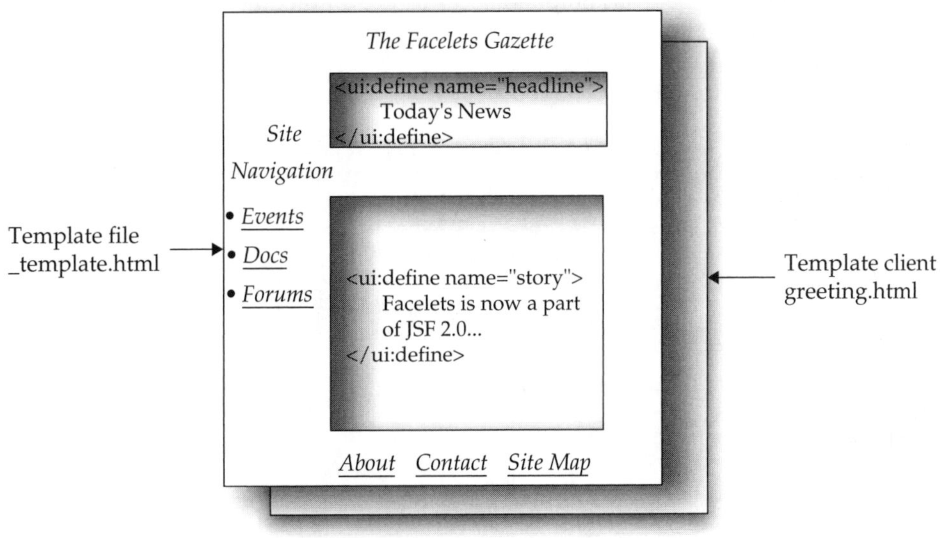

FIGURE 4-1 The template and the template client

```
<!DOCTYPE html PUBLIC "-//W3C//DTD XHTML 1.0 Transitional//EN"
"http://www.w3.org/TR/xhtml1/DTD/xhtml1-transitional.dtd"> <html
xmlns="http://www.w3.org/1999/xhtml"
      xmlns:ui="http://java.sun.com/jsf/facelets">
<head>
  <meta http-equiv="Content-Type"
        content="text/html; charset=windows-1352" />
  <title><ui:insert name="title">Placeholder Title</ui:insert></title>
  <link href="css/vt.css" rel="stylesheet" media="screen" />
</head>
<body>
  <table width="100%" border="0">
    <tr>
      <td height="89">
        <h1 align="center">
            <img src="images/logo.jpg" width="92"
                 height="110" />JSF Virtual Trainer Application</h1>
      </td>
    </tr>
    <tr>
      <ui:insert name="body">Placeholder Body</ui:insert>
    </tr>
  </table>
</body>
</html>
```

The first thing you'll notice is that this is a regular XHTML page with an additional namespace of "ui" defined, and two usages of the **ui:insert** tag from that namespace. These two **<ui:insert>** tags state that the contents of this element will be replaced with something else when the page is compiled. Let's now examine the page that contains the markup referred to by the **<ui:insert>** tags, **register.xhtml**, the template client to the **lnf-template.xml** file.

The template client from Figure 4-1 follows.

```
<!DOCTYPE html PUBLIC "-//W3C//DTD XHTML 1.0 Transitional//EN"
"http://www.w3.org/TR/xhtml1/DTD/xhtml1-transitional.dtd">
<html xmlns="http://www.w3.org/1999/xhtml"
      xmlns:ui="http://java.sun.com/jsf/facelets"
      xmlns:h="http://java.sun.com/jsf/html"
      xmlns:f="http://java.sun.com/jsf/core">
<body>
<ui:composition template="/lnf-template.xhtml">
<ui:define name="title">
   JavaServer Faces Virtual Trainer Application
   Registration </ui:define>
<ui:define name="body">
  <table width="70%">
    <tr>
      <td width="40%">First Name:</td>
      <td width="60%">
        <input type="text" jsfc="h:inputText" required="true"
               id="fname"
               value="#{UserBean.firstname}" />
        <h:message for="fname"/>
  </td>
</tr>
<tr>
  <td width="40%">Last Name:</td>
  <td width="60%">
    <input type="text" jsfc="h:inputText"
           value="#{UserBean.lastname}" required="true"
           id="lname" />
    <h:message for="lname"/>
    <span jsfc="h:message" for="fname">Message</span>
  </td>
</tr>
<tr>
  <td width="40%">Gender:</td>
  <td width="60%">
    <h:selectOneRadio type="radio"
           value="#{UserBean.gender}" required="true" id="gender">
      <input type="radio" jsfc="f:selectItem"
             itemLabel="Male" itemValue="male" />
      <input type="radio" jsfc="f:selectItem"
             itemLabel="Female" itemValue="female" />
    </h:selectOneRadio>
    <h:message for="gender"/>
  </td>
</tr>
<tr>
  <td width="40%">Date of Birth:</td>
  <td width="60%">
    <h:inputText value="#{UserBean.dob}" id="dob" required="true" >
```

```
      <f:convertDateTime pattern="mm-dd-yy"/>
    </h:inputText>(mm-dd-yy)
    <h:message for="dob"/> </td>
</tr>
<tr>
  <td width="40%">Email Address:</td>
  <td width="60%">
     <h:inputText value="#{UserBean.email}" required="true"
       validator="#{UserBean.validateEmail}" id="email"/>
     <h:message for="email"/>
  </td>
</tr>
<!-- Remainder of rows deleted for brevity -->
</table>
</ui:define>
</ui:composition>
  </body>
</html>
```

The main content of this page is enclosed in a **<ui:composition>** tag. Also note that some of the components in the page are plain old HTML with a special **jsfc** attribute. This approach is very useful for making the page directly viewable in a browser as a local file. The value of the **jsfc** attribute is the name of the jsf component that should be placed on the server side. In a template client page using **<ui:composition>**, anything outside of the bounds of a **<ui:define>** tag is ignored and is not included in the rendered output. Also, note that although this example doesn't show it, a template client file can itself act as a template and leverage other files as template clients.

The listing for the template file used by the template client follows.

```
<!DOCTYPE html PUBLIC "-//W3C//DTD XHTML 1.0 Transitional//EN"
"http://www.w3.org/TR/xhtml1/DTD/xhtml1-transitional.dtd">
<html xmlns="http://www.w3.org/1999/xhtml"
      xmlns:ui="http://java.sun.com/jsf/facelets">
<head>
<title>
  <ui:insert name="title">Placeholder Title</ui:insert></title>
<link href="css/vt.css" rel="stylesheet" media="screen" />
</head>
<body>
<table width="100%" border="0">
<tr>
  <td height="89">
    <h1 align="center">
      <img src="images/logo.jpg" width="92" height="110" />
        JSF Virtual Trainer Application
    </h1>
  </td>
</tr>
<tr>
  <td><ui:insert name="body">Placeholder Body</ui:insert></td>
</tr>
</table>
</body>
</html>
```

Guide to Facelets Templating Tags

Facelets provides six tags in the **ui:** tag library to perform templating, each with special features. This section serves as a guide and reference to these tags. Each section heading lists the general form for the tag.

ui:composition

```
<ui:composition template="optionalTemplate">
```

The **ui:composition** tag is used in files acting as a template client, and is the fundamental enabler for templating in Facelets. This tag indicates to the Facelets system that the enclosing children should be grafted into the **UIComponent** hierarchy at that point in the page. Optionally, it declares a template to which the enclosed content should be applied using the **template** attribute. Generally, **<ui:composition>** causes the child components to be created as direct children of the **UIViewRoot**, as would be the case in the example in Figure 4-2.

There's no need to explicitly use the **<f:view>** tag in Facelets, because the Facelet markup serves no other purpose than to generate the **UIComponent** tree.

As you can see in Figure 4-2, Facelets provides several tags designed for use with **<ui:composition>**. The details of these are described next.

ui:decorate

```
<ui:decorate template="requiredTemplate">
```

The **<ui:decorate>** tag provides the same feature as **<ui:composition>**, but it causes any content surrounding the **<ui:decorate>** tag to be included in the page, rather than be trimmed, as in the case of **<ui:composition>**. This enables taking any element in the page, and applying it to a template. Also, observe that the **template** attribute is required in this tag. This tag is useful when you have a series of items in one page that require the same appearance. If you were to use **ui:composition**, the output around the tags would be trimmed, which is not desirable in this case.

ui:define

```
<ui:define name="requiredName">
```

The **<ui:define>** tag is used in files acting as a template client, inside a **<ui:composition>** tag, to define a region that will be inserted into the composition at the location given by the **<ui:insert>** tag with the corresponding name for the **<ui:define>** tag. Figure 4-3 shows **<ui:define>** in action.

ui:insert

```
<ui:insert name="optionalName">
```

The **<ui:insert>** tag is used in files acting as a template to indicate where the corresponding **<ui:define>** in the template client is to be inserted. If no name is specified, the body content of the **<ui:insert>** tag is added to the view.

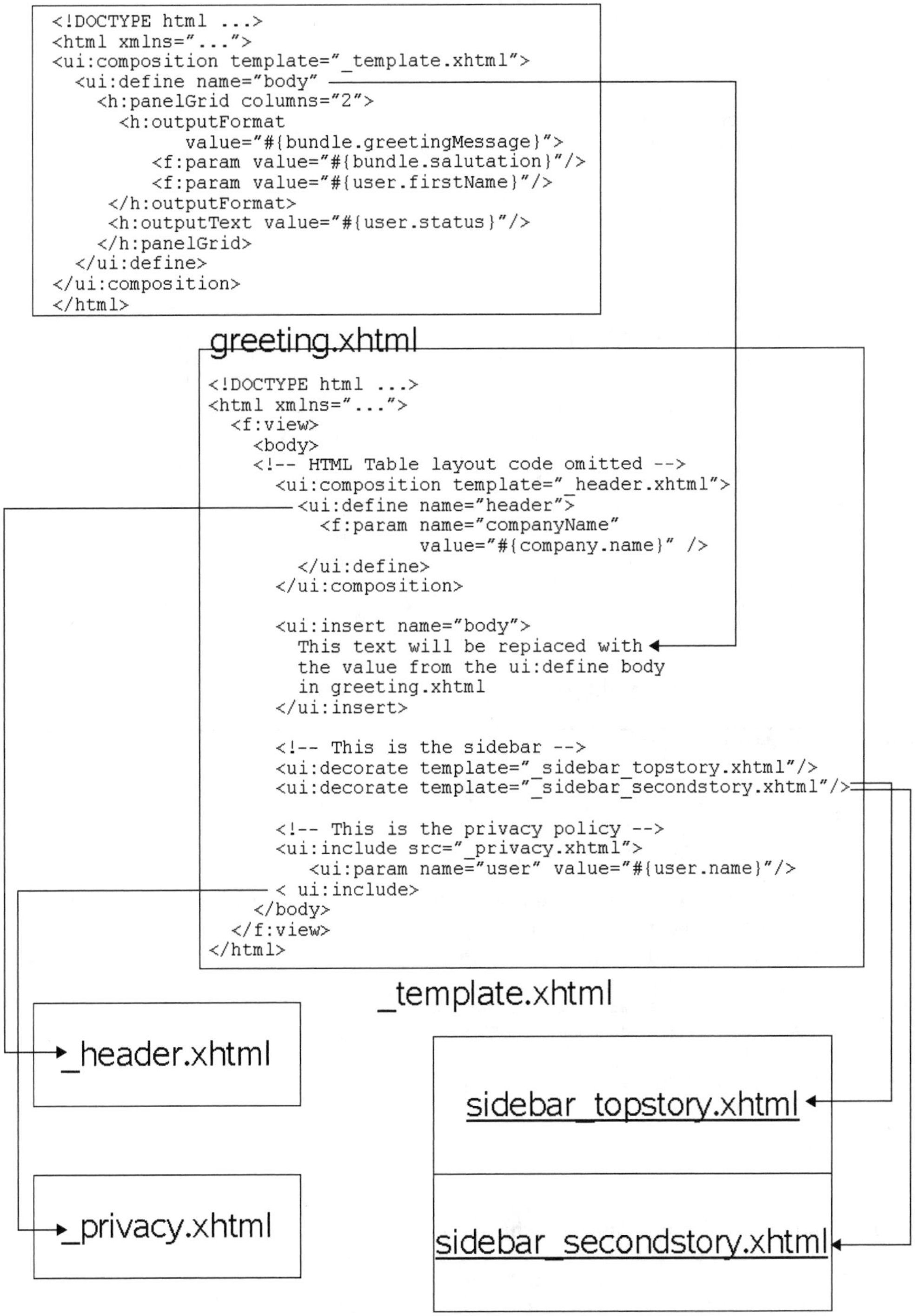

```
<!DOCTYPE html ...>
<html xmlns="...">
<ui:composition template="_template.xhtml">
  <ui:define name="body"
    <h:panelGrid columns="2">
      <h:outputFormat
            value="#{bundle.greetingMessage}">
         <f:param value="#{bundle.salutation}"/>
         <f:param value="#{user.firstName}"/>
     </h:outputFormat>
     <h:outputText value="#{user.status}"/>
    </h:panelGrid>
  </ui:define>
</ui:composition>
</html>
```

greeting.xhtml

```
<!DOCTYPE html ...>
<html xmlns="...">
  <f:view>
    <body>
    <!-- HTML Table layout code omitted -->
      <ui:composition template="_header.xhtml">
        <ui:define name="header">
          <f:param name="companyName"
                   value="#{company.name}" />
        </ui:define>
      </ui:composition>

      <ui:insert name="body">
        This text will be repiaced with
        the value from the ui:define body
        in greeting.xhtml
      </ui:insert>

      <!-- This is the sidebar -->
      <ui:decorate template="_sidebar_topstory.xhtml"/>
      <ui:decorate template="_sidebar_secondstory.xhtml"/>

      <!-- This is the privacy policy -->
      <ui:include src="_privacy.xhtml">
         <ui:param name="user" value="#{user.name}"/>
      < ui:include>
    </body>
  </f:view>
</html>
```

_template.xhtml

_header.xhtml

_privacy.xhtml

sidebar_topstory.xhtml

sidebar_secondstory.xhtml

Figure 4-2 **<ui:composition>** in action

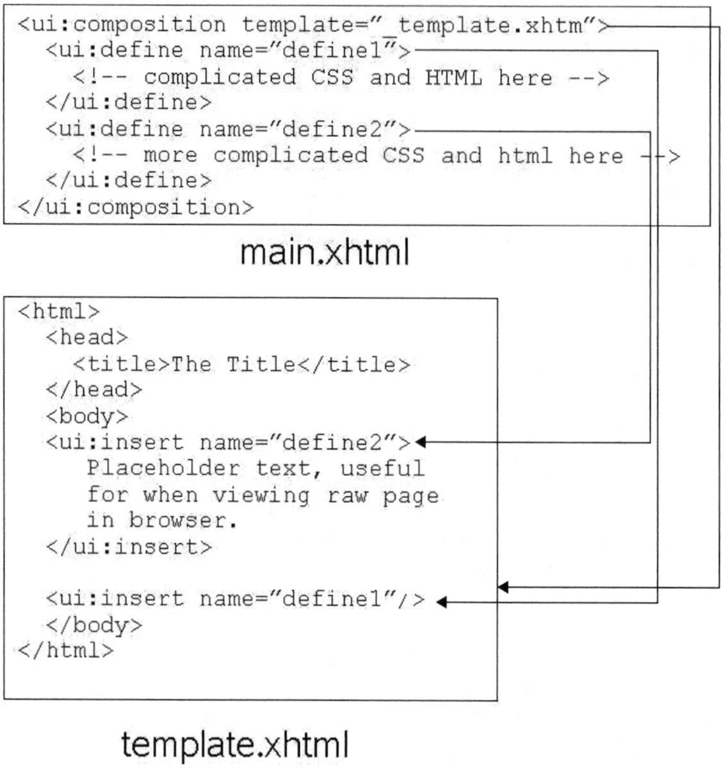

```
<ui:composition template="_template.xhtm">
  <ui:define name="define1">
    <!-- complicated CSS and HTML here -->
  </ui:define>
  <ui:define name="define2">
    <!-- more complicated CSS and html here -->
  </ui:define>
</ui:composition>
```

main.xhtml

```
<html>
  <head>
    <title>The Title</title>
  </head>
  <body>
  <ui:insert name="define2">
     Placeholder text, useful
     for when viewing raw page
     in browser.
  </ui:insert>

  <ui:insert name="define1"/>
  </body>
</html>
```

template.xhtml

FIGURE 4-3 **<ui:define>** in action

ui:include

```
<ui:include src="requiredFilename">
```

The eminently useful tag **<ui:include>** is combined with the **<ui:param>** tag to enable the parameterized inclusion of pages. This tag may be present in templates or template clients. For example, consider the following in a template file called **header.xml**:

```
<html xmlns="http://www.w3.org/1999/xhtml"
      xmlns:ui="http://java.sun.com/jsf/facelets">
<body>
  <ui:include src="userWelcome.xhtml">
    <ui:param name="details" value="#{user}"/>
  </ui:include>
</body>
</html>
```

The following is the **userWelcome.xhtml** file:

```
<html xmlns="http://www.w3.org/1999/xhtml"
     xmlns:ui="http://java.sun.com/jsf/facelets"
     xmlns:h="http://java.sun.com/jsf/html"
     xmlns:f="http://java.sun.com/jsf/core">
```

```
Welcome, #{details.honorific} #{details.firstName}
#{details.lastName}!
</html>
```

Note that the **<ui:param>** tag passes the **#{user}** expression to the **userWelcome.xhtml** file.

ui:param

```
<ui:param name="requiredName" value="requiredValue">
```

The **<ui:param>** tag is used exclusively inside **<ui:include>** tags to define name/ value pairs that are available via the EL in the included page. Both the **name** and **value** attributes may be literal strings or EL expressions. See the preceding tag for an example.

Guide to Nontemplating Facelets Tags

To complete our discussion of using Facelet tags, let's examine the remaining four tags in the Facelets **ui:** tag library—**<ui:component>**, **<ui:fragment>**, **<ui:remove>**, and **<ui:debug>**.

ui:component

```
<ui:component id="optionalComponentId"
              binding="optionalValueExpression">
```

As mentioned earlier, the **jsfc** attribute can be placed on raw HTML markup to indicate that this piece of markup corresponds to a particular **UIComponent** instance in the tree. The **<ui:component>** tag has an optional **id** attribute that will be set into the **id** property of the component. If not specified, a page-unique ID is generated. The optional **binding** attribute is a **ValueExpression** that refers to a JavaBeans property whose type is a **UIComponent**. This is exactly the same as the **binding** attribute on JSP JSF component tags. If the **ValueExpression** has no initial value, an appropriate **UIComponent** instance is created automatically and set into the **ValueExpression**. Any markup occurring outside of the **<ui:component>** tag is not included in the view.

ui:fragment

```
<ui:fragment id="optionalComponentId"
                                 binding="optionalValueExpression">
```

The **<ui:fragment>** tag is the same as **<ui:component>** except that it wraps a series of components inside a single parent component before the parent is added to the tree.

ui:remove

```
<ui:remove>
```

The **<ui:remove>** tag is mainly used during development to "comment out" a portion of the markup in order to prevent it from actually ending up in the view. **<ui:remove>** has no attributes and may appear anywhere in the page where it is valid to have a component or something that represents a component.

ui:debug

```
<ui:debug hotkey="optionalHotKey" />
```

This astoundingly useful tag will enable a hot key that pops up a new window displaying the component tree, any scoped variables currently active, and other useful debugging information. You have to set the **javax.faces.FACELETS_DEVELOPMENT context-param** in your web.xml to enable this to work. If *optionalHotKey* is not specified, pressing CTRL-SHIFT-D will pop up the debug window.

CHAPTER 5

Managed Beans and the JSF Expression Language

During the time period between the introduction of Java and its emergence as a widely popular business software platform, Java developers were fully responsible for instantiating and managing the properties of every single Java class or JavaBean in their application. This was perfectly logical because applications in the early days of Java were not multitiered, so all the logic for the entire application resided in one monolithic collection of Java Objects, often in a single virtual machine (VM).

Over time, Java matured to include server-side, distributed application technology. Lightweight Java server containers have become prevalent as the industry produced software to simplify the task of creating and maintaining enterprise applications. One key development in this regard is the notion of *Inversion of Control (IoC),* where the container takes control of managing a portion of the business logic so that the application developer needn't write the repetitive code to manage that logic. Inversion of Control was popularized by Rod Johnson with his Spring Framework. This technique is sometimes referred to as *dependency injection* because one of its main benefits is the ability to have Java Objects prepopulated with values through a declarative configuration syntax.

Because the JavaServer Faces framework runs entirely on a server in a servlet container, it is only natural that JSF comes equipped with a robust ability to offer Inversion of Control, where management of server-side JavaBeans can be done in a highly efficient and mostly automated fashion. This is exactly what JSF provides with its Managed Bean Facility.

EXPERT GROUP INSIGHT *The JSF 1.0 Expert Group decided to include the Managed Bean Facility as a core part of JSF in order to provide a complete integrated software stack for developers using JSF outside of a formal Java EE container. This decision was critical to the early success of JSF because other Web frameworks initially didn't have such a facility built in. However, like things in JSF, the Managed Bean facility is designed to be enhanced or replaced by other technologies, as will be shown in Chapter 13.*

In the previous chapters we touched on the basics of how to register managed beans in simple applications. In this chapter we will examine in detail precisely how JSF provides an IoC-enabled container: the Managed Beans Facility.

This chapter will also cover JSF's expression language (EL) in detail because the EL is the easiest way to access and manipulate managed beans and bind them to UI components in the View. The chapter concludes by explaining how to access and work on managed beans programmatically and by introducing the *backing bean* concept as well as providing a few helpful hints on how to manage backing beans and pages.

What Are Managed Beans?

Java Objects that store application data and do not implement or extend any framework-specific interfaces or classes are commonly referred to as *Plain Old Java Objects (POJOs)*. POJO-style application architectures completely decouple the view technology from the domain model of the application. This approach has numerous benefits, including resilience to changes in the kind of view technology used, better maintainability, and testability. A POJO that is declared to the JSF runtime in some way is called a *managed bean*. You never have to manually call **new( )** on a managed bean. Rather, managed beans are "lazily initialized" by the container at runtime, only when needed by the application. Any Java class with a public, no-argument constructor that conforms to the JavaBeans naming conventions for properties can be registered as a managed bean. Objects of type **java.util.List** and **java.util.Map** can also be registered as managed beans.

A Simple Managed Bean Example

Consider again from Chapter 2 the **UserBean** class, which holds the registration information of a new user. As you recall, **UserBean** was made available to a Faces application by attaching the following annotations to the class declaration:

```
import javax.faces.bean.ManagedBean
import javax.faces.bean.SessionScoped
@ManagedBean
@SessionScoped
public class UserBean {...
```

In this example, the class **com.jsfcompref.model.UserBean** is registered as a managed bean named "userBean" and has its scope set to **session**. The "scope" of a bean describes the period of time when an instance of a bean is available to other parts of the program. Scope settings are discussed later in this chapter. The "name" of the bean determines how EL expressions will refer to instances of the bean. In this example, the managed bean name is derived by convention from the simple class name. An equivalent syntax, with the new part shown in boldface, is

```
import javax.faces.bean.ManagedBean
import javax.faces.bean.SessionScoped
@ManagedBean(name="userBean")
@SessionScoped
public class UserBean {...
```

If no **name** attribute is given within the **@ManagedBean** annotation, the name is derived from the simple class name with the first letter converted to lowercase.

EXPERT GROUP INSIGHT *The author and JSF spec lead Ed Burns encouraged the expert group to bring the best ideas from the wider Web-framework community into the JSF 2.0 specification. One abundant source of good ideas was the Ruby on Rails framework, with its design principles of "Don't Repeat Yourself" and "Convention over Configuration." The latter of these two principles is exemplified here: the name of the managed bean is inferred by a naming convention in the absence of specific configuration. Other examples of ideas borrowed from Rails will be seen throughout the book.*

Alternatively, managed beans may be declared using **<managed-bean>** entries in the **faces-config.xml** file. The syntax for this declaration looks like this:

```
<managed-bean>
  <managed-bean-name>userBean</managed-bean-name>
  <managed-bean-class>com.jsfcompref.model.UserBean
    </managed-bean-class>
  <managed-bean-scope>session</managed-bean-scope>
</managed-bean>
```

JSF 2.0 TIP *Generally, for every annotation in JSF 2.0, there is a corresponding XML syntax for use in the* ***faces-config.xml*** *file. Using annotations is recommended over using XML because it leads to more cohesive and easier-to-maintain code.*

To access properties or methods of managed beans, from your JSF pages, you will use a compact, simple-to-use *expression language,* which will also be explained later in this chapter.
For example, to display the current value of the **firstName** property of **UserBean** in a JSF page, you can use an **<h:outputText>** tag (**UIOutput** component) and set its **value** attribute with the following JSF expression *#{userBean.firstName}*:

```
<h:outputText value="#{userBean.firstName}" />
```

JSF 2.0 TIP *Because JSF 2.0 includes Facelets, it is also possible to put EL Expressions directly in the page, instead of using an* ***<h:outputText>*** *tag. This is useful when there is no need to attach attributes, such as CSS or JavaScript to the* ***<h:outputText>****. For example, the preceding tag could simply be replaced by* ***#{userBean.firstName}*** *straight in the page.*

At runtime, the JSF expression allows the value of the **firstName** property to be displayed in the page. As we'll show later in the chapter, the JSF expression language allows for a shorthand way to call the **getFirstName( )** method of **UserBean** and display its value in the page using the **<h:outputText>** tag.
Recall that in addition to displaying the current properties of a managed bean, properties can also be updated if the managed bean has setter methods for those properties. To update properties of a managed bean, you can bind a property of the bean to a UI component that accepts an input value (implements **EditableValueHolder**) such as **UIInput**. Recall again the registration form used the **UIInput** component (with the JSP tag **<h:inputText>**) with its **value** attribute set with a JSF expression to accept the registrant's input values.

```
<h:inputText value="#{userBean.firstName}" />
```

In general, during a form submission, the JSF request processing lifecycle updates managed bean properties with new property values from **UIInput** components. In this example, the form submission causes the **setFirstName( )** method on **UserBean** to be called. The argument to the method is the value entered into the text field by the user.

Table 5-1 shows the basic elements used in a managed bean registration.

Initializing Managed Bean Properties

So far you have seen how to register a simple managed bean and relied on a JSF application to display or update bean properties. However, it is also possible to supply initial values to managed beans by adding a **@ManagedProperty** annotation on a field or by providing a **<managed-property>** element inside the **managed-bean** entry in the Faces configuration file.

For example, to initialize the **firstName** and **lastName** properties of the **userBean** managed bean, you can add the following to the annotation declarations:

```
@ManagedBean
@SessionScoped
public class UserBean {
@ManagedProperty(value="Jane")
private String firstName;
@ManagedProperty(value="Doe")
private String lastName;
public String getFirstName() { return firstName; }
public void setFirstName(String firstName) {this.firstName = firstName;}
public String getLastName() { return lastName; }
public void setLastName(String lastName) {this.lastName = lastName;}
}
```

or the following to the configuration:

```
<managed-bean>
  <managed-bean-name>userBean</managed-bean-name>
  <managed-bean-class>com.jsfcompref.register.UserBean</managed-bean-class>
  <managed-bean-scope>session</managed-bean-scope>
  <managed-property>
    <property-name>firstName</property-name>
    <value>Jane</value>
  </managed-property>
  <managed-property>
    <property-name>lastName</property-name>
    <value>Doe</value>
  </managed-property>
</managed-bean>
```

This has the effect of executing the setter methods for the **firstName** and **lastName** properties just after the bean is instantiated by the Faces lifecycle. Note that in both the XML and the annotation syntax, the getter and setter methods are required. At runtime the registration form in the **register.xhtml** page would no longer appear completely empty.

Element	Description	Equivalent javax.faces.bean Annotation	Target Java Language Element
<managed-bean>	Parent element of a managed bean in the Faces configuration file.	@ManagedBean	Class
<description>	Description of the purpose of the managed bean. (Optional)	NA	NA
<display-name>	A display name of the managed bean. Intended for possible development tool usage. (Optional)	NA	NA
<icon>	Icon associated with this managed bean. Also intended for development tool usage. (Optional)	NA	NA
<managed-bean-name>	The published name of the managed bean. JSF expression language uses this name.	The optional **name** attribute within the **@ManagedBean** annotation. If not specified, the value is taken to be the simple name of the class with the first letter in lowercase.	Annotation attribute
<managed-bean-class>	The fully qualified class name of the Java class being registered as a managed bean.	Implicitly derived from the class to which the annotation is attached.	NA
<managed-bean-scope>	The scope under which the newly instantiated bean will be registered. Can be: **none, request, session, application**, or an EL expression that evaluates to a **Map<String, Object>**.	@NoneScoped, @RequestScoped, @ViewScoped, @SessionScoped, @ApplicationScoped, or @CustomScoped	Class

TABLE 5-1 Elements Needed for a Basic Managed Bean Declaration

FIGURE 5-1 An initial request of the registration page with preinitialized **lastName** and **firstName**

As shown in Figure 5-1, the input fields bound to the preinitialized properties will now appear with values upon an initial (non-form submission) request.

Table 5-2 illustrates the elements required for initializing simple managed bean properties. A managed bean can have 0 to *N* sets of **<managed-property>** element trees or annotations.

In addition to initializing simple properties, managed beans containing **java.util.List** or **java.util.Map** properties can also be registered and initialized as managed properties. This is done by using either the **<list-entries>** or **<map-entries>** elements in a managed property definition.

Element	Description	Equivalent javax.faces.bean Annotation	Target Java Language Element
<managed-property>	Parent element for managed property element tree. Is a child of a **<managed-bean>**.	@ManagedProperty	field
<description>	A description of the managed property. (Optional)	NA	NA
<display-name>	A managed property display name. Intended for development tool usage. (Optional)	NA	NA
<property-name>	The case-sensitive name of the bean property to be initialized.	The optional **name** attribute within the **@ManagedProperty** annotation. If not specified, the value is taken to be the name of the field.	Annotation attribute

TABLE 5-2 The Managed Properties Elements

Element	Description	Equivalent javax.faces.bean Annotation	Target Java Language Element
<property-class>	Used to specify the type of the property. The type specified can be either a primitive or a fully qualified class type. For example, the **String** class could have been specified with **<property-class>java.lang.String </property-class>** in the previous managed property example. However, in most cases this is not needed, as the Faces runtime is able to infer the correct data type. (Optional)	Implicitly derived from the type of the field to which the annotation is attached.	NA
<value> or <null-value>	The **<value>** element provides the value with which to set the property. This value is taken as a **String** value and is converted to the corresponding data type of the property, prior to setting it to this value. When initializing a property to a **null** value, a **<null-value>** tag is used instead. Note: The **<null-value>** element cannot be used for primitive data types.	The required **value** attribute within the **@ManagedProperty** annotation	Annotation attribute

Table 5-2 The Managed Properties Elements *(continued)*

Initializing List Properties

For managed beans with a property of type **array** or of **java.util.List**, the **<list-entries>** element can initialize values for the list. There is no corresponding annotation syntax for this XML declaration. This is because most implementations of **java.util.List** are actually provided by the core JDK, and it is not recommended to make modifications (such as adding annotations) to classes in the core JDK. Consider a slight augmentation to the registration example from Chapter 2 where **UserBean** now contains a **java.util.List** property named **sportsInterests**. In keeping with the overall sports theme presented in the Virtual Trainer example application in Chapter 10, the **sportsInterests** list could keep track of the different types of sports that this user may be interested in training for.

Here is how to initialize a set of sports for this user by using a managed property for a **List**:

```
<managed-bean>
...
  <managed-property>
    <property-name>sportsInterests</property-name>
    <list-entries>
      <value>Cycling</value>
      <value>Running</value>
      <value>Swimming</value>
      <value>Kayaking</value>
    </list-entries>
  </managed-property>
</managed-bean>
```

After initializing the **sportsInterests** property, the list values can be displayed in a JSF page using **<h:dataTable>** (**HtmlDataTable** UI component), as shown here:

```
<h:dataTable value="#{userBean.sportsInterests}" var="row" >
  <h:column>
    <h:outputText value="#{row}"/>
  </h:column>
</h:dataTable>
```

Individual items from the list can also be displayed by using an array style element reference in the JSF expression, like this:

```
<h:outputText value="#{userBean.sportsInterests[0]}"/>
```

The preceding code displays "Cycling" on a JSF page because this was the first value in the **<list-entries>** list.

The different list values shown in the previous example work fine, because the default data type for **<list-entries>** is **java.lang.String**. However, if another data type is needed for the list, then a **<value-class>** is added as a child to the **<list-entries>** element and is used to specify the data type of the list items.

Consider a new property to the **UserBean** called **racePlacement** where the finishing order is recorded for different racing events. In this example a **java.lang.Integer** type is specified with a **<value-class>** element:

```
<managed-bean>
...
  <managed-property>
    <property-name>racePlacement</property-name>
    <list-entries>
      <value-class>java.lang.Integer</value-class>
      <value>23</value>
      <value>12</value>
      <value>3</value>
```

```
      <value>1</value>
    </list-entries>
  </managed-property>
</managed-bean>
```

In a more generalized form, Table 5-3 shows the elements associated with defining a managed property with **List** entries.

As mentioned before, list entries can also support array type objects. For example, if the following **states** array (and the corresponding getter and setter methods) are added to a managed bean:

```
String states[] ={ "California", "Nevada", "Oregon" };
```

it is then possible to initialize further properties of the managed bean like this:

```
<managed-bean>
...
  <managed-property>
    <property-name>states</property-name>
    <list-entries>
      <value>New York</value>
      <value>Florida</value>
      <value>Texas</value>
    </list-entries>
  </managed-property>
</managed-bean>
```

This also illustrates the fact that although initial values may have been set in the original code, adding additional managed property list items simply adds to the existing list. At runtime the superset of list values will be available to the application.

Element	Description
<managed-property>	Same as before, the parent element for managed properties.
<property-name>	The name of the property, which must be of type **array** or **java.util.List**.
<property-class>	JSF uses the default type of **ArrayList**, but any other list concrete class could be specified here.
<list-entries> (1 to N)	Parent element of the **<value-class>**, list values defined in multiple **<value>** or **<null-value>** elements.
<value-class>	When not using the default list type of **java.lang.String**, one must specify the list item data type here. (Optional)
<value> or <null-value>	The **<value>** element provides the value with which to set the property. When initializing a property to a **null** value, a **<null-value>** tag is used instead. Note: The **<null-value>** element cannot be used for primitive data types.

TABLE 5-3 Managed Property Elements for a List

Initializing Map Properties

In addition to offering the ability to initialize objects of type **array** and **java.util.List**, the JavaServer Faces Managed Bean Facility also offers a way to initialize managed beans with properties of type **java.util.Map**. Again, there is no corresponding annotation syntax, for the same reason there is no annotation syntax for **List** instances. Initializing **Map** values is very similar to initializing **List** values. Instead of **<list-entries>**, the element **<map-entries>** is used as a parent element of a series of key and value pairs.

Consider an example that uses a **java.util.Map** instead of a **java.util.List** to define a set of **sportsInterests**. In this example, the key could be a short name of the sport such as "cycling," and the actual value could be a more verbose definition of the sport: "Any competitive athletic event where a bicycle is used."

So, for a **Map** version of the **sportsInterest** example, you could use the following to initialize the **Map** values:

```
<managed-bean>
...
  <managed-property>
    <property-name>sportsInterests</property-name>
    <map-entries>
      <map-entry>
        <key>Cycling</key>
        <value>Any competitive athletic event where a
        bicycle is used.</value>
      </map-entry>
      <map-entry>
        <key>Running</key>
        <value>Any competitive athletic event where the competitors
        are running or jogging.</value>
      </map-entry>
      <map-entry>
        <key>Swimming</key>
        <value>Any competitive athletic event where the competitors
        are swimmming.</value>
      </map-entry>
      <map-entry>
        <key>Kayaking</key>
        <value>Any competitive athletic event where the competitors
        use a kayak.</value>
      </map-entry>
    </map-entries>
  </managed-property>
</managed-bean>
```

To access the individual **Map** values at runtime, simply use a JSF expression with a key. For example, to access the value associated with the "swimming" key, the following expression can be used.

```
<h:outputText value="#{userBean.sportsInterests['Swimming']}"/>
```

Incidentally, it is possible to display all of the key/value pairs for a **Map** by simply referring to the **Map** in the expression: **#{userBean.sportInterests}**. This causes the entire map to be converted to a single string that contains all keys and values.

Element	Description
<managed-property>	Same as before, the parent element for managed properties.
<property-name>	The name of the property.
<property-class>	JSF uses the default type of **HashMap**, but any other **Map** concrete class could be specified here.
<map-entries>	Parent element of **<key-class>**, **<value-class>**, and **Map** entries.
<key-class>	Element specifying data type of the keys used in the map. When not specified, a **java.lang.String** is used as a default. (Optional)
<value-class>	Element specifying data type of the values used in the map. When not specified, a **java.lang.String** is also used as a default. (Optional)
<map-entry>(1 to N)	Parent element to a **Map** key/value element pair.
<key>	The **key** value used to look up an associated **value**.
<value> or <null-value>	The **<value>** element that is retrieved when the associated key is supplied. To initialize a **Map** property to a **null** value, a **<null-value>** tag is used. Note: The **<null-value>** element cannot be used for primitive data types.

TABLE 5-4 Managed Property Elements for a Map

A more formalized listing of the elements needed for a managed **Map** property follows in Table 5-4.

In Table 5-4, notice that the type of the key and value are specified by **<key-class>** and **<value-class>**, respectively. However, both are optional, with both defaulting to **java.lang .String**. For this reason, the types of the key and value in the previous example were of the default **String** data type. The next example uses a key class of type **java.lang.Integer**. In this example, the key/value pairs consist of an integer ZIP code and the string name of the city in which that ZIP code is found.

```
<managed-bean>
...
  <managed-property>
    <property-name>cityRegistry</property-name>
    <map-entries>
      <key-class>java.lang.Integer</key-class>
      <map-entry>
        <key>94065</key>
        <value>Redwood City</value>
      </map-entry>
      <map-entry>
        <key>95118</key>
        <value>San Jose</value>
      </map-entry>
```

```
      <map-entry>
        <key>32801</key>
        <value>Orlando</value>
      </map-entry>
    </map-entries>
  </managed-property>
</managed-bean>
```

Declaring Lists and Maps Directly as Managed Beans

So far we have examined cases where existing beans had certain properties of type **List** or **Map** registered as managed properties. In fact, it is possible to declare brand new **List**s or **Map**s as managed beans entirely from the Faces configuration file. This is achieved by assigning the **<managed-bean-class>** directly as either a **List** or a **Map**.

Note *When declaring a managed bean directly as a **List** or a **Map**, you must use the concrete class types—**java.util.ArrayList** or **java.util.HashMap**—since it is impossible to call a constructor on an interface.*

The following example shows a **List** being declared entirely as a managed bean.

```
<managed-bean>
  <managed-bean-name>moreSports</managed-bean-name>
  <managed-bean-class>java.util.ArrayList</managed-bean-class>
  <managed-bean-scope>none</managed-bean-scope>
  <list-entries>
    <value>Skiing</value>
    <value>Tennis</value>
    <value>Rollerblading</value>
  </list-entries>
</managed-bean>
```

Notice that the **<managed-bean-scope>** is set to **none**. This simply means that this managed bean is not stored anywhere. Instead, it is instantiated on the fly whenever needed. The lifecycles of managed beans are examined more closely a little later in the chapter, after you have seen how managed beans can be dependent on each other.

Managed Bean Interdependence

One of the most common criteria for IoC containers is that they be able to handle interdependencies between managed objects. The JavaServer Faces Managed Bean Facility does not fall short in this regard. Setting dependencies between managed beans can easily be done using the JSF expression language.

Consider the previous example where we declared a brand new **moreSports** managed bean from scratch that listed a new set of sports as **moreSports**. This list can now be referred to in another bean through an expression. For example, you can add the values from the new list to the existing **sportsInterests** managed bean with the final result being a set of values from both lists.

```
<managed-bean>
...
  <managed-property>
    <property-name>sportsInterests</property-name>
    <list-entries>
      <value>Cycling</value>
      <value>Running</value>
      <value>Swimming</value>
      <value>Kayaking</value>
      <value>#{moreSports[0]}</value>
      <value>#{moreSports[1]}</value>
      <value>#{moreSports[2]}</value>
    </list-entries>
  </managed-property>
</managed-bean>
```

For a more general example of managed bean interdependency, consider a new custom class of type **com.jsfcompref.model.Address** that contains **String** properties for **street**, **city**, and **zipCode**. It can be registered as an independent managed bean using

```
<managed-bean>
  <managed-bean-name>addressBean</managed-bean-name>
  <managed-bean-class>com.jsfcompref.model.Address
</managed-bean-class>
  <managed-bean-scope>none</managed-bean-scope>
</managed-bean>
```

Recall that a scope of **none** means that this bean is not initialized until requested by another managed bean.

Next, you could add two new properties **homeAddress** and **shippingAddress** of type **com.jsfcompref.model.Address** to the original **UserBean**. You can then define these properties by using the following code:

```
<managed-bean>
  <managed-bean-name>userBean</managed-bean-name>
  <managed-bean-class>com.jsfcompref.model.UserBean</managed-bean-class>
  <managed-bean-scope>session</managed-bean-scope>
  <managed-property>
    <property-name>homeAddress</property-name>
    <value>#{addressBean}</value>
  </managed-property>
  <managed-property>
    <property-name>shippingAddress</property-name>
    <value>#{addressBean}</value>
  </managed-property>
  <managed-property>
    <property-name>firstName</property-name>
  </managed-property>
</managed-bean>
```

Using the Annotation syntax would look like

```
@ManaqedProperty(value="#{addressBean}")
private Address homeAddress;
@ManaqedProperty(value="#{addressBean}")
private Address shippingAddress;
```

As a request is made to a page with an expression of #{**userBean.homeAddress**}, a new instance of **UserBean** is created and stored in the **session** scope. Its properties **homeAddress** and **shippingAddress** will also be initialized as well. Subsequent postback operations could add values to the fields of the respective addresses of type **AddressBean** of the **UserBean**, using expressions that reference the address items:

```
<h:inputText value="#{userBean.homeAddress.street}"/>
```

The next question regarding managed bean interdependence is whether cyclical dependencies are possible with managed beans. Although some other IoC containers can handle cyclical dependencies, this is not the case for JSF managed beans. If two are made dependent on each other, a runtime error will occur.

Setting Managed Properties Using EL

An important point to note is that in addition to offering the ability to establish inter-bean dependencies using EL, it is also possible to set managed properties to any value accessible via EL. For example, the implicit object **param** can be used in an EL expression to set a property. This can be a handy trick that allows the application to assign a property based on an incoming **Request** parameter. As an example, consider if the previous **UserBean** had a property, **userid**, also of type **String**. It could be set as a managed property using a value from the implicit **param** object.

```
<managed-property>
  <property-name>userid</property-name>
  <value>#{param.userid}</value>
</managed-property>
```

Using the annotation syntax would look like this:

```
@ManaqedProperty(value="#{param.userid}")
private Address userid;
```

In your Facelets, you could value-bind this property to a UI component:

```
Userid entered:<h:inputText value="#{userBean.userid}"/>
```

To provide a value, of course, you would have to add the userid value as a request parameter:

```
http://host:port/yourapp/faces/yourpage.jsp?userid=cschalk
```

You can now see that it is possible to declare the entire initial state of your model tier using the managed bean facility. This makes for a very powerful and flexible system.

Controlling Managed Bean Life Spans

Much like standard procedural programming languages, JavaServer Faces provides a way to define the scope of a managed bean instance by using a **scope** setting. This setting defines the variable's lifetime and its visibility to other parts of the program. Consider this simple Java class:

```
public class ScopeExample {
  public static String global = "global";
  public void foo() {
    String local = "bar";
  }
}
```

The variable **global** can be accessed anywhere within the VM in which the **ScopeExample** class is loaded. The variable **local** may only be accessed within the **foo( )** method. Within the **foo( )** method, it is valid to say **local = global**, but outside of the **foo( )** method, the **local** variable does not exist—it is said to be "out of scope."

As you have seen in previous managed bean examples, the **<managed-bean-scope>** element of a managed bean, or the **@{Request,View,Session,Application}Scoped** annotation on the managed bean class defines how long the instance of the managed bean will be accessible to other parts of the program. Note that being inaccessible to other parts of the program does not necessarily mean the bean will be garbage-collected. There are various garbage collection algorithms employed by the Java runtime, and each has its own specific way to decide when an instance is garbage-collected. The different managed bean scopes are described in Table 5-5.

Why Not Just Use Request Scope?

One common usage of request scope in JSF applications is to simply pass data from one part of the application to another, with the guarantee that such data passing will not pollute the session and therefore risk a memory leak. Using the request scope for this purpose has a negative performance impact. The request scope, because it's a part of the Servlet specification, must adhere to the notification contract specified in the Servlet RequestAttributeListener interface. This contract enables one or more listeners to be registered to be called back for every add, remove, or replacement operation on the request scope. This has a performance impact, even if no such listeners are registered.

JSF 2.0 adds another scope, with a slightly shorter lifetime than request scope, that doesn't have this performance impact. This scope, called the FacesContext attributes scope, is active only during the running of the faces lifecycle on each request. This is shorter than the request scope, because the faces lifecycle is only active during the FacesServlet invocation. Note that it is possible to put Servlet filters before and/or after the FacesServlet. The request scope is active during those filters, whereas the FacesContext attributes scope is not.

To access the FacesContext attributes scope, you can call the getAttributes( ) method on the FacesContext or use the EL expression #{facesContext.attributes}. Like other scopes, these will give you a map interface.

(continued)

Finally, note that, thanks to the new Custom Scope feature, it is possible to store managed beans into the **FacesContext attributes** scope by declaring **<managed-bean-scope>#{facesContext.attributes}</managed-bean-scope>** in the XML declaration for the managed bean. This feature will be described in detail in Chapter 13.

EXPERT GROUP INSIGHT *The* ***page*** *scope, which is present in JSP, is conspicuous by its absence in JSF. This was intentional to avoid introducing any dependency on the JSP specification in the core JSF specification. The main reason for avoiding all such dependencies was to enable alternate page description technologies, aside from JSP, to be used with JSF. This topic is covered in detail in Chapter 12.*

When dealing with managed beans' different scopes, it is important to remember that managed beans can only reference other managed beans whose scope is either **none** or is greater than or equal to the calling bean's scope. This is also described in Table 5-5.

A final word on scopes in general: It's best to put your beans in the narrowest scope possible, preferably **request**. Doing so helps prevent memory leaks by allowing the data to be garbage-collected frequently, it encourages keeping your design lightweight because putting lots of data into the session each time is costly, and, most important, it cuts down on difficult-to-debug concurrency bugs that can happen when using session and application scope.

Scope	Description	Can Only Reference Other Managed Beans of This Scope:
none or @NoneScoped	Managed beans with a **none** scope are not instantiated nor stored in any other scope. Instead, they are instantiated on demand by another managed bean. Once created, they will persist as long as the calling bean stays alive because their scope will match the calling bean's scope.	none
request or @RequestScoped	Managed beans registered with **request** scope will be instantiated and stay available throughout a single HTTP request. This means that the bean can survive a navigation to another page, provided it was during the same HTTP request.	none, request, view, session, application

TABLE 5-5 JSF Managed Bean Scopes

Scope	Description	Can Only Reference Other Managed Beans of This Scope:
view or @ViewScoped	Managed beans registered in **view** scope remain available as long as the user stays on the same view. Navigating away from that view will cause beans registered in that view's scope to be deallocated.	none, view, session, application
session or @SessionScoped	Managed beans registered with a **session** scope will be stored on the HTTP session. This means that the values in the managed bean will persist beyond a single HTTP request for a single user. This is ideal for a shopping cart type of usage where values must be stored and made available during multiple requests.	none, session, application
application or @ApplicationScoped	Managed beans registered with an **application** scope retain their values throughout the lifetime of the application and are available to all users.	none, application
an EL Expression or a **@CustomScoped** annotation with a value attribute that is an EL expression. Note that the new **FacesContext attributes** scope, explained in a JSF 2.0 tip elsewhere in this chapter, can be used to store managed beans when you use the expression **#{facesContext.attributes}** as the value of the **<managed-bean-scope>** XML element.	If the content of the **<managed-bean-scope>** element, or the value of the **value** attribute on the **@CustomScoped** annotation is an EL Expression, and the expression evaluates to a class that implements **java.util.Map**, then the runtime uses the map itself as the scope into which the instance of the managed bean will be placed. This feature is explained in Chapter 13.	The rules for accessing other beans depend entirely on how the custom scope is defined by the application.

Table 5-5 JSF Managed Bean Scopes *(continued)*

Java EE 5 Annotations

In addition to the annotations mentioned in Table 5-5, Java EE 5 annotations are also available for use in managed beans. There are two kinds of Java EE 5 annotations you can use in a JSF managed bean: lifecycle annotations and data access annotations. Let's discuss the former first.

Any scoped managed bean method annotated with **@PostConstruct** will be called after the managed bean is instantiated, but before the bean is placed in scope. Such a method must take no arguments, must return void, and may not declare a checked exception to be thrown. The method may be public, protected, private, or package private. If the method throws an unchecked exception, the JSF implementation must not put the managed bean into service and no further methods on that managed bean instance will be called. Any scoped managed bean method annotated with **@PreDestroy** will be called before the bean is removed from the scope or before the scope in which the bean resides is destroyed, whichever comes first. The constraints placed on the method are the same as with @PostConstruct. If the method throws an unchecked exception, the implementation may log it, but the exception will not affect the execution in any way.

The data access annotations are: **@Resource**, **@Resources**, **@EJB**, **@EJBs**, **@WebServiceRef**, **@WebServiceRefs**, **@PersistenceContext**, **@PersistenceContexts**, **@PersistenceUnit**, and **@PersistenceUnits**. Usage of these annotations are beyond the scope of this book, but the **@PersistenceContext** annotation is particularly useful in gaining access to the Java Persistence API from your managed beans.

The JSF Expression Language

In the preceding examples (and in earlier chapters), you saw how to access managed bean properties and invoke managed bean custom (action) methods using special expressions with delimiters #{ and }. These expressions follow syntactic rules defined by the Expression Language Specification. Let's now take a closer look at the expression language in JavaServer Faces.

One thing to understand at the outset is that there are differences between the expression language for JSF 1.1 and the expression language for JSF 1.2. In the following discussion, the key differences between the expression language for JSF 1.1 and that for JSF 1.2 are described.

Important Expression Languages Changes Between JSF 1.1 and JSF 1.2

The most fundamental difference between JavaServer Faces versions 1.1 and 1.2 is the introduction of the Unified EL Specification. With JSF 1.1, a JSF-specific implementation of EL was created, and although very similar to other EL implementations, such as those used by JSP 2.0 and the JSP Standard Tag Library (JSTL), it still had significant differences. Because expression languages had become an increasingly popular and well-utilized technology across the Java Web tier, it was decided to generalize the EL concepts introduced specifically by JSF so that they could be used by a wider set of Java Web-tier technologies. This resulted in the creation of the *Unified EL*.

EXPERT GROUP INSIGHT *The Unified EL is now provided by the JSP 2.1 specification, though it is specified in a separate subdocument in that specification. This was done to facilitate eventually separating the Unified EL out into its own JCP specification for use by the entire Java platform Also, separating the EL from the specific technology hosting it, such as the Java Web tier, means that several important concepts that were formerly in the domain of the EL, such as the notion of scope, are now outside of the EL proper and reside only in JSP or JSF. Even so, the rest of this discussion will treat these concepts as if they were a part of the core EL.*

JSF 1.1 developers needn't worry about having to change the syntax of their expressions to upgrade to 1.2, because the Unified EL accepts syntax compatible with JSF 1.1. For example, the following still holds true:

- JSF 1.2 expressions still use delimiters #{ and }.
- Expressions starting with **#{** are still evaluated at runtime, which is referred to as *deferred evaluation*. Expressions starting with **${** are still evaluated at page compile time, in what is referred to as *immediate evaluation*.

***JSF 1.2* TIP** *The JSF 1.1 expression language is upwardly compatible with JSF 1.2.*

Examining the Evolution of the EL: Deferred vs. Immediate Expressions

The EL used in JSF 1.0 and 1.1 is an extension of the EL first used in the JSP Standard Tag Library (JSTL), and later in JSP versions 1.2 and 2.0. The main extension brought to the EL by JSF that is not present in previous versions is the concept of *deferred expressions.* In JSP, any **${}** expression that appears in the page is evaluated immediately as the page is rendered. If an expression appears as the value of a JSP tag attribute, such as

```
<c:set var="name" value="Falstaff" scope="page" />
<demo:customTag value='${pageScope.name}' />
```

then the JavaBeans property named **value** in the **CustomTag.java** tag handler class must have a type that matches the type to which the expression evaluates. Furthermore, the expression **${pageScope.name}** is evaluated immediately when the **demo:customTag** tag is encountered and the **setValue( )** method of the **CustomTag.java** tag handler receives the evaluated value.

Immediate evaluation is perfectly adequate for JSP, but JSF needed something more. JSF introduced the request processing lifecycle (described in Chapter 3), which governs what happens when the form is submitted (postback). During a postback, the JSP page that rendered the markup that is being posted back is not known and not available to the JSF runtime; therefore, any expressions in that page are not available, since they were evaluated immediately when the page was rendered.

JSF introduced the deferred expression concept to allow expressions to be useful both during the rendering of the page, and during a postback. This concept allows a deferred expression, such as **#{user.name}**, to show a value to the user, and also to be the "target" of a value entered by the user. As described earlier, JSF reserves the **#{}** delimiter to mean "deferred expression" and allows JSP to claim **${}** to mean "immediate expression." The **#{}** delimiter was chosen because it prevents the JSP runtime from evaluating the

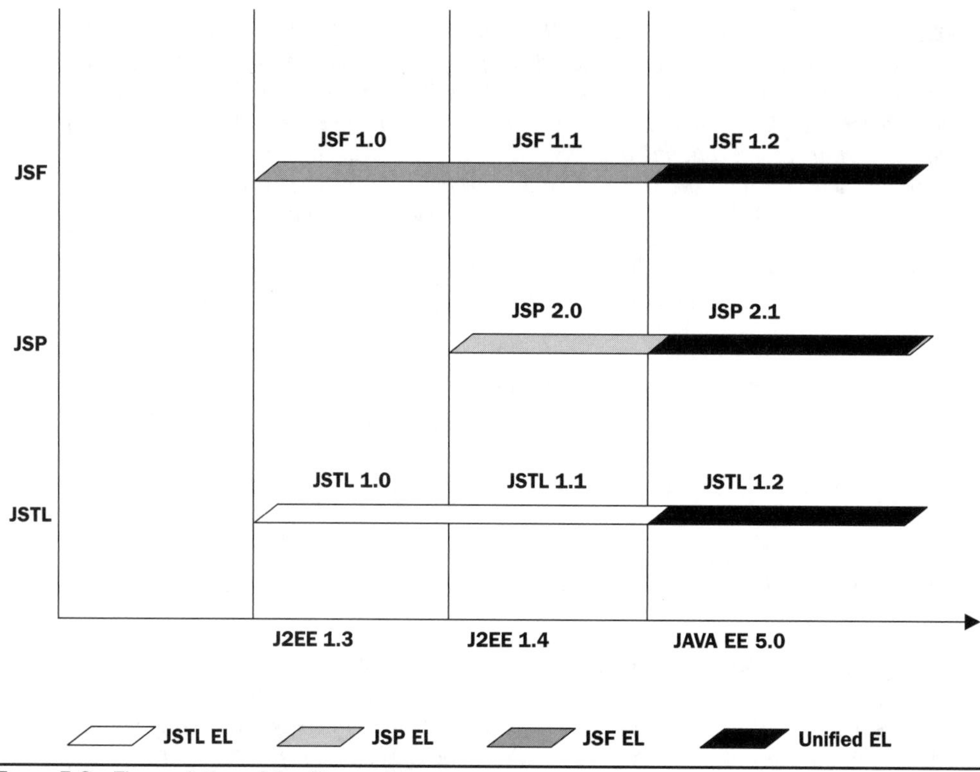

Figure 5-2 The evolution of the EL over time

expression, allowing the JSF JSP Custom Tag handler to create the expression instance and store it in the component for later evaluation.

Figure 5-2 illustrates the evolution of the EL over time. The Unified EL used in JSF 1.2, JSP 2.1, and JSTL 1.2 adds the concept of deferred expression and allows JSP to be aware of deferred and immediate expressions.

Expert Group Insight *In keeping with the design goal of being extremely extensible, it has always been possible to customize the semantics of the EL since the beginning of JSF. For more on how to do so, please see Chapter 13.*

Unified EL Concepts

The goal of having a Unified EL is to provide an easy and compact way to access application objects from any point in the application. A major force behind the need for a compact language to refer to objects was the increased usage of tag attributes in JSP or, in general, XML. Consider a tag with an attribute:

```
<MyTag attribute="value" />.
```

If *value* had to be derived dynamically at runtime, it could necessitate a long Java statement to obtain the value. Expression language provides a solution to this by

1. Eliminating the need to always refer to container-managed parent objects (**request**, **session**, and **application**).
2. Shortening the expression by omitting **get** and **set** from object properties/methods.
3. Allowing navigation of an arbitrarily complex hierarchy of JavaBeans objects.

Value Expressions

Value expressions (referred to as *Value Binding Expressions* in JSF 1.1) are by far the most common usage of expressions in JSF applications. They allow for presenting (getting) dynamically evaluated results or setting bean properties at runtime using a compact expression. Value expressions can be used to evaluate a single value such as the value of a property of a managed bean or an expression that evaluates a final value from multiple sources, including sources outside of Faces managed beans. Recall an expression used in previous examples:

```
<h:outputText value="#{userBean.firstName}"/>
```

The expression **#{userBean.firstName}** is a shorthand way to call the **getfirstName( )** method of the **userBean** managed bean. In general, value expressions are evaluated behind the scenes by a **getValue( )** method from a **ValueExpression** instance that is provided by the JSF runtime.

What Really Happens When an EL Expression Is Evaluated

As the expression **#{userBean.firstName}** is evaluated at runtime, the EL system breaks the expression down into two parts. The part before the first dot (or square bracket) is called the *base*. In this case, the base is **userBean**. The part after the first dot (or square bracket) is called a *property* and is recursively broken down into smaller parts; in this case it is just **firstName**. Generally, the base says *where to look for the bean instance*, and the property parts are interpreted as *beans properties to get* from the base. The first thing the EL does is check if the value of the base is one of the implicit objects (described shortly). In this case, it is not, so the EL sets about looking for **userBean** in progressively wider scopes. It does this by first calling **getAttribute("userBean")** on the **ServletRequest**. Because the **userBean** managed bean was declared in the **session** scope, it is not found in the **ServletRequest**. The EL then obtains the **Map** from the **getViewMap( )** method of the **UIViewRoot**. Again, because the bean was declared in **session** scope, it is not found in the **view** scope. The EL then calls **getAttribute("userBean")** on the **HttpSession**. In this case, the bean is found, so it is returned. (If the bean had not been found in the session, **getAttribute("userBean")** would have been called on the **ServletContext** for this application.) Once the EL has obtained the base, it then proceeds to resolve properties against the base. With **firstName**, the **getFirstName( )** method is called on the **UserBean** instance.

In addition to simply displaying dynamically derived values from value expressions, the output of a value expression can also be used to set an attribute of a UI component. A common usage is to set the **rendered** attribute to a value expression that evaluates to a **boolean** value. Consider the example:

```
<h:outputText rendered="#{userBean.manager}" value="#{Employee.salary}"/>
```

Notice the **rendered** attribute is defined with a value expression that derives a **boolean** value (assuming the **manager** field is of type **boolean**) by calling the method **isManager( )**.

This allows the **UIOutput** component to render conditionally, based on whether or not the user is a manager.

Using Value Expressions to Update Model Data

Using expressions to display values in a Web page is nothing new. Indeed, the original EL in early versions of JSTL had this feature. The new feature introduced by JSF is the ability to use an expression to **set** a value when a form is submitted. This means value expressions can be used for updating Model objects. For example, if an input UI component (implements **EditableValueHolder**) is value-bound to a managed bean property (Model object), upon postback the bean property will take on the updated value applied to the UI component. This occurs during the Update Model Values phase of the JSF request processing lifecycle. Recall the input example from earlier in the chapter:

```
<h:inputText value="#{userBean.firstName}"/>
```

During a postback, if the value in the input field has changed, the new value will be applied to the managed bean (**UserBean**). This is handled behind the scenes by the **setValue( )** method on the same **ValueExpression (ValueBinding)** instance calling **userBean**'s **setFirstName( )** method.

Other new features introduced by JSF include the ability to get the type of an EL expression and to determine if an EL expression is read-only or read-write.

Value Expression Syntax

So far you have seen only very basic examples of value expressions. Let's examine some more complex examples.

Recall the usage of a single dot (.) operator in previous examples. With EL it is also possible to use consecutive dot operators to traverse object hierarchies as shown in this expression:

```
<h:outputText value="#{userBean.homeAddress.street}"/>
```

In this case, the dot operator successively calls the getter methods, **getHomeAddress( )** and **getStreet( )**, as it traverses down the object hierarchy to retrieve a final value.

To access elements of an array or collection, you can use brackets ([ ]) in the expression. Recall the expressions that were used in the managed property list for **sportsInterest**:

```
...
  <value>#{moreSports[0]} </value>
  <value>#{moreSports[1]} </value>
  <value>#{moreSports[2]} </value>
```

This example also shows how JSF EL can be used outside of a JSP or a UI component. In this case, it was used in **faces-config.xml**.

In general, square brackets can be used in both JavaBeans and Maps as well. Bracket syntax is really the core, primitive way to access properties, and the dot syntax is provided as an easy-to-use alternative for simple property names.

In addition to user-created application objects, *implicit objects* are also accessible via value expressions. An *implicit object* is managed by the container. Table 5-6 lists the implicit objects along with a usage example.

Implicit Object	Type	Description
application	ServletContext or PortletContext	The **ServletContext** or **PortletContext**, depending on whether an application is running in a servlet or portlet context, respectively.
applicationScope	Map	A map for storing application-scoped data. This is the same map into which application-scoped managed beans are stored.
component (JSF 2.0 only)	UIComponent	The **UIComponent** instance being currently processed.
cc (JSF 2.0 only)	UIComponent	The top-level composite component currently being processed.
cookie	Map	A map view of values in the HTTP **Set-Cookie** header.
facesContext	FacesContext	The actual **FacesContext** instance.
flash (2.0 only)	Map	A map whose values are guaranteed to be present only on the "next" request. (A detailed explanation of **flash** is found in the text.)
header	Map	A map view of all the HTTP headers for this request.
headerValues	Map	A map view of all the HTTP headers for this request. Each value in the map is an array of strings containing all the values for that key.
initParam	Map	A map view of the init parameters for this application.
param	Map	A map view of all the query parameters for this request.
paramValues	Map	A map view of all the HTTP headers for this request. Each value in the map is an array of strings containing all the values for that key.
request	ServletRequest or PortletRequest	The **ServletRequest** or **PortletRequest**, depending on whether the code is executing in a servlet or portlet environment, respectively.
requestScope	Map	A map for storing request-scoped data. This is the same scope into which request-scoped managed beans are stored.
resource	Resource	Allow a resource reference to be rendered to the page.
session	HttpSession or PortletSession	The **HttpSession** or **PortletSession**, depending on whether code is executing in a servlet or portlet environment, respectively.
sessionScope	Map	A map view of the session-scoped attributes.
view	UIViewRoot	The current **UIViewRoot** for this view.
viewScope (JSF 2.0 only)	Map	A map view of the attributes scoped to the current view.

TABLE 5-6 Implicit Objects Available via EL

All of the properties in Table 5-6 that are of type **Map** can be accessed using the **#{MapObject['key']}** expression form. For example, to display a request parameter, **userid**, in a JSF page, you can use

```
<h:outputText value="#{param['userid']}" />
```

or

```
<h:outputText value="#{param.userid}" />
```

Also, when using Facelets, it is valid to nest expressions so that an expression can be used to look up values in a map, as in

```
<h:outputText value="#{param[cookie.currentUser]}" />
```

The EL Flash

Expert Group Insight *The name "flash" and the concept behind it are taken directly from Ruby on Rails.*

Even though more people know "flash" as a display technology from Adobe Systems Incorporated, David Heinemeier Hansson, the creator of Rails, chose the term "flash" for its usage as in "flash memory." In this sense, flash is short-term storage. Specifically, anything you put into the flash on one request will be available from the flash on the "next" request from the same browser window. This is true whether the next request is a JSF postback, a redirect, or even a simple HTTP GET for a new page. To make the concept clear, let's take the canonical example of "master-detail." The master-detail pattern shows a master object and a single detail object that gives more information about the currently selected master object. The following example uses the set of available service levels (basic, medium, premium) in the virtual trainer as the master object, and the list of subscribers to each service level as the detail objects. This example only needs one Facelets page: **master.xhtml**, shown here:

```
<!DOCTYPE html PUBLIC "-//W3C//DTD XHTML 1.0 Transitional//EN"
"http://www.w3.org/TR/xhtml1/DTD/xhtml1-transitional.dtd">
<html xmlns="http://www.w3.org/1999/xhtml"
      xmlns:h="http://java.sun.com/jsf/html"
      xmlns:f="http://java.sun.com/jsf/core">
<h:head>
  <title>A Simple JavaServer Faces 2.0 View</title>
</h:head>
<h:body>
  <h:form>
      <h1>Master</h1>
      <p><h:selectOneMenu value="#{flash.serviceLevel}">
              <f:selectItems value="#{model.keys}"/>
          </h:selectOneMenu>
      <h:commandButton value="Show Subscribers" /></p>
  </h:form>
```

```
  <h:panelGroup rendered="#{! empty flash.serviceLevel}">
      <h1>Detail</h1>
      <p>Users with Service Level: "#{flash.serviceLevel}":</p>
      <h:dataTable border="1" var="user"
                   value="#{model.data[flash.serviceLevel]}">
          <h:column>
              <f:facet name="header">First Name</f:facet>
              #{user.firstName}
          </h:column>
          <h:column>
              <f:facet name="header">Last Name</f:facet>
              #{user.lastName}
          </h:column>
          <h:column>
              <f:facet name="header">Sex</f:facet>
              #{user.sex}
          </h:column>
      </h:dataTable>
  </h:panelGroup>
</h:body>
</html>
```

The page has two regions, the **<h:form>**, which is the "master" section of the page, and the **<h:panelGroup>**, which is the "detail" section of the page. The master section has an **<h:selectOneMenu>**, which shows the available service levels and allows the user to choose one, and an **<h:commandButton>**, which submits the form. Naturally, the page could be enhanced to auto-submit the form when a selection is made from the list. The chosen service level and the available service levels are given by EL expressions:

```
<h:selectOneMenu value="#{flash.serviceLevel}">
  <f:selectItems value="#{model.keys}"/>
</h:selectOneMenu>
```

The use of **#{flash.serviceLevel}** as the **value** attribute for the **h:selectOneMenu** tag says that the chosen service level is stored into the flash under the key "serviceLevel." The use of **#{model.keys}** as the **value** attribute for the **f:selectItems** tag says that the menu should allow the user to choose one value from the **Collection** returned from the **keys** property of the managed bean named **model**.

Down in the "detail" section of the page, the **h:panelGroup** tag has a **rendered** attribute with the value **#{! empty flash.serviceLevel}**. This funny expression uses the **!** (not) and **empty** operators to cause the detail section to only display when the user has selected a service level. Also, the selected service level is echoed out with the simple expression **#{flash.serviceLevel}** and is used as the key to the **Map** returned by **model.data**, as shown in the **value** attribute of **h:dataTable**. The entries in the **Map** are instances of **List<UserData>**, which is easily displayed by **h:dataTable**.

The managed bean named **model** is shown following:

```
package com.jsfcompref;

import java.util.ArrayList;
import java.util.HashMap;
```

```
import java.util.List;
import java.util.Map;
import java.util.Set;
import javax.faces.bean.ManagedBean;
import javax.faces.bean.SessionScoped;

@ManagedBean
@SessionScoped
public class Model {

    private Map<String, List<UserBean>> data;

    public Model() {
        data = new HashMap<String, List<UserBean>>();
        // Populate the model with data in the constructor.  Naturally
        // in a real application, the model would be populated some
        // other way
        List<UserBean> users = new ArrayList<UserBean>();

        // users with "Medium" service level
        users.add(makeUser("Bob", "Biceps", "Medium", "M"));
        users.add(makeUser("Frank", "Forearms", "Medium", "M"));
        users.add(makeUser("Sherry", "Shins", "Medium", "F"));
        users.add(makeUser("Alice", "Abs", "Medium", "F"));
        data.put(users.get(0).getServiceLevel(), users);

        users = new ArrayList<UserBean>();

        // users with "Basic" service level
        users.add(makeUser("Pete", "Pectorals", "Basic", "M"));
        users.add(makeUser("Neil", "Neck", "Basic", "M"));
        users.add(makeUser("Ellen", "Elbows", "Basic", "F"));
        users.add(makeUser("Tina", "Tummy", "Basic", "F"));
        data.put(users.get(0).getServiceLevel(), users);

        users = new ArrayList<UserBean>();

        // users with "Premium" service level
        users.add(makeUser("Bernd", "Beine", "Premium", "M"));
        users.add(makeUser("Rolf", "Rückenschmerz", "Premium", "M"));
        users.add(makeUser("Bettina", "Bauch", "Premium", "F"));
        users.add(makeUser("Frauke", " Fußknöchel", "Premium", "F"));
        data.put(users.get(0).getServiceLevel(), users);


    }

    public Set<String> getKeys() {
        return data.keySet();
    }

    private UserBean makeUser(String firstName, String lastName,
            String serviceLevel, String sex) {
        UserBean result = new UserBean();
```

```
        result.setFirstName(firstName);
        result.setLastName(lastName);
        result.setServiceLevel(serviceLevel);
        result.setSex(sex);
        return result;
    }

    public Map<String,List<UserBean>> getData() {
        return data;
    }

}
```

A screen shot of the running page is shown here:

The **flash** implicit object has several other features that are closely related to navigation and will be described in a more appropriate context in the chapter that deals with navigation exclusively.

Expression Operators

In addition to the **[ ]** and **.** operators used in some previous examples, the EL specification defines several other useful operators. These operators can be categorized into the following types: arithmetic, relational, logical, conditional, and empty. Table 5-7 shows these operators.

Here are some EL operator examples:

```
<h:outputText rendered=" #{userBean.serviceLevel == 'Premium'}"
value ="Congratulations, Premium members receive a
#{Discounts.basicDiscount * 10}% discount!" />
```

The discount example renders only for Premium members and provides them with a discount percentage ten times the basic discount value.

Category	Operators
Arithmetic	+, -, *, / (or **div**), % (or **mod**)
Relational	== (or **eq**), **!=** (or **ne**), **<** (or **lt**), **>** (or **gt**), **<=** (or **le**), **>=** (or **ge**)
Logical	&& (or **and**), **||** (or **or**), **!** (or **not**)
Conditional	A ? **B : C** (Evaluate **A** to Boolean. If true, evaluates and returns **B**. Otherwise, evaluates and returns **C**.)
Empty	= **empty A** (If **A** is *null* or is an empty string, array, **Map**, or **Collection**, returns **true**. Otherwise returns **false**.)

TABLE 5-7 EL Operators

To show city temperatures in both Fahrenheit and Celsius, one can use

```
<h:outputText value="Temperature for #{cityRegistry.city.name} is:
Fahrenheit: #{cityRegistry.city.fahrenheitTemp} Celsius:
#{(cityRegistry.city.fahrenheitTemp - 32) * 5 / 9}">
```

Method Expressions

Method expressions are similar to value expressions, but instead of being used to retrieve and set managed bean (object) properties, method expressions are used to invoke public, non-static methods of managed beans. Recall the example in Chapter 2 where a method expression was bound to a **commandButton**:

```
<h:commandButton value="Confirm" action="#{userBean.addConfirmedUser}" />
```

When the Confirm button is clicked, the method **addConfirmedUser( )** is invoked.

Method expressions use a subset syntax of value expressions where only the dot operator or bracket operator([ ]) is used to traverse the object hierarchy to access a public non-static method. The other operators do not apply to method expressions.

Invocation of Methods via Method Expressions

Note that the EL does not include a way to pass arguments to methods. This is intentional to keep the EL as simple as possible.

When used from a JSP page, the arguments to the **MethodExpression** depend on the context in which the expression is used. Table 5-8 provides the method expression details of the standard tags with the **ActionSource (ActionSource2)** behavioral interface. It lists the arguments and return type to which the method pointed to by the **MethodExpression** must conform. It also lists the tags and tag attributes for the **MethodExpression**.

Table 5-9 shows the standard tags/UI components with the **EditableValueHolder** behavioral interface and their method expression details. The single tag attribute, **valueChangeListener**, is bound to a value change listener method, which accepts a **ValueChangeEvent** argument and has a return type of **void**.

Standard Tag Name	Tag Attribute	Return Type	Arguments	Description
h:commandLink, h:commandButton	action	String	none	Method to call when the **ActionSource** component is actuated. Returns a **String** for the **NavigationHandler** to determine where to navigate to.
	actionListener	void	ActionEvent	Method to call when the **ActionSource** component is actuated.

TABLE 5-8 ActionSource (ActionSource2) Standard Tags Method Expression Details

The standard tag **f:view** with its (JSF 1.2 only) attributes and method expression details is displayed in Table 5-10.

EXPERT GROUP INSIGHT *To demonstrate the value of having a diverse community of experts developing the JSF specification, the entire concept of* ***MethodExpressions*** *and making them invokeable in response to a button press on a form came from Expert Group members who are part of the tool development community. This is one example of how the design of JSF is very tool friendly, but it is by no means designed exclusively for tools.*

Standard Tag Name	Tag Attribute	Return Type	Argument	Description
h:inputHidden h:inputSecret h:inputText h:inputTextArea h:selectOneMenu h:selectOneListBox h:selectOneRadio h:selectManyMenu h:selectManyListBox h:selectManyRadio h:selectBooleanCheckbox	valueChangeListener	void	ValueChangeEvent	Called when the system detects that a component's value has changed.

TABLE 5-9 EditableValueHolder Standard Tags Method Expression Details

PART I

Standard Tag Name	Tag Attribute	Return Type	Arguments, In Order	Description
f:view	beforePhase (1.2 Only)	void	PhaseEvent	Method that will be called before every phase executes, except for the Restore View phase of the JSF request processing lifecycle
	afterPhase (1.2 Only)	void	PhaseEvent	Method that will be called after every phase executes, except for the Restore View phase of the JSF request processing lifecycle

Table 5-10 The Standard Tag f:view and Its Method Expression Details

Note that the **action** attribute of tags that represent **ActionSource** components is special in that it can accept a literal string, or a **MethodExpression** as listed in the table. If given a literal string, the EL creates a special **MethodExpression** that simply returns the literal string. In this way, you can manually specify a navigation outcome. (Navigation is covered in detail in Chapter 6.)

Invoking Arbitrary Methods Using EL

Version 2.1 of the Unified Expression Language, included in Java EE 6, now has support for invoking arbitrary methods and passing arguments to them. The feature behaves intuitively, as shown in the following XHTML and Java code. Note that if you run JSF 2.0 on a non–Java EE 6 container, you will probably not have access to this feature.

This example consists of two pages because the URL query string is used to convey arguments to the method. Note that passing unchecked query parameters directly to a method invocation is totally insecure and a production application would use the "View Parameters" feature, as described in Chapter 6. That said, the first page, **main.xhtml**, simply contains a link to the second page:

```
<!DOCTYPE html PUBLIC "-//W3C//DTD XHTML 1.0 Transitional//EN"
"http://www.w3.org/TR/xhtml1/DTD/xhtml1-transitional.dtd">
<html xmlns="http://www.w3.org/1999/xhtml"
      xmlns:h="http://java.sun.com/jsf/html"
      xmlns:f="http://java.sun.com/jsf/core">
<h:head>
  <title>A Simple JavaServer Faces 2.0 View</title>
</h:head>
<h:body>
  <h:form>
    <p>
        <h:link outcome="page02" value="Link with query parameters">
            <f:param name="word1" value="hello" />
            <f:param name="word2" value="dolly" />
        </h:link>
    </p>
  </h:form>
</h:body>
</html>
```

When the user mouses over the link, the URL shown will be: **http://localhost:8080/methodInvocation/faces/page02.xhtml?word1=hello&word2=dolly**. The second page, **page02.xhtml**, invokes the method and displays its output.

```
<!DOCTYPE html PUBLIC "-//W3C//DTD XHTML 1.0 Transitional//EN"
"http://www.w3.org/TR/xhtml1/DTD/xhtml1-transitional.dtd">
<html xmlns="http://www.w3.org/1999/xhtml"
      xmlns:h="http://java.sun.com/jsf/html"
      xmlns:f="http://java.sun.com/jsf/core">
<h:head>
  <title>Show method invocation</title>
</h:head>
<h:body>
  <h:form>
    <p>
      The text after the colon comes from the invocation of
      a method via the EL: #{model.generateSentance(param.word1,
      param.word2)}
    </p>
  </h:form>
</h:body>
</html>
```

Finally, the managed bean that contains the method to be invoked:

```
package com.jsfcompref;

import javax.faces.bean.ManagedBean;
import javax.faces.bean.RequestScoped;

@ManagedBean
@RequestScoped
public class Model {
    public String generateSentance(String word1, String word2) {
        String result = "invalid arguments";

        if (null != word1 && !word1.isEmpty() &&
            null != word2 && !word2.isEmpty()) {
            result = "The value of word1 is \"" + word1 +
                    "\" and the value of word2 is \"" + word2 + "\".";
        }

        return result;
    }
}
```

Web Application Development Details on Managed Beans

Before concluding this chapter, it is necessary to examine two important higher-level application development concepts with managed beans. The first is how to access/update managed beans programmatically from Java directly. The second is the backing bean concept.

How to Access Managed Beans Programmatically

Although you have seen many examples that access and update managed bean properties, in both pages and in the Faces configuration file, there is still one important thing to cover: how to access managed beans programmatically. To understand why this is important, consider the following scenario. Assume that a user has logged in to an application. While that user is logged in, his or her personal information is stored in a managed bean with a **scope** setting of **session**, so it will remain alive during the life of the session. If a custom method needs to access any user-specific information, such as the user's **userid** or first name/last name, this can be done programmatically using the following Java code:

```
ELContext elContext = context.getELContext( );
Application application = context.getApplication( );
String userid = (String) application.evaluateValueExpressionGet(context,
"#{userBean.userid}",String.class);
```

To set the get or set the value, use

```
ExpressionFactory expressionFactory = application.getExpressionFactory( );
ValueExpression ve =.expressionFactory.createValueExpression(elContext,
"#{userBean.userid}",String.class);
userId = (String) ve.getValue(elContext);
ve.setValue(elContext, "newUserId");
```

Note that the entire **UserBean** instance can be retrieved by using the expression **#{userBean}** without any properties, as shown here:

```
ExpressionFactory expressionFactory = application.getExpressionFactory( );
ValueExpression ve =.expressionFactory.createValueExpression(elContext,
"#{userBean }",UserBean.class);
UserBean user = (UserBean) ve.getValue(elContext);
```

Once you have the reference to an actual **UserBean** instance, you can naturally call its methods as normal.

Invoking a Method on a Managed Bean Programmatically

In addition to just accessing values of managed bean properties, JSF also provides a way to invoke a method of a managed bean. For example, if you want to execute the method **addConfirmedUser( )**, which was introduced in the JSFReg application in Chapter 2, you would use the following:

```
Application application = FacesContext.getCurrentInstance().getApplication();
ExpressionFactory expressionFactory = application.getExpressionFactory( );
MethodExpression me = expressionFactory.
  createMethodExpression(elContext,"#{UserBean.addConfirmedUser}",
                        Void.class, null);
try
  {
    me.invoke(context, null);
  }
```

```
catch (ELException e)
  {
    Throwable wrapped = e.getCause( );
  }
```

Notice in the previous code listing that the method **addConfirmedUser( )** did not take any arguments so the second argument of **invoke( )** was null. However, if the **addConfirmedUser( )** method accepted arguments that included a custom **UserInfo** object as well as an **Id** of type **String**, the method expression code would be as follows:

```
Object result = null;
MethodExpression me = expressionFactory.
  createMethodExpression(elContext,
    "#{UserBean.addConfirmedUser }", Void.class
    new Class [] { UserInfo.class, String.class} );
try
  {
    result = mb.invoke(context, new Object [] { UserInfo(),"joe.shmoe" });
  }
catch (ELException e)
  {
    Throwable wrapped = e.getCause( );
  }
```

Notice also that it is possible to retrieve the results of a method binding invocation shown here using **result** to store the return value. Here is how this method invocation is done:

```
...
elContext = context.getElContext();
MethodExpression me =
  expressionFactory.createMethodExpression(elContext,
    "#{UserBean.addConfirmedUser }", Void.TYPE,
    new Class [] { UserInfo.class, String.class});
try
  {
    result = me.invoke(elContext, new Object [] { UserInfo(), "joe.shmoe" });
  }
catch (ELException ele)
  {
    Throwable wrapped = ele.getCause();
  }
```

Note that any exception thrown by the invoked method is wrapped in an **ELException** in the Faces 1.2 Unified EL. The **cause** must be extracted from these exceptions to see what really happened in the invoked method.

Further coverage of accessing managed beans programmatically is provided in Chapter 10, where the Virtual Trainer example application is reviewed in detail.

Using Managed Beans as Backing Beans for JSF Pages

Users of Microsoft Visual Basic or ASP.Net are familiar with the notion of having an associated source code file (or class) that provides the "back-end plumbing" that handles events, updates data, and so on for a specific page. This is known as the *backing bean* concept, and although not specifically required by the Faces specification, it is fully supported and recommended in most cases. In fact, several JSF-enabled integrated development environments (IDEs) enable or, in some cases, force this programming style on the developer. (You will see examples of this in Chapter 17 when we examine JSF development with several JSF-enabled IDEs.)

To implement a backing bean approach in JSF, you can create a Java class for each JSF page and register it as a managed bean. It is recommended that backing beans be declared to be in request scope. The most preferred usage is to have a single backing bean per page although this is not enforced by any specification. A common usage is also to name the class the same name as the page. For example, **login.jsp** would have an associated backing bean of **Login.java**. Placing the backing bean classes in a subpackage of ".backing" is also useful. Finally, the backing beans can also be registered in the **faces-config.xml** file with "_Backing" added to their names so you always know which beans are backing beans.

In general, the backing bean holds the following artifacts for a page:

- Properties corresponding to input fields on a page, such as string properties for **userid** and **password**.
- Action methods and action listeners that correspond to UI components that initiate action events, such as clicking Register or Next Page.
- Declarations of UI component instances that can be directly *bound* to the UI components used on the page. (We'll drill down on this usage in more detail in Chapter 7.)

In short, it is the responsibility of the backing bean to serve as a conduit from the page to server-side application logic. In other words, it serves as the "middle man" between the page and the back-end business logic. A typical set of pages and their corresponding backing beans that link to back-end business logic is shown in Figure 5-3.

To get a better idea of how the backing bean concept works, consider a typical login example. In this example you could have a page (**login.jsp**), which is built with a collection of **UIInput** components (input fields) to accept the login credentials. In this example, the backing bean can be a Java class, **Login.java,** which has a corresponding set of JavaBean properties (of type **String**) for temporarily storing the user's login credentials. To handle the user's button click on a Login button (**UICommand**), an action method, **checkUserCredentials( )**, could be invoked. It could then call a back-end business method that performs a database or

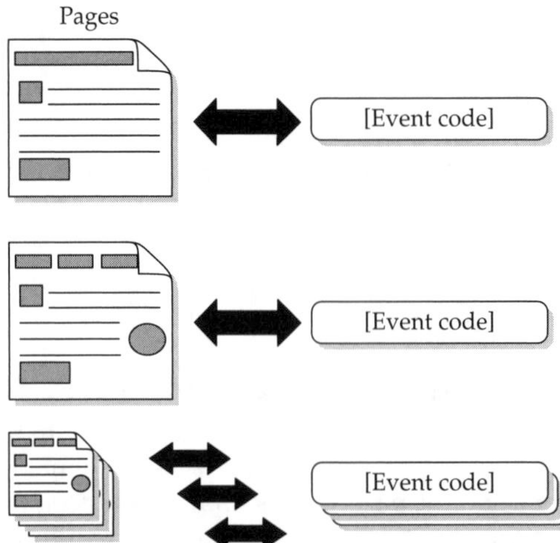

FIGURE 5-3 The backing bean concept illustrated

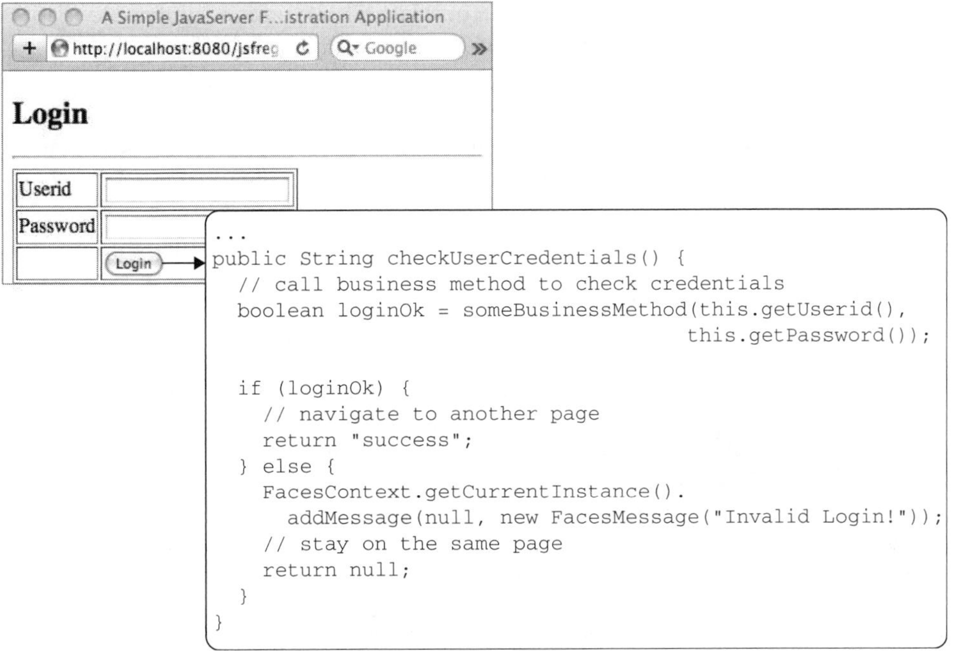

Figure 5-4 The backing bean concept shown in a login example

LDAP lookup of the user to determine whether the credentials are valid. Figure 5-4 illustrates this example.

Here is a more advanced example of backing bean usage where a page, **employees_table.jsp**, displays a scrollable table of employee information using a corresponding backing bean, **EmployeesTable.java**. In this example, the JSP page uses an **HtmlDataTable** (**<h:dataTable/>**) component to display a table of employee records. It also uses a custom **Scroller** UI component that works with methods in the backing bean to handle scrolling events such as next page, previous page, first, and last to navigate through the data being displayed by the table component. The JSP page could also have columns for row-level operations such as Edit and Delete. When the user clicks Edit, he or she would navigate to a different page to edit the row values in a form. Clicking Delete would simply delete the selected record and remain on the same page. For this example, the backing bean (**EmployeesTable.java**) would most probably have the following:

- Any JavaBean properties that are *value bound* to components in the page. In this example the **<h:dataTable> (HtmlDataTable)** component could be value bound to a JavaBean property that returns either a **List**, **Result**, **ResultSet**, or an **Array**. For example:

  ```
  <h:dataTable value="#{EmpTable_Backing.empList}" />
  ```

  This is where the tabular data is initially retrieved; however, to manipulate the data, such as scrolling and so on, the **HtmlDataTable** component on the page can also be directly bound to a declared instance of **UIData** (or **HtmlDataTable**), which has the necessary methods to navigate through the tabular data.

- At least one instance of a **UIData** (or **HtmlDataTable**) component that is *directly bound* to the **DataTable** on the page such as:

  ```
  <h:dataTable value="#{TrainingEventRegistry.eventlist}"
  binding="#{EmpTable_ Backing.tableData}" />
  ```

  In this example **EmpTable_Backing.tableData** is of type **UIData** and is used to perform data navigation operations on the tabular **(List)** data that was value bound to **HtmlDataTable**.

- An action listener method for handling table events such as scrolling through data.

Figure 5-5 illustrates our example where we have an **HtmlDataTable** component that is bound to both a **UIData** instance as well as value bound to a method that returns a **List**.

For more detailed **UIData** and **HtmlDataTable** examples, Chapter 9, which illustrates the Virtual Trainer example application, includes complete coverage of working with tabular data in Faces applications, including how to perform data navigation (scrolling) as well as inserting, updating, and deleting data associated with **HtmlDataTable** components.

Before concluding the chapter, here is a final thing to consider when using backing beans. It is possible to have more than one backing bean per page, or have multiple pages bound to properties of a single bean, as there is no specified rule on this. This is left to the developer's discretion, but having numerous dependencies between multiple pages and multiple backing beans can become very hard to manage. However, it's still technically okay to have separate request-scoped managed beans for subsections of your page that get included and reused across multiple pages. Again, these are design considerations where the Faces application architect will have to weigh the benefits of standard OOP reuse mechanisms against raising the overall application architecture complexity.

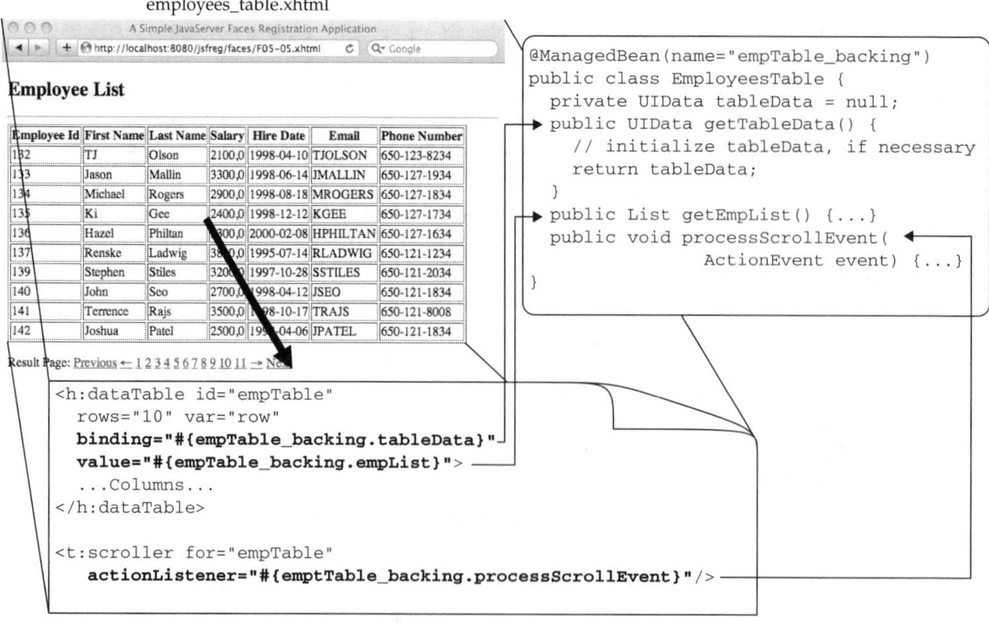

FIGURE 5-5 An **HtmlDataTable** bound to a **UIData** instance and a **List**

CHAPTER 6

The Navigation Model

One of the most elegant design aspects of JavaServer Faces is its navigation model. The JSF Navigation Model allows for the definition of a JSF application's entire page flow, which is a collection of rules governing when and how page navigation should occur in an application. As you may recall, basic navigation was introduced in Chapter 2; however, this chapter goes further and examines the JSF Navigation Model in detail by describing both the architecture behind JSF navigation as well as the different types of navigation.

The chapter begins by describing a new navigation feature added by JSF 2.0 called *implicit navigation,* which makes it very easy to add navigation to your application without adding XML configuration. Next, rule-based navigation system is described. The chapter concludes by presenting several examples of building navigation rules.

Since navigation page flow is easily portrayed visually, several JSF-enabled integrated development environments are now offering the ability to visually design the navigation page flow in a visual editor. Figure 6-1 shows Oracle JDeveloper's JSF navigation page flow designer.

Using Implicit Navigation

Most developers will find the JSF Navigation Model very easy to work with. Adding navigation to your Faces page can be as simple as hard-coding page names, such as "next," "next.xhtml," "confirmation," or "confirmation.xhtml," directly into your Facelets views, or as complex as building a collection of Faces navigation rules, complete with EL expressions for conditional navigation. The former approach, putting page names directly into the Facelets views, is called "implicit navigation" and is new in JSF 2.0. The latter approach, involving XML navigation rules, is called "rule-based navigation" and has been a part of JSF since its inception. Behind the scenes, JSF navigation relies on the familiar Java event model for its underlying architecture. As you'll see in this chapter, the overall Faces Navigation Model and its event model–based architecture provide a streamlined solution to the overall task of creating and managing an enterprise application's many navigation scenarios.

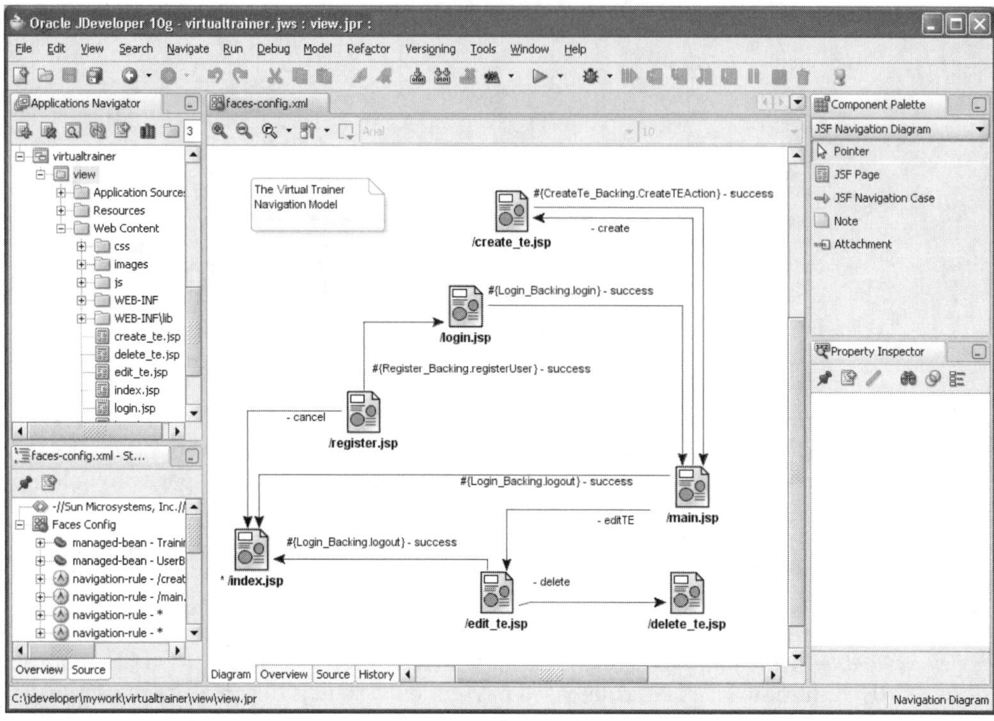

FIGURE 6-1 A JavaServer Faces navigation page flow in Oracle JDeveloper

---

EXPERT GROUP INSIGHT *Another lesson from the Ruby on Rails Web framework, and from books such as Steve Krug's* Don't Make Me Think *(New Riders, 2005), is the notion of not burdening the user with the need to understand any more complexity than necessary to actually get the job done. Ed Burns likes to refer to this as the "pay as you go complexity tax." Several key features of JSF 2.0, including page navigation, have been designed with this in mind. In the case of page navigation, a new feature called "implicit navigation" allows a very simple navigation model. Consider an application with two pages,* ***page01.xhtml*** *and* ***page02.xhtml****. If you want to put a button on* ***page01.xhtml*** *that, when pressed, submits form values and goes to* ***page02.xhtml*** *(if validation was successful, of course), you can now simply say* ***<h:commandButton value="next" action="page02" />****. Only when you need more flexibility do you need to go about using EL expressions or writing navigation rules in a separate file.*

The JSF navigation system is built on top of a simple rule system that answers the question, "which view should be shown next?" To answer this question, the rule system considers several different questions, such as "what is the current view?" "which button was pressed?" "does the view which should be shown next actually exist?" and "am I allowed to show the view which should be shown next?" and comes up with an answer, such as "page02.xhtml." It is not necessary to understand the rule system on which navigation is built in order to effectively use it. Instead, you can rely on the *implicit navigation* feature provided by JSF 2.0. This approach was illustrated by the simple registration example in Chapter 2. It provides an easy way to add navigation to your Faces application.

Let's recall the **register.xhtml** page from Chapter 2, with the important markup shown in bold face.

```
<!DOCTYPE html PUBLIC "-//W3C//DTD XHTML 1.0 Transitional//EN"
"http://www.w3.org/TR/xhtml1/DTD/xhtml1-transitional.dtd">
<html xmlns="http://www.w3.org/1999/xhtml"
      xmlns:h="http://java.sun.com/jsf/html"
      xmlns:f="http://java.sun.com/jsf/core">
<h:head>
  <title>A Simple JavaServer Faces Registration Application</title>
</h:head>
<h:body>
  <h:form>
    <h2>JSF Registration App</h2>
    <h4>Registration Form</h4>
    <table>...Irrelevant content not shown...</table>
    <p><h:messages /></p>
    <p><h:commandButton value="Register" action="confirm" /></p>
  </h:form>
</h:body>
</html>
```

When the **Register** button is pressed, the navigation rule system looks for a page within the application whose extension is the same as the current page and whose filename is **confirm**. In this case, **confirm.xhtml** does exist, and it contains the following navigation components:

```
<h:commandButton value="Edit" action="register" />
<h:commandButton value="Confirm" action="#{userBean.addConfirmedUser}" />
```

If the user clicks the **Register** button, he or she is taken back to the **register.xhtml** page. If the user clicks the **Confirm** button, an action is invoked. The **Confirm** button specifies an *action method,* **addConfirmedUser( )**, that determines the outcome programmatically in the logic of the method. This method is shown here:

```
public String addConfirmedUser() {
  boolean added = true; // actual application may fail to add user
  FacesMessage doneMessage = null;
  String outcome = null;
  if (added) {
    doneMessage = new FacesMessage("Successfully added new user");
    outcome = "done";
  } else {
    doneMessage = new FacesMessage("Failed to add new user");
    outcome = "register";
  }
  FacesContext.getCurrentInstance().addMessage(null, doneMessage);
  return outcome;
}
```

For this simple case, **addConfirmedUser( )** causes a message stating **Successfully added new user** to be displayed on the page and returns **"done"** as the outcome. This will cause the implicit navigation to take the user to the **done.xhtml** page.

The absolute minimum you need to know about JSF navigation can be listed in four bullet points.

- There are certain components you can put in the page that cause navigation to happen when they're pressed. JSF has the **h:commandButton**, **h:commandLink**, **h:button**, and **h:link** components built in.
- The markup for these components must include an **action** attribute (in the case of **h:commandButton** and **h:commandLink**) or an **outcome** attribute (in the case of **h:button** and **h:link**).
- The value of that attribute can either be a literal string, hard-coded into the page, or an EL expression that points to a method that returns a **String** (or actually any Java **Object** with a **toString( )** method).
- If a page exists for the value of the attribute, that page will be navigated to when the component was pressed.

With just this information you can get a whole lot done. This is the benefit of implicit navigation. The rest of the chapter will explain the JSF navigation feature in detail.

Overview of the JSF Navigation System

If the implicit navigation feature doesn't provide enough flexibility, the navigation rule system offers everything you need. Those familiar with Jakarta Struts will find the JavaServer Faces Navigation Model somewhat similar in that all the navigation rules can be stored in a single XML configuration file. However, where Struts defines a series of navigable application nodes in the form of Actions and Forwards in its configuration file, JavaServer Faces builds navigation rules that link actual pages directly to each other using a series of rules.

A clear benefit of having all of the JSF navigation rules residing in a single XML file is that it makes navigation very "tool friendly." In addition to the previously shown JDeveloper, there are now a growing number of JSF development tools that offer visual navigation design. These tools allow developers to design all of the navigation in a JSF application by simply "drawing" or linking the pages together in a visual environment.

Another benefit of centralized navigation rules is improved application management. Consider the classic problem when a page is renamed, such as changing **register.xhtml** to **registration.html**, and all associated links in other pages referring to the old name need to be revised with the new name. This problem does not occur when using the JSF Navigation Model, since all of the navigation rules with references to the old page name can easily be changed in one operation, in one file (**faces-config.xml**). This is obviously easier and less error-prone than editing all of the hard-coded references in multiple pages. However, there are many times, when prototyping for example, that hard-coding references is just so compellingly easy, it's the right thing to do. In that case, the implicit navigation feature is there for you.

JavaServer Faces navigation is also tightly integrated into its event model. This approach enables it to handle both *static* and *dynamic* navigations. In contrast to a static navigation (case), which is hard-coded into your **faces-config.xml**, the navigation path for a dynamic link is determined at runtime. This is done by specifying navigation conditions (or cases) into the navigation rule for the different expected results of a Java action method.

In addition to both static and dynamic navigation, the JSF Navigation Model can also handle other navigation types such as *wildcards* and HTTP *redirects.* These are examined later in the chapter, but first a little background on the exact sequence of events that occurs when a user clicks a page to initiate a navigation event. To begin, it is useful to review the Model-View-Controller (MVC) theory.

Recalling MVC—The Controller

Since the JavaServer Faces architecture is intrinsically linked to the Model-View-Controller design pattern, any user interaction with a Faces application requires that the Faces Controller handle all user interactions, or requests. As you may recall from earlier chapters, the Faces controller is a Java servlet that is able to intercept all requests to any Faces-enabled pages. It does this by using its servlet mapping defined in **web.xml**. The most common Faces mapping conventions are URLs in the form of "/faces/*" or "*.faces". This is how the JSF application is able to differentiate the Web requests that are Faces-specific. This differentiation is needed because a JavaServer Faces page must go through the request processing lifecycle where the Faces Context is prepared before the page renders itself.

In short, here is how a Faces navigation event occurs. (We'll cover the details later.) In order for a Faces page to be able to initiate a navigation event or in general submit a form, it must contain a Faces form component (**UIForm**) along with child **UIComponents**, like a Faces button or link, which implements the Faces **ActionSource** interface. When a user clicks one of these components, a navigation event will be triggered if the page contains no validation errors. The JSF request processing lifecycle handles this event with a (default) **NavigationHandler** instance that determines how to process the event based on implicit navigation and/or the navigation rules specified in **faces-config.xml**. It then returns the appropriate view or page based on the outcome of the event and its navigation rule. That's it! Now we'll drill down a bit into what actually happens behind the scenes of a navigation event.

The NavigationHandler—Behind the Scenes

The Faces **NavigationHandler** object is the heart of the navigation model for JavaServer Faces. As mentioned before, a default instance of this is provided by the JSF request processing lifecycle at runtime and is responsible for handling all navigation events. To understand the event handling process, we'll step through the exact flow of events, as shown in Figure 6-2, that occurs when a navigation event, or more specifically an **ActionEvent**, is fired and a subsequent navigation rule is processed.

As you will learn in Chapter 7, any **UIComponent** that can be activated to initiate a form submit back to the Faces server (otherwise known as a "postback") must implement the **ActionSource2** interface. Implementing this interface tells the Faces runtime that the component is the source of an **ActionEvent**. The Faces **UICommand** component implements this interface; therefore, the Faces developer can rely on an instance of this component to trigger an **ActionEvent** when clicked. An instance of a **UCommand** component is rendered to the browser as either as an **<input type="submit">** button or an **<a href>** link (with JavaScript that causes a form submit) by the standard HTML tag library. The remaining processing of this **ActionEvent** is handled automatically by the Faces runtime, but it's good to know what happens behind the scenes.

After the **ActionEvent** is triggered, if there are no conversion or validation errors in the page, the request processing lifecycle eventually arrives at the Invoke Application

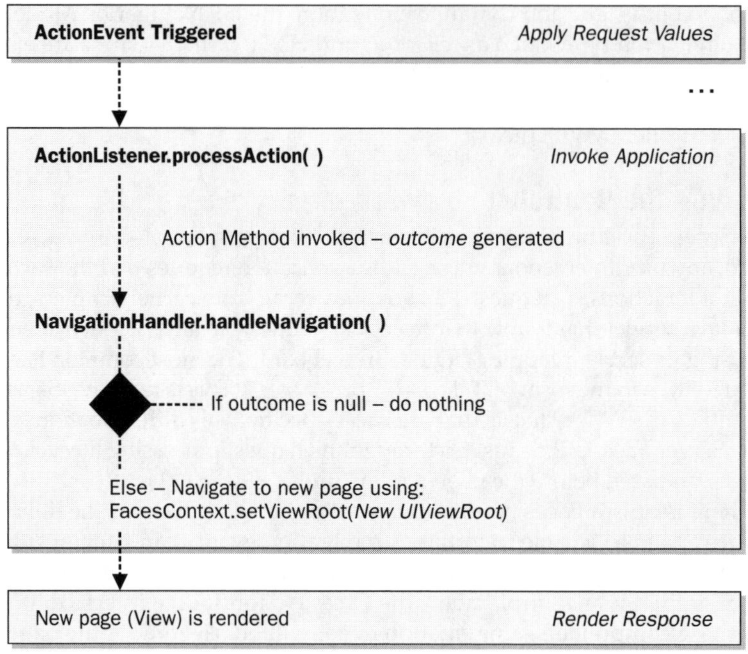

Figure 6-2 Sequence of events when a navigation occurs

phase, where the **ActionEvent** is handled by the default **ActionListener** instance and its **processAction( )** method. **ActionEvent** extends the standard Java event class **java.util .Event** and therefore has a **source** property whose value is the ID of the component that was clicked. After the **ActionListener** retrieves the **source** property that identifies the originating component that triggered the event, it processes the source component's **action** property. The value of the **action** property is provided by the page author as either a **static** string or a Faces expression that refers to an *action method*. The action method, which is an instance of **MethodExpression**, returns a **dynamically** derived string value after execution. This string outcome is then handled by the **handleNavigation( )** method of the **NavigationHandler** instance, which compares it with the set of navigation rules defined in the application's **faces-config.xml** file and/or any implicit navigation based on pages that exist in the current application. Depending on the string outcome and the logic defined in the navigation rules, the **NavigationHandler** does one of the following things:

1. Nothing. The user remains on the same page. This occurs when no navigation rule is successfully matched to the outcome of the action, or the outcome is null.
2. A navigation occurs to a new Faces page by calling **FacesContext.setViewRoot( )** with a **UIViewRoot** returned from **ViewHandler.createView( )**. This occurs when a Faces navigation rule's outcome matches the static or dynamic value of the action and is designated by the navigation rule to navigate to another Faces-enabled page using the **RequestDispatcher.forward( )** method from the Servlet API. This causes the *new* Faces page to be rendered and returned to the browser, in response to the postback. Optionally, the navigation can happen by virtue of a "redirect," explained later in the chapter.

EXPERT GROUP INSIGHT *You may notice that this event processing model is similar to the one found in standard rich-client Java applications. The similarity is intentional. The expert group wanted to make the event model as similar as possible to that found in rich clients. It was hoped this would ease development for those familiar with existing rich-client UI toolkits. Also, note the key role of the expression language* ***MethodBinding*** *in action processing and navigation. Enabling the user to easily specify a method that should be called when a button is pressed was the impetus for inventing the concept of* ***MethodBinding****.*

When the **NavigationHandler** finishes processing the navigation rule, if successful, a new page will be rendered to the client in the Render Response phase of the request processing lifecycle.

EXPERT GROUP INSIGHT *The Invoke Application phase of the request processing lifecycle was designed to be the place where other frameworks, such as Struts, could plug in to JavaServer Faces applications. This is accomplished by replacing the default* ***ActionListener*** *and calling into the Struts navigation machinery. Also, in keeping with the emphasis on extensibility, it is possible to replace or decorate the existing* ***NavigationHandler****, which allows total customization of the navigation system. One example of the usefulness of this extension point is the ability to have one part of your site built with Faces and another with a different framework, and be able to step cleanly between the two worlds.*

A Note on Faces Action Methods

As you've seen, Faces action methods are user-definable methods that process an event triggered by clicking buttons, links, or any **UIComponent** that implements **ActionSource** such as **UICommand**. As you may have noticed by now, building action methods to handle user-initiated events is a very common Faces development task. Fortunately, building Faces action methods is quite simple, as they are not defined by any specific API. Instead, any method that has the following characteristics can serve as a Faces action method:

- Must be **public**
- Can accept no arguments
- Must return an **Object** instance whose **toString( )** method will be called to get the string value for the navigation rule.

As you will see throughout the book, Faces action methods are really the glue that binds the application's user interactive components to the application's server-side logic. In a way, they can be thought of as analogous to Struts Actions in that they are the first bit of code that is executed when a user event occurs. A key difference, however, is that Faces action methods are not directly URL-accessible, such as **http://strutsapp/action.do**.

Building Navigation Rules

Now that you've seen the theory behind Faces navigation, it's time to start putting that theory into practice by defining some Faces navigation rules. JavaServer Faces navigation rules provide a precise way for the developer to define all of the application's navigations.

The rules usually reside in the **faces-config.xml** file, or they can be configured to reside in a separate file. (An example of how to do this is shown later in this chapter.)

To get a general feel for how navigation rules work, let's take an example from the real world by modeling a simple scenario with a Faces navigation rule: If I'm in the living room, and I'm feeling hungry, I go to the kitchen. If I'm in the living room, and I'm feeling sleepy, I go to the bedroom. This could be modeled with the following navigation rule.

```
<navigation-rule>
   <from-view-id>livingRoom </from-view-id>
   <navigation-case>
      <from-outcome>hungry</from-outcome>
      <to-view-id>kitchen</to-view-id>
   </navigation-case>
   <navigation-case>
      <from-outcome>sleepy</from-outcome>
      <to-view-id>bedroom </to-view-id>
   </navigation-case>
</navigation-rule>
```

As you can see, navigation rules can easily model many real-world or application scenarios. Navigation rules in a more generic form actually have the following structure:

```
<navigation-rule>
   <from-view-id>from_page.xhtml</from-view-id>
   <navigation-case>
      <from-action>#{ManagedBean.actionMethod}</from-action>
      <from-outcome>condition 1</from-outcome>
      <to-view-id>/to_page1.xhtml</to-view-id>
   </navigation-case>
   <navigation-case>
      <from-action>#{ManagedBean.actionMethod}</from-action>
      <from-outcome>condition 2</from-outcome>
      <to-view-id>/to_page2.xhtml</to-view-id>
   </navigation-case>
</navigation-rule>
```

Navigation rules have an optional, single **from-view-id**, which is where the navigation originates. As a peer of the **from-view-id** are 1 to *N* **navigation-case** entries. A **navigation-case** statement has the following child elements:

- **<from-action>** An action method that returns a custom **String** value such as "Success" or "Failure," which is usually used to indicate if the action method executed successfully. This element along with **from-outcome** is needed for *dynamic navigation* where the output of the action method specified in the **from-action** element is compared to the **from-outcome** value. If a match occurs, the corresponding **to-view-id** location will be navigated to.
- **<from-outcome>** A **String** value that is passed to the **NavigationHandler**, where it is compared with either the output of the corresponding **from-action** or the **action** attribute of a UI component with navigation support such as **commandLink** or **commandButton**.
- **<to-view-id>** The page to which the user will be navigated upon a successful match of the **from-action** and **from-outcome**.

To get a better feel for building various navigation rules, we'll take a look at a few examples starting with a simple, static navigation.

A Static Navigation Example

This first example shows how to build a simple navigation rule that just links one page to another. Before we begin, it's important to point out that although it's tempting to simply use an HTML **<a href>** tag in static navigation cases, you'll find that standardizing all navigation with JSF navigation rules (no matter how simple) will definitely make the application more manageable in the long run as application size and complexity increases.

Consider two pages, **page1.xhtml** and **page2.xhtml**. In order for **page1.xhtml** to link to a page, you will have to add a **UICommand** UI component onto **page1.xhtml**. Normally, the JSP or Facelets developer does not need to know the underlying UI component, because the standard JSF HTML JSP or Facelets tag library provides either the **<h:commandButton>** or **<h:commandLink>**, which renders either a button or link with the same **UICommand** UI component. Consider the following **commandButton** example:

```
<h:commandButton value="Proceed to Page2" action="gotopage2" />
```

The key thing to notice is the **action** attribute. For this static navigation, this is the navigation **from-outcome** value that will map to **page2.xhtml** in the navigation rule.

Here is an equivalent example using **commandLink**:

```
<h:commandLink action="gotopage2">
   <h:outputText value="Proceed to Page2"/>
</h:commandLink>
```

Notice the **commandLink** requires a child tag to produce an output similar to how the **<a href . . .>** tag also requires a body.

Now that an action of the static value **"gotopage2"** has been defined in both the button and link components on the page, the next step is to provide a navigation rule that maps this **from-outcome** value to **/page2.xhtml**. Here is the navigation rule required to do this:

```
<navigation-rule>
<from-view-id>/page1.xhtml</from-view-id>
   <navigation-case>
     <from-outcome>gotopage2</from-outcome>
     <to-view-id>/page2.xhtml</to-view-id>
   </navigation-case>
</navigation-rule>
```

Notice that for this example a **from-action** is not needed; instead, the **from-outcome** is compared to the **action** attribute of the navigation UI component (**commandLink** or **commandButton**).

And that's it. At runtime, clicking the button or link triggers a navigation to **page2.xhtml**. We can now explain how implicit navigation works. In the **handleNavigation( )** method, the **NavigationHandler** first checks the rule base if there is a **<to-view-id>** for the given **outcome**. If there is, it is used. If not, the **NavigationHandler** conjures up a value for **<to-view-id>** by taking the **outcome** and appending the current page extension, if necessary. If a page actually exists with that name, it is used.

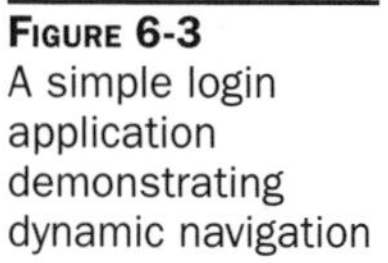

FIGURE 6-3 A simple login application demonstrating dynamic navigation

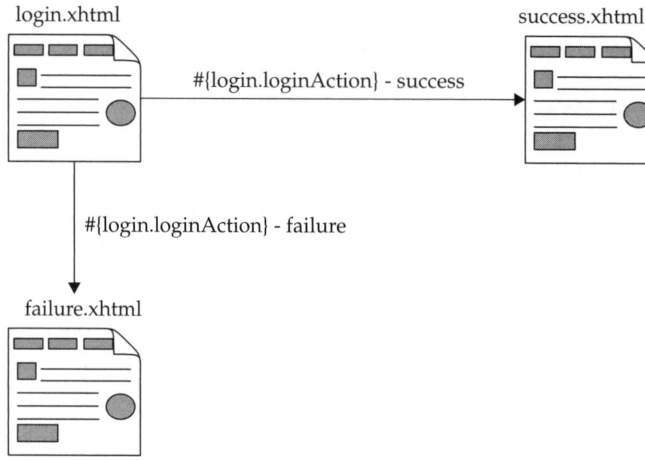

This is a case of a simple *static* navigation where nothing will change the navigation at runtime. Let's now take a look at a simple *dynamic* navigation rule where a condition will be checked by a Java method and the navigation destination will be dynamically derived.

A Dynamic Navigation Example

This next example shows a typical login example where an action method is used to dynamically determine a navigation case based on values provided in a login form. This example will have the following example pages: **login.xhtml**, **success.xhtml,** and **failure .xhtml**. It will also use **Login.java**, which will be used as a managed bean called **Login**. The **Login** bean is used to temporarily store the user ID and password. **Login** will also contain an action method that will compare the submitted user ID and password values to determine a navigation outcome. Figure 6-3 shows the navigation page flow logic of a simple login application.

Let's examine the source code for the **login.xhtml** page of this simple example. Notice the usage of two **inputText** components and a **commandButton**.

```
<!DOCTYPE html PUBLIC "-//W3C//DTD XHTML 1.0 Transitional//EN"
"http://www.w3.org/TR/xhtml1/DTD/xhtml1-transitional.dtd">
<html xmlns="http://www.w3.org/1999/xhtml"
      xmlns:h="http://java.sun.com/jsf/html"
      xmlns:f="http://java.sun.com/jsf/core">
<h:head>
    <title>Login</title>
</h:head>
<h:body>
  <h:form>
      <h:panelGrid border="1" columns="2">

          <h:outputText value="Userid:" />
          <h:inputText id="userid" value="#{login.userid}" />

          <h:outputText value="Password:" />
          <h:inputSecret id="password" value="#{login.password}" />
```

```
            <h:outputText value=" " />
            <h:commandButton value="Login" action="#{login.loginAction}" />
    </h:panelGrid>
</h:form>

</h:body>
</html>
```

The key things to notice are that the **inputText** and **inputSecret** fields have *value bindings* to properties of the **Login** managed bean. You'll also notice the **commandButton** has an action binding to a method in the **Login** bean.

The other pages for this example, **success.xhtml** and **failure.xhtml**, needn't contain any JSF content and can be as simple as

```
<!DOCTYPE html PUBLIC "-//W3C//DTD XHTML 1.0 Transitional//EN"
"http://www.w3.org/TR/xhtml1/DTD/xhtml1-transitional.dtd">
<html xmlns="http://www.w3.org/1999/xhtml">
    <head><title>Success!</title></head>
    <body>
        <p>Success!</p>
    </body>
</html>
```

The failure HTML page is identical but with a "Failure!" message.

Let's now examine the source code for the **Login** managed bean, which is shown here:

```
package com.jsfcompref;

import javax.faces.bean.ManagedBean;
import javax.faces.bean.RequestScoped;

@ManagedBean
@RequestScoped
public class Login {
  String userid;
  String password;
  public Login() { }
  public String getUserid() {
    return userid;
  }
  public void setUserid(String userid) {
    this.userid = userid;
  }
  public String getPassword() {
    return password;
  }
  public void setPassword(String password) {
    this.password = password;
  }
  // Action Method
```

```
  public String loginAction() {
      if (userid.equals("guest") && password.equals("welcome")) {
          return "success";
      } else {
          return "failure";
      }
  }
}
```

Notice the **Login** class has corresponding properties **userid** and **password** as well as an action method **loginAction( )**. The action method will be invoked when the **commandButton** is clicked. It will return a "success" **String** value if **userid** and **password** equals "guest" and "welcome," respectively. Otherwise, "failure" is returned.

Now that the user interface and the backing **Login** bean have been defined, you'll need to define the navigation rule, which is in the **faces-config.xml** file. Because this is the first time in the book when a **faces-config.xml** file is required, it is included in its entirety, including the XML schema declaration for JSF 2.0.

```
<?xml version='1.0' encoding='UTF-8'?>

<faces-config xmlns="http://java.sun.com/xml/ns/javaee"
    xmlns:xsi="http://www.w3.org/2001/XMLSchema-instance"
    xsi:schemaLocation="http://java.sun.com/xml/ns/javaee
    http://java.sun.com/xml/ns/javaee/web-facesconfig_2_0.xsd"
    version="2.0">

<navigation-rule>
  <from-view-id>/login.xhtml</from-view-id>
  <navigation-case>
    <from-action>#{login.loginAction}</from-action>
    <from-outcome>success</from-outcome>
    <to-view-id>/success.xhtml</to-view-id>
  </navigation-case>
  <navigation-case>
    <from-action>#{login.loginAction}</from-action>
    <from-outcome>failure</from-outcome>
    <to-view-id>/failure.xhtml</to-view-id>
  </navigation-case>
</navigation-rule>

</faces-config>
```

At this point the application is complete with a successful navigation to the **success.xhtml** page occurring when "guest" and "welcome" are entered in the login page, and a navigation to **failure.xhtml** when anything else is entered in the login page.

Before moving on, you may have noticed how, in addition to setting the **from-outcome** values (as was done in the static example earlier), the navigation rule for the login example also defined a **from-action,** which refers to the action method that will be returning the outcome. It is not always required to provide a **from-action**, but in cases where you have multiple action methods with the same or similar outcomes on the same page, it is best to specify the exact outcome that is expected from a **specific** action method. For example, you might have a login page that has two buttons: one that just logs you in, and a second one that logs you in and immediately performs a service such as checking your account balance. These different login buttons could be bound to two different action methods, **loginAction( )** and **loginActionCheckBalance( )**, but return the same outcome string "success." The only way to differentiate between the two buttons and correctly navigate based on their outcome is to specify the different **from-action** elements in the navigation rule. The following modified navigation rule would correctly handle this situation.

```
<navigation-rule>
  <from-view-id>/login.xhtml</from-view-id>
  <navigation-case>
    <from-action>#{login.loginAction}</from-action>
    <from-outcome>success</from-outcome>
    <to-view-id>/success.xhtml</to-view-id>
  </navigation-case>
  <navigation-case>
    <from-action>#{login.loginActionCheckBalance}</from-action>
    <from-outcome>success</from-outcome>
    <to-view-id>/showbalance.xhtml</to-view-id>
  </navigation-case>
  <navigation-case>
    <from-action>#{login.loginAction}</from-action>
    <from-outcome>failure</from-outcome>
    <to-view-id>/failure.xhtml</to-view-id>
  </navigation-case>
</navigation-rule>
```

And here is the code for the second button that is bound to the **loginActionCheckBalance( )** method:

```
<h:commandButton value="Login and Check Balance"
action="#{Login.loginActionCheckBalance}" />
```

Now that you've seen the elements of this dynamic navigation example, it's time to examine the exact sequence of events that occurs when this application is run. After the **login.xhtml** page renders the login form to the client, the user enters the values "guest" and "welcome" and then clicks Login. At this point the JSF request processing lifecycle is initiated and passes through both the Apply Request Values and Process Validation phases until it updates the Login bean's properties in the Update Model Values phase.

After updating the bean's values, the Invoke Application phase is entered and the action method **loginAction( )** is invoked, since it was bound to the **Login commandButton** and the button was clicked. The **loginAction( )** method will return "success" because the values "guest" and "welcome" satisfy its **if** condition. At this point the default **NavigationHandler** will consume the returned "success" value and then look for the navigation case that matches the **from-outcome** value of "success" with the **from-action** with the derived value of the method-binding expression **#{login.loginAction}**. As the match is found, it will select a new view (**success.xhtml**) to be rendered using the **to-view-id** value specified in the navigation case and hand the new view to the default **ViewHandler** to render back to the client. In other words, a navigation to the **success.xhtml** page will occur. Likewise, if any values are entered in the form other than "guest" and "welcome," the **loginAction( )** method would return "failure" and cause a navigation to the **failure.xhtml** to occur.

More Sophisticated Navigation Examples

In addition to the simple navigation situations just described, JSF applications usually have more detailed navigation needs. Several examples of more sophisticated navigations are shown in the following sections.

Using Wildcards

An interesting and useful feature of the JavaServer Faces Navigation Model is its ability to handle *wildcard* navigations. Wildcard navigations provide a way to establish a navigation rule for more than one page or **from-view-id**. For example, if a navigation rule has its **from-view-id** set to "*"or "/*", it means that this navigation rule applies to all pages. Another way to apply a navigation rule to all pages is to simply omit the **from-view-id** altogether and let the **NavigationHandler** process the navigation cases for all pages.

If a **from-view-id** is set to something like "/register/*", it means that this navigation rule applies to all pages residing under the **/register** directory.

Consider the example where an application needs a login page to be accessible from all pages. The navigation rule could be as follows:

```
<navigation-rule>
  <from-view-id> * </from-view-id>
  <navigation-case>
  <description>
    Global login rule for any page with a Login button/link
    or any action method
  </description>
  <from-outcome>login</from-outcome>
  <to-view-id>/login.xhtml</to-view-id>
  </navigation-case>
</navigation-rule>
```

To use this global login rule, any button or link can simply hard-code the action value to "login." Also, if any action method returns the value "login," then this rule will also be invoked.

A navigation rule could handle an error condition where a login is required for any page in the specially designated directory, such as "register/*". If the error condition "login required" is encountered, a **login-required.xhtml** page could be navigated to and displayed. For example:

```
<navigation-rule>
  <from-view-id>/register/* </from-view-id>
  <navigation-case>
  <description>
    Login Required error condition for any /register/* page.
  </description>
  <from-action>#{Login.checkLogin}</from-action>
  <from-outcome>login required</from-outcome>
  <to-view-id>/login-required.xhtml</to-view-id>
  </navigation-case>
</navigation-rule>
```

Using Conditional Navigation

Within a given **<navigation-rule>** element, the **<navigation-case>** elements are processed in the order in which they appear in the **faces-config.xml** file. The first one that matches is the one whose **<to-view-id>** will be returned for the navigation. This "first one wins" approach naturally lends itself to the "conditional navigation" feature in JSF 2.0. The idea for this feature originated in JBoss Seam and was contributed by the Seam creators to JSF 2.0. Let's take the login example from before and change the source of the success vs. failure decision to be a simple checkbox, as in this Facelets page.

```
<!DOCTYPE html PUBLIC "-//W3C//DTD XHTML 1.0 Transitional//EN"
"http://www.w3.org/TR/xhtml1/DTD/xhtml1-transitional.dtd">
<html xmlns="http://www.w3.org/1999/xhtml"
      xmlns:h="http://java.sun.com/jsf/html"
      xmlns:f="http://java.sun.com/jsf/core">
<h:head>
  <title>A Simple JavaServer Faces 2.0 View</title>
</h:head>
<h:body>
  <h:form>
      <p>If the checkbox is checked, we go to the success page,
      otherwise we go to the failure page.</p>
      <p><h:selectBooleanCheckbox value="#{model.booleanValue}" /></p>
    <p><h:commandButton value="submit" action="submit"/></p>
  </h:form>
</h:body>
</html>
```

The Java code for the model is just a simple POJO with a Boolean JavaBeans property called **booleanValue**.

```
package com.jsfcompref;

import javax.faces.bean.ManagedBean;
import javax.faces.bean.RequestScoped;

@ManagedBean
@RequestScoped
public class Model {
    protected boolean booleanValue = false;

    public boolean isBooleanValue() {
        return booleanValue;
    }
    public void setBooleanValue(boolean booleanValue) {
        this.booleanValue = booleanValue;
    }

    protected String successOutcome = "/success.xhtml";

    public String getSuccessOutcome() {
        return successOutcome;
    }
```

```
    public void setSuccessOutcome(String successOutcome) {
        this.successOutcome = successOutcome;
    }
    protected String failureOutcome = "/failure.xhtml";

    public String getFailureOutcome() {
        return failureOutcome;
    }

    public void setFailureOutcome(String failureOutcome) {
        this.failureOutcome = failureOutcome;
    }
}
```

The last piece is the most interesting, the **faces-config.xml** file.

```
<?xml version='1.0' encoding='UTF-8'?>

<faces-config xmlns="http://java.sun.com/xml/ns/javaee"
    xmlns:xsi="http://www.w3.org/2001/XMLSchema-instance"
    xsi:schemaLocation="http://java.sun.com/xml/ns/javaee
http://java.sun.com/xml/ns/javaee/web-facesconfig_2_0.xsd"
    version="2.0">

<navigation-rule>
  <from-view-id>/main.xhtml</from-view-id>
  <navigation-case>
    <from-outcome>submit</from-outcome>
    <if>#{model.booleanValue}</if>
    <to-view-id>#{model.successOutcome}</to-view-id>
  </navigation-case>
  <navigation-case>
    <from-outcome>submit</from-outcome>
    <to-view-id>#{model.failureOutcome}</to-view-id>
  </navigation-case>
</navigation-rule>

</faces-config>
```

The first **<navigation-case>** includes **<if>#{model.booleanValue}</if>**. At first it's a little strange to see EL in a place other than a JSF View, but JSF allows EL here in this case. EL is also allowed in the **<to-view-id>** element. You'll see in the next chapter that you can even include EL expressions in CSS and JavaScript files! If this expression evaluates to **true** this **<navigation-case>** will be the one whose **<to-view-id>** is selected. Otherwise, processing moves on to the next **<navigation-case>**.

Using Redirects

A **<redirect/>** option in a navigation case triggers a slightly different type of navigation. Specifically, the redirect option causes the client browser to make a new HTTP request for the specified view as opposed to just rendering the response without requiring a separate HTTP request.

A Brief HTTP Primer

At this point it is useful to take a brief aside to talk about the HTTP network protocol, on which JSF is ultimately based. HTTP stands for Hypertext Transfer Protocol, because hypertext data is the most common kind of data transferred via HTTP. As with any network protocol, there are clients and there are servers, and there are specifications for both. All popular Web browsers operate as HTTP clients and implement the client portion of the HTTP protocol. Web servers, such as servers operating according to the Java Servlet specification, operate as HTTP servers and implement the server portion of the protocol.

The basic unit of work in HTTP is the request/response transaction. In this transaction, the client makes a request and the server gives a response. An HTTP request is similar to an e-mail message in that it consists of some header information and a message body. On the other hand, an HTTP request differs from an e-mail message in that the HTTP request frequently consists of only the header information. Such a request without a body is called a GET request, while one that has a body is called a POST request. The HTTP specification describes GET and POST as two different "methods" to make a request. The response from the server is the same regardless of which method is used. The other important piece of an HTTP request is the URL to which the request is addressed. The URL can contain parameters, listed as name=value pairs.

The HTML 2.0 specification, from September 1995, defines how the GET and POST methods are to be used in Web browsers. It states, "Query Forms: METHOD=GET: If the processing of a form is idempotent (i.e., it has no lasting observable effect on the state of the world), then the form method should be GET . . . Forms with Side-Effects: METHOD=POST: If the service associated with the processing of a form has side effects (for example, modification of a database or subscription to a service), the method should be POST." This usage is still in effect today.

Recall the Login example from before, where the application did not use redirects in the navigation cases. As the user successfully "logged in" and proceeded to the **success.xhtml** page, the URL in the browser would still have the original ". . . login.xhtml . . ." page in the address bar. This is because the contents of **success.xhtml** were simply rendered to the browser without the browser specifically requesting the **success.xhtml** page. If a redirect tag is inserted in the navigation case in the form

```
<navigation-case>
  <from-action>#{Login.loginAction}</from-action>
  <from-outcome>success</from-outcome>
  <to-view-id>/success.xhtml</to-view-id>
  <redirect/>
</navigation-case>
```

then the browser is asked via the redirect to request **success.xhtml** and the user will actually see "http:// . . . /success.xhtml" in the browser's address bar.

Whether or not to use redirects largely depends on whether what is shown in the address bar of the browser matters or could be confusing if the page referenced no longer matches the page being rendered. Another important consideration of when to use redirects is performance. Using a redirect will terminate the current request and cause a new request response cycle to occur. If the page has a very large set of components, this could have a noticeable performance impact. Redirects can also necessitate an extra round trip to reinstantiate any request-scoped objects that have disappeared by the next request.

Redirects and Implicit Navigation

It is also possible to use redirects when using the implicit navigation feature, by using the **h:link** and **h:button** components.

> **Comparing h:commandButton and h:button**
>
> What's the difference between **h:commandButton/h:commandLink** and **h:button/link**? The latter two components were introduced in 2.0 to enable bookmarkable JSF pages, when used in concert with the "View Parameters" feature explained later in this chapter. There are three main differences between **h:button/h:link** and **h:commandButton/h:commandLink**.
>
> First, **h:button/h:link** causes the browser to issue an HTTP GET request, while **h:commandButton/h:commandLink** does a form POST. This means that any components in the page that have values entered by the user, such as text fields, checkboxes, etc., will not automatically be submitted to the server when using **h:button/h:link**. To cause values to be submitted with **h:button/h:link**, extra action has to be taken, using the "View Parameters" feature.
>
> The second main difference between the two kinds of components is that **h:button/h:link** has an **outcome** attribute to describe where to go next while **h:commandButton/h:commandLink** uses an **action** attribute for this purpose. This is because the former does not result in an **ActionEvent** in the event system, while the latter does.
>
> Finally, and most important to the complete understanding of this feature, the **h:button/h:link** components cause the navigation system to be asked to derive the outcome during the *rendering* of the page, and the answer to this question is encoded in the markup of the page. In contrast, the **h:commandButton/h:commandLink** components cause the navigation system to be asked to derive the outcome on the POSTBACK from the page. This is a difference in timing. Rendering always happens before POSTBACK.

Let's illustrate the difference between **h:commandButton** and **h:button**, and also the usage of redirects with implicit navigation, with a simple example. Consider this simple Facelets page.

```
<!DOCTYPE html PUBLIC "-//W3C//DTD XHTML 1.0 Transitional//EN"
"http://www.w3.org/TR/xhtml1/DTD/xhtml1-transitional.dtd">
<html xmlns="http://www.w3.org/1999/xhtml"
      xmlns:h="http://java.sun.com/jsf/html"
      xmlns:f="http://java.sun.com/jsf/core">
<h:head>
  <title>A Simple JavaServer Faces 2.0 View</title>
</h:head>
<h:body>
  <h:form>
      <p>Enter first name: <h:inputText value="#{model.firstName}" /></p>
    <p><h:button value="HTTP GET" outcome="page02" /></p>
    <p><h:commandButton value="HTTP POST with Redirect"
```

```
        action="page02?faces-redirect=true" /></p>
    <p><h:commandButton value="HTTP POST" action="page02" /></p>
  </h:form>
</h:body>
</html>
```

The first **h:commandButton** element has **action="page02?faces-redirect=true"**. In the Internet standard that defines URLs, the presence of a **?** character indicates the remainder of the URL will be an **&** or **&**–separated list of **name=value** pairs that should be submitted to the server along with the request for the URL. This is known as a "query string." JSF borrows the meaning of the **?** character here, and the meaning is exactly the same is in the Internet standard for URLs. There are two special query strings parameters recognized by JSF when it parses the outcome on the server side. The **faces-redirect** query string tells the navigation system that this implicit navigation case must be treated as if it were a real **<navigation-case>** element that included a **<redirect/>** element. The other special query string parameter, **includeViewParams**, relates to the "View Parameters" feature and will be explained in context later in the chapter. Any additional parameters not recognized by JSF are simply passed through unmodified. Let's now see what happens when each button is pressed in turn. The rendering of the view with some text entered into the text field is shown here:

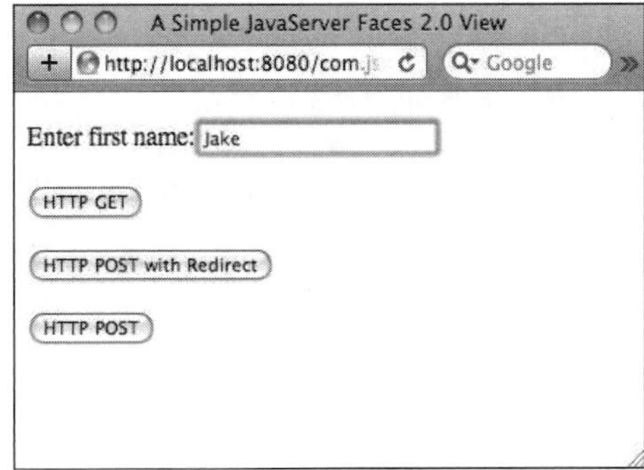

Looking at the source, you can see that all of the buttons will cause a navigation to **page02.xhtml**, the source code for which is shown here:

```
<!DOCTYPE html PUBLIC "-//W3C//DTD XHTML 1.0 Transitional//EN"
"http://www.w3.org/TR/xhtml1/DTD/xhtml1-transitional.dtd">
<html xmlns="http://www.w3.org/1999/xhtml"
      xmlns:h="http://java.sun.com/jsf/html">
<h:head>
  <title>Page 02</title>
</h:head>
<h:body>
    <p>Page 02</p>
    <p>Value of First name: &lt;#{model.firstName}&gt;.</p>

    <p>The value will be empty if either of the "HTTP POST with Redirect"
    or the"HTTP GET" buttons were pressed.  If the "HTTP POST" button was
    pressed, the value will not be empty.</p>
</h:body>
</html>
```

Finally, here is the very simple JavaBean that is the **model** managed bean:

```
package com.jsfcompref;

import javax.faces.bean.ManagedBean;
import javax.faces.bean.RequestScoped;

@ManagedBean
@RequestScoped
public class Model {

    protected String firstName;

    public String getFirstName() {
        return firstName;
    }

    public void setFirstName(String firstName) {
        this.firstName = firstName;
    }

}
```

Because **Model** has been given the **@RequestScoped** annotation, its values will not persist across multiple invocations of the JSF request processing lifecycle. Recall that the XHTML markup for the first button is **<h:button value="HTTP GET" outcome="page02" />**. Pressing this button will cause the following rendering of **page02.xhtml** to appear:

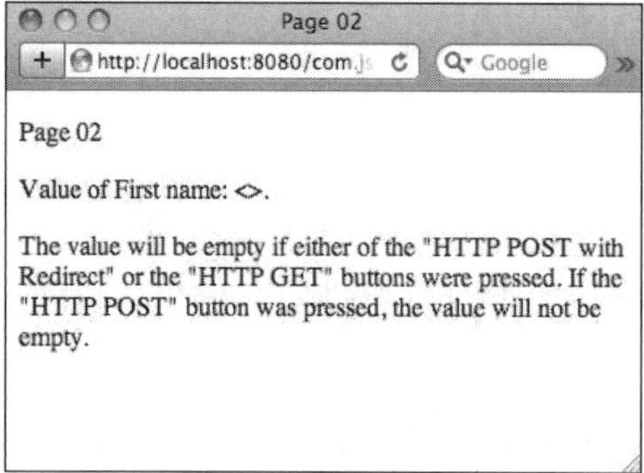

Note that the value of the **model.firstName** property is the empty string? This is because the **h:button** command does not, by default, submit any form values, so whatever is entered into the text field is lost. Returning to the first page and filling in a value for text field and pressing the second button will give us the same result, even though this time the button is coded with **<h:commandButton value="HTTP POST with Redirect" action="page02?faces-redirect=true" />**. We are, indeed, doing a POST, and the value entered into the text field is submitted, but because the **action** attribute includes **faces-redirect=true**, the implicit navigation will behave as if a **<redirect />** element was in play. Therefore, when the postback happens, and the navigation action is processed, the server tells the browser to make *another*

HTTP request to the new URL. Because the **model** Managed Bean is **@RequestScoped**, the value submitted on the first request is not retained when the server renders the page as a result of the second request. The result is the same as shown previously.

Now, returning a third time to the initial page, we once again enter a value into the text field and this time press the **HTTP POST** button. Finally, we get the expected result, as shown here.

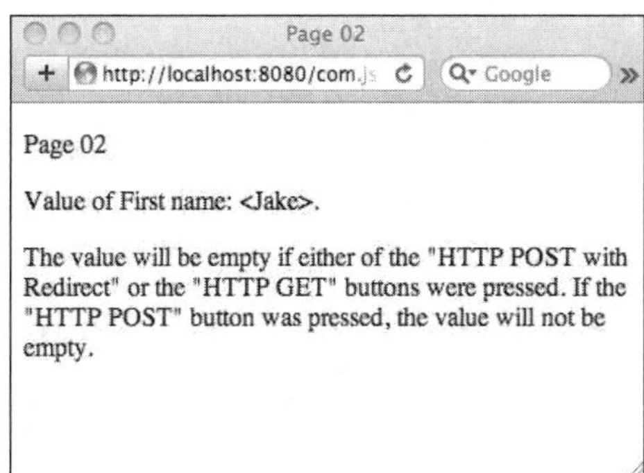

POST REDIRECT GET and JSF

Michael Jouravlev, in his influential August 2004 article on **theserverside.com**, describes the POST REDIRECT GET (PRG) pattern as follows:

> Never show pages in response to POST
>
> Always load pages using GET
>
> Navigate from POST to GET using REDIRECT

We have seen that JSF violates the first of these rules by using POST for every page navigation via the **RequestDispatcher.forward( )** method from the Servlet API. Indeed, most popular Java Servlet–based Web frameworks, including Struts, use this approach for navigation. HTTP purists rightly point out that this approach violates the first rule in the PRG pattern. Not only did JSF violate the first rule, but until JSF 2.0, it was very difficult to do it any other way. Thanks to another JSF contribution from the Seam team at JBoss, it is now much easier to do PRG with JSF. Let's rewrite the registration example from Chapter 2 using PRG. We'll do it two different ways, using the flash, and then using View Parameters.

POST REDIRECT GET Using the Flash Let's revisit the **register.xhtml** page, this time using the flash. The changed elements are shown in boldface.

```
<!DOCTYPE html PUBLIC "-//W3C//DTD XHTML 1.0 Transitional//EN"
"http://www.w3.org/TR/xhtml1/DTD/xhtml1-transitional.dtd">
<html xmlns="http://www.w3.org/1999/xhtml"
      xmlns:h="http://java.sun.com/jsf/html"
      xmlns:f="http://java.sun.com/jsf/core">
<h:head>
  <title>A Simple JavaServer Faces Registration Application</title>
</h:head>
```

```
<h:body>
  <h:form>
    <h2>JSF Registration App</h2>
    <h4>Registration Form</h4>
    <table>
      <tr>
        <td>First Name:</td>
        <td>
          <h:inputText label="First Name"
                       id="fname" value="#{flash.firstName}"
                       required="true"/>
          <h:message for="fname" />
        </td>
      </tr>
      <tr>
        <td>Last Name:</td>
        <td>
          <h:inputText label="Last Name"
                       id="lname" value="#{flash.lastName}"
                       required="true"/>
          <h:message for="lname" />
        </td>
      </tr>
... additional table rows not shown.
    </table>
    <p><h:commandButton value="Register"
       action="confirm?faces-redirect=true" /></p>
  </h:form>
</h:body>
</html>
```

The only changes necessary to the page to support PRG using the flash are: 1) change the EL expressions for the components to store their values into properties in the flash rather than on the **UserBean**, and 2) add the **faces-redirect** special query parameter to the implicit navigation to the **confirm.xhtml** page. Let's look at the **confirm.xhtml** page.

```
<!DOCTYPE html PUBLIC "-//W3C//DTD XHTML 1.0 Transitional//EN"
"http://www.w3.org/TR/xhtml1/DTD/xhtml1-transitional.dtd">
<html xmlns="http://www.w3.org/1999/xhtml"
      xmlns:h="http://java.sun.com/jsf/html"
      xmlns:f="http://java.sun.com/jsf/core">
<h:head>
  <title>A Simple JavaServer Faces Registration Application</title>
</h:head>
<h:body>
  <h:form>
    <h2>JSF Registration App</h2>
    <h4>Registration Confirmation</h4>
    <table>
      <tr>
        <td>First Name:</td>
        <td>
          <h:outputText value="#{flash.keep.firstName}" />
        </td>
      </tr>
```

```
      <tr>
        <td>Last Name:</td>
        <td>
          <h:outputText value="#{flash.keep.lastName}"/>
        </td>
      </tr>
... additional table rows not shown.
    </table>
    <p><h:commandButton value="Edit"
       action="register?faces-redirect=true" /></p>
    <p><h:commandButton value="Confirm"
       action="#{userBean.addConfirmedUser}" /></p>
  </h:form>
</h:body>
</html>
```

Again the same two kind of changes need to be made, with one difference. Instead of EL expressions such as **#{flash.firstName}** we have **#{flash.keep.firstName}**. Why is that? Be default, the flash only keeps values for a single *POST REDIRECT GET* cycle. In this case that means the user presses the **Confirm** button while viewing the **register.xhtml** page, causing the *POST*back to the Faces server. The server then sends the 302 *REDIRECT* HTTP response (with a **Location** HTTP header including **confirm.xhtml)**, causing the browser to issue a *GET* to the Faces server displaying the **confirm.xhtml** page. Because we want the values in the flash to persist for yet another PRG cycle, the flash needs to be told to keep the values, hence the special **keep** keyword.

We also make some very important changes to **UserBean**.

```
package com.jsfcompref.model;

... removed imports

@ManagedBean
@RequestScoped
public class UserBean {

... removed unchanged properties and methods

    public void pullValuesFromFlash() {
        Flash flash =
          FacesContext.getCurrentInstance().getExternalContext().
          getFlash();
        setFirstName((String) flash.get("firstName"));
        setLastName((String) flash.get("lastName"));
        setServiceLevel((String) flash.get("sex"));
        setDob((Date) flash.get("dob"));
        setEmail((String) flash.get("email"));
        setServiceLevel((String) flash.get("serviceLevel"));
    }

    public String addConfirmedUser() {

      boolean added = true; // actual application may fail to add user
      FacesMessage doneMessage = null;
```

```
        String outcome = null;
        if (added) {
            doneMessage = new FacesMessage("Successfully added new user");
            outcome = "done?faces-redirect=true";
        } else {
            doneMessage = new FacesMessage("Failed to add new user");
            outcome = "register?faces-redirect=true";
        }
          FacesContext.getCurrentInstance().addMessage(null, doneMessage);
          return outcome;
    }
}
```

First, we changed the scope to **@RequestScoped** because, in general, it is desirable to use the session as little as possible to minimize usage. Using the flash as we are doing here allows us to keep the bean in request scope. Second, we add a method **pullValuesFromFlash( )**. This method will be called when the **done.xhtml** page is rendered. Note that the return type from the call **flash.get("dob")** is **Date**. This is because the converter on **register.xhtml** has already been invoked and the value stored in the flash is already of the proper type. Finally, we modify the return from the **addConfirmedUser( )** method to tell the navigation system should be performed using a redirect, rather than the **Servlet RequestDispatcher.forward( )** method.

The last modification is to the **done.xhtml** page.

```
<!DOCTYPE html PUBLIC "-//W3C//DTD XHTML 1.0 Transitional//EN"
"http://www.w3.org/TR/xhtml1/DTD/xhtml1-transitional.dtd">
<html xmlns="http://www.w3.org/1999/xhtml"
      xmlns:h="http://java.sun.com/jsf/html"
      xmlns:f="http://java.sun.com/jsf/core">
<h:head>
  <title>A Simple JavaServer Faces Registration Application</title>
</h:head>
<h:body>
  <h:form>
    <h2>JSF Registration App</h2>
    <h4>Registration Confirmation</h4>
    <h:messages />
    #{userBean.pullValuesFromFlash( )}
    <table>
      <tr>
        <td>First Name:</td>
        <td>
          <h:outputText value="#{userBean.firstName}" />
        </td>
      </tr>
    </table>
  </h:form>
</h:body>
</html>
```

The only change necessary here is to invoke the **pullValuesFromFlash( )** method. Because this method invocation happens first thing in the page, we can be assured that the values stored in the flash because of the **keep** statements on the **confirm.xhtml** page are present for this method to use.

POST REDIRECT GET Using View Parameters The previous example reimplements the registration application using a request-scoped bean and the flash. This example does so with a request-scoped bean and the View Parameters feature.

JSF 2.0 introduced a feature similar in spirit to the "page parameters" feature found in JBoss Seam, but the JSF 2.0 incarnation of the feature is tightly integrated with the core JSF specification, making the feature easier to use and more powerful. Let's show some example code and explain how it works. The following **main.xhtml** file is a simplification of the one from the section "Redirects and implicit navigation," with the important change shown in boldface.

```
<!DOCTYPE html PUBLIC "-//W3C//DTD XHTML 1.0 Transitional//EN"
"http://www.w3.org/TR/xhtml1/DTD/xhtml1-transitional.dtd">
<html xmlns="http://www.w3.org/1999/xhtml"
      xmlns:h="http://java.sun.com/jsf/html"
      xmlns:f="http://java.sun.com/jsf/core">
<h:head>
  <title>A Simple JavaServer Faces 2.0 View</title>
</h:head>
<h:body>
  <h:form>

      <p> First name: <h:inputText id="fname"
             value="#{userBean.firstName}" /> </p>
    <p><h:commandButton value="submit"
action="page02?faces-redirect=true&amp;includeViewParams=true" /></p>

  </h:form>
</h:body>
</html>
```

Note the expression **&includeViewParams=true**. The **&** entity is a separator. JSF recognizes **&** and the single **&** character as separators within the query string. The value **includeViewParams=true** tells the navigation handler to include the view parameters when performing the navigation. But what view parameters should be included? The view parameters to be included when performing the navigation are declared on the **to-view-id** page. In this case, we are using implicit navigation, so the implicit **to-view-id** is **page02.xhtml**.

```
<!DOCTYPE html PUBLIC "-//W3C//DTD XHTML 1.0 Transitional//EN"
"http://www.w3.org/TR/xhtml1/DTD/xhtml1-transitional.dtd">
<html xmlns="http://www.w3.org/1999/xhtml"
      xmlns:h="http://java.sun.com/jsf/html"
      xmlns:f="http://java.sun.com/jsf/core">
<f:metadata>
    <f:viewParam name="fname" value="#{userBean.firstName}"/>
</f:metadata>
<h:head>
  <title>A Simple JavaServer Faces 2.0 View</title>
</h:head>
<h:body>
  <h:form>
      <p> Hello #{userBean.firstName}.</p>
      </h:form>
</h:body>
</html>
```

When the navigation handler encounters the matching **navigation-case** (implicit or explicit) that declares that view parameters should be included, it looks at the view parameters of the **from-view-id** and **to-view-id** pages and performs a match-and-copy algorithm to convey the view parameters to the new page. In this case the **navigation-case** also requested a redirect. Look at the URL bar in the following illustration of the browser after the "submit" button is pressed:

This illustration shows that the browser just fetched a URL with **fname=Zach** in the query string. This is because we declared **<f:viewParam name="fname" value="#{userBean .firstName}"/>** in the **<f:metadata>** section of the page. The presence of an **<f:viewParam>** in the page causes a **UIViewParameter** component to be added to the tree. **UIViewParameter** is a non-visible UI component that extends from **UIInput**, and therefore can accept attached objects that a **UIInput** component accepts, namely, **Converters**, **Validators** and **ValueChangeListeners**. **UIViewParameters** enable the page to accept parameters even on an initial GET request, or on a page transition request, and still preserve the security of the JSF conversion and validation model.

Let's take a more complete example, the jsfreg application, implemented to do PRG with view parameters. The **register.xhtml** page looks like this:

```
<!DOCTYPE html PUBLIC "-//W3C//DTD XHTML 1.0 Transitional//EN"
"http://www.w3.org/TR/xhtml1/DTD/xhtml1-transitional.dtd">
<html xmlns="http://www.w3.org/1999/xhtml"
      xmlns:h="http://java.sun.com/jsf/html"
      xmlns:f="http://java.sun.com/jsf/core">
<f:metadata>
    <f:viewParam name="fname" value="#{userBean.firstName}" />
    <f:viewParam name="lname" value="#{userBean.lastName}" />
    <f:viewParam name="sex" value="#{userBean.sex}" />
    <f:viewParam name="dob" value="#{userBean.dob}">
        <f:convertDateTime pattern="MM-dd-yy" />
    </f:viewParam>
    <f:viewParam name="email" value="#{userBean.email}" />
    <f:viewParam name="sLevel" value="#{userBean.serviceLevel}" />
</f:metadata>
<h:head>
  <title>A Simple JavaServer Faces Registration Application</title>
</h:head>
<h:body>
  <h:form>
    <h2>JSF Registration App</h2>
    <h4>Registration Form</h4>
```

```
    <table>
      <tr>
        <td>First Name:</td>
        <td>
          <h:inputText label="First Name"
                       id="fname" value="#{userBean.firstName}"
                       required="true"/>
          <h:message for="fname" />
        </td>
      </tr>
... remaining table rows omitted, they are the same as the
original jsfreg
    </table>

    <!-- The query parameters on the action attribute cause JSF to do the
         POST REDIRECT GET pattern -->
    <p><h:commandButton value="Register"
      action="confirm?faces-redirect=true&amp;includeViewParams=true"/></p>
  </h:form>
</h:body>
</html>
```

In the previous example, we stated that **<f:viewParam>** elements only appear on the **to-view-id** page. That is still true in this example, even though this is the first page the user sees. Recall that this particular application allows the user to go back and forth between the **register.xhtml** page and the **confirm.xhtml** page. Therefore, when the user is on the **confirm .xhtml** page, the **to-view-id** is the **register.xhtml** page and vice versa. Thus, **<f:viewParams>** is on both pages. You will need an **<f:viewParam>** for every input component on the *from* page that you wish to carry forward to the *to* page. Also note the **<f:convertDateTime>** within the **<f:viewParam>** for the **dob** property. This is necessary because, when the navigation is performed, the converter needs to be invoked to carry the value forward. If there is an explicit converter defined on the input field, then there must also be one on the corresponding **<f:viewParam>**. Finally, you can see the now familiar extra query parameters on the implicit navigation: **confirm?faces-redirect=true&includeViewParams=true**.

JSF 2.0 TIP *It is very important to point out the security implications of putting user data into URL query strings. URL query strings can be saved into browser bookmarks, stored in search engines, and cached by Web proxies and packet sniffers. Therefore it is very inadvisable to put sensitive data, such as birthdays, in URL query strings.*

Let's examine the changes to the **UserBean.java** file.

```
package com.jsfcompref.model;
... imports omitted.
@ManagedBean
@RequestScoped
public class UserBean {
... additional properties omitted.
    public String addConfirmedUser() {
      boolean added = true; // actual application may fail to add user
```

```
        FacesMessage doneMessage = null;
        String outcome = null;
        if (added) {
            doneMessage = new FacesMessage("Successfully added new user");
            outcome = "done?faces-redirect=true&amp;includeViewParams=true";
        } else {
            doneMessage = new FacesMessage("Failed to add new user");
            outcome =
"register?faces-redirect=true&amp;includeViewParams=true";
        }
          FacesContext.getCurrentInstance().addMessage(null, doneMessage);
          return outcome;
      }

}
```

The only changes to this code are to make the bean be request-scoped, for the same reason as in the flash example, and to add the query parameters to the implicit navigation string. In this case the **includeViewParams=true** parameter is added, causing whatever view parameters are declared on the **to-view-id** page to be included in the navigation.

The **confirm.xhtml** page follows:

```
<!DOCTYPE html PUBLIC "-//W3C//DTD XHTML 1.0 Transitional//EN"
"http://www.w3.org/TR/xhtml1/DTD/xhtml1-transitional.dtd">
<html xmlns="http://www.w3.org/1999/xhtml"
      xmlns:h="http://java.sun.com/jsf/html"
      xmlns:f="http://java.sun.com/jsf/core">
<f:metadata>
    <f:viewParam name="fname" value="#{userBean.firstName}" />
    <f:viewParam name="lname" value="#{userBean.lastName}" />
    <f:viewParam name="sex" value="#{userBean.sex}" />
    <f:viewParam name="dob" value="#{userBean.dob}">
        <f:convertDateTime pattern="MM-dd-yy" />
    </f:viewParam>
    <f:viewParam name="email" value="#{userBean.email}" />
    <f:viewParam name="sLevel" value="#{userBean.serviceLevel}" />
</f:metadata>
<h:head>
  <title>A Simple JavaServer Faces Registration Application</title>
</h:head>
<h:body>
  <h:form>
    <h2>JSF Registration App</h2>
    <h4>Registration Confirmation</h4>
    <table>
      <tr>
        <td>First Name:</td>
        <td>
          <h:outputText value="#{userBean.firstName}" />
        </td>
      </tr>
```

```
... additional rows omitted, they are the same as in the original
jsfreg.
    </table>

    <p><h:commandButton value="Edit"
action="register?faces-redirect=true&amp;includeViewParams=true" /></p>
  </h:form>

  <h:form>
    <h:inputHidden value="#{userBean.firstName}" />
    <h:inputHidden value="#{userBean.lastName}"/>
    <h:inputHidden value="#{userBean.sex}" />
    <h:inputHidden value="#{userBean.dob}">
        <f:convertDateTime pattern="MM-dd-yy" />
    </h:inputHidden>
    <h:inputHidden value="#{userBean.email}" />
    <h:inputHidden value="#{userBean.serviceLevel}" />

    <p><h:commandButton value="Confirm"
action="#{userBean.addConfirmedUser}" /></p>
  </h:form>

</h:body>
</html>
```

As in the **register.xhtml** page, we need the **<f:metadata>** section at the top of the page and the additional query parameters on the action string. What is new here are the additional **<h:form>** element and **<h:inputHidden>** elements, and the fact that the **Confirm** button has been moved into this new form. This is necessary because we need to carry the values forward that are passed *to* this page as view parameters to the next page as regular form submit parameters, but there are no regular input fields as there are on the **register.xhtml** page. Therefore, we use hidden fields to carry the values forward. Note also the continued necessity for the **<f:convertDateTime>** on the **dob** field. Finally, here is the **done.xhtml** page:

```
<!DOCTYPE html PUBLIC "-//W3C//DTD XHTML 1.0 Transitional//EN"
"http://www.w3.org/TR/xhtml1/DTD/xhtml1-transitional.dtd">
<html xmlns="http://www.w3.org/1999/xhtml"
      xmlns:h="http://java.sun.com/jsf/html"
      xmlns:f="http://java.sun.com/jsf/core">
<f:metadata>
    <f:viewParam name="fname" value="#{userBean.firstName}" />
    <f:viewParam name="lname" value="#{userBean.lastName}" />
    <f:viewParam name="sex" value="#{userBean.sex}" />
    <f:viewParam name="dob" value="#{userBean.dob}">
        <f:convertDateTime pattern="MM-dd-yy" />
    </f:viewParam>
    <f:viewParam name="email" value="#{userBean.email}" />
    <f:viewParam name="sLevel" value="#{userBean.serviceLevel}" />
</f:metadata>
```

```
<h:head>
  <title>A Simple JavaServer Faces Registration Application</title>
</h:head>
<h:body>
  <h:form>
    <h2>JSF Registration App</h2>
    <h4>Registration Confirmation</h4>
    <h:messages />
    <table>
      <tr>
        <td>First Name:</td>
        <td>
          <h:outputText value="#{userBean.firstName}" />
        </td>
      </tr>
... additional rows omitted
    </table>
  </h:form>
</h:body>
</html>
```

The only difference between this **done.xhtml** and the one in Chapter 2 is the now familiar **<f:metadata>** section.

XML Configuration for View Parameters

Of course, implicit navigation is not the only way to declare view parameters. It is also possible to include them in the XML navigation rules. The general form for this follows.

```
<navigation-rule>
  <from-view-id>whatever the from view id is</from-view-id>
  <navigation-case>
    <from-outcome>whatever the outcome value is</from-outcome>
    <to-view-id>whatever the to view id is</to-view-id>
    <redirect>
      ...the view-param elements are optional
      <view-param>
        <name>any string is fine here</name>
        <value>any string or value expression is fine here</value>
      </view-param>
      ...additional view-param elements may be defined
    </redirect>
  </navigation-case>
</navigation-rule>
```

The **<view-param>** elements, if present, are added to whatever query parameters are present on the action query string. The benefit of declaring them in the XML file is the ability to use EL expressions, which is not possible when including parameters in the action query string.

Bookmarkability and View Parameters

The View Parameters feature has another benefit: it enables the design of components that support *bookmarkability.* When a user directs a browser to load a page from a bookmark, the browser issues an HTTP GET request to whatever URL was in the URL bar when the bookmark was saved. Any POST data, or data that may have been in form fields in the page, is not saved as part of the bookmark. JSF includes two components, mentioned previously in this chapter, that support bookmarkability: **<h:button>** and **<h:link>**. The online code for this chapter includes an example that takes the PRG via View Parameters–enabled jsfreg application and adds a bookmarkable link to the **confirm.xhtml** page. For brevity, this looks like

```
<h:link outcome="confirm?faces-redirect=true&amp;includeViewParams=true"
        value="boomarkable link to this page"/>
```

Whatever view parameters were declared in the page will be included in the generated link. In this case the link is rendered as

```
http://localhost:8080/bookmarkableLink/faces/confirm.xhtml?
fname=Jake&lname=Trainer&sex=male&dob=11-13-
77&email=edburns%40yahoo.com&sLevel=medium
```

The **<h:button>** requires the user actually press the button to visit the page before he or she can bookmark it, but the URL, whereas with the link the user can use the "bookmark this link" feature common to most browsers.

Using JSF Components on a Servlet Error Page

The last topic that must be covered for a complete treatment of navigation is how it relates to unexpected exceptions. The Servlet specification has always had the ability to declare that a specific Java exception should cause the redirection to a specific error page. This feature also works with JSF, but you must be certain to include the Faces Servlet mapping in the declaration. This declaration must reside in the **web.xml** file. Here is an example:

```
<error-page>
  <exception-type>javax.faces.application.ViewExpiredException
  </exception-type>
  <location>/faces/sessionExpired.xhtml</location>
</error-page>
<error-page>
  <exception-type>com.jsfcompref.BadUserException
  </exception-type>
  <location>/faces/badUser.xhtml</location>
</error-page>
```

If no **<error-page>** elements are present in the **web.xml**, JSF 2.0 now provides a very useful error page that includes the following information, displayed in an attractive "show/hide" layout where the high level information is shown by default, and the detail information is easily revealed. This information includes:

- The stack trace of the **Exception**
- The **UIComponent** tree at the time the **Exception** was thrown
- All scoped variables in request, view, session, and application
- If the error happens during the execution of the Facelets page, the file on which the error happened
- The line number within that file
- Any available error messages pertaining to the content of the page
- The **viewId** at the time the **Exception** was thrown

Now that you've seen the architectural details behind JavaServer Faces Navigation Model and have stepped through several examples, it's time to look at JavaServer Faces User Interface Component Model in greater detail.

7

CHAPTER

The User Interface Component Model

From the material covered in previous chapters, you should now have a general understanding of how JavaServer Faces is a server-side, component-based architecture for building dynamic Web applications. More important, you've seen examples of how Faces Web interfaces are assembled using a collection of both visual and nonvisual components, the nonvisual ones being the components that perform validation, conversion, or other nonvisual tasks, and the visual components being the ones that render a portion of the user interface at runtime.

This chapter will now focus specifically on the Faces user interface component technology by first defining the term "UI component" and then explaining the forces that spurred the creation of component-based Web development. The chapter will then examine the JavaServer Faces user interface component architecture in detail with special attention on how to use it with JSP.

What Are UI Components?

At the outset, it is necessary to define precisely what we mean by the term "UI component." In general, a *component* is a self-contained piece of software with a well-defined usage contract that is used by another piece of software. A *user interface component* (UI component) is a specific type of component that displays user interface content which the user can modify over time. This content ranges from simple input fields or buttons to more complex items, such as trees or datagrids.

In JavaServer Faces, the term *UI component* technically refers to a specific **UIComponent** class that defines the core behavior of the component regardless of how it appears (is rendered) to the client; however, the term is more generally used to describe the entire set of software artifacts that include both the core **UIComponent** class and other related "helper" components, such as a **Renderer**, a tag handler, a **Validator**, a **Converter**, and so on. These different components work together to enable the overall UI component to run in a Faces deployment environment. The helper components, more correctly known as "attached objects" because the **UIComponent** instance maintains a Java object reference to them, are also considered Faces components, but they are not, themselves, *UI* components because they don't help in rendering the component visually.

In general, Faces components represent the time-tested abstraction technique of object-oriented programming in which the implementation details of the component are hidden from the user of the component. Instead he or she simply needs to understand the component's usage contract. It is not necessary to know the internal workings of the component. Further coverage of the different helper-components of UI components are detailed later in the chapter and numerous examples are provided in Chapter 13.

Because of its emphasis on building user interfaces from reusable and adaptable components, the Faces UI component technology is often compared to Microsoft's ASP.Net component, or *control* (as used in Microsoft's terminology) technology. This is no coincidence, since they both represent the most efficient way to build Web user interfaces. However, component-based Web development did not start with ASP.Net and JSF. The following brief history of component-based Web development shows how the trend emerged even before ASP and JSF.

The Rise of Component-Based Web Development

The main benefit of JavaServer Faces is its *standard* component model. The existence of a widely accepted standard component model enables Web developers to choose from a wide variety of components from disparate sources that are tailored to different application domains to build their applications. For example, as a developer, you could obtain a world-class reporting component from Business Objects, a production-quality GIS mapping component from ESRI, a feature-rich charting component from ILOG, and so on, and put them all together into your own application. The ability to create a true, reusable UI component, and package it together in an easily deployable form, is the distinguishing characteristic of a component-based framework. Any framework lacking this characteristic is not component-based.

Of course, Web development wasn't always so easy. Let's review a little Web development history to understand the merits of component-based development and to see why JavaServer Faces has adopted this approach.

As the Web transitioned from a predominantly static environment with simple "home page"–type Web sites to a rich and dynamic environment containing the latest e-commerce applications, Web development technologies have evolved into component-based architectures. This is primarily because of the inherent complications in providing a rich and dynamic end-user experience over a nonsynchronous Web/HTTP environment that was designed primarily for static document retrieval. For this reason, Web application development has always been a bit of an art. Because of the lack of a single standard other than HTTP/HTML, Web application development has generally been accomplished through a myriad of different approaches and technologies.

Early Web applications tended to be simplistic in nature, often just displaying small portions of dynamic data using simple CGI back-end processes. These simple back-end processes would also process incoming form values. HTTP and CGI were adequate technologies to handle these basic types of Web applications. As businesses soon saw the advantages of having business applications run over the Web or local TCP/IP intranet networks, traditional client/server applications began transitioning over to Web/HTTP-based architectures. This created an increasing need for more complex user interfaces similar to those that have been around since the beginning of client/server application development. However, because of the lack of standards for building these ever more complex user interfaces for the Web, a number of different approaches have been tried, but with mixed success.

To solve the increasing complexities of building sophisticated user interfaces for the Web, different technologies began to offer a component-centric approach to application development. Technologies such as Cold Fusion and Microsoft's Active Server Pages (ASP) began offering intelligent sets of components to assemble Web applications. With more intelligent Web components, developers could take advantage of prebuilt, sophisticated components that took on more user interface responsibilities. For example, a datagrid, which is a common yet fairly sophisticated component in many user interface technologies, can render a grid of dynamic data, possibly from a database, while handling user input gestures to scroll or page through data. Other, more sophisticated components, such as a JavaScript-enabled pop-up date picker, offered features that (in most cases) would be too time-consuming to be implemented by hand. As Web application development continued to explode, having prebuilt, sophisticated Web components reduced Web development complexity and also increased the power of the Web developer to create increasingly sophisticated user interfaces.

As both ASP and other component technologies began to simplify Web application development, the enterprise Java community began to catch up with custom JSP tag libraries and frameworks. In contrast to ASP and other non-Java Web technologies, enterprise Java component technology for Web development has largely been led by Open Source projects through the Apache Jakarta project. For example, the JavaServer Page Standard Tag Library (JSTL), which was basically an amalgamation of helpful Web development custom JSP tag libraries, was developed through the auspices of the Apache Jakarta project. JSTL includes custom tag libraries for handling basic Web development tasks such as rendering and iterating through data, and working with XML as well as SQL. JSTL, however, did not offer sophisticated user interface components, and JSTL users often had to write a fair amount of code to develop more sophisticated user interfaces using the JSTL tags.

In addition to custom tag libraries, enterprise Java also saw the introduction of complete Web development "frameworks." These provided aid to user interface development and also offered a complete infrastructure for developing Web applications that followed the Model-View-Controller design paradigm. The most notable of these technologies also came from the Apache Jakarta project and is known as Struts. With Struts, a complete infrastructure is provided within the framework, including a basic user interface or "presentation"-oriented set of components in the form of custom tag libraries. In contrast to JSTL, however, Struts also provides a Controller servlet and a complete infrastructure for building Web applications fully adherent to the MVC design methodology.

While Struts does provide an MVC framework, it cannot be said to have a true user interface component model. Yes, it is possible to drop in custom tags to do various things such as client-side validation and extended form support, but there really is no single or standard way to package specific UI functionality together into a reusable component, such as a chart or an e-mail tool. For this reason, Java Web development frameworks such as Struts (along with others, including Velocity and WebObjects) may not be considered to offer a true component-centric approach to building user interfaces, while frameworks such as JSF, Tapestry, Wicket, and Echo generally can be.

Aside from JSF, the open source Tapestry, another popular Java Web development framework, provides a component-centric development experience. Tapestry allows Web developers to work in a familiar HTML environment where additional attributes (for example, jwcid) are added to the familiar HTML tags such as **<input>** to allow a set of Java-based components to render different types of sophisticated user interface components. Tapestry also provides a small JSP tag library for integration into JSP applications.

In addition to JSF and other Java Web development frameworks, vendors have also been working hard to provide user interface component–centric development frameworks. For example, Oracle's now-deprecated UIX technology, which was originally created for the development of Oracle Applications for the Web and is a forerunner to its ADF Faces technology, provided both a rich set of user interface components as well as the backing technology for a full MVC infrastructure.

The reasons for the rise of component-based Web development frameworks are obvious. They improve productivity by allowing developers to merely assemble Web applications out of ready-to-use sophisticated components as opposed to having to constantly invent their own infrastructure and write their own user interface code.

The Goal of JavaServer Faces UI Components

JavaServer Faces UI components are intended to serve as the prime vehicle by which JavaServer Faces is expected to grow and become truly ubiquitous in Java Web development. Although the Faces specification provides a set of ready-to-use base UI components mainly to allow for building the most general types of user interfaces, the goal behind the UI component architecture is to make it completely extendable so as to empower a growing community of Faces component developers. Although JSF is still a relatively new technology, a new thriving community of Faces component developers is now emerging. These communities include both vendor-supplied and open source developers, and their component libraries complement the base (Standard) JSF components in many unique ways. There now exists a wide variety of third-party component libraries that range from those for general use to those intended for specific uses, such as for charting or mapping applications. These components all extend from base classes or implement interfaces present in the core JSF component API, presented in detail in this chapter. Therefore, it is important to have a firm understanding of the core JSF component API because by doing so, you are going a long way to understanding all present and future JSF components.

Fortunately, as the JSF component development community continues to grow, some new Web sites are starting to appear that serve as guides to the different third-party components, libraries, and Faces implementations. One of the prime community Web sites to emerge is JSFCentral.com (**http://jsfcentral.com**). At this site you'll find a thorough list of JSF components, component libraries, how-to's, and Faces-related articles. As you gain more experience with JavaServer Faces, you are definitely encouraged to experiment with the various Faces components and libraries referenced at this and other sites. You will find that the different components provide an extremely useful and thorough understanding of the power and flexibility of the JavaServer Faces technology.

Introducing the JSF UI Component Architecture

There are two main types of UI components: those that initiate an action, such as a button, and those that provide data, such as an input field. Nearly every possible JSF UI component can be placed into one of these two buckets. The behaviors of UI components are described by the distinct *behavioral interfaces* provided by the Faces specification. UI components that initiate an action—for example, invoking application logic as the result of a button click—implement the **ActionSource2** interface. The standard implementation of this interface is **UICommand**. The other UI components that provide data (that is, allow for data to be submitted to the server), such as **UIInput**, implement either the **ValueHolder** or **EditableValueHolder** interfaces. The **EditableValueHolder** interface allows for components to have their values editable by users. The raison d'être for these interfaces is to provide the highest possible abstraction to encapsulate the capabilities possessed by all possible JSF UI components. In this way, it is easier to understand all JSF components by understanding the interfaces they implement.

In addition to implementing either of these two distinct groups of interfaces, UI components (and components in general) also implement various other interfaces that further define their behaviors. Components that need to save their state between requests implement the **PartialStateHolder** interface. **Converter**s, **Validator**s, and **UIComponent**s all implement **PartialStateHolder**, since they need to be able to save their state between requests. Components that implement **NamingContainer** require that their children components' identifier IDs be unique. **UIForm** and **UIData** both implement **NamingContainer**. Table 7-1 is the complete list of behavioral interfaces required to understand the JSF component model, listed in decreasing order of importance. Only the first two rows are really important to understand to simply *use* JSF UI components. The remainder are mainly useful when creating your own JSF UI components. Deprecated interfaces and interfaces primarily used by the JSF runtime are not included.

Interface Name	A component implementing this interface . . .	Components implementing this interface include . . .
EditableValueHolder	has a "value" that can be edited by the user and submitted to the server, where it must be properly handled. Note that the editing of the value may be temporarily disabled, or "grayed out."	**UIInput**, **UISelectBoolean**, **UISelectMany**, **UISelectOne**, **UIViewParameter**, and their subclasses
ActionSource2	causes an **ActionEvent** to be fired when the component is clicked by the user.	**UICommand**, and its subclasses
PartialStateHolder	has state that needs to be maintained from request to request.	every **UIComponent** and every helper component.
ValueHolder	has a "value" that *cannot* be edited by the user. This is different than a component whose value editing capability is temporarily disabled or "grayed out."	**UIOutput** and its subclasses.
NamingContainer	provides a naming scope for its child components.	**UIForm**, **UINamingContainer**, **UIData** and their subclasses.
ClientBehaviorHolder (in the **javax.faces .component.behavior** package)	supports attaching client behavior, such as Ajax, to its runtime capabilities	all the components in the standard HTML component set.

TABLE 7-1 Behavioral Interfaces in Package javax.faces.component

Aside from understanding the behaviors of the different components, it is important to understand the overall UI component class hierarchy. First, all of the core UI component classes reside in the package **javax.faces.component** and are derived from **UIComponent**. In practice most extend from **UIComponentBase**, which itself extends from **UIComponent**. **UIComponentBase** is a convenience class that provides much of the implementation you need for building a component. Figure 7-1 shows the class hierarchy of the core UI components.

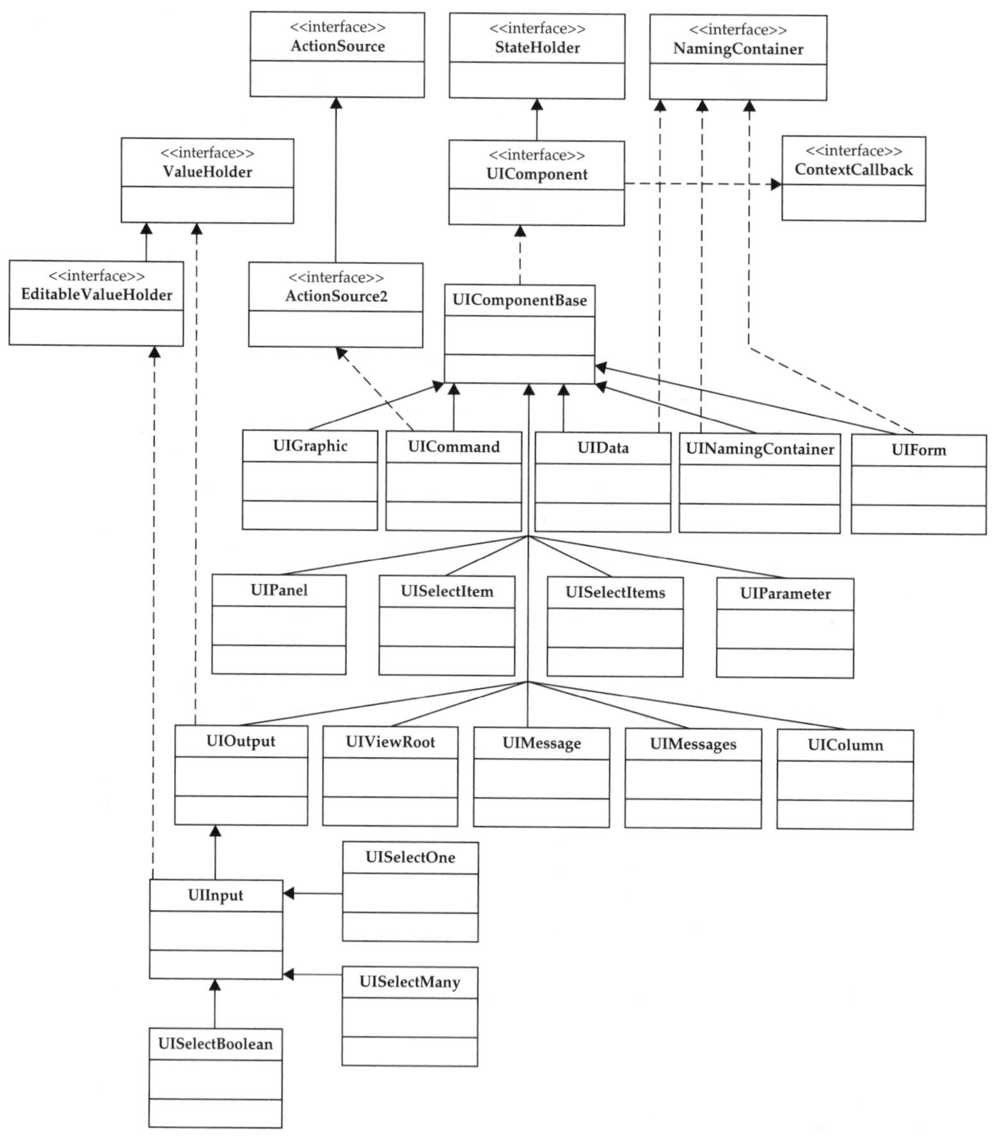

Figure 7-1 Classes and interfaces in the javax.faces.component package

By way of a quick review of object-oriented programming, the arrows in Figure 7-1 indicate "inheritance." For example, notice that **UIInput** has an arrow that points to **UIOutput**. This means **UIInput** inherits all the capabilities of **UIOutput**. Anything a **UIOutput** can do, a **UIInput** can do also, in addition to the special things that only **UIInput** can do. This also means that any instance of **UIInput** is also an instance of **UIOutput** and can be treated as such in Java code. Because **UIComponent** is at the base of the inheritance hierarchy, every UI component is a **UIComponent**.

Just as the behavioral interfaces encapsulate the capabilities of the component implementing the interface, all of the components in the core **javax.faces.component** package encapsulate the *meaning* of the component, without describing how the component appears to the user. Separating the meaning of something from its function and appearance is central to the concept of the Web itself and has been at the heart of markup-based documents and user interfaces since Charles Goldfarb's Generalized Markup Language (GML) in 1969. Table 7-2 lists the standard components and their meanings. The components are listed in decreasing order of importance of understanding, and only the first nine rows are really fundamental to understanding the JSF component API.

Component Name	Meaning
UIComponent	The true base class of all JSF UI Components.
UIComponentBase	The direct subclass of **UIComponent** from which nearly all JSF UI components extend, in practice. This class provides concrete implementations of many of the abstract methods declared on **UIComponent**.
UIInput	An instance of this component has a "value" that can be edited by the user. A **UIInput** instance also knows how to decode that value from the user and directs its conversion, validation, and transition to the model tier.
UICommand	An instance of this component causes an **ActionEvent** to be fired when the component is clicked by the user.
UIOutput	An instance of this component has a "value" that *cannot* be edited by the user.
UISelectOne	An instance of this component allows the user to select exactly zero or one value out of several values.
UISelectMany	An instance of this component allows the user to select zero, one, or many values out of several values.
UISelectBoolean	An instance of this component has a value that is either **true** or **false**.
UIData	An instance of this component contains tabular data displayed as a composition of other **UIComponent** instances.
UIForm	An instance of this component contains a composition of other **UIComponent** instances that make up a conceptual form.

TABLE 7-2 The Components in Package javax.faces.component *(continued)*

Component Name	Meaning
UISelectItem and **UISelectItems**	An instance of this component resides as a child within a **UISelectOne** or **UISelectMany** instance and represents the values from which the user may select.
UIPanel	An instance of this component contains a composition of other **UIComponent** instances that are logically grouped together in some way, other than being members of a form.
UIColumn	An instance of this component resides as a child of **UIData** and contains a composition of other **UIComponent** instances that make up a column in the tabular data.
UIMessage and **UIMessages**	An instance of this component displays one or more messages about the state of a component. Most often, these are used to display validation messages for UI components.
UIParameter	An instance of this component resides within other components that need *name=value* pairs to configure how they operate. For example, a component that renders an HTML link would need **UIParameter** children to convey URL query parameters.
UIViewParameter	Covered in detail in the preceding chapter, an instance of this component represents a **UIInput** value that needs to be conveyed across the request boundary of a POST REDIRECT GET lifecycle.
UIGraphic	An instance of this component represents an embedded image in the page.
UINamingContainer	An instance of this component provides a naming scope for its child components.
UIViewRoot	An instance of this component is automatically created to be the root node in the UI component tree.
UIOutcomeTarget	An instance of this component represents a page navigation that *does not* cause an **ActionEvent** to be fired.

TABLE 7-2 The Components in Package javax.faces.component *(continued)*

In addition to the set of core UI components in Table 7-2, Faces provides an HTML-friendly set of UI component classes that facilitate Web application development for HTML clients (browsers). The HTML set of components reside in the package **javax.faces.component.html** and are also derived from the same core UI component class hierarchy, but provide a further level of distinction for HTML clients. For example, the **HtmlCommandButton** is a button that renders in HTML and extends from the core **UICommand**, which extends **UIComponentBase**, and so on. The "HTML-ness" of the components in the **javax.faces.component.html** package is

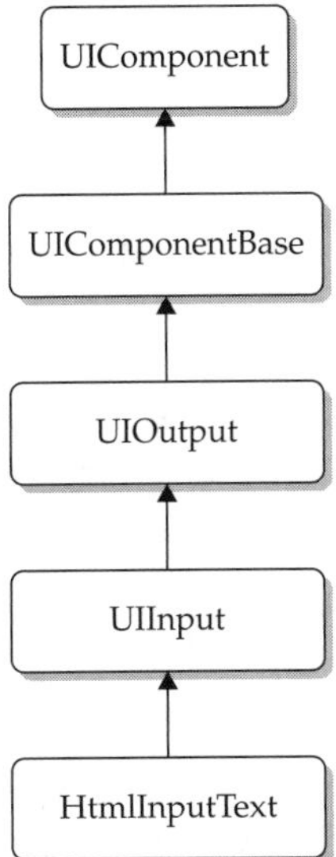

FIGURE 7-2 The class hierarchy of **HtmlInputText**

provided by another of the "moving parts" of JSF: the **Renderer**. A **Renderer** is a class that is responsible for taking a **UIComponent** instance and generating the output to show the component in a specific kind of client device, for example, a Web browser. Chapters 11 and 13 explain a **Renderer** in detail.

As another example of the hierarchical nature of UI components, Figure 7-2 shows the class hierarchy of the **HtmlInputText** UI component.

The UI Component Tree (View)

As first introduced in Chapter 3, Faces solves the inherent incompatibilities between a traditional client/server development process and the stateless Web architecture by providing an infrastructure based on a server-side UI component tree that mirrors exactly what is presented to the user in the client browser. The UI component tree is also known as the **View**. This enables the JSF developer to work on the server-side set of UI components in more of a traditional, event-based mode and let the JSF lifecycle handle the synchronization between the UI component tree on the server and what is rendered to the client browser.

To understand the notion of a server-side UI component tree that mirrors what is presented to the client, again consider the JSFReg example from Chapter 2. As a user makes an initial (nonpostback) request to view the registration form, a tree of hierarchical UI components are instantiated on the server that exactly represent what is viewed in the browser. As you recall from Chapter 3, this occurs during the Restore/Create View phase. The subsequent Render Response phase then renders the representation of the registration form to the client by calling a cascading set of **render( )** methods on each component that emit the appropriate markup for each respective component to the client. Figure 7-3 illustrates how the server-side UI component tree mirrors what is presented to the user in a client (browser).

Once the UI component tree is in memory, it is updated to reflect any changes in the client between requests, such as new values in input fields or programmatic changes written to access and manipulate any properties of the components. For example, assume

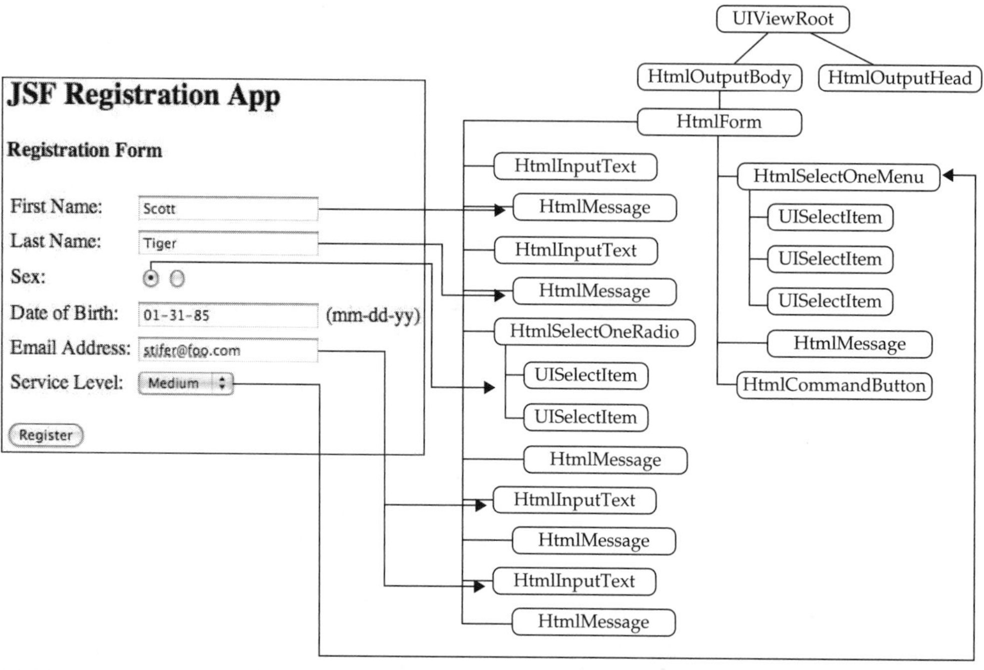

FIGURE 7-3 Faces' server-side UI component tree mirroring what the client sees

an instance (**inputText1**) of a standard Faces input field (**HTMLInputText**, which extends **UIInput**) component. If a new value is entered into the field and subsequently submitted to the server during a postback request, the new value will be applied to the server-side instance of the input field (**inputText1**) during the Apply Request Values phase. You can also alter the same component programmatically through the use of action methods, **PhaseListeners**, or any other code that is executed throughout the JSF request processing lifecycle. As an example, the **inputText1** instance can be programmatically set to read-only by calling its **setReadonly( )** method in an action method that responds to a button click:

```
inputText1.setReadonly(true);
```

As previously mentioned, the **HTMLInputText** component is an extension of the **UIInput** component that can hold a user-entered value because it implements the **EditableValueHolder** interface. In general, each component has a large set of methods that alter the behavior or settings of each component. As an example, the **HTMLInputText** component has numerous methods (both native to the class as well as inherited) that access and/or alter the component's properties. Here are some examples:

getValue( )	Returns the value of the UI component as a **java.lang .Object**. Declared in parent **UIOutput** class.
setValue(java.lang.Object *value*)	Sets the value of the UI component. Also declared in the **UIOutput** class.

To eliminate any confusion, it's important to distinguish between the class hierarchy and the server-side UI component tree hierarchy. The server-side UI component tree is a representation of the component layout in a page. It enables programmatic access to the components. For example, the parent UI component **UIForm** has a method **getChildren( )**, which returns a **List** of child UI components. Likewise, a UI component also has a **getParent( )** method to access its immediate parent component. The hierarchical nature of the component tree is how the JSF lifecycle manages all the components in one operation. Recall from Chapter 3 that the *Render Response* phase calls a cascading set of render methods on each component in order to send back a rendered response to the client. In general, during each new request, the UI component tree is constantly being altered with new values and settings based on the change in state of the UI in the client as changed by the end user or programmatically on the server.

State Management of UI Components

The UI component tree is fully managed by the **ViewHandler** between requests. However, it is the role of the **StateManager** to preserve the UI component tree in between subsequent requests. It saves the complete status of the component tree using one of several different *state-saving methods* specified as a context parameter (**javax.faces.STATE_SAVING_METHOD**) in the Web application's **web.xml** file. The different state-saving parameters are **server** and **client**.

The **server** parameter causes the application's state to be stored on the server in between requests. This is the default behavior, so this needn't be explicitly specified in **web.xml**.

The **client** parameter causes the state of the application to be saved on the client. The state information is stored in the form of rendered markup, which is sent back to the client using a hidden input field. For example, the source of the page sent back to the client will contain an input field such as

```
<input type="hidden" name="com.sun.faces.VIEW" value="H4sIknjsk...;" />
```

The state information is then included in the subsequent request as the hidden request parameter. This state-saving method allows the JSF runtime to save the entire application on the client and not on the server.

The UI Component and Its Associated "Moving Parts"

As mentioned earlier in the chapter, the term UI component is often used to describe more than just the core **UIComponent** class, but also its associated helper classes or all the other "moving parts" that work together to serve the end user in a specific capacity. The following paragraphs describe all of the software components that make up a proper JSF UI component.

The **UIComponent** class captures the abstract meaning of the component, such as: "make one choice from among several choices," "enter some input," or "display some output." Although the **UIComponent** class can optionally have code to render itself using client- or markup-specific elements (HTML, WML, and so on), it is generally not good practice, as **UIComponent**s are meant to avoid any client device–specific information. For maximum flexibility, a separate **Renderer** class is best used for this purpose.

The **Renderer** class is responsible for encapsulating client device–specific content and *rendering* it to the client. Providing this encapsulation in the request/response world of the Web requires two distinct functions: *encoding* a **UIComponent** instance to a specific client device technology, such as HTML or WML, and *decoding* information from the name value pairs in the postback and applying it back to the component for event processing.

Expert Group Insight *The Expert Group wrestled with the name* ***Renderer*** *for a long time and ultimately couldn't come up with a better name. One more descriptive but less catchy term considered was "client adapter."*

It is fundamentally important to understand that both the **UIComponent** and the **Renderer** can be fully independent and interchangeable so as to offer multiple rendering capabilities for a particular UI component. Often referred to as "pluggable" rendering, this distinguishes Faces from other Web development frameworks. As a case in point, Oracle's ADF Faces provides built-in multiple client rendering for its component set. For example, the same ADF Faces table will render in HTML when an HTML browser makes a request; however, the same UI component will render in WML when a PDA makes the same request.

The tag handler class along with an associated tag library descriptor (TLD) allows for the usage of UI components and renderers in Facelets or JSP, but more important it is the vehicle by which **Renderer**s or **Renderkit**s (which are families of **Renderer**s) are associated with **UIComponent**s. Figure 7-4 illustrates the relationship between the **UIComponent**, **Renderer**, and tag handler classes.

It is also important to understand how UI components can also be used outside the context of JSP. In this case, a **UIComponentTag** is not used. Instead, a separate **ViewHandler** can be built to allow for the usage of UI components without JSP. Chapter 13 will provide detailed coverage on how to use JSF components without JSP.

Table 7-3 summarizes the distinct "moving parts" of a usable UI component.

In Chapter 11, we will revisit the specifics of user interface components when we dive deeper into the UI component technology and show how to build custom UI components.

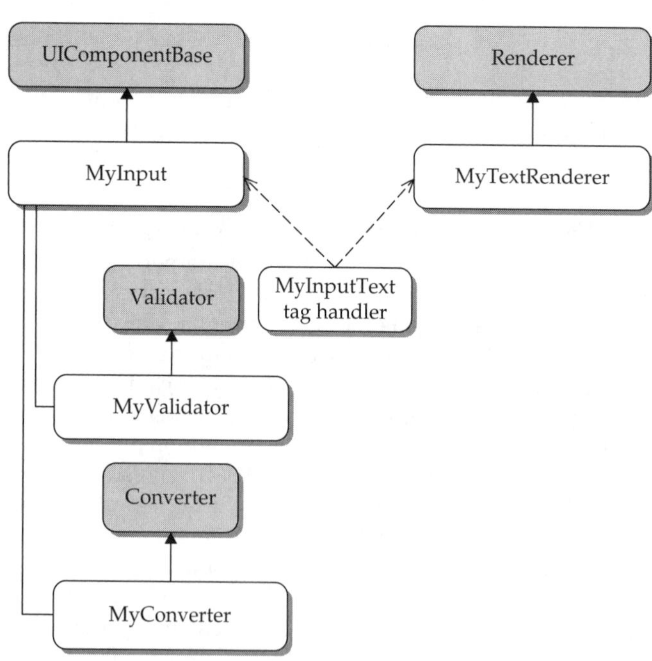

Figure 7-4 The relationship between UIComponent, Renderer, tag handler, and helper components. Shaded boxes are from the core JSF API.

Component	Purpose
UIComponent	The class that represents the abstract semantics of the component independent of the rendering of the component to a specific client device.
Renderer	An optional class that contains code to render a UI component to a specific client device.
Tag handler	An actual or conceptual class that allows a page author to place an instance of a particular kind of a component in a page. A tag handler represents a concrete pairing of a **UIComponent** and a **Renderer**.
Attached objects	An optional collection of helper components such as **Converter**s, **Validator**s, **ActionListener**s, **AjaxBehavior**s, and so on, which provide additional functionality to the UI component. These can be bound to UI components programmatically or through JSP tag attributes.

Table 7-3 The Different "Moving Parts" of a Usable JSF UI Component

Component Resources

You have seen that **UIComponent**s are Java classes and associated markup that cause a portion of a user interface to be rendered to a Web browser, and also know how to decode any value submitted by the browser in response to user action. Central to this mission, but not handled at all by the **UIComponent** itself, are files such as images, stylesheets, and JavaScript files. These kinds of files are often just as responsible for the appearance and behavior of a UI component in a Web page as the markup itself. JSF refers to these files as "resources" and has significant features to allow them to be handled cleanly by the UI component system. Component resources will be described in detail in Chapter 13, but here it is important to state that JSF supports tightly associating any number of resources with a **UIComponent**, such that when an instance of that component appears in a page, all the associated resources are also delivered to the browser so that the component can appear and behave as designed.

UI Components and Facelets

Since Facelets is the most common way to build JSF 2.0 applications, the remainder of this chapter will focus on how UI components are invoked from Facelets. Prior to JSF 2.0, JSP was also used, but JSP is no longer the recommended way of building JSF applications. The chapter concludes with helpful information on binding UI component instances to UI component tags in Facelet pages.

Accessing UI Components Programmatically

As you become more familiar with using UI components in Faces applications, you'll quickly find that working with them involves more than just using their tags in Facelet pages. Instead, Faces developers will often need to access and manipulate UI components programmatically.

To fully appreciate this point, consider the following simple example, where a Facelet page (**hello.xhtml**) has three UI components: **InputText**, **OutputText**, and a **CommandButton**. At runtime when the user enters a text value into the input field (**InputText**) and clicks the button (**CommandButton**), the output field (**OutputText**) is then updated with the value of the text entered into the input field. To meet the requirements of this situation, programmatic access to the UI components is required. Here is the source code for this example. The **hello .xhtml** JSP page is as follows:

```
<!DOCTYPE html PUBLIC "-//W3C//DTD XHTML 1.0
 Transitional//EN"
"http://www.w3.org/TR/xhtml1/DTD/xhtml1-transitional.dtd">
<html xmlns="http://www.w3.org/1999/xhtml"
      xmlns:h="http://java.sun.com/jsf/html"
      xmlns:f="http://java.sun.com/jsf/core">
<h:head>
  <title>A Simple JavaServer Faces Registration Application</title>
</h:head>
<h:body>
      <h:form>
        <h:inputText />
        <h:commandButton value="Click Me!" />
        <h:outputText value="Hello!" />
      </h:form>
    </body>
  </html>
</h:body>
```

To set the value of the **outputText** component with the value entered in the **inputText** component, an action method can be created that will programmatically get the value of the **inputText** component and set it as the value of the **outputText** field. This action method will reside in a "backing" bean, which will also contain instances of the respective UI components.

Here is the source code of **Hello.java**, which will serve as a backing bean for **hello.jsp**. You'll notice the declared instances of the UI components **HtmlInputText** and **HtmlOutputText** along with the associated getters and setters. These instances allow for programmatic access of the bound UI components.

```
package backing;


import javax.faces.component.html.HtmlCommandButton;
import javax.faces.component.html.HtmlInputText;
import javax.faces.component.html.HtmlOutputText;
import javax.faces.bean.ManagedBean;
import javax.faces.bean.RequestScoped;

@ManagedBean(name="backing_hello")
@RequestScoped
public class Hello
{
  private HtmlInputText inputText1;
  private HtmlOutputText outputText1;
```

```
  public void setInputText1(HtmlInputText inputText1)
  {
    this.inputText1 = inputText1;
  }
  public HtmlInputText getInputText1()
  {
    return inputText1;
  }
  public void setOutputText1(HtmlOutputText outputText1)
  {
    this.outputText1 = outputText1;
  }
  public HtmlOutputText getOutputText1()
  {
    return outputText1;
  }
}
```

Here is the Facelets page, but now with bindings to the UI component instances declared in the backing bean. This enables programmatic access to the actual components used in the page. It's important to understand that if the UI components in the page were not bound to component instances in a backing bean (as before), the UI component tree would still be created upon request but with separately instantiated components.

```
<h:form>
  <h:inputText binding="#{backing_hello.inputText1}"/>
  <h:commandButton value="Click Me!" />
  <h:outputText value="Hello!"
                binding="#{backing_hello.outputText1}"/>
</h:form>
```

Figure 7-5 illustrates the binding of the UI components referenced in **hello.xhtml** to the UI component tree made up of declared instances from the backing bean. Programmatic access to the UI components are enabled through binding them to the tags in the page.

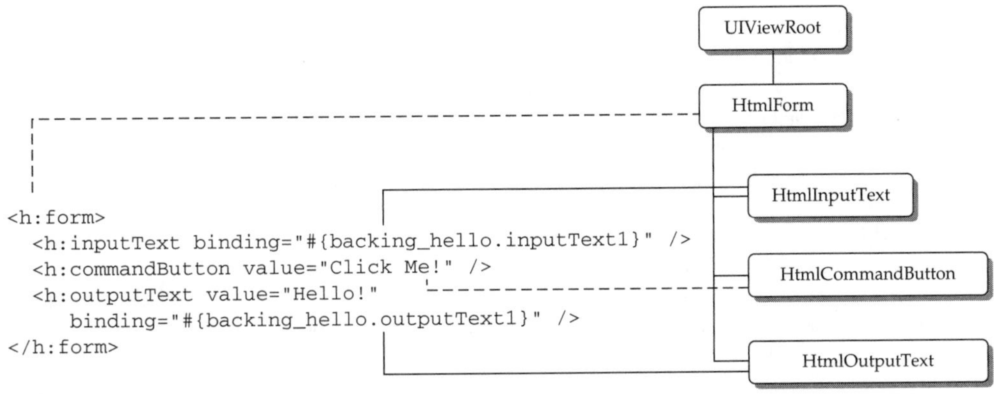

FIGURE 7-5 The UI component tree bound to the components used in the page

Now that the components used in the page are bound to component instances declared in a managed bean, you can write code to alter/manipulate the properties of the components. For this example, the **outputText** value is set to the value entered in the **inputText** component when the button was clicked. This can be achieved by creating an action method, **commandButton_action( )**, which programmatically sets the value of the **outputText** to the **inputText**'s value as a result of the button being clicked. This method can also reside in the same **Hello.java** backing bean:

```
public String commandButton_action()
{

  outputText1.setValue(inputText1.getValue());
  return "success";
}
```

The final step needed for this small application to work is to set the **action** attribute of the **commandButton** to the expression referring to the action method. This will ensure that the action method **commandButton_action( )** is invoked when the button is clicked. (As you recall from Chapter 3, action methods are actually invoked during the Invoke Application phase of the request processing lifecycle):

```
<h:commandButton value="Click Me!"
           action="#{backing_hello.commandButton_action}"/>
```

Let's review precisely what happens at runtime with this simple application. The end-user makes an initial, non-postback request to view the page **hello.jsp**. The Faces controller servlet handles the request by creating a **UIViewRoot** component and storing it in the **FacesContext**. It then redirects to the **hello.xhtml** JSP page. As shown in Figure 7-5, the execution of the Facelets page causes the **UIViewRoot** to be populated (into a tree) with children components, as well as causing those components to be rendered to the client as they are added to the component tree. The user then sees the rendered page with an input field, a button, and an output field with an initial "Hello!" value. The component tree is saved for future requests.

TIP *In JSF 1.2 and 2.0, the execution of the Facelets or JSP page only builds the view. This differs from JSF 1.0, which built the view and rendered the view as it was being built. In JSF 1.2 and 2.0, the act of rendering the view happens after the Facelets or JSP page executes. This is important—the knowledge that the entire tree has been built before rendering enables components to avoid problems such as not being able to access another component in the view because it hasn't yet been added to the view.*

The end user then enters a text value such as "Hello JSF!" into the input field and then clicks the "Click Me!" button, resulting in a postback request being submitted to the JSF application. It again enters the initial Create/Restore phase, but this time it restores the tree from before. It then updates the server-side **InputText1** component with the value "Hello JSF!" during the Apply Request Value phase. Since no validation or conversion is involved nor is a Model bean's property updated (since the component was not *value* bound using its **value** attribute), we pass on through to the Invoke Application phase. In this phase the action method **commandButton_action( )** is invoked and the **inputText1** component's value is then applied to the **outputText1** component's value. The subsequent Render Response phase renders the current state of the components back to the user. Since no navigation rule was created to handle the "success" value returned from the action method, the same page is rendered.

To get even a better feel for working with UI components programmatically, you could add a call to make the input field read-only as the action method executes.

```
outputText1.setValue(inputText1.getValue());
inputText1.setReadonly(true);
return "success";
```

This will change how the input field renders after the submit and it will no longer be editable.

Helpful Advice for Binding UI Components in JSF Views

The first bit of helpful advice to consider when binding UI components in JSF views concerns deciding when and how to use *value binding* and/or *component binding.*

In the previous "Hello JSF" example we took a slight departure from our earlier examples of always value binding to Model bean properties. Recall that JSFReg directly bound the components to the Model **UserBean** by setting the **value** attribute of the UI component to **#{userBean.firstName}**. This is definitely the right approach if you always want to apply the value of a UI component to a certain Model bean property, but in simple cases you can often work with just the UI components themselves without having to always apply their values to Model bean properties. When a JSF tag representing a UI component is directly bound to an instance of the same type of UI component in a backing bean, direct component binding is preferable. Instead of setting the **value** attribute as before, the **binding** attribute is set with the JSF expression of the instance of the UI component in the backing bean. The same "Hello JSF" example showed that value binding to a Model bean property was not needed. Instead, it was possible to simply work with the values of the components themselves as opposed to value binding them to a separate Model bean property. This is often the case when only working with transient values that do not need to be passed on to the Model.

Using Component Binding—Revisiting the Login Example from Chapter 6

To better understand the difference between value binding and component binding, consider the simple login example presented in Chapter 6. This example contained a login page with UI components value bound to Model bean properties for **userid** and **password** that are both of type **String**:

```
<h:inputText id="userid" value="#{login.userid}" />
```

and

```
<h:inputSecret id="password" value="#{login.password}" />
```

As an alternative to value binding the input fields on the page to Model properties, we could instead simply declare **UIInput** properties in a backing bean using

```
    private HtmlInputText userid;
    private HtmlInputSecret password;
//  Getters and setters for these properties not shown
```

(Both **HtmlInputText** and **HtmlInputSecret** directly extend from **UIInput**.)

In this manner the Facelet page would instead use component binding to establish a link from the UI components on the page to the UI components declared in the backing bean. The JSF View code for this is

```
<h:inputText id="userid" binding="#{login_Backing.userid}" />
```

and

```
<h:inputSecret id="password" binding="#{login_Backing.password}" />
```

In this example the backing bean is registered with the name "login_Backing" and contains the **UIInput** declarations.

Similar to the example in Chapter 6, a **loginAction( )** action method is also needed to check the login field values, except it would now be placed in the backing bean. Its code compares the values of the UI component input fields as opposed to comparing the **String** properties of the original **Login** Model bean.

```
  // Revised loginAction Method from Chapter 6
  public String loginAction() {
    if (userid.getValue().equals("guest") &&
        password getValue().equals("welcome"))
      return "success";
    else
      return "failure";
  }
```

Notice the usage of **getValue( )**. This is because the code has to extract the value from the UI components, **userid** and **password**, whereas before in Chapter 6 it was simply comparing **String** properties in the Model bean. As you can see, this component binding variation of the login example shows how it is possible to simply use UI components in backing beans to hold transient values (such as login credentials) as opposed to passing these values directly onto Model beans. It also shows that placing event handling code, such as **loginAction( )**, into a backing bean is a better coding practice than placing it in a Model bean, which is not really supposed to contain UI-related code.

Final Component Binding Recommendations

The final bit of advice to consider deals with how and when to declare instances of UI components in backing beans. In short, only declare an instance of a UI component in a backing bean when you absolutely need it. You do not need to declare instances for all of the UI components in a page. Doing so tends to overcomplicate your backing bean code.

For example, in the earlier "Hello JSF!" example, the UI components **commandButton** and **form** were used in the page along with the **inputText** and **outputText** components. However, the **commandButton** and **form** components did not have any specific code associated with them, so backing bean instances for them were not necessary.

In general, it's important to understand that you do not have to declare instances of all the UI components in a backing bean that are used in a page. You should declare UI component instances in a backing bean only when you need programmatic access to the components referenced in the page. You'll find this practice helpful in keeping your backing bean code as clean as possible.

Here's a final word of caution for those using JSF-enabled IDEs. Several JSF-enabled development environments have the ability to auto-generate UI component instances in backing beans as you drag and drop components onto a page. Although it is often helpful to have the component instances in backing beans generated as you drop them onto a page, you must keep track of this code, as it can quickly become hard to manage, especially when numerous components are being used. Pruning of unused (auto-generated) UI component instances is often recommended to keep the backing beans easy to manage.

8

CHAPTER

Converting and Validating Data

This chapter examines in detail two important topics for all Web applications: data conversion and validation. JSF has software components to handle this aspect of Web application development. Data conversion is handled by *converters,* while validation is handled by *validators.* The main point of conversion is to guarantee that the application's business logic only deals with data that is of the expected Java language type. The main point of validation is to assure that the properly typed data has been validated against the application's specific constraints. Systems that make such a guarantee allow for easier-to-develop business logic, since most of the tedious error checking and error handling is done outside of the model tier. Such systems are also more secure and easier to maintain. You can think of validation and conversion as a protective layer around your business logic that doesn't permit unchecked data to pass through. You saw an example of validation and conversion failures in the sample application in Chapter 2.

At some level, every computer program boils down to data transformation and processing. For example, traditional rich-client development frameworks such as Swing or Motif for the X Window System convert keyboard and mouse input into events delivered to the program's event loop. Batch processing programs read data from files, possibly employing character set transformations, before processing the data. Web applications are no different; they need to convert the value entered by the user, such as "Jan 12, 2003," to a **java.util.Date**. Since the primary transfer protocol between a Web browser and the server is text-based HTTP, Web applications receive most of their data as ASCII text over a TCP socket. In the case of Faces applications, the Servlet API converts this data to the Java Unicode **String** type. While having a Java **String** is an improvement over raw ASCII, more needs to be done to bridge the gap between **String** and the domain model of the application, which deals in terms of objects, such as **Integer**, **Float**, and **java.util.Date**, or primitives, such as **double**, **long**, and **char**. This is the job of the *Faces Converter system.* Conversion is a two-way process by which data is converted from the **String**-based representation of the Servlet API to the representation demanded by the application business logic and back again. Conversion is completely customizable and language-specific, and takes into account the **Locale** in which your application is running.

Getting the data converted into the proper form expected by your application is one thing, but that's still not enough to provide the previously mentioned correctness guarantee to the business logic. It is also necessary to ensure that the data has been validated against some application-specific constraints. This is the job of the *Faces Validation system.*

While conversion is a two-way transformation process, validation doesn't transform the data; it only asserts that the data is "correct" given some constraint. Validation is the process by which a piece of converted data has one or more correctness checks applied to it, yielding a Boolean result of whether the data is valid or not. Some basic examples of validation constraints are "this piece of data is required," "this number must be between 1 and 10," and "this credit card number must not be expired."

Some Validation and Conversion Examples

Before describing the details associated with validation and conversion, it's useful to examine some examples that illustrate how the major elements in the conversion and validation system interact with each other, and with the user.

We begin with a simple example that uses a text field with a label and a button, shown next. Assume the data type of the **number** JavaBeans property referred to in the expression **#{bean.number}** is **java.lang.Long**.

```
<p>Enter a number from 1 to 10:
<h:inputText value="#{bean.number}" id="numberField" required="true">
   <f:validateLongRange minimum="1" maximum="10" />
</h:inputText></p>
<h:messages for="numberField" />
<h:commandButton value="Submit" />
```

This produces the following HTML output, which, of course, is rendered by the browser.

```
<p>Enter a number from 1 to 10:
<input type="submit" id="numberField"></input></p>
<input type="submit" value="Submit"></input>
```

If the user clicks Submit with no value entered, the page will be redisplayed with this message stating that a value must be provided, as shown here.

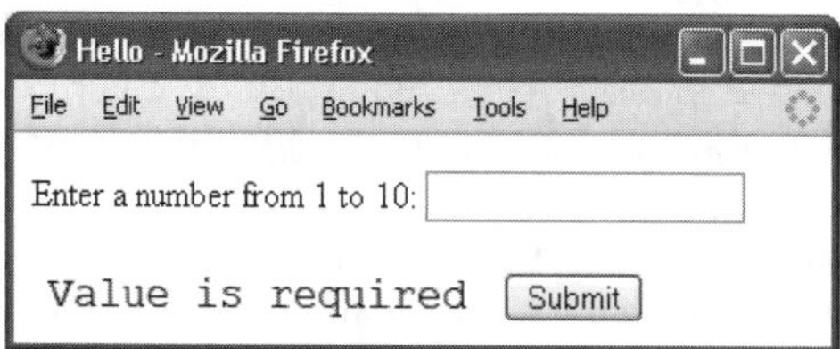

This is an example of the "**required**" validation facility in action, described later in the chapter. If the user enters a non-number value, the page will be redisplayed with this message stating that the value must be a number, as shown here.

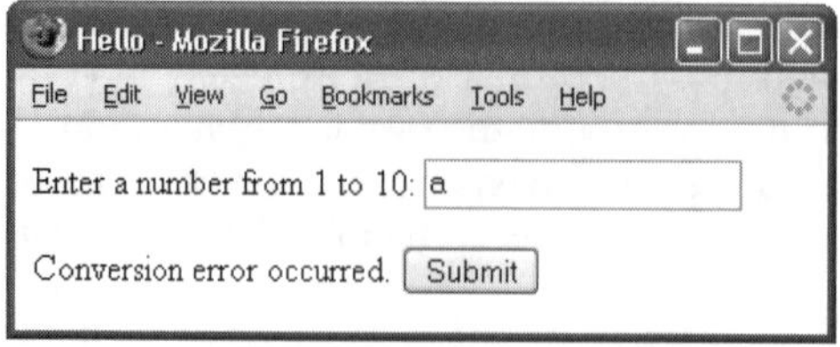

This is an example of the implicit conversion facility, described later in the chapter. Because the value entered by the user is stored in the value expression **#{bean.number}**, the system knows the expected type is **java.lang.Long**. Therefore, it is able to apply the **LongConverter** to the value before performing the validation. Implicit converters are available for all Java language primitives and their respective wrapper types, though the set of implicit converters may be extended as described in the later section "Custom Converters."

If the user enters a number that is not between 1 and 10, the page will be redisplayed with a message stating that the value must be between 1 and 10, as shown here.

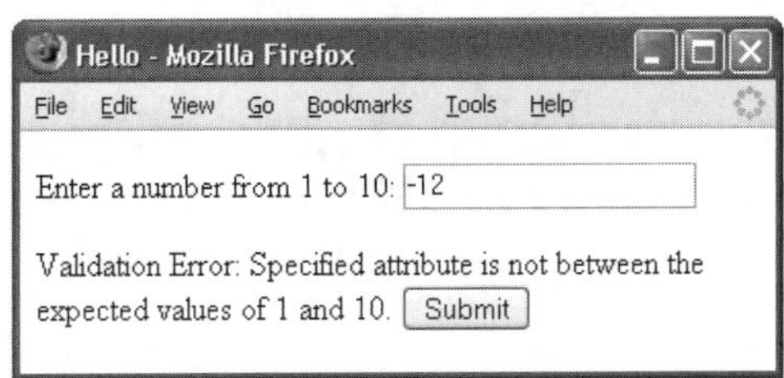

This is an example of using one of the four standard validator tags provided by Faces. The standard validator tags are covered in the section "Using Markup to Associate a Validator with a UIComponent Instance" later in this chapter.

In all cases, the invalid data remains in the text field to aid the user in correcting the error. Also, note that both validation and conversion failures appear to the user in the same way: with a specific message stating what is wrong and how to fix it. While the user doesn't know or care that conversion and validation are distinct processes, it is important for you to understand the distinction: conversion guarantees the data is in the expected type, and validation guarantees that it is valid given the application-specific constraints.

EXPERT GROUP INSIGHT *Some frameworks, such as Tapestry, do not have a separate conversion facility. The Expert Group felt that the expressive power offered by having a separate conversion concept outweighed the complexity it introduced, especially since the implicit conversion facility substantially mitigated the complexity by hiding conversion in many cases.*

The next example uses one of the three standard converter tags.

```
<p>Interest Rate: <h:outputText value="#{rates.prime}}">
  <f:convertNumber type="percentage"/>
</h:outputText>.</p>
```

The following HTML is rendered from this example:

```
<p>Interest Rate: 5.22%.<p>
```

Although all three standard converter tags are explained in detail in the section "Explicit Conversion via Markup Tags" later in the chapter, it is useful to note one point now: Converters can be associated with input or output components, but validators may only be associated with input components. This makes sense because it is impossible for invalid data to enter the system if the developer has properly used the validation system; therefore, there is no need to validate data on output.

The final example in this section shows a reasonably complex application of conversion and validation for an inventory tracking system. The user has to enter a valid Stock Keeping Unit, or SKU, that actually is in the inventory.

```
<h:outputText value="#{bundle.skuLabel}" />
<h:inputText value="#{product.sku}" required="true" id="sku" size="8">
   <f:validator validatorId="skuConverter" />
   <f:converter converterId="skuValidator" />
</h:inputText>
<h:message styleClass="errorMessage" for="sku" />
```

This example again shows the "**required**" facility and a *custom validator* that looks for the item in the inventory. It renders a simple label and text field. A custom validator is simply a JSF validator that is not included in the core JSF implementation. Frequently a custom validator is written specifically to go along with a particular application. Notice that two validators and a converter are attached to the text field. The explicit **skuConverter** ensures that the user has entered something that can be considered an SKU. The required attribute simply states that a value is required, and the **skuValidator** ensures that the item is in the inventory. The **<h:message>** tag directs the system to place the error message pertinent to this text field, if any, at that point in the page. This example shows that you can extend the Faces framework by providing custom converters and validators that are specific to your business logic needs. Custom converters and validators are dealt with in turn later in the chapter.

Conversion and Validation Under the Covers

Chapter 3 covered the Faces request processing lifecycle in considerable detail, but the portions of the lifecycle that deal with conversion and validation bear repeating here.

Converters are instances of **javax.faces.convert.Converter**, and validators are (usually) instances of **javax.faces.validator.Validator**. As shown in Figures 8-1 and 8-2, conversion (from **String** to **Object**) and validation normally happen during the Process Validations phase of the request processing lifecycle (unless the component has its **immediate** property set to true, in which case they happen during the Apply Request Values phase). Conversion (from **Object** to **String**) happens during the Render Response phase of the request processing lifecycle.

Conversion and validation can be said to have an outcome: success or failure. The outcome alters the flow through the lifecycle. When performing validation, the entire view is traversed by the system and each **UIInput** component is asked to validate itself, which includes performing data conversion. Figure 8-3 shows the components attached to the UI component for validation and conversion.

The diagram in Figure 8-3 shows that a **UIOutput** component may have zero or one **Converter** instances associated with it, while a **UIInput**, which is a subclass of **UIOutput**, may have zero or more **Validator** instances associated with it. The means by which these instances are associated with each other may be direct via an instance variable, or indirect, by lookup, or through a **ValueBinding**.

Following are the essential elements of the algorithm for doing conversion and validation. Throughout the course of this chapter, the various elements of this algorithm will be examined in detail. At this point, it is necessary to understand only in a general way how the various pieces fit together during the validation process. Keep in mind that this

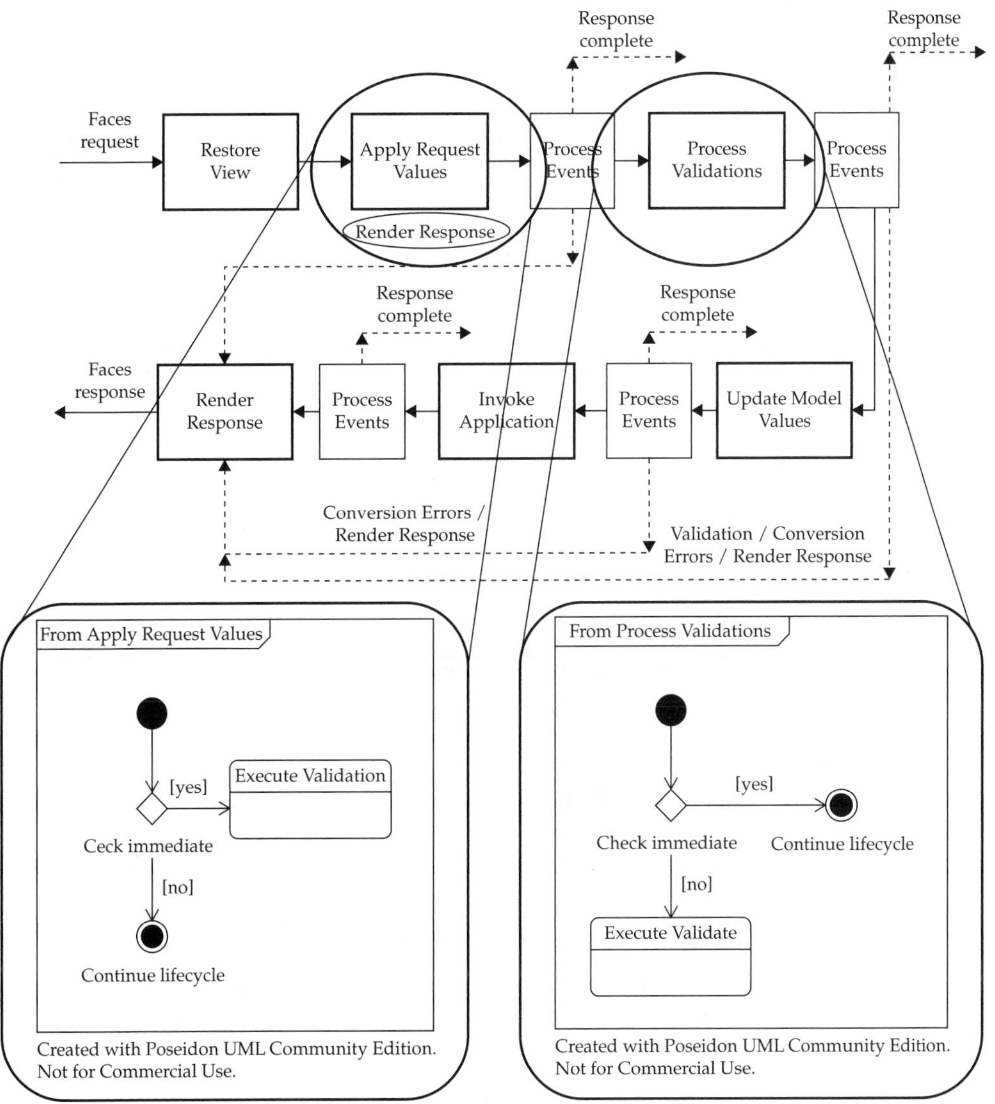

FIGURE 8-1 When conversion and validation happen during the request processing lifecycle

algorithm is performed on each **EditableValueHolder** node in the UI component hierarchy in the page, regardless of the outcome of performing the algorithm on previous nodes.

There is no way to abort validation processing midway through a view traversal, because the system needs to collect *all* of the error messages in one pass.

1. Obtain the value submitted by the user by calling **getSubmittedValue( )** on the **EditableValueHolder** instance of this component. This value was originally retrieved from the incoming request during the Apply Request Values phase of the request processing lifecycle, which is discussed in detail in Chapter 3.

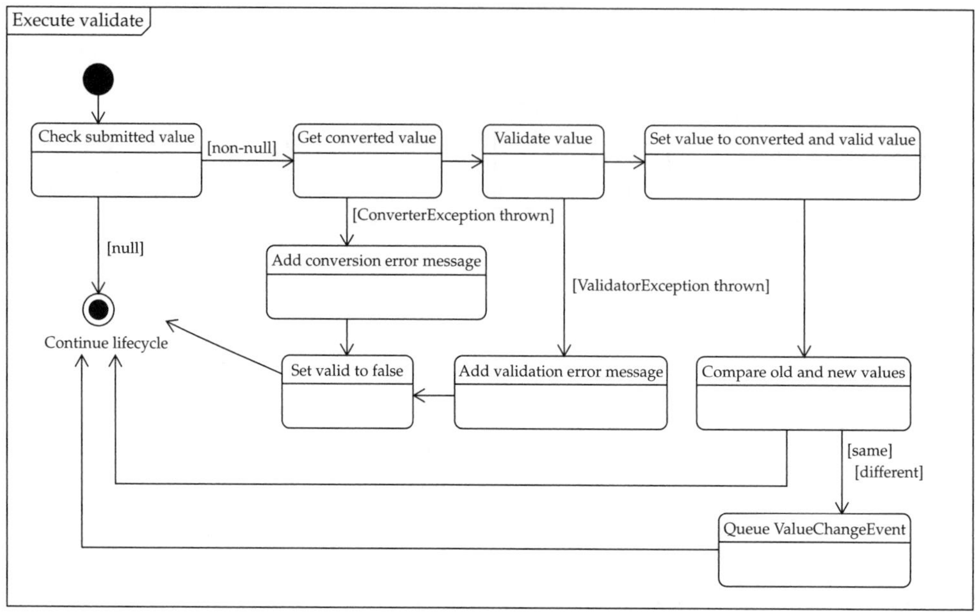

FIGURE 8-2 How conversion and validation are performed

2. Obtain the **Converter** instance to use.
   a. If this component has a **Renderer**, ask it to convert the value.
   b. Otherwise, see if there is a **Converter** instance attached to this component. If so, use it.
   c. Otherwise, if this component's value is bound via a **ValueBinding**, use the type of the **ValueBinding** to create a **Converter** by type.
   d. If none of the previous finds a **Converter**, assume the submitted value is already properly converted and return.

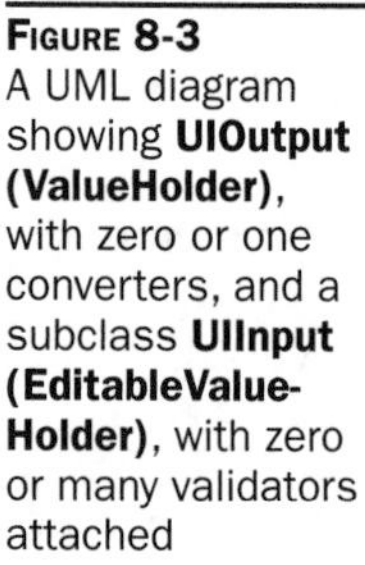

FIGURE 8-3 A UML diagram showing **UIOutput (ValueHolder)**, with zero or one converters, and a subclass **UIInput (EditableValue-Holder)**, with zero or many validators attached

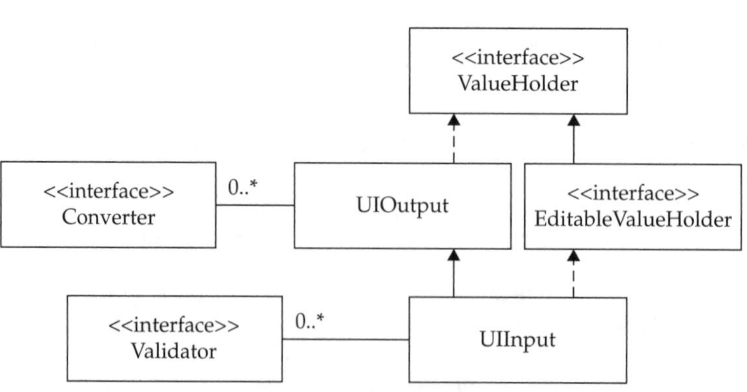

3. Convert the submitted value by calling the **getAsObject( )** method on the **Converter** instance.
4. If a **ConverterException** occurs when trying to convert the value, queue the error message, mark the value as invalid, and abort the algorithm.

TIP *The **converterMessage** property was added to **UIInput** to allow the page author to override the standard conversion message enclosed in the **ConverterException**. This feature, combined with either the **f:loadBundle** tag (described in Chapter 16) or the **resource-bundle** element in the **faces-config.xml** file (described in Chapter 15), allows the page author to provide fully internationalized conversion messages on a per-instance basis.*

5. Otherwise, proceed to validate the value.
   a. If the value has been marked as "required," yet is empty, queue the required validator failed message, mark the component as invalid, and abort the algorithm. If the value is empty and not required, proceed to Step 6.

TIP *As mentioned earlier for **ConverterException**, a **requiredMessage** property was added to **UIInput** in JSF 1.2. This allows the page author to override the standard, and not very user-friendly, message shown in response to a failure in the required state of a value.*

   b. Otherwise, call the **validate( )** method on each of the **Validator** instances attached to this component instance. If **ValidatorException** is thrown, queue the error message, mark the component as invalid, and abort the algorithm.
   c. If there is a **MethodBinding** for a **Validator** on this instance, invoke it. If the invocation causes an **EvaluationException**, get the cause of the exception. If the cause is an instance of **ValidatorException**, queue the message from the exception, mark the component as invalid, and abort the algorithm.

TIP *As mentioned earlier for **ConverterException**, a **validatorMessage** property was added to **UIInput** in JSF 1.2.*

6. If the value is still valid at this point, compare the valid value with the previous value in the component. If the previous value is different from the new value, queue a **ValueChangeEvent**. (Event handling is discussed in Chapter 9.)
7. If the value is not valid, signal a skip to the Render Response phase by calling **renderResponse( )** on the current **FacesContext**.

EXPERT GROUP INSIGHT *The initial state of every **UIInput** instance is "valid," and the conversion and validation algorithm simply seeks to mark the component as "invalid."*

There are many ways to attach a **Converter** instance, or one or more **Validator** instances, to a **UIInput** component. These are described in detail later in the chapter. Before moving on, it's necessary to mention the final piece of the conversion and validation puzzle: *the message system.* This system allows the page author to control all aspects of the display of conversion and validation error messages in the page in a very flexible manner by using one or more **<h:message>** or **<h:messages>** tags. After explaining converters and validators in detail, we'll conclude by exploring the message components.

The Faces Converter System

At the core of the Faces converter system is the **javax.faces.convert.Converter** interface. This interface must be implemented by all objects that want to function as a converter. This section covers in detail the lifetime of converter instances, the standard converters that are available "out-of-the-box," and how converters are associated with **UIComponent** instances. An example of how to write a custom converter is also presented.

The **javax.faces.convert.Converter** interface defines the two methods shown next.

```
public Object getAsObject(FacesContext context,
                          UIComponent component,
                          String value)


public String getAsString(FacesContext context,
                          UIComponent component,
                          Object value)
```

The *context* parameter is the **FacesContext** instance for this request. The *component* parameter is the component whose value is being converted. It is useful for converters to have access to the component so that they can query the component's attribute set for any parameters necessary to perform the conversion. The *value* parameter is the value to be converted. Note that it is *not* the responsibility of the converter to modify the component with the converted value. It is advisable that converter implementations don't modify the state of the component.

For all converters, the **getAsString( )** method is called during rendering to get the **String** version of the data that is suitable for display in the current rendering technology. The **getAsObject( )** method is called during the input processing to convert the value from **String** to the correct model type. If a **ConverterException** is thrown by this method, the component is marked as invalid and the message is extracted from the exception and added to the set of messages on the current **FacesContext**. Afterward, processing continues.

A **Converter** instance is registered with the system according to the type of data it can convert, or by a *converter ID,* which is a logical name by which you can refer to the converter. Table 8-1 lists the standard converters, the class they can convert, and their converter ID.

All of the converters shown in Table 8-1 can be used from markup via the **<f:converter>** tag, described later, in the section "Associating a Converter with a UIComponent Instance." The **DateTimeConverter** and **NumberConverter** have their own **<f:convertDateTime>** and **<f:convertNumber>** tags that allow complex configuration parameters to be expressed directly in markup. These two converters are special in that they provide a gateway to the text formatting capabilities of the **java.text** package. The internal details of these converters as they apply to the calling of their **getAsString( )** and **getAsObject( )** methods are described in the following sections. These two converters have several JavaBeans properties that control the conversion process. When using Faces with markup, the setters for these properties are called by the markup tag that represents the converter in the page.

Class in javax.faces.convert	Converts Values of Type	Converter ID
BigDecimalConverter	java.math.BigDecimal	javax.faces.BigDecimal
BigIntegerConverter	java.math.BigInteger	javax.faces.BigInteger
BooleanConverter	java.lang.Boolean boolean	javax.faces.Boolean
ByteConverter	java.lang.Byte byte	javax.faces.Byte
CharacterConverter	java.lang.Character char	javax.faces.Character
DateTimeConverter	java.util.Date java.sql.Date	javax.faces.DateTime
DoubleConverter	java.lang.Doubledouble	javax.faces.Double
FloatConverter	java.lang.Float float	javax.faces.Float
IntegerConverter	java.lang.Integer int	javax.faces.Integer
LongConverter	java.lang.Long long	javax.faces.Long
NumberConverter	java.lang.Number (for currencies, percentages, and so on)	javax.faces.Number
ShortConverter	java.lang.Short short	javax.faces.Short

TABLE 8-1 The Standard Converters

DateTimeConverter

The **getAsObject( )** method parses a **String** into a **java.util.Date** using an algorithm similar to the following:

1. Examine the argument string. If **null**, return **null**; otherwise, call **trim( )** on the argument. If the string ends up being zero length after trimming, return **null**.
2. Use the **Locale** JavaBeans property of this **Converter** instance, if non-**null**. Otherwise, if **Locale** is **null**, use the one from the **UIViewRoot** for this view. This **Locale** will inform the rest of the processing for this method call.
3. If a **pattern** JavaBeans property is specified on this converter instance (by virtue of the converter's **setPattern( )** method being called), it must conform to the rules of **java.text.SimpleDateFormat**. The **pattern** property takes precedence over the **type**, **dateStyle**, and **timeStyle** JavaBeans properties.
4. If **pattern** is not specified, parsing takes place based on the value of the **type** property, which must be **date**, **time**, or both.

EXPERT GROUP INSIGHT *Parsing is nonlenient! The given string must conform exactly to the formatting parameters. Failure to conform causes a conversion error. The Expert Group decided that the original implementation of lenient parsing in the **SimpleDateFormat** class of the JDK was incorrect and inconsistently implemented across Java platform vendors. In addition, the so-called "leniency" isn't really lenient in any useful way. Thus, the decision was made to disallow the use of lenient parsing in JSF.*

The **getAsString( )** method converts the model tier **Object** to a **String** for rendering using an algorithm very similar to the one described earlier, except that a **null** model tier value is converted to a zero-length **String**.

NumberConverter

The **getAsObject( )** method parses a **String** into a **java.lang.Number** subclass using an algorithm that is the equivalent of the following:

1. Examine the argument string. If **null**, return **null**; otherwise, call **trim( )** on the argument string. If the string ends up being zero length after trimming, return **null**.
2. Use the **Locale** property of this **Converter** instance, if non-**null**. Otherwise, if **Locale** is **null**, use the one from the **UIViewRoot** for this view. This **Locale** will inform the rest of the processing for this method call.
3. If a **pattern** JavaBeans property is specified (by virtue of the **setPattern( )** being called), it must conform to the rules of **java.text.DecimalFormat**. The **pattern** property takes precedence over the **type** property.
4. If a **pattern** JavaBeans property is not specified, parsing takes place based on the value of the **type** property, which must be **number**, **percentage**, or **currency**.
5. If the **integerOnly** property is set to true, only the integer part of the **String** is parsed.

The **getAsString( )** method converts the model tier **Object** to a **String** for rendering using an algorithm very similar to the one described earlier, except that a **null** model tier value is converted to a zero-length string, and the **groupingUsed**, **maxFractionDigits**, **maxIntegerDigits**, **currencyCode**, and **currencySymbol** properties are applied before formatting.

Associating a Converter with a UIComponent Instance

As described in the preceding section, each **UIOutput** instance in the view may have zero or one **Converter** associated with it. There are several ways to make that association, and we'll cover each in this section. Since Faces was designed with ease of development in mind, most users will not need to manually associate a converter with a component instance due to the comprehensive list of standard converters that automatically are associated with the component, depending on its current value. We call these "implicit converters." In addition to the implicit converter association, there are a number of ways a converter can manually be associated with a component instance: by using one of the standard markup converter tags, by using a custom converter tag, or programmatically in Java code by calling **setConverter( )** on the component instance.

Implicit Conversion

Table 8-2 lists the implicit converters by class. For each entry, there is a corresponding converter instance in the package **javax.faces.convert**. For example, the class **java.lang.Double** has an implicit converter with the fully qualified class name of **javax.faces.convert.DoubleConverter**.

Value Class	Converter
java.math.BigDecimal	javax.faces.convert.BigDecimalConverter
java.math.BigInteger	javax.faces.convert.BigIntegerConverter
java.lang.Boolean	javax.faces.convert.BooleanConverter
java.lang.Byte	javax.faces.convert.ByteConverter
java.lang.Character	javax.faces.convert.CharacterConverter
java.lang.Double	javax.faces.convert.DoubleConverter
java.lang.Float	javax.faces.convert.FloatConverter
java.lang.Integer	javax.faces.convert.IntegerConverter
java.lang.Long	javax.faces.convert.LongConverter
java.lang.Short	javax.faces.convert.ShortConverter

TABLE 8-2 The Implicit Converters

EXPERT GROUP INSIGHT *To help with the JSR goal of making JSF as useful as possible within tools, all of the standard converters adhere to JavaBeans naming conventions for properties. This allows tools to easily add converters to a palette and provide property inspectors for easy customization.*

In order for implicit conversion to occur, the system must be able to discern the type of the value. As you learned in Chapter 3, each **EditableValueHolder** component instance has a "local value" property, as well as an optional "value binding." The local value is not type-safe and is always known to the system as being of type **Object**. It is only when a component instance has a value binding that its type is discoverable by the system, thanks to the **getType( )** method of the Expression Language API. Components that don't have a value binding cannot have implicit conversion. For example, the first of the two following text fields will have an implicit **Integer** converter associated with it, while the second will not.

```
<h:inputText id="age" value="#{user.age}" />
<h:inputText id="weight" value="10"/>
```

Assuming the **age** JavaBeans property of the **user** managed bean is of type **Integer**, the system will automatically create and use a **javax.faces.convert.IntegerConverter** whenever conversion is required. Conveniently, as you will soon see, it is easy to install additional converters to extend or modify the set of types for which implicit conversion can be performed. Note the absence of an implicit converter for dates. This is because we have no way of knowing if the number should be a Date, a Time, or a Date and Time.

Explicit Conversion via Markup Tags

If you require greater control over conversion than that afforded by implicit conversion, three markup tags are provided in the **jsf_core** tag library: **<f:convertDateTime>**, **<f:convertNumber>**, and **<f:converter>**. The general form of these tags is shown next.

For brevity, some attributes have been omitted. Chapter 16 contains the complete reference. Most of the tag attributes in the following have corresponding JavaBeans properties on the converter instance that sits behind the tag. The setter methods of these properties are called as appropriate.

```
<f:convertDateTime dateStyle="dateStyle"
  locale="locale" pattern="formatPattern" timeZone="timeZone"
  type="type"
  binding="valueExpression"/>
<f:convertNumber currencyCode="code"
  currencySymbol="symbol"
  groupingUsed="boolean" locale="locale"
  pattern="formatPattern" type="type"
  binding="valueExpression" />
<f:converter converterId="converter-id"
  binding="valueExpression" />
```

For **<f:convertDateTime>**, the **dateStyle** attribute must be **short**, **medium**, **long**, **full**, or **default**. If not specified, **default** is assumed. If specified, **locale** must be a value binding expression that evaluates to an instance of **java.util.Locale**, or a literal string that is valid to pass as the first argument to the constructor for **java.util.Locale(String language, String country)**. In this case, the empty string will be passed as the second argument. If locale is not specified, the return value of **FacesContext.getCurrentInstance( ).getViewRoot( ) .getLocale( )** will be used. If pattern is specified, its value must be a format pattern as used in **java.text.SimpleDateFormat**, or an expression that evaluates to the same. If **timeZone** is specified, its value must be a literal string that is a timezone ID as in the Javadocs for **java .util.TimeZone.getTimeZone( )**, or a value binding expression that evaluates to an instance of **java.util.TimeZone**. If not specified, the system timezone is used. If **type** is specified, its value must be **date**, **time**, or **both**. This tells the converter to format or parse the value as a date, a time, or a **DateTime**, respectively. If not specified, **both** is assumed. If **binding** is specified, its value must be a value binding expression that evaluates to an instance of **javax.faces.convert.DateTimeConverter**.

For **<f:convertNumber>**, the **currencyCode**, if specified, must be a literal string that is a valid ISO 4217 currency code (such as USD or EUR), or a value binding expression that evaluates to the same. If not specified, the system currency code is used. If specified, the **currencySymbol** is the actual currency symbol used, such as "$" or "€", or an expression that evaluates to the same. If not specified, the system symbol is used. If specified, the **groupingUsed** must be either true or false. If not specified, **true** is assumed. If specified, **pattern** must be a literal string that is used as the pattern for the underlying **java.text .DecimalFormat** instance, or an expression that evaluates to the same. If not specified, no pattern is used. If specified, the **type** parameter must be **number**, **currency**, or **percentage**. If not specified, **number** is assumed. If specified, the **binding** attribute must be an expression that evaluates to a **javax.faces.convert.NumberConverter** instance.

For **<f:converter>**, the **converterId** attribute is the converter identifier as specified in the config file, such as **faces-config.xml**, or as the **value** attribute of the **@FacesConverter** annotation. In Faces 1.0 and 1.1, **converterId** was a required attribute, but in 1.2 and 2.0 either the **binding** or **converterId** attribute must be specified. If both are specified, **converterId** is used to create the converter, and the **setValue( )** method of the binding is used to store the created converter.

The **<f:convertDateTime>** tag leverages the conversion facilities provided by **java.text .SimpleDateFormat**, the **<f:convertNumber>** tag leverages the conversion facilities provided by **java.text.DecimalFormat**, and **<f:converter>** provides a markup gateway to look up a converter by its **converter-id**. These three tags are sufficient to cover the conversion needs for all possible datatypes. They are described in detail in Chapter 16, but the following discussion explains how they can be used to control conversion.

The usage pattern for all of the converter tags is to nest them inside the markup for the component to which they should be attached. For example:

```
<h:outputText id="date" value="#{transaction.date}">
  <f:convertDateTime dateStyle="short"/>
</h:inputText>
```

This example associates a **DateTimeConverter** instance with the **HtmlOutputText** instance with the ID **date**. The same pattern is true for the other converter tags.

TIP *Beginning with JSF 1.2, all of these* ***Converter*** *tags provide a* ***binding*** *attribute that functions similar to the* ***binding*** *attribute on* ***UIComponent*** *instances (and the tags that expose them), as described in Chapter 7. Briefly, the* ***binding*** *attribute allows you to say that the actual* ***Converter*** *instance must come from the result of evaluating an EL expression. This feature enables programmatically configuring a converter instance directly from Java code, and then allows that converter instance to be referred to in many different places. This means you only have to configure the converter attributes once, avoiding the class of bugs that comes from duplicating information in multiple places. Also, the* ***binding*** *attribute makes it very easy to add custom converters and validators, as opposed to going through the hassle of adding them to a faces-config.xml file and the attendant markup tags.*

Before jumping into the tags themselves, let's review the basics of date formatting using **java.text.SimpleDateFormat**. This class is a concrete implementation of **java.text.DateFormat**, which allows parsing dates or times in a language-independent manner. **SimpleDateFormat** applies user-specified parameters to convert a string into a **java.util.Date** instance and back again. These parameters are applied to the **SimpleDateFormat** instance by a variety of methods, as described next. The most basic element of **SimpleDateFormat** is *style*, which is inherited from the superclass, **DateFormat**. The *style* parameter is a symbolic constant passed to the static **getDateInstance( )** or **getTimeInstance( )** method on **DateFormat**. This parameter provides a useful abstraction by saying the formatted value will be in **SHORT**, **LONG**, **MEDIUM**, or **FULL** style. The exact meaning of the *style* parameter depends on whether you are dealing with a date, a time, or a date and time. A **SHORT**-styled date is 05/26/03, while a **LONG**-styled time is 12:30:45 pm. When the maximum level of control is required, use the *pattern* parameter of **SimpleDateFormat**. The pattern is supplied to the instance by calling the **applyPattern( )** method. This allows you to specify a format string to control how the date, time, or date and time are output. For example, the pattern string

```
"HH:mm:ss on EEEE ',' MMMM dd ',' yyyy"
```

will produce an output such as this:

```
13:24:21 on Tuesday, April 15, 1997
```

See the Java platform API documentation for **SimpleDateFormat** for the complete specification of the pattern language. The *timezone* parameter of **DateFormat** allows you to state in which time zone this time should be treated. This is passed as an argument to the **setTimeZone( )** method.

The **<f:convertDateTime>** tag exposes the power of the **SimpleDateFormat** class to the markup Faces user. All of the tag attributes for this tag are value expression enabled. Briefly, the most useful tag attributes are **type**, **style**, and **pattern**. The **type** tag attribute allows you to choose to treat the value as a date, a time, or both. This is used to determine whether **getDateInstance( )**, **getTimeInstance( )**, or **getDateTimeInstance( )** should be used to create the underlying **DateFormat** instance, respectively. The **style** parameter for the underlying **SimpleDateFormat** is specified by providing a **dateStyle** or **timeStyle** tag attribute with a value of **SHORT**, **MEDIUM**, **LONG**, or **FULL**. The value of the **pattern** attribute is passed through directly to the underlying **SimpleDateFormat** instance. If you want to force conversion to be a specific **Locale**, the **locale** attribute is provided.

Let's also review the use of **java.text.DecimalFormat** for formatting numbers, including currencies. This class is a concrete implementation of **java.text.NumberFormat** that allows parsing numbers in a language-independent manner. **DecimalFormat** applies user-specified parameters to convert a string into a **java.lang.Number** instance and back again. **DecimalFormat** has many elements, but the main ones of interest to conversion are **pattern** and **groupingUsed** (defined on a superclass, **NumberFormat**). As in the **SimpleDateFormat**, the **pattern** parameter provides complete control over the appearance of the number and is applied to the underlying **NumberFormat** instance by calling its **applyPattern( )** method. For example, the **pattern** "\u00A4 #.00" says this number should be output as a currency with any number of digits before the decimal separator, and exactly two after it. The currency symbol and decimal separator are, of course, locale-sensitive. The **groupingUsed** JavaBeans property specifies whether a locale-sensitive grouping delimiter should be used—for example, "3,147,295".

The **<f:convertNumber>** tag exposes **java.text.DecimalFormat** to the markup Faces user. As mentioned earlier, all tag attributes are value expression enabled. The most useful attributes are shown next:

- type
- pattern
- currencyCode
- currencySymbol
- groupingUsed

The **type** attribute can be **number**, **currency**, or **percentage**. The value of this attribute is used to determine if the underlying **NumberFormat** instance should be created using **getNumberInstance( )**, **getCurrencyInstance( )**, or **getPercentInstance( )**, respectively. The **currencyCode** attribute is an ISO 4217 currency code, such as "USD" for U.S. dollar, and "EUR" for European Union Euro. The **currencySymbol** can be used to directly specify the currency symbol, but in JDK 1.4 and beyond, the **currencyCode** takes precedence if specified. The **groupingUsed** attribute is a **boolean** that functions as mentioned in the preceding paragraph.

The last of the three standard markup tags for conversion is **<f:converter>**. This tag allows associating an arbitrary converter with a component using the converter ID lookup mechanism. Previously, we mentioned that converters can be registered and looked up by class. They can also be registered and looked up by **converter-id**, registered in the **faces-config.xml** file for the application. Table 8-1 lists the standard converters and their converter IDs. While it's certainly possible to use the **<f:converter>** tag with the standard converters, it is really intended to provide a gateway to custom converters without requiring the creation of a custom converter tag. For example, the Virtual Trainer example uses a custom **WeightConverter** that consults the user's preferences and displays weights in either metric or English units. For example:

```
<h:inputText id="targetWeight" value="#{user.targetWeight}">
  <f:converter converterId="weight"/>
</h:inputText>
```

Programmatically Associating a Converter with a UIComponent

The final way to associate a **Converter** with a **UIComponent** is programmatically. Nearly all of the markup tags in Faces serve only to expose the underlying component model to the markup page author. In the case of the converter tags, this can mean that the **setConverter( )** method of a **ValueHolder** instance is called. The existence of a **setConverter( )** method means that you can call it directly, if you are so inclined. When using this approach, you must be aware of when in the request processing lifecycle your code is executing. Also, this approach violates the separation of controller from view in the MVC paradigm because a priori knowledge of the view is required to find the components on which to install the converters. With these cautions, we include this approach here for completeness.

As mentioned earlier, conversion happens twice during the lifecycle, once during the Apply Request Values or Process Validations phase, and again during the Render Response phase.

Beginning with JSF 1.2, if you want your **Converter** to be used during the whole lifecycle, try using a **UIViewRoot PhaseListener** registered for the **beforePhase** event of the Render Response phase. This will ensure that the **Converter** is installed before the first rendering and that it remains installed throughout the life of the view thanks to the state management APIs. Once you know when in the lifecycle your converter installing code will execute, it's a matter of creating and installing it in the desired component.

The following example shows how to programmatically create and install a converter on two components in the view. One component uses by-type converter lookup, and the other uses by-class converter lookup.

```
FacesContext context = FacesContext.getCurrentInstance( );
Converter intConverter = null;
Converter floatConverter = null;
UIComponent component1 = null;
UIComponent component2 = null;
UIViewRoot root = context.getViewRoot( );
// Find the components on which we'll install the Converters.
component1 = (ValueHolder) root.findComponent("form"
+                                  NamingContainer.SEPARATOR_CHAR +
                                 "intComponent");
```

```
component2 = (ValueHolder) root.findComponent("form"
+                              NamingContainer.SEPARATOR_CHAR +
                             "floatComponent");
// Create the Converters, one by type, the other by Class.
intConverter =
  context.getApplication( ).createConverter("javax.faces.Integer");
floatConverter =
  context.getApplication( ).createConverter(Float.class);
// Install the converters.
component1.setConverter(intConverter);
component2.setConverter(floatConverter);
```

The main point of this example is to show the two variants of **createConverter( )** and the use of **setConverter( )**.

The Lifetime of a Converter

Even though the Java platform provides automatic memory management in the form of garbage collection, it is still very important to be mindful of the memory implications of the design decisions that you make as you develop your application. This is particularly important when using a framework, where objects are frequently instantiated on the user's behalf without the user's knowledge. As described in the preceding section, each **UIComponent** instance in the view may have zero or one **Converter** associated with it, and there are several ways to make that association. The lifetime implications of these different ways are the subject of this section.

Implicit Conversion

Converters associated with *implicit* conversion are dynamically created each time they are needed. This might give the appearance of being an unnecessary performance penalty, but actually, implicit conversion is a good thing for performance. The cost of instantiating these kinds of converters is very small, and because they are not attached to the component, there is no state saving and restoring penalty.

Explicit Conversion

All methods of *explicit* conversion boil down to calling **setConverter( )** on the **UIComponent** instance, which makes the converter a part of the component's state, thereby ensuring it will be saved and restored across requests by the state management system. With this approach, the lifetime of the converter is the same as the lifetime of the component instance itself, which is configurable by the application author by setting the server's session timeout value.

Conversion Done by Validators

Some validators also use converters to aid in performing validation. Depending on the implementation of the **Validator**, this may cause a **Converter** instance to be created.

Custom Converters

The real power of the Faces conversion model is its extensibility. In this section, we will provide a complete converter for the Virtual Trainer example. This converter looks up the value of the **weightUnits** preference in the **preferences** object and uses it to convert the weight from the domain model unit, which is kilograms, to the user's preference, which may be kilograms or pounds. We'll start with the converter class and close with the configuration information necessary to hook up the converter to the system.

The converter class for Virtual Trainer is called **WeightConverter**. It implements the **Converter** interface and is shown next.

```
package com.jsfcompref.trainercomponents.convert;

import javax.faces.convert.Converter;
import javax.faces.convert.ConverterException;
import javax.faces.context.FacesContext;
import javax.faces.application.Application;
import javax.faces.component.UIComponent;

import java.util.Locale;
import java.text.NumberFormat;
import java.text.ParseException;
import javax.el.ValueExpression;
import javax.faces.component.UIViewRoot;
import javax.faces.convert.FacesConverter;

@FacesConverter(value="com.jsfcompref.Weight")
public class WeightConverter extends Object implements Converter {

    public static final int UNIT_KILOGRAMS = 0;
    public static final int UNIT_POUNDS = 1;

    private Locale locale = null;

    private NumberFormat formatter = null;


    public WeightConverter() {
      formatter = null;
      locale = null;
    }

    private int getUnitFromUserPreferences(FacesContext context) {
      if (null == context) {
          return -1;
      }
      Integer result = null;
      int unit = -1;
        Application application = context.getApplication();

        if (null == application) {
            return unit;
        }

      // look up the user's preference
      ValueExpression ve = application.getExpressionFactory().
                createValueExpression(context.getELContext(),
                "#{user.preferences.weightUnits}", Integer.class);
```

```
      try {
          result = (Integer) ve.getValue(context.getELContext());
      }
      catch (Throwable e) {
      }
        if (null == result) {
            result = new Integer(UNIT_KILOGRAMS);
        }

      if (null != result) {
          unit = result.intValue();
      }

      return unit;
    }

    private NumberFormat getNumberFormat(FacesContext context) {
      if (null == formatter) {
          formatter = NumberFormat.getNumberInstance(getLocale(context));
      }
      return formatter;
    }

    private Locale getLocale(FacesContext context) {
        Locale locale = this.locale;
        if (locale == null) {
            UIViewRoot root = null;
            if (null != (root = context.getViewRoot())) {
                locale = root.getLocale();
            }
            else {
                locale = Locale.getDefault();
            }
        }
        return (locale);
    }


    public Locale getLocale() {
        if (this.locale == null) {
            this.locale =
                getLocale(FacesContext.getCurrentInstance());
        }
        return (this.locale);
    }

    public void setLocale(Locale locale) {
        this.locale = locale;
    }

    public Object getAsObject(FacesContext context,
                              UIComponent component, String value) {
        if (context == null || component == null) {
            throw new NullPointerException();
        }
```

```
  // this example doesn't use the component parameter but we will
  // use it later in the chapter when we explore conversion
  // messages.

  if (null == value || 0 == value.length()) {
      return null;
  }

  int units = getUnitFromUserPreferences(context);
  float floatValue;

  try {
      floatValue = getNumberFormat(context).parse(value).floatValue();
  }
  catch (ParseException e) {
      throw new ConverterException(e.getMessage());
  }

  // if the user's preference is English, this String is in
  // pounds.  Get the float value of the pounds
  if (UNIT_POUNDS == units) {
      floatValue /= 2.2; // convert to kilograms
  }

  return new Float(floatValue);
}

public String getAsString(FacesContext context, UIComponent component,
                          Object value) {
    if (context == null || component == null) {
        throw new NullPointerException();
    }
  // this example doesn't use the component parameter but we will
  // use it later in the chapter when we explore conversion
  // messages.

  if (null == value || 0 == value.toString().length()) {
      return null;
  }

  String result = null;

  float floatValue = ((Float)value).floatValue();
    int units = getUnitFromUserPreferences(context);

  if (UNIT_POUNDS == units) {
      floatValue *= 2.2; // convert to pounds
  }

  result = getNumberFormat(context).format(new Float(floatValue));

  if (UNIT_POUNDS == units) {
      result = result + " lbs.";
  }
```

```
        else {
            result = result + " kg.";
        }

        return result;
    }
}
```

In **WeightConverter**, the **getAsObject( )** method uses the number parsing provided by classes in the **java.text package** to perform the conversion from **String** to **float**. If the user has requested that weights be shown in pounds, the **float** value of pounds is converted to kilograms. The kilogram **float** value is then wrapped in an instance of **java.lang.Float** and returned.

The **getAsString( )** method extracts the **float** primitive from the **Float** wrapper object. If the user has requested that weights be shown in pounds, the **float** value is converted to pounds and the number formatting classes from the **java.text** package are used to format the value into a string, with the units appended.

Helper methods are provided to get the **NumberFormat** and **Locale** instances to use. Pay special attention to the private **getLocale( )** method. It takes a **FacesContext** as a parameter and extracts a **Locale** from the **UIViewRoot** for this view. This is important because the Faces internationalization system ensures that the **UIViewRoot**'s **Locale** is the correct one to use for all language-sensitive operations.

WeightConverter uses the **@FacesConverter** annotation to declare itself to the runtime system. Alternatively, the following XML code can be added to the **faces-config.xml** to achieve the same effect:

```
<converter>
  <description>
    Registers the weight converter using the converter id weight
  </description>
  <converter-id>com.jsfcompref.Weight</converter-id>
  <converter-class>
    com.jsfcompref.trainer.convert.WeightConverter
  </converter-class>
</converter>
```

The XML markup for **WeightConverter** simply identifies the converter by ID and a fully qualified Java class name. This enables the use of the **<f:converter>** tag to attach the converter to **UIComponent** instances in the view. Instead of registering the converter by ID, it is also possible to register the converter by the type of object it can convert. Here is an example of the annotation syntax for registering a converter by type:

```
package converter;
import javax.faces.convert.FacesConverter;
import javax.faces.convert.FacesConverter;

@FacesConverter(forClass="java.lang.Byte")
SpecialByteConverter implements Converter ...
```

The equivalent XML syntax is shown next:

```
<converter>
  <description>
    Registers the weight converter using the converter id weight
  </description>
  <converter-for-class>java.lang.Byte</converter-for-class>
  <converter-class>
    converter.SpecialByteConverter
  </converter-class>
</converter>
```

Converters registered in this way can be discovered for use in implicit conversion, which was explained earlier.

The **WeightConverter** can be used from markup through the **<f:converter>** tag, as shown next:

```
<p>Current Weight <h:outputText value="#{user.currentWeight}">
  <f:converter id="com.jsfcompref.Weight" /> </h:outputText> </p>
```

Note that the **binding** attribute could also be used to good effect in the following:

```
<p>Current Weight <h:outputText value="#{user.currentWeight}">
  <f:converter binding="#{converters.weightConverter} /> </h:outputText> </p>
```

where the expression **#{converters.weightConverter}** points to an instance of our **WeightConverter**.

Now that you've learned about conversion, let's examine validation, which happens immediately after conversion in the flow of the request processing lifecycle.

The Faces Validation System

The **javax.faces.validator.Validator** interface is the foundation of the JSF validation system. As a general rule, this interface is implemented by objects that want to function as a **Validator**. (However, as explained later in this section, not all objects that function as a **Validator** must implement this interface.) This section covers in detail the lifetime of validator instances, the standard validators that are available "out-of-the-box," how validators are associated with **UIComponent** instances, and an example of how to write a custom **Validator**.

The javax.faces.validator.Validator interface defines a single method called **validate( )**, which is shown next:

```
public void validate(FacesContext context,
                     UIComponent component,
                     Object value)
```

As with the converter methods, the *context* parameter is the **FacesContext** instance for this request, the *component* parameter is the component whose value is being validated, and the *value* parameter is the value on which to perform the validation.

This method is called during the Apply Request Values phase if the component has the **immediate** property set, or during the Process Validations phase otherwise. Before calling **validate( )**, the component is marked as invalid. The **validate( )** method is then passed a value that has been successfully converted. This method must throw a **ValidatorException** if the validation fails. If no such exception is thrown, the system assumes validation has succeeded and marks the component as valid. If the exception is thrown, its message is extracted and added to the set of messages on the current **FacesContext** and processing continues. Standard Faces validators run on the server, though it's possible to write a validator that executes entirely on the client. Even when using client-side validation, it is strongly advisable to perform server-side validation as a double-check against malicious code in the browser.

As with converters, Faces provides a small but useful set of standard **Validator** implementations, listed in Table 8-3. Unlike converters, **Validator** instances are not registered by class, only by **validator-id**. This is because the concept of validation is not tied tightly to an object's type. For example, it is possible for a number to be a valid credit card number but still be expired. Expired credit cards are of no use to an e-commerce system!

In addition to the validators shown in Table 8-3, Faces also provides a facility to specify that a value is "required," but since this feature is so commonly used, it has been implemented for maximum correctness and simplicity and does not use the regular validation system. Let's examine the standard validators and the "required" facility in detail. The validation messages used in this section paraphrase the meaning of the message. The real messages will be dealt with later in this chapter, in the section "Tie It All Together: Messages in a View."

validator-id	Tag Handler	Description
javax.faces.DoubleRange	f:validateDoubleRange	Validates that data of type **java.lang.Double** is within a specified range.
javax.faces.Length	f:validateLength	Validates that data of type **String** has a length that is within a specified range.
javax.faces.LongRange	f:validateLongRange	Validates that data of type **java.lang.Long** is within a specified range.
javax.faces.Bean	f:validateBean	Causes the local value pointed to by the component to be validated by Java EE bean validation. (This feature will be described later in this chapter.)
javax.faces.RegularExpression	f:validateRegex	Allows the usage of the powerful Java Regular Expression feature within JSF pages.
javax.faces.Required	f:validateRequired	A nestable validator that does the same thing as the required tag attribute.

TABLE 8-3 The Standard Validators

LongRangeValidator

LongRangeValidator.validate( ) verifies that the value of the component to which it is attached is within a specified range using an algorithm similar to the following:

1. The argument value has already been converted. This means that it is an instance of **java.lang.Long**. Therefore, the primitive **long** value is extracted.
2. If the user set a maximum parameter for this **Validator** instance, the value is checked against the configured maximum. If the value is greater than the maximum, one of two exceptions must be thrown. First, if the user configured a minimum parameter, then the value is not within the specified range. In this case, a **ValidatorException** with a "not in range" message is thrown. Second, if no minimum parameter is specified, then a **ValidatorException** with a "greater than the specified maximum" message is thrown.
3. If the user set a minimum parameter for this **Validator** instance, the value is checked against the configured minimum. If the value is less than the minimum, one of two exceptions must be thrown. First, if the user configured a maximum parameter, then the value is not in the specified range. In this case, a **ValidatorException** with a "not in range" message is thrown. Second, if no maximum parameter is specified, then a **ValidatorException** with a "less than the specified minimum" message is thrown.
4. If a **NumberFormatException** was thrown during processing, a **ValidatorException** with a "there was a type error during validation" message is thrown.

This class also implements the **equals( )** method to allow comparing two instances. The **equals( )** method returns true if the other **Validator** is configured with the same parameter values for maximum and minimum. The following example illustrates the use of the **f:validateLongRange** tag, which exposes the **LongRangeValidator** to the markup page author.

```
<p>Enter a California Zip Code:
  <h:inputText value="#{user.address.zip}" id="zip">
    <f:validateLongRange minimum="90000" maximum="99999" />
  </h:inputText>
<h:message for="zip" /></p>
```

This example asks the user to enter a Zip code in California, which means they must enter a number from 90000 to 99999. A more robust example would also have a custom validator that checks that the Zip code entered is indeed a valid Zip code, since not all numbers between 90000 and 99999 are valid Zip codes in California.

DoubleRangeValidator

The **DoubleRangeValidator** class behaves exactly like the **LongRangeValidator**, except that it operates on **Double** instances instead.

LengthValidator

LengthValidator.validate( ) verifies that the string length of the data is within a specified range using an algorithm similar to the following:

1. The value has already been converted, which means that you can safely call **toString( )** on it.

2. If the user has specified a maximum-length parameter and the length of the value is greater than that maximum, throw a **ValidatorException** with the "string is too long" message.
3. If the user has specified a minimum-length parameter and the length of the value is greater than that minimum, throw a **ValidatorException** with the "string is too short" message.

This class also implements the **equals( )** method to allow two instances to be compared. The **equals( )** method returns true if the other **Validator** is configured with the same parameter values for maximum and minimum.

The following example illustrates the use of the **f:validateLength** tag, which exposes the **LengthValidator** to the markup page author.

```
<p>Credit Card Number:
  <h:inputText value="#{user.creditCard}" id="cc">
    <f:validateLength minimum="16" maximum="16" />
  </h:inputText>
</p>
```

In this example, we require that the user enter exactly 16 characters. Again, a more robust example would include a custom validator that handles things like interspersed dashes and/or spaces and validates the number against a credit card database.

The "required" Facility and the RequiredValidator

The notion of a value being "required" for the user to enter is so common that it receives special treatment in Faces. Recall that any **UIComponent** in the view that can possibly have a user-entered value implements the **EditableValueHolder** interface. This interface has a **boolean** property called **required** whose default value is **false**. The validation processing in **UIInput** checks this property, and if no value has been provided by the user, a "value is required" message is added to the set of messages for this **FacesContext** and the component is marked as invalid. If the field is not required, and no value has been provided, no further validation processing happens.

***JSF 2.0* TIP** *Prior to JSF 2.0, validation was simply not run at all on fields whose values were empty or null. JSF 2.0 changes this default behavior slightly. If the JSF runtime is executing in an environment that supports bean validation, empty fields are validated by default. Otherwise, the behavior is the same as it was prior to JSF 2.0: empty fields are not validated. Bean validation is covered in detail later in this chapter. To force JSF to not validate empty fields, add this **<context-param>** to your **web.xml** file:*

```
<context-param>
  <param-name>javax.faces.VALIDATE_EMPTY_FIELDS</param-name>
  <param-value>false</param-value>
</context-param>
```

As an alternative to the **required** attribute, it is possible to nest an **<f:validateRequired />** element within any input component to achieve the same effect.

RegExValidator

RegExValidator.validate( ) ensures the value of the component being validated is a **String** that matches the *regular expression* given by the value of this validator's **pattern** property. Regular expressions are a powerful concept from theoretical computer science that enables programs to tell if a given string matches a "pattern" written in a special syntax. A full treatment of regular expressions is beyond the scope of this book, but the Javadocs for class **java.util.regex.Pattern** are a very good place to start. The following example illustrates the use of the **f:validateRegex** tag, which exposes the **RegExValidator** to the page author. This example is included in the online code for this chapter.

```
<h:panelGrid border="1" width="60%" columns="2">
    <h:outputText value="Enter password.  Must be between six and ten
characters in length contain at least one special character from the
list &#8220;!&#34;#$%&amp;&#39;()*+,-./:;&lt;=&gt;?@[\]^_`{|}~&#8221;
(not including the quotes), two digits, and exactly one upper case
character" />
    <h:panelGroup>
    <h:inputSecret id="password" value="#{flash.password}">
        <f:validateLength minimum="6" maximum="10" />
        <f:validateRegex pattern=".*\p{Punct}.*" />
        <f:validateRegex pattern=".*\d.*\d.*" />
        <f:validateRegex pattern=".*[A-Z].*" />
    </h:inputSecret>
    <h:message for="password" />
    </h:panelGroup>

</h:panelGrid>
```

For the record, a valid password in this example is "!!!!95A" without the quotes.

BeanValidator

This validator is explained in the later section titled "Using Bean Validation from JSF." A brief code example is included here for completeness.

```
<h:inputText value="#{user.name}">
  <f:validateBean validationGroups="com.jsfcompref.groups.Minimal" />
</h:inputText>
```

How to Associate a Validator with a UIComponent Instance

As shown in the UML diagram in Figure 8-2, each **EditableValueHolder** instance in the view may have zero or many **Validator** instances associated with it. There are several ways to make that association, and each is described in this section. Unlike in the case of **Converters**, there is no implicit **Validator** association mechanism. This is because **Validators** don't have the concept of type as a part of their external contract, though **Validator**s may indeed need to be aware of the type of the data they are validating to function properly.

Two methods are provided for explicitly associating a **Validator** with a **UIComponent** instance: via markup tags or programmatically. Each **EditableValueHolder** instance maintains a list of **Validator** instances, as well as a special **MethodBinding** property that points to a method that acts like a **Validator**. These two data stores for **Validator** instances provide lots of flexibility in how to validate your Web application.

Using Markup to Associate a Validator with a UIComponent Instance

There are two ways to associate a **Validator** with a **UIComponent** instance from markup: using one of the tags from **jsf_core** or using a **MethodBinding** (or **MethodExpression** in Faces 1.2 and 2.0) as the value of the **validator** attribute on one of the component tags directly. This section covers each style in turn.

Faces provides a markup tag in the **jsf_core** tag library for each of the standard validators. The **<f:validateDoubleRange>**, **<f:validateLongRange>**, and **<f:validateLength>** tags attach the **DoubleRangeValidator**, the **LongRangeValidator**, and the **LengthValidator**, respectively, to the component represented by the component tag in which they are nested. For example:

```
<h:inputText id="zipcode" value="#{user.zipCode}">
  <f:validateLength maximum="5" minimum="5" />
  <f:validateLongRange minimum="90000" maximum="99999" />
</h:inputText>
```

This attaches one **LengthValidator** and one **LongRangeValidator** to the **HtmlInputText** component associated with the **<h:inputText>** tag. The **LengthValidator** has been configured to ensure that the user enters exactly five characters in the text field. The **LongRangeValidator** has been configured to ensure the Zip code is between 90000 and 99999. If the **zipcode** property of the **user** bean is of type **Integer**, implicit conversion will take place as well.

JSF 2.0 adds the ability to turn this inside out, placing the components *inside* the validator. The following example is taken from the online code for this chapter, in the sample called **validatorWrapping**. This example simply modifies the **JSFReg** example from Chapter 2 and modifies the **register.xhtml** page to enclose the table within an **<f:validateRequired>** element, rather than having individual **required="true"** attributes on every component. The following is an excerpt from the **register.xhtml** page showing this style of validator usage:

```
<h2>JSF Registration App</h2>
<h4>Registration Form</h4>
<f:validateRequired>
    <table>
      <tr>
        <td>First Name:</td>
        <td>
          <h:inputText label="First Name"
                       id="fname" value="#{userBean.firstName}"/>
          <h:message for="fname" />
        </td>
      </tr>
Intervening rows deleted
    </table>
    </f:validateRequired>
```

It's very important to note that, when nesting, any validators, or settings on validators, that happen *inside* of the nesting take precedence over whatever validators or settings are specified on the wrapping validator(s).

For each of the standard validators, JSF 2.0 adds a **boolean** property, **disabled**. If the value of this property is **true**, or if it is an EL expression that evaluates to **true**, the validator will not be installed on the component. This property is also inherited from any enclosing validators in the markup. This feature is important when considering the new **default-validators** feature in JSF 2.0, described in the section "Using Bean Validation from JSF." Even though this feature was introduced for use with bean validation, it is perfectly usable with regular JSF validators.

As with converters, Faces also provides a generic **<f:validator>** tag that allows you to associate any **Validator** with the component in which it is nested by giving the **validator-id**. Also, similar to converters and **UIComponent** tags in general, the **Validator** tags offer a "binding" attribute to state that the actual **Validator** instance should come from evaluating an EL expression. (See Chapter 16 for full details on the **Validator** tags and all their attributes.)

Using Markup and the validator Attribute to Associate a Validator with a UIComponent Instance

Unlike conversion, validation is a one-way process, and it happens only once during a run through the request processing lifecycle. These constraints open up the possibility of using the Expression Language to point to a method on an arbitrary JavaBean that adheres to the contract and signature of **Validator.validate( )**. The **MethodBinding** class from the EL makes this possible. For example:

```
<h:inputText validator="#{user.validateAge}" value="#{user.age}" />
```

assuming the **user** bean has a method defined like

```
public void validateAge(FacesContext context, UIComponent component,
                        Object value) {
  // Validation code here
}
```

During the Process Validations phase, when it comes time to validate this component, call the method **validateAge( )** on the bean named **user** and assume that it will fulfill the contract of a **Validator**. This late-binding approach saves the instantiation of separate **Validator** instances and can greatly simplify application design by allowing you to put the business logic, and the method to validate it, in the same class.

All of the tags in the **html_basic** tag library that map to **UIComponent**s and that implement the interface **javax.faces.component.EditableValueHolder** honor the **validator** attribute. They are

inputHidden	inputSecret	inputText
inputTextarea	selectBooleanCheckbox	selectManyCheckbox
selectManyListbox	selectManyMenu	selectOneListbox
selectOneMenu	selectOneRadio	

Note that using this method of association allows only one **Validator** to be added to the component, but you can still attach multiple validators using the other methods of association.

Programmatically Associating a Validator with a UIComponent Instance

As with converters, the markup layer for validators is merely a façade around the component model. The markup tags all result in a call to **addValidator( )** on the underlying component instance, and the **required** attribute results in a call to **setRequired(true)** on the component. It is certainly possible to call these methods directly, but as with converters, you must be aware of when in the request processing lifecycle your code to add the validator or set the required attribute will execute.

TIP *If you want your **Validator** to be used during the whole lifecycle, try using a **UIView RootPhaseListener** registered for the **beforePhase** event of the Render Response phase. This will ensure that the **Validator** is installed before the first rendering and that it remains installed throughout the life of the view thanks to the state management APIs.*

Once you know when in the lifecycle your validator installing code will execute, it's a matter of creating and adding it to the desired component. The following example shows how to programmatically create and add two different **Validator** instances on a component in the view.

```
FacesContext context = FacesContext.getCurrentInstance( );
Validator progressValidator = null;
MethodBinding pointerToValidatorMethod = null;
EditableValueHolder component = null;
UIViewRoot root = context.getViewRoot();
// Find the component on which we'll add the Validator.
component = (EditableValueHolder) root.findComponent("form" +
NamingContainer.SEPARATOR_CHAR + "userComponent");
// Ensure that this component doesn't already have a
// progressValidator.
Validator [] validators = component.getValidators( );
boolean found = false;
for(int i = 0; i < validators.length && !found; i++) {
  found = (validators[i] instanceof ProgressValidator);
}
if(found) {
  return;
}
// Create the progressValidator.
progressValidtor = context.getApplication().createValidator("progressValida
tor");
// Add it to the component.
component.addValidator(progressValidator);
// Ensure that this component doesn't already
// have a validator in its MethodBinding slot.
if(null != component.getValidator()) {
  return;
}
Class params = {FacesContext.class, UIComponent.class, Object.class};
```

```
pointerToValidatorMethod =
context.getApplication().createMethodBinding("#{user.validateAge}",
                                            params);
component.setValidator(pointerToValidatorMethod);
```

The main point of this example is to show the use of the **createValidator( )**, **addValidator( )**, and **setValidator( )** methods. Note that we had to take extra care to check if the validator was already added. This is necessary because validators are additive, whereas converters are not.

The Lifetime of a Validator

As shown previously, the Faces converter system will implicitly associate a **Converter** with a component based on the Java language type of the model property to which the component's value is bound. There is no such implicit concept for validation. Due to the lack of implicit validation, it's easier to be aware of the lifetime implications of validators because you always have to take some kind of action to add a **Validator**. In all cases, once you take that action, the **Validator** instance persists for the lifetime of the **UIComponent** instance, which is generally limited by the lifetime of the session. If you're worried about excessive object instantiation, a good approach is to use the **MethodBindingValidator** technique as shown in the section "Writing a validation( ) Method That Is Pointed to by a MethodBinding." This places the lifetime constraints squarely into the realm of managed beans.

Custom Validators

Creating custom **Validator** implementations is even more common than creating custom **Converter** instances, partly because the set of standard validators provided by Faces is relatively small, and partly because it is very easy to write a **Validator**. In this section, we'll cover the two ways of implementing a **Validator** and discuss the pros and cons of each.

Implementing the Validator Interface

The first way that you can create a validator is to implement the **Validator** interface. With this approach, it is recommended to keep the validator in its own separate class, since you must register it by **validator-id**. Also, instances of the **Validator** can be created automatically, so it's best to keep it lightweight. For the Virtual Trainer example, one can imagine a **Validator** that ensures that the client has met all the fitness requirements for participation in an event, according to the opinion of the virtual trainer.

The following class, called **EventRequirementValidator**, provides such an implementation.

```
package com.jsfcompref.trainercomponents.validator;

import javax.el.ValueExpression;
import javax.faces.application.Application;
import javax.faces.application.FacesMessage;
import javax.faces.validator.Validator;
import javax.faces.validator.ValidatorException;
import javax.faces.component.UIComponent;
import javax.faces.context.FacesContext;

import javax.faces.validator.FacesValidator;
```

```
@FacesValidator(value="com.jsfcompref.EventRequirements")
public class EventRequirementValidator extends Object implements Validator {

    public void validate(FacesContext context,
                         UIComponent  component,
                         Object       value) throws ValidatorException {
      Boolean hasMetRequirements = null;
      Boolean newHasMetRequirements = null;
        Application application = context.getApplication();

      ValueExpression ve = application.getExpressionFactory().
                createValueExpression(context.getELContext(),
                "#{currentUser.status.qualified}", Boolean.class);
      try {
            // This is an example of programmatically
            // invoking a ValueExpression.
            // It is not used in the validator calculation,
            // but it is left in
            // for illustration.
          hasMetRequirements = (Boolean) ve.getValue(context.
              getELContext());
          newHasMetRequirements = (Boolean) value;
      }
      catch (Throwable e) {
          // log error
      }

      if (!newHasMetRequirements.booleanValue()) {
            FacesMessage message =
              new FacesMessage("You still have more work to do!");
          throw new ValidatorException(message);
      }

    }


}
```

EventRequirementValidator uses the **@FacesValidator** annotation to declare itself to the runtime system. Alternatively, the following XML code can be added to the **faces-config.xml** to achieve the same effect:

```
<validator>
  <description>
    Validates that the current user has met the requirements for the event.
  </description>
  <validator-id>eventRequirements</validator-id>
  <validator-class>
    com.jsfcompref.validator.EventRequirementValidator
  </validator-class>
</validator>
```

Note that this **EventRequirementValidator** has no configuration parameters, and thus it is essentially stateless. The **validate( )** method simply looks up the **qualified** property in the user's **status** bean and throws a **ValidatorException** if it is false. The markup for the validator allows the use of the **<f:validator>** tag to add this validator to any **UIComponent** instance in the view.

Writing a validation( ) Method That Is Pointed to by a MethodExpression

The second approach to validation allows any managed bean in your application to function as a **Validator**, without implementing the **Validator** interface or registering the **Validator** in the **faces-config.xml** file. This approach is very useful when you have existing code that you want to retrofit to JSF. You need add only one method, and then any **UIComponent** can use that method to perform validation. An example of this approach was shown earlier in this chapter, in the section "Using Markup and the validator Attribute to Associate a **Validator** with a UIComponent Instance."

Using Bean Validation from JSF

A good technology shouldn't force its users to understand where it came from and how it was developed in order to use it in practice. For most features in JSF, this is true, but when one tries to use JSF in concert with other Java EE technologies, knowledge of the provenance of each technology is sometimes required. For example, it is perfectly valid to use JSF 2.0 on top of a non–Java EE 6–compliant container, such as Apache Tomcat version 6, or Jetty version 6. However, those containers do not include support for EJB, JPA, or the feature described in this section: bean validation. The online code samples for the book include information on getting JSF to run with bean validation on Tomcat 6 and Jetty. The remainder of this section describes how to use bean validation with JSF 2.0.

What Is Bean Validation?

The name "bean validation" comes from how the feature leverages JavaBeans naming conventions so that the objects being validated are our old friends, POJOs. Bean validation is a new feature in Java EE 6, specified as JSR-303, which generalizes the concept of validation so that it can be used beyond JSF. In fact, the bean validation feature is so general that it can be used in standalone Java Swing applications, with no server involved at all. However, because the process of including new features into the core JDK is so difficult and laborious, and because the main use-case for bean validation is server-side applications, it is delivered as a part of Java EE 6. In fact, the most popular expected usage of bean validation is within JSF applications, so the two expert groups, JSF and bean validation, worked very closely together during development to ensure sensible and intuitive interoperability between these two technologies.

The following three fundamental observations underlie both JSF validation and bean validation.

- Good application design includes separation of concerns, including use of the Model-View-Controller paradigm.
- The application needs a way to ensure that the model is "valid" according to arbitrary constraints defined by the application.

- In the spirit of separation of concerns, the logic that defines and performs this validation is best kept separated, but closely related to, the model itself. In other words, the validation can be seen as metadata[1] for the model.

JSF and bean validation have different ways of specifying the validation logic that goes along with, but is separate from, the model.

Differences Between JSF Validation and Bean Validation

There are two main differences between JSF validation and bean validation. The first is that in bean validation, the primary way to declare that a validation should be applied to a POJO is to attach an annotation to a field or a JavaBeans getter method on the POJO. The following example, taken from the **validateBean** sample application in the online code for this book, uses bean validation to validate the **UserBean** in the **JSFReg** application, instead of JSF validation.

```
package com.jsfcompref;

import java.util.Date;
import javax.faces.application.FacesMessage;
import javax.faces.context.FacesContext;
import javax.faces.bean.ManagedBean;
import javax.faces.bean.SessionScoped;

@ManagedBean
@SessionScoped
public class UserBean {

    @NotEmpty(message="You must supply a first name")
    protected String firstName;
    @NotEmpty(message="You must supply a last name")
    protected String lastName;
    @NotEmpty(message="You must supply a birthday")
    protected Date dob;
    protected String sex;
    @NotEmpty(message="You must supply an email address")
    @Email
    protected String email;
    protected String serviceLevel = "medium";

    public String getFirstName() {
        return firstName;
    }

public void setFirstName(String firstName) {
// ...additional code not shown.  It's the same as in chapter 2.
```

The **@NotEmpty** and **@Email** annotations are custom bean validation *constraints*. Like JSF standard validators, a core set of constraints are built into bean validation, but, also like

[1]Metadata is a potentially confusing term that literally means "data about data." In this usage, it simply means that the validation logic, that is, the constraints to apply and how to apply them, are data that goes alongside the model data.

JSF validators, they often fall short of what you need to get real work done. The steps required to implement a custom constraint will be covered later in this chapter, but for now it is sufficient to know that the preceding code says that the **firstName**, **lastName**, **dob**, and **email** fields are not empty, and that the **email** field must be a valid e-mail address. Contrast this with JSF, where the association between the validation and the model is done in the JSF page.

This brings us to the second main difference between JSF validation and bean validation: where the validation happens. In JSF validation, the model itself is not validated, but rather, the individual fields are validated *before* they are pushed into the model during the Update Model Values lifecycle phase. Because bean validation was designed for use in any kind of application, it doesn't have a lifecycle to define when the validation happens. Rather, bean validation requires the validation to be performed on the model itself, *after* it has been populated with input data. Therefore, to use JSF and bean validation together, a technique was devised to resolve the differences between these two models. Features were added to the core bean validation API that essentially answer the questions, "*If* I were to push this value into the model, would it be valid?" and "If the value is not valid, what validation message should I present to the user?"

This section does not provide a complete description of bean validation. While it is entirely possible to use every aspect of bean validation in an application that uses JSF, this section will only describe those aspects that are directly included in the JSF-to-bean validation integration feature set. For complete information on bean validation, consult the specification, which may be downloaded from **http://jcp.org/en/jsr/summary?id=303**.

Details on Using Bean Validation from JSF

Let's now look more closely at the details associated with bean validation. At the core of the process is the concept of a "constraint."

In bean validation, a constraint is a Java annotation that is annotated with the annotation **javax.validation.Constraint**. The definition of the **@Email** constraint from the example is shown here. The **@Constraint** annotation is shown in boldface. The **validatedBy** attribute will be explained shortly.

```
package com.jsfcompref;

import java.lang.annotation.Documented;
import java.lang.annotation.ElementType;
import java.lang.annotation.Retention;
import java.lang.annotation.RetentionPolicy;
import java.lang.annotation.Target;
import javax.validation.Constraint;

@Documented
@Constraint(validatedBy = EmailConstraintValidator.class)
@Target({ElementType.METHOD, ElementType.FIELD})
@Retention(RetentionPolicy.RUNTIME)
public @interface Email {
    String message() default "{validator.email}";

    Class<?>[] groups() default {};

    Class<? extends ConstraintPayload>[] payload() default {};
}
```

The act of using a **Constraint** on a POJO is called a *constraint declaration.* Taking an excerpt from the **UserBean** in the preceding section, it looks like this.

```
@Email
protected String email;
```

This is exactly analogous to the use of the e-mail validator on the **<h:inputText>** field in the **registration.xhtml** page, as shown here:

```
<h:inputText label="Email Address"
  id="email" value="#{userBean.email}" required="true"
  validator="#{userBean.validateEmail}"/>
```

In both cases, we are declaring that the e-mail field should be validated by a piece of code that answers the question, "is this data a valid e-mail address?" In bean validation, that code lives in the class (or classes) listed on the right-hand side of the **validatedBy** attribute within the **@Constraint** annotation. Such a class must implement the **ConstraintValidator** interface, which uses generics for maximal type safety. This is called a **ConstraintValidator** implementation. The **EmailConstraintValidator** class looks like this:

```
package com.jsfcompref;

import javax.validation.ConstraintValidator;
import javax.validation.ConstraintValidatorContext;

public class EmailConstraintValidator
      implements ConstraintValidator<Email, String> {

    public void initialize(Email parameters) {
    }

    public boolean isValid(String value,
                           ConstraintValidatorContext ctxt) {

        boolean result = true;
        if (-1 == value.indexOf("@")) {
            result = false;
        }

        return result;
    }

}
```

It is very important to understand the use of generics in this class declaration.

```
public class EmailConstraintValidator
      implements ConstraintValidator<Email, String> {
```

The first generic must be the actual annotation that is annotated with **@Constraint**, in this case **Email**. The second generic is the type of the value that is to be validated. The **initialize( )** method will always be called before **isValid( )** and can be used to perform any setup necessary for the forthcoming validation. The **isValid( )** method is exactly analogous to our validator method in the original **JSFReg** version of **UserBean**. In fact, the code was copied and pasted directly. The only change is that, instead of throwing a **ValidatorException**, the **isValid( )** method returns **true** if the value is valid, and returns **false** otherwise. The last remaining difference to explore is how the validation messages get defined and placed into the view. You will see how to do this in the context of Faces messages, later in the chapter, but for now just know that the line

```
String message() default "{validator.email}";
```

on the **Email** annotation can either be a resource bundle key enclosed with **{ }**, or an actual literal string, such as

```
String message() default "You must include a valid email";
```

Now that you know what a **Constraint** is, and how to define a **ConstraintValidator** implementation for it, it's time to show how these are used with JSF.

Validating JSF Managed Bean Properties with Bean Validation

Like Ed Burns for JSF, Emmanuel Bernard, the team leader for the bean validation specification, was very keen on reducing or eliminating any extra configuration that users must do in order to use his technology. Emmanuel devised a new feature in JSF, the **default-validators**, and declared some rules about how this new feature was to be used in the case of bean validation. This element can be included within the existing **<application />** element. The syntax for this element looks like this:

```
<faces-config>
  <application>
    <default-validators>
      <validator-id>whatever.validator.id.you.want</validator-id>
    </default-validators>
  </application>
</faces-config>
```

Any validators declared in this way are automatically added to every **EditableValueHolder** component, on every page in the application. The magic with respect to bean validation is that if you are running in a container that supports bean validation, the **javax.faces.Bean** validator is automatically included among the **default-validators**. Because of the way the **javax.faces.Bean** validator is defined, this means any fields annotated with bean validation **Constraint**s that are pointed to by EL expressions in the Facelet page are automatically validated according to those **Constraint**s.

For example, the **JSFReg** e-mail field that previously looked like this:

```
<h:inputText label="Email Address"
  id="email" value="#{userBean.email}" required="true"
  validator="#{userBean.validateEmail}"/>
```

can simply be rewritten as this:

```
<h:inputText label="Email Address" id="email" value="#{userBean.email}" />
```

Note that the **validator** and **required** attributes have been removed. You can rest assured that the **@NotEmpty** and **@Email** constraints will be applied to the e-mail field when the **<h:inputText />** does its **validate( )** processing.

***JSF 2.0* Tip** *Of course, it is possible to disable bean validation, even on containers that support it. One way to do so is to declare an empty **<default-validators />** element in your **faces-config**. This is shown in the online example for this chapter called **emptyFields**. The other way is to add the **javax.faces.validator.DISABLE_BEAN_VALIDATOR <context-param>** in your **web.xml** file and set its value to **true**.*

The **<f:validateBean>** can be used in the page, either as a nested validator, or wrapping other input components, to pass additional parameters to control bean validation, such as **groups**. The topic of **groups** is beyond the scope of this book.

Tie It All Together: Messages in a View

The previous sections covered the mechanics of conversion and validation, when they happen, their impacts on the request processing lifecycle, the ways to create converters and validators, and how to associate them with the components in your view, but all of that would be for naught were it not for giving user feedback. After all, the point of all this is to tell users they've done something wrong, and hopefully how to fix it. The way this information flows from the source of the error (a conversion or validation error) to the user is through the **javax.faces.application.FacesMessage** class, the **FacesContext**, and the **UIMessage** or **UIMessages** components. This section covers messages in detail, including how they're created, how to control their display, how to customize the standard messages, and how to add custom messages. The chapter will close with the special factors that must be considered regarding messages and bean validation.

As explained in Chapter 3, the **FacesContext** instance is the per-request object that is the entry point to all of the Faces-specific context information relating to the current run through the request processing lifecycle. The two properties of particular import to conversion and validation are messages and the **UIViewRoot**. The page author doesn't interact with these properties directly, but rather by using the **<h:message>** and **<h:messages>** tags from the **html_basic** tag library. In the interest of completeness, we cover the **FacesContext** message and **UIViewRoot** properties as they relate to conversion and validation.

FacesMessage-Related Methods on FacesContext

The **FacesMessage** class encapsulates a single, localized, human-readable message, typically associated with a particular component in the view, and typically describing a problem in the process of conversion or validation. In addition to the message string itself, a **FacesMessage** has three properties of interest: **severity**, **summary**, and **detail**.

The **severity** property is defined as an inner class of **FacesMessage** with the following logical values: **INFO**, **WARN**, **ERROR**, and **FATAL**. The **severity** property provides additional information to the user about the error and has no effect on the lifecycle. The **summary** and **detail** properties are the actual localized, human-readable messages.

The **FacesContext** instance maintains two logical collections of **FacesMessage** instances: a collection of messages that are associated with a component, and those that are not associated with a component. The former is usually the garden-variety conversion and validation message, and the latter may be a message that applies to the form as a whole. These two collections are accessed by the different variants of the **getMessages( )** method on **FacesContext**. The variant that takes no arguments returns an **Iterator** of all messages, associated with a component or not. The variant that takes a **clientId** gets only messages associated with the component of that **clientId**, or, if the **clientId** is **null**, gets only messages that are *not* associated with a specific **clientId**. The **FacesContext** also provides a method to return the severity of the most severe message it currently has—**getMaximumSeverity( )**, and a method to return an **Iterator** of **clientIds** for which it has messages: **getClientIdsWithMessages( )**. Most markup applications won't need to call these methods directly, but an example to illustrate their use is in order. As you can imagine, the implementations of the renderers for the **h:message** and **h:messages** tags use the **getMessages(**) method to get the message or messages to render. Let's go a step further and show an example that directs the application to a special page if there are any messages with a severity of **Severity.FATAL**. To make this happen, we need to hook up an action method to a **UICommand** component. This is the standard way to do navigation in Faces, and is covered in detail in Chapter 6. First, here is the markup fragment for the button that submits the form:

```
<h:commandButton action="#{bean.checkForFatalError}" />
```

As explained in Chapter 6, this will cause the **public String checkForFatalError( )** method on the managed bean named **bean** to be called when the button is pressed. The return value from this method is fed into the navigation system to determine the next view to display. The implementation of the **checkForFatalError( )** method follows.

```
public String checkForFatalError() {
    FacesContext context = FacesContext.getCurrentInstance();


    // Test method, queue some errors
    context.addMessage(null, new FacesMessage(FacesMessage.SEVERITY_WARN,
            "warning", "warning"));
    context.addMessage(null, new FacesMessage(FacesMessage.SEVERITY_INFO,
            "info", "info"));
    context.addMessage(null, new FacesMessage(FacesMessage.SEVERITY_FATAL,
            "fatal", "fatal"));

    FacesMessage.Severity severity = context.getMaximumSeverity();
    String result = "checkForFatalError2";

    if (null != severity) {
        if (severity == FacesMessage.SEVERITY_FATAL) {
            result = "fatalError";
        }
    }
    return result;
}
```

This method gets the **FacesContext** for this request, extracts its **maximumSeverity** JavaBeans property, and examines it. If the value is **FacesMessage.Severity.SEVERITY_FATAL**, it returns the value **fatalError**; otherwise, it returns the value **"checkForFatalError2"**. These values are fed into the navigation system and the implicit navigation feature is used to discern the appropriate page to show. The messages that are queued by this method are for illustration purposes only. In practice, the messages would be queued by application code.

The UIViewRoot and Its Locale Property

The **FacesContext** is the place where you obtain the **UIViewRoot** for the current view. This **UIComponent** subclass is the root node of the tree structure that *is* the view. All of the components in your page are arranged as a tree of children of this root node. This root node has several properties, but its **locale** property is of special interest to conversion and validation. The **locale** property is an instance of **java.util.Locale** that is guaranteed to be the right locale for any language-specific processing in this view. Chapter 14 explains how the **locale** property is set by the user and/or by the system, but at this point you need to know only that it is the correct **Locale** to use.

Converters use the locale for many of their methods. For example, the **DateTimeConverter** couldn't get very far unless it knew what separator it should use between numbers in a **SHORT**-styled date, or where the year should go. For example, Europeans tend to use 14.05.1995, while Americans prefer 05/14/1995. Because messages are human-readable text, they are localized using the **ResourceBundle** mechanism of the Java platform.

When and How FacesMessage Instances Are Created and Added to the FacesContext

There are exactly three times in the request processing lifecycle when the standard components will create a **FacesMessage** instance and add it to the **FacesContext**: when conversion fails, when validation fails, or when the converted and validated data cannot be pushed to the model during the Update Model Values phase. This last case is not likely due to user error, but the user needs to be informed nonetheless. Each case is examined in turn.

A **Converter** signals an error by throwing a **ConverterException**. When creating the exception, the converter has the option of giving a **FacesMessage** to the constructor directly, providing a simple string message, or including no message at all. If no **FacesMessage** is provided to the **ConverterException**, a standard "conversion failed" **FacesMessage** is generated. If the **ConverterException** has a string **message** property, its value is used as the **detail** property of the **FacesMessage**. The **severity** of a **Converter FacesMessage** instance is always **ERROR**.

A **Validator** signals an error by throwing a **ValidatorException**. Unlike the **ConverterException**, the **ValidatorException** must take a **FacesMessage** in its constructor. The severity of a **Validator FacesMessage** instance is always **ERROR**.

Finally, if an EL exception is thrown when trying to propagate the value to the model during the Update Model Values phase, the message of the exception is examined. If non-null, a new **FacesMessage** is created with the exception message as the summary. If **null**, a **FacesMessage** is created with a generic error message.

EXPERT GROUP INSIGHT *In all of the preceding cases, we have glossed over how the content of the* **FacesMessage** *is localized for messages that are built into the specification. The EG intentionally avoided providing a factory API for* ***FacesMessage*** *instances because a generic factory pattern may be included in a future release of the Java platform, and it would be preferable to use that when it is available. Instead of the factory, the EG specified the exact manner in which the Java platform's* ***ResourceBundle*** *mechanism must be used to create and populate a* ***FacesMessage*** *instance with its localized message content. The following is the algorithm:*

1. *Call the* ***getMessageBundle( )*** *method on the application. This returns the fully qualified name of the* ***ResourceBundle*** *to be used for this application, or null if no such bundle has been set. If null, use* ***javax.faces.Messages*** *as the name of the* ***ResourceBundle****.*
2. *Use the Java platform* ***ResourceBundle*** *lookup methods, and the* ***Locale*** *from the current* ***UIViewRoot*** *to obtain the* ***ResourceBundle*** *named from Step 1.*
3. *Look in the* ***ResourceBundle*** *for a value under the key given by the value of the* ***messageId*** *for this* ***FacesMessage****. If none is found, there is no localized content for this message. Otherwise, use the value as the summary property of the* ***FacesMessage****. Append the string "_detail" to the* ***messageId*** *and look in the* ***ResourceBundle*** *for a value under that key. If one is found, use the value as the detail of the* ***FacesMessage****.*
4. *Make sure to perform any parameter substitution required on the localized content—for example, if the returned* ***ResourceBundle*** *is "Validation Error: Specified attribute is not between the expected values of {0} and {1}," the proper values must be substituted for {0} and {1}, perhaps using* ***java.text.MessageFormat****.*

How FacesMessages Are Rendered

At long last we have come to the place where the users enter the picture: showing them the errors in their input and how to correct them. In keeping with the JSF component model, there are two standard components that serve as placeholders in the view for messages to appear: **UIMessage** and **UIMessages**. Along with these components, there are renderers in the standard HTML render-kit: **javax.faces.Message** and **javax.faces.Messages**, respectively. Naturally, to show the valid combinations of these components and renderers, there are the **<h:message>** and **<h:messages>** tags in the **html_basic** tag library. As with all of the components in the standard HTML component set, the heavy lifting is done by the renderers, so we'll briefly describe those in this section. We then list the standard message keys for converters and validators, and show how to customize messages and add new ones.

Rendering a Message for a Specific Component in the Page

The **<h:message>** tag places into the view a **UIMessage** component associated with a **javax.faces.Message** renderer. Whenever the user places a **<h:message>** tag in the page, the user is required to provide a **for** attribute that gives the **componentId** of the component for which this tag will display messages. This gives the page author complete freedom to display the messages however he or she likes in the page. Beginning in JSF1.2, a **dir** attribute has been included that lets the page author give a cue to the **Renderer** about the direction of the text, either left to right (LTR) or right to left (RTL). This **Renderer** gets an **Iterator** of messages from the **FacesContext** by calling its **getMessages( )** method, and passing the value of the **for** attribute. Only the first message in the **Iterator** is rendered. (See Chapter 16 for complete information on **<h:message>**.)

Rendering All the Messages in a Page

The **<h:messages>** tag places into the view a **UIMessages** component associated with a **javax.faces.Messages** renderer. Whenever the user places a **<h:messages>** tag, all messages in the **FacesContext** are displayed, unless the **globalOnly** attribute is set, in which case only messages that are not associated with a given component are displayed. The **layout** attribute can be either **table** or **list**. If **table**, the messages are displayed in an HTML table; if **list**, they are displayed in an HTML unordered list. (Again, see Chapter 16 for complete information on **<h:message>**.)

The Standard Message Keys

Table 8-4 lists the standard message keys in JSF. The **FacesMessage** instances around which these messages are built are all generated during the Apply Request Values phase if the component has its **immediate** property set, and during the Process Validations phase otherwise. The severity of all these **FacesMessage** instances is **Severity.ERROR**.

Customizing the Content of One of the Standard Messages

The default content for the standard messages is pretty dry and may not be what you want in your application. For example, the standard message for **javax.faces.validator .LengthValidator.MINIMUM** is "Validation Error: Value is less than allowable maximum of "{0}"", which can be pretty cryptic to some. Because of the specification for how **FacesMessage** instances are produced, it is possible to provide your own **ResourceBundle** that is consulted before the standard one, thus allowing you to override any of the standard messages, as well as provide your own for any custom **Converter** or **Validator** implementations you may have. To do this, simply create an **<application>** element in your **faces-config.xml** file (if you don't have one already) and add a **<message-bundle>** element inside of it. Note that DTD and Schema are very ordering-dependent, so you must place the message-bundle element in the right order if you have other elements in your **<application>** element. Full details of the element ordering can be found in Chapter 15.

The following is the **<application>** element for the Virtual Trainer:

```
<application>
  <message-bundle>com.jsfcompref.Messages</message-bundle>
  <locale-config>
    <default-locale>en</default-locale>
    <supported-locale>de</supported-locale>
   </locale-config>
</application>
```

This states that the application resource bundle should be **com.jsfcompref.Messages** and that the default locale for the application is English, but German is supported also. (See Chapter 14 for details on internationalizing JSF applications.) All that remains now is to author the **Messages.properties** and **Messages_de.properties** files. The following is a snippet from the **Messages.properties** file. Notice the use of the standard **LengthValidator** to ensure the user's password is at least six characters long.

```
javax.faces.validator.LengthValidator.MINIMUM=\
  Not long enough. Make it longer!
```

messageId
javax.faces.component.UIInput.CONVERSION
javax.faces.component.UIInput.REQUIRED
javax.faces.component.UISelectOne.INVALID
javax.faces.component.UISelectMany.INVALID
javax.faces.converter.BigDecimalConverter.DECIMAL
javax.faces.converter.BigIntegerConverter.BIGINTEGER
javax.faces.converter.BooleanConverter.BOOLEAN
javax.faces.converter.ByteConverter.BYTE
javax.faces.converter.CharacterConverter.CHARACTER
javax.faces.converter.DateTimeConverter.DATE
javax.faces.converter.DateTimeConverter.TIME
javax.faces.converter.DateTimeConverter.DATETIME
javax.faces.converter.DateTimeConverter.PATTERN_TYPE
javax.faces.converter.DoubleConverter.DOUBLE
javax.faces.converter.FloatConverter.FLOAT
javax.faces.converter.IntegerConverter.INTEGER
javax.faces.converter.LongConverter.LONG
javax.faces.converter.NumberConverter.CURRENCY
javax.faces.converter.NumberConverter.PERCENT
javax.faces.converter.NumberConverter.NUMBER
javax.faces.converter.NumberConverter.PATTERN
javax.faces.converter.ShortConverter.SHORT
javax.faces.converter.STRING
javax.faces.validator.NOT_IN_RANGE
javax.faces.validator.DoubleRangeValidator.MAXIMUM
javax.faces.validator.DoubleRangeValidator.MINIMUM
javax.faces.validator.DoubleRangeValidator.NOT_IN_RANGE
javax.faces.validator.DoubleRangeValidator.TYPE
javax.faces.validator.LengthValidator.MAXIMUM
javax.faces.validator.LengthValidator.MINIMUM
javax.faces.validator.LongRangeValidator.MAXIMUM
javax.faces.validator.LongRangeValidator.MINIMUM
javax.faces.validator.LongRangeValidator.NOT_IN_RANGE
javax.faces.validator.LongRangeValidator.TYPE

TABLE 8-4 The Standard Message Keys

TIP *In Faces 1.2, a feature was added where the label of the component with which the message is associated is incorporated in the message string. If you want to support this feature when overriding a standard message, you must keep in mind that element {1} will be substituted with the label. Doing this doesn't make sense for the preceding example, but it's important to keep this in mind.*

There are, of course, cases when you just want to override a standard message for one specific usage of one of the standard **Validator**s in your application. This can easily be accomplished using the **MethodBinding** validator approach, as described earlier. In the method functioning as a **Validator**, you can manually call the appropriate standard **Validator**, catch the **ValidatorException**, create your own **FacesMessage** instance with your own message, and pass that to the constructor of a new **ValidatorException**, which you then throw.

TIP *You can also override the message using the **requiredMessage**, **converterMessage**, or **validatorMessage** property of **UIInput**. This is exposed as a tag attribute on all of the tags that expose **UIInput** components to the page author.*

Creating Your Own Messages

Creating your own messages is as simple as adding a message key to your properties file, and then following the algorithm in the section "When and How **FacesMessage** Instances Are Created and Added to the **FacesContext**" earlier in this chapter to create the **FacesMessage** instance, and pass it to the constructor of your **ConverterException** or **ValidatorException**. In Chapter 10, you will see how to create a **FacesMessageMaker** class to encapsulate this process. Alternatively, your custom **Validator** could simply just pull the **String** off of a **ResourceBundle** manually in an application-specific manner.

Messages and Bean Validation

Because bean validation was designed for broader use than just JSF, it does not directly leverage the JSF message mechanism described in the preceding section, but not to worry. The integration feature makes sure everything works just fine, including localization just as it works in JSF. First recall that a constraint declaration must have a message property, which looks like this (as shown in boldface).

```
package com.jsfcompref;

import java.lang.annotation.Documented;
import java.lang.annotation.ElementType;
import java.lang.annotation.Retention;
import java.lang.annotation.RetentionPolicy;
import java.lang.annotation.Target;
import javax.validation.Constraint;

@Documented
@Constraint(validatedBy = EmailConstraintValidator.class)
@Target({ElementType.METHOD, ElementType.FIELD})
@Retention(RetentionPolicy.RUNTIME)
```

```
public @interface Email {
    String message() default "{validator.email}";

    Class<?>[] groups() default {};

    Class<? extends ConstraintPayload>[] payload() default {};
}
```

This property is either a literal string or a **ResourceBundle** property key enclosed in curly braces. The message can be optionally overridden at the site of the constraint declaration, like this usage on **UserBean**:

```
@Email(message="Silly user, your email is invalid")
private String email;
```

If the value of the message is not a literal string, then the **ValidationMessages ResourceBundle**, in the default Java package, is consulted for a key. If there is a value for that key, it is used as the localized value for the message. In the **validateBean** online example, this file is stored at **ch08/validateBean/src/main/java/ValidationMessages_en.properties** and contains the entry

```
validator.email=Invalid email address
```

It is not possible to customize the location or name of the **ValidationMessages** properties file. It must be named **ValidationMessages**, and it must reside in the root (or default) Java package.

Finally, it is possible to interpolate properties from the constraint declaration within the validation message. Let's expand our **Email** constraint definition to have a property for the e-mail domain that must be used. The new declaration simply adds this property to the annotation:

```
String domain;
```

And the constraint declaration looks like this:

```
@Email(domain=".org")
private String email;
```

The entry in the **ValidationMessages_en.properties** file is shown next:

```
validator.email=Invalid email address. Must end in {domain}.
```

Now that you've learned the details of conversion and validation, and how to use bean validation in JSF, let's examine in depth the Faces Event system in the next chapter.

9

CHAPTER

The JSF Event Model

JavaServer Faces differs from most other Web development technologies in that it provides an event-based programming model that is similar to the one used in traditional, thick-client development with Swing or AWT. This enables a much finer degree of control when dealing with complex user interfaces and is well suited for use by traditional client developers. Web developers who may not be fully familiar with this type of event model, which is considerably different than basic HTTP request event (GET/POST) processing, will soon appreciate the level of granularity provided by the Faces event model when dealing with more complex user interfaces.

A High-Level Overview of the JSF Event Model

Before the advent of sophisticated user interfaces, programs tended to execute in a serial fashion. That is, they would start, process data, and exit. When human input was required, the program would prompt the user, using a phrase such as "Enter your name:" and then wait until the data was entered. This simple "question/answer" mechanism constituted programming's first widely deployed user interface paradigm. Although conceptually simple, the effectiveness of this approach was inherently limited. As program/user interactions became more complex, a better approach was needed. This need gave rise to the *graphical user interface (GUI).*

The GUI offers a substantially more sophisticated system that is based on user-initiated changes to the various interface elements. To manage these interactions, the "event/listener" model was devised. There are two concepts in this model: events and listeners. Each kind of event is an abstraction that answers the questions "what happened?" and "to whom?" The listener instances are provided by the application and answer the question "what is the application going to do about the occurrence of this event?"

The programming model for event/listener frameworks works like this. The framework describes a set of events, each with its own specific meaning regarding the state of the application. For example, an event is generated when the value of a field is changed or when a button is clicked. You program an event/listener framework by understanding the set of available events and deciding which ones are of interest to your specific application. For the events of interest, you register one or more listeners, effectively telling the framework, "If this event happens, call me back at this listener implementation." The listener implementations are where you put your application-specific code.

For example, let's say the application designer wants to automatically update the City and State fields when the user changes the Zip Code field. To implement this feature on top of an event/listener framework, the designer needs to understand that the framework publishes a "value change" event whenever the value of a field changes. The designer would then register a listener for this event on the Zip Code field. The implementation of the listener would be handed a reference to the Zip Code field, from which it could extract the value and take the action necessary to update the City and State fields. The art of programming an event/listener framework is simply a matter of understanding the set of available events, the meaning of each one, and mapping that to the needs of your specific application as a collection of listeners for those events.

As graphical user interface technologies ranging from the X Window System and the Apple Macintosh to Microsoft Windows began emerging in the late 1980s and early 1990s, they all had one thing in common: an event-based mechanism for dealing with state changes of user interface elements. In the years preceding the explosion of the Web, these were the dominant technologies for building software user interfaces.

As the Web became the dominant platform for application development, rich, event-based user interface development took a step backward. Because of the loosely connected nature of the Web where clients communicate asynchronously in a much lighter fashion than the traditional user interface technologies, the familiar event-based model regressed to a more primitive form of basic input and output in which a sequence of name-value pairs (parameters) are submitted to a server and the application code mainly deals with a single GET or POST event. Gone was the notion of being able to respond to intricate user interface changes.

As the Web gained in popularity, client-based technologies such as JavaScript and DHTML were introduced to improve the end-user experience by allowing the client browser the ability to react to more intricate changes in the state of a user interface element. However, using JavaScript and DHTML has always been a bit of an art, mainly because of the dual nature of dealing with client events and dealing with server Get/Post events. There was also the myriad of challenges inherent in getting the application to run in different Web browsers.

NOTE *Clever use of JavaScript and DHTML in the form of asynchronous calls to the server to pass data back and forth independent of page delivery is becoming popular; it is known as Asynchronous JavaScript and XML (Ajax). Examples of how to use Ajax in custom JavaServer Faces components are provided in Chapter 12.*

As mentioned at the start of this chapter, JavaServer Faces distinguishes itself among the different Web technologies by providing an event model that supports a rich, event-based user interface programming style that is similar to that used when developing for AWT or Swing. Using the JSF event model, which is part of the overall JSF request processing lifecycle, you no longer need to be concerned with processing large sets of name/value pairs provided in HTTP Get and Post requests. Instead, you can program to a more traditional event model where user interface elements broadcast changes in state (events) to a respective set of listener objects that then perform the tasks required.

Some Event Examples

There are two broad categories of events in JSF, *application events* and *lifecycle events*. These will be explained completely later in the chapter, but some quick examples will greatly aid in understanding the big picture.

First, let us examine an example of an application event by revisiting the master-detail example from Chapter 5. This example allowed the user to select a service level to view from a drop-down list and then see the subscribers at that service level. In the earlier version of this example, we used the flash to convey the value of the selected service level to show in the detail view. Here, we will listen for the **ValueChangeEvent** and take the appropriate action to update the model. Here is the new markup for the **master.xhtml** page.

```
<h:form>
  <h1>Master</h1>
      <p><h:selectOneMenu valueChangeListener="#{model.menuValueChanged}"
              value="#{model.serviceLevel}">
              <f:selectItems value="#{model.keys}"/>
          </h:selectOneMenu>
          <h:commandButton value="Show Subscribers" /></p>
</h:form>

<h1>Detail</h1>

<p>#{flash.valueChangeMessage}</p>

<h:dataTable border="1" var="user"
             value="#{model.data[model.serviceLevel]}">
    <h:column>
        <f:facet name="header">First Name</f:facet>
               #{user.firstName}
    </h:column>
The rest of the rows are not shown because they are the same as in chapter 5.
</h:dataTable>
```

The substantive changes are shown in boldface. Rather than storing the value in the Flash, we are now storing it directly on the model object. We also must change the data table to pull its value from the new location. Also, we have added a **valueChangeListener** method expression. This expression points to the following method in the managed bean:

```
public void menuValueChanged(ValueChangeEvent vce) {
  FacesContext context = FacesContext.getCurrentInstance();
  Flash flash = context.getExternalContext().getFlash();
  String
          oldValue = vce.getOldValue().toString(),
          newValue = vce.getNewValue().toString();
  flash.put("valueChangeMessage", "Value changed from " + oldValue +
          " to " + newValue);
  this.setServiceLevel(newValue);
}
```

Finally, the EL Expression **#{flash.valueChangeMessage}** is used to output the message.

The second example expands the preceding example to listen for the **PreRenderComponentEvent**, which is in the category of events called *lifecycle events.* Let's say we want to perform a check of the U.S. Government's "Denied or Restricted Parties List" when the detail view is shown. Some large companies operating in the U.S. are required to check all visitors to their facilities against this list and take appropriate action before granting access. A simple change to the **master.xhtml** page is one way to inject this behavior into the application without changing very much at all. The new **master.xhtml** page is shown here, with changed regions in boldface.

```
<h:form>
      <h1>Master</h1>
      <p><h:selectOneMenu valueChangeListener="#{model.menuValueChanged}"
              value="#{model.serviceLevel}">
              <f:selectItems value="#{model.keys}"/>
          </h:selectOneMenu>
          <h:commandButton value="Show Subscribers" /></p>
   </h:form>
   <h1>Detail</h1>
   <p>#{flash.valueChangeMessage}</p>
   <h:dataTable border="1" var="user"
               value="#{model.data[model.serviceLevel]}">
      <h:column>
          <f:facet name="header">First Name</f:facet>
                #{user.firstName}
      </h:column>
       <h:column>
          <f:facet name="header">Last Name</f:facet>
          <h:outputText value="#{user.lastName}">
              <f:event type="preRenderComponent"
                       listener="#{model.checkDRPL}" />
          </h:outputText>
       </h:column>

       <h:column>
          <f:facet name="header">Sex</f:facet>
                #{user.sex}
       /h:column>
  </h:dataTable>

<p><span style="color:red">#{drplMessage}</span></p>
```

First, note that the simple **#{user.lastName}** expression was changed to an **<h:outputText>** with a nested **<f:event>** element. This useful element will be described in detail later in the chapter, but for now just know that its purpose is to install a special kind of listener called a **ComponentSystemEventListener** on the parent **UIOutput** component. We want our listener to be called before this component renders; therefore we use the "preRenderComponent" value for the **type** attribute. Because this component is in a table, note that it will get called once for every row in the table. We are using our old trick of pushing a message into request scope and showing it later in the page, in this case with the EL expression **#{dprlMessage}**. The implementation of the **checkDRPL** method is shown here:

```
public  void  checkDRPL(ComponentSystemEvent  cse)
throws  AbortProcessingException  {
  ValueHolder  lastName  =  (ValueHolder)  cse.getComponent();
  FacesContext  context  =  FacesContext.getCurrentInstance();
  Map<String,Object>  requestMap  =  context.getExternalContext().
              getRequestMap();
```

```
    // check the government "Denied or Restricted Person's
    // List" for this last name
    String restrictedName = "Abs";
    if (restrictedName.equals(lastName.getValue())) {
            String message =
             "Warning, record lookup for restricted person " +
              lastName.getValue().toString();
      requestMap.put("drplMessage", message);
    }
}
```

The preceding two examples convey the essence of the Faces event system: the system has many different ways to tell your application, "what happened?" Your job as the designer is to decide what to do about it.

How JSF Events Work

Similar to AWT and Swing, the JavaServer Faces event model architecture borrows concepts from the event model of the JavaBeans specification, where "events are a mechanism for propagating state change notifications between a source object and one or more target *listener* objects." So, for example, if the source object were a button and if it were clicked, it would broadcast an event indicating its change in state (i.e., that it was clicked) and a corresponding listener object would be able to respond to the event, provided it was designated to listen for the specific type of event that occurred.

When using JSF, it's important to understand that although buttons are pressed or field values are being altered, nothing really happens on the client regarding application state at the instant these changes occur, as far as JSF is concerned. Instead, these changes are evaluated by the request processing lifecycle and are processed according to the rules defined by the lifecycle.

In general, Faces events are used to signify when state changes occur within UI components or within the request processing lifecycle and process them accordingly. Recall from Chapter 7 that all UI components can be broken down into two main branches. The first are those that *initiate an action,* such as a button. These implement the interface **ActionSource2**. The second are those that *hold a value,* such as an output or input field. These implement **ValueHolder** or **EditableValueHolder**. The two most common Faces events are patterned after these types of UI components. For **ActionSource2** components, an *action event* and a corresponding *action listener* are used to fire and then process events originating from **ActionSource2** components, such as when a button is clicked. For UI components that actually hold a value (implement **ValueHolder** or **EditableValueHolder** interfaces), a *value change event* and its associated *value change listener* are used. A value change event and listener can be programmed to react when a value of an input field has changed. Both action events and value change events extend from the generic Faces event **FacesEvent**, which extends from **java.util.EventObject**.

JSF provides another category of event and listener that goes beyond the scope of events that originate from UI components. This category of events and listeners is intended to give insight to the lifetime of the application and the execution of the request processing lifecycle. To record and process state changes that occur in the request processing lifecycle, *phase events* and *phase listeners* are used. Phase events are fired before and after each request

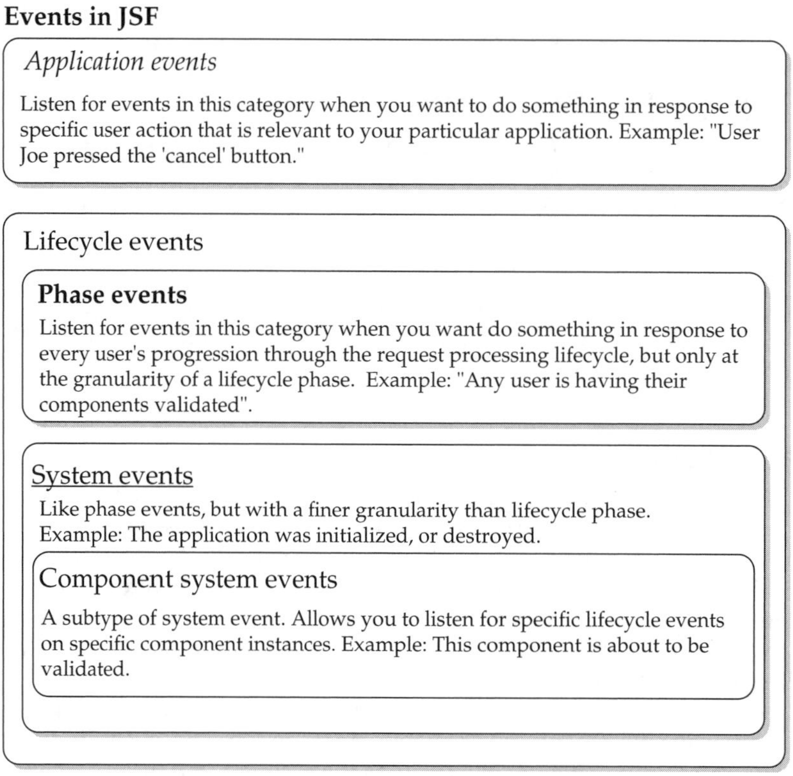

Events in JSF

Application events

Listen for events in this category when you want to do something in response to specific user action that is relevant to your particular application. Example: "User Joe pressed the 'cancel' button."

Lifecycle events

Phase events

Listen for events in this category when you want do something in response to every user's progression through the request processing lifecycle, but only at the granularity of a lifecycle phase. Example: "Any user is having their components validated".

System events

Like phase events, but with a finer granularity than lifecycle phase. Example: The application was initialized, or destroyed.

Component system events

A subtype of system event. Allows you to listen for specific lifecycle events on specific component instances. Example: This component is about to be validated.

FIGURE 9-1 Categories of events in JSF and meaning of each category

processing lifecycle phase. Phase listeners can be written to listen for and react to the different phase events that occur during the processing of the lifecycle. *System events,* new in JSF 2.0, provide a deeper insight into the lifecycle by allowing you to listen, on a per-component level, for events such as "validation is about to occur on this component" and "this component is about to be rendered." Figure 9-1 illustrates the categories of events offered by JSF and adds some descriptive information about the events that are conceptually grouped into each category. Each category is shown with a different typeface to help you understand what each kind of event means in the context of when they are delivered, as shown later in Figures 9-4 and 9-5.

The Faces Event Listener Interfaces and Event Classes

To listen to the Faces events, a set of Java interfaces are provided by the Faces environment. Faces event listeners must implement these interfaces, which are illustrated in Figure 9-2.

EXPERT GROUP INSIGHT *Note that **PhaseEvent** extends **java.util.EventObject** directly, while **ValueChangeEvent** and **ActionEvent** extend from **FacesEvent**. The **PhaseListener** concept came after the core event model was defined, and it was decided to keep the two kinds of events separate in the class hierarchy because the **FacesEvent** subclasses all have a **UIComponent** as their source, while a **PhaseEvent** has the **Lifecycle** as its source.*

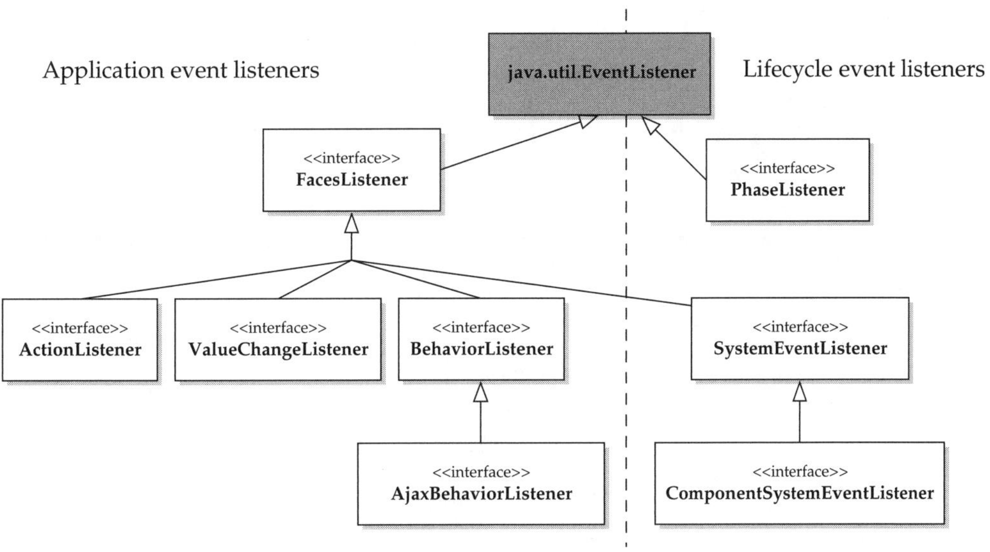

FIGURE 9-2 Faces event listener interfaces

As we'll explain shortly, exactly when and how Faces events are fired and processed is managed entirely by the JSF request processing lifecycle and there are even ways to manipulate the order of when certain types of events are processed.

After understanding the events and their corresponding listener interfaces, it's important to understand the kinds of classes to which these listeners can be attached. This information is shown in Figure 9-3. This diagram makes the following statements:

- The **Lifecycle** instance may have zero or more **PhaseListeners** attached to it.
- A **UIViewRoot** instance may have from zero to two **PhaseListeners** attached to it.
- Every **UIComponent** instance may have zero or more **SystemEventListeners** attached to it.
- Every instance of a component in the **javax.faces.component.html** package may have zero or more **ClientBehaviors** attached to it, and to each of those may be attached zero or more **BehaviorListener** interfaces. (The behavior system will be explained completely in Chapter 12.)
- Every **UIInput** instance may have zero or more **ValueChangeListeners** attached to it.
- Every **UICommand** may have zero or more **ActionListeners** attached to it.

When Are Faces Events Processed?

Faces events can be published throughout the lifetime of the JSF application. This lifetime can be broken down into three stages: startup, running the request processing lifecycle, and shutdown. Most of the time the application is running, it's in this middle stage:

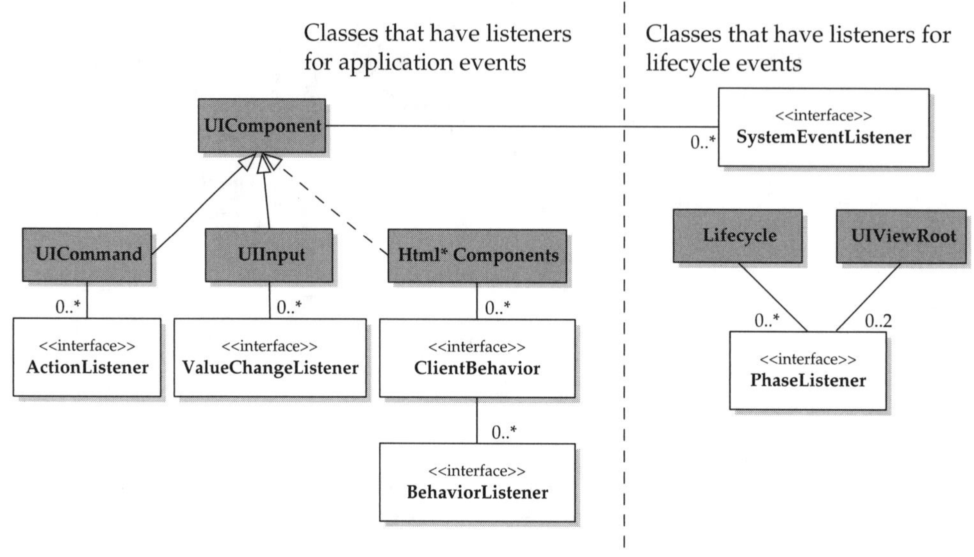

Figure 9-3 Faces classes that have listeners

processing requests. The events published during this stage, and more important, exactly when they are published, are shown in Figure 9-4.

The events that happen during startup and shutdown, as well as events that can happen at any point in the lifecycle, are shown in Figure 9-5.

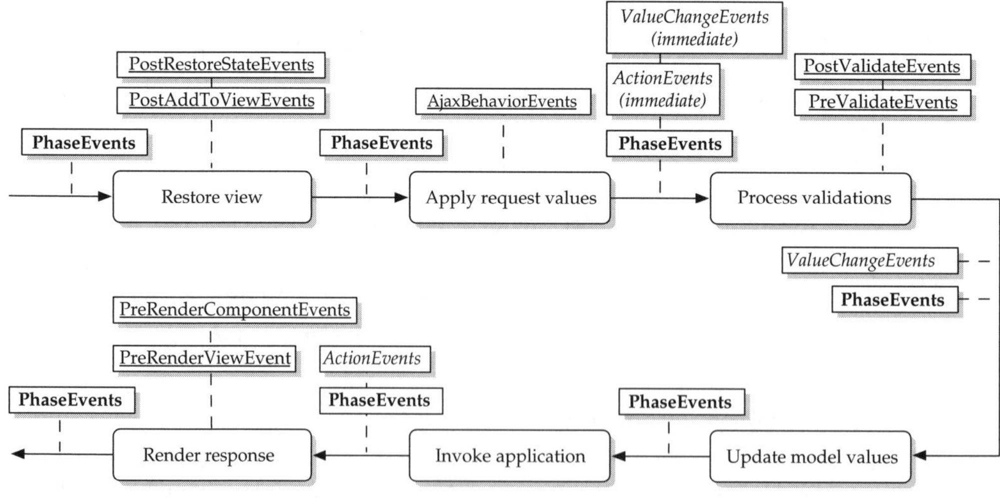

Figure 9-4 Faces events published during the request processing lifecycle

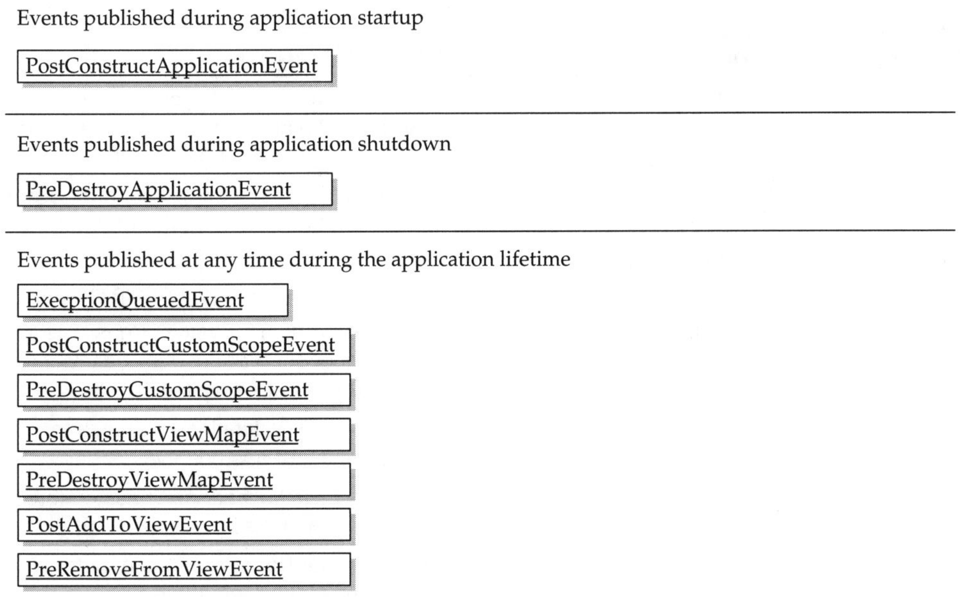

Events published during application startup

PostConstructApplicationEvent

Events published during application shutdown

PreDestroyApplicationEvent

Events published at any time during the application lifetime

ExecptionQueuedEvent

PostConstructCustomScopeEvent

PreDestroyCustomScopeEvent

PostConstructViewMapEvent

PreDestroyViewMapEvent

PostAddToViewEvent

PreRemoveFromViewEvent

FIGURE 9-5 Faces events published at other times during the application lifetime

Table 9-1 summarizes the different types of events and when they are processed in the request processing lifecycle.

Event Category	Event Type	When It Is Processed
Application Events	ActionEvent	At the completion of the Invoke Application phase unless the **immediate** flag is **true**; then it is processed at the end of the Apply Request Value phase.
	ValueChangeEvent	At the completion of the Process Validations phase unless the **immediate** flag is **true**; then it is processed at the end of the Apply Request Value phase.

TABLE 9-1 The Standard Event Types in JSF *(continued)*

Event Category	Event Type	When It Is Processed
Lifecycle Events	PhaseEvent	Before or after each lifecycle phase. Can write **PhaseListener** to listen and execute for specific lifecycle phase events.
	PostRestoreStateEvent	During the Restore View Phase, after every component has had its state restored.
	PostAddToViewEvent	During Restore View Phase, after a component has been added to a view.
	AjaxBehaviorEvent	During Apply Request Values Phase, as each component that has Ajax behavior has its **decode( )** method called.
	PostValidateEvent	During Process Validations Phase, after each component has been validated.
	PreValidateEvent	During Process Validations Phase, before each component has been validated.
	PreRenderComponentEvent	During Render Response Phase, before each component is rendered.
	PreRenderViewEvent	During Render Response Phase, before the entire view is rendered.
	PostConstructApplicationEvent	Before the first request has started through the request processing lifecycle.
	PreDestroyApplicationEvent	After the application has been directed to shut down by the container.
	ExeceptionQueuedEvent	During any phase, when an exception is queued for the **ExceptionHandler**.
	PostConstructCustomScopeEvent	During any phase, when a custom scope has been created. Custom scopes are discussed in Chapter 13.
	PreDestroyCustomScopeEvent	During any phase, when a custom scope is about to be destroyed.
	PostConstructViewMapEvent	During any phase, at the first point in time when the view scope is accessed. For example, via the evaluation of an EL expression that starts with **viewScope**, such as **#{viewScope.user}**.
	PreDestroyViewMapEvent	After the end of the Render Response phase.
	PreRemoveFromViewEvent	During any phase when a component is programmatically removed from the view. This happens when **remove( )** is called on the **List<UIComponent>** returned from **UIComponent.getChildren( )**.

Table 9-1 The Standard Event Types in JSF *(continued)*

TIP *It is possible to register* ***PhaseListeners*** *on the* ***UIViewRoot*** *of the view.* ***PhaseEvents*** *sent to listeners registered in this way still have the* ***Lifecycle*** *as their source and have the benefit of being scoped to a particular view rather than for every view in the application. Phase listeners can be registered on the* ***UIViewRoot*** *using the* ***<f:phaseListener>*** *tag or programmatically by calling the* ***addPhaseListener( )*** *method or the* ***setBeforePhaseListener( )*** *or* ***setAfterPhaseListener( )*** *methods. These latter two take a* ***MethodExpression*** *that points to a method whose signature matches that of the* ***afterPhase( )*** *method of the* ***PhaseListener*** *interface. The* ***<f:view>*** *tag also has attributes* ***beforePhaseListener*** *and* ***afterPhaseListener****, which accept method expression arguments with signatures* ***javax.faces.event.PhaseListener.beforePhase( )*** *and* ***javax.faces.event.PhaseListener.afterPhase( )****, respectively.*

Application Events

The following two sections examine the most important category of events in JSF, *application* events. These are important because they are the most convenient way to react to the user's manipulation of the UI components in the application.

The Anatomy of an Action Event

Consider the simple case of a Faces button (**<h:commandButton/>** or **UICommand**) being clicked on a page. As with any Web application, when the Faces button is clicked, the form is submitted and an HTTP Post is sent to the application server where the JSF application is running. As the JSF request processing lifecycle processes the request, it is in the Apply Request Values phase that the event generated by the button click is queued as an action event. If the HTTP request contains a component ID that matches the ID of the **UICommand** button that was clicked, then the Faces lifecycle knows that the button was clicked.

At this point, the only thing that can be done is to record that the button click occurred, since other UI components may still be receiving their updates from other incoming request values. To record the button click event, the Faces lifecycle instantiates an **ActionEvent** object and passes it as an argument to the **UICommand**'s **queueEvent( )** method. The event has now been queued for future processing. The Apply Request Values phase will complete and proceed to the other phases, Process Validations and Update Model Values. It isn't until the Invoke Application phase is reached successfully (providing no validation, conversion, or model update errors are encountered) that a corresponding **ActionListener** will process the **ActionEvent**.

NOTE *An* ***ActionEvent*** *can actually be processed immediately, that is, during the Apply Request Values phase (instead of waiting until the Invoke Application phase), but only if the* ***UICommand****'s* ***immediate*** *attribute was set to* ***true****. More information on the effects of setting the* ***immediate*** *attribute is provided later in the chapter.*

So far, what has taken place has occurred behind the scenes, being handled automatically by the Faces lifecycle. At this point the **ActionEvent** has been recorded and queued. It is now time for your code to take over. Following the standard operating procedure as per the JavaBeans specification, you must provide an associated **ActionListener** that is listening for the incoming **ActionEvent**.

In general, to handle events in Faces you can write a custom listener class that implements the appropriate interface (**javax.faces.event.ActionListener** for action events) and then bind it to the UI component (in this case, **UICommand**). For action events, it is also possible to just write either an action method or an action listener method. An *action method* is simply a Java method that you can place in a backing bean that takes no arguments and returns a **String**. Action methods are actually handled by a built-in *default* **ActionListener** that takes the returned **String** value from the action method and passes it to the **NavigationHandler** in order to determine if a navigation is warranted. If no navigation is needed after an action event, you can write an action listener method. In contrast to an action method, an *action listener method* simply executes and no navigation is expected as a result of the execution of the method. As a result, the action listener method returns **void** and accepts a single **ActionEvent** as an argument.

An action method is bound to a **UICommand** (or any component that implements **ActionSource**) by setting the **action** attribute with the method expression of the action method. An action listener method is bound in a similar way but to the component's **actionListener** attribute instead. To see examples of both an action method and an action listener method, recall the **confirm.jsp** page in the example application from Chapter 2. In the page there is a **commandButton** whose **action** attribute contains the method expression to invoke the **addConfirmedUser( )** method:

```
<h:commandButton value="Confirm" action="#{UserBean.addConfirmedUser}" />
```

The source code for the action method is as follows:

```
public String addConfirmedUser() {
  // This method would call a database or other service and
  // add the confirmed user information.
  System.out.println("Adding new user…");
  return "success";
}
```

As you can see, it follows the standard signature of an action method with no arguments and returns a **String** value. In this example, it simply prints a message to the console and returns "success," but in a real application it would probably call another method that interacts with a database and the returned result would be based on whether the operation succeeded. This returned value is then used to determine if a navigation is needed. For example, if the addition of a new user somehow failed, a "failure" **String** value could be returned and a navigation to an error page could occur. (Of course, a corresponding navigation case would have to be added to **faces-config.xml** for the **NavigationHandler** to handle this.) The key point to remember with an action method is that it relies on the built-in default **ActionListener** to invoke it and then pass this value to the **NavigationHandler** in order to determine if a navigation is needed.

If no navigation was needed after the action event was processed, an action listener method could be used instead of an action method. As mentioned earlier, in contrast to an action method, an action listener method takes a single argument of type **ActionEvent** and has a **void** return type. And instead of binding to the **action** attribute, the action listener method is bound to the UI component's **actionListener** attribute. The following line shows how to bind an action listener method to a Faces **UICommand** button:

```
<h:commandButton value="Confirm"
actionListener="#{UserBean.addConfirmedUserListenerAction}" />
```

And the action listener method could look like this:

```
public void addConfirmedUserListenerAction(ActionEvent ae) {
  // This method would call a database or other service
  // and add the confirmed user information.
  System.out.println("Adding new user…");
}
```

Notice the action listener method takes an **ActionEvent** as its single argument and has a return type of **void**. Other than the fact that an action method has the ability to incur a Faces navigation after execution, uses of action methods and action listener methods are basically identical.

Handling an Action Event Earlier in the Faces Lifecycle

As you recall from earlier in the chapter, action events are normally processed during the Invoke Application phase; however, there are times when you would want the action (or action listener) method to execute earlier, such as before validation during the Apply Request Values phase. For example, you may want to provide a Cancel button that calls a method before validating the field values. To short-circuit the processing of the action event, one simply sets the UI component's **immediate** attribute to **true**.

For example:

```
<h:commandButton value="Confirm"
action="#{UserBean.addConfirmedUser}" immediate="true" />
```

Upon execution, the **addConfirmedUser( )** method will execute at the end of the Apply Request Values phase instead of the Invoke Application phase. This short-circuits the normal flow of events and immediately causes the action event to be processed before any validation occurs.

NOTE *An important point about setting a button's **immediate** attribute to **true** is that when retrieving another input component's value (using **getValue( )** in an action/action listener method) as a result of clicking the button, getting the correct value of that input component is not guaranteed unless the input component's **immediate** attribute is also set to **true**.*

The Anatomy of a Value Change Event

Having stepped through what happens during an action event, we'll now step through what happens during a value change event. As you recall from earlier in the chapter, a *value change event* is an event that is used to indicate when a value of a UI component, such as an input field, has changed. In general, value change events handle changes in the values of UI components that implement either **ValueHolder** or **EditableValueHolder** interfaces. A common example of a value change event is when an input field (**UIinput**) has been updated. Recall the scenario earlier in the chapter, where you might want to capture the event when the Zip Code field has been filled in so that the server can auto-fill a City field. Another common example is when implementing dependent lists of values in drop-down menus—for example, when an item such as a particular state has been selected in one menu, then the dependent select menu could display the appropriate cities that reside in the chosen state. Handling change events improves the overall usability of a Faces application, and when coupled with a small JavaScript callout (**onchange** or **onclick**) on the client to auto-submit when the change occurs, the user interface can react based on small value change events as opposed to the usual submitting a form or clicking a button.

The behind-the-scenes plumbing of a value change event is basically the same as the action event described earlier. Consider a simple example where a JSP page has a single input field (**UIInput**) and a button (**UICommand**). If the page is run and some text is entered and then the button is clicked to submit the form, a value change event will be fired. Similar to the action event, the JSF request processing lifecycle will automatically fire a value change event by instantiating a **ValueChangeEvent** object and passing it as an argument to the **UIInput**'s **queueEvent( )** method.

Even though the value change event has been fired, there is no code yet to handle the event. Similar to an action event, a value change event can be handled in several ways, ranging from writing a custom value change listener class that implements the **ValueChangeListener** interface, to simply writing a value change listener method that uses the default value change listener provided by the Faces runtime. To react to a value change event, the following method can be used by the default value change listener.

```
public void valueChangeMethod(ValueChangeEvent vce) {
  System.out.println("In valueChangeMethod: A value was changed!");
}
```

This method can reside in a managed bean and be value-bound to an input field (or any UI component that holds a value) using

```
<h:inputText valueChangeListener="#{backing_bean.valueChangeMethod}"/>
```

When the application is run and a value is entered into the input field and the form is submitted by clicking the button, the **valueChangeMethod( )** will be executed because the value of the input field was changed from its initial empty value to a new value with the entered text. However, unlike the action event in which the event is processed during the Invoke Application phase, value change events are processed in the Process Validations phase. A subsequent resubmission of the form without changing the value in the input field will not cause the value change listener method to execute.

You can cause the value of an input component to be set immediately, before any other input components during the Apply Request Values phase, by setting its **immediate** attribute to **true**. This is needed in certain cases to avoid validation errors when processing value change events. You will see an example of this later in the chapter.

Writing Custom Action and Value Change Listeners

So far you have seen how to write methods that use the default action and value change listeners. These methods were directly associated with UI components by using their **action** or **actionlistener** JSP tag attributes, like this:

```
<h:commandButton value="Confirm" action="#{UserBean.addConfirmedUser}" />
```

or like this:

```
<h:commandButton value="Confirm" actionlistener="#{UserBean.addConfirmedUser}" />
```

In addition to using the default listeners, you can write your own action or value change listener classes. These classes simply implement either the **ActionListener** or **ValueChangeListener** interface. The following code is an example of a simple custom action listener class. Notice the **process Action( )** method that is overridden to process the actual action event.

```
package com.jsfcompref;
import javax.faces.event.ActionListener;
import javax.faces.event.ActionEvent;
public class MyActionListener implements ActionListener {
  public MyActionListener() {
    }
  public void processAction(ActionEvent ae) {
    System.out.println("MyActionListener is processing an action event!");
  }
}
```

To use the custom action listener class, **MyActionListener**, you can associate it with a UI component using a nested **<f:actionlistener />** tag as follows.

```
<h:commandButton value="Click Me!">
  <f:actionListener type="com.jsfcompref.MyActionListener"/>
</h:commandButton>
```

Notice that in this case the action listener tag uses the **type** attribute to refer directly to the full Java classpath of the custom action listener. As expected, when this page is run and when the button is clicked, the **processAction( )** method will execute and print a message to the console.

In a similar fashion, a custom value change listener class that implements the **ValueChangeListener** interface could also be created like this:

```
package com.jsfcompref;
import javax.faces.event.ValueChangeListener;
import javax.faces.event.ValueChangeEvent;
public class MyValueChangeListener implements ValueChangeListener {
  public MyValueChangeListener() {
  }
  public void processValueChange(ValueChangeEvent vce) {
    System.out.println("MyValueChangeListener is processing a " +
                       "value change event!");
  }
}
```

To use the custom value change listener **MyValueChangeListener** class, you can associate it with any UI component that holds a value using a nested **<f:valueChangelistener />** tag as follows.

```
<h:inputText value="foo">
  <f:valueChangeListener type="com.jsfcompref.MyValueChangeListener"/>
</h:inputText>
<h:commandButton value="Click me!"/>
```

Similar to the action listener tag, **valueChangeListener** also uses a **type** attribute to refer directly to the value change listener class using its full Java classpath. When the page containing this code is run, the user can then change the current value (from "foo") in the input field and click the submit button to issue a postback request. During the Apply Request Value phase of the request processing lifecycle, the Faces runtime will see that the value of the input field was changed between the initial and postback requests and **MyValueChangeListener**'s. The **processValueChange( )** method will execute and print a message to the console.

Many times it is useful to submit a form without requiring the user to click a submit button. For example, consider the situation in which you want to auto-fill the city and state after a user has entered a Zip code. In this case, setting the JavaScript callout **onchange** attribute of the Zip Code input field to "**this.form.submit( )**" will cause the form to be submitted automatically when the field on the client has changed without requiring the user to click a submit button.

```
<h:inputText value="foo" onchange="this.form.submit();">
  <f:valueChangeListener type="com.jsfcompref.MyValueChangeListener"/>
</h:inputText>
```

After the user enters a value and tabs out of the input field, the JavaScript callout **onchange** will execute the JavaScript function **this.form.submit( )** and the form will be submitted by the browser client. Since a value was changed in the field, the custom value change listener (**MyValueChangeListener**) will also execute its **processValueChange( )** method as well.

Table 9-2 summarizes the alternate ways to work with action and value change events showing examples using both **<h:commandButton/>** and **<h:inputText/>** UI components:

Listener Type	Code Usage Sample
Default action listener with action method	`<h:commandButton value="Click me!" **action**="#{*ManagedBean.actionMethod*}" />`
Default action listener with action listener method	`<h:commandButton value="Click me!" **actionlistener**="#{*ManagedBean .actionListenerMethod*}" />`
Custom action listener class	`<h:commandButton value="Click me!" > <f:**actionlistener** type="*package .CustomActionListener*" /> </h:commandButton>`
Default value change listener with value change listener method	`<h:inputText value="foo" **valuechangelistener**=" #{*ManagedBean.valueChangeListenerMethod*}" />`
Custom value change listener class	`<h:inputText value="foo" > <f:**valueChangeListener** type="*package.CustomValueChangeListener* "/> </h:inputText>`

Table 9-2 Alternative Ways to Use Action and Value Change Listeners

More Faces Event Examples

To gain a firm understanding of value change listeners, it will be useful to work through more examples. These examples are based on the Zip code scenario mentioned earlier in the chapter in which City and State fields are automatically filled in after the user provides a value in the Zip Code input field and then tabs out of the Zip Code field. As explained, this mechanism lets the user avoid entering the city and state manually. The first example shows how to implement the basic, auto-fill functionality by using a value change event and listener. This example also shows how to avoid triggering a validation error by using the **immediate** attribute. The second example expands on the first by showing how to conditionally render a portion of the UI also by using a value change listener where a UI component's **rendered** property is toggled when a checkbox is clicked.

Using a Value Change Event to Auto-Fill Fields

For this first example, consider a form with the following input fields: Name, Zip Code, City, and State, like the one shown in Figure 9-6. When the user fills in a value in the Zip Code field and moves the cursor out of that field, the City and State fields are automatically populated with the correct values.

Building this example requires the processing of a value change event that is associated with the Zip Code input field. The event is triggered when the user enters or changes a value, and then tabs out of the field. For this example, we'll use the default value change listener along with a value change listener method.

The initial source code for the facelet page **main.xhtml** with the four fields is as follows:

```
<!DOCTYPE html PUBLIC "-//W3C//DTD XHTML 1.0 Transitional//EN"
"http://www.w3.org/TR/xhtml1/DTD/xhtml1-transitional.dtd">
<html xmlns="http://www.w3.org/1999/xhtml"
      xmlns:h="http://java.sun.com/jsf/html"
      xmlns:f="http://java.sun.com/jsf/core">
<h:head>
  <title>A Simple JavaServer Faces 2.0 View</title>
</h:head>
<h:body>
  <h2>Address Form</h2>
  <h:form prependId="false">
    <h:panelGrid columns="2">
      <h:outputLabel value="Name:"/>
      <h:inputText id="inputname" binding="#{zipAutoFill.inputName}"/>
      <h:outputLabel value="Zip Code:"/>
      <h:inputText id="inputzip" binding="#{zipAutoFill.inputZip}"
                   valueChangeListener="#{zipAutoFill.zipAutoFillListener}"
                   onchange="this.form.submit()"/>
      <h:outputLabel value="City:" />
      <h:inputText id="inputcity" binding="#{zipAutoFill.inputCity}"/>
      <h:outputLabel value="State:"/>
      <h:inputText id="inputstate" binding="#{zipAutoFill.inputState}"/>
      <h:commandButton value="Submit"/>
    </h:panelGrid>
   </h:form>
</h:body>
</html>
```

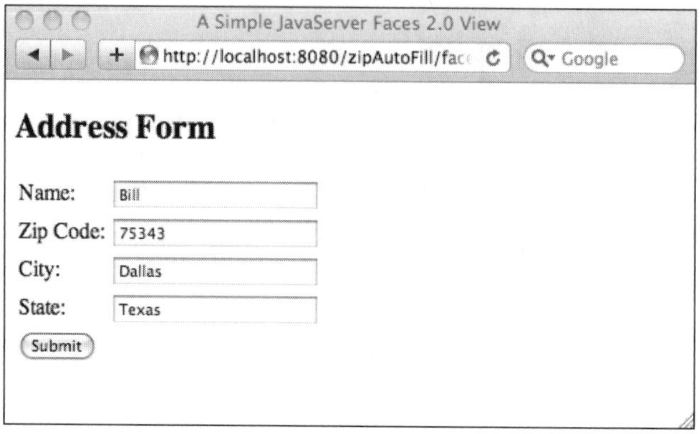

FIGURE 9-6 An example name and address form, with the City and State automatically populated

Note that we are using the **binding** attribute to cause the actual **UIComponent** instances to be pushed into the **zipAutoFill** managed bean. This approach allows the backing bean code to manipulate the state of the UI directly, but it should be used with caution. Caution is necessary because using the **binding** attribute can be seen as a violation of the separation of concerns in the Model-View-Controller pattern: by using the **binding** attribute, you are directly inserting View information into a class that would otherwise contain only model information. On the other hand, this "violation" of the MVC pattern is really a matter of perspective. If you consider this particular managed bean, **zipAutoFill**, to be a part of the View logic, then such violations disappear. The important lesson is: always be aware of how you are using your managed beans. If you are using the **binding** attribute, that's fine, but avoid having both value-bound and component-bound properties in a single managed bean class.

The first thing to notice is that each **inputText** component is bound to a set of **HtmlInputText** UI components that are declared in a backing bean Java class registered as a managed bean named **zipAutoFill**. Here is the source code for the **zipAutoFill** managed bean:

```
package com.jsfcompref;

import javax.faces.bean.ManagedBean;
import javax.faces.bean.RequestScoped;
import javax.faces.component.html.HtmlInputText;
import javax.faces.event.ValueChangeEvent;

@ManagedBean(name="zipAutoFill")
@RequestScoped
public class ZipAutoFillBackingBean {

  private HtmlInputText inputName, inputZip, inputCity, inputState;
  public void zipAutoFillListener(ValueChangeEvent vce) {
    String zip = vce.getNewValue().toString();

    StringBuilder city = new StringBuilder();
    StringBuilder state = new StringBuilder();
    performLookup(zip, city, state);
```

```
    inputCity.setValue(city.toString());
    inputState.setValue(state.toString());
  }

  private void performLookup(String zip, StringBuilder city,
        StringBuilder state) {
    // Production code would actually perform the lookup.
    // For now, we assume that every possible zip code is
    // in Dallas, Texas.
    city.append("Dallas");
    state.append("Texas");

  }
  // JavaBeans getters and setters are required but are omitted here.

}
```

In order to trigger the automatic lookup and filling in of the City and State input fields when a Zip code is entered, a value change listener method is added to the **zipAutoFill** managed bean. This method is **zipAutoFillListener( )** in the preceding code. The logic to actually look up the city and state based on a Zip code is left as a task for the reader and is outside the scope of this exercise, so in this example the value change listener method will just set hard-coded city and state names to the **HtmlInputText** city and state components. This listener is added to the **inputzip** text field via the **valueChangeListener** attribute.

Notice the addition of a JavaScript callout **onchange( )** with a value of "**this.form .submit( )**". Recall that this enables the form to auto-submit itself using JavaScript when the user changes a value and tabs out of the field.

The example will now perform as expected. When a value is entered into the Zip Code field, the form auto-submits itself and values are automatically provided for the City and State fields by the value change listener method.

This example works fine as is, but if any validations are added to any of the input fields, the auto-submit could cause a validation error to appear as the user tabs out of the Zip Code field. For example, if the Name field (**inputName**) is changed to be a required field (by setting its **required** attribute to **true**), a validation error will be triggered if the Name field is empty when the form is auto-submitted. This situation is shown in Figure 9-7.

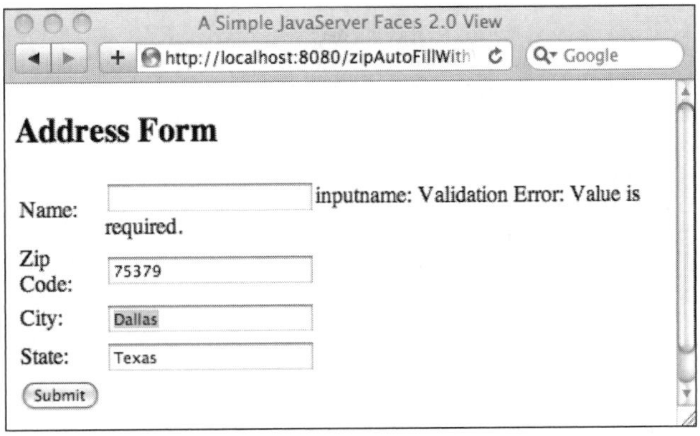

FIGURE 9-7 The form with a validation error appearing

Also, in order to show the validation error message, the *inputname* field will need a corresponding **<h:message />** component associated with it.

```
<h:inputText id="inputname" required="true"
binding="#{zipAutoFill.inputName}"/>
<h:message for="inputname"/>
```

Now the form has an annoying validation error that is triggered whenever a value is entered into the Zip Code field even before the submit button is clicked. This is exactly the situation that the **immediate** attribute was designed to avoid. The **immediate** attribute allows you to bypass validation for a subset of the components in the view. The best way to use the **immediate** attribute is to think of the components in the view as two logical groups: those that need partial validation, and those that do not. By placing **immediate="true"** on every component that should participate in the partial validation, and by *not* having this attribute on the rest of the components, validation is bypassed for those components that do not have the attribute.

The form input fields now have the following changes:

```
<!DOCTYPE html PUBLIC "-//W3C//DTD XHTML 1.0 Transitional//EN"
"http://www.w3.org/TR/xhtml1/DTD/xhtml1-transitional.dtd">
<html xmlns="http://www.w3.org/1999/xhtml"
      xmlns:h="http://java.sun.com/jsf/html"
      xmlns:f="http://java.sun.com/jsf/core">
<h:head>
  <title>A Simple JavaServer Faces 2.0 View</title>
</h:head>
<h:body>
  <h2>Address Form</h2>
  <h:form prependId="false">
    <h:panelGrid columns="2">
      <h:outputLabel value="Name:"/>
      <h:panelGroup>
          <h:inputText id="inputname" binding="#{zipAutoFill.inputName}"
                       required="true"/>
          <h:message for="inputname" />
      </h:panelGroup>
      <h:outputLabel value="Zip Code:"/>
      <h:inputText id="inputzip" binding="#{zipAutoFill.inputZip}"
                   valueChangeListener="#{zipAutoFill.zipAutoFillListener}"
                   immediate="true"
                   onchange="document.getElementById('autofill').click();"/>
      <h:outputLabel value="City:" />
      <h:inputText id="inputcity" binding="#{zipAutoFill.inputCity}"
                   immediate="true" />
      <h:outputLabel value="State:"/>
      <h:inputText id="inputstate" binding="#{zipAutoFill.inputState}"
                   immediate="true" />
      <h:commandButton value="Submit"/>
    </h:panelGrid>
```

```
    <h:commandButton style="visibility: hidden" id="autofill"
                     value="autofill" immediate="true" />
  </h:form>
</h:body>
</html>
```

We have added **required="true"** to **inputname**. We have added **immediate="true"** to **inputzip**, **inputcity**, and **inputstate**, and we have added a new **h:commandButton** with id **autofill**. This button is hidden from the user using the **style="visibility: hidden"** CSS attribute, but it still exists in the page for the sole purpose of commencing the partial validation when the **onchange** event happens. Because this button has **immediate="true"**, clicking it, even when done via JavaScript as shown here, causes the form to be submitted in such a way that only components that also have **immediate="true"** are validated, while the others are excluded from validation.

NOTE *The example shown can be implemented so that its behavior is more user-friendly by using* Ajax. *This will prevent the entire page from having to be resubmitted to the client just to see the values of the dependent fields being auto-filled. Techniques for implementing Ajax applications are covered in Chapter 12.*

Extending the Value Change Example

The preceding example illustrated a common user interface behavior in which values of one or more input fields are updated as a result of information provided by another input field. Another very common user interface behavior is to simply change a user interface element property, such as to **readonly** or **disabled**. In Faces, this behavior is even easier to implement than the preceding example but is achieved in largely the same manner.

Consider the following enhancement to the Zip code example. To enable the user to enter additional information into the form, another input field called More Info is added. However, this input field will not display initially. Instead, a checkbox labeled "Add more info?" will be included. When the user clicks the box, it renders the More Info input field (using a new text area) to receive more information.

To implement this new functionality onto the same form in the preceding example, you first add the following UI components to the page in between the last field and the submit button:

```
<h:outputLabel value="Add more Info"/>
<h:selectBooleanCheckbox />
<h:outputLabel value="More Info" rendered="#{zipAutoFill.infoRendered}"/>
<h:inputTextarea />
```

NOTE *In a production application, the* ***for*** *attribute of* ***h:outputLabel*** *should be set to the* ***id*** *of the associated input component for accessibility.*

Because the new UI component tags are added to the Facelet page, you must also add declarations for the new components in the **zipAutoFill** backing bean.

```
private HtmlInputTextarea moreInfo;
private HtmlSelectBooleanCheckbox moreInfoCheckbox;
```

To keep track of the render state of the More Info field, add a **boolean** variable called **infoRendered** and set it initially to **false**:

```
boolean infoRendered = false;
```

In addition to the declarations, you must also add the associated JavaBean getter and setter accessors for each new bean property in order to be able to access/update the properties in the application.

In order to toggle the **infoRendered boolean** variable when the checkbox is clicked, a value change listener method is added to the backing bean. Similar to before, once the value change event is processed, the Render Response phase must be initiated, by calling **renderResponse( )**, in order to avoid validations.

```
public void toggleMoreInfo(ValueChangeEvent vce) {
  setInfoRendered((Boolean) vce.getNewValue());
}
```

In the Facelet page, the new UI component tags are bound to the declarations in the backing bean. The **<h:selectBooleanCheckbox>** tag will have the following modifications:

```
<h:selectBooleanCheckbox binding="#{zipAutoFill.moreInfoCheckbox}"
              immediate="true"
              onchange="document.getElementById('autofill').click();"
              valueChangeListener="#{zipAutoFill.toggleMoreInfo}"/>
```

Explanations of the attribute settings follow:

- **binding** UI component binding to declared instance of **HtmlSelectBooleanCheckbox** in backing bean
- **immediate** Immediacy setting, which avoids validation processing
- **valueChangeListener** Bound to value change listener method that toggles the **infoRendered boolean** variable to render the More Info field in backing bean
- **onchange** JavaScript method to auto-submit the form when the checkbox is clicked.

The More Info output label and text area components must now be modified to render conditionally based on the value of the **infoRendered boolean** variable, as shown next:

```
<h:outputLabel value="More Info" rendered="#{zipAutoFill.infoRendered}"/>
<h:inputTextarea id="moreinfo" binding="#{zipAutoFill.moreInfo}"
                 rendered="#{zipAutoFill.infoRendered}"/>
```

The resultant view is shown in Figure 9-8.

This example has shown how through proper usage of value change events in Faces, one can implement a very useful user interface behavior.

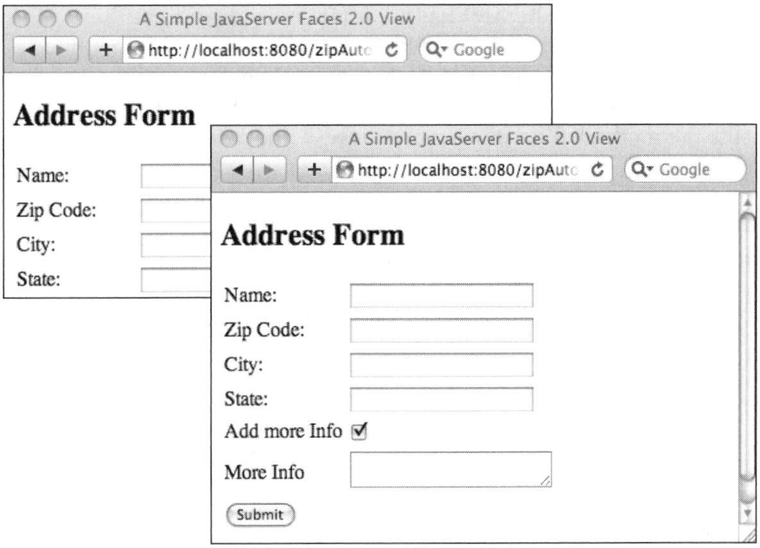

FIGURE 9-8 Toggling the More Info text box with a checkbox

Working with Phase Events and Listeners

Recall that in addition to application events, the other category of event in Faces is the lifecycle event. Within this category are two kinds of events: *phase events* and *system events.* Phase events are events that are processed in between each phase of the Faces request processing lifecycle. Since they have the ability to execute in between the different phases, phase events and their respective phase listeners provide a unique way to jump into the execution of the lifecycle and check or alter values/properties of any object in a Faces application. System events will be discussed in the section following this one.

Using a PhaseListener to Observe the Faces Lifecycle in Action

One of the most useful things to do is to write a phase listener that executes at every phase in the Faces lifecycle and reports to either a logging facility (or even just to the console) when the different phases of the lifecycle are processed. This type of phase listener is very easy to write, and it can be used as a tool to confirm the correct execution of events and phases based on different criteria, such as when certain UI components have their **immediate** property set to **true,** or if a certain listener method short-circuits the lifecycle directly by calling the **RenderResponse( )** method of the Faces context.

To build a phase listener to process the phase events that are emitted by the changing of lifecycle phases, simply create a Java class that implements the **PhaseListener** interface. We begin by creating the following skeleton, called **MyPhaseListener**:

```
package com.jsfcompref;
import javax.faces.event.PhaseListener;
public class MyPhaseListener implements PhaseListener {
  public MyPhaseListener() {
  }
  // Implement PhaseListener methods here.
}
```

Next, the methods **beforePhase( )**, **afterPhase( )**, and **getPhaseId( )** must be overridden and implemented. Both the **beforePhase( )** and **afterPhase( )** methods accept a single argument of type **PhaseEvent** and execute either before or after the phase event is passed to the methods. Each phase event has an associated phase ID and can be used to pick when to execute the method. Since the **beforePhase( )** and **afterPhase( )** methods execute for all phase events, if you want to perform a specific action for a single phase of the lifecycle, you can provide some simple logic to check the phase ID of the incoming phase event and then conditionally execute your code based on that check. For example, the following **beforePhase( )** method will print a message "Processing new Request!" to the console, but only when it processes a **RESTORE_VIEW** phase event. The subsequent statement will print a message "before - ..*phase id*." for all phase events of the lifecycle:

```
public void beforePhase(PhaseEvent pe) {
  if (pe.getPhaseId() == PhaseId.RESTORE_VIEW) {
    System.out.println("Processing new Request!");
  }
  System.out.println("before - " + pe.getPhaseId().toString());
}
```

A subsequent **afterPhase( )** method can be similarly coded as

```
public void afterPhase(PhaseEvent pe) {
  System.out.println("after - " + pe.getPhaseId().toString());
  if (pe.getPhaseId() == PhaseId.RENDER_RESPONSE) {
    System.out.println("Done with Request!\n");
  }
}
```

Notice how this method prints an *after phase* message for all phases. It also prints a special "Done with Request!" when it encounters the final Render Response phase.

The final method to implement is **getPhaseId( )**, which is used to determine which phase this phase listener will process events for. Since it must execute during every phase change, it returns **ANY_PHASE**.

```
public PhaseId getPhaseId() {
  return PhaseId.ANY_PHASE;
}
```

The code to the phase listener is now complete, but to use it in the Faces application, its full classpath must be registered. One way is to specify it in the **faces-config.xml** as follows:

```
<lifecycle>
  <phase-listener>com.jsfcompref.MyPhaseListener</phase-listener>
</lifecycle>
```

TIP *Beginning with Faces 1.2, it is also possible to register phase listeners directly on the **UIViewRoot** and avoid the necessity of including them in the **faces-config.xml** file.*

Once registered in a Faces application, the phase listener will report all of the lifecycle phases being entered during execution of the application. For example, upon an initial, nonpostback request to a Faces application, the output in the console will look like this:

```
...
Processing new Request!
before - RESTORE_VIEW 1
after - RESTORE_VIEW 1
before - RENDER_RESPONSE 6
after - RENDER_RESPONSE 6
Done with Request!
```

The text in boldface is what is returned from **getPhaseId().toString()**. This confirms what was presented in Chapter 3 in that during an initial Faces request, where no data is being posted back to the application, the request processing lifecycle simply creates a new view of UI components (in the Restore View phase) and then renders a response to the client.

A subsequent request that now posts form information back to the application will cause the following output, since the entire lifecycle will be processed.

```
...
Processing new Request!
before - RESTORE_VIEW 1
after - RESTORE_VIEW 1
before - APPLY_REQUEST_VALUES 2
after - APPLY_REQUEST_VALUES 2
before - PROCESS_VALIDATIONS 3
after - PROCESS_VALIDATIONS 3
before - UPDATE_MODEL_VALUES 4
after - UPDATE_MODEL_VALUES 4
before - INVOKE_APPLICATION 5
after - INVOKE_APPLICATION 5
before - RENDER_RESPONSE 6
after - RENDER_RESPONSE 6
Done with Request!
```

Once a phase listener like this has been installed, you can observe the effects of several changes that can affect the processing order of the Faces lifecycle. For example, a page with a single **commandButton** that is bound to an action method, which prints out a message "in action method," could have its **immediate** property set to **true**. When the application is run, it will execute the action method at the end of the Apply Request Values phase, as opposed to the Invoke Application phase, where it would normally execute, as shown next:

```
Processing new Request!
before - RESTORE_VIEW 1
after - RESTORE_VIEW 1
before - APPLY_REQUEST_VALUES 2
Action event processed...
after - APPLY_REQUEST_VALUES 2
before - RENDER_RESPONSE 6
after - RENDER_RESPONSE 6
Done with Request!
```

In addition to tracking action events, a phase listener such as this could track exactly when a value change listener method executes by simply using a print statement such as "In value change listener method." You can then observe where it executes in the lifecycle. Also recall that in the Zip code example, the value change listener methods also jumped directly to the Render Response phase by calling the **RenderResponse( )** method on the Faces context. This will be observable with the same phase listener example.

More detailed examples of the **PhaseListener** facility will be shown in Chapter 13.

Working with SystemEvents and Listeners

The last major kind of events in Faces are the **SystemEvent** and its cousin **ComponentSystemEvent**. These events are similar to phase events in that they provide insight into the application as it runs, but **SystemEvent**s allow a much more detailed insight than offered by **PhaseEvent**s.

EXPERT GROUP INSIGHT *The system event facility, and the events published using it, were originally designed to enable other major new features in JSF 2.0, such as composite components, resource loading, and Ajax. This facility had a general utility, however, so the expert group decided to expose it as a publicly accessible feature.*

At a high level, the system event facility is a simple publish/subscribe event bus. Like "flash," the term "event bus" is another term borrowed from computer hardware. In hardware, a bus is the name given to the hardware that transfers data between different parts of the computer system, such as moving instructions from memory to the CPU. In JSF, the event bus is a software model that allows you to register one or more listeners for various kinds of system events, shown earlier in Table 9-1, and receive notifications when the events occur. The system event bus differs from application events in that system events are delivered as soon as they are published, whereas application events are queued and delivered later.

Take a moment and review the master-detail example from the beginning of this chapter. That example used the **<f:event type="preRenderComponent" listener="#{model .checkDRPL}"/>** tag nested inside of an **<h:outputText>** component. This caused the following method to be called before the component is rendered:

```
public void checkDRPL(ComponentSystemEvent cse) throws AbortProcessingException {
  ValueHolder lastName = (ValueHolder) cse.getComponent();
  // ...
}
```

Note that we are able to ask the argument **ComponentSystemEvent** for the UI component that is the source of the event. Let's take another example that shows the use of **SystemEvent**, which is the base class for **ComponentSystemEvent** and is intended for those system events that do not necessarily pertain to individual component instances.

We return to the **ZipAutoFill** example and use the **PostConstructApplicationEvent** to populate the Zip Code database, while we use the **PreDestroyApplicationEvent** to deallocate this database. First, let's create a **faces-config.xml** file and add the following content to it:

```
<faces-config xmlns="http://java.sun.com/xml/ns/javaee"
    xmlns:xsi="http://www.w3.org/2001/XMLSchema-instance"
    xsi:schemaLocation="http://java.sun.com/xml/ns/javaee
```

```
http://java.sun.com/xml/ns/javaee/web-facesconfig_2_0.xsd"
    version="2.0">
  <application>
    <system-event-listener>
        <system-event-listener-class>
com.jsfcompref.ApplicationListener</system-event-listener-class>
        <system-event-class>
javax.faces.event.PostConstructApplicationEvent</system-event-class>
    </system-event-listener>
    <system-event-listener>
        <system-event-listener-class>
com.jsfcompref.ApplicationListener</system-event-listener-class>
        <system-event-class>
javax.faces.event.PreDestroyApplicationEvent</system-event-class>
    </system-event-listener>
  </application>
</faces-config>
```

These **<system-event-listener>** entries declare two **SystemEventListener** instances. Within the first, the **<system-event-class>** element states that the instance would like to listen for the **PostConstructApplicationEvent**, while within the second the **<system-event-listener>** states that the instance would like to listen for the **PreDestroyApplicationEvent**. It makes sense to have the same class for both instances because their uses are closely related, though any class that implements **SystemEventListener** is valid for the inside of the **<system-event-listener-class>** element.

The source code for the **ApplicationListener** is shown next.

```
package com.jsfcompref;

import java.util.HashMap;
import java.util.Map;
import javax.faces.application.Application;
import javax.faces.context.FacesContext;
import javax.faces.event.AbortProcessingException;
import javax.faces.event.PostConstructApplicationEvent;
import javax.faces.event.PreDestroyApplicationEvent;
import javax.faces.event.SystemEvent;
import javax.faces.event.SystemEventListener;

public class ApplicationListener implements SystemEventListener {

  public boolean isListenerForSource(Object app) {
    boolean result = false;
    result = (app instanceof Application);
    return result;
  }

  public void processEvent(SystemEvent event)
      throws AbortProcessingException {
      Map<String, Object> appMap =
        FacesContext.getCurrentInstance().getExternalContext().
        getApplicationMap();
    if (event instanceof PostConstructApplicationEvent) {
        appMap.put("zips", createZipDatabase());
```

```
    } else if (event instanceof PreDestroyApplicationEvent) {
      Map<String, Map<String, Object>> zips =
                   (Map<String, Map<String, Object>>)
                    appMap.remove("zips");
      zips.clear();
    }
  }

  public Map<String, Map<String, Object>> createZipDatabase() {
    Map<String, Map<String, Object>> result =
              new HashMap<String, Map<String, Object>>(1);

    Map<String, Object> innerMap = new HashMap<String, Object>(2);
    innerMap.put("city", "Dallas");
    innerMap.put("state", "Texas");

    String dallasZips[] = { "75201", "75202", ...};
    for (String zip : dallasZips) {
      result.put(zip, innerMap);
    }
    return result;
  }
}
```

The first two methods shown here are required for **SystemEventListener** implementations. The **isListenerForSource( )** method is called by the runtime to ask the listener, "here is the source of the event, are you interested in it?" This is an opportunity to differentiate among different kinds of event source classes. The **processEvent( )** method is called when the event actually fires. In this case, we interrogate the type of the **event** argument and take the appropriate action. The specifications for the **PostConstructApplicationEvent** and **PreDestroyApplicationEvent** guarantee that this **processEvent( )** will be called exactly twice, once at startup and once at shutdown. Therefore, it is safe to use the higher-performance **HashMap** class rather than the concurrency-safe **ConcurrentHashMap** because we know that the application will only be doing reads from the map. Finally, we need to modify the **zipAutoFill** bean's **performLookup( )** method to use this new database.

```
private void performLookup(String zip, StringBuilder city,
    StringBuilder state) {
  Map<String, Object> appMap =
    FacesContext.getCurrentInstance().getExternalContext().
    getApplicationMap();
  Map<String, Map<String, Object>> zips =
      (Map<String, Map<String, Object>>) appMap.get("zips");
  Map<String, Object> dataForZip = zips.get(zip);
  if (null != dataForZip) {
    city.append((String) dataForZip.get("city"));
    state.append((String) dataForZip.get("state"));
  } else {
    city.append("Unknown City");
    state.append("Unknown State, maybe Texas?");
  }

}
```

How SystemEvents Are Published

The system event facility was inspired by utilities such as Solaris dtrace, and GNU/Linux truss. These command-line UNIX utilities enable one to observe the operation of a program as it runs. For example, it is possible to trace all system calls that open files from the file system. The implementation of the system in Faces was designed to be very fast, so that calls to publish events, which will likely happen very frequently, do not bog down the running of the lifecycle. System events are published by calling the **publishEvent( )** method on the **javax .faces.application.Application** instance. This is a singleton class that can easily be accessed from anywhere using the **FacesContext.getCurrentInstance( ).getApplication( )** method.

There are two forms of **publishEvent( )**. The first form is shown here:

```
public void publishEvent(FacesContext context,
              Class<? Extends SystemEvent> systemEventClass,
            Object source);
```

The second argument is the **.class** for a Java class that extends the **SystemEvent** base class. Any such classes must have a public zero-argument constructor. The third argument is the source of the event. When the event is published, whatever you pass here is set as the **source** member of the **SystemEvent** instance, and passed to the listener.

The second form of **publishEvent( )** is shown next:

```
public void publishEvent(FacesContext context,
              Class<? Extends SystemEvent> systemEventClass,
            Class<?> sourceBaseType,
            Object source);
```

This second form has an additional argument, **sourceBaseType**. For performance reasons, the specification for the **publishEvent( )** method specifically excludes implementations from walking up the inheritance hierarchy of the source object. However, it is sometimes necessary to manually tell the system the base type of the source argument. This variant covers such cases.

How to Subscribe to SystemEvents

The other side of the **SystemEvent** equation is, naturally, how to subscribe to these events. Like many things in JSF, there is a Java API, a markup API, and an XML API that allow subscribing to events. The latter two APIs are built on top of the former. Let's examine the Java API first.

The Java API to Subscribe to SystemEvents

There are two classes that have **subscribeToEvent( )** methods: **Application**, and **UIComponent**. Use the **Application** version when you want to listen for direct **SystemEvent** subclasses. Use the **UIComponent** version when you want to listen for **ComponentSystemEvent** subclasses. The general form for **Application.subscribeToEvent( )** looks like this:

```
public void subscribeToEvent(Class< ? extends SystemEvent> systemEventClass,
              SystemEventListener yourListener);
```

The first argument is the type of event for which you want your listener to be called. The last argument is your listener instance. Another variant allows you to restrict your listener to be notified only if the source class matches a specific class.

```
public void subscribeToEvent(Class< ? extends SystemEvent> systemEventClass,
              Class<? sourceClass>,
              SystemEventListener yourListener);
```

The first and last arguments are the same as before. The second argument, which may be **null**, indicates the class that you would like to allow as the source for events.

As an alternative to manually calling **subscribeToEvent( )**, the **@ListenerFor** annotation may be placed on any **UIComponent** or **Renderer** class. The system scans for the presence of these annotations at the point in time when a **UIComponent** is created. The use of this annotation on a custom **UIComponent** looks like this:

```
@ListenerFor(systemEventClass=PreValidateEvent.class)
public class MyInput extends UIInput {
...
public void processEvent(ComponentSystemEvent event)
  throws AbortProcessingException {
  super.processEvent(event);
  // do any pre-validate stuff here
}
}
```

Note that **UIComponent** already implements **ComponentSystemEventListener** so every component instance is eligible to be a listener for **ComponentSystemEvent**s. Any time an instance of **MyInput** is used in a view, a call is made to **subscribeToEvent( )** on the **MyInput** instance, passing **PreValidateEvent.class** as the first argument and the **MyInput** instance as the second argument.

If you want to have a single class listen for multiple **ComponentSystemEvent**s, you can wrap your **@ListenerFor** annotation within **@ListenersFor**, as shown here:

```
@ListenersFor({
  @ListenerFor(systemEventClass=PostAddToViewEvent.class)
  @ListenerFor(systemEventClass=PostConstructViewMapEvent.class)
})
public class MyInput extends UIInput {
...
```

In this case your **processEvent( )** method must be capable of processing all the different kinds of **ComponentSystemEvent** subclasses listed in the **@ListenerFor** annotations.

The Markup API to Subscribe to SystemEvents

The **<f:event>** element was show earlier in the chapter; here is its general form.

```
<f:event type="one of the types listed below, or mentioned in @NamedEvent"
     listener="an EL expression that points to a method that
                returns void and takes a ComponentSystemEvent" />
```

Valid values for **type** are: **preRenderComponent**, **postAddToView**, **preValidate**, **postValidate**, or the value of the **shortName** attribute (implicit or explicit) on a class annotated with **@NamedEvent**. How to use **@NamedEvent** will be explained in the following section. The **<f:event>** element causes **subscribeToEvent( )** to be called on the parent **UIComponent** instance.

The XML API to Subscribe to SystemEvents

As shown earlier in the **ApplicationListener** example, it is possible to declare listener classes in the **faces-config.xml** file. The general form for this is shown here.

```
<faces-config>
  <application>
  <system-event-listener>
    <system-event-listener-class>fully qualified class name of a class
      that implements SystemEventListener</system-event-listener-class>
    <system-event-class>fully qualified class name of a class that
        extends javax.faces.event.SystemEvent</system-event-class>
    <source-class>OPTIONAL fully qualified class name of a class
     that will be the sourceClass argument to subscribeToEvent( )
    </source-class>
  </system-event-listener>
  </application>
</faces-config>
```

This code will cause **Application.subscribeToEvent( )** to be called with the specified arguments. If **<source-class>** is given, the variant of **subscribeToEvent( )** that takes a **sourceClass** argument is called instead.

General Rules for Creating Custom Application Events and Listeners

As you may have gathered by now, JavaServer Faces is extremely flexible, allowing for customization in numerous ways. Faces events and listeners are no exception, and building custom events and listeners is a fairly straightforward process. You will seldom need to do so, though, because most common Web application development tasks can be handled by the core Faces and phase events provided by the specification. Most often, when a specific need is found for a custom event type, it is within the context of building a complete custom Faces UI component and associated classes because the custom event type and listener are often tightly coupled.

If the situation does arise in which you must build custom event types and event listeners, here are the steps that you will follow:

1. Decide on a specific purpose for the custom event and listener type. For example, this could be a specialization of a common action or value change event, which fits into the context of usage of the custom component. For instance, a custom table component could implement a custom row change event and listener.
2. Create the custom event type, which must extend, directly or indirectly, **javax .faces.event.FacesEvent**. The event's constructor will contain the component (usually custom) with which this event should be associated. Most important, the **isAppropriateListener(FacesListener listener)** method must be overridden to inspect the argument **listener** and see if this event applies to the listener.

If so, this method returns **true**; otherwise, **false**. This is the single most important method in the custom event and listener API because it alone allows the core JSF runtime to deal with your custom event without knowing the specifics of the event or listener type.

3. Create the custom event listener interface that defines the behavior of the listener. It will extend, directly or indirectly, **FacesListener**.

The details of how an event is bound to specific types of components require an understanding of custom JSF component development, which is covered in Chapters 11, 12, and 13.

Creating Custom SystemEvent and ComponentSystemEvent Classes

Because **SystemEvent**s and **ComponentSystemEvent**s all use the same **SystemEventListener** and **ComponentSystemEventListener** interfaces, respectively, it is not necessary to create a custom listener interface when customizing system events. Therefore the task of creating custom system events involves only two steps.

1. If your event is specific to a **UIComponent,** subclass from **ComponentSystemEvent**; otherwise, subclass from **SystemEvent**.
2. Decide when you want to publish your event and place a call to **Application .publishEvent( )** or **UIComponent.publishEvent( )** at that point in the code.

If you are creating a **ComponentSystemEvent** subclass, and you want to make it available for use in the **<f:event>** element, you must attach a **@NamedEvent** annotation to your class. The general form for this is shown here:

```
package com.jsfcompref;
@NamedEvent(shortName="this optional element is what the user
            must put as the value of the type attribute
            on the f:event element")
public class RegistrationProcessedEvent extends ComponentSystemEvent {
...
```

If the **shortName** attribute is missing, the runtime derives it according to the following rules:

1. Get the unqualified class name, for example, **RegistrationProcessedEvent**.
2. Strip of the trailing "Event" characters, if present, for example, **RegistrationProcessed**.
3. Convert the first character to lowercase, for example, **registrationProcessed**.
4. Prepend the package name, for example, **com.jsfcompref.registrationProcessed**.

This value can then be used in the page as shown here:

```
<h:myCommandButton>
  <f:event type="com.jsfcompref.registrationProcessed"
          listener="#{myBean.listener}" />
</h:myCommandButton>
```

Then, at the appropriate point in the component's lifecycle, a call is made to **publishEvent( )**, for example,

```
public void doSpecialProcessing(FacesContext context) {
  // Custom code here
  Application app = context.getApplication( );
  app.publishEvent(context,
  com.jsfcompref.RegistrationProcessedEvent.class, this);
}
```

You now have an understanding of the Faces event system. In the next chapter, we tie together everything you've learned thus far in the Virtual Trainer example application.

II

PART

Extending JavaServer Faces

CHAPTER 10

Applying JSF: Introducing the Virtual Trainer Application

In the preceding chapters, you've seen several smaller examples of JavaServer Faces. Now it's time to examine a complete, though small, JSF application that ties together all of the topics covered so far. This example will also provide a firm conceptual foundation that will help you understand the more advanced concepts in the following chapters. It is important to understand that this application was created to demonstrate concepts and is not intended to be an example of the best way to craft a scalable production application. In particular, the database interactions are not at all optimized and would probably perform poorly given a large number of concurrent users. Also, the application ignores one of the most basic techniques regarding persistence: using a data access layer between the view layer and the database. The art of building a scalable persistence layer is a topic well beyond the scope of this book, but the area is well covered in the literature.

The application is called Virtual Trainer. It is a JSF-based Web application that helps an athlete or casual sports enthusiast train for an event. Virtual Trainer provides a robust introduction to building a complete JSF application because it neatly integrates all of the concepts presented so far, while introducing some new important topics. These include

- Using page templates in practice, including role-specific content and navigation
- Using composite components to abstract a part of the application for maximal reuse
- Displaying and editing tabular data with **dataTables**
- Building drill-down row editing from a **dataTable**
- Constructing a persistence layer using the Java Persistence Architecture
- Using the Flash and View Parameters to implement the entire site using the proper GET REDIRECT POST web pattern, with minimal use of the session.
- Use implicit navigation exclusively. No **<navigation-rules>**.
- Use a custom **ExceptionHandler** to gracefully handle **ViewExpiredException** events, which happen when the user's session expires due to inactivity. This is a common occurrence in Web applications, so any production application must handle such things in a way that doesn't break the user's experience with the application.

The Virtual Trainer application presented in this chapter is also downloadable from **http://jsfcompref.com/**.

A Quick Tour of the Virtual Trainer Application

Before looking at exactly how this application was coded, an overview of the Virtual Trainer application is in order. The Virtual Trainer application gives a sports or fitness enthusiast the ability to plan their workout sessions and have them directly relate to actual upcoming athletic events. For example, if you are a runner who wants to train for an upcoming marathon, you can create a customized training routine that has a personalized set of individual training sessions to follow. As you fulfill each workout session, you can comment on your progress. A human online trainer advisor will also be able to comment and offer you encouragement/advice.

The following sections present a quick tour of Virtual Trainer in order to acquaint you with its functionality. It guides you through the following tasks in the application:

- Registering, logging in, and browsing through some of the precreated training events
- Selecting an event for which you would like to train
- Creating and deleting a training sessions
- Logging out and logging back in as the user **jake**, who is a training advisor
- Creating and updating training events
- Updating the training event workout comments that were previously edited by the guest user account

Registering and Logging In to the Virtual Trainer Application

There are eleven pages in the Virtual Trainer application. It must be said that this style of having lots of pages is very out of fashion right now. A more current approach would be to have a single-page application using Ajax. This is certainly possible and very easy to do with JSF 2.0, but because we haven't addressed Ajax yet, we'll stick with the "Web 1.0" style of application design. For more on Ajax, please see Chapter 12. The complete traversal of the application we will follow in this section is shown in Figure 10-1.

Any attempt to access any of the pages in the Virtual Trainer application when not already logged in will cause the login page to be shown. This is shown in Figure 10-2.

Assuming this is your first time to the Virtual Trainer site, you'll click Register to establish a new account for yourself. This will bring you to the registration page for new accounts. Figure 10-3 shows a properly filled-out registration form for a new account.

After you complete the registration and click Register (and assuming no validation errors have occurred), you are automatically logged in to the application with your new account.

After entering the credentials, you'll then see the main page (shown later in Figure 10-6), where you can choose which of the available events to train for by clicking the checkbox next to those events and clicking the Update Event Subscriptions button.

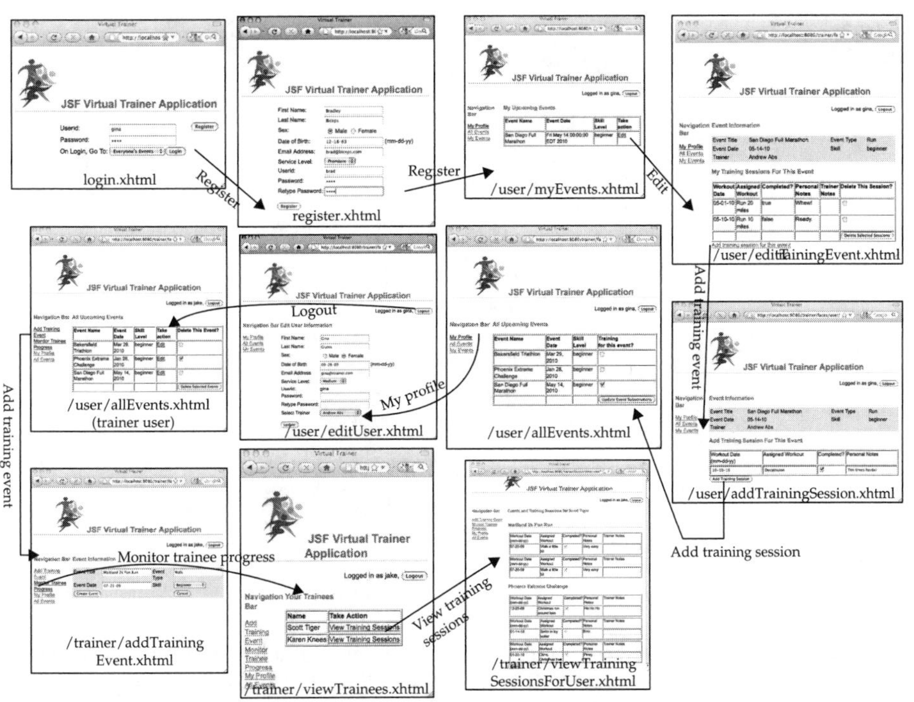

FIGURE 10-1 A sample traversal of Virtual Trainer

Creating a New Training Event Workout Plan

Once you have chosen which events you want to train for, you are taken to the **My Upcoming Events** page. This page lists the events you selected from the main page, with an **Edit** link next to each one that allows you to create the training event workout plan for that event.

Selecting an event to edit brings you to the detail page for your participation in that event. This page, shown in Figure 10-4, allows you to create a workout training plan for an upcoming athletic event that was added into the system by a trainer. Virtual Trainer has already generated

FIGURE 10-2 The Virtual Trainer login page

FIGURE 10-3 The Virtual Trainer registration page

a set of workout sessions based on your age and skill level to help you prepare for the event. You can add more training sessions to this plan, as well as delete any of the ones that have already been added. To add a training session, click **Add training session for this event**. This takes you to the **Add Training Session For This Event** page, shown in Figure 10-5. At this point, you'll begin your workout routine based on the workout sessions assigned for the event.

FIGURE 10-4 The **Event Details** page

FIGURE 10-5
Adding a training session

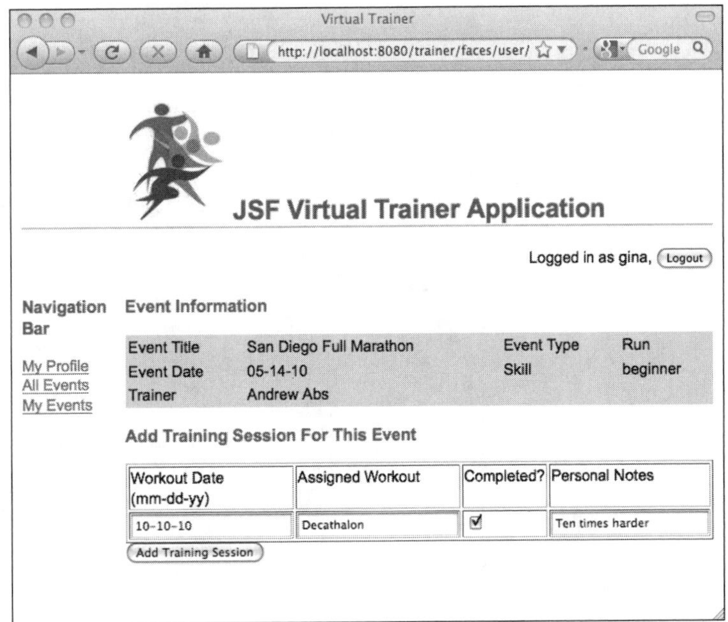

As you perform your workouts, you'll return to the application to log your progress as each workout session is completed. After you complete a specific workout session, you can check it off and enter any comments about the workout. This page is shown in Figure 10-5.

In order to get a better feel for dealing with larger sets of training events without having to enter all the information manually, the downloadable version of the Virtual Trainer application provides a guest account that allows anyone to log in and work with preloaded training events and individual workout sessions.

After logging out and logging back in using the guest account, you'll see a preloaded set of training events on the main page, shown in Figure 10-6.

Choosing Your Trainer

At any point during your interaction with the Virtual Trainer, you can update your chosen human trainer by clicking the **My Profile** link in the left-hand navigation menu. This takes you to a page that looks very similar to the registration page but has one additional field: **Select Trainer**. This page is shown in Figure 10-7.

Actions Available Only to Trainers

Users that have been created as trainers have access to additional pages not shown to users who are not trainers. The application has an account created with userid and password **jake** who is a trainer. Other trainer userids are **andrew**, and **frauke**, with passwords **andrew** and **frauke**, respectively. The main page looks slightly different for trainer users than regular users. The trainer version of the main page is shown in Figure 10-8. The differences include

- Additional links in the navigation menu for **Add Training Event** and **Monitor Trainee Progress**.
- Additional columns in the table: **Take action** and **Delete This Event?**

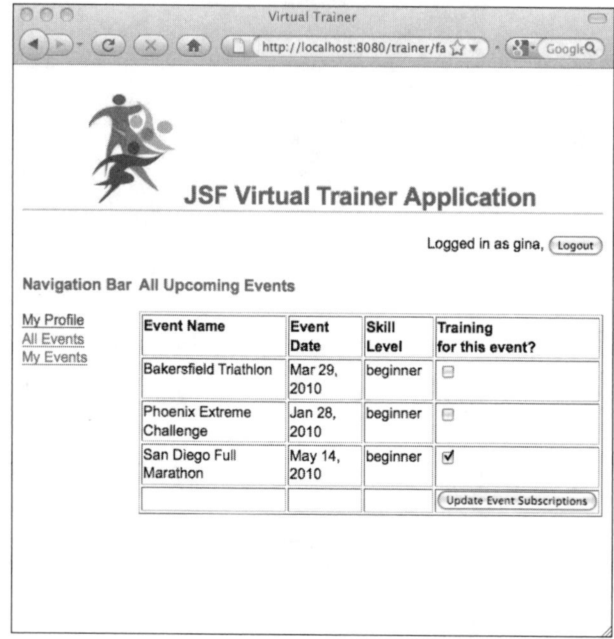

FIGURE 10-6 Browsing multiple training events on the main page

Clicking an **Edit** link in the **Take action** column allows you to update the details of the training event. Trainers can delete one or more events by clicking the checkboxes next to the events and clicking the **Delete Selected Events** button. This will cascade the delete to remove the event from the list of events from any users who are training for it.

Clicking the **Add Training Event** link takes you to the page shown in Figure 10-9. Here trainers can fill in the details about a new event so that users can start training for it.

FIGURE 10-7 The **My Profile** page

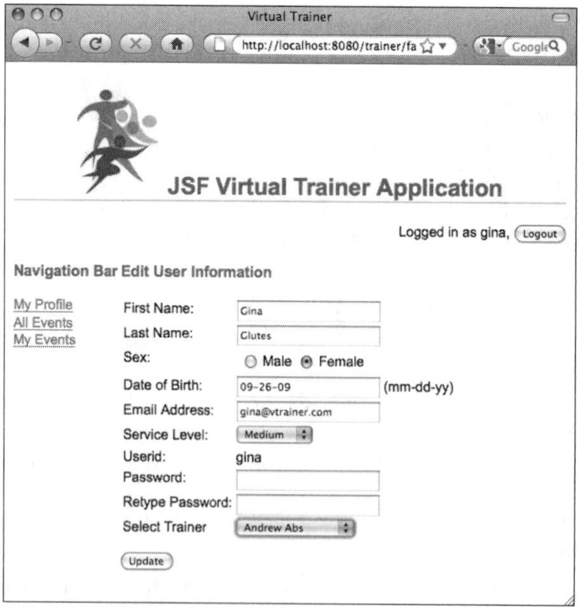

FIGURE 10-8 The main page as seen by any user who is a trainer

Clicking the **Monitor Trainee Progress** link takes you to a page where you see the users who have listed you as their trainer, as shown in Figure 10-10. Clicking the **View Training Sessions** link next to one of the names takes you to the **Events and Training Sessions for <User>** page, shown in Figure 10-11, where <User> is replaced with the name of the user you have selected. On this page, the trainer can offer some notes on the training sessions undertaken by the user, clicking the **Update** button to store those comments so the user can see them. This page is actually an example of using a data table within a data table. Such a design is frequently used in enterprise applications, so we will examine this page later in detail.

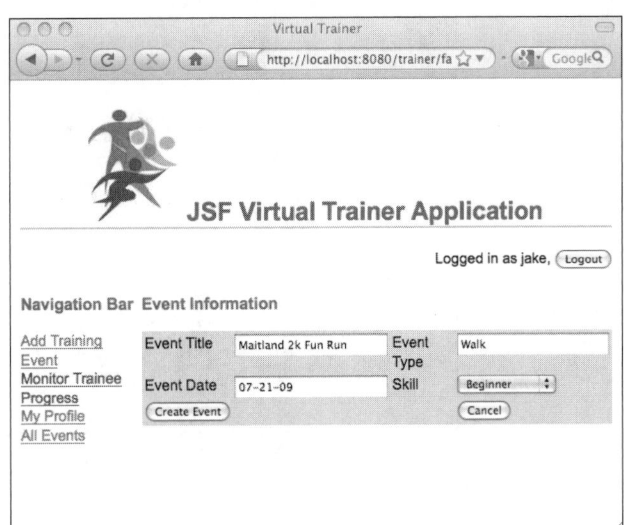

FIGURE 10-9 The Add Training Event page

Figure 10-10 The Monitor Trainee Progress page

As you complete the individual workout sessions and fill in your progress, you can click the Update Event button to update your progress in the application. Your designated online trainer also has the ability to log in to the application and view your progress. The online trainer will be able to provide comments or encouragement throughout your training.

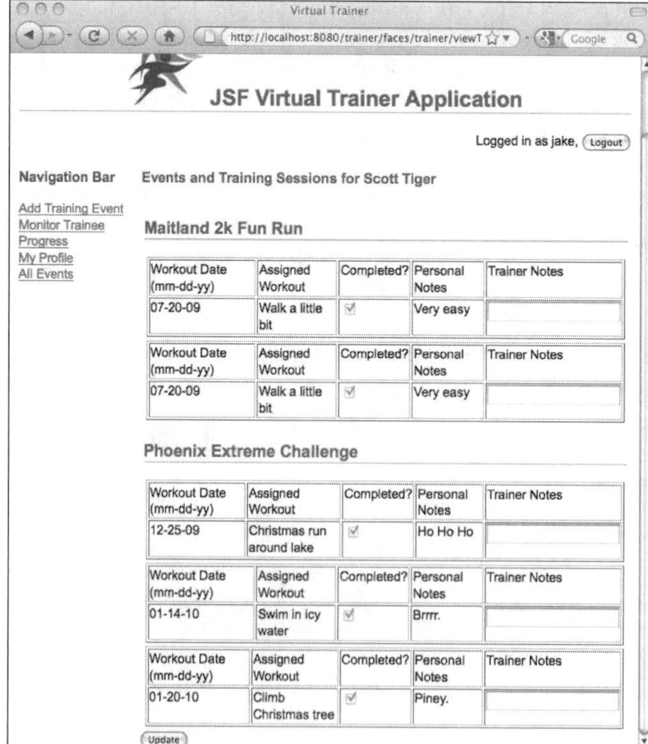

Figure 10-11 The Events and Training Sessions for <User> page

This concludes the brief walkthrough of the Virtual Trainer application. It is now time to discuss how the application was built by first describing the application requirements and then showing how the individual pages and backing technology were created.

The Virtual Trainer Application Requirements

The following lists the key requirements for the application:

- Application users will have the ability to register new accounts for themselves and log in to the application.
- Users who are trainers are not created using the Web user interface.
- Trainers will have the ability to create a set of athletic events for which users will be able to train.
- Users can opt in or opt out of training for specific events at any point in time.
- The user also will be able to select an online training advisor who will be able to monitor his or her progress and provide helpful comments along the way.
- Once the athletic training events have been created, an individually customized set of training sessions are generated for each athletic event. These represent individual date-based workout sessions that the user can follow.
- Each individualized training session is assigned with a specific date and will be rendered with a checkbox allowing the user to check off whether he or she performed the specific training session.
- In addition to the checkbox, the user will have an input text field to log any specific comments about the training session.
- The online training advisor will also be able to enter comments for each training event as well as to provide guidance.
- At all times the URL bar must reflect the page that users thinks they are on. There must never be a time where the URL in the URL bar confuses the user by seeming to be "out of step" with the application.

The Virtual Trainer Application Architecture

In a very simple sense, the application is a *master-detail* application where the user can edit a set of items that are related to each other in a master-detail fashion. Figure 10-12 is a UML diagram that provides visual representation of the data model entities of the application. A **User** can train for zero or more **Events**. Independent of training for an event, a **User** has zero or more **TrainingSessions**, each of which corresponds to exactly one **Event**. A **User** may have exactly one trainer, which is just a special **User** instance. A **User** that is a trainer may have zero or more **Users** as trainees. There is a **UserRegistry** that handles Create, Read, Update, and Delete (CRUD) operations for **TrainingSession** and **User** instances. There is an **EventRegistry**, which handles CRUD for **Event** instances. Code for the **UserRegistry** and **EventRegistry** classes will be shown after most of the other aspects of the trainer have been explained.

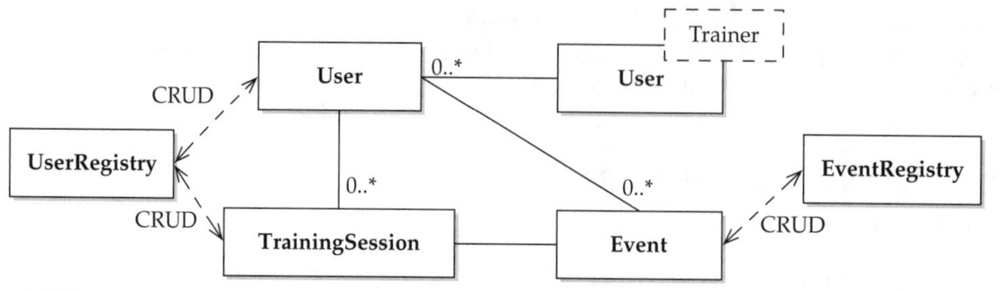

Figure 10-12 The data model of the Virtual Trainer application

The Virtual Trainer application uses the following elements to implement the application architecture described in the preceding paragraph:

- Facelet pages and backing beans
- Entities representing the data model
- Helper classes for accessing and persisting the entities

Each is described in the following sections.

Facelet Pages

The Facelet pages and backing beans used by Virtual Trainer are listed next. The pages are spread across four directories, including the top-level directory, also known as the Web application root. The following four sub-sections explain the purpose of each file.

Pages in the Web Application Root

- **/template.xhtml** All of the other Facelet pages in the application use this page as a template client. This page includes common style elements and a navigation menu that appears on the left side of every page.
- **/login.xhtml** The login page, it is made much simpler through the use of a JSF 2 composite component. This will be explained in more detail later in the chapter.
- **/register.xhtml** Reached only by coming from the **login.xhtml** page, this page is used to allow new users to join the Virtual Trainer.

Pages in the /user Directory

Pages in this directory are shown for all logged-in users, though some of them are not used for users who are trainers.

- **/user/allEvents.xhtml** Linked from the navigation menu defined in the top-level **template.xhtml** file, and redirected to by many actions throughout the application, this is the main page for the application. It shows a list of all events in the system and offers different options based on whether the current user is a trainer or not.

- **/user/myEvents.xhtml** Linked from the navigation menu, this page shows the events for which the current user is training and allows the user to take further action on any such event.
- **/user/editTrainingEvent.xhtml** Reached when a user selects an event on the **myEvents.xhtml** page, this page allows users to view the event details, including their training schedule for the selected event. Users can delete multiple training sessions with one form submission. There is a link to the **addTrainingSession.xhtml** page.
- **/user/addTrainingSession.xhtml** Reached only from the **editTrainingEvent.xhtml** page, this page lets you add an individual training session to the training plan for a particular event.
- **/user/editUser.xhtml** Reached only from the **My Profile** link in the navigation menu, this page allows users to update their profile information, including selecting their online trainer from the list of available trainers.

Pages in the /trainer Directory

Pages in this directory are only shown to users who are trainers.

- **/trainer/addTrainingEvent.xhtml** Linked from the navigation menu, this page allows a trainer to add a new event so that users may start training for it.
- **/trainer/editTrainingEvent.xhtml** Linked from the navigation menu, this page allows a trainer to update the details of an existing event.
- **/trainer/viewTrainees.xhtml** Linked from the navigation menu, this page allows the trainer to see the list of users that have selected them as their trainer, and to click on each such user to perform additional actions.
- **/trainer/viewTrainingSessionsForUser.xhtml** Linked from the **viewTrainees.xhtml** page, this page allows trainers to provide advice to the users as they progress through their training plans.

Pages in the /resources Directory

Files in this directory are treated specially by the JSF runtime. This special treatment will be discussed during the detailed explanation of JSF 2 Composite Components, a powerful new feature in JSF 2.0. This feature is described in Chapter 11. For now, just know that files and directories within the **/resources** directory are intended to be included in other pages in the application. Content here can be images, stylesheets, and composite components.

- **/resources/style/logo.jpg** A simple logo included in the **template.xhtml** page
- **/resources/style/vt.css** A CSS stylesheet, used in the **template.xhtml** page
- **/resources/trainer/loginPanel.xhtml** A JSF 2 composite component that is a self-contained "login panel." Users of this component must supply a POJO model object with specific properties and methods to fill out the behavior of the login panel.

This version of the Virtual Trainer entirely uses implicit navigation and therefore has no explicit navigation rules in the **faces-config.xml** file. In fact, the only reason this application needs a **faces-config.xml** file at all is to declare the custom **ExceptionHandler** that is used to gracefully handle session timeouts.

Backing Beans

The term "backing bean" describes a request-scoped JSF managed bean that is conceptually bound to a specific JSF page. Even though a backing bean is declared as a JSF managed bean, it is not considered a true "model object" because it has intimate knowledge of the view.

EXPERT GROUP INSIGHT *Even though it would be useful to formalize the concept of backing bean by including an abstract class containing all the common functionality for such beans, it was decided not to put the concept into the specification.*

The following utility class is the base class for all the backing beans in the Virtual Trainer application. If the JSF Expert Group were to include a backing bean base class in the specification, it would probably look something like this. Because this class is the abstract base class for all backing beans in Virtual Trainer, we will examine it in detail now, even though detailed descriptions for the concrete subclasses will appear later in the chapter in the context of the Facelet pages they back.

```
package com.jsfcompref.trainer.backing;

import com.jsfcompref.trainer.entity.User;
import java.util.Map;
import javax.faces.bean.ManagedProperty;
import javax.faces.bean.RequestScoped;
import javax.faces.context.FacesContext;
import javax.faces.context.Flash;


@RequestScoped
public abstract class AbstractBacking {

  @ManagedProperty(value="#{facesContext}")
  private FacesContext facesContext;

  @ManagedProperty(value="#{requestScope}")
  private Map<String, Object> requestMap;

  @ManagedProperty(value="#{sessionScope}")
  private Map<String, Object> sessionMap;

  public User getCurrentUser() {
    return (User) getSessionMap().get("currentUser");
  }

  public void setCurrentUser(User currentUser) {
    getSessionMap().remove("currentUser");
    if (null != currentUser) {
```

```
      getSessionMap().put("currentUser", currentUser);
    }
  }

  public boolean isUserLoggedIn() {
    return getSessionMap().containsKey("currentUser");
  }

  // The compiler can optimizes calls such as this into plain
  // field accesses.
  // Therefore, there is no performance penalty for always using the
  // accessor.
  public FacesContext getFacesContext() {
    return facesContext;
  }

  public void setFacesContext(FacesContext context) {
    this.facesContext = context;
  }

  public Flash getFlash() {
    return getFacesContext().getExternalContext().getFlash();
  }

  // getters and setters for properties annotated with
  // @ManagedProperty are omitted for brevity, but are required
  // for the @ManagedProperty annotation to work.
}
```

The first thing to note is the presence of the **@RequestScoped** annotation, which is a bit unusual for the absence of a corresponding **@ManagedBean** annotation on the class declaration. This is because the **@ManagedBean** annotation may never appear on an abstract class. As you will soon see, the **@ManagedBean** annotation appears on each of the subclasses of **AbstractBacking**, which are shown in Figure 10-13.

The most useful thing about this design is the use of the **@ManagedProperty** annotation to inject the current **FacesContext** and the request and session scopes. The class also provides a getter for the **Flash**, which is used heavily in this version of the Virtual Trainer. Finally, the one and only aspect of this class that is closely tied to the architecture of the Virtual Trainer is contained in the **currentUser** and **userLoggedIn** JavaBeans properties. For simplicity, this application stores the **User** object in the session scope. Also, the setter for the **currentUser** property takes the liberty of removing any previously stored user from the session before setting the new one. The new user is stored if and only if it is non-null. Therefore, it's possible to call **setCurrentUser(null)** from any subclass to remove the user from the session. The getter for the **boolean userLoggedIn** property simply checks for the "currentUser" key in the session scope.

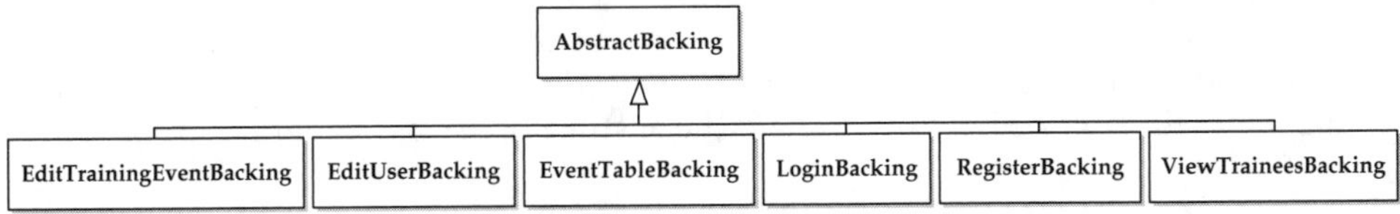

Figure 10-13 The backing beans of the Virtual Trainer application

The concrete subclasses of **AbstractBacking** are summarized in the following table. Detailed descriptions of the important aspects of each class will be discussed in the appropriate context later in the chapter.

Backing Bean Name	An Instance of This Class Backs the . . .
LoginBacking	**login.xhtml** page and has a utility method that is used on the **template.xhtml** page. Thus an instance of this class is created for every request made to the application.
EventTableBacking	two pages that need to display a table of training events: **allEvents.xhtml** and **myEvents.xhtml**.
EditUserBacking	**editUser.xhtml** page.
RegisterBacking	**register.xhtml** and **editUser.xhtml** pages.
ViewTraineesBacking	**viewTrainingSessionsForUser.xhtml** and **viewTrainees.xhtml** pages.
EditTrainingEventBacking	**editTrainingEvent.xhtml** pages in the **user** and **trainer** directories, the **viewTrainees.xhtml** and **viewTrainingSessionsForUser.xhtml** pages in the **trainer** directory, and the **addTrainingSession.xhtml** page in the **user** directory.

Persistence and Transaction Architecture

Any real-world application must have an industrial-strength persistence and transaction architecture. Persistence and transactions are absolutely crucial aspects of any real enterprise application. For example, performance problems stemming from the persistence layer can completely cripple an application. Also, any multiuser application must consider transactionality. Therefore it's very important to get the persistence and transaction layers right. Thankfully, these problems are very well understood and there are many good books available on these topics. The Virtual Trainer application has a persistence and transaction architecture, but the author makes no guarantees as to its scalability or suitability for use in a real-world application. Rather, the persistence and transaction architecture in the Virtual Trainer is intended to illustrate one way to approach filling this important role in your application, with a specific view toward JSF.

One popular and standard way to handle persistence in enterprise Java applications is the Java Persistence Application Programming Interface, or simply JPA. JPA has been a standard part of enterprise Java since Java EE 5. In the same way that JSF took the best ideas from the community and synthesized them into the standard, JPA took ideas from Hibernate, Spring, Service Data Objects, Java Data Objects, and EJB Container Managed Persistence and standardized the way enterprise Java applications handle persistence to a relational database.

Likewise, for transactions, there is the Java Transaction Architecture, or JTA.

The persistence and transaction architecture in Virtual Trainer is taken from a design by Alberto Lemos (more commonly known as Dr. Spock). Mr. Lemos is an expert software developer and trainer currently working at Globalcode, a leading provider of technology training in Brazil. This design uses JPA and the abstract base class pattern, as shown in Figure 10-14.

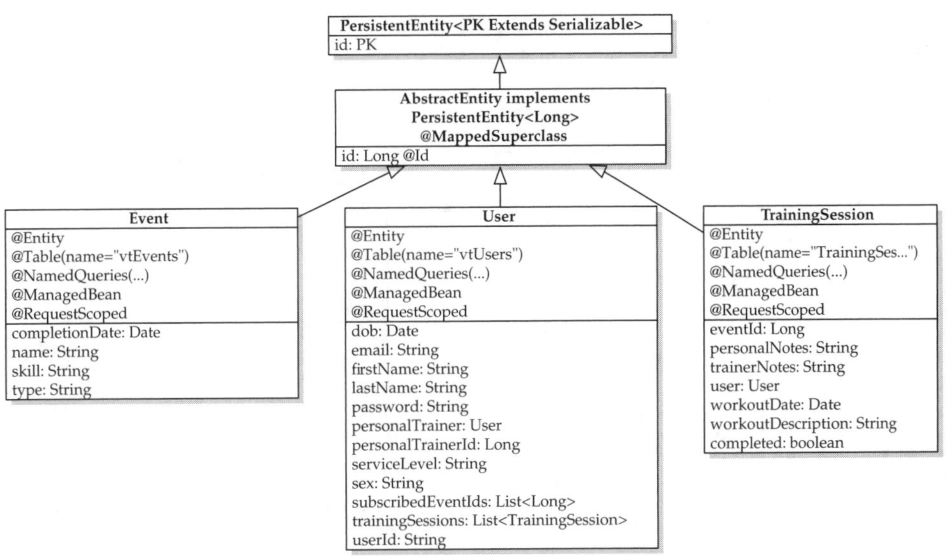

FIGURE 10-14 The persistence architecture of the Virtual Trainer application

As in managed beans, annotations are a very important aspect of JPA. (Though the one configuration file, **persistence.xml**, is absolutely vital, we defer discussing that until much later in the chapter.) At the top of Figure 10-14, we see a simple Java interface, **PersistentEntity**. This interface enforces two practical requirements of any objects stored using JPA: implementing **Serializable**, and having a primary key. The abstract class **AbstractEntity** implements **PersistentEntity** and declares the type of the primary key to be **Long**. It also tells JPA that the field **id**, of type **Long**, is to be the primary key by adding the **@Id** annotation to the field. As the accompanying box shows, there are three concrete subclasses of **AbstractEntity**, each of them with a number of attributes and each annotated with the same set of JPA annotations.

AbstractEntity Subclasses

@Entity allows JPA to manage the persistence of instances of this class. Naturally, there are some conditions that must be met by classes with this annotation, but those conditions are beyond the scope of this book.

@Table names the physical database table used to store instances of this class. With JPA this means that every field in the class will correspond to a column in the table. This is where the conditions on what kind of fields are valid are very important.

@NamedQueries contains a list of **@NamedQuery** annotations, each of which contains a String written in the JPA Query Language (JPAQL). JPAQL is very similar to SQL. An example of JPAQL from the Virtual Trainer is "select u from User as u where u.trainer = TRUE".

JPA Entities can also be JSF managed beans, as shown by the presence of the **@ManagedBean** and **@RequestScoped** annotations.

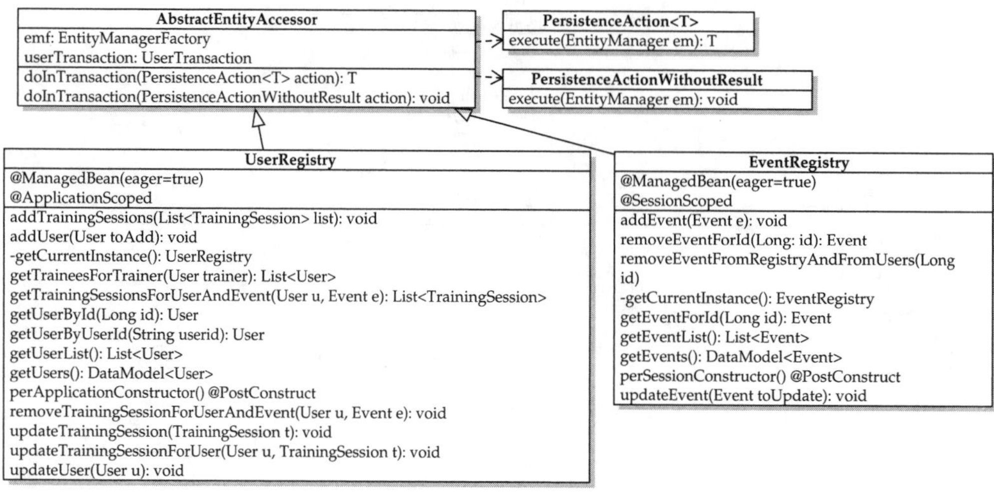

FIGURE 10-15 The transaction and entity accessor architecture of the Virtual Trainer application

Entities are not useful on their own. You need some way to manage them and expose them to the parts of your application that need access to them. For that, we have the **AbstractEntityAccesor** base class and its concrete subclasses, shown in Figure 10-15.

This is the most novel and interesting part of Spock's design. **AbstractEntityManager** handles all the JPA and JTA interaction and offers one simple overloaded method with two variants: one for when you need a result and one for when you do not. The highlights of the source code for **AbstractEntityManager** are shown here:

```
package com.jsfcompref.trainer.entity.accessor;

import java.util.logging.Level;
import java.util.logging.Logger;
import javax.annotation.Resource;
import javax.persistence.EntityManager;
import javax.persistence.PersistenceUnit;
import javax.persistence.EntityManagerFactory;
import javax.transaction.UserTransaction;

public abstract class AbstractEntityAccessor {

  @PersistenceUnit
  private EntityManagerFactory emf;
  @Resource
  private UserTransaction userTransaction;

  protected final <T> T doInTransaction(PersistenceAction<T> action)
  throws EntityAccessorException {
    EntityManager em = emf.createEntityManager();
    try {
      userTransaction.begin();
```

```
      T result = action.execute(em);
      userTransaction.commit();
      return result;
    } catch (Exception e) {
      try {
        userTransaction.rollback();
      } catch (Exception ex) {
        Logger.getLogger(AbstractEntityAccessor.class.getName()).
         log(Level.SEVERE, null, ex);
      }
      throw new EntityAccessorException(e);
    } finally {
      em.close();
    }

  }

  protected final void doInTransaction(
      PersistenceActionWithoutResult action)
        throws EntityAccessorException {
    EntityManager em = emf.createEntityManager();
    try {
      userTransaction.begin();
      action.execute(em);
      userTransaction.commit();
    } catch (Exception e) {
      try {
        userTransaction.rollback();
      } catch (Exception ex) {
        Logger.getLogger(AbstractEntityAccessor.class.getName()).
          log(Level.SEVERE, null, ex);
      }
      throw new EntityAccessorException(e);
    } finally {
      em.close();
    }
  }

  protected static interface PersistenceAction<T> {

    T execute(EntityManager em);
  }

  protected static interface PersistenceActionWithoutResult {

    void execute(EntityManager em);
  }

}
```

An example of using **doInTransaction( )**, the **addUser( )** method of **UserRegistry**, is shown here:

```
public void addUser(final User toAdd) throws EntityAccessorException {
  doInTransaction(new PersistenceActionWithoutResult() {
     public void execute(EntityManager em) {
      em.persist(toAdd);
    }
  });
}
```

The two concrete subclasses of **AbstractEntityAccessor** are listed and summarized in the following table.

Class Name	Purpose
UserRegistry	Manages create, read, and update operations on the **User** entity. Also has some helper methods to access the **TrainingSession**s associated with a user. Using helper methods for this purpose was a design choice. An alternative would be to have a separate **TrainingSessionRegistry** class.
EventRegistry	Manages create, read, update, and delete operations on the **Event** entity.

The next section explains in detail how the Virtual Trainer application is built, starting with the basic page design and culminating with advanced data operations.

Navigation Concerns

A very useful approach to follow when starting a Web development project is to first design a prototype in old-fashioned HTML. This approach was used for Virtual Trainer. It was during this phase that a custom Cascading Style Sheet, **vt.css**, was also created to define a consistent look and feel for the entire application. As you'll see shortly, JSF components also come pre-equipped to work well with CSS. It should be noted that in addition to merely providing a look and feel for an application, CSS can also be used to specify the layout of the items on the page. For the most part, however, HTML tables are still widely used to initially define a page layout.

Once the HTML prototype conveys the general design of the user interface, the HTML pages can then be transformed into JSF-enabled Facelet pages. Facelets makes this transition exceedingly simple. (Please see Chapter 4 for more about Facelets.) It is also possible to continue using HTML tables for layout in your final JSF applications; however, for maximum accessibility it's generally a good practice to use JSF layout/container components.

Another commonly used practice during the design phase of an application is to create a single page template that all other pages will be derived from. While there are many techniques and technologies for page templating, a simple and common approach is to design a single master, or parent template page, that will be used as a starting template for all other pages, thus ensuring a consistent page design and layout. This is the approach that was used for the Virtual Trainer application.

The following is the general page design template for Virtual Trainer:

```
<!DOCTYPE html PUBLIC "-//W3C//DTD XHTML 1.0 Transitional//EN"
"http://www.w3.org/TR/xhtml1/DTD/xhtml1-transitional.dtd">
<html xmlns="http://www.w3.org/1999/xhtml"
```

```
    xmlns:h="http://java.sun.com/jsf/html"
    xmlns:f="http://java.sun.com/jsf/core"
    xmlns:c="http://java.sun.com/jsp/jstl/core"
    xmlns:ui="http://java.sun.com/jsf/facelets">
<ui:insert name="metadata"/>
<f:event type="preRenderView"
        listener="#{loginBacking.forwardToLoginIfNotLoggedIn}" />
<h:head>
  <title><ui:insert name="title">Virtual Trainer</ui:insert></title>
  <h:outputStylesheet library="style" name="vt.css" />
</h:head>
<h:body>

<table width="100%" border="0">
<tr><td height="89"><h1 align="center">
  <img src="#{resource['style:logo.jpg']}" alt="Virtual Trainer Logo" />
  JSF Virtual Trainer Application</h1>
</td></tr>
<c:if test="#{loginBacking.userLoggedIn}">
  <tr><td align="right"><h:form>
    Logged in as #{sessionScope.currentUser.userid},
    <h:commandButton value="Logout" action="#{loginBacking.performLogout}" />
  </h:form></td></tr>
</c:if>
</table>
<!-- WARNING: Using tables for non-tabular data violates the
   Web Content Accessibility Guidelines (WCAG).
   Do not copy this practice in your real application.
   Use CSS instead. A gem of a site for WCAG compliance is
   http://worksperfectly.net/wcag/ -->
<table border="0">
<tr><td width="20%">
<c:if test="#{loginBacking.userLoggedIn}">
  <h3>Navigation Bar</h3>
  <c:if test="#{loginBacking.currentUser.trainer}">
    <h:link outcome="/trainer/addTrainingEvent">Add Training Event</h:link><br/>
    <h:link outcome="/trainer/viewTrainees">Monitor Trainee Progress</h:link><br/>
  </c:if>
  <h:link outcome="/user/editUser">My Profile</h:link> <br />
  <h:link outcome="/user/allEvents">All Events</h:link> <br />
  <c:if test="#{!loginBacking.currentUser.trainer}">
    <h:link outcome="/user/myEvents">My Events</h:link> <br />
  </c:if>
</c:if>
</td>
<td><ui:insert name="content" /></td>
</tr>
</table>
</h:body>
</html>
```

The preceding Facelet page is **template.xhtml**. It exposes three spots for templated content: **metadata**, at the very top of the page, **content** at the very bottom of the page, and **title**, which is simply the content of the HTML **<title>** element. The meaning of the **metadata** section will become clear when we describe how this application uses GET REDIRECT POST as its navigation paradigm.

After the metadata insertion, we have **<f:event type="preRenderView" listener="#{loginBacking.forwardToLoginIfNotLoggedIn">**. The **<f:event>** element is described in detail in Chapter 9. In this case, the **<f:event>** element forces a call to the method **forwardToLoginIfNotLoggedIn( )** on class **LoginBacking** before the page is rendered. This method ensures that the only pages that can be shown without the user being logged in are **login.xhtml** and **register.xhtml**. The code for this method is shown here:

```
public void forwardToLoginIfNotLoggedIn(ComponentSystemEvent cse) {
  String viewId = getFacesContext().getViewRoot().getViewId();
  if (!isUserLoggedIn() && !viewId.startsWith("/login") &&
    !viewId.startsWith("/register")) {
    getFacesContext().getApplication().getNavigationHandler().
        handleNavigation(getFacesContext(), null,
        "/login?faces-redirect=true");
  }
}
```

This method is essentially a single if statement that says, "if the user is not already logged in, and we're not already on the login or registration pages, then redirect to the login page." Note the use of implicit navigation here. This feature is described in detail in Chapter 6.

The **preRender** event is used in a very similar fashion on all pages that should only be viewable by users who are trainers. For example, the **addTrainingEvent.xhtml** page has this code near the top: **<f:event type="preRenderView" listener="#{editTrainingEventBacking .forwardToMainIfNotTrainer}" />**. The code behind this method is shown here:

```
public void forwardToMainIfNotTrainer(ComponentSystemEvent cse) {
  User user;
  if (null != (user = getCurrentUser()) && !user.isTrainer()) {
    getFacesContext().getApplication().getNavigationHandler().
        handleNavigation(getFacesContext(), null,
        "/user/allEvents?faces-redirect=true");
  }
}
```

Continuing through **template.xhtml**, we come to the **<h:head>** section. This section has a **<ui:insert>** for the title, with a default value of **Virtual Trainer**, and it includes a stylesheet using **<h:outputStylesheet library="style" name="vt.css" />**. This is an example of a usage of a resource library.

Following the head is a table that spans the width of the page. This table provides a common page header for application pages. Within this header, this same resource is used to render the logo image using the EL syntax for referring to resources: **<img src="#{resource['style:logo.jpg']}" alt="Virtual Trainer Logo" />**. Also in the header, if the user is logged in, we provide a button to allow that user to log out using the following code:

```
<c:if test="#{loginBacking.userLoggedIn}">
  <tr><td align="right"><h:form>
    Logged in as #{sessionScope.currentUser.userid},
    <h:commandButton value="Logout"
                     action="#{loginBacking.performLogout}" />
  </h:form></td></tr>
</c:if>
```

Beneath the header we have another table, with a single row. The first column contains a very simple navigation bar populated with **<h:link>** elements pointing to various places within the application. The second column is simply **<ui:insert name="content" />**. Let's take a closer look at the navigation bar.

```
<c:if test="#{loginBacking.userLoggedIn}">
  <h3>Navigation Bar</h3>
  <c:if test="#{loginBacking.currentUser.trainer}">
    <h:link outcome="/trainer/addTrainingEvent">Add Training Event</h:
link><br/>
    <h:link outcome="/trainer/viewTrainees">Monitor Trainee Progress</h:
link><br/>
  </c:if>
  <h:link outcome="/user/editUser">My Profile</h:link> <br />
  <h:link outcome="/user/allEvents">All Events</h:link> <br />
  <c:if test="#{!loginBacking.currentUser.trainer}">
    <h:link outcome="/user/myEvents">My Events</h:link> <br />
  </c:if>
</c:if>
```

First, note that the navigation bar isn't even shown unless the user is logged in. This is necessary because the login page itself uses the **template.xhtml** and we certainly don't want to show the links to a user who is not logged in. Second, note that some of the links are displayed only if the user is a trainer, using **<c:if test="#{loginBacking.currentUser.trainer}">**, and in similar fashion the **myEvents** link is *not* shown if the user is a trainer. Finally, note the values of the **outcome** attributes. This is an example of implicit navigation, described in detail in Chapter 6.

Another important thing to note about navigation in Virtual Trainer is the near complete use of the POST REDIRECT GET pattern. This pattern, and its desirable properties, are also described in Chapter 6.

The following section describes the mechanics of how login and logout work.

Creating a Simple Authentication System

As you'll see in Chapter 14, creating a truly secure enterprise Web application takes careful planning and coding. However, it is often useful to begin with a simple authentication system that provides basic application-level authentication that can later be enhanced to a more robust architecture without completely redesigning the architecture. This is the approach used by Virtual Trainer.

The application-based authentication employed in Virtual Trainer consists of a login form on a page (**login.xhtml**) that obtains user credentials and then checks them against a registry of users. If the user credentials do not exist in the registry, a Faces invalid login message is displayed on the form and the user is not permitted to log in to the application. Virtual Trainer uses a new feature in JSF 2.0, Composite Components, to encapsulate the login panel into a reusable component. This approach, combined with the use of Facelets, makes the login page extremely simple:

```
<!DOCTYPE html PUBLIC "-//W3C//DTD XHTML 1.0 Transitional//EN"
"http://www.w3.org/TR/xhtml1/DTD/xhtml1-transitional.dtd">
<html xmlns="http://www.w3.org/1999/xhtml"
```

PART II

```
  xmlns:h="http://java.sun.com/jsf/html"
  xmlns:f="http://java.sun.com/jsf/core"
  xmlns:ui="http://java.sun.com/jsf/facelets"
  xmlns:vt="http://java.sun.com/jsf/composite/trainer">
<body>
<ui:composition template="template.xhtml">

<ui:define name="metadata">
  <f:event type="preRenderView"
           listener="#{loginBacking.forwardToMainIfLoggedIn}" />
</ui:define>

<ui:define name="content">
  <table width="100%" border="0">
  <tr><td width="90%">
  <h:form>
    <vt:loginPanel model="#{loginBacking}">
      <f:facet name="loginOutcomeChoiceList">
        <h:selectOneMenu binding="#{loginBacking.loginOutcomeChoiceList}" >
          <f:selectItem itemLabel="Everyone's Events"
                        itemValue="allEvents" />
          <f:selectItem itemLabel="My Events" itemValue="myEvents" />
        </h:selectOneMenu>
      </f:facet>
    </vt:loginPanel>
  </h:form>
  </td>
  <td align="right">
  <h:form>
    <h:commandButton value="Register"
                     action="register?faces-redirect=true" />
  </h:form>
  </td></tr></table>
</ui:define>
</ui:composition>
</body>
</html>
```

Once again, we are using the **preRenderView** event to bypass the login page if the user is already logged in. The code for this method is available in the complete online version of the Virtual Trainer. Also, we have a simple **<h:commandButton>** that goes to the **register .xtml** page.

The heart of this page is usage of the **<vt:loginPanel>** component. This component is bundled with the Virtual Trainer application as a JSF 2 composite component, which is simply a special kind of Facelet file that acts as a true JSF **UIComponent** when it appears in a Facelet page. This powerful feature of JSF 2 is covered extensively in Chapter 11, and indeed the loginPanel example will be the basis for explaining this feature. As for all object-oriented components, the only thing you need to know to use a composite component in your page is the usage contract exposed by the component. Composite components encode this information directly in the Facelet page using a new Facelet tag library, but for now, the usage contract will be conveyed in simple text.

Login Panel Usage Contract

You must pass a value for the **model** attribute. This value must evaluate to a POJO that has the following methods.

```
public boolean useridIsValid(String userid);
public boolean passwordIsValid(String password);
```

Your POJO must also have the following read-only JavaBean String property: **successOutcome**. Optionally, the POJO may have a read-only JavaBean String property named **failureOutcome**.

Optionally, you may pass a facet into the component, named **loginOutcomeChoiceList**. This facet should contain a menu of choices for where the navigation should go after a successful login.

The model's **useridIsValid( )** method will be called first. If it returns **true**, **passwordIvValid( )** will be called next. If it returns **true**, the model's **successOutcome** property will be looked up and navigation will proceed to that outcome. If it returns **false** and the model has a **failureOutcome** property, navigation will proceed to that outcome. If the model has no **failureOutcome** property, no navigation will be performed. This two-step approach allows the component to display nice error messages such as "userid <user> does not exist" or "userid <user> is valid, but the password is incorrect", where <user> is replaced by the value submitted by the user.

In light of this contract, we will now show the full source for the **LoginBacking** class, but first notice the **<h:selectOneMenu binding="#{loginBacking.loginOutcomeChoiceList}" />** element. This element causes the actual **UIInput** that is associated with the markup to be stored into the **loginOutcomeChoiceList** property of **LoginBacking**. This is an example of the "component binding" feature described in detail in Chapter 7.

```
package com.jsfcompref.trainer.backing;

import com.jsfcompref.trainer.entity.accessor.UserRegistry;
import com.jsfcompref.trainer.entity.User;
import javax.faces.bean.ManagedBean;
import javax.faces.component.UIInput;
import javax.faces.event.ComponentSystemEvent;

@ManagedBean
public class LoginBacking extends AbstractBacking {
  private UIInput loginOutcomeChoiceList;
  private User nonAuthenticatedUser;

  public boolean useridIsValid(String toTest) {
    boolean result = false;
    UserRegistry registry = UserRegistry.getCurrentInstance();
    result = (null != (nonAuthenticatedUser =
                   registry.getUserByUserid(toTest)));
    return result;
  }
```

```
  public boolean passwordIsValid(String toTest) {
    boolean result = false;
    if (null != nonAuthenticatedUser) {
      String userPassword = nonAuthenticatedUser.getPassword();
      if (null != userPassword && userPassword.equals(toTest)) {
        // Put the current user in the session
        setCurrentUser(nonAuthenticatedUser);
        result = true;
      }
    }
    nonAuthenticatedUser = null;
    return result;
  }

  public String getSuccessOutcome() {
    String choice = (String) getLoginOutcomeChoiceList().getValue();
    return "/user/" + choice + "?faces-redirect=true";
  }

  public String performLogout() {
    String result = "/login?faces-redirect=true";
    setCurrentUser(null);
    getFacesContext().getExternalContext().invalidateSession();
    return result;
  }
  // getter and setter for loginOutcomeChoiceList omitted for brevity.
  // forwardToLoginIfNotLoggedIn() and forwardToMainIfLoggedIn() omitted
  // because they appeared earlier in the text.
}
```

First, note that we extend **AbstractBacking**. By doing so, we are declaring that we are a request scoped managed bean, because the **@RequestScoped** annotation is present on the **AbstractBacking** class. This bean simply fills out the usage contract of the composite component. In our case, we see if a user exists for the provided userid, in the **useridIsValid( )** method. If so, we store the **User** instance in an ivar. In the **passwordIsValid( )** method, we simply ask the **User** instance we saved in **useridIsValid** for its password and compare it with the submitted password. Finally, the getter for the **successOutcome** property consults the value of the **loginOutcomeChoiceList** and includes it into the outcome. This simple approach enables the user to navigate to either the "all events" or the "my events" page. Finally, the **performLogout( )** method, which serves as the action for the **logout** button on the **template.xhtml** page, simply removes the user from the session and invalidates the sesson. Figure 10-16 shows the login component in action in a number of different scenarios.

This simple application-based login/logout functionality works great for prototypes; however, as previously mentioned, enterprise security is usually handled in a more robust manner with a more sophisticated security mechanism that could rely on several layers of security. Again, enterprise security with JSF is detailed in Chapter 14.

Before continuing on to the main browse and edit pages, let's review the registration portion of the application, which you'll find is simply an extension from Chapter 2's JSFReg application with a few enhancements.

FIGURE 10-16 The Virtual Trainer Login page with validation errors

Revisiting JSFReg: Building the Registration System

Now that we have a simple authentication system, it makes sense to offer functionality that lets people register themselves as valid users of the application. In building a registration system, recall from Chapter 2 the simple JSFReg application. It is now time to incorporate this simple example into the more comprehensive Virtual Trainer application. In short, all we really have to do is import the form onto a **register.xhtml** page and provide a comparable backing bean that processes the input and calls a **registerUser** method.

The code for the registration form, which also resides in the central content area defined by the page template, is shown next:

```
<h:form prependId="false">
<h:panelGrid columns="3">
    <h:outputLabel for="fname" value="First Name:" />
    <h:inputText label="First Name"
                 id="fname" value="#{user.firstName}"
                 required="true"/>
```

```
    <h:message for="fname" />

    <h:outputLabel for="lname" value="Last Name:" />
    <h:inputText label="Last Name"
                 id="lname" value="#{user.lastName}"
                 required="true"/>
    <h:message for="lname" />

    <h:outputLabel for="sex" value="Sex:" />
    <h:selectOneRadio label="Sex"
                       id="sex" value="#{user.sex}" required="true">
        <f:selectItem itemLabel="Male" itemValue="male" />
        <f:selectItem itemLabel="Female" itemValue="female" />
    </h:selectOneRadio>
    <h:message for="sex" />

    <h:outputLabel for="dob" value="Date of Birth:" />
    <h:panelGroup>
        <h:inputText label="Date of Birth"
                 id="dob" value="#{user.dob}" required="true">
            <f:convertDateTime pattern="MM-dd-yy" />
        </h:inputText> (mm-dd-yy)
    </h:panelGroup>
    <h:message for="dob" />

    <h:outputLabel for="email" value="Email Address:" />
    <h:inputText label="Email Address"
                 id="email" value="#{user.email}" required="true" />
    <h:message for="email" />

    <h:outputLabel for="slevel" value="Service Level:" />
    <h:selectOneMenu label="Service Level" id="slevel"
                     value="#{user.serviceLevel}">
        <f:selectItem itemLabel="Medium" itemValue="medium" />
        <f:selectItem itemLabel="Basic" itemValue="basic" />
        <f:selectItem itemLabel="Premium" itemValue="premium" />
    </h:selectOneMenu>
    <h:message for="slevel" />

    <h:outputLabel for="userid" value="Userid:" />
    <h:inputText required="true" id="userid" value="#{user.userid}" />
    <h:message for="userid" />

    <h:outputLabel for="password" value="Password:" />
    <h:inputSecret required="true" id="password"
                     validator="#{registerBacking.validatePassword1}"
                     value="#{requestScope.password1}" />
    <h:message for="password" />

    <h:outputLabel for="password2" value="Retype Password:" />
    <h:inputSecret required="true" id="password2"
                                 value="#{requestScope.password2}"
                                validator="#{registerBacking.validatePassword2}" />
    <h:message for="password2" />
</h:panelGrid>
```

```
<p><h:commandButton  value="Register"
                action="#{registerBacking.registerUser}"  /></p>
</h:form>
```

There are two practical differences between this page and the one in Chapter 2. First, a simple multifield validator approach is employed to ensure the two password fields match. Second, the processing that happens when the form is submitted is quite different for having to work with the persistence layer. We'll start by examining the **RegisterBacking** bean.

```
package com.jsfcompref.trainer.backing;

import com.jsfcompref.trainer.entity.accessor.EntityAccessorException;
import com.jsfcompref.trainer.entity.accessor.UserRegistry;
import com.jsfcompref.trainer.entity.User;
import javax.faces.application.FacesMessage;
import javax.faces.bean.ManagedBean;
import javax.faces.component.UIComponent;
import javax.faces.context.FacesContext;
import javax.faces.validator.ValidatorException;

@ManagedBean
public class RegisterBacking extends AbstractBacking {
  private Object password1;

  public void validatePassword1(FacesContext context,
      UIComponent component,
      Object password1) throws ValidatorException {
    this.password1 = password1;
  }

  public void validatePassword2(FacesContext context,
      UIComponent component,
      Object password2) throws ValidatorException {
    if (!(password1.equals(password2))) {
      throw new ValidatorException(
          new FacesMessage("Passwords must match."));
    }
  }

  /**
   * <p>If this method is called, we know that the user is valid and
   * safe to persist</p>
   * @return
   */
  public String registerUser() {
    String result = null;
    User newUser = (User) getRequestMap().get("user");
    // set the password into the user, because we know the
    // validator was successful if we reached here.
    newUser.setPassword((String) getRequestMap().get("password1"));
    try {
      UserRegistry.getCurrentInstance().addUser(newUser);
      // Put the current user in the session
      setCurrentUser(newUser);
      // redirect to the main page
```

```
        result = "/user/allEvents?faces-redirect=true";
      } catch (EntityAccessorException ex) {
        getFacesContext().addMessage(null,
            new FacesMessage("Error when adding user" +
            ((null != newUser) ? " " + newUser.toString() : "") +
              "."));
      }
      return result;
    }
}
```

The **register.xhtml** page uses a combination of JSF validation and JSR-303 Bean Validation. The former is used for the **password1** and **password2** fields. By storing the value of the **password1** field in the **validatePassword1( )** method, we are able to compare it to the value of **password2** in the **validatePassword2( )** method. If the passwords do not match, we throw a **ValidatorException** as all JSF validators must. Invoking JSR-303 bean validation is as simple as attaching the **@Email** and **@UseridUniquenessConstraint** annotations on the **getEmail( )** and **getUserid( )** methods of the **User** bean. The **@Email** constraint and validator are taken directly from Chapter 8. The **@UseridUniquenessConstraint** is very important because the system must ensure that no two users are registered with the same userid. The constraint annotation is defined as shown here:

```
package com.jsfcompref.trainer.entity;

import java.lang.annotation.Documented;
import java.lang.annotation.ElementType;
import java.lang.annotation.Retention;
import java.lang.annotation.RetentionPolicy;
import java.lang.annotation.Target;
import javax.validation.Constraint;
import javax.validation.ConstraintPayload;

@Documented
@Constraint(validatedBy = UseridUniquenessConstraintValidator.class)
@Target({ ElementType.METHOD, ElementType.FIELD })
@Retention(RetentionPolicy.RUNTIME)
public @interface UseridUniquenessConstraint {
  String message() default "A user with that userid already exists";
  Class<?>[] groups() default {};
  Class<? extends ConstraintPayload>[] payload() default {};
}
```

As with all JSR-303 constraints, a validator must be associated, in this case **UseridUniquenessConstraintValidator**, shown here:

```
package  com.jsfcompref.trainer.entity;

import  com.jsfcompref.trainer.entity.accessor.UserRegistry;
import  javax.validation.ConstraintValidator;
import  javax.validation.ConstraintValidatorContext;

public  class  UseridUniquenessConstraintValidator  implements
  ConstraintValidator<UseridUniquenessConstraint,  String>  {
```

```
  public boolean isValid(String value, ConstraintValidatorContext ctx){
    return (null == UserRegistry.getCurrentInstance().
            getUserByUserid(value));
  }

  public void initialize(UseridUniquenessConstraint arg0) { }
}
```

Note that the **isValid( )** method calls **UserRegistry.getUserByUserid( )**. This method causes JPA actions to be taken. Because the **User** class is a JPA **Entity**, and also has a JSR-303 Constraint applied to it, care must be taken when using JPA within the actual constraint implementation, as we do here. To prevent nested transactions, we have added a **<validation-mode>NONE</validation-mode>** element to the **persistence.xml**. This file is shown later in the chapter.

We can now look to the submit button for the form, whose **value** attribute is **#{registerBacking.registerUser}**. The JSF lifecycle ensures that **registerUser( )** will only be called if all the submitted values are valid and in the proper Java language type.

Before reviewing the **registerUser( )** method, a very important subtlety becomes apparent when we examine the **value** attribute for all of the input fields on the **register.xhtml** page. For example, **<h:inputText label="First Name" id="fname" value="#{user.firstName}" required="true"/>**. This stores a value to the **firstName** property on a managed bean called **user**. Recall from Figure 10-14 that the **User** entity also is declared as a managed bean. This approach allows the JSF managed bean facility to instantiate the entity so that it can be persisted in the **registerUser( )** method. To do so, we simply can get it out from request scope, store the password into it, and call the **addUser( )** method on **UserRegistry**. If the persistence attempt fails, we add a message and redirect to the main page.

Building the Core Pages of the Virtual Trainer Application

When you log in to the application, the page chosen by the user from the drop-down list on the login page is displayed. Let's first look at **allEvents.xhtml**. This page allows you to browse through a list of training events in tabular form. The actions a user can take on the page depend on whether the user is a trainer or not. Users see this page as the list of available events, with the events they are training for indicated with a checked checkbox. Trainers see can either edit one event at a time or click multiple events to delete them with the **Delete Selected Events** button.

Creating the allEvents.xhtml Page

Many of the pages in this application rely on the use of the **h:dataTable** component and its underlying **UIData** object. Let's examine how this works on the **allEvents.xhtml** page. Because this page is a template client of **template.xhtml** but only defines the **content** part, we only need to show the **content** part here.

```
<ui:define name="content">
<h3>All Upcoming Events</h3>
<h:form>
<h:dataTable value="#{eventRegistry.events}" var="event"
    binding="#{eventTableBacking.events}"
    rendered="#{eventRegistry.events.rowCount > 0}"
    border="1">
```

```
<h:column>
    <f:facet name="header">Event Name</f:facet>#{event.name}
</h:column>
<h:column>
    <f:facet name="header">Event Date</f:facet>
        <h:outputText value="#{event.completionDate}">
            <f:convertDateTime timeStyle="short" />
        </h:outputText>
    </h:column>
    <h:column>
        <f:facet name="header">Skill Level</f:facet>#{event.skill}
    </h:column>
    <h:column>
        <c:if test="#{currentUser.trainer}">
            <f:facet name="header">Take action</f:facet>
                <h:link outcome="/trainer/editTrainingEvent">
                    <f:param name="id" value="#{event.id}"/>
                Edit</h:link>
        </c:if>
        <c:if test="#{!currentUser.trainer}">
            <f:facet name="header">Training<br/>
                for this event?</f:facet>
            <h:selectBooleanCheckbox
               value="#{eventTableBacking.subscribedToEvent}"/>
            <f:facet name="footer">
                <h:commandButton value="Update Event Subscriptions"
                         action="myEvents?faces-redirect=true"/>
            </f:facet>
        </c:if>
    </h:column>
    <c:if test="#{currentUser.trainer}">
        <h:column>
            <f:facet name="header">Delete This Event?</f:facet>
            <h:selectBooleanCheckbox
              value="#{eventTableBacking.deleteEvent}"/>
            <f:facet name="footer">
                <h:commandButton value="Delete Selected Events"
                         action="allEvents?faces-redirect=true"/>
            </f:facet>
        </h:column>
    </c:if>
</h:dataTable>
</h:form>
<p><h:messages/></p>
</ui:define>
```

The rendering of this page is straightforward; it employs the **<c:if>** technique used in **template.xhtml** to render different content, depending on whether the user is a trainer or not. The actions taken in these two cases are notable. First, let's take the case of a regular user, who is allowed to update the set of events for which they are training by checking (or clearing) the checkboxes and clicking the **Update Event Subscriptions** button. The markup for the checkbox looks like this **<h:selectBooleanCheckbox value="#{eventTableBacking .subscribedToEvent}"/>**. Let's examine the **boolean subscribedToEvent** read/write JavaBeans property on **EventTableBacking**.

```
private UIData events; // getter and setter omitted for brevity
private List<Long> subscribedEventIds;

public List<Long> getSubscribedEventIds() {
  if (null == subscribedEventIds) {
    subscribedEventIds = getCurrentUser().getSubscribedEventIds();
  }
  return subscribedEventIds;
}

public boolean isSubscribedToEvent() {
  Event currentEvent = (Event) getEvents().getRowData();
  boolean result = false;
  result = getSubscribedEventIds().contains(currentEvent.getId());
  return result;
}

public void setSubscribedToEvent(boolean subscribedToEvent) {
  Event currentEvent = (Event) getEvents().getRowData();
  Long id = currentEvent.getId();
  boolean isCurrentlySubscribed = getSubscribedEventIds().contains(id);
  boolean doPersist = false;
  if (true == subscribedToEvent) {
    if (!isCurrentlySubscribed) {
      getSubscribedEventIds().add(id);
      doPersist = true;
    }
  } else if (isCurrentlySubscribed) {

    getSubscribedEventIds().remove(id);
    doPersist = true;
  }
  if (doPersist) {
    try {
      UserRegistry.getCurrentInstance().updateUser(getCurrentUser());
    } catch (EntityAccessorException ex) {
      Logger.getLogger(EventTableBacking.class.getName()).log(Level.SEVERE,
                        null, ex);
    }
  }
}
```

The first line in the getter and the setter of the **subscribedToEvent** property that backs the checkbox is **Event currentEvent = (Event) getEvents().getRowData()**. This is a very common pattern with data tables, and it is the way you get access to the POJO that is exposed by the **var** attribute on **<h:dataTable>**. The getter for **subscribedToEvent** simply returns **true** if the **id** of the **Event** for the current row is among the list of events the current user is subscribed to. The setter is more involved. If the checkbox is checked, but we are not currently subscribed to the event, we add the event's **id** to the list of subscribed events. If the checkbox is not checked, we remove the **id** from the list. If the list is modified in either case, we need to persist the change with a call to **UserRegistry.getCurrentInstance( ) .updateUser(getCurrentUser( )**.

PART II

NOTE *Hitting the database when rendering or updating every row in the table is a very bad idea for performance. A production application would batch these operations. However, the simplicity of this approach allows the* **Update Event Subscriptions** *button to be a simple* **action** *without any backing method.*

Let's now take a look at how the actions available to the trainer are handled. First, the **Edit** link: **<h:link outcome="/trainer/editTrainingEvent"><f:param name="id" value="#{event.id}"/>Edit</h:link>**. Recall from Chapter 6 that the new **<h:link>** element renders a plain old, non-JavaScript HTML anchor element with query params for each of the nested **<f:param>** elements. The elements **<h:link>** and **<h:button>** are nearly always used in concert with View Parameters, also described in Chapter 6. We'll cover the other side of the **Edit** link after showing how the **Delete Selected Events** button works. As expected, this works in a very similar way to the **Update Event Subscriptions** button on the user's version of the page, but it is much simpler because the checkboxes are never checked when the page renders, since the act of checking them deletes them from the database. The markup for the checkbox is **<h:selectBooleanCheckbox value= "#{eventTableBacking.deleteEvent}"/>**. Because the checkboxes never start out checked, we simply return **false** from the getter. The setter looks like this:

```
public void setDeleteEvent(boolean deleteEvent) {
  if (deleteEvent) {
    Event currentEvent = (Event) getEvents().getRowData();
    Long id = currentEvent.getId();
    EventRegistry.getCurrentInstance().
      removeEventFromRegistryAndFromUsers(id);
  }
}
```

The same caution about performing a database update for every row in the table applies here. Don't do it in a production application.

Because the act of deleting a training event, as done in the preceding code, is so similar to the act of deleting a training session from a user's workout plan, the **/user/editTrainingEvent.xhtml** page will not be examined in the book. Of course, it is available in the online code.

The Trainer Version of editTrainingEvent.xhtml

Now we quickly come to the **/trainer/editTrainingEvent.xhtml** page, reached when a trainer clicks the **Edit** link next to one of the events. This page uses the **template.xhtml** and has **<ui:define>** elements for the **metadata** and **content** spots. Let's look at the **metadata** first.

```
<ui:define name="metadata">
  <f:metadata>
    <f:viewParam name="id" required="true"
          value="#{editTrainingEventBacking.selectedEventId}"
          requiredMessage="No training event selected"
          validatorMessage="Invalid training event id selected">
      <f:validateLongRange minimum="1" />
    </f:viewParam>
  </f:metadata>
```

```
  <f:event type="preRenderView"
       listener="#{editTrainingEventBacking.forwardToMainIfNotTrainer}" />
  <f:event type="preRenderView"
       listener="#{editTrainingEventBacking.loadTrainingEvent}" />
</ui:define>
```

First, and most important, we have an **<f:metadata>** section that declares a **<f:viewParam>** named **id**. This is the other side of the **<h:link>** on the **allEvents.xhtml** page. Second, we have **forwardToMainIfNotTrainer**, as mentioned earlier. Finally, we have the **editTrainingEventBacking.loadTrainingEvent** element. This works in concert with **<f:viewParam>** to convey the selected event so that it can be edited in the page. The code for **loadTrainingEvent( )** on class **EditTrainingEventBacking** is shown here:


```
// Getters and setters for these fields omitted for brevity.
private Long selectedEventId;
private Event selectedEvent;
private UIData trainingSessionData;

public void loadTrainingEvent(ComponentSystemEvent cse) {
  // if the event has not yet been set
  if (null == getSelectedEvent()) {
    Long eventId = getSelectedEventId();
    if (null == eventId) {
      // Try to get it from the flash
      eventId = (Long) getFlash().get("selectedEventId");
    }

    if (null == eventId) {
      getFacesContext().addMessage(null,
          new FacesMessage("The training event you requested is invalid"));
      getFlash().setKeepMessages(true);
      getFacesContext().getApplication().getNavigationHandler().
          handleNavigation(getFacesContext(), null,
                           "/user/allEvents?faces-redirect=true");
    } else {
      Event event = EventRegistry.getCurrentInstance().
          getEventForId(eventId);
      if (null == event) {
        getFacesContext().addMessage(null,
          new FacesMessage("The training event you requested does " +
                           "not exist"));
        getFlash().setKeepMessages(true);
        getFacesContext().getApplication().getNavigationHandler().
            handleNavigation(getFacesContext(), null,
                           "/user/allEvents?faces-redirect=true");
      } else {
        getFlash().put("selectedEvent", event);
        setSelectedEvent(event);
      }
    }
  }
}
```

This code loads the **Event** from the database given its **id**. It stores the **Event** both using the **selectedEvent** setter, and also in the Flash. This is necessary to enable postbacks to the **editTrainingEvent.xhtml** page. If, for any reason, the event cannot be loaded, we add a helpful message and redirect back to the **allEvents.xhtml** page.

Now that we have examined the **metadata** section of **editTrainingEvent.xhtml**, let's look at the **content**.

```
<ui:define name="content">
<h3>Event Information</h3>
<h:form>

<c:if test="#{! empty editTrainingEventBacking.selectedEvent}">
  <c:set target="#{flash}" property="selectedEvent"
         value="#{editTrainingEventBacking.selectedEvent}" />
</c:if>
<c:if test="#{! empty flash.selectedEvent}">
  <c:set target="#{editTrainingEventBacking}" property="selectedEvent"
         value="#{flash.selectedEvent}" />
</c:if>

<h:panelGrid columns="4" width="100%" border="0" class="form-bkg">
  <h:outputText value="Event Title" />
  <h:inputText value="#{editTrainingEventBacking.selectedEvent.name}"
               required="true"></h:inputText>

  <h:outputText value="Event Type" />
  <h:inputText value="#{editTrainingEventBacking.selectedEvent.type}"
               required="true" />

  <h:outputText value="Event Date" />
  <h:inputText value="#{editTrainingEventBacking.selectedEvent.completionDate}"
               required="true">
    <f:convertDateTime pattern="MM-dd-yy" />
  </h:inputText>

  <h:outputText value="Skill" />
  <h:selectOneMenu label="Skill" id="slevel"
                   value="#{editTrainingEventBacking.selectedEvent.skill}">
    <f:selectItem itemLabel="Beginner" itemValue="beginner" />
    <f:selectItem itemLabel="Intermediate" itemValue="intermediate" />
    <f:selectItem itemLabel="Advanced" itemValue="advanced" />
  </h:selectOneMenu>

  <h:commandButton
     action="#{editTrainingEventBacking.updateExistingTrainingEvent}"
     value="Update Event" />

<h:outputText value=" " />
<h:outputText value=" " />

  <h:button outcome="/user/allEvents?faces-redirect=true"
            value="Cancel" />
</h:panelGrid>
</h:form>
</ui:define>
```

The first two **<c:if>** statements cause the selected event to be pushed to the flash when the page renders, and pulled from the flash when the page posts back. This is necessary to avoid putting the **Event** object in the session. The **<h:panelGrid>** is just a simple form field, except that the fields point to the **selectedEvent** property of the **EventTableBacking** bean. This is the **Event** that was looked up by **id** on the previous page; it is either looked up from the **loadTrainingEvent( )** method when the page initially renders or looked up from the flash when the page posts back. Once we have the **selectedEvent** properly being loaded, it's easy to update it with this button: **<h:commandButton action="#{editTrainingEventBacking .updateExistingTrainingEvent}" value="Update Event" />**. The code for the method pointed to by this markup is shown here:

```
public String updateExistingTrainingEvent() {
  String result = null;

  EventRegistry eventRegistry = EventRegistry.getCurrentInstance();
  Event newEvent = getSelectedEvent();
  try {
    eventRegistry.updateEvent(newEvent);
    result = "/user/allEvents?faces-redirect=true";
  } catch (EntityAccessorException ex) {
    Logger.getLogger(EditTrainingEventBacking.class.getName()).
         log(Level.SEVERE, null, ex);
  }
  getFlash().clear();

  return result;
}
```

Once we update the modified event, we simply redirect back to the **allEvents** page.

The technique just shown, that of using view parameters in concert with the flash in **/user/allEvents.xhtml** and **/trainer/editTrainingEvent.xhtml**, is applied in exactly the same way between the **/user/editTrainingEvent.xhtml** and **/user/addTrainingSession.xhtml** pages. In the interest of brevity, this code is not present in the text, but it is available in the online sample. The final two pages to examine are **/trainer/viewTrainees.xhtml** and **/trainer/viewTrainingSessionsForUser.xhtml**.

Creating the viewTrainees.xhtml and viewTrainingSessionsForUser.xhtml Pages

The navigation bar in **template.xhtml** includes a link, visible only to trainers, to **/trainer/viewTrainees.xhtml**. This page lists the users for whom the current user is a trainer, offering a link to another page where the workout plans for the selected user can be viewed and modified. Like other trainer pages, **viewTrainees.xhtml** includes a **metadata** section that calls the **forwardToMainIfNotTrainer** method. The very simple **content** section is shown here:

```
<ui:define name="content">
  <h3>Your Trainees</h3>
  <h:form>
    <h:dataTable value="#{viewTraineesBacking.traineesForCurrentUser}"
       var="user"
       rendered="#{viewTraineesBacking.traineesForCurrentUser.rowCount > 0}"
       border="1">
```

```
      <h:column><f:facet name="header">Name</f:facet>
        #{user.firstName} #{user.lastName}
      </h:column>

      <h:column>
        <f:facet name="header">Take Action</f:facet>
        <h:link outcome="viewTrainingSessionsForUser">
          <f:param name="id" value="#{user.id}"/>
          View Training Sessions
        </h:link>
      </h:column>

    </h:dataTable>
  </h:form>
</ui:define>
```

Note that the **<h:dataTable>** does not have a **binding** attribute. This is because we don't need to access the row data from Java code; we're simply generating a list of links. The relevant code for the **ViewTraineesBacking** class is shown next.

```
public DataModel<User> getTraineesForCurrentUser() {
  DataModel<User> users = new ListDataModel<User>(UserRegistry.
        getCurrentInstance().getTraineesForTrainer(getCurrentUser()));
  return users;
}
```

The **/trainer/viewTrainingSessionsForUser.xhtml** page is more interesting. Like **/trainer/editTrainingEvent.xhtml**, it has a **metadata** and **content** section. The former is nearly identical to the one in **editTrainingEvent.xhtml**. There are only two differences between these two pages. First, the **id** view parameter refers to the **id** field of the selected **User**. Second, we have a **preRenderView** method called **loadUser** instead of **loadTrainingEvent**. This method uses the **id** to load the selected user. The **content** section is very different, however, and is shown here:

```
<ui:define name="content">
  <h3>Events and Training Sessions for
      #{viewTraineesBacking.selectedUser.firstName}
      #{viewTraineesBacking.selectedUser.lastName}</h3>
  <h:form>
    <c:if test="#{! empty flash.selectedUser}">
      <c:set target="#{viewTraineesBacking}" property="selectedUser"
           value="#{flash.selectedUser}" />
    </c:if>
    <h:dataTable value="#{viewTraineesBacking.selectedUser.myEvents}"
           var="event"
           rendered="#{viewTraineesBacking.selectedUser.myEvents.
                     rowCount > 0}"
           border="0">
      <h:column>
        <h2>#{event.name}</h2>
        <h:dataTable value="#{viewTraineesBacking.selectedUser.
                          getTrainingSessionsForEvent(event)}"
              binding="#{viewTraineesBacking.trainingSessions}"
```

```
              var="trainingSession"
              border="0">
          <h:column>
            <h:panelGrid columns="5" border="1">
              <h:outputText value="Workout Date (mm-dd-yy)" />
              <h:outputText value="Assigned Workout" />
              <h:outputText value="Completed?" />
              <h:outputText value="Personal Notes" />

              <h:outputText value="Trainer Notes" />
              <h:outputText value="#{trainingSession.workoutDate}">
                <f:convertDateTime pattern="MM-dd-yy" />
              </h:outputText>
              <h:outputText value="#{trainingSession.workoutDescription}"/>
              <h:selectBooleanCheckbox disabled="true"
                  value="#{trainingSession.completed}"/>
              <h:outputText value="#{trainingSession.personalNotes}"/>
              <h:inputText value="#{trainingSession.trainerNotes}"/>
            </h:panelGrid>
          </h:column>
        </h:dataTable>
      </h:column>
    </h:dataTable>

    <h:commandButton action="/user/allEvents?faces-redirect=true"
           value="Update"/>
    <c:if test="#{! empty viewTraineesBacking.selectedUser}">
      <c:set target="#{flash}" property="selectedUser"
          value="#{viewTraineesBacking.selectedUser}" />
    </c:if>
  </h:form>
</ui:define>
```

This is the page that uses the nested data table approach mentioned earlier. The outer table iterates over the **Events** for which the current user is training. For each event, there is an inner table that shows all of the training sessions for that event such that the trainer can make comments in the **Trainer Notes** field. Note that the method invocation feature new to the Unified EL in Java EE 6 is employed to arrive at the **DataModel** over which the inner table iterates. This **DataModel** is returned when the EL expression **#{viewTraineesBacking .selectedUser.getTrainingSessionsForEvent(event)}** is evaluated. The **event** argument is actually the **var** from the outer table. The Java code for this method is shown here:

```
public DataModel<TrainingSession> getTrainingSessionsForEvent(Event e) {
  // lazily initialize training sessions
  if (!sessionsInitialized) {
    populateTrainingSessions();
    sessionsInitialized = true;
    try {
      UserRegistry.getCurrentInstance().updateUser(this);
    } catch (EntityAccessorException ex) {
      Logger.getLogger(User.class.getName()).log(Level.SEVERE, null, ex);
    }
  }
```

```
    DataModel<TrainingSession> sessionsForEvent = null;
    List<TrainingSession> sessionList = UserRegistry.getCurrentInstance().
       getTrainingSessionsForUserAndEvent(this, e);

    sessionsForEvent = new ListDataModel<TrainingSession>(sessionList);

    return sessionsForEvent;
}
```

The initial **if** statement is simply there to ensure that the training sessions are automatically populated for demonstration purposes. You can see that this method delegates the hard work to the **UserRegistry**, the code for which will follow this section.

Let's return once more to **viewTrainingSessionsForUser.xhtml**. The technique of using view parameters in concert with the flash, as in **/user/allEvents.xhtml** and **/trainer/editTrainingEvent.xhtml**, is once again employed, this time between **/trainer/viewTrainees.xhtml** and **/trainer/viewTrainingSessionsForUser.xhtml**. We will not belabor the point by repeating the code once again. The next section concludes our examination of the core functionality of the Virtual Trainer by exploring the code in **UserRegistry** and **EventRegistry**.

The UserRegistry and EventRegistry

These two classes extend the aforementioned **AbstractEntityAccessor** class and thus know how to manage the JPA entities **User**, **TrainingSession**, and **Event**. Let's start with **UserRegistry** because the notion of **User** is common to nearly every Web application.

UserRegistry has three responsibilities:

- Initialize the **UserRegistry** instance itself and provide access to it via a static method that can be called from anywhere.
- Read and write **User** instances to/from persistence.
- Read and write **TrainingSession** instances to/from persistence.

To minimize the conceptual burden of digesting a great big block of code, we'll examine each responsibility in turn, but know that all of the following methods are on the **UserRegistry** class.

Accessing and Initializing the UserRegistry Instance

The **UserRegistry** class is designed here to be an application singleton. In this section you will learn one way to initialize and access such a class in a JSF application.

```
@ManagedBean(eager = true)
@ApplicationScoped
public class UserRegistry extends AbstractEntityAccessor implements Serializable {
public static UserRegistry getCurrentInstance() {
  UserRegistry result = null;
  Map<String, Object> appMap = FacesContext.getCurrentInstance().
      getExternalContext().getApplicationMap();
  result = (UserRegistry) appMap.get("userRegistry");
  assert(null != result);
```

```
  return result;
}
@PostConstruct
public void perApplicationConstructor() {
  try {
    doInTransaction(new PersistenceActionWithoutResult() {

      public void execute(EntityManager em) {
        Query query = em.createNamedQuery("user.getAll");
        List<User> results = query.getResultList();
        if (results.isEmpty()) {
          populateUsers(em);
          query = em.createNamedQuery("user.getAll");
          results = query.getResultList();
          assert(!results.isEmpty());
        }
      }
    });
  } catch (EntityAccessorException ex) {
    Logger.getLogger(UserRegistry.class.getName()).log(Level.SEVERE, null, ex);
  }
}
// the populateUsers() method is for demonstration purposes
// and is omitted from the text, but is present in the online code.
```

First and most important, note that this class is an application-scoped managed bean, and note the **eager=true** attribute on the **@ManagedBean** annotation. This attribute advises the JSF runtime that this bean instance, of which there is only one per application, must be instantiated at startup time, before the container has served any requests. Furthermore, the presence of the **@PostConstruct** annotation on the **perApplicationConstructor( )** method requires the system call that method immediately after the class's constructor is called. This method is responsible for populating the user database at startup time with an initial set of users. Naturally, a production application would not have this sort of requirement. It is useful to understand the **user.getAll** named query. This is an example of a JPA named query, one of the most powerful and commonly used features in JPA. Named queries are declared as annotations on the entity class, in this case **User**. We'll examine the entity classes briefly after this section, but for now, just understand that queries are really the heart of JPA. Understand queries, and Java Persistence Query Language (JPQL), and you understand the most important thing about JPA.

Reading and Writing User Instances

This is the largest collection of methods on the class. It's quite likely that the number of methods could be reduced with a little refactoring.

```
public DataModel<User> getUsers() {
  DataModel<User> users = new ListDataModel<User>(getUserList());
  return users;
}

public User getUserByUserid(final String userid) {
  User result = null;
```

```
    // PENDING do a query to get this information, don't iterate over
    // the list
    List<User> users = getUserList();
    for (User user : users) {
      if (user.getUserid().equals(userid)) {
        result = user;
        break;
      }
    }

    return result;
  }

  public User getUserById(final Long id) {
    User result = null;
    try {
      result = doInTransaction(new PersistenceAction<User>() {

        public User execute(EntityManager em) {
          return em.find(User.class, id);
        }
      });
    } catch (EntityAccessorException ex) {
      Logger.getLogger(UserRegistry.class.getName()).log(Level.SEVERE,
                       null, ex);
    }
    return result;
  }

  public List<User> getUserList() {
    List<User> result = Collections.emptyList();
    try {
      result = doInTransaction(new PersistenceAction<List<User>>() {

        public List<User> execute(EntityManager em) {
          Query query = em.createNamedQuery("user.getAll");
          List<User> results = query.getResultList();
          return results;
        }
      });
    } catch (EntityAccessorException ex) {
      Logger.getLogger(UserRegistry.class.getName()).log(Level.SEVERE,
                       null, ex);
    }

    return result;
  }

  public List<User> getTrainerList() {
    List<User> result = Collections.emptyList();
    try {
      result = doInTransaction(new PersistenceAction<List<User>>() {

        public List<User> execute(EntityManager em) {
          Query query = em.createNamedQuery("user.getTrainers");
```

```
          List<User> results = query.getResultList();
          return results;
        }
      });
    } catch (EntityAccessorException ex) {
      Logger.getLogger(UserRegistry.class.getName()).log(Level.SEVERE,
                        null, ex);
    }

    return result;
  }

  public List<User> getTraineesForTrainer(final User trainer) {
    List<User> result = Collections.emptyList();
    try {
      result = doInTransaction(new PersistenceAction<List<User>>() {

        public List<User> execute(EntityManager em) {
          Query query = em.createNamedQuery("user.getUsersForTrainerId");
          query.setParameter("theId", trainer.getId());
          List<User> results = query.getResultList();
          return results;
        }
      });
    } catch (EntityAccessorException ex) {
      Logger.getLogger(UserRegistry.class.getName()).log(Level.SEVERE,
                        null, ex);
    }

    return result;
  }
```

The first six methods read **User** instances from the persistence layer, in one way or another. The last two methods write **User** instances to the persistence layer.

Reading and Writing TrainingSession Instances

Because **TrainingSession** is a JPA **@Entity** and has its own **@Table**, a more correct design would have a separate **TrainingSessionRegistry**. However, as shown in Figure 10-12, **TrainingSession** is intimately related with **User**, and therefore it is acceptable to allocate the responsibility for managing **TrainingSession** instances to the **UserRegistry**.

```
public void addTrainingSessions(final List<TrainingSession> toAdd)
       throws EntityAccessorException {
  doInTransaction(new PersistenceActionWithoutResult() {

    public void execute(EntityManager em) {
      for (TrainingSession t : toAdd) {
        em.persist(t);
      }
    }
  });
}
```

```
public void updateTrainingSession(final TrainingSession toUpdate)
  throws EntityAccessorException {
  doInTransaction(new PersistenceActionWithoutResult() {

    public void execute(EntityManager em) {
      em.merge(toUpdate);
    }
  });
}

public void removeTrainingSessionForUserAndEvent(final User user,
    final Event e, final TrainingSession trainingSession) {
  try {
    doInTransaction(new PersistenceActionWithoutResult() {

      public void execute(EntityManager em) {
        em.remove(em.contains(trainingSession) ? trainingSession :
          em.merge(trainingSession));
        user.getTrainingSessions().remove(trainingSession);
        em.merge(user);
      }
    });
  } catch (EntityAccessorException ex) {
    Logger.getLogger(UserRegistry.class.getName()).log(Level.SEVERE,
                    null, ex);
  }
}

public void updateTrainingSessionForUser(final User user,
    final TrainingSession trainingSession) {
  try {
    doInTransaction(new PersistenceActionWithoutResult() {

      public void execute(EntityManager em) {
        em.merge(trainingSession);
        em.merge(user);
      }
    });
  } catch (EntityAccessorException ex) {
    Logger.getLogger(UserRegistry.class.getName()).log(Level.SEVERE,
                    null, ex);
  }
}
```

Now let's examine the smaller **EventRegistry**. This class only deals with one kind of entity, **Event**.

EventRegistry has two responsibilities.

- Initialize the **EventRegistry** instance itself and provide access to it via a static method that can be called from anywhere.
- Read and write **Event** instances to/from persistence.

Accessing and Initializing the EventRegistry Instance

As with the **UserRegistry**, the **EventRegistry** is a singleton, but this class is designed to be a session-scoped singleton. Even so, we use the same techniques to initialize and access the instance as with **UserRegistry**.

```
@ManagedBean(eager = true)
@SessionScoped
public class EventRegistry extends AbstractEntityAccessor implements Serializable {

public static EventRegistry getCurrentInstance() {
  EventRegistry result = null;
  FacesContext context = FacesContext.getCurrentInstance();
  Map<String, Object> sessionMap = context.getExternalContext().getSessionMap();
  if (null == (result = (EventRegistry) sessionMap.get("eventRegistry"))){
    result = context.getApplication().
             evaluateExpressionGet(context, "#{eventRegistry}",
                                   EventRegistry.class);
  }
  assert(null != result);

  return result;
}

@PostConstruct
public void perSessionConstructor() {
  try {
    doInTransaction(new PersistenceActionWithoutResult() {

      public void execute(EntityManager em) {
        Query query = em.createNamedQuery("event.getAll");
        List<Event> results = query.getResultList();
        if (results.isEmpty()) {
          populateEvents(em);
          query = em.createNamedQuery("event.getAll");
          results = query.getResultList();
          assert(!results.isEmpty());
        }
      }
    });
  } catch (EntityAccessorException ex) {
    Logger.getLogger(EventRegistry.class.getName()).log(Level.SEVERE, null, ex);
  }

}
// populate events omitted for brevity
```

As with **UserRegistry**, **EventRegistry** is an eager managed bean; however, **EventRegistry** is in session scope. There is also a static accessor method and an **@PostConstruct** annotated initialization method.

Reading and Writing Event Instances

Continuing the discussion of **EventRegistry**, let's examine the methods that deal with reading and writing **Event** instances.

```
public DataModel<Event> getEvents() {
  DataModel<Event> Events = new ListDataModel<Event>(getEventList());
  return Events;
}

public Event getEventForId(final Long id) {
  Event result = null;

  try {
    result = doInTransaction(new PersistenceAction<Event>() {

      public Event execute(EntityManager em) {
        return em.find(Event.class, id);
      }
    });
  } catch (EntityAccessorException ex) {
    Logger.getLogger(EventRegistry.class.getName()).log(Level.SEVERE,
                     null, ex);
  }

  return result;
}

public List<Event> getEventList() {
  List<Event> result = Collections.emptyList();
  try {
    result = doInTransaction(new PersistenceAction<List<Event>>() {
      public List<Event> execute(EntityManager em) {
        Query query = em.createNamedQuery("event.getAll");
        List<Event> results = query.getResultList();
        return (List<Event>) results;
      }
    });
  } catch (EntityAccessorException ex) {
    Logger.getLogger(EventRegistry.class.getName()).log(Level.SEVERE,
                     null, ex);
  }

  return result;
}

public Event removeEventForId(final Long id) {
  Event result = null;

  try {
    result = doInTransaction(new PersistenceAction<Event>() {

      public Event execute(EntityManager em) {
        Event result = em.find(Event.class, id);
```

```
        if (null != result) {
          em.remove(result);
        }

        return result;
      }
    });
  } catch (EntityAccessorException ex) {
    Logger.getLogger(EventRegistry.class.getName()).log(Level.SEVERE,
                     null, ex);
  }


  return result;
}

public void removeEventFromRegistryAndFromUsers(final Long id) {
  this.removeEventForId(id);
  UserRegistry userRegistry = UserRegistry.getCurrentInstance();
  List<User> userList = userRegistry.getUserList();
  for (User u : userList) {
    List<Long> subscribedIds = u.getSubscribedEventIds();
    if (subscribedIds.contains(id)) {
      subscribedIds.remove(id);
      try {
        userRegistry.updateUser(u);
      } catch (EntityAccessorException ex) {
        Logger.getLogger(EventRegistry.class.getName()).
                         log(Level.SEVERE, null, ex);
      }
    }
  }
}


public void addEvent(final Event toAdd) throws EntityAccessorException {
  doInTransaction(new PersistenceActionWithoutResult() {
    public void execute(EntityManager em) {
      em.persist(toAdd);
    }
  });
}

public void updateEvent(final Event toAdd) throws EntityAccessorException {
  doInTransaction(new PersistenceActionWithoutResult() {
    public void execute(EntityManager em) {
      em.merge(toAdd);
    }
  });
}
```

By this time, the patterns used in this application should be very familiar and you should be acquainted with the basic JPA techniques. We complete our discussion of the core Virtual Trainer by briefly surveying the entity classes for their persistence implications.

PART II

JPA and the Entity Classes in Virtual Trainer

Recall from Figure 10-14 that there are three **JPA** entity classes in Virtual Trainer, and these are also exposed as request-scoped JSF managed beans. Let's first take a look at the declaration of **User**.

```
package com.jsfcompref.trainer.entity;

import java.io.Serializable;
import javax.faces.bean.ManagedBean;
import javax.faces.bean.RequestScoped;
import javax.persistence.Entity;
import javax.persistence.NamedQueries;
import javax.persistence.NamedQuery;
import javax.persistence.Table;


@Entity
@Table(name = "vtUsers")
@NamedQueries({
  @NamedQuery(name = "user.getAll", query = "select u from User as u"),
  @NamedQuery(name = "user.getTrainers", query =
             "select u from User as u where u.trainer = TRUE"),
  @NamedQuery(name = "user.getUsersForTrainerId",
             query =
             "select u from User as u where u.personalTrainerId = :theId")
})
@ManagedBean
@RequestScoped
public class User extends AbstractEntity implements Serializable {
  protected String firstName;
  protected String lastName;
  @Temporal(TemporalType.DATE)
  protected Date dob;
  protected String sex;
  protected String email;
  private String serviceLevel = "medium";
  @Column(name="userid", nullable=false)
  private String userid;
  private String password;
  private boolean trainer;
  private List<Long> subscribedEventIds;
  private Long personalTrainerId;
  @OneToMany(mappedBy = "user", cascade = CascadeType.ALL)
  private List<TrainingSession> sessions;
  private boolean sessionsInitialized = false;
```

The most interesting thing about this declaration is the **@NamedQueries** declaration. An introduction to JPQL is beyond the scope of this book, but this sample code should give you an idea of what it's all about. JPA automatically handles mapping all the fields in this class to the database. Special care has to be given to the **TrainingSession** list, however, because this is a reference to another entity class. A more proper way to do this might involve a secondary table, but this was not explored for the Virtual Trainer.

Now we'll show the similar declaration for **Event**.

```
@Entity
@Table(name = "vtEvents")
@NamedQueries({@NamedQuery(name = "event.getAll",
query = "select e from Event as e")})
@ManagedBean
@RequestScoped
public class Event  extends AbstractEntity implements Serializable
{
  @Column(nullable = false, unique = true)
  String name;
  @Temporal(TemporalType.DATE)
  @Column(name = "completion_date", nullable = false)
  Date completionDate;
  String skill;
  String type;
```

And finally, the **TrainingSession**.

```
@Entity
@Table(name = "vtEvents")
@NamedQueries({@NamedQuery(name = "event.getAll", query = "select e from
Event as e")})
@ManagedBean
@RequestScoped
public class Event  extends AbstractEntity implements Serializable
{
  @Column(nullable = false, unique = true)
  String name;

  @Temporal(TemporalType.DATE)
  @Column(name = "completion_date", nullable = false)
  Date completionDate;
  String skill;
  String type;
```

JPA XML Configuration File: persistence.xml

For all the automatic configuration that JPA does for you, you still have a small amount of manual configuration to do. This is mostly a side effect of the business reality that there are multiple vendors that provide JPA runtimes. The version of the trainer that is available online is designed to run nicely in Sun's open source Glassfish V3 application server, which bundles the Eclipselink JPA implementation. The **persistence.xml** file, which must reside in the deployed Web app's classpath under **/META-INF/persistence.xml**, is shown here:

```
<?xml version="1.0" encoding="UTF-8"?>
<persistence version="2.0" xmlns="http://java.sun.com/xml/ns/persistence"
xmlns:xsi="http://www.w3.org/2001/XMLSchema-instance"
xsi:schemaLocation="http://java.sun.com/xml/ns/persistence
http://java.sun.com/xml/ns/persistence/persistence_2_0.xsd">
  <persistence-unit name="trainerPU" transaction-type="JTA">
    <provider>org.eclipse.persistence.jpa.PersistenceProvider</provider>
    <jta-data-source>trainer</jta-data-source>
```

PART II

```
    <class>com.jsfcompref.trainer.entity.User</class>
    <class>com.jsfcompref.trainer.entity.Event</class>
    <class>com.jsfcompref.trainer.entity.TrainingSession</class>
    <validation-mode>NONE</validation-mode>
    <properties>
      <property name="eclipselink.target-database" value="Auto"/>
      <property name="eclipselink.ddl-generation" value="create-tables"/>
    </properties>
  </persistence-unit>
</persistence>
```

A Custom ExceptionHandler Example

Software development is an exercise in ignorance reduction: you try to account for all the requirements and address all the possible cases that can arise as users use the software. Recognizing that it is impossible for complex software to realistically account for **all** possible cases, JSF provides an **ExceptionHandler**, whose purpose is to handle any exceptions that arise that are not explicitly handled elsewhere in either the framework or your application. This section covers the steps necessary to add an **ExceptionHandler** to the Virtual Trainer.

First, adding a custom **ExceptionHandler** requires some content in the **faces-config.xml**. Because this is the first time in the development of the Virtual Trainer that we needed a **faces-config.xml** file, it is included in its entirety here.

Expert Group Insight *For every new feature in JSF 2.0, the expert group had to decide if it was worthwhile, and practical, to introduce an annotation to prevent the need for the feature to rely on content in the **faces-config.xml** file. The main criterion taken into consideration in this decision was frequency of use. If the EG felt a feature was going to be used frequently, they tried to expose it as simply as possible, usually via an annotation. **ExceptionHandler** did not make the cut, so you have to use **faces-config.xml** to access this feature.*

```
<?xml version='1.0' encoding='UTF-8'?>
<faces-config xmlns="http://java.sun.com/xml/ns/javaee"
  xmlns:xsi="http://www.w3.org/2001/XMLSchema-instance"
  xsi:schemaLocation="http://java.sun.com/xml/ns/javaee
  http://java.sun.com/xml/ns/javaee/web-facesconfig_2_0.xsd"
  version="2.0">
<factory>
  <exception-handler-factory>
    com.jsfcompref.trainer.extras.ExceptionHandlerFactory
  </exception-handler-factory>
</factory>
</faces-config>
```

This is an example of the abstract factory pattern, which is frequently used in JSF to enable extending the capability of the base framework. This pattern, described in detail in Chapter 13, requires a class whose sole purpose is to create instances of another class. Think of it as a way to make the constructor pluggable. The **ExceptionHandlerFactory** for the trainer is shown here.

```
package com.jsfcompref.trainer.extras;

import javax.faces.context.ExceptionHandler;
```

```
public class ExceptionHandlerFactory extends
javax.faces.context.ExceptionHandlerFactory {

  private javax.faces.context.ExceptionHandlerFactory parent;

  public ExceptionHandlerFactory(
      javax.faces.context.ExceptionHandlerFactory parent) {
    this.parent = parent;
  }

  @Override
  public ExceptionHandler getExceptionHandler() {
    ExceptionHandler result = parent.getExceptionHandler();
    result = new CustomExceptionHandler(result);

    return result;
  }

}
```

The next and final step is the **CustomExceptionHandler**, shown here.

```
package com.jsfcompref.trainer.extras;

import java.util.Iterator;
import java.util.Map;
import javax.faces.FacesException;
import javax.faces.application.NavigationHandler;
import javax.faces.application.ViewExpiredException;
import javax.faces.context.ExceptionHandler;
import javax.faces.context.ExceptionHandlerWrapper;
import javax.faces.context.FacesContext;
import javax.faces.event.ExceptionQueuedEvent;
import javax.faces.event.ExceptionQueuedEventContext;

class CustomExceptionHandler extends ExceptionHandlerWrapper {

  private ExceptionHandler parent;

  public CustomExceptionHandler(ExceptionHandler parent) {
    this.parent = parent;
  }

  @Override
  public ExceptionHandler getWrapped() {
    return this.parent;
  }

  @Override
  public void handle() throws FacesException {
    for (Iterator<ExceptionQueuedEvent> i =
         getUnhandledExceptionQueuedEvents().iterator();
         i.hasNext();) {
```

PART II

```
        ExceptionQueuedEvent event = i.next();
        ExceptionQueuedEventContext context =
          (ExceptionQueuedEventContext) event.getSource();
        Throwable t = context.getException();
        if (t instanceof ViewExpiredException) {
          ViewExpiredException vee = (ViewExpiredException) t;
          FacesContext fc = FacesContext.getCurrentInstance();
          NavigationHandler nav =
              fc.getApplication().getNavigationHandler();
          try {
            // Push some useful stuff to the flash scope for
            // use in the page
            fc.getExternalContext()getFlash().put("currentViewId",
                                                  vee.getViewId());
            nav.handleNavigation(fc, null, "/login?faces-redirect=true");
            fc.renderResponse();
          } finally {
            i.remove();
          }
        }
      }
      // At this point, the queue will not contain any ViewExpiredEvents.
      // Therefore, let the parent handle them.
      getWrapped().handle();
    }
}
```

Note that we take advantage of the **ExceptionHandlerWrapper** convenience class. This is one of many wrapper classes, the usage of which is described in detail in Chapter 13. The heart of this class is how we iterate over the unhandled exceptions with the call to **getUnhandledExceptionQueuedEvents( )**. This particular example takes action on the **ViewExpiredException**, which happens when the user tries to access a page when their session has expired, a very common occurrence. In this case, we extract some information from the exception and place it in flash scope, and then redirect to the login page, which now includes the following text, shown only when the view has expired.

```
<c:if test="#{! empty flash.expiredViewId}">
  <p>To protect your security, your session has expired.
  The page you were last looked at was #{flash.expiredViewId}.</p>
</c:if>
```

To round up our discussion of the Virtual Trainer, we take a look at the issues surrounding internationalization.

Internationalizing the Virtual Trainer Application

This section covers two features important to the creation of any production Web application: localization and accessibility. When effectively applied, both enable your Web application to be accessed by large numbers of users throughout the global marketplace. Localization and accessibility are examined together because they both share some common implementation techniques.

Localization

Localization is the process by which an application is adapted to meet the requirements of a specific geographic region of the world, also known as a *locale.* This includes a wide range of considerations, including culture, language, currency, typesetting, and so on. Localization is often abbreviated L10n because there are ten letters between the "l" and the "n" in the word "localization."

A closely related term to localization is *internationalization,* which is commonly abbreviated as i18n. (Localization is abbreviated with a capital *L,* but internationalization is abbreviated with a lowercase *i* because the lowercase *l* looks like a number 1, but there is no such confusion with the letter *i.*) Internationalization is what happens during software development to ease the process of localization; ideally, localization should require no programming at all. With JavaServer Faces, all of the internationalization work has already been done for you, so localizing your application is literally as easy as authoring your **ResourceBundle**s and possibly setting some **dir** and **lang** attributes on your markup. This section covers how to perform localization on a Faces application, including an example of localizing the Virtual Trainer application.

Some Benefits of the Localization Facilities Provided by JavaServer Faces

Let's begin by examining some of the benefits of the internationalization facility provided by Faces. Like many things in JSF, the way to handle localization is the same as for any other Java applications—Web-based or otherwise: using **ResourceBundle**s. Unlike desktop Java applications, though, the Web offers unprecedented reach, allowing users from all around the globe to concurrently access a single instance of an application. Faces takes advantage of the user-configurable language information sent by a Web browser with each request to choose the best locale among the choices available to the application. The Faces internationalization system allows you to declare exactly which locales are supported by your application, even down to different variants of the same language. For example, you could have an application localized for Austrian German and German German such that users from Austria would see a greeting of "*Gruß Gott*", while users from Germany would see "*Guten Tag*".

In addition to the standard Java platform techniques of using **ResourceBundle**s, Faces provides several ways to expose your **ResourceBundle**s to the Faces runtime via the Expression Language. A simple Facelet example shows how easy it is:

```
<h:form>
  <p><h:outputText value="#{bundle.greeting}" />
  <h:outputText value="#{user.firstName}" />
</h:form>
```

If this looks like regular JSF code, that's because it is. Code in the **faces-config.xml** file simply exposes a resource bundle as something that can be accessed via the EL. This is one case where a **faces-config.xml** file is still necessary. Create one and add the following code:

```
<application>
  <resource-bundle>
    <base-name>com.jsfcompref.trainer.Messages</base-name>
    <var>bundle</var>
  </resource-bundle>
</application>
```

Previous versions of JSF recommended using the **f:loadBundle** tag to associate a request-scoped variable called **bundle** with the **ResourceBundle** that uses the base name of **com.jsfcompref.trainer.Messages**. Since JSF 1.2, this is no longer recommended because it fails in the case of Ajax and partial page updates because the **f:loadBundle** tag may not always be executed in those cases.

In this example, the resource bundle is located under **com/jsfcompref/trainer** in the file **Resources.properties**. The general form for defining a **ResourceBundle** in a properties file is **<basename>_<language>_<country>_<variant>**. The **basename** portion is a fully qualified Java class name. As with actual **.java** files, the real filename is only the last part of the fully qualified class name; the previous parts of the fully qualified Java class name come from the directory structure. The meaning of the **language**, **country**, and **variant** extensions is explained later in the chapter, but for now, just know that these extensions tell the Java runtime to what **Locale** object this **ResourceBundle** applies. Also, note that the **language**, **country**, and **variant** parameters are optional. Their absence means this **ResourceBundle** is to be used as a fallback in case no better match for the requested locale can be found. For this example, the different resource files for this example could look like this:

Resources.properties:

```
greeting=Hello
titleMale=Mr.
...
```

Resources_fr.properties:

```
greeting=Bon Jour
titleMale=Monsieur.
...
```

Resources_de.properties:

```
greeting=Guten Tag
titleMale=Herr
...
```

Resources_de_at.properties:

```
greeting= Gruß Gott
titleMale=Herr
...
```

Once this association is made, you can refer to any key within that bundle using an EL expression that starts with **bundle** (or whatever you choose for the value of **var**). The text after the first dot is interpreted as the key in the bundle. You may wonder how to refer to **ResourceBundle** keys that contain dots. No worries; the square bracket EL syntax can be used in that case. For example, if there were a bundle key called **home.directory**, you could refer to it with the expression **#{bundle.home['directory']**.

A JSF Localization Example

Before looking at the details of localization with JSF, it's helpful to work through a complete example. This section shows how to localize the JSFReg example from Chapter 2. Because localization is best kept to the presentation layer, let's start by examining the localization

Application Page	Localization Needs
register.xhtml	Title, Sub title, First Name label, Last Name label, Sex label, Male label, Female Label, Date of Birth label, Email address label, Date of Birth pattern, Date of Birth pattern label, Service Level label, Service Level labels, Button label
confirm.xhtml	In addition to the localization needs from **register.xhtml**, **confirm .xhtml** requires a Confirmation label, and button labels for "edit" and "confirm"
done.xhtml	Labels for First Name, Last Name, Sex, Date of Birth, Email Address, and Service Level

TABLE 10-1 The Localization Needs of the JSFReg Application

needs of the three Facelet pages that compose the JSFReg application. Table 10-1 lists the pages and their localization needs.

When localizing an existing application, it's a good practice to perform a similar analysis to determine the localization needs. Of course, it is preferable that the application be developed with localized labels to begin with, but this is not always possible. From the analysis, we see that the localization needs of JSFReg are pretty simple and can all be addressed with a **ResourceBundle**. A real-world application will likely have more complex needs, such as the capability to dynamically switch locales while using the application, and also support right-to-left text, such as Arabic. Figure 10-17 portrays the various elements of a localized JSF application.

Creating the ResourceBundles The way localization is done in Java is through the use of the **java.util.ResourceBundle** class. Several ways exist to create an instance of **ResourceBundle** and make it available to your application. This chapter only explains the use of a properties file as the means for authoring a **ResourceBundle**, while the act of making it available to

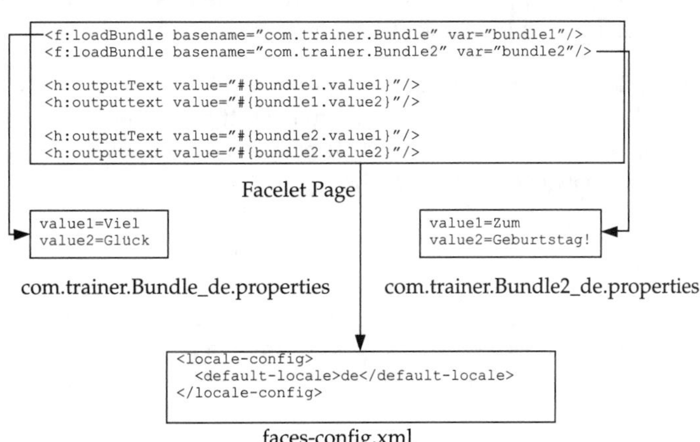

FIGURE 10-17 A localized JSF application

your application is handled by the Faces runtime, as described next. The following **Resources_de.properties** file shows the keys and values for the German version of the localized messages.

```
title=Ein Einfaches JavaServer Faces Ausrichtung Anwendung
subtitle= Ausrichtung Anwendung
inviteRegistriationLink=Klicken Sie Hier um anzumelden
registrationLabel=Anmeldeformular
firstName=Vorname:
lastName=Nachname:
sexLabel=Sex:
sexMale=Mann
sexFemale=Frau
birthday=Geburtstag:
datePattern=dd.MM.yy
emailAddress=Email Adresse:
serviceLevel=Bedienungsqualit\u00e4t
serviceLevelBasic=einfach
serviceLevelMedium=mittlerer
serviceLevelPremium=erstklassig
registerButton=anmelden
confirmationLabel=Best\u00e4tigung
editButton=\u00c4ndern
confirmationButton= Best\u00e4tigen
```

Simple applications can afford to put all the localized resources in one bundle, but more complex applications may want to break out the bundles by page or function.

Making the ResourceBundles Available to the Application Recall from the section "Assembling the JSFReg Application" in Chapter 2 the list of files and where they reside in the directory structure of the Web application. **ResourceBundle** instances are loaded into the VM using the regular Java **ClassLoader** facility; therefore, they must reside in a subdirectory of the **WEB-INF/classes** directory that matches the package hierarchy in which the **ResourceBundle** is to reside. In this example, the bundle will reside in the classpath at **com.jsfcompref.trainer .Resources**.

A more complex application requiring multiple **ResourceBundle**s would probably have all the bundles in a separate package, such as **com.jsfcompref.trainer.bundles**.

Declaring the Supported Locales for the Application In order for Faces to find the right **Locale** instance for the user, given his or her language settings in the browser, you must tell the Faces runtime what is the default locale and supported locales. This is done in the **<application>** method of the **faces-config.xml** file.

```
<application>
  <locale-config>
    <default-locale>en</default-locale>
    <supported-locale>de</supported-locale>
    <supported-locale>fr</supported-locale>
    <supported-locale>es</supported-locale>
  </locale-config>
</application>
```

The preceding declaration states that the default locale is English, while German, French, and Spanish are supported. The ordering of elements in the **<locale-config>** element is important, as described next in the section on how Faces chooses the right locale.

Localizing the Facelet Pages The final step in localizing the application is to modify the JSP files to use the **ResourceBundle** instead of hard-coded label values. We will only include the **register.xhtml** page, because the process of changing the rest of the pages is exactly the same.

```
<!DOCTYPE html PUBLIC "-//W3C//DTD XHTML 1.0 Transitional//EN"
"http://www.w3.org/TR/xhtml1/DTD/xhtml1-transitional.dtd">
<html xmlns="http://www.w3.org/1999/xhtml"
    xmlns:h="http://java.sun.com/jsf/html"
    xmlns:f="http://java.sun.com/jsf/core">
<h:head>
  <title>#{bundle.title}</title>
</h:head>
<h:body>
  <h:form>
  <h2>#{bundle.title}</h2>
  <h4>#{bundle.subtitle}</h4>
  <table>
    <tr>
    <td>#{bundle.firstName}</td>
    <td>
      <h:inputText label="#{bundle.firstName}"
             id="fname" value="#{userBean.firstName}"
             required="true"/>
      <h:message for="fname" />
    </td>
    </tr>
    <tr>
    <td>#{bundle.lastName}</td>
    <td>
      <h:inputText label="#{bundle.lastName}"
             id="lname" value="#{userBean.lastName}"
             required="true"/>
      <h:message for="lname" />
    </td>
    </tr>
    <tr>
    <td>#{bundle.sexLabel}</td>
    <td>
      <h:selectOneRadio label="#{bundle.sexLabel}"
              id="sex" value="#{userBean.sex}" required="true">
      <f:selectItem itemLabel="#{bundle.sexMale}" itemValue="male" />
      <f:selectItem itemLabel="#{bundle.sexFemale}" itemValue="female" />
      </h:selectOneRadio>
      <h:message for="sex" />
    </td>
    </tr>
    <tr>
    <td>#{bundle.birthday}</td>
    <td>
      <h:inputText label="#{bundle.birthday}"
             id="dob" value="#{userBean.dob}" required="true">
```

```
        <f:convertDateTime pattern="#{bundle.datePattern}" />
        </h:inputText> (mm-dd-yy)
        <h:message for="dob" />
      </td>
      </tr>
      <tr>
      <td>#{bundle.emailAddress}</td>
      <td>
        <h:inputText label="#{bundle.emailAddress}"
               id="email" value="#{userBean.email}" required="true"
               validator="#{userBean.validateEmail}"/>
        <h:message for="email" />
      </td>
      </tr>
      <tr>
      <td>#{bundle.serviceLevel}</td>
      <td>
        <h:selectOneMenu label="#{bundle.serviceLevel}"
                 value="#{userBean.serviceLevel}">
        <f:selectItem itemLabel="#{bundle.serviceLevelMedium}" itemValue="medium" />
        <f:selectItem itemLabel="#{bundle.serviceLevelBasic}" itemValue="basic" />
        <f:selectItem itemLabel="#{bundle.serviceLevelPremium}" itemValue="premium" />
        </h:selectOneMenu>
      </td>
      </tr>
    </table>
    <p><h:commandButton value="#{bundle.registerButton}" action="confirm" /></p>
    </h:form>
  </h:body>
  </html>
```

Note that all the English text has been replaced by EL expressions pointing to the **bundle** declared in the **faces-config.xml**. Also, the value of the **itemLabel** attribute in the **<h:selectOneRadio>** and **<h:selectOneMenu>** tags has been replaced with similar EL expressions. Finally, note the value of the **pattern** attribute on the **<f:convertDateTime>** also comes from the bundle. If you opt not to use the **pattern** attribute, you can use the **dateStyle** attribute, which will derive a **pattern** value from the **Locale**.

The Details Behind Faces Localization and Internationalization

Now that you have worked through an example, it is time to examine the details of localization. Let's begin by reviewing the string representation of a **Locale** and how that concept applies to the name of a **ResourceBundle**. A **Locale** is broken down into three parts: language, country, and variant. The string representation of a **Locale** uses a two-letter ISO 639 code for the language, a two-letter ISO 3166 code for the country, and a vendor-specific code for the variant, all separated by dashes or underscores. For example, **fr_CA** indicates the French language as spoken in Canada. A filename for a **ResourceBundle** defined as a properties file consists of four parts, a required **basename**, and optional language, country, and variant parts. For example, the **ResourceBundlecom.jsfcompref.trainer.Resources_de_AT.properties** has **com.jsfcompref.trainer.Resources** as the basename, **de** as the country, and **at** as the language.

Now let's take a closer look at the **<locale-config>** element, shown next:

```
<application>
  <locale-config>
    <default-locale>en</default-locale>
    <supported-locale>de_at</supported-locale>
    <supported-locale>de_de</supported-locale>
    <supported-locale>fr</supported-locale>
    <supported-locale>es</supported-locale>
  </locale-config>
</application>
```

The **<locale-config>** element is the one place where the developer tells the JSF runtime which languages are supported by the application. This differs from JSP and JSTL, where the presence or absence of bundles for a particular locale is used to determine which languages are supported.

EXPERT GROUP INSIGHT *The **<locale-config>** element is used to make the determination because no **ResourceBundles** will have been loaded by the time the determination is needed; therefore, they cannot be examined for their locality. Also, it's possible that the JSF implementation may be localized for more languages than your application, and you don't want the application to display messages for any languages other than the ones you know your application supports.*

How the Correct Locale Is Determined It is useful to understand the details of the algorithm for determining the correct locale based on the user's preferences sent by the browser. Most browsers allow the user to configure a priority list of languages in which pages should be rendered. Figure 10-18 illustrates this configuration in the Firefox Web browser.

These settings are sent to the server in the **Accept-Language** and **Accept-Charset** HTTP headers, which are exposed to the JSF runtime via the Servlet API.

During the *Restore View* phase of the request processing lifecycle, the **calculateLocale( )** method is called on the **ViewHandler**, which causes the following algorithm to be performed and the result set as the **locale** property of the **UIViewRoot** for this view. Note that if you need to provide a different algorithm for selecting the locale, it is very easy to do so using the custom **ViewHandler** techniques described in Chapter 13.

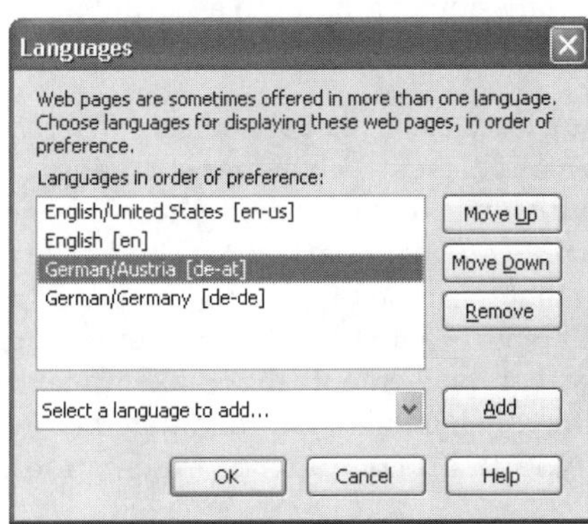

FIGURE 10-18 The languages and character encoding dialog in Firefox

For each language entry "**preferred**" sent in the **Accept-Language** header by the browser:

For each entry "**supported**" in the list of **supported-locale**s from the **faces-config .xml** file:

If **preferred** is exactly equal to **supported**, consider it a match and return.

If the language portion of **preferred** is equal to the language portion of **supported**, and **supported** has no country defined, consider it a match and return.

If no match is found in the **supported-locale**s list:

If preferred is exactly equal to the **default-locale**, consider it a match and return.

If the language portion of **preferred** is equal to the language portion of **default-locale**, and **default-locale** has no country defined, consider it a match and return.

If no match is found with the previous algorithm for any of the **preferred** languages sent in the **Accept-Language** header, and if there is a **<default-locale>**, use it. Otherwise, just use **Locale.getDefault( )**.

Let's work through some examples to clarify the algorithm. Let's say the user prefers **de_ch**, **en**, and **fr** as his or her language priorities, and the **<locale-config>** is as listed previously. First, we consider **de_ch**. It's not exactly equal to any of the **supported-locale**s or the **default-locale**, so we continue on to **en**. This doesn't match any of the **supported-locale**s, but it does match the **default-locale**, so it is considered a match and the page is rendered in English. Let's remove the **default-locale** from the **locale-config** and re-evaluate the algorithm. Again, **de_ch** has no match, so we continue. The same goes for **en**. We now come to **fr**. There is an exact match in the **supported-locale** list, so the page is rendered in French.

The user can override the **Locale** determined by the previous algorithm either by calling **setLocale( )** on the **UIViewRoot** directly or by giving a **locale** attribute to the **<f:view>** tag, as in the following:

```
<f:view locale="en_US" >
```

The **locale** attribute is **ValueExpression**-enabled, so the following is also valid:

```
<f:view locale="#{prefs.locale}">
```

provided that the expression evaluates to a **Locale** instance or a string representation of a **Locale** instance as described earlier.

How the Correct Character Encoding Is Determined There is considerable confusion regarding meanings of the terms "charset," "character encoding," and "character code." Let's clear up some of that confusion before explaining how these terms relate to Web applications in general and Faces applications in particular. The whole point of localization is to display your application so that it can be understood by users from specific geographic regions. Since the Web is still mainly a textual medium, the elements that make up text are very important. Let's say that the elements that make up text in a natural language are called *characters*. A collection of characters grouped together in some logical fashion is called a *character repertoire*. No specific computer representation or even sort order is implied by the concept of a character repertoire; it's purely a human concept. A character repertoire is usually presented by giving the names of the characters and a visual representation of each one. A *character code* is a big list of the characters in a character repertoire, with a non-negative integer number, known as a *code position,* assigned to each character. Synonyms for code position are *code point, code number, code element,* and *code set value.* With the introduction of the concept of character code comes the notion of the characters being sorted. For example, Morse code lists each letter in the English alphabet in alphabetical order, followed by the numerals 0 through 9, followed by some control characters. Finally, a *character encoding* is another big list, this time of the *code positions* in a *character code* with a sequence of binary numbers known as *octets* associated with each. ASCII is probably the best known character encoding. It is also a character code because each code position is also its encoding—for example, the letter *a* is at code position 97, and it is also encoded as the number 97. Figure 10-19 illustrates the concepts of repertoire, code, and encoding.

Generally, the only concept you have to understand is character encoding. The declaration of a character encoding is what allows the big sequence of bytes that compose a Web page to be turned into meaningful localized human-readable text. Without a character encoding, the browser would have no way to know how it should interpret the bytes for display. The most common encoding for computer systems is, of course, ASCII, but this encoding doesn't travel well because it only contains characters for English. The most common character encoding for the Web is called ISO-8859-1, also known as Latin 1. This encoding is a superset of ASCII, but it also includes characters for Western and Northern European Languages.

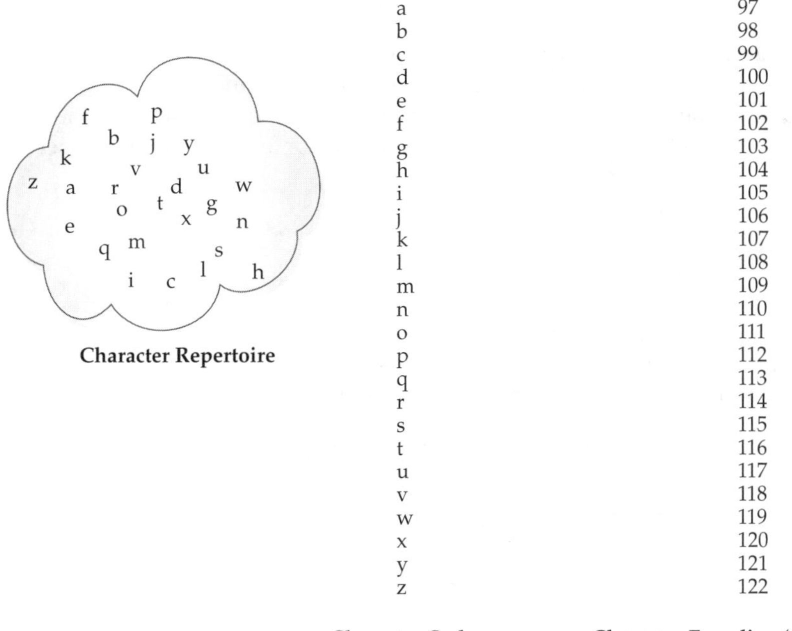

FIGURE 10-19 Character repertoire, character code, and character encoding

Other popular encodings are Shift_JIS for Japanese, Big5 for Chinese, ISO-8859-6 for Arabic, and UTF-8 for the Unicode encoding. UTF-8 is growing in popularity because it allows a single document to use nearly any world language without having to switch encodings.

Now that you understand why character encodings are important in general, let's see why they are important to the Web. Because the HTTP protocol of the Web is a request/ response protocol, it is vitally important that the character encoding used to render a Web page with an HTML **form** element to the browser be the same as the character encoding used to submit the form to the browser. This is done by passing character encoding information along with the request and response. As with the language of the document, the character encoding is sent via an HTTP header. In this case, the encoding is sent as a parameter to the **Content-Type** header. Generally, for the Web, **Content-Type** is **text/html** for HTML pages, **application/xhtml+xml** for XHTML documents, and **text/xml** for XML documents. So, to say that a Web page is presented as HTML using the UTF-8 encoding, the **Content-Type** header would be

```
Content-Type: text/html; charset=UTF-8
```

Note that the name of the parameter is **charset** even though it refers to a character encoding. This header travels along with the Web page when it is sent from the server to the browser, and with the form submit when it is sent from the browser back to the server.

In addition, it is often useful to include a **meta** tag in the **<head>** element with the same information:

```
<meta http-equiv="Content-Type" content="text/html; charset=UTF-8" />
```

These actions cause the response character encoding to be set as desired. The JSF framework will discover the character encoding value set in this manner and store it in the session. When the form postback occurs, the request character encoding is set with the information stored in the session *before* the request is interpreted. In this way, the proper interpretation of the postback is achieved.

Final Comments on Virtual Trainer

As mentioned at the start of this chapter, the purpose of this walk through the Virtual Trainer development process is to solidify your understanding of the core JSF technologies that are used when building a real Web application. As you move on to the more advanced topics in this book, you may find it helpful to refer back to this chapter, thinking of ways to apply the more advanced techniques to Virtual Trainer.

Readers are also encouraged to download the source code to Virtual Trainer and experiment with the code itself. The downloadable version can be obtained at McGraw-Hill's Web site at **www.mhprofessional.com/computingdownload**.

CHAPTER 11

Building Custom UI Components

One of the most compelling and powerful aspects of JavaServer Faces is the development of custom JSF User Interface (UI) components. This is an essential topic for advanced JSF developers because it enables you to extend JavaServer Faces by creating your own JSF components that are tailored to the specific demands of your application. JSF 2.0 provides a powerful new feature, called "composite components" that makes it easier than ever before to create custom UI components. You will learn everything there is to know about building composite components in this chapter, as well as the pre-JSF 2.0 way of building UI components, on top of which the composite component feature is built.

One of the early goals of JavaServer Faces was to provide a component-centric foundation that the Java community could extend as needed. At the time of this writing, a large and growing marketplace of JSF component developers is available that extends the original base components provided in the JSF specification. A quick look at **http://jsfcentral.com** confirms this fact. The new components being created come from both open source and independent vendors. Leading vendors such as Oracle, Exadel, ICEsoft, ESRI, JSCAPE, Business Objects, and Infragistics all have production-quality professional JSF component libraries ready for use in your applications.

Writing a JSF custom UI component can be as simple as writing a Facelet page or as complex as providing support for multiple client device types such as Web browsers, PDAs, and smart phones. When the Expert Group set out to design the experience developers would have when they created custom components, they were guided by the notion of a "pay as you go complexity tax." This concept states that the user should have to know only *just enough* to get the job done, but no more. If the job is more complex, then you need to know more to get it done. By following this concept, it is hoped the act of creating custom UI components becomes more commonplace when developing JSF applications.

Deciding When to Build a Custom UI Component

Before examining the process of building a custom component, it is necessary to emphasize that it is something that you won't always need to do. Before deciding to build a custom component, you should first check to see that you are not reinventing the wheel. You should consider the following before embarking on custom development:

- Customization may not be necessary because the JSF community may already have a solution fulfilling your needs. Consult the component directory section of **http://jsfcentral.com/** or do a Web search for "jsf component libraries."
- Your requirements may not rise to a level that requires a custom component. Remember, a component is something that has a behavior and an appearance. If the goal is to simply create a dynamic portion of content, and you don't need listeners, events, or other behaviors, Facelet templating may be all you need.
- Certain customization can also be attained without having to build an entirely new UI component. In many cases it is possible to write some custom logic such as a **Validator** or a **Converter** that can then be applied to one of the existing (standard) UI components.

Once an adequate amount of research has been performed and a solution that fits your requirements is still not found, then it is logical to proceed with custom JSF component development.

JSF 2.0 Tip *The experience of writing custom UI components in JSF was dramatically simplified in JSF 2.0 with a feature known as "composite components." Most of this chapter is spent on this feature. However, it's important to recognize that this feature is built on top of the existing JSF UI component infrastructure, and that custom UI components built with earlier versions of JSF will work just fine in JSF 2.0.*

What Are UI Components?

As stated in Chapter 7, a *user interface component* (UI component) is a specific type of component that *displays user interface content* that the user can *modify over time*. This content ranges from simple input fields or buttons to more complex items, such as trees or datagrids. The part of the definition that reads "content that the user can modify over time" is the most important difference between something that *is* a UI component and something that *is not* a UI component. For example, when a user checks a checkbox, he expects it to stay checked until he unchecks it, but when the user views a page with a navigation menu on the left, that navigation menu generally stays the same regardless of what the user is doing elsewhere in the page. In other words, the component has a "current state." Of course, it's not hard to imagine a dynamic navigation menu whose contents depend on other parts of the page, but the minute your navigation menu needs such behavior, it ceases being a mere part of the page and becomes a UI component. In the simplest terms, a UI component is something that has appearance, state, and behavior, and that can be reused in a variety of different contexts.

Let's take a step back and get some perspective. Most JSF end users don't really care so much about what is and is not a component. They have a page they see in the browser, and some of the things in the page respond to mouse clicks and keystrokes and some of the things in the page do not. JSF page authors see a component as a tag they can stick in the page and have it display something useful, such as the login panel in the preceding chapter, which is shown by putting the tag **<vt:loginPanel />** in the page. JSF component authors see a component as a collection of other JSF elements, such as a **UIComponent** class, a **Converter**, zero or more **Validators**, and maybe a separate **Renderer**. These associated components working together as a usable UI component can be described as the *moving parts* of a UI component, but rather than burden you with the details right now, let's take a simple example.

A Simple JSF UI Component

Here is a page that uses the login panel component from the Virtual Trainer. A page that uses a component is called, unsurprisingly, a *using page*. The text in boldface will be specifically discussed following the code.

```
<!DOCTYPE html PUBLIC "-//W3C//DTD XHTML 1.0 Transitional//EN"
"http://www.w3.org/TR/xhtml1/DTD/xhtml1-transitional.dtd">
<html xmlns="http://www.w3.org/1999/xhtml"
  xmlns:h="http://java.sun.com/jsf/html"
  xmlns:f="http://java.sun.com/jsf/core"
  xmlns:ui="http://java.sun.com/jsf/facelets"
  xmlns:vt="http://java.sun.com/jsf/composite/trainer">
<body><h:form>
  <vt:loginPanel />
</h:form></body>
</html>
```

As with any Facelet tag, the UI components must live inside of a Facelet tag library, which must be declared with an XML namespace declaration, in this case **xmlns:vt="http://java.sun.com/jsf/composite/trainer"**. The characters after the **xmlns:** but before the = are arbitrary, but because those same characters must be used throughout the page to refer to components from the library, it's a good idea to keep it short. In this case, we use **vt**. The URL on the right-hand side of the = is important. Any URL that starts with **http://java.sun.com/jsf/composite/** is taken to be the name of a special Facelet tag library called a *JSF Composite Component Library*. There must be one and only one path segment after the last '/' character in the namespace URL. The system will interpret this to be the name of the composite component library, in this case **trainer**. Once the composite component library is declared, any components within that library may be used in the page, as shown by the usage of **<vt:loginPanel />**.

Now let's look at the markup for the login panel component, formally known as the *defining page*. This markup *must* be in a file whose filename matches the tag name on the using page, in this case, **loginPanel.xhtml**, and the file must reside in a resource library whose name matches the part of the namespace URL after **http://java.sun.com/jsf/composite/**, in this case, **trainer**. This arrangement is shown in Figure 11-1. In the case of the maven-based project for the Virtual Trainer, that means the file is **src/main/webapp/resources/trainer/loginPanel.xhtml**. When the Web application is built, the actual file ends up as **resources/trainer/loginPanel.xhtml** in the **trainer.war**. Following is a simplified version of the login panel. This code renders something recognizable as a login panel, but it doesn't do anything yet—it doesn't have any behavior.

```
<!DOCTYPE html PUBLIC "-//W3C//DTD XHTML 1.0 Transitional//EN"
"http://www.w3.org/TR/xhtml1/DTD/xhtml1-transitional.dtd">
<html xmlns="http://www.w3.org/1999/xhtml"
  xmlns:h="http://java.sun.com/jsf/html"
  xmlns:cc="http://java.sun.com/jsf/composite">
<cc:interface/>
```

```
<cc:implementation>
<h:panelGrid columns="3">
  <h:outputLabel for="#{cc.clientId}:userid" value="Userid:" />
  <h:inputText required="true"
        requiredMessage="Userid is required" id="userid" />
  <h:message for="#{cc.clientId}:userid" />

  <h:outputLabel for="#{cc.clientId}:password" value="Password:" />
  <h:inputSecret required="true"
          requiredMessage="Password is required" id="password" />
  <h:message for="#{cc.clientId}:password" />
  <h:outputText value="On Login, Go To:"
         rendered="#{! empty cc.facets.loginOutcomeChoiceList}"/>

  <h:commandButton id="loginButton" value="Login" />
  <h:messages for="#{cc.clientId}" />

</h:panelGrid>
</cc:implementation>
</html>
```

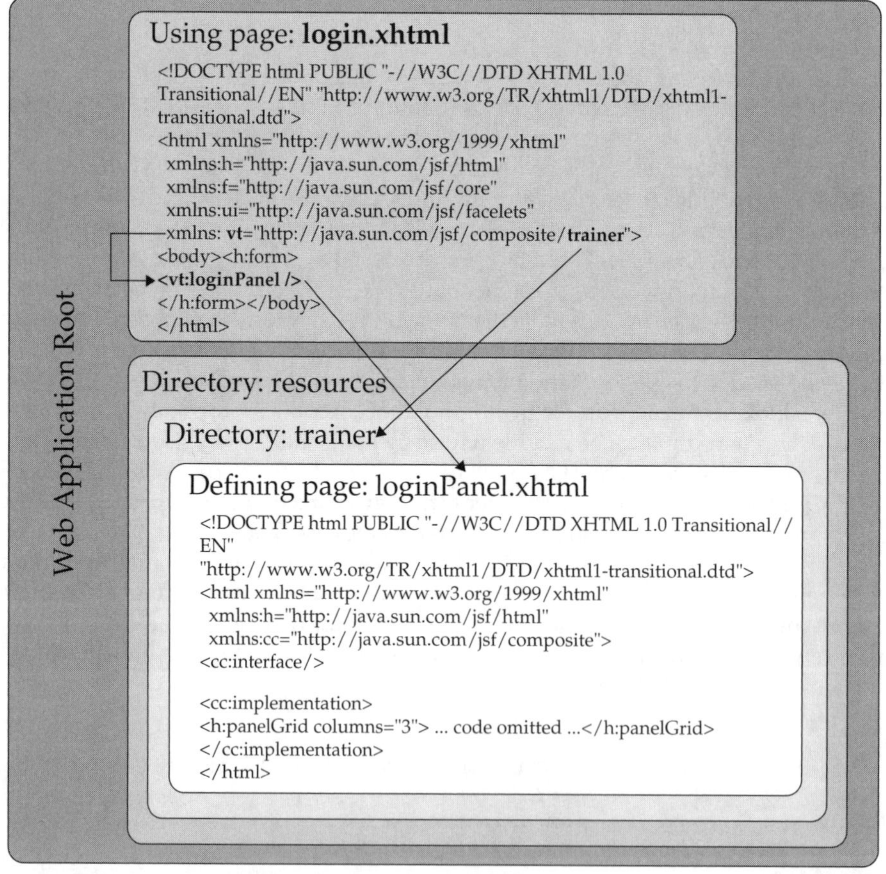

FIGURE 11-1 The arrangement of files in the example application

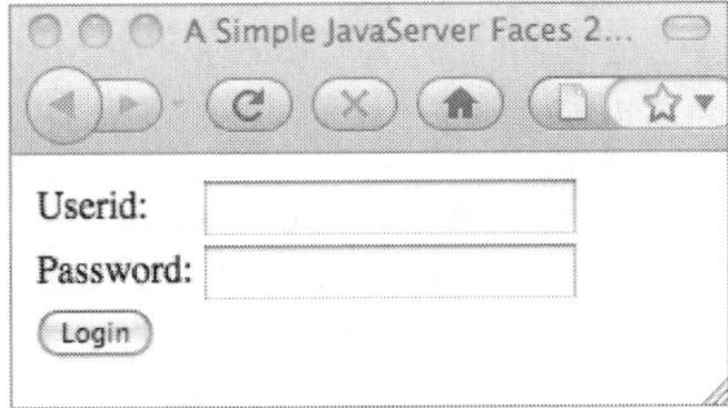

Figure 11-2 The simple login panel, rendered in Firefox

Aside from the text in boldface, this is nothing more than a regular Facelet page, which is rendered as shown in Figure 11-2. The meaning of the new text will be completely explained in the following sections.

The Code Behind the Markup of This Simple JSF UI Component

Notice that we wrote no Java code, yet we're calling this a true JSF UI component. In fact, the preceding component is an example of a *JSF Composite Component*, a new feature in JSF 2.0. As far as the page author is concerned, **<vt:loginPanel>** *is* a real, live JSF UI Component. It can have listeners attached to it, it can emit events, and it can have facets and child content. A composite component can be made to do everything a real UI Component can, from the page author's perspective. In reality, there are several **UIComponent** instances in the page, as shown in Figure 11-3.

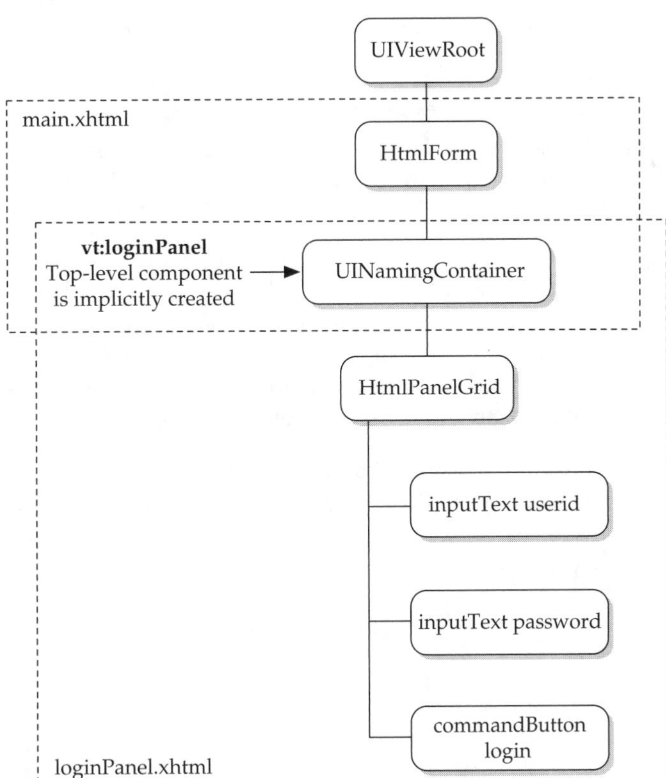

Figure 11-3 UIComponent instances in the simple login panel

EXPERT GROUP INSIGHT *The Expert Group specifically emphasized the page author's perspective as the most important viewpoint for the feature.*

This figure shows the page author's perspective on things. On the **main.xhtml** page there are exactly two components: **h:form**, and **vt:loginPanel**. On the **loginPanel.xhtml** page are more components than are shown in Figure 11-3, but the important ones are shown to give you an idea of what is going on. Most important, the **UINamingContainer** component is automatically created to serve as the *top-level component* parent of all the components in the **loginPanel.xhtml** page. It is very important to understand that even though no top-level component is explicitly declared in **loginPanel.xhtml**, one is automatically created for you to serve as the parent of the components in that page. This is very similar to how, in **main.xhtml**, no **<f:view>** is declared, but nonetheless, one is created for you. Later on you will see how to explicitly declare the top-level component, which can be written as Java code, or even as a Groovy script.

Introduction to Resource Libraries

Resource libraries, which were hinted at in Chapter 10 and in the preceding simple example, are one of two key enabling features for composite components, the other being Facelets itself. Resource libraries will be described completely in Chapter 13, but it's important to understand the basics now, before continuing. As far as the JSF runtime is concerned, a resource library is just a directory on disk. (Technically, it's a directory *or* something accessible to the classpath). The default JSF runtime supports two kinds of locations for directories that are considered to be resource libraries:

- Directories that are subdirectories of the **resources** directory in the top-level Web application root, for example **resources/trainer**, as shown in Figure 11-1.
- Directories that are available to the Classloader under **META-INF/resources**, such as **META-INF/resources/trainer** in a jar file named **trainer.jar** that resides in **WEB-INF/lib**. Note that an equivalent location is **WEB-INF/classes/META-INF/resources/trainer** because the Servlet spec requires that the **WEB-INF/classes** directory be loaded as a classpath root on the application Classloader.

Resource libraries can be localized and versioned, and there are rules for how the runtime must always use the latest version it can find, but these and other subtleties of resource libraries will be discussed in Chapter 13. These are the two most important facts to understand about resource libraries and composite components:

- The name of the resource library is what comes after the **http://java.sun.com/jsf/composite/** in the XML namespace declaration on the using page.
- The names of the Facelet files within the resource library are usable as JSF components on the using page.

Adding Behavior to a Composite Component

A component isn't a **UIComponent** until it has some behavior. This section explains how to add behavior to the **vt:loginPanel** component. Recall that the defining page for a composite component has two top-level elements, both from the **http://java.sun.com/jsf/composite/** tag library: **cc:interface** and **cc:implementation**. Anyone who has programmed in Objective-C will recognize these sections, and their meaning in JSF composite components is the same as in that venerable old binary-compiled programming language.

cc:interface Declares everything the page author needs to know to use this component. This is more formally known as the *usage contract*.

cc:implementation Defines the implementation of the contract declared in the **cc:interface** section.

It is exactly appropriate to think of the **cc:interface** section as an abstraction of what is inside the **cc:implementation** section in the same way that the image on the left side of Figure 11-4 is an abstraction of the image on the right side.

When performing any kind of abstraction, one must separate what is important from what is not, and this decision is entirely dependent on the audience. For example, let's say that we know the user of the login panel component wants to be able to attach **Validator**s to the userid and password fields to enforce various rules, and it wants control the action of where to go next when the validation succeeds. The using page for such a variant of the component is shown here:

```
<!DOCTYPE html PUBLIC "-//W3C//DTD XHTML 1.0 Transitional//EN"
"http://www.w3.org/TR/xhtml1/DTD/xhtml1-transitional.dtd">
Bcc: b_edward@bellsouth.net
<html xmlns="http://www.w3.org/1999/xhtml"
    xmlns:h="http://java.sun.com/jsf/html"
    xmlns:f="http://java.sun.com/jsf/core"
    xmlns:vt="http://java.sun.com/jsf/composite/trainer">
<h:head>
  <title>A Simple JavaServer Faces 2.0 View</title>
</h:head>
<h:body>
  <h:form>
    <vt:loginPanel passwordValidatorMessage="Enter password.
          Must be between six and ten characters in length."
          action="next">
      <f:validateLength for="userid" minimum="6" />
      <f:validateLength for="password" minimum="6" maximum="10" />
    </vt:loginPanel>
  </h:form>
</h:body>
</html>
```

Figure 11-4
An abstraction

The using page is straightforward. We're telling the login panel

- Where to go if login succeeds (the **action** attribute)
- What message to display if the password is invalid (the **passwordValidatorMessage** attribute)
- What validators to attach to the userid and password fields (the **f:validator** children)

The using page conforms to the usage contract, in file **resources/trainer/loginPanel.xhtml**:

```
<!DOCTYPE html PUBLIC "-//W3C//DTD XHTML 1.0 Transitional//EN"
"http://www.w3.org/TR/xhtml1/DTD/xhtml1-transitional.dtd">
<html xmlns="http://www.w3.org/1999/xhtml"
  xmlns:h="http://java.sun.com/jsf/html"
  xmlns:cc="http://java.sun.com/jsf/composite">
<cc:interface>
    <cc:attribute name="useridValidatorMessage" default="Invalid userid"/>
    <cc:attribute name="passwordValidatorMessage"
                  default="Invalid password"/>
    <cc:attribute name="action" targets="loginButton"
                  default="next?faces-redirect=true" />
    <cc:editableValueHolder name="userid" />
    <cc:editableValueHolder name="password" />
    <cc:actionSource name="loginButton" />
</cc:interface>
The implementation section has not changed from the previous code listing,
so it is not repeated here.
</html>
```

We're declaring that the **<vt:loginPanel>** tag supports the following attributes:

- **useridValidationMessage**, with default value "Invalid userid"
- **passwordValidationMessage**, with default value "Invalid Password"
- **action**, with default value "next?faces-redirect=true"

We are also declaring that there are two **EditableValueHolder** instances and one **ActionSource** instance that can be the target of attached objects appropriate to those kinds of components. This design effectively leverages the existing capabilities of JSF, and enables the following features and more:

- Attach any valid combination of validators or converters to any combination of the userid and password fields.
- Attach action listeners to the button.
- Customize the action that will happen when the button is pressed.
- Customize the validation messages for the userid and password fields.
- Allow the user to provide absolutely no values at all and just conform to the defaults: convention over configuration!

A First Look into the Details of Composite Components

Let's now examine how the declarations in the **<cc:interface>** section are wired up to the components within the **<cc:implementation>** section. First, the attributes: **useridValidatorMessage**, **passwordValidatorMessage**, and **action**.

Composite component authors use one or more **<cc:attribute>** elements within the **<cc:interface>** section to declare that the composite component supports one or more XML attributes. The complete reference material for this and all other tags can be found in Chapter 16, but here is the general form of **<cc:attribute>**, with only the most important attributes included:

```
<cc:attribute name="name of the attribute in the using page"
              default="optional default value for the attribute"
              required="true or false.  If true, there must be a value
                        for this attribute in the using page."
              type="optional Java language type for the attribute"
              method-signature="optional and mutually exclusive with the
                                type attribute this attribute is a Java
                                method signature of the method pointed
                                at by this attribute"
              targets="optional list of component ids within the
                       cc:implementation that should receive this attribute"
              displayName="optional information to describe the attribute"
              shortDescription="more optional information.">
```

NOTE *It is perfectly legal to nest* ***<cc:attribute>*** *elements within* ***<cc:attribute>*** *elements, and an example of this usage will be shown later in the chapter.*

Let's examine the **<cc:attribute>** declarations. The value of the **name** attribute is what the user must use to assign a value to this attribute in the using page, for example **<vt:loginPanel action="next">**. Within the defining page, the "trick" is telling the runtime how to "retarget" the attributes from the using page to specific components within the **<cc:implementation>** section, for example taking that **action="next"** and putting it on the **<h:commandButton value="Login" id="loginButton" />**.

Expert Group Insight *An unfortunate side effect of software that espouses the "convention over configuration" and "don't repeat yourself" philosophy is that its implementation has to do a lot of complex work to infer the user's meaning from the given (or more frequently, not given) input. Complexity has to live somewhere, but it's better that it live under the covers of the framework than be exposed to the user.*

We will describe this "trick" as a set of rules that the JSF runtime must follow.

Composite Component Processing Rules

Rule for Processing <cc:attribute> Elements

For each **<cc:attribute>** element in the **<cc:interface>** section, determine the nature of the attribute and take the appropriate action. If the value of the attribute is a **MethodExpression**, or the name of the attribute is **action**, **actionListener**, **validator**, or **valueChangeListener**, find the target for the attribute within the **<cc:implementation>** section (using the following rule) and move the **MethodExpression** from the top-level component to the target. Otherwise, assume the value of the attribute is a **ValueExpression** and simply store the attribute into the attributes map of the top-level component.

Rule for Retargeting Attributes and Attached Objects from the Using Page to the Defining Page

Look for a **targets** attribute. If you find one, interpret its value as a space-separated list of client IDs, relative to the top-level component. For each entry in the list, find the actual **UIComponent** instance within the **<cc:implementation>** section and retarget the attribute or attached object in the appropriate way. If there is no **targets** attribute, interpret the value of the **name** attribute as the client ID, relative to the top-level component, and find that **UIComponent** instance within the **<cc:implementation>** section and retarget the attribute or attached object in the appropriate way.

With the preceding rules in mind, it is easy to understand what is done with the two **<cc:editableValueHolder>** elements and the **<cc:actionSource>** element. Because none of these elements declares a **targets** attribute, the runtime will find the **<h:inputText id="userid" />**, **<h:inputText id="password" />**, and **<h:commandButton id="loginButton" />** as the targets for those elements, respectively. In this case, the **<f:validateLength>** validators in the using page are retargeted to each input field. This example doesn't use the **loginButton** for anything, because the **action** attribute does all we need. This arrangement is shown here:

Defining page: loginPanel.xhtml

```
<cc:interface>
  <cc:attribute name="useridValidatorMessage" default="Invalid userid"/>
  <cc:attribute name="passwordValidatorMessage" default="Invalid password"/>
  <cc:attribute name="action" targets="loginButton" default="next?faces-redirect=true" />
  <cc:editableValueHolder name="userid" />
  <cc:editableValueHolder name="password" />
  <cc:actionSource name="loginButton" />
</cc:interface>

<cc:implementation>
<h:panelGrid columns="3">
  <h:outputLabel for="#{cc.clientId}:userid" value="Userid:" />
  <h:inputText required="true" validatorMessage="#{cc.attrs.useridValidatorMessage}"
    requiredMessage="Userid is required" id="userid" />
  <h:message for="#{cc.clientId}:userid" />

  <h:outputLabel for="#{cc.clientId}:password" value="Password:" />
  <h:inputSecret  required="true"  id="password"
     validatorMessage="#{cc.attrs.passwordValidatorMessage}"
     requiredMessage="Password is required" />
  <h:message for="#{cc.clientId}:password" />
  <h:outputText value="On Login, Go To:"
    rendered="#{! empty cc.facets.loginOutcomeChoiceList}"/>

  <h:commandButton value="Login" id="loginButton" />
  <h:messages for="#{cc.clientId}" />
</h:panelGrid>
</cc:implementation>
```


The #{cc} Implicit Object

The last concept to meet in our introduction to composite components is the very useful **#{cc}** implicit object. This expression resolves to the top-level component for the defining page in which the expression appears. This is the **UINamingContainer** instance from Figure 11-3. Because **UIComponent** and its subclasses conform to JavaBeans naming conventions, it is possible to get lots of information from the **#{cc}** expression. For example **<h:outputLabel for="#{cc.clientId}:userid" value="Userid:" />** causes the label to have the correct absolute client ID to the actual userid text field. The most common usage of **#{cc}**, however, is the special **#{cc.attrs}** expression. We can see this is how the **useridValidatorMessage** and **passwordValidatorMessage** attributes are conveyed to the implementation section.

```
<h:inputText required="true"
        validatorMessage="#{cc.attrs.useridValidatorMessage}"
        requiredMessage="Userid is required" id="userid" />
  <h:message for="#{cc.clientId}:userid" />
  <h:outputLabel for="#{cc.clientId}:password" value="Password:" />
  <h:inputSecret  required="true"
          validatorMessage="#{cc.attrs.passwordValidatorMessage}"
          requiredMessage="Password is required" id="password" />
  <h:message for="#{cc.clientId}:password" />
```

This concludes our introduction to JSF components and composite components. The following sections will give you a deeper understanding of what's going on under the covers.

The Parts of a UI Component

The various parts that constitute a JSF UI component, as shown in Figure 11-5, are a collection of some subset of the following artifacts. Artifacts in italic text are required but are auto-generated for you. Artifacts in gray in the figure are optional and are *not* auto-generated. You can see that every box is either in italic text or in gray, meaning that custom components can be made without creating any of these kinds of artifacts, as shown previously.

- **UIComponent subclass** A Java class derived from either **UIComponentBase** or directly from **UIComponent**. You can also extend from an existing base **UIComponent** class, such as **UIOutput**. This is the Java class that represents the core behavior of the component. It can optionally contain logic to render itself to a client, or rendering logic can reside in a separate renderer class. It's important to note the distinction between **UIComponent** and "UI component." The first is the actual Java class that provides the core behavior of the component, and the latter is the generic term used by convention to describe all of the elements working together to offer the usage of the overall component to the user (such as an input field rendered in HTML with built-in validation and conversion).
- **Renderer class** A class that contains code to render a **UIComponent**. It can also contain code to decode the incoming data from a form post. Different rendering classes can provide multiple renderings for the same **UIComponent**. For example, the **UICommand** component can be rendered as a button or a link, depending on the renderer associated with the component. In the former case, a **ButtonRenderer** is used, and in the latter a **LinkRenderer** is used. Renderers can also provide different rendering options for the same **UIComponent** for different client types that accept different markup flavors. For example, a radio button list looks different in a Web browser than it does in a mobile phone.

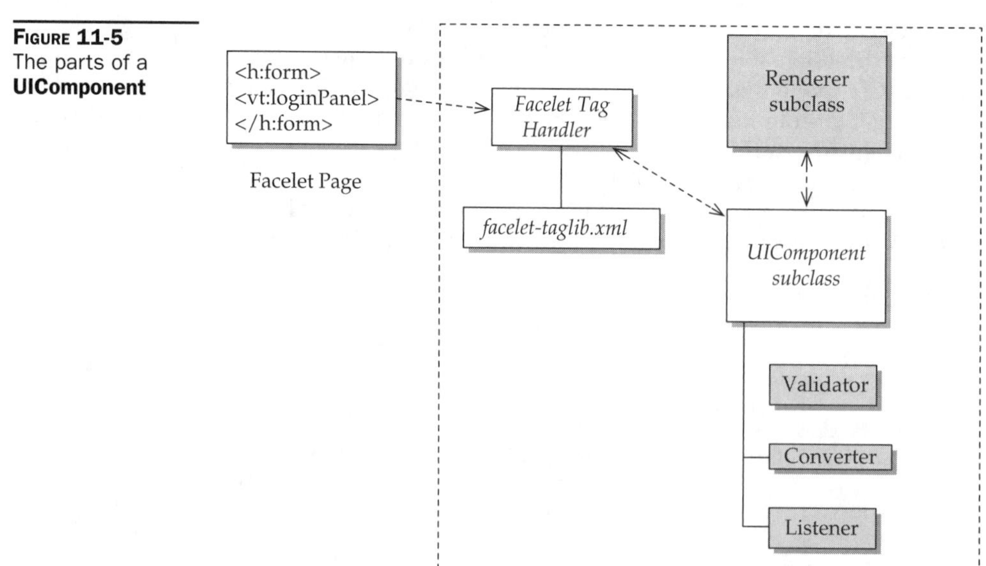

FIGURE 11-5 The parts of a **UIComponent**

- **Facelet Tag Handler** A Facelet tag handler class that allows the UI component to be used in a Facelet page. It provides a way for the page author to direct where in the page the component should appear, and it allows the page author to customize its appearance by passing attributes in the familiar way one does with HTML. It associates a separate **Renderer** class with a **UIComponent** class. There is an analogous concept for JSP, but this concept is deprecated in JSF 2.0.
- **facelet-tablib.xml** A Facelet tag library that declares the allowable tags and what **UIComponent** class should be used for each one.
- **Attached Objects** A collection of standard (included in the JSF RI) or custom helper classes such as **Converter**, **Validator**, and **ActionListener** that can be programmatically bound to UI components (in addition to being associated from inside of a JSP page). For example, a JSF UI input field component can be associated with a built-in number range **Validator** that ensures that a number is within a certain range. These helper classes can also be customized to extend any behavior not provided out of the box with the JSF reference implementation. For example, a custom credit card **Validator** could be used with a JSF input field to validate credit card numbers, or a custom **Converter** could be used to convert currencies.

A Noncomposite JSF Custom UIComponent

The composite component feature will cleanly address most of your custom component needs. Therefore, in most cases, you will not need to write an entirely Java based custom **UIComponent**., However, to provide a deeper understanding of what's really happening, let's examine how to develop a JSF custom **UIComponent** without using composite components.

Often the best way to learn a new technology is to begin with a simple, working example—in other words, a "Hello World" program. This is the approach used here. In this section you will see how to build a simple, yet fully functional custom JSF UI component. Although quite short, it introduces the main issues surrounding custom, non-composite UI component development.

Before showing the actual code needed for our "Hello World" example, let's examine how the component will be used. The name of the component is **HtmlHelloWorld**. A page author will be able to add the custom **HtmlHelloWorld** component to a Facelet page, and it will render a short message that displays the current date and time. Later, you'll see how to customize it to provide a custom message via one of its properties.

Building the HtmlHelloWorld Example

The **HtmlHelloWorld** component consists of the following subcomponents:

- An **HtmlHelloWorld UIComponent** Java class. This is the heart of the UI component. It provides the core functionality of the component, which is to display its message, rendered in HTML.
- The file **helloworld-taglib.xml**, a Facelet tag library descriptor (TLD) file for the component.

You'll notice that there is no **Renderer** class. For this example, the code that displays (i.e., renders) the hello message is actually embedded in the **HtmlHelloWorld** class. Later examples will show custom UI components with separate **Renderer** classes along with explanations of why and how you would want the rendering code to be in separate classes under certain circumstances.

The source code for the UI component class **HtmlHelloWorld.java** is as follows:

```
package com.jsfcompref.components.component;

import java.io.IOException;
import javax.faces.component.FacesComponent;
import javax.faces.component.UIComponentBase;
import javax.faces.context.FacesContext;
import javax.faces.context.ResponseWriter;

@FacesComponent(value="HtmlHelloWorld")
public class HtmlHelloWorld extends UIComponentBase {

  @Override
  public String getFamily() {
    return null;
  }

  @Override
  public void encodeAll(FacesContext context) throws IOException {
    ResponseWriter writer = context.getResponseWriter();
    writer.startElement("div", this);
    writer.writeAttribute("style", "color : red", null );
    writer.writeText("HelloWorld! today is: " +
                     new java.util.Date(), null);
    writer.endElement("div");
  }
}
```

The first thing to notice is the name of the class, **HtmlHelloWorld**. This is by convention because this component's default rendering is for an HTML client. It bears repeating that the preceding approach of hard-coding literal strings in Java code to generate HTML is no longer necessary thanks to composite components. Nonetheless, as you'll see later in the chapter, UI components and their respective **Renderers** (whether they're embedded in the component or not) have the ability to render in multiple markups such as HTML, WML, and so on.

Referring back to the code, you can see the most important method in this class, **encodeAll( )**, contains the code to render itself to the client. The actual generation of markup (rendering) is performed with a **ResponseWriter** object, which is available from the **FacesContext**. The **ResponseWriter** has various methods to output markup including the ones used here: **startElement( )**, **writeAttribute( )**, **writeText( )**, and **endElement( )**. You'll notice the extra **null** arguments in the example. When defined, these extra arguments provide additional component information to development tools to improve the design-time experience. For now you can leave them with **null** values. In addition to the aforementioned **ResponseWriter** methods, it is also possible to use a generic **write( )**

method that literally dumps any markup directly to the page without requiring writing the elements and attributes separately. This works fine, but it can be a bit problematic when having to escape quote characters. For example:

```
writer.write("<div style=\"color : blue\">HelloWorld!</div>");
```

EXPERT GROUP INSIGHT *As mentioned here, the* ***ResponseWriter*** *concept allows design-time JSF tools to better integrate with the components in the page by allowing the component developer to give hints to the design time environment about the association between the markup in the page and the components in the view. Design-time tools will commonly replace the standard* ***ResponseWriter*** *with one that "intercepts" this extra information and conveys it to the user in some fashion.*

In general, the set of rendering methods, including **encodeBegin( )**, **encodeEnd( )**, and **encodeChildren( )** (which are an older way of accomplishing the same thing as **encodeAll( )**), are the methods for rendering all markup to the client in a hierarchical manner. For example, the **HtmlHelloWorld** component could have had a separate child component to render the date. In this case, all three methods could be used in sequential order to render content ahead of the child component, render the child component, and then render content after the child component.

NOTE *As a general tip, although not shown in these preliminary examples, it is considered good practice to also encode an ID attribute for the component. This allows for greater usability with client-side code (JavaScript) that may need to refer or operate on the component by referencing its ID. To render an ID for a component, use:* ***writer.writeAttribute("id", getClientId(context), null);***

The other method to notice is the **getFamily( )** method. This method returns the general category of which this component is a member. For example, the **UIInput** component belongs to the family **javax.faces.Input**, while the **UICommand** component belongs to the family **javax.faces.Command**. The **family** value is combined with the **rendererType** property to select a **Renderer** from a **RenderKit**. In the case of a component/renderer pairing that renders an HTML input field, the family would be **javax.faces.Input** and the renderer-type would be **javax.faces.Text**. In the case of a component/renderer pairing that renders an HTML button, the family would be **javax.faces.Command** and the renderer-type would be **javax.faces.Button**. In a custom component, the family and renderer-type values can be any string but must match the corresponding values in the **faces-config** declaration for the component and the renderer. The simple **HtmlHelloWorld** example doesn't create a new family of components and renderers, so it can just return a **null** value for now.

Finally, notice the **@FacesComponent** annotation. This annotation is an alternative for the following XML in the **faces-config.xml** file:

```
<component>
  <component-type>HtmlHelloWorld</component-type>
  <component-class>
    com.jsfcompref.components.component.HtmlHelloWorld
  </component-class>
</component>
```

The point of either syntax is to establish an entry in the runtime component registry for the component type **HtmlHelloWorld**. The component registry will be covered in Chapter 13, but it is essentially a data structure that enables the construction of **UIComponent** instances in many different scenarios.

NOTE *As you become more experienced in developing non-composite, custom UI components, you'll want to create fully qualified names for component types, such as* ***com.jsfcompref .HtmlHelloWorld****. Similar to Java packages, this provides greater naming possibilities with its hierarchical structure.*

Now that we have a Java class, and that class has been entered into the runtime component registry, under the string **HtmlHelloWorld**, the last piece of the puzzle is to make the component available to page authors by including it in a Facelet tag library.

```
<?xml version='1.0' encoding='UTF-8'?>
<facelet-taglib xmlns="http://java.sun.com/xml/ns/javaee"
   xmlns:xsi="http://www.w3.org/2001/XMLSchema-instance"
   xsi:schemaLocation="http://java.sun.com/xml/ns/javaee
   http://java.sun.com/xml/ns/javaee/web-facelettaglibrary_2_0.xsd"
   version="2.0">
  <namespace>http://jsfcompref.com/example</namespace>
  <tag>
    <tag-name>helloworld</tag-name>
    <component><component-type>HtmlHelloWorld</component-type></component>
  </tag>
</facelet-taglib>
```

In this example, the preceding code resides in **WEB-INF/classes/META-INF/ helloworld.taglib.xml** at runtime. There are two ways to make the JSF runtime aware of such tag libraries:

- Make it available to the Web application Classloader as just done here.
- Set the **<context-param>** in the **web.xml**, such as **<name> javax.faces.FACELETS_ LIBRARIES</name> <value>/WEB-INF/helloworld.taglib.xml</value>**. This value is a semicolon (;)–separated list of paths, starting with slash (/), relative to the Web application root. Such files do not need to be in **WEB-INF**, but they are often placed there by convention.

Finally, to use the component, it can be placed in a Facelet page with the following source:

```
<!DOCTYPE html PUBLIC "-//W3C//DTD XHTML 1.0 Transitional//EN"
"http://www.w3.org/TR/xhtml1/DTD/xhtml1-transitional.dtd">
<html xmlns="http://www.w3.org/1999/xhtml"
      xmlns:h="http://java.sun.com/jsf/html"
      xmlns:vt="http://jsfcompref.com/example">
<h:head>
  <title>A Simple JavaServer Faces 2.0 View</title>
</h:head>
```

```
<h:body>
  <h:form>
    <p><vt:helloworld /></p>
  </h:form>
</h:body>
</html>
```

Notice that the taglib URI, **http://jsfcompref.com/example**, must match the URI defined in the tag library descriptor file. Since **HtmlHelloWorld** doesn't require any attributes, the tag **<vt:helloworld/>** is all that is needed.

Now that we've created a simple, but fully functional component, we can begin adding attributes to the component. Because **HtmlHelloWorld** extends from **UIComponentBase**, **UIComponent** properties from the superclass such as **id**, **binding**, **rendered** are already available for use in the Facelet page.

For example, to test the **rendered** attribute, one can set the value to be false:

```
<vt:helloworld rendered="false"/>
```

This will cause the UI component to not render in the page.

With Facelets, there is no need to add any getters or setters on the **UIComponent** subclass when adding custom attributes. Any attributes added by the page author are automatically available in the **Map** returned from **getAttributes( )**. Let's add an attribute, **hellomsg**, which allows the user to specify a custom message to the component.

The **encodeAll( )** method can then use the **hellomsg** value in the **responseWriter** methods to display the message when rendered.

```
...
@Override
public void encodeAll(FacesContext context) throws IOException {
  ResponseWriter writer = context.getResponseWriter();
  writer.startElement("div", this);
  writer.writeAttribute("style", "color : red", null );
  String message =
    (String) this.getAttributes().get("hellomsg");
  if (null == message) {
    writer.writeText("HelloWorld! today is: " +
      new java.util.Date(), null);
  } else {
    writer.writeText(message, null);
  }
  writer.endElement("div");
}...
```

The Facelet page can now define a custom message in the tag.

```
<vt:helloworld hellomsg="Hello JSF! "/>
```

As the page is run again, the custom message then appears.

Facelets automatically supports EL for all attributes. For example, the code

```
<vt:helloworld hellomsg="#{param.msg}"/>
```

will evaluate the expression, allowing the user to provide a request parameter, **msg**, at runtime and have it display as the message. When the page is run with the URL **http://localhost:port/faces/contextroot/hello.xhtml?msg=HelloAgain!!**, the message in the request parameter will be displayed in the page with the UI component.

Now that **HtmlHelloWord** can accept an attribute, a possible next step is to use the attribute to do something. For example, instead of just printing the value of the **hellomsg** attribute on the JSP page, a new attribute such as **stocksymbol** could be added to the component and it could be used as a parameter to a Web service. The returned stock value could then be displayed on the page.

A HelloWorld UI Component That Accepts Form Input

So far, **HtmlHelloWorld** can retrieve attributes provided by the tag and can render (encode) itself to a client. In this next example, we'll create a new version of the component that accepts form input. This new version, called **HtmlHelloInput**, renders an input field and a button. It then processes the incoming value from the input field. In general, the process of handling incoming form values from a UI component is known as *decoding*.

HtmlHelloInput allows a user to enter some text into the input field and the component will immediately render the entered text onto the page. **HtmlHelloInput** will extend **UIInput** instead of **UIComponentBase**. It also no longer needs to override the **getFamily( )** method, since it's extending **UIInput**. We will need to declare that this component does not have a specific external renderer because it renders itself. The declaration of the UI component is now

```
public class HtmlHelloInput extends UIInput {
  public HtmlHelloInput() {
    setRendererType(null); // this component renders itself
  }
...
```

The new **HtmlHelloInput** has an **encodeEnd( )** method that calls three submethods to render the respective subelement of the UI component.

NOTE *An **encodeEnd( )** method was used in this case as opposed to an **encodeBegin( )** from before. In general, when a component accepts input, it is best to use an **encodeEnd( )** because **encodeBegin( )** can be called before a necessary **Converter** is attached.*

```
@Override
public void encodeEnd(FacesContext context) throws IOException {
  String clientId = getClientId(context);
  char sep = UINamingContainer.getSeparatorChar(context);
  encodeInputField(context, clientId + sep + "inputfield");
  encodeSubmitButton(context, clientId + sep + "submit");
  encodeOutputField(context);
}
```

Notice that each subelement is supplied with a unique identifier. The identifier as derived from the clientId of the root component by appending the naming container separator char and an appropriate literal string.

JSF 2.0 Tip *This version of JSF allows the application developer to customize the character that is used to separate the parts of a client ID. The default value of this character is ':', but it can be changed by setting the **javax.faces.SEPARATOR_CHAR** context-param in the **web.xml** file. This is necessary when using CSS style sheets that want to use the IDs as CSS pseudoclasses.*

The main point of the client ID, in all components, is to allow the UI component to identify them later during the *decode* process (which parses the incoming submitted data). Let's examine the source for these methods, beginning with **encodeInputField( )**, shown here:

```
private void encodeInputField(FacesContext context, String clientId)
    throws IOException {
  // Render a standard HTML input field
  ResponseWriter writer = context.getResponseWriter();
  writer.startElement("input", this);
  writer.writeAttribute("type", "text", null);
  writer.writeAttribute("name", clientId, "clientId");
  Object value = getValue();
  if (value != null) {
    writer.writeAttribute("value", value.toString(), "value");
  }
  writer.writeAttribute("size", "6", null);
  writer.endElement("input");
}
```

Notice the call to **getValue( )**. While rendering the input field, the value of the rendered HTML input field is set if the UI component's underlying value is not **null**. Later, in the **decode( )** method, you will see how to set a UI component's value.

The code for **encodeSubmitButton( )** and **encodeOutputField( )** is shown next:

```
private void encodeSubmitButton(FacesContext context, String clientId)
    throws IOException {
  // render a submit button
  ResponseWriter writer = context.getResponseWriter();
  writer.startElement("input", this);
  writer.writeAttribute("type", "Submit", null);
  writer.writeAttribute("name", clientId, "clientId");
  writer.writeAttribute("value", "Click Me!", null);
  writer.endElement("input");
}

private void encodeOutputField(FacesContext context)
    throws IOException {
  ResponseWriter writer = context.getResponseWriter();
  String hellomsg = (String) getAttributes().get("value");
  writer.startElement("p", this);
  writer.writeText("You entered: " + hellomsg, null);
  writer.endElement("p");
}
```

Notice that **encodeOutputField( )** uses an alternate way to retrieve the value of the **hellomsg** attribute, which differs from retrieving the actual value of the overall component, as was done in the **encodeInputField( )**.

The final new method is the **decode( )** method, which parses the incoming **Request** data after a postback occurs.

```
@Override
public void decode(FacesContext context) {
  Map requestMap = context.getExternalContext().getRequestParameterMap();
  String clientId = getClientId(context);
  char sep = UINamingContainer.getSeparatorChar(context);
  String submitted_hello_msg =
      ((String) requestMap.get(clientId + sep + "inputfield"));
  setSubmittedValue(submitted_hello_msg);
}
```

Notice how the decode method uses the unique field identifier **clientId + sep + "inputfield"** to look up the specific parameter that contains the submitted value in the **requestMap**. Recall that this was assigned in the **encodeInputField( )** method.

Finally, we need to make an entry in the **helloworld.taglib.xml** file.

```
<tag>
  <tag-name>helloinput</tag-name>
  <component><component-type>HtmlHelloInput</component-type></component>
</tag>
```

Using the **helloinput** tag in JSP is also trivial:

```
<vt:helloinput />
```

At runtime, the **HtmlHelloInput** component now renders the input, as shown in Figure 11-6.

A JSF Stock Quote Component

To make the original **HtmlHelloInput** component more interesting, the component could be altered, or a new component based on **HtmlHelloInput** could be created. This new component would present an input field as before but would accept it as a stock symbol and then pass it as an argument in a call to a stock quote Web service. To build a stock quote variation of the **HtmlHelloInput** component, the following tasks need to be done:

- A Web service proxy (or client) has to be created that allows a Java application to make a call to a Web service that returns a current stock quote. Since the Java code needed for Web service proxies/clients tends to be a bit cryptic and somewhat

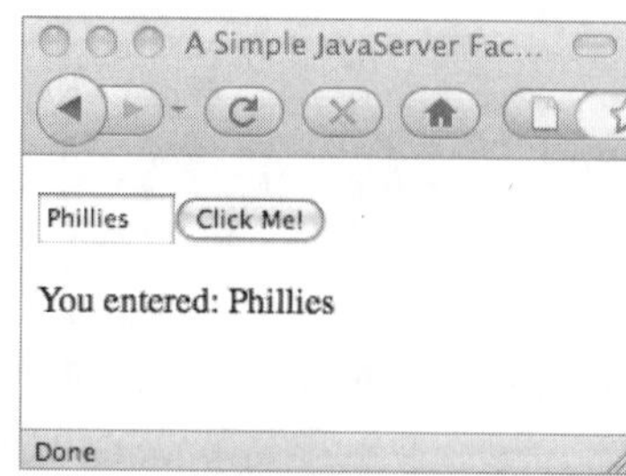

Figure 11-6 The **HtmlHelloInput** component in action

repetitive, it is best to use automatic Web service proxy/client generators, which are provided in many popular Java integrated development environments such as Oracle's JDeveloper or Sun's NetBeans IDE. Once the proxy class is created, it can be instantiated and used in the **UIComponent** code directly, or it can be registered as a Faces-managed bean, making its methods accessible to the Faces application via method binding.

- Once the proxy has been created, the **UIComponent** code can be altered to process a stock **symbol** attribute (as opposed to hellomsg). Instead of just displaying a simple message, the current stock price can be displayed. This is accomplished by using the stock symbol as an argument to the stock quote Web service using the proxy.
- Once retrieved, the quote information could be displayed in HTML (or in whatever markup is desired) during the encode process.
- The overall architecture for a Web service–enabled stock quote component (**HtmlStockInput**) is illustrated in Figure 11-7.

After generating a proxy for the Web service, the decode method can be written to parse the input value and save the stock symbol into the component:

```
public void decode(FacesContext context) {
  Map requestMap = context.getExternalContext().getRequestParameterMap();
  String clientId = getClientId(context);
  char sep = UINamingContainer.getSeparatorChar(context);
  String symbol = ((String) requestMap.get(clientId + sep + "inputfield"));
  setSubmittedValue(symbol);
 }
```

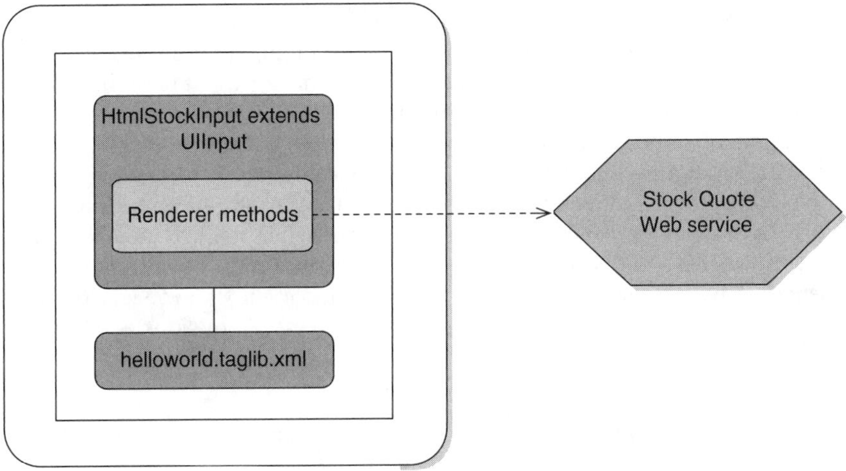

FIGURE 11-7 A Web service–enabled JSF stock quote component

In the **encodeOutputField** method, a call is then made to the Web service proxy code.

```
public void encodeOutputField(FacesContext context)
  throws IOException {
  ResponseWriter writer = context.getResponseWriter();
  String symbol = (String)getAttributes().get("value");
  float currentPrice = 0;
  if (null != symbol) {
  // Use symbol in call to Web Service to get currentPrice
    NetXmethodsServicesStockquoteStockQuotePortClient client = null;
    try {
      client = new NetXmethodsServicesStockquoteStockQuotePortClient();
    } catch (Exception ex) {
       ex.printStackTrace();
    }
    currentPrice = client.getQuote(symbol);
    writer.startElement("p", this);
    writer.writeText("Current stock price for " + symbol + " is: " +
      currentPrice, null);
    writer.endElement("p");
  }
}
```

NOTE *The code for the Web service proxy for this example was auto-generated by Oracle JDeveloper 10g. Since Web service proxy code can have application server dependencies, this step is left to the reader. This Web service at* ***http://services.xmethods.net/soap/urn:xmethods-delayed-quotes.wsdl*** *was active during the writing of this book and is for U.S. stock markets only.*

State Management with Custom Components

Of all the various aspects of JSF custom component development, the one that causes the most confusion is state management. JSF 2.0 simplifies state management with the introduction of the Partial State feature. Prior to JSF 2.0, component state was typically stored in instance variables on the **UIComponent** subclass. For example, the **UIInput** component has a **valid** property, which indicates whether this component is valid or not. This value would be stored in a simple **boolean** instance variable, accessed via a JavaBeans getter and setter and handled explicitly in the **saveState( )** and **restoreState( )** methods. JSF 2.0 introduces the **StateHelper** interface to make this sort of activity easier and less error prone. This interface and its implementation were designed by Sun JSF Expert Group member and Mojarra team leader Ryan Lubke. The getter and setter for this method on **UIInput** now look like this:

```
enum PropertyKeys {
/**
  * <p>Flag indicating whether or not this component is valid.</p>
  */
  valid
}
public boolean isValid() {
  return (Boolean) getStateHelper().eval(PropertyKeys.valid, true);
}
```

```
public void setValid(boolean valid) {
  getStateHelper().put(PropertyKeys.valid, valid);
}
```

There is no instance variable named **valid**; rather, the value is stored in the data structure within the implementation of the **StateHelper** interface, accessed via the **UIComponent.getStateHelper( )** method. Because all **UIComponent**s ultimately extend from **UIComponent**, they have access to this method and should use it to store anything that needs to be preserved across requests. The following sections show how to perform write, read, and remove operations on a **StateHelper**.

Writing to a StateHelper

The **StateHelper** interface has three different methods that write to the internal data structure.

- **Object put(Serializable *key*, Object *value*)** is intended for the simple instance variable case, as shown previously.
- **Object put(Serializable *key*, String *mapKey*, Object *value*)** is intended to store values that would otherwise be stored in a **Map** instance variable. An example from **UIComponent** is found in the implementation of its **setValueExpression(String *name*, ValueExpression *binding*)** method. This method, and its corresponding getter, need a **Map** data structure to store the expression, as shown here:

```
enum PropertyKeys {
/**
  * key in the StateHelper map data structure that backs the
  * setValueExpression( ) and getValueExpression( ) methods
  */
  bindings
}
public void setValueExpression(String name, ValueExpression binding) {
  // intervening code omitted...
  getStateHelper().put(UIComponentBase.PropertyKeys.bindings,name,binding
);
  // code omitted...
}
```

- **void add(Serializable *key*, Object *value*)** is intended to store values that would otherwise be stored in a **List** instance variable. An example from **UIViewRoot** is found in the **addPhaseListener( )** method.

```
enum PropertyKeys {
/**
  * key in the StateHelper map data structure that backs the
  * addPhaseListener( ) methods
  */
  phaseListeners
}
public void addPhaseListener(PhaseListener newPhaseListener) {
  getStateHelper().add(PropertyKeys.phaseListeners, newPhaseListener);
}
```

In all of these cases, the first argument to the **StateHelper** method is an **enum**. There is no strict requirement for the first argument to be an **enum**, but it is very convenient and natural to use an **enum** for this purpose.

Reading from a StateHelper

Values are read from a **StateHelper** in two ways:

- **Object eval(Serializable *key*)** or **Object eval(Serializable *key*, Object *defaultValue*)**. This is by far the most common approach, as was shown previously in the **isValid( )** method. It is used for values that were stored with a call to **put(Serializable *key*, Object *value*)**.
- **Object get(Serializable *key*)**. This method is used when the value was stored with a call to **put(Serializable *key*, Object *value*)** or **void add(Serializable *key*, Object *value*)**.

Removing Values from a StateHelper

Values are removed from a **StateHelper** in two ways:

- **Object remove(Serializable *key*)** This variant removes the underlying **Map** data structure that is written to when **Object put(Serializable *key*, String *mapKey*, Object *value*)** is called.
- **Object remove(Serializable *key*, Object *valueOrKey*)** This variant is used when you want to remove an entry from an underlying **List** or **Map** data structure.

There is currently no need to remove simple values stored with a call to **Object put(Serializable *key*, Object *value*)**, so no way to do so is provided. You know how to use **StateHelper** to automatically managed any persistent state required in your custom **UIComponent**. Let's continue the exploration of custom components by examining how to extract rendering code into a **Renderer**.

Extracting Rendering Code into a Renderer

One powerful feature that JSF has always had is the pluggable rendering concept. The rationale for this feature is the fundamental principle that rendering logic should be separated from behavior. The composite component feature exemplifies this principle more cleanly, but there is still value in learning to use the **Renderer** feature. As stated in Chapter 7, a **Renderer** is a class that is responsible for taking a **UIComponent** instance and generating the output to show the component in a specific kind of client device, for example, a Web browser. Let's do a trivial refactoring of the rendering code in **HtmlHelloInput** into the new **HtmlHelloWorldRenderer**.

```
package com.jsfcompref.components.renderer;

import java.io.IOException;
import java.util.Map;
import javax.faces.component.EditableValueHolder;
import javax.faces.component.UIComponent;
import javax.faces.component.UINamingContainer;
```

```
import javax.faces.context.FacesContext;
import javax.faces.context.ResponseWriter;
import javax.faces.render.FacesRenderer;
import javax.faces.render.Renderer;

@FacesRenderer(componentFamily="javax.faces.Input",
               rendererType="HtmlHelloWorld")
public class HtmlHelloWorldRenderer extends Renderer{

  @Override
  public void decode(FacesContext context, UIComponent component) {
    // The only difference between this method and the variant in
    // HtmlHelloInput is the additional UIComponent argument.
  }

  @Override
  public void encodeEnd(FacesContext context, UIComponent component) throws
IOException {
    // The only difference between this method and the variant in
    // HtmlHelloInput is the additional UIComponent argument,
    // which is also passed through to the encodeInputField(),
    // encodeSubmitButton(), encodeOutputField() methods
  }
}
```

A **Renderer** is responsible for encapsulating the client device dependent aspects of a **UIComponent**, all of which happen to be related to the component's appearance, hence the name renderer. In a similar fashion to **UIComponent**s, there is a runtime registry for **Renderers**, called a **RenderKit**. The details behind **RenderKit**s are discussed in detail in Chapter 13, but for now it is sufficient to know that a **RenderKit** is a data structure that contains **Renderer** instances and that this data structure is consulted by JSF when it comes time to send the HTML to the browser. The **@FacesRenderer** annotation declares the **HtmlHelloWorldRenderer**, with a specific **componentFamily**, and **rendererType**. The equivalent XML syntax for the **faces-config.xml** file is shown here.

```
<render-kit>
  <renderer>
    <component-family>javax.faces.Input</component-family>
    <renderer-type>HtmlHelloWorldRenderer</renderer-type>
    <renderer-class>
      com.jsfcompref.components.renderer.HtmlHelloWorldRenderer
    </renderer-class>
  </renderer>
</render-kit>
```

NOTE *In the accompanying code sample, we didn't add either a **<render-kit-id>** or a **<render-kit-class>** as child elements of **<render-kit>**. Omitting these simply means that the new renderer class will be added to the default render-kit at runtime. More details on creating custom render-kits will be provided in Chapter 13. Similarly, with the **@FacesRenderer** annotation, the **renderKit** attribute is optional, and omitting it has the same result.*

Note that the component family is listed as **javax.faces.Input**. By declaring this value for the component family, you can be assured that the component instance handed to all the methods on **HtmlHelloWorldRenderer** will be an instance of **UIInput**. In this case there is no longer any need for the custom **HtmlHelloInput** class. The only other configuration you need is in the **helloworld.taglib.xml** file, shown here:

```
<tag>
  <tag-name>hellorenderer</tag-name>
  <component>
      <component-type>javax.faces.Input</component-type>
      <renderer-type>HtmlHelloWorld</renderer-type>
  </component>
</tag>
```

With these configuration steps in place, simply replacing **<vt:helloinput>** with **<vt:hellorenderer />** will cause the **HtmlHelloWorldRenderer** to be used instead of the **HtmlHelloInput** component.

Creating a Custom Facelet Tag Library TagHandler

The custom component featured in the preceding section included a **helloworld.taglib.xml** file that declared a custom tag for the component by declaring its **component-type** and **renderer-type**. In the great majority of cases, this is all that will be needed to make your custom UI components (and their **Renderers**) available for use in JSF pages. However, there are times when having access to the Facelet page execution process is helpful, and in these cases a custom **handler-class** is useful. The first change we must make is to declare the java class in the **helloworld.taglib.xml** file, as shown here.

```
<tag>
  <tag-name>hellorenderer</tag-name>
  <component>
      <component-type>javax.faces.Input</component-type>
      <renderer-type>HtmlHelloWorld</renderer-type>
      <handler-class>com.jsfcompref.trainer.taglib.HelloHandler</handler-class>
  </component>
</tag>
```

Because this particular tag handler corresponds to a **UIComponent** subclass, **HelloHandler** must extend **javax.faces.view.facelets.ComponentHandler**. Similar classes are available for tags that correspond to **Validator** or **Converter** instances. The Java code for **HelloHandler** is shown next.

```
package com.jsfcompref.trainer.taglib

import javax.faces.component.UIComponent;
import javax.faces.view.facelets.ComponentConfig;
import javax.faces.view.facelets.ComponentHandler;
import javax.faces.view.Facelets.FaceletContext;

public class HelloHandler extends ComponentHandler {
```

```
  public HelloHandler(ComponentConfig config) {
    super(config);
    // The config argument provides access to all the information
    // given by the page author, the componentType, the rendererType,
    // the attributes, and even the Location of the tag in the page.
  }

  @Override
  public void onComponentCreated(FaceletContext ctx, UIComponent c,
                                 UIComponent parent) {
    // this will be called when the UIComponent instance corresponding
    // to this particular tag in the page is created, but before
    // the component has been populated with its UIComponent children.
    super.onComponentCreated(ctx, c, parent);
   }

  @Override
  public void onComponentPopulated(FaceletContext ctx, UIComponent c,
                                   UIComponent parent) {
    // this will be called when the UIComponent has been populated
    // with its child components.
    super.onComponentPopulated(ctx, c, parent);
  }
}
```

The preceding **HelloHandler** class shows how you can gain access to the way the Facelet runtime builds the page. It simply delegates to the superclass implementation. Those wishing for even more control can override the **getTagHandlerDelegate( )** method on their class that extends **ComponentHandler**. Some additional imports are needed:

```
import javax.faces.view.facelets.MetaRuleset;
import javax.faces.view.facelets.TagHandlerDelegate;
```

The method you need to override looks like this.

```
@Override
protected TagHandlerDelegate getTagHandlerDelegate( ) {
  final TagHandlerDelegate parent = super.getTagHandlerDelegate( );
  TagHandlerDelegate result = new TagHandlerDelegate( ) {

    @Override
    public MetaRuleset createMetaRuleset(Class type) {
      // The MetaRuleset class handles setting tag attributes
      // in the page to properties on the UIComponent instance.
      return parent.createMetaRuleset(type);
    }

    @Override
    public void apply(FaceletContext ctx, UIComponent comp)
      throws IOException {
      // This is called when the actual tag is executed in the page.
      // For most people that were writing custom Facelet tag handlers
```

```
        // prior to JSF 2.0, this is the method they needed most.
        parent.apply(ctx, comp);
      }
    };
    return result;
}
```

The preceding code uses the decorator pattern to gain access to the **TagHandlerDelegate** instance provided by the JSF runtime. This design allows the implementation to continue to do most of the work, while allowing the developer the ability to customize only the aspects of the class where the default implementation is insufficient.

Using a RenderKit to Support Multiple Client Device Types

In this section, we will extend the simple example to support an additional client device type. This particular example only adds support for one additional client device type, the kind used on Internet-enabled handheld devices from Apple Computer Inc. such as the iPhone or iPod Touch, but the example is written in such a way as to make it easy to support additional client device types. The result will be that the same Facelet page will appear differently when viewed in a desktop Web browser and on the Apple mobile device, as shown in Figure 11-8.

To make this possible, we rely on two basic concepts: a JSF **PhaseListener** and class decoration. This example will provide a foundation for a more complete customization, as well as showing how to automatically deliver a client device–specific CSS style sheet to the user agent, and allow you to tailor how individual markup elements are displayed.

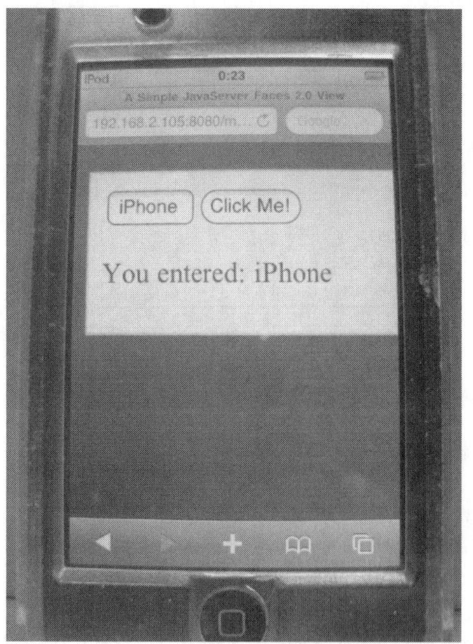

FIGURE 11-8 The same page on different devices, with different **RenderKit**s.

PhaseListeners are described in more detail in Chapter 9, but for now just know that a **PhaseListener** is an interface you implement when you want to have the system call back your application code as a request moves through the JSF lifecycle. In this case, we want our **PhaseListener** to inspect the **User-Agent** header after the restore view phase and set the **RenderKit** appropriately, on a per-request basis, as shown here in this inner class:

```
public class RenderKitSelectorPhaseListener implements PhaseListener {

  public PhaseId getPhaseId() {
    return PhaseId.RESTORE_VIEW;
  }

  private void setRenderKitFromUserAgent(FacesContext context,
      String userAgent) {
    // To implement this kind of feature in a robust way requires a lot
    // of research and will result in lots of heuristics.  This version
    // is very simple and just looks for the strings iPod or iPhone
    // to determine if the User-Agent is coming from an iPhone or iPod
    // touch.
    if (userAgent.contains("iPod") || userAgent.contains("iPhone")) {
      context.getViewRoot().setRenderKitId(
              AppleMobileRenderKit.RENDER_KIT_ID);
    }
  }

  public void afterPhase(PhaseEvent event) {
    setRenderKitFromUserAgent(event.getFacesContext(),
        event.getFacesContext().getExternalContext().
        getRequestHeaderMap().get("User-Agent"));
  }

  public void beforePhase(PhaseEvent event) {
  }
}
```

This simple phase listener is declared to the runtime in the **faces-config.xml** file.

```
<lifecycle>
  <phase-listener>com.jsfcompref.components.renderer.applemobile.
  RenderKitSelectorPhaseListener</phase-listener>
</lifecycle>
```

This code exposes a very important subtlety with our choice of setting the **RenderKit** on a per-request basis. We made this choice because we didn't want to push the awareness of which **RenderKit** to use into the session. This is a trade-off between server memory and runtime speed performance. In this case we chose to save server memory (and complexity) in favor of a sacrificing a little runtime speed. The subtlety comes from how we *must* take action in the **afterPhase( )** method of restore view because this is the earliest time in the lifecycle when **context.getViewRoot( )** returns non-**null**. We need access to the **UIViewRoot** so that we can set its **renderKitId** property. At this point, we have a working phase listener that sets the **RenderKit** to use on this run through the lifecycle.

Decorating the HTML_BASIC RenderKit

Now we will show how to decorate the standard HTML_BASIC **RenderKit**, which all JSF implementations must provide. This will give us the ability to provide a **RenderKit** that is exactly the same as the standard one, but only override specific **Renderer**s to provide content for a specific client device type.

```
package com.jsfcompref.components.renderer.wrapper;

import java.util.HashMap;
import java.util.Map;
import javax.faces.FactoryFinder;
import javax.faces.context.FacesContext;
import javax.faces.render.RenderKit;
import javax.faces.render.RenderKitFactory;
import javax.faces.render.RenderKitWrapper;
import javax.faces.render.Renderer;

public abstract class BaseRenderKitWrapper extends RenderKitWrapper {

  private RenderKit basic;
  private Map<String, Map<String, Renderer>> myFamilies =
    new HashMap<String, Map<String, Renderer>>();

  public BaseRenderKitWrapper() {
    RenderKitFactory factory = (RenderKitFactory)
      FactoryFinder.getFactory(FactoryFinder.RENDER_KIT_FACTORY);
    basic = factory.getRenderKit(FacesContext.getCurrentInstance(),
                     "HTML_BASIC");
  }

  @Override
    public RenderKit getWrapped() {
    return basic;
  }

  @Override
    public void addRenderer(String family, String rendererType, Renderer
renderer) {
    Map<String, Renderer> renderersForFamily = myFamilies.get(family);
    if (null == renderersForFamily) {
      renderersForFamily = new HashMap<String, Renderer>();
      myFamilies.put(family, renderersForFamily);
    }
    renderersForFamily.put(rendererType, renderer);
  }

  @Override
    public Renderer getRenderer(String family, String rendererType) {
    Renderer result = null;
    Map<String, Renderer> renderersForFamily = myFamilies.get(family);
    if (null != renderersForFamily) {
      result = renderersForFamily.get(rendererType);
```

```
      if (result instanceof BaseRendererWrapper) {
        ((BaseRendererWrapper)result).setBaseRenderKit(this);
      }
    }
    if (null == result) {
      result = basic.getRenderer(family, rendererType);
    }
    return result;
  }

  public Renderer getBaseRenderer(String family, String rendererType) {
    Renderer result = null;
    result = basic.getRenderer(family, rendererType);
    return result;
  }

}
```


This class extends **javax.faces.render.RenderKitWrapper**. The wrapper concept is explained in Chapter 13. This concept boils down to extending a "wrapper" base class, overriding the abstract **getWrapped( )** method, and then overriding only the minimum number of other methods as needed. In the constructor, we obtain a reference to the thread-safe singleton HTML_BASIC **RenderKit**, which we also return from the **getWrapped( )** method. The other methods we override are **getRenderer( )** and **addRenderer( )**. These two methods fulfill the basic contract of a **RenderKit** as a data structure that stores **Renderer** instances, as shown in the preceding **HtmlHelloWorldRenderer** example. The data structure within a **RenderKit** implementation is commonly implemented as a two-level **Map**. The keys in the outer map are component family identifiers. Each key in the outer map is associated with an inner **Map**, in which the keys are renderer-type identifiers and the values are the actual **Renderer** instances. In the preceding code, this data structure is the **myFamilies** instance variable. In **getRenderer( )** and **addRenderer( )**, we check **myFamilies** first when access to a **Renderer** is needed, and if no matching **Renderer** is found there, we call through to the **RenderKit** returned from **getWrapped( )**. In this way, we can override as many or as few of the **Renderer**s from the standard HTML_BASIC **RenderKit** as needed.

Now that you understand how our **RenderKit** decoration works, it is time to show a concrete **BaseRenderKitWrapper** subclass, called **AppleMobileRenderKit**.

```
package com.jsfcompref.components.renderer.applemobile;

import com.jsfcompref.components.renderer.wrapper.BaseRenderKitWrapper;
import javax.faces.context.FacesContext;

public class AppleMobileRenderKit extends BaseRenderKitWrapper {

  public static final String RENDER_KIT_ID = "HTML_APPLEMOBILE";
  public static final String RESOURCE_LIBRARY_NAME = "applemobile";

  static String getRequestPathForResource(FacesContext context,
                                String resourceName) {
    String result = null;
    String expressionString = "#{resource['" + RESOURCE_LIBRARY_NAME + ":" +
```

```
      resourceName + "']}";
    result = context.getApplication().evaluateExpressionGet(context,
                             expressionString, String.class);
    return result;
  }
}
```

The only thing needed in addition to what is provided in the base class is the **getRequestPathForResource( )** method. The design of the **AppleMobileRenderKit** assumes the existence of a corresponding resource library, named by the constant **RESOURCE_LIBRARY_NAME**. Renderers within the **RenderKit** can refer to resources from this library by calling this method.

Finally, because there is no annotation for adding a **RenderKit**, you must declare it in the **faces-config.xml** file.

```
<render-kit>
  <render-kit-id>HTML_APPLEMOBILE</render-kit-id>
  <render-kit-class>com.jsfcompref.components.renderer.applemobile.
  AppleMobileRenderKit</render-kit-class>
</render-kit>
```

Decorating an Individual Renderer

Just as we decorate the HTML_BASIC **RenderKit**, we also need the ability to decorate the individual **Renderer**s of which it consists. Because there is no wrapper class for actual **Renderer** instances in the JSF specification, we have to invent our own, which turns out to be very simple. Two pieces of information are required: 1) a reference to the **BaseRenderKitWrapper** and 2) awareness of the renderer's component family and renderer type. We encapsulate this information in the **BaseRendererWrapper** abstract class. The reference to the **BaseRenderKitWrapper** is stored ino the individual **BaseRendererWrapper** instance in **BaseRenderKitWrapper.getRenderer( )**, shown in the preceding code. The second piece of information is hard-coded into the concrete subclass of **BaseRendererWrapper**. In this example, we are decorating the **Renderer** that writes out the HTML **<body>** element, so our **AppleMobileBodyRenderer** class, which extends **BaseRendererWrapper**, knows that its component family is **javax.faces.Output** and its renderer type is **javax.faces.Body**. First, the base class:

```
package com.jsfcompref.components.renderer.wrapper;

import java.io.IOException;
import javax.faces.component.UIComponent;
import javax.faces.context.FacesContext;
import javax.faces.convert.ConverterException;
import javax.faces.render.Renderer;

public abstract class BaseRendererWrapper extends Renderer {

  public abstract String getFamily();

  public abstract String getRendererType();

  private BaseRenderKitWrapper baseRenderKit;
```

```
  public BaseRenderKitWrapper getBaseRenderKit() {
    return baseRenderKit;
  }

  public void setBaseRenderKit(BaseRenderKitWrapper appleMobileRenderKit) {
    this.baseRenderKit = appleMobileRenderKit;
  }

  @Override
  public String convertClientId(FacesContext context, String clientId) {
    return getBaseRenderKit().getBaseRenderer(getFamily(),
                getRendererType()).convertClientId(context, clientId);
  }

  @Override
  public void decode(FacesContext context, UIComponent component) {
    getBaseRenderKit().getBaseRenderer(getFamily(),
              getRendererType()).decode(context, component);
  }
  // the remaining methods from Renderer are exactly the same
  // as the ones shown previously.  All of them simply call
  // getBaseRenderKit().getBaseRenderer(getFamily( ), getRendererType( ))
  // and then call the appropriate method.
```

Now we can finally show the concrete **AppleMobileBodyRenderer** class. This class simply calls the base **Renderer** and adds a **style** attribute to the generated **<body>** element that has a background image that looks nice on mobile devices from Apple Computer, Inc. It also causes a CSS style sheet tailored to the needs of these mobile devices to be rendered into the document's **<head>** section by using the resource relocation feature. This feature will be covered in detail in Chapter 13.

```
package com.jsfcompref.components.renderer.applemobile;

import com.jsfcompref.components.renderer.wrapper.BaseRendererWrapper;
import java.io.IOException;
import java.io.StringWriter;
import javax.faces.application.ResourceDependency;
import javax.faces.component.UIComponent;
import javax.faces.context.FacesContext;
import javax.faces.context.ResponseWriter;
import javax.faces.render.FacesRenderer;

@FacesRenderer(componentFamily="javax.faces.Output",
               rendererType="javax.faces.Body",
               renderKitId=AppleMobileRenderKit.RENDER_KIT_ID)
@ResourceDependency(name = AppleMobileRenderKit.RESOURCE_LIBRARY_NAME +
                           ".css",
                    library = AppleMobileRenderKit.RESOURCE_LIBRARY_NAME)
public class AppleMobileBodyRenderer extends BaseRendererWrapper {

  @Override
  public String getFamily() {
    return "javax.faces.Output";
  }
```

PART II

```
  @Override
  public String getRendererType() {
    return "javax.faces.Body";
  }

  @Override
  public void encodeBegin(FacesContext context, UIComponent component)
    throws IOException {
    ResponseWriter writer = context.getResponseWriter();
    StringWriter buf = new StringWriter();

    // Allow the base class writer to actually write out the body element
    try {
      ResponseWriter clonedWriter = writer.cloneWithWriter(buf);
      context.setResponseWriter(clonedWriter);
      super.encodeBegin(context, component);

      // write out a background attribute with an
      // Apple mobile specific image
      String requestPath = AppleMobileRenderKit.
              getRequestPathForResource(context, "bg.gif");
      // check if the body element already has a style attribute.
      if (buf.toString().contains("style=")) {
        // exercise for the reader
      } else {
        // It does not have one, we can simply write it.
        clonedWriter.writeAttribute("style", "background: url(" +
                                    requestPath +
                                    ") repeat top center;", "style");
      }
      clonedWriter.close();
    } finally {
      context.setResponseWriter(writer);
    }

    if (null != buf) {
      writer.write(buf.toString());
    }

  }
}
```

First, let's cover the annotations. By now you know that **@FacesRenderer** declares a **Renderer** class to the runtime. In this case, we are using all the attributes, including **renderKit**, whose value comes from the constant defined on the **AppleMobileRenderKit** class. The next annotation, **@ResourceDependency**, causes the runtime to ensure that the CSS style sheet **applemobile.css** is delivered to any page that includes a component that is rendered by this **Renderer**. This means that whenever anyone using an Apple mobile device browses to a page that contains an **<h:body>** element, the rendered **<head>** element on that same page will contain the following markup:

```
<link type="text/css" rel="style sheet"
      href="/htmlHelloWorld/faces/javax.faces.resource/
            applemobile.css?ln=applemobile" />
```

The lines are broken to accommodate the book print layout, but the value of the **href** attribute is what the browser needs to know to fetch the CSS resource. With **@FacesRenderer** and **@ResourceDependency** in place, let's continue with the code for **AppleMobileBodyRenderer**.

The actual CSS style sheet in this example is really just a placeholder. A production solution would obviously have more content. For completeness, it is shown here:

```
/*
 * Please consult
http://developer.apple.com/safari/library/documentation/InternetWeb/
Conceptual/iPhoneWebAppHIG/Introduction/Introduction.html
 * for more details
 */
P { font-size: 500% }
```

The **getFamily( )** and **getRendererType( )** methods are abstract in the base class, so we must override them here with concrete values. Finally, we can cover **encodeBegin( )**. We need to call into the HTML_BASIC version of the body **Renderer**, but we have to do so in such a way that we can inject our own **style** attribute into the rendered **<body>** element. In this case, we're writing out markup to tell the browser to use **bg.gif** from the resource library as the background image for the **<body>**. The rendered markup is show here:

```
<body style="background: url(/htmlHelloWorld/faces/javax.faces.resource/
            bg.gif?ln=applemobile) repeat top center;">
```

Again, the lines are broken to accommodate the book print layout.

Customizing the HtmlHelloWorldRenderer

The last element in our working example is to add the existing **HtmlHelloWorldRenderer** to the **AppleMobileRenderKit**. We could either modify the **@FacesRenderer** annotation on the existing Java code or simply declare it in the XML. For extensibility, let's use the latter approach. The complete **faces-config.xml** example is shown here:

```
<?xml version='1.0' encoding='UTF-8'?>

<faces-config xmlns="http://java.sun.com/xml/ns/javaee"
              xmlns:xsi="http://www.w3.org/2001/XMLSchema-instance"
              xsi:schemaLocation="http://java.sun.com/xml/ns/javaee
http://java.sun.com/xml/ns/javaee/web-facesconfig_2_0.xsd"
              version="2.0">

<lifecycle>
  <phase-listener>com.jsfcompref.components.renderer.applemobile.
                  RenderKitSelectorPhaseListener</phase-listener>
</lifecycle>
```

```
<render-kit>
  <render-kit-id>HTML_APPLEMOBILE</render-kit-id>
  <render-kit-class>com.jsfcompref.components.renderer.applemobile.
                    AppleMobileRenderKit</render-kit-class>
  <renderer>
    <component-family>javax.faces.Input</component-family>
    <renderer-type>HtmlHelloWorld</renderer-type>
    <renderer-class>com.jsfcompref.components.renderer.
                    HtmlHelloWorldRenderer</renderer-class>
  </renderer>
</render-kit>
</faces-config>
```

This completes our discussion of Java-based custom **UIComponent**s and **Renderer**s. The remainder of the chapter will return to composite components and end with the complete **vt:loginPanel** example, including how to package this example into a self-contained jar that can simply be dropped into the **WEB-INF/lib** of any JSF2 application.

Advanced Composite Component Development

The preceding discussion on composite components included a simple login panel component. In this section, we will revisit composite components and describe the more advanced aspects of this feature.

Creating a Backing Class for <vt:loginPanel>

When the page author includes **<vt:loginPanel>** tag in the page, the author is actually including a whole subtree of components, rooted at the top-level component, that stands behind the actual **<vt:loginPanel>** tag. When developing advanced custom components, it is frequently necessary to implement behavior using actual programming language code, and not just XHTML markup. In such cases, it is useful to create a "backing" class for the composite component. This is exactly analogous to the backing bean concept introduced in Chapter 5; the only difference is the backing object must be an actual **UIComponent** instead of a POJO. The **<vt:loginPanel>** included in Chapter 10 does exactly this.

Facelets Insight *It might seem tempting to just put the Java code for the backing class straight into the page, as with JSP Scriptlets. Rather than pollute the design of Facelets by introducing something like Scriptlets, Jacob Hookom, the inventor of Facelets, made a different choice: just don't provide the feature. This is consistent with the philosophy that Facelets is simply a way to let page authors lay out and configure* ***UIComponent*** *instances. If you want programming language code, put it in a programming language source file, not an XML file. The Composite Component feature honors Jacob's design choice by making it very easy to associate code with a composite component.*

As with many things in JSF2, there is a convention that can be followed to associate a real Java class as the top-level component for a composite component. The accompanying sidebar shows you the rules for how the top-level component is created.

Rules for Creating the Top-Level Component for a Composite Component

When the JSF runtime encounters a composite component tag in a page, it follows these steps to create the top-level Java component that will serve as the root of the subtree of components. In all of the following cases, it is assumed that the top-level component is a **UIComponent** that implements **javax.faces.component.NamingContainer** and returns **javax.faces.NamingContainer** from its **getFamily( )** method.

- See if there is a **component-type** attribute on the **<cc:interface>** element. If so, interpret it to be the component type of a component already registered with the JSF runtime and create an instance of that component.
- If there is no **component-type** attribute, look for a script-based **UIComponent** implementation that corresponds to the composite component Facelet page. Sun's Mojarra implementation supports the Groovy programming language. If Groovy is enabled, Mojarra looks for a file with the same name as the composite component Facelet page, but with the extension **.groovy**, in the same directory as the composite component Facelet page, for example, **trainer/loginPanel.groovy**.
- If no such script can be found, create a fully qualified Java class name by taking the library name of the resource library that contains the composite component Facelet page and appending the dot character "." and the name of the Facelet page without the extension. For example, **trainer/loginPanel.xhtml** becomes **trainer.loginPanel**. In this case, we look for a Java class named **trainer.loginPanel** and instantiate it, assuming it conforms to the previously stated requirements.
- If no such class can be found, we simply ask the JSF runtime to create a component with the component type **javax.faces.NamingContainer**.

The **<vt:loginPanel>** component uses these rules to have the **loginPanel.java** file serve as the top-level component. To see how this works, let's view the complete source for the **trainer/loginPanel.xhtml** component. We'll look at the interface section, and then the implementation section.

The Interface Section for <vt:loginPanel>

The interface declares a single attribute, **model**, which is a POJO with a number of useful properties. It also supports a facet that lets users control where they want to go once the navigation is successful.

```
<cc:interface>
  <cc:attribute name="model" required="true">
    <cc:attribute name="useridIsValid" required="true"
        method-signature="boolean f(java.lang.String)" />
    <cc:attribute name="passwordIsValid" required="true"
        method-signature="boolean f(java.lang.String)" />
    <cc:attribute name="successOutcome" required="true"
        type="java.lang.String" />
    <cc:attribute name="failureOutcome" type="java.lang.String" />
  </cc:attribute>
```

PART II

```
  <cc:facet name="loginOutcomeChoiceList"
      shortDescription="This facet should contain a menu of choices
        for where the navigation should go after a successful login."/>
</cc:interface>
```

The POJO passed into the top-level component as the value of the **model** attribute must have the following Java methods:

- **boolean userIdIsValid(String *toTest*)**
- **boolean passwordIsValid(String *toTest*)**

It must also have the following **String** JavaBean property: **successOutcome**. Optionally, it may have a **String** JavaBean property: **failureOutcome**.

The using page markup may have a facet nested within **<vt:loginPanel>** named **loginOutcomeChoiceList**. Here is the using page markup from the Virtual Trainer.

```
<vt:loginPanel model="#{loginBacking}">
  <f:facet name="loginOutcomeChoiceList">
    <h:selectOneMenu binding="#{loginBacking.loginOutcomeChoiceList}" >
      <f:selectItem itemLabel="Everyone's Events" itemValue="allEvents" />
      <f:selectItem itemLabel="My Events" itemValue="myEvents" />
    </h:selectOneMenu>
  </f:facet>
</vt:loginPanel>
```

The Implementation Section for <vt:loginPanel>

This section makes extensive use of the **binding** attribute in combination with the **#{cc}** EL implicit object and the knowledge that there is a top-level component that implements specific methods. The Java class will be shown following the Facelet markup.

```
<cc:implementation>
  <h:panelGrid columns="3">
    <h:outputLabel for="#{cc.clientId}:userid" value="Userid:" />
    <h:inputText binding="#{cc.userid}" required="true"
           requiredMessage="Userid is required" id="userid" />
    <h:message for="#{cc.clientId}:userid" />
    <h:outputLabel for="#{cc.clientId}:password" value="Password:" />
    <h:inputSecret binding="#{cc.password}" required="true"
            requiredMessage="Password is required" id="password" />
    <h:message for="#{cc.clientId}:password" />
    <h:outputText value="On Login, Go To:"
           rendered="#{! empty cc.facets.loginOutcomeChoiceList}"/>
    <h:panelGroup>
      <cc:renderFacet name="loginOutcomeChoiceList"/>
      <h:commandButton value="Login" action="#{cc.action}"
              actionListener="#{cc.actionListener}" />
    </h:panelGroup>
    <h:messages for="#{cc.clientId}" />
  </h:panelGrid>
</cc:implementation>
```

Note the **for** attribute for all the **<h:outputLabel>** elements. This is essential because the label must have the absolute client ID of the actual **Userid** field, which, of course, depends on where you place the **<vt:loginPanel>** in the page. This is why the top-level component must be a naming container, because it provides a naming scope for all of its children.

Next note all the **binding** attributes. Recall from Chapter 7 that the **binding** attribute tells the system to use that EL expression as the way to get the actual **UIComponent** for the markup. As you will shortly see, there are JavaBeans properties named **userid** and **password** on the custom top-level component that serve as the target for these **binding** expressions.

Next, note the conditional rendering of the **"On Login, Go To:"** text. This text will only be rendered if the facet is actually provided in the using page. The **<cc:renderFacet>** element can be included without any sort of conditional check because it will automatically take no action if there is no such facet. Finally, and most important, notice the **action** and **actionListener** attributes on the button. These attributes point directly to methods on the top-level component.

The Backing Component for <vt:loginPanel>

The discussion for this component will proceed in two parts. The first part, shown next, accounts for the **binding** statements in the **<cc:implementation>** section. The second part accounts for the **<h:commandButton>** attributes.

```
package trainer;

import java.util.Map;
import javax.el.ELContext;
import javax.el.ELResolver;
import javax.el.PropertyNotFoundException;
import javax.faces.application.FacesMessage;
import javax.faces.component.UIInput;
import javax.faces.component.UINamingContainer;
import javax.faces.context.FacesContext;
import javax.faces.event.ActionEvent;

public class loginPanel extends UINamingContainer {
  private UIInput userid;
  private UIInput password;

  public UIInput getPassword() {
    return password;
  }

  public void setPassword(UIInput password) {
    this.password = password;
  }

  public UIInput getUserid() {
    return userid;
  }

  public void setUserid(UIInput userid) {
    this.userid = userid;
  }
```

Note that the package is **trainer** and the name of the class is **loginPanel**. This is an unusual name for a Java class. Most Java classes start with an uppercase letter. However, to match the naming convention that allows the system to automatically discover this component when the **trainer/loginPanel.xhtml** file is loaded as a result of **<vt:loginPanel>** appearing in the page, we need to name it exactly the same as the **.xhtml** file. Also note that the class extends **UINamingContainer**, which is a handy way of meeting the requirements of a top-level component. Observe that this component has JavaBeans properties of type **UIInput** named **userid** and **password** as required by the **<cc:implementation>** section.

TIP *Because the backing class is an actual **UIComponent**, it is often very useful to override specific methods, such as **decode( )** and **validate( )**. This gives you a lot of power to leverage the design of JSF to your advantage.*

Now we can examine the **action** and **actionListener** attributes.

```
private String action;

public String action() {
  return action;
}

public void actionListener(ActionEvent e) {
  FacesContext context = FacesContext.getCurrentInstance();
  FacesMessage message = null;
  ELContext elContext = context.getELContext();
  ELResolver resolver = elContext.getELResolver();
  Map<String, Object> attrs = this.getAttributes();
  Class paramTypes[] = { String.class };
  Object params[] = new Object[1];
  boolean useridIsValid, passwordIsValid;

  Object model = attrs.get("model");
  params[0] = getUserid().getValue();
  useridIsValid = (Boolean) resolver.invoke(elContext, model,
      "useridIsValid", paramTypes, params);

  // failureOutcome is not a required attribute
  try {
    action = (String) resolver.getValue(elContext, model,
        "failureOutcome");
  } catch (PropertyNotFoundException pnfe) {
    action = null;
  }

  if (!useridIsValid) {
    message = new FacesMessage("Userid " + params[0].toString() +
        " is not recognized.");
    context.addMessage(getUserid().getClientId(context), message);
  } else {
    params[0] = getPassword().getValue();
    passwordIsValid = (Boolean) resolver.invoke(elContext, model,
        "passwordIsValid", paramTypes, params);
```

```
        if (!passwordIsValid) {
          message = new FacesMessage("Password for userid " +
              (String) getUserid().getValue() + " is incorrect.");
          context.addMessage(password.getClientId(context), message);
        } else {
          action = (String) resolver.getValue(elContext, model,
              "successOutcome");
        }
      }
    }
  }
```


The **action( )** method simply returns the **action** instance variable. The really interesting code is in the **actionListener( )** method. In this method we call the **useridIsValid( )** and **passwordIsValid( )** methods, and access the **successOutcome** and **failureOutcome** properties of the **model** object provided by the page author. First, we obtain a reference to the **model** object by calling **attrs.get("model")**. Model object in hand, we get the value of the **userid** field and call **useridIsValid( )** on the model object. We are using a new feature in the unified EL here. In preparation for an invalid login, we try to store the value of the **failureOutcome** property from the model into our **action** instance variable, but because this property is not required, we must do so in a **try-catch** block. If the **userid** turns out not to be valid, we add an appropriate error message for the **userid** component. Otherwise, we check the **password** using a similar approach to how we checked the **userid**. Finally, if both the **userid** and **password** are valid, we access the component's **successOutcome** property and set it as the value of the **action** instance variable. Using the **action** and **actionListener** methods in this way is only possible because the **actionListener** is always called *before* the **action**.

Composite Component Feature Review

Now that you have seen the important capabilities of the Composite Component feature, it is worthwhile to review what you have learned:

- A composite component is a special Facelet page, with a **<cc:interface>** and **<cc:implementation>** section, that resides in a resource library.
- Using a composite component in a page is the same as using a regular component: you have to declare the proper XML namespace in the **<html>** element.
- A composite component always has a top-level component that stands behind the markup, which is automatically created for you. It is easy to provide your own top-level component class when you need to add behavior to the composite component.

The chapter will now conclude with a detailed discussion of how to package up your custom components into an easy-to-deploy jar file.

Packaging JSF Components into a Self-Contained Jar

The core benefit of JSF components is only realized if they are easy to deploy into an application. By following some simple naming conventions, it is possible to produce a single jar file that can properly describe itself to the JSF runtime. In this case, the only installation necessary is to drop a jar file into **WEB-INF/lib** and declare the Facelet tag library at the top of any Facelet page that uses one of the components.

Packaging a Composite Component into a Jar

Recall that a composite component can be as simple as a single Facelet file in a resource directory, or as complex as a Facelet file with a backing class (possibly written in Groovy) and associated scripts and style sheets. In all of these cases, the actions required to package the component into a jar file are simple. Let's start with the simplest case, the single Facelet file, and then progress to the more involved cases. This simple case is required for all other cases as well, so it's a good place to start.

Packaging a Composite Component Facelet File

This task is no different than packaging any resource in a resource library into a jar file: simply put the Facelet file into the jar under the **META-INF/<libname>** directory, where **<libname>** is the name of the resource library. For example, the **trainer/loginPanel.xhtml** file would go into **META-INF/trainer/loginPanel.xhtml** in the **trainer.jar**. Any other resources needed by any of your composite components can be packaged in the same manner.

Declaring a Custom Namespace URL for a Composite Component Library

Because the Composite Component feature was designed with convenience in mind, it is not necessary to declare an actual Facelet tag library descriptor if you simply use the **http://java.sun.com/jsf/composite/** URL prefix. However, for reuse it is necessary to allow developers to package their composite components into a Facelet tag library with an arbitrary URL. To do so, we need a **.taglib.xml** file. Recall that the JSF runtime automatically scans the **META-INF** directory in the Web application classpath for all files that end with **.taglib.xml** and loads them as Facelet tag libraries. Therefore, placing the following content in the file named **META-INF/trainer.taglib.xml** in the **trainer.jar** will declare the composite component library to the JSF runtime.

```
<facelet-taglib xmlns="http://java.sun.com/xml/ns/javaee"
   xmlns:xsi="http://www.w3.org/2001/XMLSchema-instance"
   xsi:schemaLocation="http://java.sun.com/xml/ns/javaee
   http://java.sun.com/xml/ns/javaee/web-facelettaglibrary_2_0.xsd"
   version="2.0">
<facelet-taglib>
  <namespace>http://jsfcompref.com/trainer</namespace>
  <composite-library-name>trainer</composite-library-name>
</facelet-taglib>
```

Now, instead of saying

```
<html xmlns="http://www.w3.org/1999/xhtml"
  xmlns:vt="http://java.sun.com/jsf/composite/trainer">
```

in your Facelet pages that want to use the **<vt:loginPanel>** component, you would say

```
<html xmlns="http://www.w3.org/1999/xhtml"
  xmlns:vt="http://jsfcompref.com/trainer">
```

Packaging Backing Classes for a Composite Component

This task is no different than packaging a regular JSF **UIComponent** into a jar, as explained in the next section.

Packaging a Noncomposite Component into a Jar

In all cases, with a noncomposite component, it is necessary to include the **.taglib.xml** file into the **META-INF** directory of the component jar file. If you are using annotations on your component class, this is all the configuration you need. Otherwise, you need to include a **faces-config.xml** file into the **META-INF** directory of the jar. Note that this particular usage of the **faces-config.xml** file is different than the normal case, where it contains configuration information for the whole application. In the case of a component library, **faces-config.xml** should only contain configuration information for the components themselves; it should not have any outside dependencies. These "component-centric" **faces-config.xml** files can indeed contain any valid elements from the **faces-config.xml** syntax, including **phase-listener** and **managed-bean**. This flexibility makes it possible to build very powerful components.

How the JSF Runtime Loads faces-config.xml Files

When a JSF application starts up, the runtime must perform the following steps to load the application configuration resources (**faces-config.xml** files) pertaining to this application. Before doing so, however, it must configure the standard render-kit and any other default behavior such as the **ViewHandler**, **StateManager**, default **ActionListener**, and so on.

1. For each jar in **WEB-INF/lib**, look inside the jar and load any **faces-config.xml** files that appear in the **META-INF** directory of that jar.

EXPERT GROUP INSIGHT *The order in which these jars will be encountered by the runtime, and therefore the order in which the **faces-config.xml** files will be loaded, is unspecified. An attempt was made to specify this for JSF 1.2, but arriving at a high-quality solution was beyond the scope of the requirements for JSF 1.2. The issue was resolved by reaching an agreement between the Sun and MyFaces implementations to alphabetize the jar files before they are inspected for their **META-INF/faces-config.xml** files.*

2. Look at the value of the servlet initialization parameter called **javax.faces.CONFIG_FILES**. This value is interpreted to be a comma-separated list of context-relative resource paths that should be loaded as **faces-config.xml** files. Note that the elements of this list can be any resource path, enabling you to name your configuration files anything you like.
3. Look in the Web application for a resource called **/WEB-INF/faces-config.xml**. Load the resource, if present.

If any errors occur anywhere in this process, loading of the files stops and the application does not deploy. If the same definition exists in two different files, either the last one loaded takes precedence, or the contents of the files are merged, depending on the semantics of each individual element. For example, let's say you wanted to override the standard text renderer.

You could declare a renderer of type **javax.faces.Text** in the **META-INF/faces-config.xml** file in your **components.jar**. Since the implementation loads the standard render-kit *before* processing the configuration file, the definition would effectively replace the standard one. On the other hand, if you have several files that contain navigation rules listed in the **javax .faces.CONFIG_FILES** initialization parameter, any **navigation-case** elements in those files would be merged in an additive fashion.

JSF 2.0 Tip *JSF 2.0 allows* ***faces-config.xml*** *files to direct the order in which the runtime will load and process the artifacts defined within. This is done via the* ***<absolute-ordering>*** *or* ***<ordering>*** *elements. These attributes are described in detail in Chapter 16.*

How the JSP Runtime Loads TLD Files

Even though the use of JSP files is strongly discouraged in JSF 2.0, the JSP JSP tag library descriptor (TLD) file is still useful for the listeners that it can declare to the system. Like the **faces-config.xml** files, any files that reside in the **META-INF** directory of any jar in **WEB-INF/lib** must be loaded by runtime. In JSP this means the tags in the TLD are made available to the JSP pages in the application via the taglib URI given in the TLD. Another useful mechanism is the ability to declare **listener** elements that cause any of the listeners defined by the servlet specification to be loaded and called at the appropriate time in the application's lifecycle. Table 11-1 lists the **Listeners** provided by the servlet specification that can be declared in a TLD.

You have now been exposed to a significant depth and breadth of subject matter regarding the world of JSF custom **UIComponent**s. With the knowledge you now have, you can build localizable, reuseable, and, most important, easy-to-use custom **UIComponent**s for a wide array of client device types. The next chapter will build on this knowledge and show how to add Ajax capabilities to your applications and your components.

Listener Name	Description
javax.servlet.ServletRequestEvent	Notifies on the creation or destruction of a **ServletRequest**
javax.servlet.http.HttpSessionListener	Called upon the creation or destruction of a **HttpSession**
javax.servlet.ServletContextListener	Called upon the creation or destruction of a **ServletContext**
javax.servlet.ServletRequestAttributeListener	Called upon the addition or removal of attributes on the **ServletRequest**
javax.servlet.http.HttpSessionAttributeListener	Called upon the addition or removal of attributes on the **HttpSession**
javax.servlet.ServletContextAttributeListener	Called upon the addition or removal of attributes on the **ServletContext**

Table 11-1 **Listeners** That Can Be Declared in a TLD

12

CHAPTER

JSF and Ajax

If you came to JSF looking for Ajax support, you'll be happy to learn that no other Web framework has as comprehensive, well-integrated, and easy-to-use Ajax capabilities. If you are an existing JSF user and want to add Ajax to your application, you'll be happy to know that everything you've learned so far about JSF still applies when using Ajax. In fact, the object-oriented design of JSF was ready for Ajax before the term had ever been coined. In this chapter, you will be exposed to a brief overview of Ajax followed by a simple example, built on the JSFReg application from Chapter 2. The middle of the chapter will give you an understanding of the fundamentals of JSF and Ajax. The chapter will close by touching on some advanced topics.

Ajax Overview

The term "Ajax" was coined by web user experience expert Jesse James Garrett in February 2005. Ajax has come to be known as an acronym that stands for *A*synchronous *J*avaScript *A*nd *X*MLHttpRequest, but more generally it has come to stand for a specific technique that makes Web applications behave more responsively for users. To that end, the most important letter in Ajax is the *A* for Asynchronous. In a non-Ajax application, the only way to send data to the server is via an HTML form submission that locks up the browser until the server responds. The following JSF page would do exactly that:

```
<!DOCTYPE html PUBLIC "-//W3C//DTD XHTML 1.0 Transitional//EN"
  "http://www.w3.org/TR/xhtml1/DTD/xhtml1-transitional.dtd">
<html xmlns="http://www.w3.org/1999/xhtml"
      xmlns:h="http://java.sun.com/jsf/html">
<h:head>
  <title>A Simple JavaServer Faces 2.0 View</title>
</h:head>
<h:body>
  <h:form>
    You entered: #{requestScope.input}.
    <h:inputText id="input" value="#{requestScope.input}" />
    <p><h:commandButton value="submit" /></p>
  </h:form>
</h:body>
</html>
```

There is nothing wrong with this JSF page nor the HTML it renders. This simple example renders a form with a text field and a button. When the user enters some text and presses the button, the text that user entered in the field is shown back to him or her. Since the advent of the ISINDEX tag in 1992, people have accepted that all Web applications basically worked like this example, the essence of which is captured in the following steps:

1. Visit a Web page.
2. Fill in some data.
3. Press a button.
4. Wait.
5. Repeat from Step 1.

Seventeen years later Mr. Garrett observed that *enough people* had browsers that were *new enough,* and computers that were *powerful enough* to run them, that the tyranny of this workflow could be broken. Of course, the converse to people having *new enough* browsers is that their old browser, usually Netscape 4, faded from widespread use. Three important capabilities that these "new enough" browsers had were 1) JavaScript, 2) the DOM, and 3) the XMLHttpRequest JavaScript object. *JavaScript* you already know: it's the scripting language supported, in some form or another, by all Web browsers shipped after 1997. *DOM* stands for Document Object Model. It's the Web standard that browsers use to allow JavaScript to dynamically manipulate a web page that is being displayed in the browser. **XMLHttpRequest** is a name for a collection of programming language functions that you can call from JavaScript to make synchronous or asynchronous HTTP requests to a web server and read the responses without doing a form submit.[1] By combining JavaScript and XMLHttpRequest, and using the asynchronous capabilities of both to update the DOM when the server responds with data, the workflow can now look like this:

1. Visit a Web page.
2. Fill in some data (and the browser automatically submits just enough of it to do some work and update the web page).
3. Repeat Step 2.

Of course, it is quite common to mix the old and new workflows, even for applications that use Ajax very heavily. By now you can see that Ajax isn't a technology, it's a technique that, when used properly, allows the developer to deliver a more responsive user experience, with far less unproductive waiting than otherwise possible.

---

[1]Like everything in enterprise software, the business case is what drives adoption of new technology. The biggest barrier to adoption is building up a big enough "installed base" to make the technology successful. Ajax is a special case because the work of building up the installed base was already done. As mentioned in the text, JavaScript had been around since 1997, and DOM came out around that same time. The **XMLHttpRequest** object was introduced into Microsoft Internet Explorer 5 in 1999 and quickly copied by the other leading browser, Mozilla Firefox. The technology pieces in place, the last element required to assure the popularity of Ajax was "the killer app." This app was Google Maps, offered by Google starting in February 2005.

To bring the example back to JSF, it's very easy to convert the preceding example to use Ajax, as shown here:

JSF 2.0* Tip** *All of the examples in this chapter show the built-in Ajax support in JSF 2.0. If you are using a version of JSF prior to 2.0, please see the first edition of this book, or consult the excellent reference Web site:* ***http://jsfmatrix.net/*. This site lists all the known JSF+Ajax frameworks in existence, most of which were designed to work with JSF 1.2.*

```
<!DOCTYPE html PUBLIC "-//W3C//DTD XHTML 1.0 Transitional//EN"
  "http://www.w3.org/TR/xhtml1/DTD/xhtml1-transitional.dtd">
<html xmlns="http://www.w3.org/1999/xhtml"
      xmlns:h="http://java.sun.com/jsf/html"
      xmlns:f="http://java.sun.com/jsf/core">
<h:head>
  <title>A Simple JavaServer Faces 2.0 View</title>
</h:head>
<h:body>
  <h:form>
    You entered: #{requestScope.input}.
    <h:inputText id="input" value="#{requestScope.input}">
      <f:ajax render="@form" />
    </h:inputText>
  </h:form>
</h:body>
</html>
```

We simply deleted the button and nested an **<f:ajax>** element within the input text. Now whenever the user moves the cursor out of the input field, the effect will be the same as if that user pressed the button, with the all important exception that the contents of the form will update asynchronously, without a full page refresh. That's what the **rendered="@form"** attribute on the **<f:ajax>** tag means. The **<f:ajax>** tag will be fully explained later in the chapter, along with its corresponding JavaScript functions. To enable this ease of use, there is a whole lot of work being done for you behind the scenes, and you don't need to understand any of it to make great use of Ajax in JSF.

A Simple Ajax Example from JSFReg

Let's continue with a more practical example from JSFReg: asynchronous validation. Let's say we want to add a **userid** field to the **register.xhtml** page, and make it so that the availability of the userid is checked automatically as the user fills out the form. The beginning lines of the new **register.xhtml** file are shown here:

```
<!DOCTYPE html PUBLIC "-//W3C//DTD XHTML 1.0 Transitional//EN"
"http://www.w3.org/TR/xhtml1/DTD/xhtml1-transitional.dtd">
<html xmlns="http://www.w3.org/1999/xhtml"
      xmlns:h="http://java.sun.com/jsf/html"
      xmlns:f="http://java.sun.com/jsf/core">
<h:head>
  <title>A Simple JavaServer Faces Registration Application</title>
</h:head>
```

```
<h:body>
  <h:form>
    <h2>JSF Registration App</h2>
    <h4>Registration Form</h4>
    <table>

      <tr>
        <td>Userid:</td>

        <td>
          <f:ajax render="useridMessage">
            <h:inputText label="Userid" id="userid"
                         value="#{userBean.userid}" required="true"/>
            <h:message id="useridMessage" for="userid" />
          </f:ajax>
        </td>
      </tr>
```

The system is designed so that the **<f:ajax>** tag has an awareness of the kinds of components it is wrapping so that it can take the appropriate action to best imbue each particular component with Ajax capability.

Note that there is no explicit validator attached to the field. This is because we are using JSR-303 Bean Validation, as shown in the Virtual Trainer from Chapter 10. To recall how this works, we simply need to define a **Constraint** and annotate the setter for the **userid** property in the **UserBean** class, as shown here:

```
private String userid;

@UseridUniquenessConstraint
public String getUserid() {
  return userid;
}

public void setUserid(String userid) {
  this.userid = userid;
}
```

The constraint definition is looks like this:

```
package com.jsfcompref.model;

import java.lang.annotation.Documented;
import java.lang.annotation.ElementType;
import java.lang.annotation.Retention;
import java.lang.annotation.RetentionPolicy;
import java.lang.annotation.Target;
import javax.validation.Constraint;
import javax.validation.ConstraintPayload;

@Documented
@Constraint(validatedBy = UseridUniquenessConstraintValidator.class)
@Target({ ElementType.METHOD, ElementType.FIELD })
@Retention(RetentionPolicy.RUNTIME)
public @interface UseridUniquenessConstraint {
```

```
        String message() default "A user with that userid already exists";

        Class<?>[] groups() default {};

      Class<? extends ConstraintPayload>[] payload() default {};
}
```

And the last piece is the **ConstraintValidator** class:

```
package com.jsfcompref.model;

import javax.validation.ConstraintValidator;
import javax.validation.ConstraintValidatorContext;

public class UseridUniquenessConstraintValidator implements
    ConstraintValidator<UseridUniquenessConstraint, String> {
  public boolean isValid(String value, ConstraintValidatorContext ctx) {
    boolean result = (null != value && 3 < value.length());
    return result;
  }
  public void initialize(UseridUniquenessConstraint arg0) {
  }
}
```

Now, the presence of the **<f:ajax>** tag wrapping the input field and its corresponding message will cause the form to be submitted, processed, and rendered, partially. In this case, only the value of the **userid** field is submitted, and only the necessary components that need to process the **userid** field are processed in the JSF lifecycle. To clarify your understanding of partial submits, processing, and rendering, compare the full submit lifecycle, shown in Figure 12-1, with the partial submit lifecycle shown in Figure 12-2.

Figures 12-1 and 12-2 illustrate the basic principle underlying the way Ajax is supported in the JSF standard: Ajax is just a way to take action on discrete subtrees of a complete server-side view.

While this is not the only way to use JSF and Ajax, it is the only way supported by the standard and therefore is the easiest way to use JSF and Ajax. More advanced JSF and Ajax usage is possible, and examples abound on the Internet. For example, Direct Web Remoting (DWR) is a popular Ajax framework that has some extension points for using it with JSF. More on DWR can be found at **http://directwebremoting.org/**. Finally, no discussion on JSF and Ajax would be complete without a reference to **http://jsfmatrix.net/**. This site is a table of all the JSF+Ajax frameworks in existence, most of which are suitable for use with JSF 1.2, and therefore most of which don't use the new Ajax support in the JSF standard as of JSF 2.0.

Now that you have a basic understanding of Ajax in the JSF standard, let's take a quick look under the covers to see how the preceding JSFReg example actually works. Once we have traversed the inner workings of this demo, I will explain the full details and usage of the **<f:ajax>** tag and the underlying **jsf.ajax** JavaScript object on top of which this tag is built.

Ajax JSFReg Behind the Scenes

Even though the only mention of Ajax in the entire JSFReg example is the single usage of the **<f:ajax>** tag, there is a lot of work going on behind the scenes to make it possible.

PART II

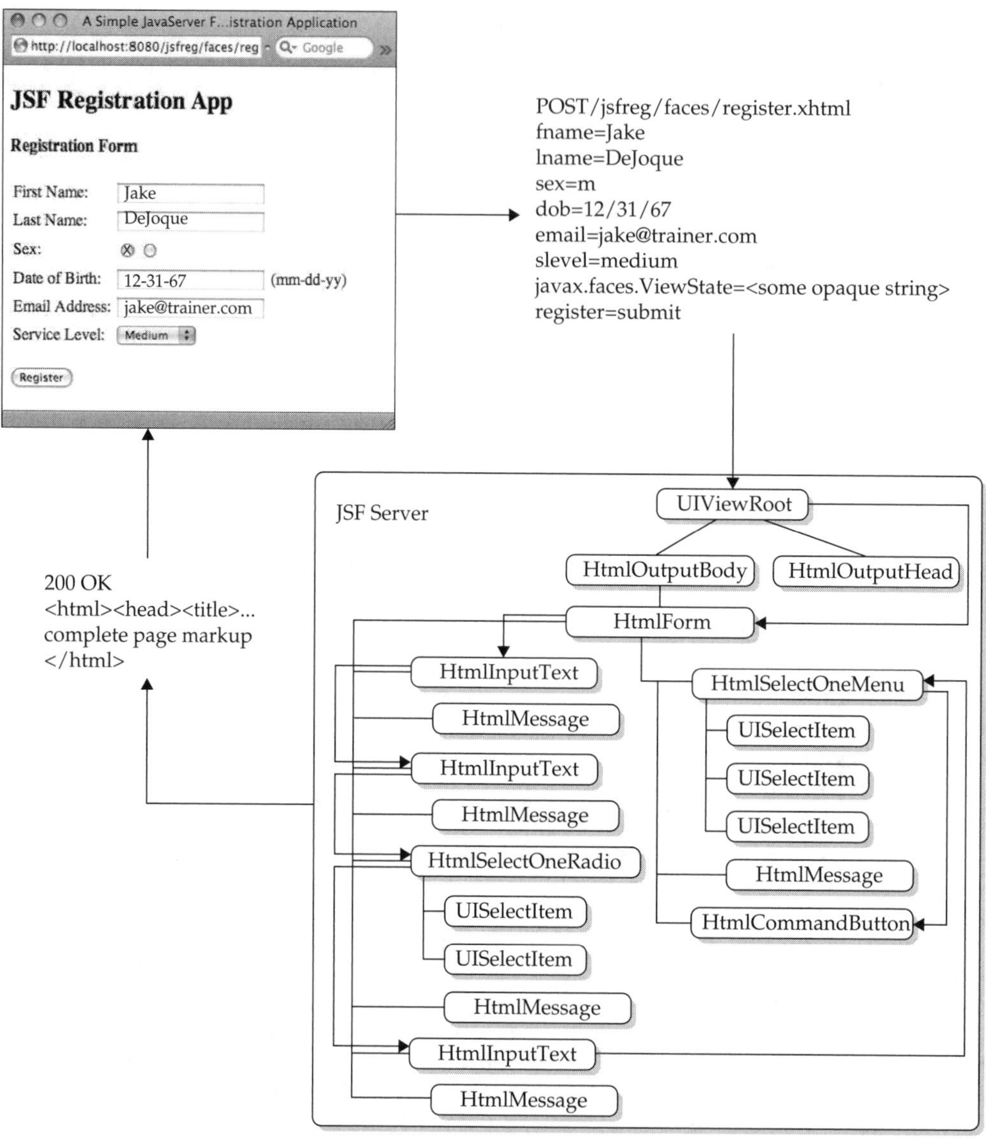

FIGURE 12-1 Full submit

This section will explain all of the inner workings in detail, but first it is necessary to direct you to install the essential tool for all Web developers, and Ajax developers in particular: Firebug. Firebug is an extension for Mozilla Firefox that enables you to debug JavaScript, track HTTP transactions, and much more.

Installing Firebug and Using It to Understand Ajax JSFReg

The examples in this section are executed with Mozilla Firefox 3.5 and Firebug version 1.4.0, which can be downloaded from **http://getfirebug.com/**. Once you have installed the **.xpi** file

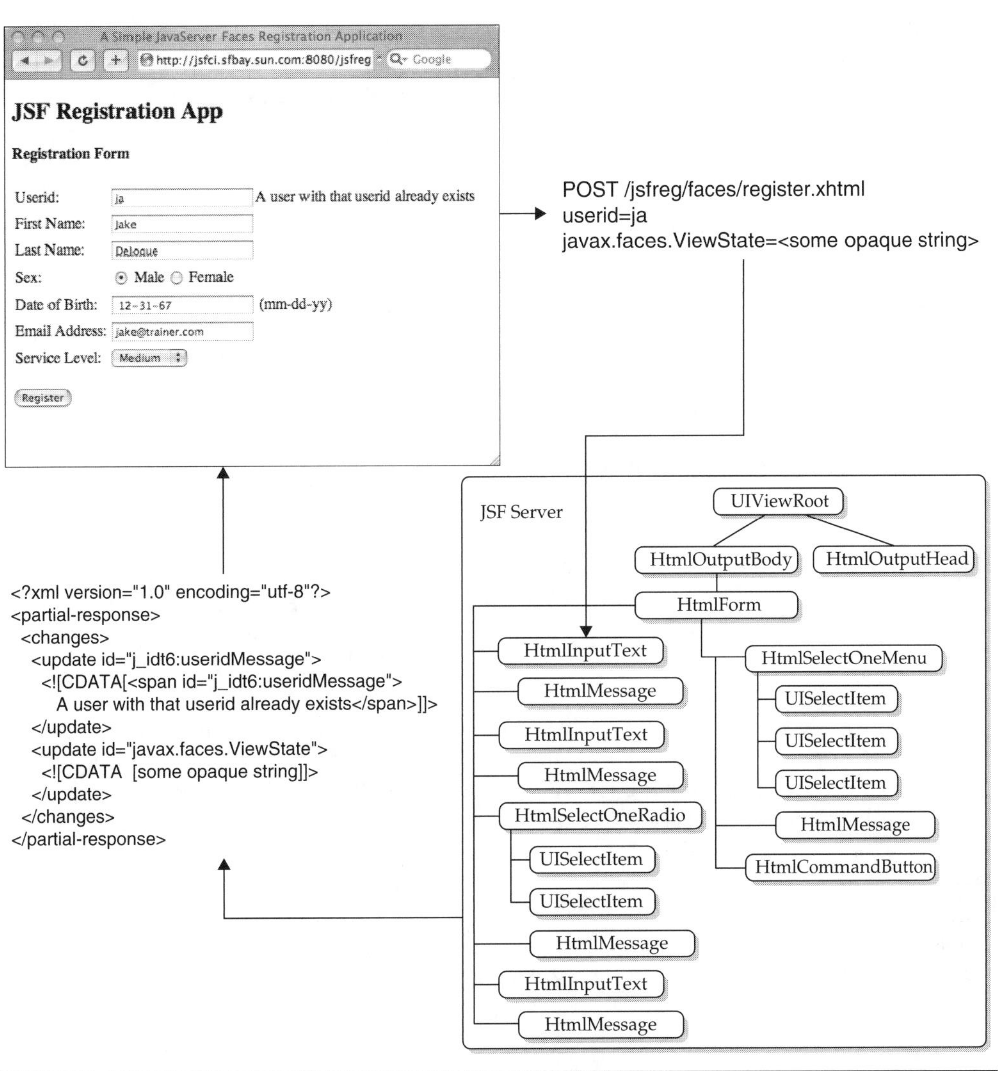

FIGURE 12-2 Partial submit

and restarted your Firefox, visiting the Ajax JSFReg example will cause the browser to appear as shown in Figure 12-3.

Clicking the lovely beetle icon will expose the Firebug window. Click the word **Net** in the topmost Firebug toolbar (item 1 in Figure 12-4), then click the word **All** on the line below the topmost Firebug toolbar (item 2), and then reload the page (item 3). The window should look something like Figure 12-4.

Now, click the **Clear** button, type in two characters into the **Userid** field, and press TAB to move the keyboard focus out of the text field (item 1 in Figure 12-5). The Firebug window should update. Expand the **POST register.xhtml** node in the Firebug window (item 2) and click the **Response** tab (item 3). You will now see the **<partial-response>** XML content that

FIGURE 12-3 Firebug installed, but not activated

If this icon is gray, it indicates Firebug is installed, but not enabled.

causes the browser to dynamically update the changed portions of the page in response to the JSR-303 **ConstraintValidator**. This is illustrated in Figure 12-5. You have now been exposed to the very basics of using Firebug to understand JSF and Ajax. The following sections will explain how the simple Ajax JSFReg example works.

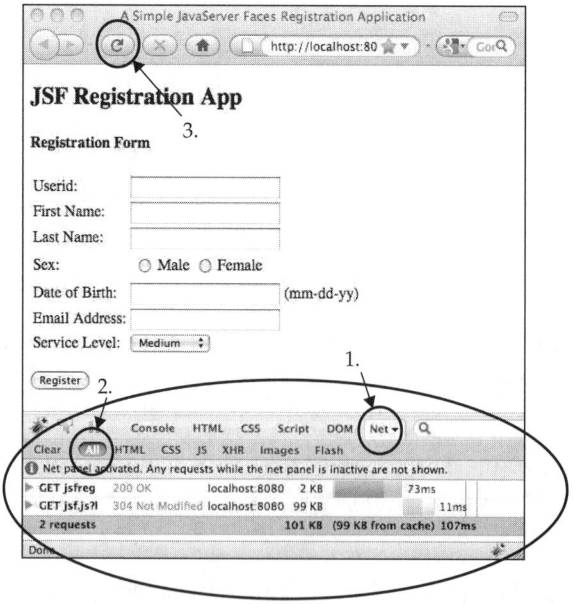

FIGURE 12-4 Firebug, activated with the Net panel showing the result of loading the JSFReg page

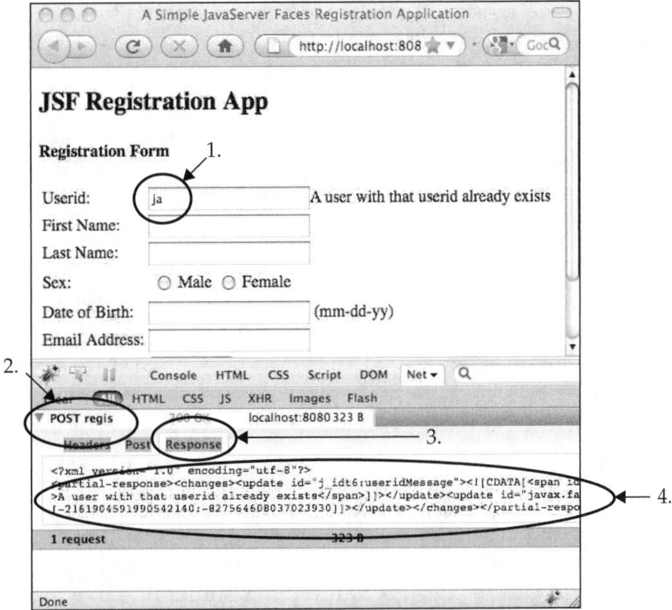

FIGURE 12-5 Firebug, showing Ajax HTTP traffic

Ajax JSFReg Step-by-Step

The following steps must be taken in order to use the built-in Ajax in JSF. If you use the **<f:ajax>** tag, they are taken for you automatically, but it is helpful to know what's happening on your behalf.

1. The user requests a JSF page that has a component that has a dependency on the built-in Ajax functionality, as well as one or more components that uses that dependency in some way, for example **http://server/jsfreg/faces/register.xhtml**. This dependency can be indicated in one of the following ways

   - The component or its **Renderer** has a **@ResourceDependency** annotation with the resource name **jsf.js** and library name **javax.faces**.
   - The page contains **<h:outputScript library="javax.faces" name="jsf.js" />**.
   - A component or tag handler in the page has code equivalent to the following:

     ```
     UIOutput output = new UIOutput();
     output.setRendererType("javax.faces.resource.Script");
     output.getAttributes().put("name", "jsf.js");
     output.getAttributes().put("library", "javax.faces");
     context.getViewRoot().addComponentResource(context, output, "head");
     ```

   This last method is what the **<f:ajax>** tag does.

   Any one of these steps will cause the following markup to be rendered into the page delivered in response to this render request. The script may end up in the **<head>**, **<body>**, or **<form>**, depending on options passed to the specific technique for indicating the resource dependency.

   ```
   <script type="text/javascript"
   src="/jsfreg/faces/javax.faces.resource/jsf.js?ln=javax.faces"></script>
   ```

2. The browser renders the page with the preceding script reference and thus makes a separate HTTP request to get the JavaScript file. This JavaScript file is known as the "Standard JavaScript Resource," and all JSF implementations are required to include it in a resource library named **javax.faces** with a resource name **jsf.js**. Resources are described in detail in Chapter 11. For now, it is sufficient to know that the **jsf.js** file has all the JavaScript code necessary to use the standard Ajax JSF features. Note that no matter how many components on the page declare a dependency on the standard JavaScript resource, it will only be referenced once in the page.
3. The user takes action in the page that causes the script to execute. In the case of **register.xhtml**, this action is to move the keyboard focus out of the **Userid** field. The markup rendered for this field my Sun's Mojarra implementation is shown here:

   ```
   <input type="text" onchange="mojarra.ab(this,event,'valueChange',0,
   'j_idt6:useridMessage')" name="j_idt6:userid" id="j_idt6:userid"/>
   ```

   The **mojarra.ab( )** function is nonstandard but allowable within by the specification. This function ultimately calls through to the **jsf.ajax.request(s, e, op)** JavaScript function, which *is* defined in the Standard JavaScript Resource.
4. When the browser delivers the **onchange** event to the JavaScript function, and **jsf.ajax.request( )** is called, this function makes a POST to the JSF server, via Ajax. The actual content of the request looks something like the following:

   ```
   POST /jsfreg/faces/register.xhtml
   Host: localhost:8080
   User-Agent: Mozilla/5.0 (Macintosh; U; Intel Mac OS X 10.5; en-US;
   rv:1.9.1.3) Gecko/20090824 Firefox/3.5.3
   Accept: text/html,application/xhtml+xml,application/xml;q=0.9,*/*;q=0.8
   Accept-Language: en-us,en;q=0.5
   Accept-Encoding: gzip,deflate
   Accept-Charset: ISO-8859-1,utf-8;q=0.7,*;q=0.7
   Keep-Alive: 300
   Connection: keep-alive
   Faces-Request: partial/ajax
   Content-Type: application/x-www-form-urlencoded; charset=UTF-8
   Referer: http://localhost:8080/jsfreg/
   Content-Length: 431
   Cookie: JSESSIONID=e324d6413179e3c4eea8d77503a7
   Pragma: no-cache
   Cache-Control: no-cache
   j_idt6=j_idt6
   j_idt6:dob=
   j_idt6:email=
   j_idt6:fname=
   j_idt6:j_idt22=medium
   j_idt6:lname=
   j_idt6:userid=ja
   javax.faces.ViewState=-2250254750720751792:391987019164050210
   javax.faces.behavior.event=valueChange
   javax.faces.partial.ajax=true
   javax.faces.partial.event=change
   javax.faces.partial.execute=j_idt6:userid j_idt6:userid
   javax.faces.partial.render=j_idt6:useridMessage
   javax.faces.source=j_idt6:userid
   ```

5. The JSF server receives the Ajax request, recognizes it as such due to the content in the request shown in boldface in the preceding step, and performs the partial lifecycle processing shown in Figure 12-2. Note that this particular example does not narrow the traversal as much as it could be narrowed. Later in the chapter, I'll show how to do that. As a result of the partial processing, the JSF server delivers the following XML to the client:

```
<?xml version="1.0" encoding="utf-8"?>
<partial-response>
  <changes>
    <update id="j_idt6:useridMessage">
      <![CDATA[<span id="j_idt6:useridMessage">A user with that userid
           already exists</span>]]>
    </update>
    <update id="javax.faces.ViewState">
      <![CDATA[-2250254750720751792:3919870191640502l0]]>
    </update>
  </changes>
</partial-response>
```

6. The Standard JavaScript Resource, which initiated the Ajax request in Step 4, receives the response and takes the action prescribed by the JSF standard to update the appropriate portions of the page using innerHTML or some other implementation specific technique.

The preceding six-step process is taken for you automatically when you use the **<f:ajax>** tag in the page. Now that you have been introduced to the work done by the **<f:ajax>** tag, it's time to explore the options this tag gives you for use in the page.

The <f:ajax> Tag and Its Attributes

This section explains the options available on the **<f:ajax>** tag and gives some insight into how to use them.

EXPERT GROUP INSIGHT *As JavaScript expert Douglas Crockford likes to say, JavaScript is the world's most misunderstood programming language. This is probably why it's in the running for being considered the world's most feared and avoided programming language, at least for certain classes of programmers. Acknowledging this reality, the Expert Group strove for two entry points for Ajax functionality: one for those that dislike JavaScript (the* ***<f:ajax>*** *tag) and one for those that at least don't mind it so much (the JavaScript functions on the* ***jsf.ajax*** *JavaScript object).*

The general form for the **<f:ajax>** tag is shown in Figure 12-6. All of the attributes are optional. The action taken in the case of missing attributes is explained in the accompanying sidebar.

Like most of the tags in the **f:** library, the **<f:ajax>** tag cannot be used in isolation; it has to be nested within, or wrapped around, a tag that corresponds to a server side **UIComponent**. This code wraps the input field and the button and applies Ajax capabilities to each component:

```
<f:ajax>
  <h:inputText value="#{model.username}" />
  <h:commandButton action="next" />
</f:ajax>
```

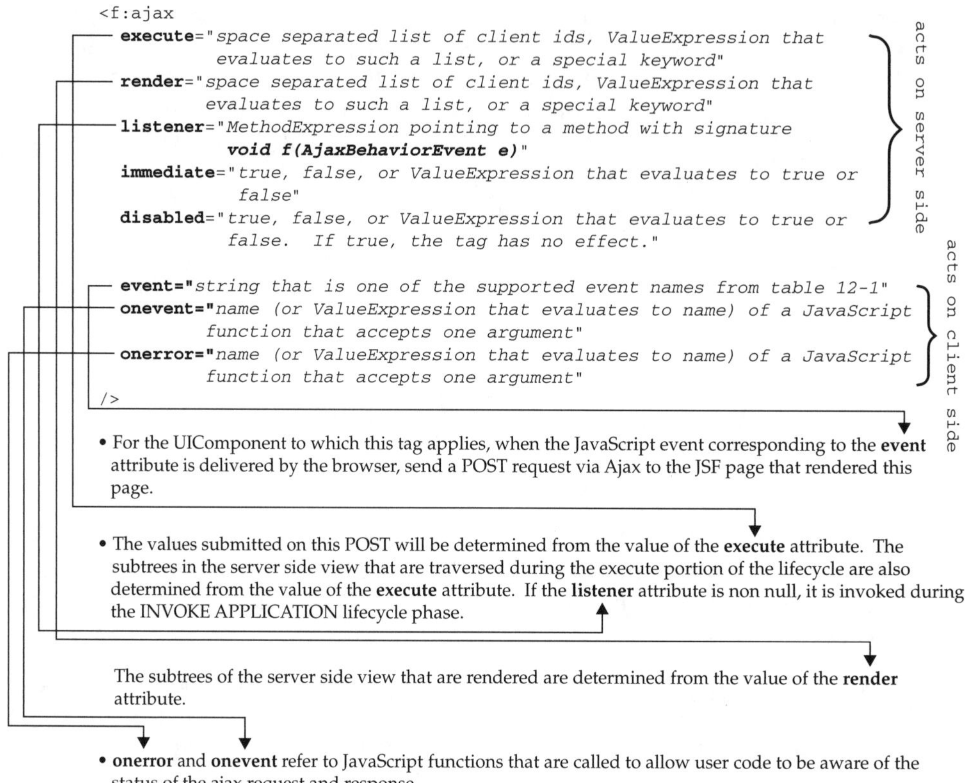

Figure 12-6 The general form of the <f:ajax> tag

This code does the same thing but using the nesting syntax:

```
<h:inputText value="#{model.username}">
  <f:ajax />
</h:inputText>
<h:commandButton action="next">
  <f:ajax />
</h:commandButton>
```

You may well ask, "If both variants do the same thing, why have two variants?" The answer comes when you need to customize the attributes for each specific usage. In this case, the fine granularity of nesting the **<f:ajax>** within individual components is probably what you want. Note that it is possible to wrap and nest the same component, as shown here:

```
<f:ajax event="mouseout">
  <h:inputText value="#{model.username}">
    <f:ajax event="dblclick" />
  </h:inputText>
  <h:commandButton action="next" />
</f:ajax>
```

In such cases, the attributes effectively are the union of the wrapping tag and the wrapped tag. In the preceding example, the **<h:inputText>** would have Ajax behavior applied for the **mouseout** and **dblclick** events, while the **<h:commandButton>** would only have Ajax behavior for **mouseout**.

Figure 12-6 tells what happens when the **<f:ajax>** tag is applied to a **UIComponent** tag. The accompanying simple rules describe to which **UIComponent** tags the **<f:ajax>** tag applies.

Rules to Determine Which UIComponent Tag Is Imbued with Ajax Behavior

This sidebar lists the rules the JSF runtime follows to determine to which **UIComponent** tag the **<f:ajax>** tag applies.

- If the **<f:ajax>** tag has no **UIComponent** tag children and is nested immediately inside of a **UIComponent** tag, the parent **UIComponent** is imbued with Ajax behavior as described in Figure 12-6.
- If the **<f:ajax>** tag has **UIComponent** children (and any children of those children, and so on) are imbued with Ajax behavior as described in Figure 12-6.

Optional Arguments and <f:ajax>

As mentioned previously, all of the attributes on the **<f:ajax>** tag are optional and have sensible default values, described here.

- If **execute** is not specified, the client ID of the **UIComponent** to which the **<f:ajax>** tag applies is the default. This means that only one name=value pair will be submitted in the POST data and only one **UIComponent** will be processed during the postback.
- If **render** is not specified, no components will be traversed during the Render Response phase.
- If **listener** is not specified, the only action that will be invoked during the Invoke Application phase will be the one that corresponds to an **ActionSource** component listed in the **execute** attribute, if the **execute** attribute refers to such a component. This attribute makes the **<f:ajax>** tag cause potentially any component to act like an **ActionSource**.
- If **immediate** is not specified, the action happens during the Invoke Application phase; otherwise, the action happens during the Apply Request Values phase. This attribute is semantically equivalent to the attribute of the same name on other components in JSF.
- If **disabled** is not specified, the Ajax behavior performs as planned. This is useful for conditionally turning off Ajax, for example, if the application is aware of whether or not JavaScript is supported in the browser.
- If **event** is not specified, the value returned from the **getDefaultEventName( )** method on the **UIComponent** is used. If specified, the event name must be one of the values returned from the **getEventNames( )** method on the **UIComponent**. Later Table 12-1 lists the default and additional supported event names for each component in the Standard HTML RenderKit.

(continued)

- If **onevent** is not specified, no JavaScript function is called to provide status updates.
- If **onerror** is not specified, in **Development** mode, for Sun's Mojarra JSF implementation only, a modal alert dialog is raised sent. In all other modes, the error is unhandled if no **onerror** is specified.

Special Keywords for Use in the execute and render Attributes

The **execute** and **render** keywords accept a set of special keywords, each with the meaning shown in this table.

Keyword	Meaning When Used in execute	Meaning When Used in render
@all	Every component on the page is submitted and processed. This is useful when you want to do a full-page submit.	Every component on the page is rendered. This is useful when you just want to rerender the whole page asynchronously. This behavior is useful if you want to update the page and keep some client side state outside of JSF.
@none	Execute the lifecycle, including its phase listeners, but no components will be traversed.	Perform the Render Response phase, including firing any **preRenderView** events, but don't actually render anything.
@this	Submit and process only the component to which the **<f:ajax>** is applied.	Render only the component to which the **<f:ajax>** is applied.
@form	Submit and process the entire **<h:form>** in which the component that has the **<f:ajax>** is nested.	Render the entire **<h:form>** in which the component that has the **<f:ajax>** is nested.

To round out our description of the **<f:ajax>** tag, Table 12-1 lists the default and supported values for the **event** attribute for all of the tags in the Standard HTML RenderKit. Before this complete list, there are two important global default events value that override those listed in Table 12-1.

- The default event value for any component that is an **EditableValueHolder** is **change**. This corresponds to the **onChange** JavaScript event and means that the Ajax transaction will commence when the browser detects that the user has changed the value of the field. This is very similar to the **onBlur** JavaScript event with subtle differences between browsers
- The default event value for any component that is an **ActionSource** is **action**. This event maps to the **onClick** JavaScript event. The word "action" was chosen over "click" to be more general and to account for an **ActionSource** component that may not support a "click" concept. However, the **<h:commandButton>** and **<h:commandLink>** components do support the "click" concept, and thus **action** is a synonym for **click** on those components.

Tag Name	Default Event Attribute Value	Supported Event Attribute Values
<h:body>	none	click dblclick keydown keypress keyup load mousedown mousemove mouseout mouseover mouseup unload
<h:commandButton>	action	blur change click action dblclick focus keydown keypress keyup mousedown mousemove mouseout mouseover mouseup select
<h:commandLink>	action	blur click action dblclick focus keydown keypress keyup mousedown mousemove mouseout mouseover mouseup
<h:dataTable>	none	click dblclick keydown keypress keyup mousedown mousemove mouseout mouseover mouseup
<h:form>	none	click dblclick keydown keypress keyup mousedown mousemove mouseout mouseover mouseup
<h:graphicImage>	none	click dblclick keydown keypress keyup mousedown mousemove mouseout mouseover mouseup
<h:inputSecret>	valueChange	blur change valueChange click dblclick focus keydown keypress keyup mousedown mousemove mouseout mouseover mouseup select
<h:inputText>	valueChange	blur change valueChange click dblclick focus keydown keypress keyup mousedown mousemove mouseout mouseover mouseup select
<h:inputTextArea>	valueChange	blur change valueChange click dblclick focus keydown keypress keyup mousedown mousemove mouseout mouseover mouseup select
<h:button>	none	blur click dblclick focus keydown keypress keyup mousedown mousemove mouseout mouseover mouseup
<h:link>	action	blur click action dblclick focus keydown keypress keyup mousedown mousemove mouseout mouseover mouseup
<h:outputLabel>	none	blur click dblclick focus keydown keypress keyup mousedown mousemove mouseout mouseover mouseup
<h:outputLink>	action	blur click action dblclick focus keydown keypress keyup mousedown mousemove mouseout mouseover mouseup
<h:panelGrid>	none	click dblclick keydown keypress keyup mousedown mousemove mouseout mouseover mouseup

Table 12-1 Default and Supported Event Values for the Standard HTML RenderKit Components *(continued)*

Tag Name	Default Event Attribute Value	Supported Event Attribute Values
<h:selectBooleanCheckbox>	valueChange	blur change click valueChange dblclick focus keydown keypress keyup mousedown mousemove mouseout mouseover mouseup select
<h:selectManyCheckbox>	valueChange	blur change click valueChange dblclick focus keydown keypress keyup mousedown mousemove mouseout mouseover mouseup select
<h:selectManyListbox>	valueChange	blur change valueChange click dblclick focus keydown keypress keyup mousedown mousemove mouseout mouseover mouseup select
<h:selectManyMenu>	valueChange	blur change valueChange click dblclick focus keydown keypress keyup mousedown mousemove mouseout mouseover mouseup select
<h:selectOneListbox>	valueChange	blur change valueChange click dblclick focus keydown keypress keyup mousedown mousemove mouseout mouseover mouseup select
<h:selectOneMenu>	valueChange	blur change valueChange click dblclick focus keydown keypress keyup mousedown mousemove mouseout mouseover mouseup select
<h:selectOneRadio>	valueChange	blur change click valueChange dblclick focus keydown keypress keyup mousedown mousemove mouseout mouseover mouseup select

TABLE 12-1 Default and Supported Event Values for the Standard HTML RenderKit Components *(continued)*

TIP *One subtle but potentially very useful syntax to use with the* ***execute*** *and/or* ***render*** *attributes is the fact that the clientId elements in the lists for those attributes may be given as a search expression as used in* ***UIComponent.findComponent( )****. Please see the JavaDocs for that method for details on how to use* ***findComponent( )****.*

The onevent and onerror Attributes

Two of the attributes are special in that they allow you to pass the name of a JavaScript function to the **<f:ajax>** tag so that the system can call you back in various cases as the Ajax transaction progresses. JavaScript is a dynamically typed language with lots of functional language capabilities. Therefore, it is very easy to pass around references to functions, and the signatures for those functions are dynamic. So when Figure 12-6 states that **onerror** and **onevent** refer by name to a function that takes one argument, a function that takes no arguments will work as well, you just won't have access to the useful information passed in that argument. The rest of the section assumes that you do in fact have JavaScript functions with one argument when you use the **onevent** and **onerror** callback facility.

Property Name	Meaning
Type	The value of the **event** attribute that this callback is describing. For example, "click".
Status	**Begin** when the request has not yet been sent. **complete** when the Ajax response has been received but has not yet been processed. A **complete** status will be delivered even in the case of an error. **success** after the **complete** status has been shared and after the response has successfully been processed.
responseCode	The HTTP status code from the response, such as 404 or 200.
responseXML	The actual XML response, beginning with **<partial-response>**, such as shown in Figure 12-5.
responseText	A String, not XML, version of responseXML.
source	The DOM element that caused the Ajax transaction to be sent.

TABLE 12-2 The Data Argument to the JavaScript Callback Function

First, let's cover the **onevent** attribute. The JavaScript function you name in the **onevent** attribute will be called three times during the course of the Ajax transaction. Each time it will be passed a JavaScript Object with the properties shown in Table 12-2.

The following simple code can be used to put up a nice animated GIF that appears when the Ajax transaction is processing. First, make sure the following JavaScript code is accessible to the page.

```
// This code is derived with permission from work done by
// Jim Driscoll on his blog at <http://weblogs.java.net/blog/driscoll/>.
// First, get a nice animated gif from <http://www.ajaxload.info/>.
// Put it into the page and set its visibility to hidden initially.
var spinnerElement = getSpinnerElement( ) // reference to the DOM element
if (!window["busystatusdemo"]) {
  var busystatusdemo = {};
}

busystatusdemo.onStatusChange = function onStatusChange(data) {
  var status = data.status;
  if (status === "begin") { // turn on busy indicator
    spinnerElement.style.display = "inline";
  } else {  // turn off busy indicator, on either "complete" or "success"
    spinnerElement.style.display = "none";
  }
};
```

Then, any time you want to make it so that the spinner shows and hides during the Ajax transactions, you simply need to add **onevent="busystatusdemo.onStatusChange"** to your **<f:ajax>** element.

The **onerror** function takes the same kind of argument, but it's only called in the case of an error on the XMLHttpRequest. One common case is when there is a **ViewExpiredException**.

You have now been exposed to the entire breadth and depth of the **<f:ajax>** tag. The remainder of the chapter will examine the JavaScript functions in the Standard JavaScript Resource that ultimately do the work for the **<f:ajax>** tag, and close with some brief thoughts on advanced Ajax applications in JSF.

The Standard JavaScript Resource

The JSF 2 standard requires that implementations provide a JavaScript resource with library name **javax.faces** and resource name **jsf.js**. The content of this JavaScript resource must be a JavaScript source file that defines a globally scoped JavaScript object called **jsf**. This globally scoped JavaScript object must have exactly two properties, **ajax** and **util**, each of which is a JavaScript object with even more properties defined. This section will explain the contents of each of these JavaScript objects in terms of the preceding discussion on **<f:ajax>**.

Standard JavaScript Resource: jsf.ajax

The top-level **jsf** object must have a property named **ajax** that must have the JavaScript functions shown in Table 12-3.

Because **addOnError** and **addOnEvent** are so similar to their tag counterparts, no further discussion of these functions is required. Likewise because the user never needs to call **response( )**, it is called for you by the system when the Ajax response is received, no further discussion of this function is required. This leaves the **request( )** function, which provides the second of the two entry points to Ajax functionality for JSF page authors. One very simple example of the usage of this function is shown with the familiar JSFReg example.

```
<!DOCTYPE html PUBLIC "-//W3C//DTD XHTML 1.0 Transitional//EN"
  "http://www.w3.org/TR/xhtml1/DTD/xhtml1-transitional.dtd">
<html xmlns="http://www.w3.org/1999/xhtml"
      xmlns:h="http://java.sun.com/jsf/html"
      xmlns:f="http://java.sun.com/jsf/core">
<h:head>
  <title>A Simple JavaServer Faces 2.0 View</title>
</h:head>
<h:body>
  <h:form>
    You entered: #{requestScope.input}.
    <h:inputText id="input" value="#{requestScope.input}"
      onchange=
  "jsf.ajax.request(this, event, { render: '@form'}); return false"
    />
  </h:form>
</h:body>
</html>
```

Function Name and Signature	Meaning
addOnError(*callback*)	This provides the implementation of the **onerror** attribute for **<f:ajax>**.
addOnEvent(*callback*)	This provides the implementation of the **onevent** attribute for **<f:ajax>**.
request(*source*, *event*, *options*)	This provides the implementation of "request kickoff" part of the Ajax functionality provided by **<f:ajax>**.
response(*request*, *context*)	This provides the implementation of the response handling portion of the Ajax functionality of the **<f:ajax>** tag.

TABLE 12-3 The JavaScript Functions on the jsf.js JavaScript Object

Property Name	Meaning
execute	Equivalent to the attribute of the same name on **<f:ajax>**
render	Equivalent to the attribute of the same name on **<f:ajax>**
onevent	Equivalent to the attribute of the same name on **<f:ajax>**
onerror	Equivalent to the attribute of the same name on **<f:ajax>**
params	A JavaScript object that contains name, value pairs that will be sent in the POST data for the request.

TABLE 12-4 The Meaning of Various Properties in the Final Argument to jsf.ajax.request

The preceding code is equivalent to the one that started out the chapter. The only subtleties are in the arguments to the **jsf.ajax.request** function. The first argument, **this**, is the JavaScript DOM element that will be set as the **source** in the **onevent** callback. The second argument, **event**, is the JavaScript DOM event object. This will be passed to the **jsf.ajax.request** function directly from the browser. The last argument is a JavaScript object with properties for most of the tag attributes on **<f:ajax>**, as shown in Table 12-4.

Even though the behavior and API for the JavaScript way of accessing JSF Ajax capabilities is very similar to the tag way of accessing these features, the fact that you can access the features from anywhere within JavaScript gives you enormous power.

Advanced Topics on JSF and Ajax

This chapter has exposed you to everything you need to know to get work done with JSF and Ajax. Most applications can do quite a lot with just these fundamentals. The advanced user would be well served by exploring the following topics in greater depth.

- Using a flashy JavaScript effects library with JSF, such as Script.aculo.us. This library can be found at **http://script.aculo.us/**. A great example of the power of combining such a library with JSF can be found in the **PrimeFaces JSF Component Library at http://primefaces.prime.com.tr/en/**.
- Using the published XML schema for the Ajax response format to talk directly with the server-side component tree. Because both the HTTP POST request format and the XML schema for the response are fully specified, it is possible to go very deep into manipulating the server-side components with JavaScript or other client technologies such as JavaFX.
- Exploring how iterating components, such as **<ui:repeat>** and **<h:dataTable>**, can benefit from Ajax interagtion. For example, it is pretty simple to make it so a single cell in a data table can be updated in a very attractive style using effects from Script .aculo.us and the JSF Ajax library.

13

CHAPTER

Building Non-UI Custom Components

Chapter 11 presented the easiest way to extend Faces, by providing custom UI components that page authors can easily use. In addition to allowing custom UI components, Faces has many non-UI component extension points that have no visual representation for the end user. These non-UI component extension points are far less frequently used, but when you need to use them, you *really* need to use them. For example, if the existing set of validators and converters doesn't meet your requirements, you need to provide a custom solution, as shown in Chapter 8. In a more advanced case, if you want to seamlessly integrate JSF into an existing dependency injection scheme, such as Spring, implementing a custom EL resolver is the easiest approach. An example of this scenario is shown later in this chapter. Both of these examples can only be accomplished by using one of the non-UI custom component mechanisms described in this chapter.

Non-UI Custom Components and Decoration in JSF

Table 13-1 shows the complete alphabetical listing of the non-UI custom component classes and interfaces defined in the JSF specification. The Decoratable? column indicates whether this particular class or interface enables "decorating" the existing implementation rather than wholly replacing it.

The decorator pattern enables a developer to override as much, or as little, functionality of an existing class as desired, while leaving the "rest" to the "real" implementation. The pattern may as well have been named "customizer," but that word already had too many meanings in the software lexicon. The particular implementation of decoration practiced in the JSF specification uses the presence of a single argument constructor in the decorating class to decide if the user wants to leverage decoration or not. For example, the code to decorate the standard **ResourceHandler** is shown next.

```
import javax.faces.application.ResourceHandler;
import javax.faces.application.ResourceHandlerWrapper;
```

```
private ResourceHandler parent = null;
public CustomResourceHandler(ResourceHandler parent)
  extends ResourceHandlerWrapper {
  this.parent = parent;
}

public ResourceHandler getWrapped( ) {
  return this.parent;
}
```

Class to Extend, or Interface to Implement	Purpose	Decoratable?
ActionListener	Alters what happens when an **ActionEvent** is fired. This occurs when the user presses a button or clicks a link.	Yes
ApplicationFactory	Gains access to the creation of the singleton **Application** instance to alter the way it serves the system.	Yes
Converter	Adds a new way to convert from **String** to a model tier type and back again.	No
Custom Scope	Enables applications to easily define new scopes with customizable start and end times.	No
ELResolver	The replacement for **VariableResolver** and **PropertyResolver** in the Unified EL (used by JSF 1.2).	No
ExceptionHandlerFactory	Enables applications to have a single point of control for handling unexpected exceptions.	Yes
FacesContextFactory	Takes control of the creation of **FacesContext** instances to alter the way they interact with the rest of the system.	Yes
LifecycleFactory	Adds a new implementation of the request processing lifecycle, or extends or replaces the existing one.	Yes
NavigationHandler	Alters the way navigation between pages is performed.	Yes
PhaseListener	Provides an execution entry point at any particular phase in the request processing lifecycle.	No
PartialViewContextFactory	Enables applications to control how the view is traversed during Ajax requests.	Yes
PropertyResolver	In JSF 1.1, handles resolving each part of a JSF EL Expression after the initial part.	Yes
RenderKit	Defines a collection of **Renderer** classes designed to adapt a collection of **UIComponent** classes for use in a specific client device type.	No

Table 13-1 The Complete List of Non-View-Related Customizable Components in JSF

Class to Extend, or Interface to Implement	Purpose	Decoratable?
RenderKitFactory	Gains access to the creation of **RenderKit** instances to alter the way it serves **RenderKit** instances to the system.	Yes
ResourceHandler	Allows JSF to handle image and script requests from the browser.	Yes
StateManager	Alters the way view state is saved and restored between requests.	Yes
VariableResolver	In JSF 1.1, handles resolving the first part of a JSF EL Expression.	Yes
Validator	Adds a new way to validate correctly converted user-provided data based on application-specific constraints.	No
ViewDeclaration LanguageFactory	Allows the replacement or decoration of the way JSF views are declared.	Yes
ViewHandler	Replaces JSP as the view description technology. A custom **ViewHandler** is also useful for other tasks, such as selecting a **RenderKit**, choosing a **Locale**, or gaining access to the timing of view creation.	Yes
VisitContextFactory	Enables controlling how the tree is visited during the execution of the lifecycle.	Yes

TABLE 13-1 The Complete List of Non-View-Related Customizable Components in JSF *(continued)*

The XML markup in the **faces-config.xml** file to declare this class to the JSF runtime is as follows:

```
<faces-config>
  <!-- intervening content omitted -->
  <application>
     <resource-handler>
        com.jsfcompref.extras.CustomResourceHandler</resource-handler>
  </application>
</faces-config>
```

When the JSF runtime is starting up, the presence of XML elements for any of the decoratable classes from Table 13-1 (such as **resource-handler** in the preceding example) will cause the implementation class to be scanned for the presence of a public one-argument constructor with the proper argument type. If one is found, this constructor is used to create the instance, and the "previous" instance is passed to the constructor. It is up to the custom class to choose to save or discard the passed-in "previous" instance. For example, during JSF startup, the **ResourceHandler** returned from **Application.getResourceHandler( )** is an instance of **com.sun.faces.application.ResourceHandlerImpl**. As the **faces-config.xml** file is loaded, when the custom **<resource-handler>** element is encountered, the JSF implementation calls the **CustomResourceHandler** constructor, passing in the **ResourceHandlerImpl** instance.

When the constructor returns, **Application.getResourceHandler( )** now returns **CustomResourceHandler**. If no public one-argument constructor of the proper type is found, a public zero-argument constructor is used to create the instance. If there is no public zero-argument constructor for the specified class, an error is thrown and the application will not start.

EXPERT GROUP INSIGHT *Adam Winer, Oracle's representative on the JSF 1.0 Expert Group, was very adamant about the inclusion of decorators wherever possible. His design foresight has significantly helped the extensibility of JSF.*

Wrapper Classes

To aid in the task of decorating, JSF provides a number of "wrapper" classes. They all work the same way, as shown with the previous **ResourceHandlerWrapper** example. All of the following classes implement the **javax.faces.FacesWrapper** interface.

AppliactionFactory	AppliactionWrapper	ExceptionHandlerFactory
ExceptionHandlerWrapper	ExternalContextFactory	ExcetnalContextWrapper
FacesContextFactory	FacesContextWrapper	LifecycleFactory
PartialResponseWriter	PartialViewContextFactory	PartialViewContextWrapper
PreJsf2ExceptionHandlerWrapper	RenderKitFactory	RenderKitWrapper
ResourceHandlerWrapper	ResourceWrapper	ResponseWriterWrapper
StateManagerWrapper	ViewDeclarationLangugeFactory	ViewHandlerWrapper
VisitContextFactory	VisitContextWrapper	

Decorating a Class That Implements FacesWrapper

For any class **Base** that implements **javax.faces.FacesWrapper<Base>**, use this pattern to decorate the class:

```
public class DecorateBase extends Base {
  private Base parent;
  public DecorateBase(Base parent) {
    this.parent = parent;
  }

  public Base getWrapped( ) {
    return parent;
  }
...
```

Now, as many or as few methods from **Base** can be overridden in your **DecorateBase** class.

Non-View Custom Components Explained

The remainder of this chapter provides information or references to information elsewhere in the book for the preceding non-view custom components. The **faces-config** declaration for all of these components is covered in detail in Chapter 15. These components are listed in the order in which it makes the most sense to present them, with the more commonly used extension points first.

PhaseListener

PhaseListeners provide JSF developers with a capability to insert code at any point in the request processing lifecycle. As you saw in Chapters 8 and 10, **PhaseListener**s can be used in multiple ways. Their usages can be purely for analysis by allowing the developer to listen for any application changes at any point in the lifecycle. **PhaseListener**s can also be employed in a production application, such as how a **PhaseListener** was used in Chapter 11 to aid in dynamic **RenderKit** selection. This section lists the ways to add a **PhaseListener** to the application, including the new "per-view PhaseListener" feature in JSF.

Interface to Implement

In JSF 1.0 and 1.1, a **PhaseListener** is simply a Java class that implements the interface **javax.faces.event.PhaseListener**. This interface defines three methods:

```
public PhaseId getPhaseId( )
public void beforePhase(PhaseEvent event)
public void afterPhase(PhaseEvent event)
```

The method **getPhaseId( )** is called by the runtime to determine which lifecycle phase this listener instance applies to. There are constants in the class **PhaseId** for each of the lifecycle phases, as well as **ANY_PHASE**. Returning **PhaseId.ANY_PHASE** tells the runtime that this listener instance should be called before and after all lifecycle phases. For example:

```
public PhaseId getPhaseId() {
  return PhaseId.ANY_PHASE;
}
```

Likewise, returning **PhaseId.RENDER_RESPONSE** allows the runtime to invoke this **PhaseListener** instance specifically during the Render Response phase. In addition to using **getPhaseId( )** to associate a **PhaseListener** with a specific (or any) phase, the interface defines the other methods, **beforePhase( )** and **afterPhase( )**, which execute both before and after the associated phase, respectively. The developer can then provide custom code inside these methods. For example, the code

```
public void beforePhase(PhaseEvent pe) {
  if (pe.getPhaseId() == PhaseId.RESTORE_VIEW)
    System.out.println("before - " + pe.getPhaseId().toString());
}
```

will first check to see if the current phase is the Restore View phase, and then will print a simple message to the console indicating that it is executing just before the phase.

Obviously, just printing a message indicating the current phase merely scratches the surface of what is possible with a **PhaseListener**. Having access to the entire application at a specific moment in time allows for more creative uses for **PhasesListeners**. In addition to the examples already shown, in Chapter 15 a **PhaseListener** is used to check if a user is logged in when attempting to view a page—if not, the user is redirected to a login page. (Please see Chapter 15 for the full implementation details.) In general, when writing a JSF-centric application, please consider using a **PhaseListener** instead of a Servlet Filter. Nearly anything that can be done in a filter can also be done in a **PhaseListener**, yet **PhaseListener**s have the added benefit of providing access to the entire JSF framework, including the components in the current view, the Expression Language, and the lifecycle itself.

Registering a PhaseListener

When implementing a **PhaseListener**, you must register it by using a **phase-listener** XML element in the **faces-config.xml** file. This element contains a fully qualified Java class name of your **PhaseListener** implementation class. This element is a child of the **lifecycle** element. See Chapter 15 for the **faces-config.xml** syntax for registering a **PhaseListener**.

JSF 1.2 Tip *JSF 1.2 introduced a new tag to the jsf-core tag library,* ***f:phaseListener****. The general form for this tag is shown in Chapter 16, but a usage example is included here for completeness.*

```
<f:phaseListener binding="#{page1.phaseListener}" />
```

A per-view ***PhaseListener*** *is guaranteed only to be invoked when the particular view on which it is declared is going through the lifecycle. The* ***f:view*** *tag in JSF 1.2 also defines two new* ***MethodExpression*** *attributes called* ***beforePhase*** *and* ***afterPhase*** *that must point to public methods that take a* ***PhaseEvent*** *and return void. These methods are then invoked for every phase except restore view.*

Converter and Validator

Chapter 8 covered converters and validators in detail. (Please refer to Chapter 8 for complete information.) This section is included here as a reference to the API for providing a custom **converter** or **validator**.

Interfaces to Implement

The interface **javax.faces.convert.Converter** defines the two methods shown next.

```
public Object getAsObject(FacesContext context,
UIComponent component,
String value)
public String getAsString(FacesContext context,
UIComponent  component,
Object value)
```

The **javax.faces.validator.Validator** interface defines a single method called **validate( )**, which follows:

```
public void validate(FacesContext context,
UIComponent component,
Object value)
```

Registering a Converter or Validator

When implementing a custom converter or validator, you may register them declaratively using **converter** or **validator** elements in the **faces-config.xml** file, or you may register them dynamically at runtime using the API. The **converter** and **validator** elements are direct children of the root **faces-config** element and must be the fully qualified Java class name of the class extending **Converter** or **Validator**, respectively. See Chapter 15 for the **faces-config.xml** syntax for registering a **Converter** or **Validator**. See Chapter 7 for any other converter or validator information.

ViewHandler

This section is included here as a reference to the API for providing a custom **ViewHandler**.

Abstract Class to Extend

The abstract class **javax.faces.application.ViewHandler** defines the following methods:

```
public Locale calculateLocale(FacesContext context);
public String calculateRenderKitId(FacesContext context);
public UIViewRoot createView(FacesContext context, String viewId);
public String getActionURL(FacesContext context, String viewId);
public String getResourceURL(FacesContext context, String path);
public void renderView(FacesContext context, UIViewRoot viewToRender)
       throws IOException, FacesException;
public UIViewRoot restoreView(FacesContext context, String viewId);
public void writeState(FacesContext context) throws IOException;
```

Registering a ViewHandler

When implementing a custom **ViewHandler**, you may register it declaratively using the **view-handler** element in the **faces-config.xml** file, or you may register it dynamically by calling the **setViewHandler( )** method on the **Application** instance. (See the following for more on the **Application** instance.) The **view-handler** element is a child of the **application** element in the **faces-config.xml** file. The contents of the **view-handler** element must be the fully qualified Java class name of your **ViewHandler** implementation class. (See Chapter 15 for the **faces-config.xml** syntax for registering a **ViewHandler**.)

Note that there is a **ViewHandlerWrapper** class to make it easier to decorate the existing **ViewHandler** implementation.

VariableResolver and PropertyResolver

In JSF 1.0 and 1.1, the JSF runtime has default singleton instances of **VariableResolver** and **PropertyResolver** that fulfill the specified requirements to allow JSF EL expressions to be resolved. In JSF 1.2, these two classes have been deprecated with the introduction of the **javax.el.ELResolver** class in the Unified EL. This section covers what these two classes do in JSF 1.0 and 1.1, while the following section covers **ELResolver** in JSF 1.2.

The following example illustrates the central role the **VariableResolver** and **PropertyResolver** play in JSF. For discussion, let's say that the JSF runtime maintains a reference to the **VariableResolver** and **PropertyResolver** using variables **myVariableResolver** and **myPropertyResolver**, respectively. Also, the signatures of the **resolveVariable( )** and **getValue( )** methods on these classes have been abbreviated for convenience in the discussion shown next. Consider the following JSF EL expression:

```
#{requestScope.user.firstName}
```

To resolve this expression and get its value, the EL implementation in JSF 1.0 and 1.1 breaks this expression down into two parts: **requestScope** and **user.firstName**. The JSF runtime calls **myVariableResolver.resolveVariable("requestScope")**. This method takes the argument string and "resolves" it. In this case, "**requestScope**" is one of the implicit objects, listed in Table 5-6 of Chapter 5, so the **VariableResolver** instance must return a **java.util.Map** implementation that wraps the attribute set for the current **javax.servlet .ServletRequest**. For the purposes of discussion, let's call this **requestMap**.

With "**requestScope**" successfully resolved to **requestMap**, the JSF runtime further breaks down the **user.firstName** part of the expression into its individual parts: **user** and **firstName**. The JSF runtime calls **myPropertyResolver.getValue(requestMap, "user")**. This method will look in the Map for a value under the key "user" and return it. Because we're in the Virtual Trainer example, the **requestMap** has such a value under the key "user", and this value is an instance of **com.jsfcompref.trainer.model.UserBean**. For discussion, let's call this the **userBean**. Finally, the last step in the evaluation of the expression happens when **myPropertyResolver.getValue(userBean, "firstName")** is called. Because **UserBean** is a plain old JavaBean, the **PropertyResolver** looks for a JavaBeans property with the name "**firstName**", which it finds, and invokes the **getFirstName( )** method, thus returning the first name of the user.

You can now see the pattern of how the expression is continually broken down stepwise into parts, with the result of evaluating step *N* being fed into the evaluation of step *N* + 1.

If we were trying to set a value into the expression—for example, as the value of an **h:inputText** field—the last part of the expression would have its **setFirstName( )** method called instead of **getFirstName( )**. Any expression parts between the first and last parts, however, would still be evaluated exactly as in the "get" case.

You can now see that by enabling the overriding or decoration of **PropertyResolver** and **VariableResolver**, JSF allows extreme customization of the behavior of the EL. Implicit objects can be intercepted or changed. The operation of EL operators "." and [ ] can be changed. The list of things you can do is open-ended. The most important aspect to remember when doing a custom **VariableResolver** or **PropertyResolver** is to save and use the previous instance passed into the constructor per the decorator pattern. Failure to do so will cause the EL to stop working.

JSF 1.2 TIP *This loophole was closed in JSF 1.2, where it is impossible to override the behavior of the predefined implicit objects, though it is still possible to introduce new ones. Also, the dependency on the decorator pattern for* ***VariableResolver*** *and* ***PropertyResolver*** *leaves the developer open to the possibility of introducing serious and difficult-to-understand bugs when he or she tries to decorate one or both of these classes. Neglecting to save and/or use the previous* ***VariableResolver*** *or* ***PropertyResolver*** *instance when implementing a custom one will cause the entire JSF EL to stop working! This problem has been solved in JSF 1.2 by using a chain of responsibility pattern for* ***ELResolver*** *instances instead of the decorator pattern in JSF 1.0 and 1.1.*

Abstract Classes to Extend

For **PropertyResolver**, the abstract class **javax.faces.el.PropertyResolver** must be extended. It defines the following methods:

```
public abstract Object getValue(Object base, Object property)
       throws EvaluationException, PropertyNotFoundException;
public abstract Object getValue(Object base, int index)
       throws EvaluationException, PropertyNotFoundException;
public abstract void setValue(Object base, Object property, Object value)
       throws EvaluationException, PropertyNotFoundException;
public abstract void setValue(Object base, int index, Object value)
       throws EvaluationException, PropertyNotFoundException;
public abstract boolean isReadOnly(Object base, Object property)
       throws EvaluationException, PropertyNotFoundException;
public abstract boolean isReadOnly(Object base, int index)
       throws EvaluationException, PropertyNotFoundException;
public abstract Class getType(Object base, Object property)
       throws EvaluationException, PropertyNotFoundException;
public abstract Class getType(Object base, int index)
       throws EvaluationException, PropertyNotFoundException;
```

For **VariableResolver**, the abstract class **com.sun.faces.el.VariableResolver** must be extended. It defines the following method:

```
public abstract Object resolveVariable(FacesContext context, String name)
throws EvaluationException;
```

Let's take a real-world example of **VariableResolver** decorating from the source code of the Spring Framework. The following code has been abbreviated. The full version can be downloaded from **www.springframework.org/**. This example allows any JSF EL expression to reference POJOs (plain old Java objects) created by Spring's **BeanFactory** as well as regular JSF managed beans.

```
/*
 * Copyright 2002-2005 the original author or authors.
 *
...
package org.springframework.web.jsf;
import org.springframework.web.context.WebApplicationContext;
/**
 * JSF VariableResolver that first delegates to the original
 * resolver of the underlying JSF implementation, then to the
```

```
 * Spring root WebApplicationContext.
 *
 * @author Juergen Hoeller
 */
public class DelegatingVariableResolver extends VariableResolver {
  protected final VariableResolver originalVariableResolver;
  public DelegatingVariableResolver(VariableResolver
                                   originalVariableResolver) {
    this.originalVariableResolver = originalVariableResolver;
  }
  protected final VariableResolver getOriginalVariableResolver() {
    return originalVariableResolver;
  }
  public Object resolveVariable(FacesContext facesContext,
                               String name)
      throws EvaluationException {
    // Ask original resolver.
    Object originalResult = getOriginalVariableResolver().
                          resolveVariable(facesContext, name);
    if (originalResult != null) {
      return originalResult;
    }
    // Ask Spring root context.
    WebApplicationContext wac =
      getWebApplicationContext(facesContext);
    if (wac.containsBean(name)) {
      return wac.getBean(name);
    }
    return null;
  }
  protected WebApplicationContext
    getWebApplicationContext(FacesContext facesContext) {
      return FacesContextUtils.
          getRequiredWebApplicationContext(facesContext);

}
```

The heart of this class is the **resolveVariable( )** method required by the **VariableResolver** interface. This method first asks the existing JSF implementation if it can resolve the variable. If not, the Spring **WebApplicationContext** is consulted. Once this **VariableResolver** has been installed in the application, any EL expressions can leverage it without even knowing they are doing so. For example, let's say the bean **shoppingCart** is supplied to the system via Spring's **BeanFactory** and that there is no JSF managed bean with the name **shoppingCart**. Then this expression would cause the **DelegatingVariableResolver** to be consulted: **#{shoppingCart.items}**.

Registering a VariableResolver or PropertyResolver

A custom **VariableResolver** or **PropertyResolver** may be registered declaratively in the **faces-config.xml** file using the **variable-resolver** and **property-resolver** XML elements, or dynamically at runtime using the **setVariableResolver( )** or **setPropertyResolver( )** methods on **Application**. The declarative registration is most common and recommended. Both **variable-resolver** and **property-resolver** elements are children of the **application** element in the **faces-config.xml** file. These elements both must contain the fully qualified Java class name of the implementation class for your **VariableResolver** or **PropertyResolver**, respectively. See Chapter 15 for the **faces-config.xml** syntax for registering a **VariableResolver**.

Overriding **PropertyResolver** is much the same as that just shown, but it is less common to do so in practice. As such, this feature is not documented further here.

NOTE *In JSF 1.1, it is perfectly valid to have multiple* ***property-resolver*** *or* ***variable-resolver*** *elements but not in the same* ***faces-config.xml*** *file. The way to work around this restriction is to leverage one of the ways to tell the JSF runtime that there are multiple XML files that should be treated as* ***faces-config.xml*** *files. See the section titled "How the JSF Runtime Loads faces-config.xml Files" in Chapter 11.*

ELResolver (JSF 1.2)

The preceding section covered how the EL can be augmented in JSF 1.1 through the Spring Framework example. In JSF 1.2, **VariableResolver** and **PropertyResolver** have been deprecated, but of course they are still supported for backward compatibility. In JSF 1.2, the concepts of **PropertyResolver** and **VariableResolver** have been merged into the Unified EL class **javax.el.ELResolver**. Basically, an **ELResolver** functions as a **VariableResolver** if the first argument to its **getValue( )** or **setValue( )** method is **null**. Otherwise, it functions as a **PropertyResolver**.

This section shows how to use the JSF 1.2 class **ELResolver** in place of the now deprecated **PropertyResolver** or **VariableResolver** classes, which were used with JSF 1.1.

The ELResolver Chain of Responsibility

Another change in JSF 1.2 is the removal of the decorator pattern in favor of a *chain of responsibility (CoR)* pattern for extending the EL. The use of the CoR pattern makes it impossible to accidentally break the EL by forgetting to delegate to the existing implementation, as well as making it impossible to redefine implicit objects already defined in the specification. The EL implementation maintains a chain of **ELResolver** instances for various kinds of expression elements. When presented with an expression, the EL implementation walks down the chain for each part of the expression until one of the resolvers in the chain successfully resolves the expression part. This success is signaled by setting a flag: the resolver calling **setPropertyResolved(true)** on the **ELContext** that is passed to every call on every **ELResolver** in the chain. The EL implementation checks the flag by calling **getPropertyResolved( )** on the **ELContext** after every call on every resolver in the chain, and if it returns **true**, the next part of the expression is evaluated, starting again at the head of the chain. The **ELResolver** chain is shown in Figure 13-1.

Let's take a generic example (not relating to the Virtual Trainer example) to clarify the resolution process. Let's say we have a request-scoped managed bean named **user** that has a **friends** property whose value is a **Map** of names to other **user** instances. Also, the **user** bean also has a property called **address** that is a **String**. Such an expression could look like **#{user .friends.jeff.address}**. Assume this is the first time the **user**-managed bean is being resolved and therefore it hasn't yet been instantiated. Before diving into the resolution process for this expression, first some terminology. Each part of the expression is seen by the EL as a **base** object, and a **property** object. For example, when evaluating the last part of the expression,

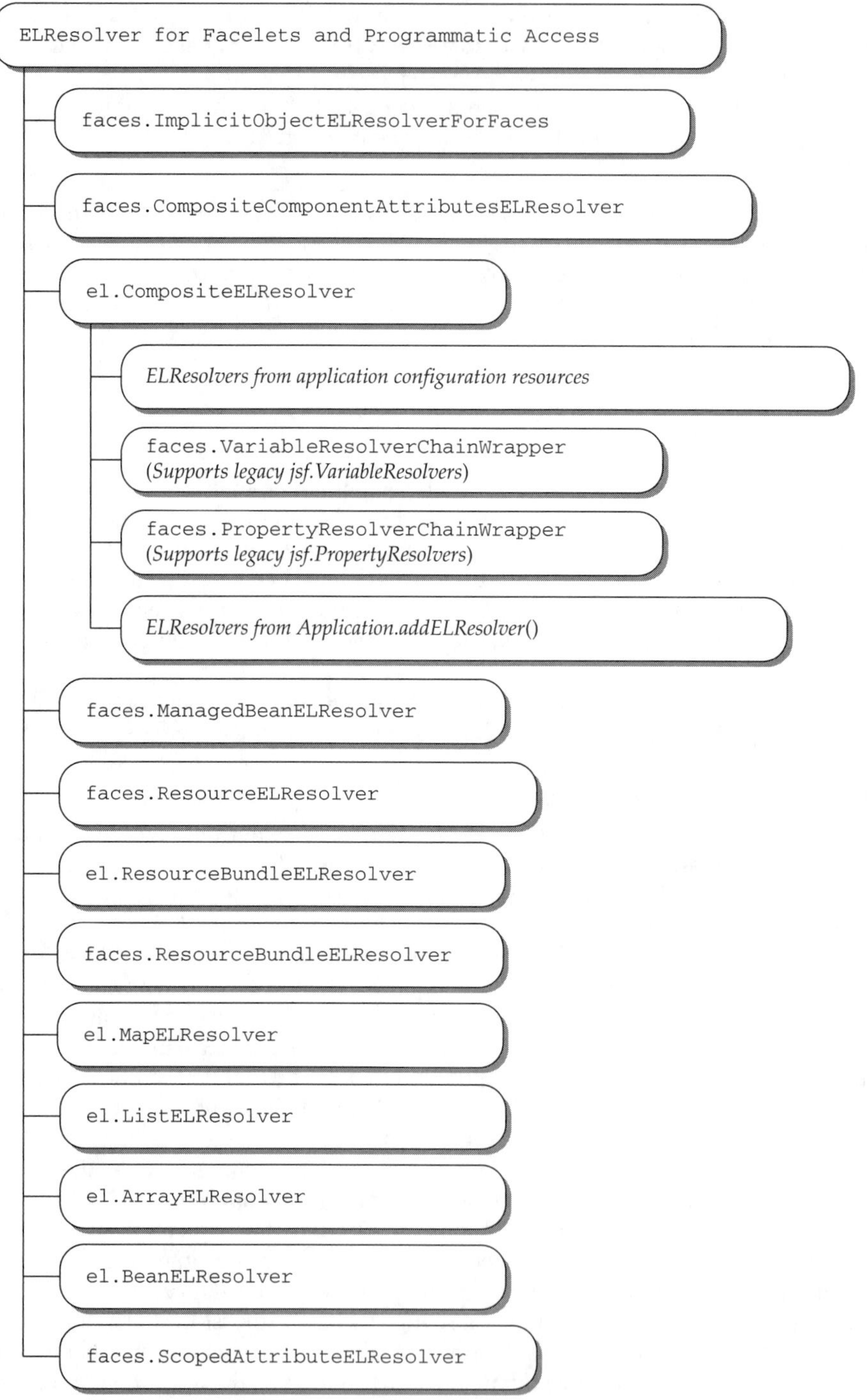

Figure 13-1 The **ELResolver** chain from JSF 2.0

jeff is the **base**, while **address** is the property. A special case is the first part of the expression, for which the **base** is **null**.

EXPERT GROUP INSIGHT *Allowing* ***base*** *to be* ***null*** *for the first part of the expression is the key enabling concept that permits the JSF 1.1 concepts of* ***VariableResolver*** *and* ***PropertyResolver*** *to be combined into the* ***ELResolver****. If the* ***base*** *is null, an* ***ELResolver*** *functions much like a* ***VariableResolver****. Otherwise, it functions as a* ***PropertyResolver****.*

The resolution of **#{user.friends.jeff.address}** is as follows:

1. To begin, **base** is **null**; **property** is **user**.
2. The **ImplicitObjectELResolverForFaces** is consulted. Since **user** is not an implicit object, no action is taken and flow continues down the chain.
3. The **CompositeComponentAttributesELResolver** is consulted. Since **user** is not equal to **cc.attrs**, flow continues.
4. The JSF implementation's **CompositeELResolver** is consulted. This instance is the head of a subchain of resolvers. It doesn't resolve anything on its own.
   a. Any **ELResolver** instances declared in the **faces-config.xml** files are consulted. In this case, we assume there are none, so flow continues.
   b. Any custom **VariableResolver** or **PropertyResolver** instances in the **faces-config.xml** files are consulted. Again, there are no such classes in this case, so flow continues.
5. JSF's **ManagedBeanELResolver** is consulted. Finally, some action is taken! Because **user** is listed as a **managed-bean-name** in the **faces-config.xml** file, this resolver will tell the EL implementation that some action was taken by calling **setPropertyResolved(true)** on the **ELContext** instance, instantiate the managed bean, place it in the proper scope, and return it.
6. Now **base** is **user**; **property** is **friends**. Now that we have the **user** bean in hand, it's time to resolve its **friends** property. A managed bean is simply a plain old Java object (POJO), but the JSP spec treats POJOs as **JavaBean** instances. Starting again at the top of the chain, each link in the chain is consulted until the **javax.el.BeanELResolver** is reached to perform this resolution. This will call **setPropertyResolved(true)** on the **ELContext**, call the **getFriends( )** method on the user bean, and return.
7. Now **base** is **friends**; **property** is **jeff**. Recall that the **getFriends( )** method on the user bean returns a **Map**. Starting at the top, again, we reach the **el.MapELResolver**, which knows how to resolve things on **Map** instances. This resolver calls **setPropertyResolved(true)** on the **ELContext**, looks up the **friends** key in the **Map**, and returns it.
8. Now **base** is **jeff**; **property** is **address**. Once again, we have a POJO as our base, so the **BeanELResolver** again does the job. It's important to note that the only way the implementation knows to treat the **base** as a POJO is that every other possible way of treating it has yielded no results. In other words, if it's not an implicit object, managed bean, **Map**, **ResourceBundle**, **List**, or **Array**, then treat it as a POJO and see if it works. The **scopedAttributeELResolver** is a special case because it only operates when **base** is **null**.

ELResolver in package javax.el	Description	Usage Example
ArrayELResolver	Resolves expression segments that are arrays.	#{user.accounts[0]}
BeanELResolver	Resolves JavaBean properties.	#{user.name}
CompositeELResolver	Maintains a chain of nested **ELResolvers**.	Not Applicable
ImplicitObjectELResolver	Resolves the implicit objects from the JSP specification.	#{cookie.userName}
ListELResolver	Resolves expression segments that are **java.util.List** instances.	#{user.accounts[0]}
MapELResolver	Resolves expression segments that are **java.util.Map** instances.	#{user.propertyMap}
ResourceBundleELResolver	Resolves expression segments that are **java.util.ResourceBundle** instances.	#{bundle.key}
ScopedAttributeELResolver	Performs scope search: request, page, session, application.	#{user}

TABLE 13-2 **ELResolver** Instances Defined by the EL 1.0 Specification

The **ELResolvers** in Figure 13-1 are defined by the EL specification and the JSF specification. Their ordering is defined by the JSF specification. The meaning of these resolvers is shown in Tables 13-2 and 13-3.

Expert Group Insight *The resolvers in Table 13-3 are defined by the JSF 1.2 specification, and no public implementation of these classes is provided. This was intentional because the Expert Group didn't want anyone extending the JSF 1.2 resolvers to allow for maximum flexibility in implementation.*

Abstract Class to Extend

An **ELResolver** must extend the abstract class **javax.el.ELResolver** and implement the following methods:

```
public Object getValue(ELContext context,
                Object base,
                Object property);
public Class getType(ELContext context,
                Object base,
                Object property);
public void setValue(ELContext context,
                Object base,
                Object property,
                Object value);
public boolean isReadOnly(ELContext context,
                  Object base,
                  Object property);
```

```
public Iterator getFeatureDescriptors(ELContext context,
                          Object base);
public Class getCommonPropertyType(ELContext context,
             Object base);
```

ELResolver from Faces Specification	Description	Usage Example
CompositeComponentAttributes ELResolver	Resolves expressions that need access to the attributes map of a composite component.	#{cc.attrs.loginButtonLabel}
ImplicitObjectELResolverForFaces	Resolves only the implicit objects defined by JSF.	#{FacesContext. viewRoot.locale}
ManagedBeanELResolver	Responsible for instantiating **managed-bean** instances and placing them in the proper scope for future resolution with a scoped attribute **ELResolver**.	#{user.name}
VariableResolverChainWrapper	Responsible for allowing JSF 1.1–style **VariableResolver** instances to continue to work.	#{customImplicitObject. value}
PropertyResolverChainWrapper	Responsible for allowing JSF 1.1–style **PropertyResolver** instances to continue to work.	#{user.name}
ResourceELResolver	Allows getting the request path for a resource from the EL	#{resource['trainer:bg.gif']}
ResourceBundleELResolver	Responsible for returning and/or creating a **ResourceBundle** from information in the **faces-config.xml**. Actual resolution of the key in the bundle happens in the **javax.el.ELResolver**.	#{bundle.name}
ScopedAttributeELResolver	Just like the **javax.el .Scop edAttributeELResolver**, but doesn't resolve page scope.	#{user.name}

TABLE 13-3 ELResolver Instances Defined in the JSF Specification

Registering an ELResolver

When implementing an **ELResolver**, you must register it using the **el-resolver** element in the **faces-config.xml** file. The contents of this element must be a fully qualified Java class name of a class that extends **ELResolver**. In JSF 1.2, the **el-resolver** element is a child of the **application** element in the **faces-config.xml** file. See Chapter 15 for the **faces-config.xml** syntax for registering an **ELResolver**.

To illustrate a custom **ELResolver**, and explain how to implement each of the preceding methods, let's examine the **ShaleELResolver** from the Shale framework. Though the Shale framework is no longer actively developed, it does provide a good example of ELResolver decoration. This **ELResolver** adds the **jndi** implicit object to the EL. For more on Shale, please see **http://shale.apache.org/shale-core/jndi-integration.html**.

The **ShaleELResolver** begins as shown next:

```
/*
 * Copyright 2004-2005 The Apache Software Foundation.
 *
 * License document omitted
 *
 */
package org.apache.shale.faces;
import java.beans.FeatureDescriptor;
import java.util.ArrayList;
import java.util.Iterator;
import javax.el.ELResolver;
import javax.el.ELContext;
import javax.el.PropertyNotFoundException;
import javax.el.EvaluationException;
import javax.faces.el.EvaluationException;
import javax.naming.Context;
import javax.naming.InitialContext;
import javax.naming.Name;
import javax.naming.NameClassPair;
import javax.naming.NameNotFoundException;
import javax.naming.NamingEnumeration;
import javax.naming.NamingException;
/**
 * <p>Shale-specific ELResolver for evaluating JavaServer Faces
 * value and method expressions. The following special
 * variable names are recognized, and evaluated as indicated:</p>
 * <ul>
 * <li><strong>jndi</strong> - Returns the JNDI context at name
 *   <code>java:comp/env</code> (relative to the initial context
 *   supplied by the container.</li>
 * </ul>
 * <p>All other evaluations are delegated to <code>ELResolver</code>
 * chain.</p>
 *
 */
public class ShaleELResolver extends ELResolver {
  /**
   *<p>Construct a new {@link ShaleELResolver} instance.</p>
   *
   */
```

```
 public ShaleELResolver() {
 }
/**
 * <p>Variable name to be resolved to our JNDI environment context.</p>
 */
private static final String JNDI_VARIABLE_NAME = "jndi";
// Prevent returning a huge number of results
// from getFeatureDescriptor()
private static final int MAX_TOP_LEVEL_NAMES = 1000;
// ------------------------------ VariableResolver Methods
/**
 * <p>Resolve variable names known to this resolver; otherwise,
 * delegate to the ELResolver chain.</p>
 *
 * @param name Variable name to be resolved
 */
public Object getValue(ELContext elContext, Object base,
                       Object property) {
  Object result = null;
 // If we have a non-null base object, function as a PropertyResolver
 if (null != base) {
   if (base instanceof Context) {
     elContext.setPropertyResolved(true);
     Context context = (Context) base;
     try {
       if (property instanceof Name) {
       result = context.lookup((Name) property);
       } else {
         if (null != property) {
           result = context.lookup(property.toString());
         }
       }
     } catch (NameNotFoundException e) {
       // Mimic standard JSF/JSP behavior when base is a Map
       // by returning null
       return null;
     } catch (NamingException e) {
       throw new EvaluationException(e);
     }
   }
 }
 else {
   // function as a VariableResolver
   if (null == property) {
     throw new PropertyNotFoundException("ShaleELResolver: name must
                                          not be null");
   }
   if (JNDI_VARIABLE_NAME.equals(property)) {
     elContext.setPropertyResolved(true);
     try {
       InitialContext ic = new InitialContext();
         result = (Context) ic.lookup("java:comp/env");
       } catch (NamingException e) {
         throw new EvaluationException(e);
```

PART II

```
        }
      }
    }
    return result;
  }
```

Pay special attention to the **getValue( )** method. It is the most often called method on **ELResolver**. Because the **ShaleELResolver** simply adds JNDI capabilities to the EL, a **null base** argument means that it must look at the value of the **property** argument. If it is equal to the string "**jndi**", it sets the **ELResolver**'s **propertyResolved** property to **true**, consults the **InitialContext** from JNDI, and obtains its "java:comp/env" **Context** value and returns it. A non-**null base** argument must be of type **javax.naming.Context**. In this case, the **propertyResolved** property is set to **true**, the **lookup( )** method is called on the **Context**, and the value is returned.

Next is the **getType( )** method:

```
public Class<?> getType(ELContext elContext, Object base,
                        Object property){
  if (null != base && base instanceof Context) {
    elContext.setPropertyResolved(true);
    return Object.class;
  }
}
```

The **getType( )** method is called by the implementation to determine if a subsequent call to **setValue( )** is safe to call without causing a **ClassCastException** to be thrown. In this case, if the base is an instance of **javax.naming.Context**, then any **Object** may be passed as the value.

EXPERT GROUP INSIGHT *A better name for the **getType( )** method is **getTypeForSet( )**, but for historical reasons it is simply called **getType( )**.*

The next method is **setValue( )**:

```
public void setValue(ELContext elContext, Object base,
       Object property,
       Object value) {
  if (null != base && base instanceof Context) {
      Context context = (Context) base;
    elContext.setPropertyResolved(true);
    try {
      // Mimic standard JSF/JSP behavior when base is a Map
      // by calling rebind() instead of bind()
      if (property instanceof Name) {
        context.rebind((Name) property, value);
      } else {
        context.rebind(property.toString(), value);
      }
    } catch (NamingException e) {
      throw new EvaluationException(e);
    }
  }
}
```

The **setValue( )** method is used to enable the all-important "left-hand-side" operation of an expression, discussed in Chapter 4. In this case, it is only valid to set a value in an existing **Context** instance, so the **rebind( )** method is called to set the value.

The **isReadOnly( )** method, shown next, is called to tell if it is safe to call **setValue( )** without fear of a **PropertyNotWritableException** being thrown.

```
public boolean isReadOnly(ELContext elContext,
        Object base,
        Object property) {
  if (base instanceof Context) {
    elContext.setPropertyResolved(true);
    // Mimic standard JSF/JSP behavior when base is a Map
    // by returning false if we cannot tell any better
    return false;
  }
}
```

Next comes the **getFeatureDescriptors( )** method:

```
public Iterator getFeatureDescriptors(ELContext elContext,
    Object base) {
  String name = null;
  InitialContext ic = new InitialContext();
  Context context = (Context) ic.lookup("java:comp/env");
  NamingEnumeration<NameClassPair> names = null;
  ArrayList<FeatureDescriptor> featureDescriptors =
      new ArrayList<FeatureDescriptor>();
  if (null == base) {
    name = "";
  } else {
    name = base.toString();
  }
  names = context.list(name);
  try {
    NameClassPair cur = null;
    FeatureDescriptor curDescriptor = null;
    int i = 0;
    while (names.hasMoreElements() && i++ <       MAX_TOP_LEVEL_NAMES) {
      cur = names.nextElement();
      curDescriptor = new FeatureDescriptor();
      curDescriptor.setName(cur.getName());
      curDescriptor.setDisplayName(cur.getNameInNamespace());
      curDescriptor.setExpert(true);
      if (null != cur.getClassName()) {
        curDescriptor.setValue(ELResolver.TYPE,
            Class.forName(cur.getClassName()));
      }
      curDescriptor.setValue(ELResolver.RESOLVABLE_AT_DESIGN_TIME,
          true);
      featureDescriptors.add(curDescriptor);
    }
    if (MAX_TOP_LEVEL_NAMES <= i) {
      // log error
    }
```

PART II

```
    } catch (NamingException e) {
      throw new EvaluationException(e);
    }
    return featureDescriptors.iterator();
}
```

The **getFeatureDescriptors( )** method is used by a design-time tool to allow code completion of expressions at design time. A well-designed custom **ELResolver** will properly implement this method to enable itself to function optimally inside of tools.

Finally, **ShaleELResolver** ends with **getCommonPropertyType( )**, shown next. It is also designed to assist tools by returning the "highest" **Class** that this resolver can resolve against the given **base** instance.

```
public Class<?> getCommonPropertyType(ELContext context,
                                     Object base) {
      if (null == base) {
        return Context.class;
      }
      return Object.class;
    }
}
```

NavigationHandler

The default **NavigationHandler** provided by the JSF implementation is adequate in most cases, but one can imagine some scenarios where supplementing its behavior can be useful. For example, let's suppose you don't like the XML navigation syntax provided by the JSF specification. A custom **NavigationHandler** could be installed to allow for an alternate navigation syntax, for example by using annotations on JSP pages. Such an approach is being investigated for a future version of the JSF specification.

Abstract Class to Extend

A custom **NavigationHandler** must extend the class **javax.faces.application .NavigationHandler** and must define the following method:

```
public void handleNavigation(FacesContext context,
String fromAction,
String outcome);
```

An implementation of this method must call **context.getViewRoot( ).getViewId( )** and look at the **fromAction** and **outcome** arguments to determine the **viewId** of the next view to be shown, then create it by calling **context.getApplication( ).createView( )**. Before returning, the new **UIViewRoot** is installed by calling **context.setViewRoot( )**.

Showing the details of annotation-based **NavigationHandler** as an example of how to implement one is beyond the scope of this section, but a basic description follows. Require the user to provide a backing bean for each page in the application, as is enforced with the Sun JavaStudio Creator tool. Introduce a class-level **@FromViewId** annotation to attach to each backing bean class. Introduce a method-level **@NavigationCase** annotation, with

fromOutcome and **toViewId** parameters to attach to each action method in a backing bean. Provide a **ServletContextListener** in your custom component's TLD file that uses the annotation processing tool (apt) included in JDK 1.5 to discover the annotations present in the backing beans. Perhaps you can use a naming convention to make it easier to discover the complete set of backing bean classes. This annotation processor would then build up a data structure that is used by the custom navigation handler to satisfy **handleNavigation( )** requests.

JSF 2.0 TIP *JSF 2.0 introduced* ***ConfigurableNavigationHandler****, which extends* ***NavigationHandler****. This class allows the runtime to interrogate the navigation rule base, and is the way implicit navigation works.*

If you're going to go to the trouble of decorating **NavigationHandler**, and you're on JSF 2.0, you may as well just make your class extend **ConfigurableNavigationHandler**. Here are the methods defined on this class:

```
public NavigationCase getNavigationCase(FacesContext context,
String fromAction,
String outcome);
public Map<String, Set<NavigationCase>> getNavigationCases( );
public void performNavigation(String outcome);
```

Registering a NavigationHandler or ConfigurableNavigationHandler

A custom **NavigationHandler** or **ConfigurableNavigationHandler** may be registered declaratively in the **faces-config.xml** file using the **navigation-handler** element, or dynamically using the **setNavigationHandler** method on the **Application**. The former is recommended and must contain the fully qualified Java class name of the class extending **NavigationHandler**. The **navigation-handler** element is a child of the **application** element in the **faces-config.xml**. See Chapter 15 for the **faces-config.xml** syntax for registering a **NavigationHandler**.

ActionListener

The **ActionListener** is where the outcome of executing a user action, such as pressing a button, is derived. Once the outcome is obtained, the **ActionListener** is responsible for calling the **NavigationHandler**, which executes the decision-making process based on that outcome. Thus, the **ActionListener** works closely with the **NavigationHandler**, but it makes sense to allow them both to be independently replaced. As shown in the preceding section, it is sometimes desirable to replace how the navigation decision is made, without changing how the outcome is derived that is passed into the navigation decision-making process. Likewise, it can be convenient to replace just the outcome derivation process without replacing the navigation decision-making process.

Chapter 14 provides an example of how to replace the default **ActionListener** with one that consults the Java platform security model before performing the action. This example only allows the action to complete if the user is properly authenticated and has the proper permissions to execute the action. See the section "Using JAAS Authentication in the Virtual Trainer" in Chapter 14 for details and source code.

Interface to Implement

A custom **ActionListener** must implement the interface **javax.faces.event.ActionListener**, which defines the following method:

```
public void processAction(ActionEvent event)
throws AbortProcessingException;
```

The **processAction( )** method receives the **ActionEvent** emitted from an **ActionSource** component (such as a button), invokes the method binding returned as the value of the **action** property of the **ActionSource** to arrive at the outcome value, and calls the **NavigationHandler** with the resultant outcome.

Registering an ActionListener

A custom **ActionListener** may be registered declaratively using the **action-listener** element in the **faces-config.xml** file, or dynamically using the **setActionListener( )** method on **Application**. The former is recommended and must contain the fully qualified Java class name of a class implementing **ActionListener**. The **action-listener** element is a child of the **application** element in the **faces-config.xml**. See Chapter 15 for the **faces-config.xml** syntax for registering an **ActionListener**.

StateManager

A Web Application Framework must provide a solution for managing view state across HTTP requests as the user moves through the application. A *good* Framework will allow the design and implementation of this solution to be customizable, and Faces does just that with the **StateManager** API.

View state management is a complex business, and few application developers will have to worry about customizing it. In fact, most use cases for customizing state management arise for JSF implementers or those taking an existing JSF implementation and customizing it to their needs. For example, one use case for a custom **StateManager** would be replacing the default implementation with a high-performance one that relies on a database and supports object pooling. Therefore, only a brief overview of the **StateManager** API is provided.

Abstract Class to Extend in JSF 1.1 and 1.0

A custom **StateManager** must extend the abstract class **javax.faces.application.StateManager** and decorate or replace the following methods:

```
public SerializedView saveSerializedView(FacesContext context);
protected Object getTreeStructureToSave(FacesContext context);
protected Object getComponentStateToSave(FacesContext context);
public void writeState(FacesContext context, SerializedView state)
    throws IOException;
public UIViewRoot restoreView(FacesContext context, String viewId,
                              String renderKitId);
protected UIViewRoot restoreTreeStructure(FacesContext context,
                                          String viewId,
                                          String renderKitId);
```

```
protected void restoreComponentState(FacesContext context,
                                         UIViewRoot viewRoot,
                                         String renderKitId);
public boolean isSavingStateInClient(FacesContext context);
```

A default implementation of **isSavingStateInClient( )** is provided that consults the JSF specification–defined **javax.faces.STATE_SAVING_METHOD** servlet context **init** parameter to determine if the state is to be saved in the page (the default) or on the server. The intent of the previous methods is explained by examining the state saving and state restoring process in the context of the request processing lifecycle.

JSF 1.2 TIP *A bug in the JSF 1.1 specification is that the* ***SerializedView*** *class itself is not* ***Serializable****! When saving the state on the server, this poses problems with containers that need to do session failover within a cluster. This problem was fixed in JSF 1.2 with a redesign of the* ***StateManager*** *API, which included deprecating all of the JSF 1.1 methods of this class.*

State Saving Using the StateManager in JSF 1.0 and 1.1 As part of the Render Response lifecycle phase, the JSF runtime must call the **saveSerializedView( )** method of the **StateManager**. This method returns an instance of the inner class **javax.faces.application .StateManager.SerializedView,** which is a simple structure that encapsulates the tree structure and component state of a view in two **Object**s obtainable from the **getTreeStructure( )** and **getComponentState( )** methods of **SerializedView**, respectively. The protected helper method **getTreeStructureToSave( )** and **getComponentStateToSave( )** can be implemented to aid in the creation of the **SerializedView** instance. The meaning of the **treeStructure** and **componentState** properties is implementation-dependent, but tree structure is generally the parent-child relationships of each node in the tree, while component state is the in-depth state of each node of the tree.

Once the **SerializedView** instance is created, the JSF runtime passes it to the **writeState( )** method. This method delegates to the **writeState( )** method of the **ResponseStateManager** from the current **RenderKit** to write the state in a rendering technology–specific manner—for example, when the **HTML_BASIC RenderKit** writes this state out to a hidden field in the page.

State Restoring Using the StateManager in JSF 1.1 and 1.0 The JSF runtime must call the **restoreView( )** method of the **StateManager** to inspect the incoming request and restore the view so that postback processing can occur. As with state saving, the implementation can use the **restoreTreeStructure( )**, **restoreComponentState( )**, **getTreeStructureToRestore( )**, and **getComponentStateToRestore( )** methods to aid in the process of restoring the view. The **restoreTreeStructure( )** method builds the **UIViewRoot** rooted tree of components. The **restoreComponentState( )** method traverses that tree and restores the component state of each node. The respective getters for tree structure and component state may call through to the **ResponseStateManager** to inspect the request in a rendering technology–specific way—for example, the **HTML_BASIC RenderKit** will know to look for a hidden field.

JSF 1.2 TIP *The following sections deal with state management in JSF 1.2.*

Abstract Class to Extend in JSF 1.2

In JSF 1.2, all of the methods of **StateManager** except for **restoreView( )** and **isSavingStateInClient( )** have been deprecated. The inner class **SerializedView** has also been deprecated.

EXPERT GROUP INSIGHT *Special care was taken to ensure that existing, 1.1-style* ***StateManager*** *implementations will continue to function properly.*

Developers wishing to follow the JSF 1.2 patterns must implement the following methods:

```
public Object saveView(FacesContext context);
public void writeState(FacesContext context, Object state)
     throws IOException;
```

These methods leave considerably more up to the implementation than their 1.1 counterparts by not declaring the concepts of tree structure and component state at the API level. As such, no specific description is required for the "save view" and "restore view" behavior, as was the case for the 1.1 versions explained earlier. All you need to know is that **saveView( )** is called during the Render Response phase, and **restoreView( )** is called during the Restore View phase. Both of these methods must rely on the **ResponseStateManager** from the current **RenderKit** to perform the rendering technology–specific actions regarding state management. The **ResponseStateManager** is covered in the section on **RenderKitFactory** that follows.

Registering a StateManager

A custom **StateManager** may be registered declaratively using the **state-manager** element in the **faces-config.xml** file, or dynamically by calling **setStateManager( )** on the **Application**.

The former is recommended and must contain the fully qualified Java class name of a class extending **StateManager**. The **state-manager** element is a child of the **application** element in the **faces-config.xml**. See Chapter 15 for the **faces-config.xml** syntax for registering a **StateManager**.

Note that JSF 2.0 includes a **StateManagerWrapper** class to make it easier to decorate the **StateManager**.

RenderKit

Chapter 11 demonstrated how to add individual **Renderer** definitions to the standard render-kit, making them immediately available for use by components. A more reusable and well-encapsulated solution is to provide a self-contained **RenderKit**. A **RenderKit** is simply a collection of **Renderers** (usually designed to support the same kind of client device) that is able to render a collection of **UIComponent** classes. A component library may bundle custom components along with the **RenderKit**, or it may simply allow the **Renderers** to render the standard components in the **javax.faces.component** package. In terms of separation of concerns, the JSF architecture allocates the responsibility for all of the rendering technology–specific code to the **RenderKit** and its **Renderers**, while the rendering technology–independent code is the responsibility of the **UIComponent** subclass.

An example of rendering technology–specific code is, in HTML, a text field that happens to be encoded as **<input type="text" />**, where its value is decoded from the postback as a name=value pair in the POST data or GET query string of the request. An example of rendering technology–independent code is the notion that a component is a "select one choice from many choices" component and therefore needs some way to represent the selected choice and the possible choices.

There are two main steps to creating a custom **RenderKit**:

1. Defining the **RenderKit** and **Renderer** classes themselves, as well as the XML markup to define them to the JSF runtime
2. Indicating which views in the application use which **RenderKit**

Each is examined in the following.

Defining the RenderKit and Renderer Classes More than anything else, a **RenderKit** is a data structure that returns a **Renderer** instance given two pieces of information: the component family and the renderer type. These terms were introduced in Chapter 11, but let's recap their meaning. The component family is a logical group of components—for example, "input", "output", or "selectOne". It captures the semantic intent of a component, and in the JSF specification there is exactly one component family declaration for each of the 18 components in the package **javax.faces.component**. The renderer type captures the appearance of the component that this **Renderer** renders. The JSF specification defines renderer types for things like button, checkbox, menu, and text area. Therefore, the combination of these two pieces of information to select a **Renderer** is the key to JSF's client device independence.

Abstract Class to Extend to Implement a RenderKit A custom **RenderKit** must extend the abstract class **javax.faces.render.RenderKit** and provide implementations for the following abstract methods.

```
public void addRenderer(String family, String rendererType,
                          Renderer renderer);
public Renderer getRenderer(String family, String rendererType);
public ResponseStateManager getResponseStateManager( );
public ResponseWriter createResponseWriter(Writer writer,
                                              String contentTypeList,
                                             String characterEncoding);
public ResponseStream createResponseStream(OutputStream out);
```

JSF 2.0 provides the class **RenderKitWrapper** to make it easier to decorate the standard **RenderKit**.

Factories in JSF

The architecture of JSF takes great advantage of several design patterns, as shown earlier in the use of the decorator pattern. A related pattern is the *abstract factory* pattern, which provides an interface for creating families of related or dependent objects without specifying their concrete classes. In JSF, this pattern is implemented in the class **javax.faces.FactoryFinder**, which sends references to factories for creating instances of the following four kinds of classes: **RenderKit**, **FacesContext**, **Lifecycle**, and **Application**. The design of **FactoryFinder** enables replacing the implementation of any of the four kinds of factories.

PART II

Factory Class Name	Creates Instances of Class	Returns Singleton?
javax.faces.application .ApplicationFactory	javax.faces.application.Application	Yes
javax.faces.context .ExceptionHandlerFactory	javax.faces.context.ExceptionHandler	No
javax.faces.context .FacesContextFactory	javax.faces.context.FacesContext	No
javax.faces.lifecycle .LifecycleFactory	javax.faces.lifecycle.Lifecycle	Yes
javax.faces.context .PartialViewContextFactory	javax.faces.context.PartialViewContext	No
javax.faces.render .RenderKitFactory	javax.faces.render.RenderKit	No
javax.faces.component.visit .VisitContextFactory	javax.faces.component.visit.VisitContext	No
javax.faces.view .ViewDeclarationLanguage Factory	javax.faces.view.ViewDeclaration Language	Yes

TABLE 13-4 Types of Factories Available from **FactoryFinder**, and the Kinds of Classes They Create

Table 13-4 lists the types of factories that can be obtained through the **FactoryFinder**, along with the kinds of classes each knows how to create. Table 13-4 also shows which kinds of factories will always return the exact same instance when called any number of times (known as singletons), and those that will return a new and different instance when called.

To motivate this discussion, recall the initial design requirement of JSF that applications built with JSF must run in a Servlet *or* Portlet container. To enable this, all of the Servlet- or Portlet-specific methods have been extracted in the **ExternalContext** instance that is obtained from the **getExternalContext( )** method of **FacesContext**. The **ExternalClass** has many methods that call for different, yet similar, actions to be taken when the container is a Servlet container versus a Portlet container. However, the default **FacesContext** implementation required by the JSF specification is only suitable for use in Servlet environments. How then to achieve this required portability? Custom implementations of **FacesContextFactory** and **LifecycleFactory** come to the rescue. The JSF Portlet integration library provides such a class, which we will examine later in this chapter, in the section titled "FacesContextFactory." For now, it's necessary to understand the concepts behind these pluggable factories.

Registering a Factory

As will be later shown in Chapter 15, the **faces-config.xml** file may contain a **<factory>** element with subelements for any of the four factory classes. This is the primary means by which one would replace a factory instance with a custom implementation. For example, in the Portlet integration library case, we have

```
<factory>
  <faces-context-factory>
    com.sun.faces.portlet.FacesContextFactoryImpl
  </faces-context-factory>
  <lifecycle-factory>
    com.sun.faces.portlet.LifecycleFactoryImpl
  </lifecycle-factory>
</factory>
```

For completeness, we must also mention a last-resort factory replacement mechanism used by the **FactoryFinder**. If a file exists in the **META-INF/services** directory of any jar in the classpath whose name is equal to any of the fully qualified factory class names in Table 13-4, the contents of that file will be assumed to contain a first line that is a fully qualified class name of a Java class that implements that specific factory. So, to continue the Portlet library example, let's say we have a jar called **factories.jar** that has the following contents:


```
META-INF/MANIFEST.MF
META-INF/services/javax.faces.context.FacesContextFactory
META-INF/services/javax.faces.lifecycle.LifecycleFactory
com/jsfcompref/FacesContextFactoryImpl.class
com/jsfcompref/LifecycleFactoryImpl.class
```

Note that there is no **META-INF/faces-config.xml** file. Further, let's assume that the file **META-INF/services/javax.faces.context.FacesContextFactory** in the jar is a text file that contains only the line

```
com.jsfcompref.FacesContextFactoryImpl
```

and that the file **META-INF/services/javax.faces.lifecycle.LifecycleFactory** in the jar is a text file that contains only the line

```
com.jsfcompref.LifecycleFactoryImpl
```

Because there is no **faces-config.xml** file in the jar, the JSF runtime is unable to replace the factory instances using the standard XML mechanism. Therefore, when the runtime asks the **FactoryFinder** to return an instance of **FacesContextFactory**, the **META-INF/services/javax.faces.context.FacesContextFactory** file is consulted and the custom class **com.jsfcompref.FacesContextFactoryImpl** is returned instead.

Finally, note that methods on **FactoryFinder** are generally never called by developer code. Rather, **FactoryFinder** methods are only invoked by the JSF runtime, though there is no prohibition on user code calling **FactoryFinder**. To that end, we list the methods of **FactoryFinder** next for reference.

```
public static Object getFactory(String factoryName) throws FacesException;
public static void setFactory(String factoryName, String implName);
public static void releaseFactories( ) throws FacesException;
```

The first method returns a factory instance that extends the class given by the **factoryName** argument, as long as the argument is one of the values in the first column in Table 13-4. The second method can be called to replace the factory implementation at runtime whenever needed before the first call to **getFactory( )** on that particular factory type. The last method is called to tell the **FactoryFinder** to release all instances of all factories it has created.

RenderKitFactory

Let's examine **RenderKitFactory** first to follow on from the custom **RenderKit** example shown earlier. One use case for creating a custom **RenderKitFactory** is when you cannot, or do not want to, declare the entire **RenderKit** in XML using the **<render-kit>** and **<renderer>** elements.

Abstract Class to Extend An instance of **RenderKitFactory** must extend the abstract class **javax.faces.render.RenderKitFactory** and implement the following methods:

```
public void addRenderKit(String renderKitId, RenderKit renderKit);
public RenderKit getRenderKit(FacesContext context, String renderKitId);
public Iterator getRenderKitIds( );
```

This class also implements **FacesWrapper**, meaning it has a **public RenderKitFactory getWrapped( )** method. For example, suppose you wanted to create a custom **RenderKit** that extended the **HTML_BASIC RenderKit** and replaced just the **OutputText Renderer** as shown previously, but without specifying any of the XML. The following custom **RenderKitFactory** does just this:

```
package com.jsfcompref.trainercomponents.renderer;
import com.jsfcompref.trainercomponents.renderer.BasicRenderKit;
import java.util.Iterator;
import javax.faces.context.FacesContext;
import javax.faces.render.RenderKit;
import javax.faces.render.RenderKitFactory;
public class ExtendHtmlBasicRenderKitFactory extends
RenderKitFactoryWrapper {
  private String [][] standardRenderKit = {
// The OutputText renderer is intentionally commented out.
//    { "javax.faces.Output", "javax.faces.Text" },
    { "javax.faces.Command", "javax.faces.Button" },
    { "javax.faces.Command", "javax.faces.Link" },
    { "javax.faces.Data", "javax.faces.Table" },
    { "javax.faces.Form", "javax.faces.Form" },
    { "javax.faces.Graphic", "javax.faces.Image" },
    { "javax.faces.Input", "javax.faces.Hidden" },
    { "javax.faces.Input", "javax.faces.Secret" },
    { "javax.faces.Input", "javax.faces.Text" },
    { "javax.faces.Input", "javax.faces.Textarea" },
    { "javax.faces.Message", "javax.faces.Message" },
    { "javax.faces.Messages", "javax.faces.Messages" },
    { "javax.faces.Output", "javax.faces.Format" },
    { "javax.faces.Output", "javax.faces.Label" },
    { "javax.faces.Output", "javax.faces.Link" },
    { "javax.faces.Panel", "javax.faces.Grid" },
    { "javax.faces.Panel", "javax.faces.Group" },
    { "javax.faces.SelectBoolean", "javax.faces.Checkbox" },
    { "javax.faces.SelectMany", "javax.faces.Checkbox" },
    { "javax.faces.SelectMany", "javax.faces.Listbox" },
    { "javax.faces.SelectMany", "javax.faces.Menu" },
    { "javax.faces.SelectOne", "javax.faces.Listbox" },
    { "javax.faces.SelectOne", "javax.faces.Menu" },
    { "javax.faces.SelectOne", "javax.faces.Radio" }
  };
```

```
  /** Creates a new instance of ExtendHtmlBasicRenderKitFactory */
  public ExtendHtmlBasicRenderKitFactory(RenderKitFactory parent) {
    this.parent = parent;
  }

  public RenderKitFactory getWrapped( ) {
    return this.parent;
  }

  private RenderKitFactory parent = null;
  public RenderKit getRenderKit(FacesContext facesContext,
                               String renderKitId) {
    RenderKit result = null;
    // First, ask the parent.
    if (null == (result = parent.getRenderKit(facesContext, renderKitId))) {
      // Note that we don't care if renderKitId is null, because we're
      // supposed to throw a NullPointerException if it is.
      if (renderKitId.equals("com.jsfcompref.CustomRenderKit")) {
          result = createAndPopulateBasicRenderKitInstance(facesContext);
          parent.addRenderKit("com.jsfcompref.CustomRenderKit", result);
    }
  }
  return result;
 }
 private RenderKit createAndPopulateBasicRenderKitInstance(FacesContext context) {
   RenderKit result = new BasicRenderKit();
   RenderKit standard = parent.getRenderKit(context,
           RenderKitFactory.HTML_BASIC_RENDER_KIT);
   int i = 0;
   // For all renderers except outputText, copy from the standard RenderKit.
   for (i = 0; i < standardRenderKit.length; i++) {
     result.addRenderer(standardRenderKit[i][0],
         standardRenderKit[i][1],
         standard.getRenderer(standardRenderKit[i][0],
           standardRenderKit[i][1]));
 }
 // Replace just the outputText renderer.
 result.addRenderer("javax.faces.Output", "javax.faces.Text",
     new SpecialOutputTextRenderer());
 return result;
}
}
```

In the constructor, you see the now familiar decorator pattern at work. The **getRenderKit( )** method first delegates to the parent **RenderKitFactory** to satisfy the request. If no **RenderKit** is found for the argument **renderKitId** and the argument is equal to the literal string **com.jsfcompref.CustomRenderKit**, the **createAndPopulateBasicRenderKitInstance( )** method is called. This method creates an instance of the class **BasicRenderKit** and leverages the private data structure called **standardRenderKit** to populate it with renderers from the standard **HTML_BASIC RenderKit** for all renderers *except* the **OutputText Renderer**. This one is handled specifically by adding an instance of **SpecialOutputTextRenderer**. The new **BasicRenderKit** is returned where it is added to the list of **RenderKits** stored in the parent.

ExceptionHandlerFactory

Chapter 10 includes a complete example of **ExceptionHandlerFactory**, but it is included here for completeness.

Abstract Class to Extend A custom implementation of **ExceptionHandlerFactory** must extend the abstract class **javax.faces.context.FacesContextFactory** and implement the following method:

```
public ExceptionHandler getExceptionHandler( );
```

This class also implements FacesWrapper, meaning it has a public **ExceptionHandlerFactory getWrapped( )** method.

```
public class MyExceptionHandlerFactory extends ExceptionHandlerFactory {
  private ExceptionHandlerFactory parent;
  public MyExceptionHandlerFactory(ExceptionHandlerFactory parent) {
    this.parent = parent;
  }

  public ExceptionHandlerFactory getWrapped( ) {
    return this.parent;
  }

  public ExceptionHandler getExceptionHandler( ) {
    final ExceptionHandler parentHandler = getWrapped( ).
      getExceptionHandler( );
    ExceptionHandler result = new ExceptionHandlerWrapper( ) {
      public ExceptionHandler getWrapped( ) {
        return parentHandler;
      }
      // implement as many or as few methods from
      // ExceptionHandler
    };
  }
```

FacesContextFactory

As mentioned at the beginning of this section, one good use case for providing a custom **FacesContextFactory** is adapting JSF to the Portlet environment. However, this is certainly not the only conceivable use case. One could also imagine adapting JSF to run inside of a pure Swing application environment, though no one has yet taken this approach. Any such attempt would most likely choose to provide a custom **FacesContextFactory**.

Abstract Class to Extend A custom implementation of **FacesContextFactory** must extend the abstract class **javax.faces.context.FacesContextFactory** and implement the following method:

```
public FacesContext getFacesContext(Object context, Object request,
                                    Object response, Lifecycle lifecycle)
    throws FacesException;
```

Let's examine the simple implementation of this method in the Sun JSF-Portlet integration library, shown next:

```
public FacesContext getFacesContext(Object context,
    Object request,
    Object response,
    Lifecycle lifecycle)
  throws FacesException {
  if ((context == null) || (request == null) ||
      (response == null) || (lifecycle == null)) {
    throw new NullPointerException();
  }
  ExternalContext econtext =
    new ExternalContextImpl((PortletContext) context,
    (PortletRequest) request,
    (PortletResponse) response);
  return (new FacesContextImpl(econtext, lifecycle));
}
```

Here, **getFacesContext( )** simply creates an **ExternalContextImpl** instance, casts the **context**, **request**, and **response** arguments to their Portlet interface classes, and passes them on to the **FacesContextImpl** constructor. The implementation details of these classes are not pertinent to this discussion and have been omitted from the text.

ExternalContextFactory

New in JSF 2.0, it is possible to decorate just the **ExternalContext**. Prior releases required you to decorate the **FacesContextFactory** and produce a custom **FacesContext** class, even if you just wanted to decorate the **ExternalContext**. Here's how it works in JSF 2.0:

```
public class MyExternalContextFactory extends ExternalContextFactory {
  private ExternalContextFactory parent;

  public MyExternalContextFactory(ExternalContextFactory parent) {
    this.parent = parent;
  }

  public ExternalContextFactory getWrapped( ) {
    return this.parent;
  }

  public ExternalContext getExternalContext(Object context,
    Object request, Object response) {
    final ExternalContext parentContext = getWrapped( ).
      getExternalContext(context, request, response);
    ExternalContext result = new ExternalContextWrapper( ) {
      public ExternalContext getWrapped( ) {
        return parentContext;
      }
      // implement as many or as few methods from
      // ExternalContext.
    };
```

LifecycleFactory

The capabilities of this particular JSF extension point are also used in the JSF Portlet integration library; however, the full power of providing additional lifecycles has not yet been fully explored as of this writing.

Abstract Class to Extend A custom **LifecycleFactory** must extend the class **javax.faces.lifecycle .LifecycleFactory** and implement the following methods:

```
public abstract void addLifecycle(String lifecycleId, Lifecycle lifecycle);
public abstract Lifecycle getLifecycle(String lifecycileId);
public abstract Iterator getLifecycleIds( );
```

Like the **RenderKitFactory**, the **LifecycleFactory** maintains a **Map** of **lifecycleIds** to **Lifecycle** instances. In order to take advantage of using a custom **LifecycleFactory**, you must examine the API of the **Lifecycle** class.

```
public void addPhaseListener(PhaseListener listener);
public void removePhaseListener(PhaseListener listener);
public PhaseListener[] getPhaseListeners( );
public void execute(FacesContext context) throws FacesException;
public void render(FacesContext context) throws FacesException;
```

The first three methods are simply an implementation of a JavaBeans listener property for **PhaseListener**. The **execute( )** method is responsible for running the postback part of the lifecycle, as described in Chapter 3. The **render( )** method is responsible only for rendering.

Expert Group Insight *Initially, there was only an* ***execute( )*** *method, but during development of the specification we realized that a postback to a Portlet limited the postback portion of the request processing lifecycle to only the one Portlet in the page that actually is experiencing the form submit, while every Portlet in the page must re-render itself. Breaking these out into two separate phases allowed this design to be possible.*

Please see Chapter 3 for details on the request processing lifecycle, which will give you insight into ways to provide your own implementation, if desired. Finally, note that **LifecycleFactory** implements **FacesWrapper**, making it easier to decorate the existing lifecycle.

JSF 1.2 Tip *In JSF 1.2, Expert Group member Jacob Hookom, inventor of Facelets, introduced a new way to specify the* ***lifecycleId*** *for an application with a potential use in AJAX applications: having a different lifecycle for different* ***FacesServlet*** *instances in the same application. Prior to JSF 1.2, every* ***FacesServlet*** *in a single Web application was required to share the same* ***LifecycleFactory*** *and therefore the same kind of lifecycle. This was because the only way to specify an alternate lifecycle was through a* ***lifecycleId context-param*** *in the* ***faces-config.xml*** *file. Jacob's idea was to also allow an* ***init-param*** *element to contain a* ***lifecycleId****. By doing this, it's possible to write a custom Lifecycle implementation that is optimized for handling AJAX requests and responses.*

PartialViewContextFactory

Decorating this class allows you to affect how the runtime processes partial traversals of the view, most importantly during Ajax requests.

Abstract Class to Extend A custom PartialViewContextFactory must extend the class **javax.faces.context.PartialViewContextFactory** and implement the following method:

```
public PartialViewContext getPartialViewContext(FacesContext context);
```

This class implements **FacesWrapper**, so really it's only necessary to override the **getWrapped( )** method as shown in the introductory section on decoration. It is convenient to use the inner class decorator pattern shown in the section **ExceptionHandlerFactory** to implement the **getPartialViewContext( )**, as shown here:

```
public class MyPartialViewContextFactory extends PartialViewContextFactory {
  private PartialViewContextFactory parent;
  public MyPartialViewContextFactory(PartialViewContextFactory parent) {
    this.parent = parent;
  }

  public PartialViewContextFactory getWrapped( ) {
    return this.parent;
  }

  public PartialViewContext getPartialViewContext(FacesContext context) {
    final PartialViewContext parentContext = getWrapped( ).
      getPartialViewContext( );
    PartialViewContext result = new PartialViewContextWrapper( ) {
      public PartialViewContext getWrapped( ) {
        return parentContext;
      }
      // implement as many or as few methods from
      // PartialViewContext
    };
  }
```

The class **PartialViewContext** has methods that control nearly every aspect of how Ajax requests are processed. Please see Chapter 12 for a more detailed discussion of Ajax and JSF.

ViewDeclarationLanguageFactory

Decorating this class allows you to affect how the runtime takes an input file and produces a tree of **UIComponent** instances against which the JSF lifecycle can be run.

Abstract Class to Extend A custom ViewDeclarationLanguageFactory must extend the class **javax.faces.view.ViewDeclarationLanguageFactory** and implement the following method:

```
public ViewDeclarationLanguage getViewDeclarationLanguage(String viewId);
```

This class implements **FacesWrapper**, so really it's only necessary to override the **getWrapped( )** method as shown in the introductory section on decoration. It is convenient to use the inner class decorator pattern shown in the section **ExceptionHandlerFactory** to implement the **getViewDeclarationLanguage( )**, as shown here:

```
public class MyViewDeclarationLanguageFactory extends ViewDeclarationLanguageFactory {
  private ViewDeclarationLanguageFactory parent;
  public MyViewDeclarationLanguageFactory(ViewDeclarationLanguageFactory parent) {
    this.parent = parent;
  }

  public ViewDeclarationLanguageFactory getWrapped( ) {
    return this.parent;
  }

  public ViewDeclarationLanguage getViewDeclarationLanguage(String viewId) {
    final ViewDeclarationLanguage parentVDL = getWrapped( ).
      getViewDeclarationLanguage( );
    ViewDeclarationLanguage result = new ViewDeclarationLanguageWrapper( ) {
      public ViewDeclarationLanguage getWrapped( ) {
        return parentVDL;
      }
      // implement as many or as few methods from
      // ViewDeclarationLanguage
    };
  }
```

A developer would decorate the **ViewDeclarationLanguageFactory** if she wanted to provide a new VDL for JSF. For example, it would be very useful if the Jamon templating engine (**www.jamon.org/**) could be used as a View Declaration Language for JSF.

VisitContextFactory

Decorating this class allows you to affect how the runtime takes an input file and produces a tree of **UIComponent** instances against which the JSF lifecycle can be run.

Abstract Class to Extend A custom **VisitContextFactory** must extend the class **javax.faces .VisitContextFactory** and implement the following method:

```
public VisitContext getVisitContext(FacesContext context,
          Collection<String> ids, Set<VisitHint> hints);
```

This class implements **FacesWrapper**, so really it's only necessary to override the **getWrapped( )** method as shown in the introductory section on decoration. It is convenient to use the inner class decorator pattern shown in the section **ExceptionHandlerFactory** to implement the **getVisitContext( )**, as shown here:

```
public class MyVisitContextFactory extends VisitContextFactory {
  private VisitContextFactory parent;
  public MyVisitContextFactory(VisitContextFactory parent) {
    this.parent = parent;
  }

  public VisitContextFactory getWrapped( ) {
    return this.parent;
  }
```

```
public VisitContext getVisitContext(FacesContext context,
     Collection<String> ids, Set<VisitHint> hints) {
  final VisitContext parentVDL = getWrapped( ).
    getVisitContext( );
  VisitContext result = new VisitContextWrapper( ) {
    public VisitContext getWrapped( ) {
      return parentVDL;
    }
    // implement as many or as few methods from
    // VisitContext
  };
}
```

A developer would decorate the **VisitContextFactory** if he wanted to control or observe the way the JSF runtime traverses the view during the execution of the lifecycle.

Application Factory

The final factory class you can replace is the **ApplicationFactory**. The **Application** instance is really the heart of the JSF runtime. It is an application singleton that holds references to many core JSF classes. Some possible use cases for decorating the **ApplicationFactory** include

- Gaining access to the process by which new **UIComponent** instances are created by overriding or decorating the **createComponent( )** method
- Gaining access to the process by which new **Converter** instances are created by overriding or decorating the **createConverter( )** method
- Gaining access to the process by which new **Validator** instances are created by overriding or decorating the **createValidator( )** method
- Supplementing the **Locale** awareness afforded by the **getSupportedLocales( )** method to include other **Locales** without using the XML configuration syntax of the **<locale-config>** element described in Chapter 15. For example, if an application needs to dynamically support a changeable set of **Locale**s at runtime without restarting, decorating the **ApplicationFactory** would provide one way to meet this requirement.

In JSF 1.1, **Application** has the JavaBeans properties shown in Table 13-5. Recall that a JavaBeans property is really just a pair of "getter/setter" methods that conform to the following naming conventions. For Read Only properties, only the getter method exists. For Write Only properties, only the setter method exists. For Read/Write methods, both a getter and a setter exist. To derive the name of the getter or setter method given a property name, capitalize the first letter of the property and prefix it with get or set, respectively. For example, for the Read/Write property **actionListener**, the getter is **getActionListener( )** and the setter is **setActionListener( )**. The type of the property is the return type of the getter method, which must be the same as the argument type of the setter method. Finally, the getter must take no arguments, and the setter method must take only one argument—the same type as the return type of the getter method.

In addition to providing the properties shown in Table 13-5, **Application** also defines the following methods: **createComponent( )**, **createConverter( )**, **createMethodBinding( )**, **createValidator( )**, and **createValueBinding( )**.

JavaBeans Property	Type	Read Only (RO) or Read/Write (RW)	Description
actionListener	ActionListener	RW	Holds the class responsible for handling actions
componentTypes	Iterator of String	RO	The component types for **UIComponent** instances this application can create on a call to **createComponent(String)**
converterIds	Iterator of String	RO	The converterIds for **Converter** instances this application can create on a call to **createConverter(String)**
converterTypes	Iterator of Class	RO	The types for **Converter** classes this application can create on a call to **createConverter(Class)**
defaultLocale	Locale	RW	The default **Locale** for this application
defaultRenderKitId	String	RW	The default **RenderKitId** for this application
messageBundle	String	RW	The name of the **ResourceBundle** used for application error messages
navigationHandler	NavigationHandler	RW	The **NavigationHandler** for this application
propertyResolver	PropertyResolver	RW	The **PropertyResolver** for this application
stateManager	StateManager	RW	The **StateManager** for this application
supportedLocales	Iterator (on get) Collection (on set)	RW	A **Collection** or **Iterator** of **Locale** instances that are supported by this application
validatorIds	Iterator of String	RO	The validatorIds for **Validators** that can be created by this application on a call to **createValidator(String)**
variableResolver	VariableResolver	RW	The **VariableResolver** for this application
viewHandler	ViewHandler	RW	The **ViewHandler** for this application

TABLE 13-5 Application Properties in JSF 1.1

JSF 1.2 adds the properties shown in Table 13-6 and deprecates the **propertyResolver** and **variableResolver** properties. In JSF 1.2, the **createMethodBinding( )** and **createValueBinding( )** methods are deprecated, and the **evaluateExpressionGet( )** has been added. JSF 2.0 adds the methods shown in Table 13-7.

JavaBeans Property	Type	Read Only (RO) or Read/Write (RW)	Description
ELContextListeners	ELContextListener	RW	Allows applications to add a listener to be notified when a new **ELContext** instance is created
ELResolver	ELResolver	RW	Returns the singleton **ELResolver** to be used for resolving all expressions
ExpressionFactory	ExpressionFactory	RO	Returns the **javax.el .ExpressionFactory** for creating **ValueExpression** and **MethodExpression** instances

TABLE 13-6 **Application** Properties Added in JSF 1.2

Method	Arguments	Description
void addBehavior	String behaviorId, String behaviorClass	Declare a new **Behavior** class that can be returned from **createBehavior( )**
void addDefaultValidatorId	String validatorId	Add a new **validator-id** so that it will be set as one of the validators for every **EditableValueHolder** component on every page in the application.
Behavior createBehavior	String behaviorId	Return a new instance of the one of the known behavior classes.
UIComponent createComponent	FacesContext context, Resource componentResource	This is how the runtime instantiates a composite components from Facelet page in a resource library.
UIComponent createComponent	FacesContext context, String componentType, String rendererType	Like **createComponent(String)**, but it causes the created component to be inspected for JSF-related annotations.
UIComponent createComponent	ValueExpression ve, FacesContext context, String componentType, String rendererType	Like **createComponent(ValueExpression, FacesContext, String)**, but it causes the Renderer to be inspected for JSF related annotations.
Map<String, String> getDefaultValidatorInfo	none	Allows the runtime to inspect the currently configured Validators
ProjectStage getProjectStage	none	Returns the ProjectStage for this application instance
void setProjectStage	ProjectStage stage	Sets the ProjectStage
ResourceHandler getResourceHandler	none	Returns the ResourceHandler for this application
void setResourceHandler	ResourceHandler handler	Sets the ResourceHandler for this application
event related methods	NA	These are described in detail in Chapter 9

TABLE 13-7 **Application** Methods Added in JSF 2.0

Abstract Class to Extend A custom **ApplicationFactory** class must extend the abstract class **javax.faces.application.ApplicationFactory** and must implement the following methods:

```
public Application getApplication( );
public void setApplication(Application application);
```

This is simply a Read/Write JavaBeans property of type **Application**. Also, as a final note, it is inadvisable to override the **ApplicationFactory** without using the decorator pattern, because the core nature of the implementation of the **Application** class leads to the introduction of implementation-specific code. Therefore, please use the decorator pattern when overriding the **Application**. This is made easier in JSF 2.0 because **Application** implements **FacesWrapper.**

Additional Non-UIComponent Topics

Two topics remain to complete our discussion of non-UIComponent extensions to JSF, both of which are new features in JSF 2.0: the **ProjectStage** feature and the Custom Scope feature.

Telling the JSF Runtime Where You Are in the Software Development Lifecycle: ProjectStage

Another idea taken from Ruby on Rails is the notion of telling the runtime where you are in the software development lifecycle. In Rails, this is done by setting the **RAILS_ENV** environment variable. In JSF 2.0, it is done by setting the **javax.faces.PROJECT_STAGE** context param in the web.xml, as shown here.

```
<context-param>
  <param-name>javax.faces.PROJECT_STAGE</param-name>
  <param-value>Development</param-value>
</context-param>
```

Alternatively, the value may be set into the JNDI key **java:comp/env/jsf/ProjectStage**. If both a **context-param** and the JNDI key are set, the value in the JNDI key takes precedence.

Either method causes the **projectStage** property to be set on the application instance. Various parts of the JSF runtime will query the value of this property and take action based on its value. The valid values for this property, and some actions that are taken by Sun's Mojarra implementation when they are set, are shown next.

ProjectStage.Development

This value means the project is in active development. This will cause the runtime to display extra verbose log messages, helpful tips in the page, and make other simplifying assumptions that make sense only during development.

Sun's Mojarra JSF runtime takes the following actions.

- All **UIComponents** in the view will have an entry in their attributes **Map** under the key **javax.faces.component.VIEW_LOCATION_KEY**. The value for that entry is the **javax.faces.view.Location** instance describing the location of that component in the view.

- Resources are not cached. This makes it easier to dynamically modify resources, such as scripts and stylesheets, without redeploying the application, something you don't need to do in Production.
- If a composite component is trying to load a backing groovy class, and the groovy class is not found, a message is logged.
- The default **ExceptionHandler** will ensure that a nice error page is shown if one is not manually set by the developer.
- The Facelet compiler will cause helpful debugging messages to be added to the page if taglib declarations are omitted.
- The standard JavaScript resource is served to the client uncompressed. This is very helpful when debugging Ajax applications. For values other than **ProjectStage .Development**, the standard JavaScript resource is compressed to reduce download size and optimize performance.
- If the value is not **ProjectStage.Production**, the **<h:button>** and **<h:link>** elements will cause a message to be rendered to the page if the outcome to which they point is not found.

Other implementantions make take additional action if the **ProjectStage** is **Development**.

ProjectStage.Production

This value means the project is running in production, so the runtime disables helpful hints and takes shortcuts to improve performance. If no value for **ProjectStage** is defined, this is the default.

ProjectStage.SystemTest and ProjectStage.UnitTest

The JSF specification says nothing about what should happen if the value is **SystemTest** or **UnitTest**, these are open for application developers and component developers to exploit.

Custom Scopes

This advanced topic is discussed briefly here; more details on this topic can be found in the online code samples for the book.

Any EL Expression that resolves to class that implements **Map** can be used as the scope of a managed bean. For example, this bean uses the **@CustomScoped** annotation.

```
package com.jsfcompref;
import javax.faces.bean.ManagedBean;
import javax.faces.bean.CustomScoped;
@ManagedBean
@CustomScoped("#{shoppingCart.items}")
public class CartItems {
   // ... properties omitted
}
```

The equivalent XML syntax is shown next.

```
<managed-bean>
  <managed-bean-name>CartItems</managed-bean-name>
  <managed-bean-class>com.jsfcompref.CartItems</managed-bean-class>
  <managed-bean-scope>#{shoppingCart.items}")</managed-bean-scope>
</managed-bean>
```

It is up to the application developer to ensure that the POJO that vends the custom scope, in this case another managed bean called named **shoppingCart**, takes responsibility for beginning and ending the scope, and expiring entries in the scope as appropriate. The class that manages the scope must ensure that the **PostConstructCustomScope** and **PreDestroyCustomScope** events are published at the appropriate times. Details on how to publish events are in Chapter 9. By publishing these events, managed bean methods annotated with **@PostConstruct** and **@PreDestroy** will be invoked as for normal managed beans.

14

CHAPTER

Securing JavaServer Faces Applications

This chapter explains how to secure your JavaServer Faces application. At the outset, it is important to state that computer security in general, and Web security in particular, are very large topics. In this chapter, we examine the issue only as it relates to JSF. We begin with an introduction to some high-level security concepts, followed by a review of the fundamentals of the security features provided by the Java EE Platform Web tier. Fortunately, everything you already know about Java EE Platform Security applies to JSF applications as well. The chapter will close by presenting a simple JSF-based framework for securing a JSF Web application, using the Virtual Trainer as an example. Throughout, you'll see how effectively leveraging JSF streamlines the process of adding security.

Aspects and Implementation of Web Application Security

Web application security can be broken down into three main aspects:

- **Authentication** Proving to the system that a user's identity is authentic. In other words, "you are who you say you are."
- **Authorization** Granting access to certain parts of the system based on the user's identity. This is sometimes referred to as *role-based access control* because each user is associated with one or more roles, and the roles dictate what actions the user may take. In other words, "we know who you are; now, what are you allowed to do?"
- **Data security** Ensuring that interactions between the user and the system cannot be observed by unauthorized parties. In other words, "we know who you are and what you're allowed to do; now, let's prevent people from snooping on you while you do it."

Not all applications need all three aspects; customer requirements will dictate which of the three are needed. For example, an intranet application that runs on a secure LAN does not require data security because all the communications on the LAN are already assumed to be secure. Also, some of the aspects may be combined. Consider an application that doesn't require authentication for general use yet has a portion of the application that only administrators may access. In this case, the user must be *authenticated* as an administrator, and then *authorized* to perform functions that normal users cannot. You can see that applying security to a Web application is an art that requires merging customer requirements with the aspects of authentication, authorization, and data security.

The implementation of the aspects of Web security is generally broken down into two areas: *container managed* and *application managed*. An application is said to use container-managed security when it relies on the security features provided by the container. For many applications, this is all that is needed. This chapter will cover the fundamentals of container-managed security in the following section. Application-managed security is when the application itself provides some or all of the security features. Application-managed security is often built on top of the features of container-managed security and is used when container-managed security alone fails to meet the security requirements. Application-managed security will be covered at the end of the chapter, in the section "Application-Managed Security with JavaServer Faces."

Container-Managed Security

This section provides an overview of the security features provided by the Java EE Platform Web tier. The discussion will be guided by presenting each of the three aspects of Web application security and how each is addressed in the Web tier. All of the container-managed security features are configured using entries in the Web deployment descriptor, the **web.xml** file.

Container-Managed Authentication

Many applications require only container-managed authentication security. The Web tier provides three features to implement this aspect: basic, form-based, and client certificate. (A fourth version of authentication is provided, called digest, but it is not widely supported and therefore is not discussed further.) You tell the container which kind of authentication you are using by placing a **<login-config>** element inside of the **<web-app>** element in the **web.xml** file. Recall that the ordering of elements inside of the **<web-app>** element is significant and the application may fail to deploy if you don't follow the proper ordering as dictated in the DTD or schema. The following example configures basic authentication for the application:

```
<web-app>
  <!-- intervening elements omitted -->
  <security-constraint>
    <!-- contents omitted, see discussion on Authorization -->
  </security-constraint>
  <login-config>
    <auth-method>BASIC</auth-method>
    <realm-name>file</realm-name>
  </login-config>
  <!-- intervening elements omitted -->
</web-app>
```

The details of the **<security-constraint>** element are left to the section on authorization, but for now, just know that this element allows you to control which parts of your application are subject to authentication.

The Servlet API provides several methods on **HttpServletRequest** to interface with the container-managed authentication system, regardless of which method (basic, form, digest, or client certificate) is used. These are shown in Table 14-1.

These methods provide one way to build application-managed security on top of the existing security infrastructure of the Web tier. We'll revisit these API methods in the section "Container-Managed Authorization and the Concept of Roles" with an example of how to integrate container-managed security elements into application-managed security.

Let's examine each of the four implementations of container-managed authentication in the Java EE Web tier.

Basic Authentication and the Concept of a "Realm"

Basic authentication has been around since the beginning of the Web. Indeed, it was defined in the HTTP 1.0 specification way back in 1996. The basic authentication scheme also introduced the notion of "realm," which you saw earlier as **<realm-name>** in the **web.xml** excerpt. A *realm* is an opaque string interpreted by the server to identify a data store for resolving username and password information. The *implementation of the realm concept is not*

Method Name	Return Type	Purpose	New in JavaEE 6
authenticate(Http-ServletResponse *response*)	boolean	Leverage the current return values from **getUserPrincipal( )**, **getAuthType( )**, and **getRemoteUser( )** to perform container-managed authentication. Returns **true** if this authentication is successful, **false** otherwise.	Yes
getAuthType( )	String	Returns a string showing which authentication type is in use, or **null** if the request is unauthenticated.	No
getRemoteUser( )	String	Returns the username of the user making this request, or **null** if the request is unauthenticated.	No
getUserPrincipal( )	Principal	Returns a **java.security.Principal** instance representing the current user. **Principal** is a simple interface, implementations of which are provided by the underlying security system to represent the user while allowing a flexible security implementation.	No
isUserInRole(String *role*)	boolean	Returns **true** if the user making this request is included in the argument **role**. Otherwise, it returns **false**.	No
login(String userid, String *password*)	void	Throws **ServletException** if the login is unsuccessful	Yes
logout( )	void	Make it so that future calls to **getUserPrincipal( )**, **getAuthType( )**, and **getRemoteUser( )** return **null**.	Yes

TABLE 14-1 HttpServletRequest Authentication Methods

standard; different containers implement it differently. In the Apache Tomcat container, a simple plain text XML file is used to configure the **UserDatabase** realm, the **<TOMCAT-HOME>/conf/tomcat-users.xml** file:

```
<tomcat-users>
  <role name="trainer" />
  <role name="user" />
  <user name="administrator" password="admin" roles="trainer" />
  <user name="edburns"  password="pass" roles="user" />
</tomcat-users>
```

The Sun Java System Application server provides **file**, **admin-realm**, and **certificate** realms, as well as support for JAAS (Java Authentication and Authorization Service), all of which have their own configuration mechanisms. Oracle's OC4J (Oracle Containers for J2EE) has its own **jazn-data.xml** configuration file, which is also a JAAS Descriptor. All of these files contain realm definitions with associated users and roles.

Basic authentication is not secure because the username and password information are sent via Base64 encoded plain text as the value of the **Authorization** HTTP header. (Unfortunately, the name of the header is "Authorization," but the service it performs is authentication.) Base64 encoding is a well-known algorithm that converts binary data into plain ASCII text by breaking the binary data down into six-bit chunks and converting each one to an ASCII character. There is no encryption element to the Base64 encoding algorithm; therefore, this data can easily be examined by packet sniffers and other network intrusion technologies.

To make basic authentication secure, a secure transport layer must be employed. Please see the section "Container-Managed Data Security" for more on this topic. When using basic authentication, the browser presents a pop-up dialog to users asking them to provide their username and password, as shown in Figure 14-1.

While basic authentication may not be secure, there are some instances in which it is sufficient for user requirements, such as when the entire application resides on a secure network and when prototyping.

Form-Based Authentication

Form-based authentication is so called because you must author a Web page with a form in it that provides the UI to the login page of the application. Form-based authentication was designed well before JSF came along and makes assumptions about the server-side processing of the authentication that are not entirely compatible with the design of JSF. It is certainly possible to use the standard form-based authentication technique to provide authentication to a JSF application, but an ideal solution would use a custom component to hide the details from the page author. This section will show one way to build such a component. We will use

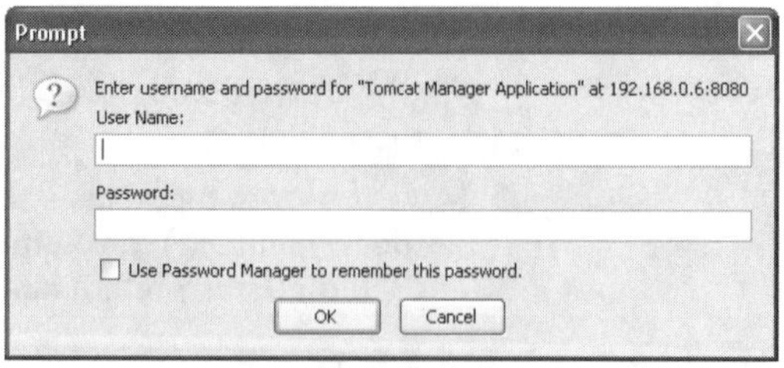

FIGURE 14-1 A browser's basic authentication dialog

Prompt

Enter username and password for "Tomcat Manager Application" at 192.168.0.6:8080

User Name:

Password:

Use Password Manager to remember this password.

OK Cancel

the component to illustrate the use of form-based authentication. First though, let's return to the **<login-config>** element of the **web.xml** file.

```
<login-config>
  <auth-method>FORM</auth-method>
  <realm-name>file</realm-name>
  <form-login-config>
    <form-login-page>/faces/login.xhtml</form-login-page>
    <form-error-page>/faces/loginError.xhtml</form-error-page>
  </form-login-config>
</login-config>
```

Assuming the **<security-constraint>** element is correctly defined to cover the parts of the application that you want to be subject to authentication, any attempts to access these pages without first going through the login page will fail, and the user will be redirected to the login page. Let us now show the portion of the **login.xhtml** page using a form-based login of the **vt:loginPanel** composite component. This component hides the details of the container-managed, form-based login mechanism. Most notably, it hides the awkward and non-JSF-based **j_security_check** syntax required for container-managed form-based login.

```
<!DOCTYPE html PUBLIC "-//W3C//DTD XHTML 1.0 Transitional//EN"
"http://www.w3.org/TR/xhtml1/DTD/xhtml1-transitional.dtd">
<html xmlns="http://www.w3.org/1999/xhtml"
  xmlns:h="http://java.sun.com/jsf/html"
  xmlns:vt="http://java.sun.com/jsf/composite/trainer">
<h:head>Login</h:head>
<h:body>
<p>Please login to access this part of the site.</p>
<vt:loginPanel/>
</h:body>
</html>
```

The **loginError.xhtml** page is just a plain old Web page (it need not be a JSF or even Facelet) that is shown when the login has failed for some reason. It is useful to provide a "try again" link that allows the user to try to log in again, as shown here:

```
<!DOCTYPE html PUBLIC "-//W3C//DTD XHTML 1.0 Transitional//EN"
"http://www.w3.org/TR/xhtml1/DTD/xhtml1-transitional.dtd">
<html xmlns="http://www.w3.org/1999/xhtml"
  xmlns:h="http://java.sun.com/jsf/html">
<body>

  <p>A login error has occurred.</p>
  <h:link outcome="login">Return to login page</h:link>

</body>
</html>
```

Let's now take a look at the **trainer/loginPanel.xhtml** composite component page. Composite components are described in Chapter 11.

```
<cc:interface>
  <cc:attribute name="useridLabel" default="Userid:" />
```

PART II

```
    <cc:attribute name="passwordLabel" default="Password:" />
    <cc:attribute name="loginButtonLabel" default="Login" />
    <cc:attribute name="resetButtonLabel" default="Reset" />
  </cc:interface>

  <cc:implementation>
    <form method="post" action="j_security_check">
    <h:panelGrid columns="2">
      <h:outputLabel for="j_username" value="#{cc.attrs.useridLabel}" />
      <input type="text" name="j_username"  />

      <h:outputLabel for="j_password" value="#{cc.attrs.passwordLabel}" />
      <input type="password" name="j_password" />

      <h:outputText value=" " /> <!--this is necessary for layout -->
      <input type="reset" name="reset" value="#{cc.attrs.resetButtonLabel}" />
      <input type="submit" name="submit" value="#{cc.attrs.loginButtonLabel}" />
    </h:panelGrid>
    </form>
  </cc:implementation>
```

The important thing to note is that **vt:loginPanel** must not be nested within an **<h:form>** tag because the component itself generates the HTML **<form method="post" action="j_security_check">**. The **j_security_check**, **j_username**, and **j_password** HTML attribute values are required by container-managed authentication.

The online code for this sample is fully functional, but in the interest of time, let's say that the two top-level directories from the Chapter 10 version of Virtual Trainer are carried forward here: **user** and **trainer**. Let's assume these directory names correspond to container-defined authorization roles, and therefore any files within these directories will require authentication before they can be displayed. For example, an attempt to access **http://trainerhost/faces/user/userPage.xhtml** will cause the server to redirect you to the **<form-login-page>**, in this case, **http://trainerhost/faces/login.xhtml**. Entering in a userid/ password pair that is known to the container will bring you to the page you originally requested, **userPage.xhtml**, which is shown here:

```
<?xml version='1.0' encoding='UTF-8' ?>
<!DOCTYPE html PUBLIC "-//W3C//DTD XHTML 1.0 Transitional//EN"
"http://www.w3.org/TR/xhtml1/DTD/xhtml1-transitional.dtd">
<html xmlns="http://www.w3.org/1999/xhtml"
    xmlns:h="http://java.sun.com/jsf/html">
<h:head>User Page</h:head>
<h:body>

<p>This is a user page.</p>
<h:form>
<h:commandButton action="#{securityBacking.logout}" value="Logout" />
</h:form>

</h:body>
</html>
```

As shown in Table 14-1, Servlet 3.0, which is new in Java EE 6, now has a method called **logout( )**, which we call from the backing bean, **SecurityBacking**, shown next.

```
package com.jsfcompref.trainer.backing;

import java.util.logging.Level;
import java.util.logging.Logger;
import javax.faces.bean.ManagedBean;
import javax.faces.bean.RequestScoped;
import javax.faces.context.FacesContext;
import javax.servlet.ServletException;
import javax.servlet.http.HttpServletRequest;

@ManagedBean
@RequestScoped
public class SecurityBacking {

  public String logout() {
    String result = "/login?faces-redirect=true";

    FacesContext context = FacesContext.getCurrentInstance();
    HttpServletRequest request = (HttpServletRequest) context.
        getExternalContext().getRequest();
    try {
      request.logout( );
    } catch (ServletException ex) {
      Logger.getLogger(SecurityBacking.class.getName()).
          log(Level.SEVERE, null, ex);
      result = "/loginError?faces-redirect=true";
    }
    return result;
  }
}
```

The only interesting thing about this page is the call to **request.logout( )**. This method will make the container unaware of the authentication credentials, thus requiring the container to forward the user to the login page when that user tries to access a forbidden page.

Certificate Authentication

Client *certificate* authentication is the most secure of the standard forms of container-managed security. Unfortunately, even though parts of setting up certificate authentication are standardized, a complete implementation requires significant vendor-specific configuration steps. Therefore, this section presents a higher-level view of performing authentication using certificates than was provided for basic or form-based authentication.

We must first introduce the concept of public key cryptography before we can explain the concept of an identity certificate. The easiest way to share data securely is to encrypt it using some scheme and share the password with the party with whom you want to share the data. Of course, the matter of sharing the password securely is a problem, but let's just say you can tell the person directly. While the shared password scheme is easy to understand and implement, it doesn't scale to large numbers of users without compromising security.

Public key cryptography, also called public key infrastructure, or PKI, solves the problem by breaking the concept of a password into two parts, a "public key" and a "private key." The archetypal analogy to describe PKI involves two people—Alice and Bob—who want to send messages to each other through the postal mail. In order for Alice to send a message to Bob securely, Alice asks Bob to send her his open padlock, to which only Bob has the key. Alice then puts the message in the box and locks it with Bob's padlock, sending it in the mail. When Bob receives the box he can open the box with his key and see the message. Conversely, when Bob wants to send a message to Alice, he needs Alice's open padlock. In PKI, the padlock is the public key, and the key for the padlock is the private key. This situation is depicted in Figure 14-2.

In order to share data with someone, you need their public key and your private key; therefore, it is desirable to distribute your public key as widely as possible. That's where the "infrastructure" in public key infrastructure really comes in. When padlocks (public keys)

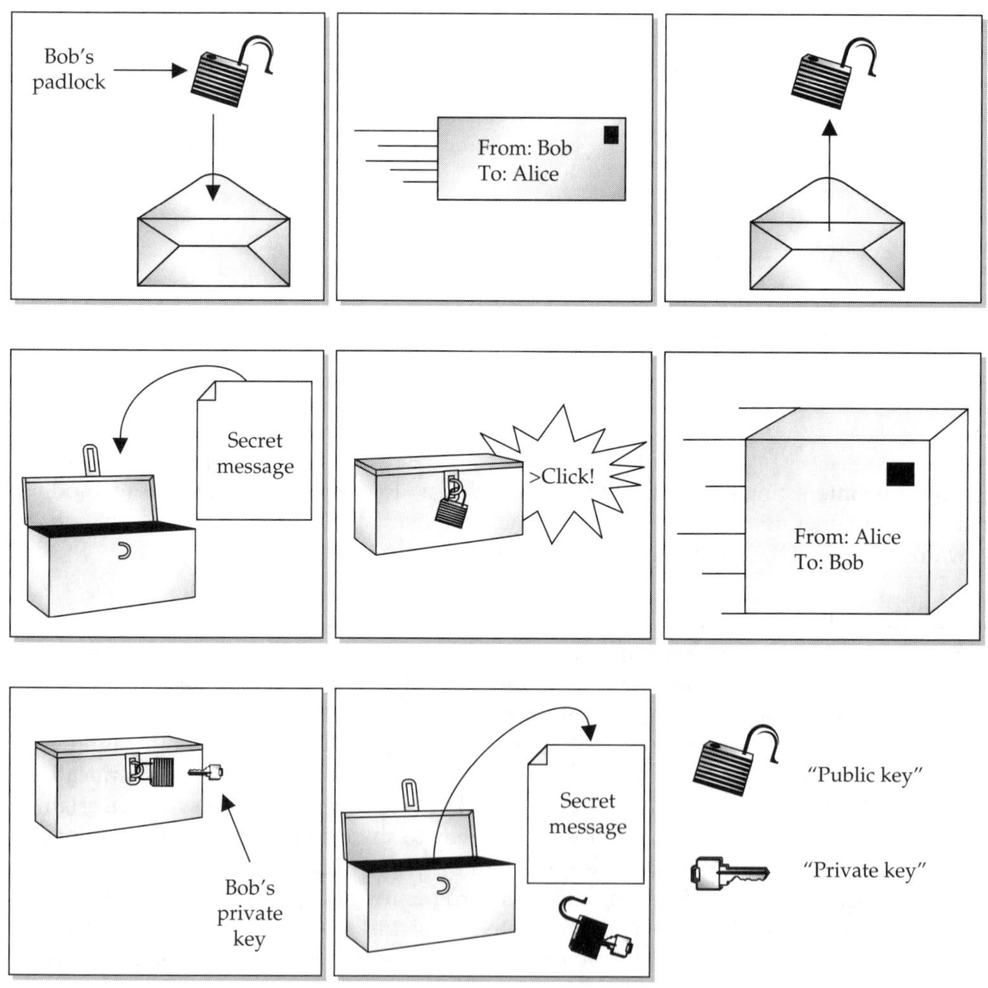

Figure 14-2 Public key infrastructure

are freely distributed, the problem is verifying that Alice's padlock really belongs to Alice and not some malicious postman who opened the mail and replaced Alice's padlock with his own, only to intercept the return package and open the box. The authenticity of a public key is determined using an "identity certificate."

When speaking of Internet security, an "identity certificate" is an electronic document originating from a trusted source that vouches for the authenticity of a public key. The source from which the certificate originates is known as the certificate authority (CA), and there are a handful of such bodies in business around the world today. CACert, Thawte, and VeriSign are three popular CAs. To bring the matter back to Web applications, servers and clients may possess their own public keys, and identity certificates to vouch for them, to encrypt all the traffic between client and server. Because Web applications are by nature interactive, clients must authenticate themselves to servers as well as servers to clients. This is known as two-way authentication and is the standard practice when using client certificate authentication. Once the certificates have been authenticated, the public keys are used to establish a secure transport connection, such as with the Secure Sockets Layer (SSL). Whenever you see a URL that begins with **https:**, you're using SSL.

To enable client certificate authentication, you need to put the following in your **loginconfig** element:

```
<login-method>
  <auth-method>CLIENT-CERT</auth-method>
  <realm-name>admin-realm</realm-name>
</login-method>
```

Unfortunately, this is where the standardization ends. Please consult your container's documentation for how to complete the implementation of client certificate authentication.

Container-Managed Authorization and the Concept of Roles

Now that we have discussed how users prove their identities to the Web application, let's examine how the Web application designer can restrict access to various parts of the application. The **<security-constraint>** element in the **web.xml** file is used to provide this feature.

```
<?xml version="1.0" encoding="UTF-8"?>
<web-app version="3.0" xmlns="http://java.sun.com/xml/ns/javaee"
  xmlns:xsi="http://www.w3.org/2001/XMLSchema-instance"
  xsi:schemaLocation="http://java.sun.com/xml/ns/javaee
                      http://java.sun.com/xml/ns/javaee/web-app_3_0.xsd">
  <!-- context-params and Faces Servlet mappings omitted for brevity. -->
  <welcome-file-list>
    <welcome-file>faces/user/userPage.xhtml</welcome-file>
  </welcome-file-list>
  <security-constraint>
    <web-resource-collection>
      <web-resource-name>trainer pages</web-resource-name>
      <url-pattern>/trainer/*</url-pattern>
    </web-resource-collection>
    <auth-constraint>
      <role-name>trainer</role-name>
    </auth-constraint>
  </security-constraint>
```

PART II

```
  <security-constraint>
    <web-resource-collection>
      <web-resource-name>user pages</web-resource-name>
      <url-pattern>/user/*</url-pattern>
    </web-resource-collection>
    <auth-constraint>
      <role-name>user</role-name>
    </auth-constraint>
  </security-constraint>
  <login-config>
    <auth-method>FORM</auth-method>
    <realm-name>file</realm-name>
    <form-login-config>
      <form-login-page>/faces/login.xhtml</form-login-page>
      <form-error-page>/faces/loginError.xhtml</form-error-page>
    </form-login-config>
  </login-config>
</web-app>
```

The preceding XML states the following about the application. This Web application may have zero or more security constraints. Each security constraint contains zero or more collections of pages, and access to any of the pages is predicated on the user being a member of the specified role. A user's membership in a role is determined using some form of authentication method. The previous **web.xml** excerpt says, "Users that try to access any page inside of the top-level **trainer** directory must be authenticated using form-based authentication, with the authentication database being provided by the container-specific **file** realm. Once authenticated, they must be a member of the **trainer** group in order to be allowed to see the page." Each of the elements related to authorization in **<security-constraint>** is described in Table 14-2.

You may ask, if the only interesting element inside of **<auth-constraint>** is **<role-name>**, why do we need the **<auth-constraint>** element? This is to distinguish the role from the **<user-data-constraint>** element, which dictates which transport-level security is to be used to protect the resources in the collection. More on **<user-data-constraint>** in the next section.

Container-Managed Data Security

The last aspect of Web application security is **Data Security**. Generally, this aspect builds on top of **authentication** and **authorization**, but this need not necessarily be the case. For example, any user may view the Web page for Sun's Mojarra on **java.net** at **https://javaserverfaces.dev.java.net/**, but in order to file issues in the issue tracker, or take any other actions, the user must have the appropriate authentication and authorization. As with all aspects of container-managed security, data security is configured using the **web.xml** file. Let's complete our example from the trainer by stating that all trainer pages be transmitted between server and client using data security.

```
<web-app>
  <!-- intervening elements omitted -->
  <security-constraint>
    <web-resource-collection>
      <web-resource-name>trainer modules</web-resource-name>
      <url-pattern>/trainer/*</url-pattern>
    </web-resource-collection>
```

```
    <auth-constraint>
      <role-name>trainer</role-name>
    </auth-constraint>
    <user-data-constraint>
      <transport-guarantee>CONFIDENTIAL</transport-guarantee>
    </user-data-constraint>
  </security-constraint>
  <login-config>
    <auth-method>BASIC</auth-method>
    <realm-name>form</realm-name>
  </login-config>
  <!-- intervening elements omitted -->
</web-app>
```


Element Name	Contained in Element	Description
web-resource-collection	security-constraint	A collection of content in your Web application. Typically, this means a collection of JSP pages and the images, scripts, and other content used by those pages. You must have at least one **<web-resource-collection>** inside your **<security-constraint>** element.
web-resource-name	web-resource-collection	A human-readable name you can attach to the collection. There must be exactly one **<web-resource-name>** per **<security-constraint>** element.
url-pattern	web-resource-collection	A pseudo-regular-expression-style syntax for grouping pages together. Take, for example, the **url-pattern /admin/*includes** pages inside the **admin** directory. You can also use a file extension as a url-pattern—for example, **/*.xhtml** is a url-pattern that identifies all JSP files in the root directory of the Web application. There may be zero or more **<url-pattern>** elements in the **<web-resource-collection>** element. The absence of a **<url-pattern>** means the constraint doesn't apply to any resource.
auth-constraint	security-constraint	Contains zero or more **<role-name>** elements. If any of the elements is the asterisk character (*), all users are granted access to the resources defined in the **<web-resource-collection>**.
role-name	auth-constraint	The name of a role defined in a container-specific fashion, for example, in elements in the **tomcat-users.xml** file as described earlier.

Table 14-2 Elements in **<security-constraint>**

The only new element here is **<user-data-constraint>**, with its child **<transport-guarantee>**. Valid values for **<transport-guarantee>** are **NONE, INTEGRAL,** and **CONFIDENTIAL**. Generally, the latter two imply SSL. In order to use SSL on your server, you must give it an identity certificate and public/private key pair (described earlier in the section titled "Certificate Authentication") using container-specific techniques.

A Small Security Improvement in the Virtual Trainer

Now that you understand container-managed security, let's look at a simple example that shows how to integrate it into your application. Recall the four security methods on **HttpServletRequest** from Table 14-1: **getAuthType( )**, **getRemoteUser( )**, **getUserPrincipal( )**, and **isUserInRole(String *role*)**. Let's take the common example of showing or hiding content on the page based on whether or not the user is in a certain role. In the Virtual Trainer application, let's say we want to provide an "edit" link for the list of events only if the user is in the "trainer" role. The easiest way to do this is to provide a Boolean read-only JavaBeans property in a request-scoped managed bean that uses the **isUserInRole( )** method of the Servlet API. For example, consider the **isUserIsTrainer( )** method shown next:

```
public boolean isUserIsTrainer( ) {
  FacesContext context = FacesContext.getCurrentInstance();
  Object request = context.getExternalContext().getRequest();
  boolean result = false;
  if (request instanceof HttpServletRequest) {
    result = (HttpServletRequest)request).isUserInRole("trainer");
  }
  else if (request instanceof PortletRequest) {
    result = ((PortletRequest)request).isUserInRole("trainer");
  }
  return result;
}
```

Notice that we are taking care to consider that this application may run in a Portlet environment. The **ExternalContext** class is intended to handle this for you by wrapping commonly used methods.

Once you have the **userIsTrainer** JavaBeans property, you can access it via the EL as the value of the **rendered** attribute to show or hide parts of the page:

```
<h:dataTable value="#{events.data}" var="event">
  <h:column>
    <h:outputText value="#{event.name}" />
  </h:column>
  <h:column rendered="#{user.userIsTrainer}">
    <h:commandLink action="editEvent" />
  </h:column>
</h:dataTable>
```

Note that we had to name the method **isUserIsTrainer** in order to be able to refer to it as **#{user.userIsTrainer}** from the EL. This is because of JavaBeans naming conventions. Specifically, for Boolean properties the leading "is" in the method name is omitted.

Application-Managed Security with JavaServer Faces

Container-managed security provides several advantages over application-managed security. Perhaps the two most important are convenience and peace of mind. The convenience comes from just using what the specifications and containers provide. The peace of mind comes from using features that have been implemented by security professionals and vetted by the competitive marketplace. However, if the constraints of container-managed security don't fit your customer's requirements, or if you are simply the type of person who likes to control all the variables yourself, application-managed security is for you. Obviously, it is possible and advisable to build your application-managed security solution on top of existing container-managed facilities.

The application-managed security implementation in Chapter 10, where the **preRenderView** event is used to prevent unauthenticated and unauthorized access to the application, and to specific pages within the application, is a fine example of application-managed security. One possible improvement would be to make it tie in to the container-managed security for login and logout. Such an example is beyond the scope of this chapter.

Leveraging JAAS from a JSF Application

We will conclude this chapter by showing how to enhance the Virtual Trainer example by leveraging the standard security infrastructure of the Java platform. From its inception, the Java platform has treated security as a first-class concern. Indeed, one of the first benefits of Java was to securely bring dynamic behavior to Web-deployed applications. Over the years, the implementation and API to security has evolved, but the core principals have improved and become steadily more secure. Therefore, choosing to build your application-managed security on top of the standard Java security features is a very safe bet.

A term often applied to Java security is JAAS, which is short for Java Authentication and Authorization Service. JAAS started out as an optional package in JDK 1.3 but has become a core part of the Java platform as of JDK 1.4. As the name implies, JAAS covers the first two of the three main aspects of security: authentication and authorization. Let's explore one way to integrate JAAS-style authentication and authorization into the Virtual Trainer application.

Using JAAS Authentication in the Virtual Trainer

While it would certainly be possible to call into the JAAS layer directly from the Virtual Trainer's application logic—for example, from the **UserRegistry** bean—a more reusable solution is to encapsulate the JAAS interface in a custom **ActionListener**. This approach decouples the security completely from your application and takes advantage of the intended use of the **ActionListener** extension hook.

The mechanics of providing such an **ActionListener** are described in Chapter 12, but let's review them briefly here. The first step is to modify the **faces-config.xml** file for the **trainercomponents** reusable component library so that it includes the **action-listener** declaration, as shown next.

```
<application>
  <action-listener>
    com.jsfcompref.trainercomponents.util.JAASActionListener
  </action-listener>
</application>
```

Then, leverage the decorator pattern, as described in Chapter 12, to delegate most of the work to the "real" **ActionListener** by providing a constructor that saves a reference to it. Following the constructor, the **processAction( )** method must be implemented, as described in the following:

```
...
  private ActionListener parent = null;
  public void processAction(ActionEvent event)
    throws AbortProcessingException {
    FacesContext context = FacesContext.getCurrentInstance();
    ValueHolder comp = null;
    String userid = null, password = null;
    JAASHelper jaasHelper = new JAASHelper();
    // Check to see if they are on the login page.
    boolean onLoginPage = (-1 != context.getViewRoot().getViewId().
        lastIndexOf("login")) ? true : false;

    if (onLoginPage) {
      if (null != (comp = (ValueHolder)
        context.getViewRoot().findComponent("form:userid"))) {
        userid = (String) comp.getValue();
      }
      if (null != (comp = (ValueHolder)
        context.getViewRoot().findComponent("form:password"))) {
        password = (String) comp.getValue();
      }
      // If JAAS authentication failed
      if (!jaasHelper.authenticate(userid, password)) {
        context.getApplication().getNavigationHandler().
            handleNavigation(context, null, "login");
        return;
      } else {
        // Subject must not be null, since authentication succeeded
        assert(null != jaasHelper.getSubject());
        // Put the authenticated subject in the session.
        context.getExternalContext().getSessionMap().put(JAASSubject,
            jaasHelper.getSubject());
      }
    }
  }

  parent.processAction(event);
  // use JAAS to perform viewId level authorization
  // The ForcedLoginPhaseListener already forced the user to log in
  // before reaching this page.
  Subject subject = (Subject) context.getExternalContext().
      getSessionMap().get(JAASSubject);
  assert(null != subject);
  // If the user doesn't have permission to view this viewId
  if (!jaasHelper.hasPermissionToAccessViewId(subject, context.
      getViewRoot().getViewId())) {
    // Put error messages in the request
    Map requestMap = context.getExternalContext().getRequestMap();
    requestMap.put("userid", userid);
```

```
      requestMap.put("requiredPermission", "trainer");
      requestMap.put("viewId", context.getViewRoot().getViewId());
      // Redirect to the insufficientPermissions page
      context.getApplication().getNavigationHandler().
          handleNavigation(context, null, "insufficientPermissions");
    }
}
```

The first thing to note is that part of the usage contract for **JAASActionListener** is the requirement that the username and password components be nested inside a **UIForm** named "form" and be named "userid" and "password", respectively. This expedient measure allows the **JAASActionListener** to easily extract the user-provided values for username and password so that they can be passed on to the **JAASHelper** class. The second thing to note about the usage contract is the requirement that the application provide a navigation rule for the outcome "login" that causes the user to be directed to the login page if the authentication failed. In the failure case, **processAction( )** is not called until after redirecting to the "login" outcome using **NavigationHandler**. If authentication succeeded, the **Subject** is stored in the session for later access. The **java.security.Subject** is the Java class that represents the user to the runtime. (We'll cover **Subject** in greater detail in the section on JAAS authentication.) Finally, the parent **processAction( )** method is called to do the normal action handling. Note that this causes the existing application-managed authentication, as described in Chapter 9, to take place. A production-quality implementation would probably remove the application-managed authentication in favor of using JAAS, rather than just supplementing it, as we have done here.

Let's examine the **JAASHelper** class.

```
public class JAASHelper {
  LoginContext loginContext = null;
  public JAASHelper() {
  }
  public boolean authenticate(String userid, String password) {
    boolean result = false;
    try {
      loginContext = new LoginContext("FileLogin",
          new LoginCallback(userid, password));
      loginContext.login();
      result = true;
   }
   catch (LoginException e) {
     // A production-quality implementation would log this message
     result = false;
   }
   return result;
}

public Subject getSubject () {
  Subject result = null;
  if (null != loginContext) {
    result = loginContext.getSubject();
  }
  return result;
}
```

PART II

```
public static class LoginCallback implements CallbackHandler {
  private String userName = null;
  private String password = null;

public LoginCallback(String userName, String password) {
  this.userName = userName;
  this.password = password;
}

public void handle(Callback[] callbacks) {
  for (int i = 0; i< callbacks.length; i++) {
    if (callbacks[i] instanceof NameCallback) {
      NameCallback nc = (NameCallback)callbacks[i];
      nc.setName(userName);
    } else if (callbacks[i] instanceof PasswordCallback) {
      PasswordCallback pc = (PasswordCallback)callbacks[i];
      pc.setPassword(password.toCharArray());
    }
   }
  }
 }
}
```

The **authenticate( )** method uses the class **java.security.auth.login.LoginContext** to perform the login. The **login( )** method of this class will throw a **LoginException** if the login fails for any reason. This exception is caught by **authenticate( )**, and it responds by setting **result** to **false**. If no exception is thrown, **result** is set to **true**. **authenticate( )** ends by returning the value of **result**.

The two arguments to the **LoginContext** constructor are the most important part of this example. The first, the literal string "FileLogin", refers to an implementation of the **javax .security.auth.spi.LoginModule** interface. This interface is implemented by a provider of a particular implementation of authentication technology—for example, JNDI, LDAP, or database. In this example, we use a free software implementation called "tagish" that provides a simple file-based authentication scheme. The implementation comes from John Gardner and can be found at **http://www.thekirschners.com/software/jass-login-modules/tagish-jaas-login-modules.html**. Providing a **LoginModule** implementation is beyond the scope of this chapter, but we must illustrate how to use one, once it has been provided. This is the beauty of JAAS—the authentication technology itself is separated from the rest of the system. In other words, if you want to plug in LDAP, do it by providing a custom **LoginModule**.

The JVM is made aware of the existence of a **LoginModule** implementation either through a **-D** flag or via a modification to the **JAVA_HOME/jre/lib/java.security** file. In our case, we use the former option:

```
-Djava.security.auth.login.config==
<absolute-file-path>/tagish.login
```

Note the use of forward slashes instead of the standard Windows backslashes. Also note the "= =" instead of just one "=". The format of this file is prescribed by JAAS:

```
FileLogin
{
  com.tagish.auth.FileLogin required
pwdFile="<absolute-file-path>passwd";
};
```

The **FileLogin** identifier must match the argument to the **LoginContext** constructor. The first element inside the **FileLogin** declaration is the fully qualified class name of the class implementing **LoginModule**. In our application, we have bundled **tagish.jar**, which contains this class, into the **WEB-INF/lib** directory of the application. The **required** flag tells the system that the login must succeed; and whether it succeeds or fails, the login must still proceed down the **LoginModule** chain. Other valid values for this flag are **requisite**, **sufficient**, and **optional**; they are described in the Javadocs for the class **javax.security.auth.login.Configuration**. The **pwdFile** argument is an implementation-specific parameter to the code in **tagish.jar** that tells it where to find its password file. The format of this file is also implementation-specific; for the trainer application, it looks like

```
username:MD5 Hash Of Password:group*
```

The specific file for the Virtual Trainer follows:

```
# Passwords for com.tagish.auth.FileLogin
jfitness:5a64edabc9358c603103053a3c600a88:user
stiger:40be4e59b9a2a2b5dffb918c0e86b3d7:user
guest:084e0343a0486ff05530df6c705c8bb4:user
jake:1200cf8ad328a60559cf5e7c5f46ee6d:user:trainer
```

Obviously, a simple MD5 hash of the password is not at all secure and a production-quality implementation would use an actual encryption algorithm. For the purposes of security, MD5 is just as secure as Base64 encoding, described earlier in the chapter, which is to say, not at all secure. A handy MD5 hash calculator can be found at **http://bfl.rctek.com/tools/?tool=hasher**. Note that user **jake** is a member of the **user** and **trainer** groups, while all the other users are simply members of the **user** group. Groups will come into play in the next section.

The second argument to the **LoginContext** constructor is an implementation of the **javax.security.auth.callback.CallbackHandler** interface. The **LoginCallback** implementation saves the username and password ultimately originating from the **userid** and **password** components in its constructor and uses standard boilerplate code to propagate them to the JAAS system.

Using JAAS Authorization in the Virtual Trainer

A detailed review of JAAS authorization is beyond the scope of this book, but we will show just enough to get you started. These classes are displayed in Figure 14-3. After authentication, the logged-in user is associated with an instance of **Subject.** As shown in the preceding section, the **Subject** is stored in the session for easy access elsewhere in the application. A **Subject** has a set of **Principal**s, otherwise known as groups. Each **Principal** has zero or more **Permission**s associated with it that govern what a **Subject** with that **Principal** is allowed to do. In the Virtual Trainer example, the subject **jake** has the **user** and **trainer** principals. Users with the **trainer** principal are allowed to access pages that normal users may not access.

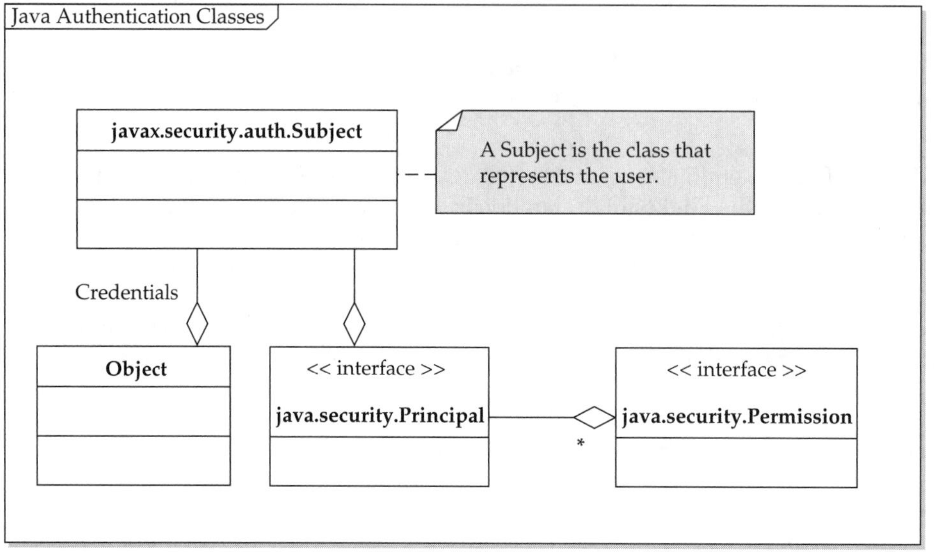

Figure 14-3 Java authorization classes

Subject instances can also have **Credential**s associated with them for things such as public/private key pairs for a public key infrastructure, or certificates for certificate-based authentication.

The **tagish** library provides an implementation of **Principal** sufficient for our needs in the form of the **com.tagish.auth.TypedPrincipal** class. The Java platform provides a concrete **BasicPermission** class that applications can extend to define their own subclass. In our case, we define **ViewIdPermission** to represent permission to access a given view ID.

A production-quality implementation will want to extend **Permission** directly and provide robust behavior for view ID pattern matching. The listing for **ViewIdPermission** follows.

```
public class ViewIdPermission extends BasicPermission {
  public ViewIdPermission(String viewId) {
    super(viewId);
  }

  public ViewIdPermission(String viewId, String actions) {
    super(viewId, actions);
  }
}
```

You can see that this subclass adds no value over the **BasicPermission** class; it is included here mainly to show where a production implementation would extend.

The valid principal types, and the permissions each one has, are defined in a policy file declared to the VM in a similar manner to the way the login configuration was declared earlier, via a **-D** option, or via modifying the **java.security** file. As in the preceding section, we choose the former option.

```
-Djava.security.auth.policy==
<absolute-path>/web/WEB-INF/trainer.policy
```

The format of the file is defined by JAAS:

```
grant Principal com.tagish.auth.TypedPrincipal "trainer" {
  permission
com.jsfcompref.trainercomponents.util.ViewIdPermission "*";
};
grant Principal com.tagish.auth.TypedPrincipal "user" {
  permission
com.jsfcompref.trainercomponents.util.ViewIdPermission "/main.xhtml";
};
```

The preceding policy file defines two **Principal**s, "trainer" and "user", and grants some **ViewIdPermission**s to each. The trainer is allowed to access any view ID as indicated by the "*" declaration. The user is only allowed to access the "/main.xhtml" view ID. Note that we don't need to list the login and logout view IDs because they are explicitly excluded from the authorization scheme by the **JAASActionListener** implementation. The limitation of our simple **ViewIdPermission** implementation is evident here because we have to modify this policy file to explicitly grant the "user" access to any view IDs they must view.

Once the **Principal**s and **Permission**s have been defined and declared, the **JAASActionListener** and **JAASHelper** classes must be extended to use them. First, let's rewrite the **processAction( )** method to include this feature.

```
public void processAction(ActionEvent event)
  throws AbortProcessingException {
  FacesContext context = FacesContext.getCurrentInstance();
  UIOutput comp = null;
  String userid = null, password = null;
  JAASHelper jaasHelper = new JAASHelper();

  // Check to see if they are on the login page.
  boolean onLoginPage = (-1 != context.getViewRoot().getViewId().
      lastIndexOf("login")) ? true : false;
  if (onLoginPage) {
    if (null != (comp = (UIOutput)
      context.getViewRoot().findComponent("form:userid"))) {
      userid = (String) comp.getValue();
    }
    if (null != (comp = (UIOutput)
      context.getViewRoot().findComponent("form:password"))) {
      password = (String) comp.getValue();
    }
    // If JAAS authentication failed
    if (!jaasHelper.authenticate(userid, password)) {
      context.getApplication().getNavigationHandler().
          handleNavigation(context, null, "login");
      return;
    }
    else {
      // Subject must not be null, since authentication succeeded
      assert(null != jaasHelper.getSubject());
      // Put the authenticated subject in the session.
      context.getExternalContext().getSessionMap().put(JAASSubject,
```

PART II

```
          jaasHelper.getSubject());
      }
  }

  parent.processAction(event);
  // use JAAS to perform viewId level authorization
  // The ForcedLoginPhaseListener already forced the user to log in
  // before reaching this page.
  Subject subject = (Subject) context.getExternalContext().
      getSessionMap().get(JAASSubject);
  assert(null != subject);

  // If the user doesn't have permission to view this viewId
  if (!jaasHelper.hasPermissionToAccessViewId(subject, context.
      getViewRoot().getViewId())) {
    // Redirect to the insufficientPermissions page
    context.getApplication().getNavigationHandler().
        handleNavigation(context, null, "insufficientPermissions");
  }
}
```

The first part of the method is unchanged from the previous section. We have added code after the **parent.processAction(event)** call to handle authorization. First, the **Subject** is retrieved from the session. Then, the static **hasPermissionToAccessViewId( )** method is called on **JAASHelper**, passing the **Subject** and the view ID. If **hasPermissionToAccessViewId( )** returns false, we navigate to the "insufficientPermissions" outcome using the **handleNavigation( )** method of **NavigationHandler**. Note that the last argument to the **handleNavigation( )** is hard-coded to the value "insufficientPermissions". This constitutes an implicit usage contract requirement in the necessity of the user to declare an **insufficientPermissions navigation-rule outcome** and associated JSP page to show when the user doesn't have permission to access the given view ID. Let's now examine the implementation of **hasPermissionToAccessViewId( )**.

```
public static boolean hasPermissionToAccessViewId(Subject subject,
                                                  String viewId) {
  boolean result = true;
  final Permission perm = new ViewIdPermission(viewId);
  final SecurityManager sm;

  if (System.getSecurityManager() == null) {
    sm = new SecurityManager();
  } else {
    sm = System.getSecurityManager();
  }
  try {
    Subject.doAsPrivileged(subject, new PrivilegedExceptionAction() {
      public Object run() {
        sm.checkPermission(perm);
        return null;
      }
    },null);
    result = true;
  } catch (AccessControlException ace) {
```

```
      result = false;
    } catch (PrivilegedActionException pae) {
      result = false;
    }
      return result;
}
```

This standard code obtains or creates a **SecurityManager** for use later in the method. It then calls the static **doAsPrivileged( )** method, passing the argument **Subject** and an inner class **PrivilegedExceptionAction** subclass that asks the **SecurityManager** if the currently executing code has the argument **Permission**. If the code does not have the permission, either an **AccessControlException** or **PrivilegedActionException** will be thrown, in which case it returns false from **hasPermissionToAccessViewId( )**. Otherwise, it returns **true**.

To Learn More about Security

As mentioned at the beginning of the chapter, computer/network security is a very large topic. This book covers only the part that relates to JSF. Those readers who are interested in gaining broader knowledge of the subject should read *Hacking Exposed, Sixth Edition* (McGraw-Hill, 2009) by Stuart McClure et al.

III

PART

JavaServer Faces Tools and Libraries

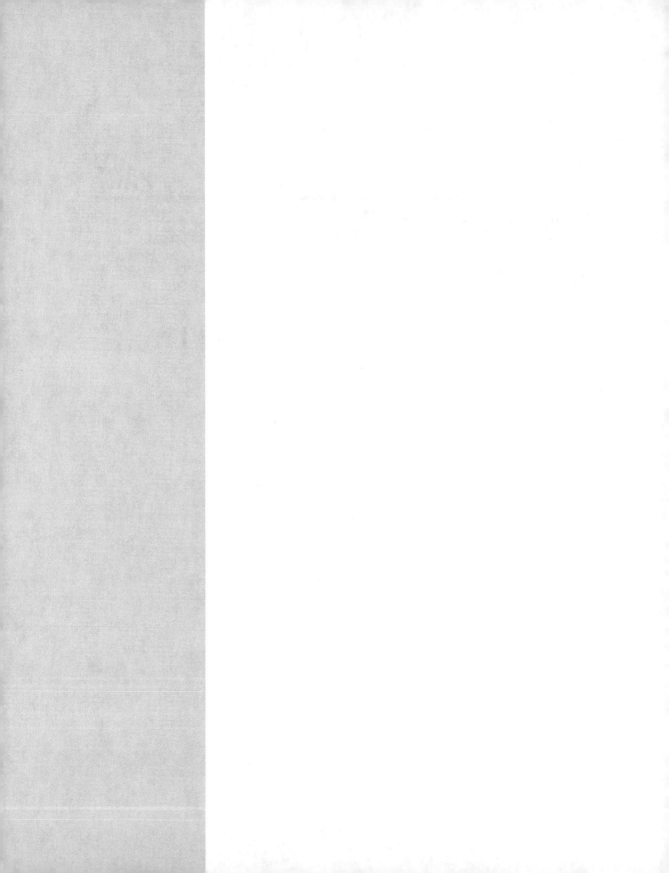

15

CHAPTER

Configuring JavaServer Faces Applications

Most server-side software technologies, Java or otherwise, require some kind of "configuration code" in addition to the actual application code. In the Java world, this configuration code is frequently written in an external XML file. One benefit of this approach is that configuration changes can be accomplished without having to recompile Java code. Another benefit is that it provides a central location for application configuration. For example, this can be especially helpful to developers who need to get an overview of managed bean interdependence within the application.

In the JavaServer Faces 2.0 release, Java annotations can be used as an alternate (or complimentary) configuration approach, entirely eliminating XML configuration code. This is the recommend approach for JSF applications. The benefit of this approach is that annotations can be used to eliminate some or all of the XML. Also, coming back to the lessons from Ruby on Rails, you get the benefits of a "Don't Repeat Yourself" design. The act of placing an annotation on a Java class makes an explicit link between the annotation and the class. In XML, this would have to be done with a separate XML element listing the fully qualified class name of the Java class, which has already been written in the Java source file. The drawback of using annotations is that changes to annotations will require the recompilation of Java code. Although this chapter focuses mostly on the XML configuration approach, annotation equivalents to XML elements are listed wherever they exist.

Upon application startup, JavaServer Faces loads its configuration file(s), if any, and scans all compiled classes for annotations. It then creates a series of configuration objects that correspond to the discovered settings. JavaServer Faces then uses those configuration objects to guide its behavior.

If present, the JavaServer Faces configuration file is XML-based and its format is governed by either a Document Type Definition (DTD) file or an XML schema file, depending on the version of JSF in use. JSF versions 1.0 and 1.1 use a DTD to govern the format of their configuration files; versions 1.2 and later use an XML schema. The DTDs and XML schema specify how the configuration elements must be ordered in the file, what settings are required, and so on. Each JSF configuration file declares its conformance to a DTD or XML schema by having either a **DOCTYPE** definition or an XML schema definition at the top of the file.

Following is the **DOCTYPE** definition for JSF version 1.0 configuration files that makes use of the 1.0 DTD:

```
<!DOCTYPE faces-config PUBLIC
  "-//Sun Microsystems, Inc.//DTD JavaServer Faces Config 1.0//EN"
  "http://java.sun.com/dtd/web-facesconfig_1_0.dtd">
<faces-config>
  <!-- Configuration file contents go here. -->
</faces-config>
```

Next is the **DOCTYPE** definition for JSF version 1.1 configuration files:

```
<!DOCTYPE faces-config PUBLIC
  "-//Sun Microsystems, Inc.//DTD JavaServer Faces Config 1.1//EN"
  "http://java.sun.com/dtd/web-facesconfig_1_1.dtd">
<faces-config>
  <!-- Configuration file contents go here. -->
</faces-config>
```

The definition shown next specifies the XML schema for JSF version 1.2 configuration files:

```
<faces-config xmlns="http://java.sun.com/xml/ns/javaee"
  xmlns:xsi="http://www.w3.org/2001/XMLSchema-instance"
  xsi:schemaLocation=
"http://java.sun.com/xml/ns/javaee/web-facesconfig_1_2.xsd"
  version="1.2">
  <!-- Configuration file contents go here. -->
</faces-config>
```

Finally, the following definition specifies the XML schema for JSF version 2.0 configuration files:

```
<faces-config xmlns="http://java.sun.com/xml/ns/javaee"
  xmlns:xsi="http://www.w3.org/2001/XMLSchema-instance"
  xsi:schemaLocation=
"http://java.sun.com/xml/ns/javaee/web-facesconfig_2_0.xsd"
  version="2.0">
  <!-- Configuration file contents go here. -->
</faces-config>
```

Notice that for XML schema there is no **DOCTYPE** declaration. The XML schema being used is defined via the **xmlns:xsi** and **xsi:schemaLocation** attributes of the root element (**<faces-config>**) of the configuration file. Also note that all of the other Java EE config files, such as **web.xml**, and Tag Library Descriptors (TLDs) are now governed by XML schema instead of DTDs as of Java EE version 5.

When JSF reads a configuration file, its XML parser uses the **DOCTYPE** definition to determine the DTD or schema with which the XML file must conform. If configured to do so, the XML parser will validate the XML file's conformance to the DTD or XML schema and prevent application startup if an error occurs, such as out of order elements, or poorly formed XML markup.

Understanding XML Schemas

XML Schema was developed by W3C and made an official recommendation in 2001. XML Schema was developed to solve some problems with DTDs, such as providing an XML syntax for describing the document itself, rather than the different, non-XML notation of the DTD, and providing a way to associate concrete data types with markup elements. Unfortunately, W3C XML Schema ended up being very obtuse and difficult to understand, and went way beyond solving just these problems. Nevertheless, it is the standard chosen for describing XML documents in Java EE 5, so it's important to understand how it works. Thankfully, most modern IDEs, including NetBeans, have support for visual editing of XML schema files.

XML schemas specify a set of elements and attributes that make up a specific XML document type along with specifying the order in which elements must be placed in the file, and the relationship between elements. Additionally, XML schemas define which element attributes are required and which are optional. The main difference between a DTD and an XML schema is that XML schemas are themselves XML documents. Because of this, XML schemas offer a much richer format for defining an XML document type. This allows for a more specific definition of the format that an XML document type must have.

Understanding How Configuration Files Are Processed

At Web application startup, JSF implementations use a standardized algorithm for locating and loading configuration files. The locating and loading of configuration files is completed before any requests can be processed by the Web application. If any of the configuration files being loaded causes an XML parsing error, the application startup process will be aborted and the application will not be accessible.

Following is the process and order in which configuration files are located and loaded:

- Check for the existence of a **/META-INF/faces-config.xml** file in each **.jar** file accessible by the servlet context class loader and load it if it exists. JSF 2.0 also will load any file in META-INF that ends in .faces-config.xml, for example **META-INF/my.faces-config.xml**. This means all **.jar** files in the **WEB-INF/lib** directory will be scanned, and this is how custom JSF components can declare themselves to the JSF runtime. (See Chapter 10 for more on building a self-contained JSF component library jar.) The "drop your jar into **WEB-INF/lib** and it will automatically be configured and loaded" feature has been a part of JSF since its first release.
- Check for the existence of a **javax.faces.CONFIG_FILES** context parameter in the application's **web.xml** deployment descriptor and, if it exists, load the list of comma-delimited files it specifies. The following example configuration file illustrates the use of the **javax.faces.CONFIG_FILES** context parameter:

```
<!DOCTYPE web-app PUBLIC
  "-//Sun Microsystems, Inc.//DTD Web Application 2.3//EN"
  "http://java.sun.com/dtd/web-app_2_3.dtd">
<web-app>
    <display-name>Example</display-name>
    <description>Example Application</description>
    <context-param>
      <param-name>javax.faces.CONFIG_FILES</param-name>
      <param-value>
```

```
        /WEB-INF/test1-faces-config.xml,
        /WEB-INF/test2-faces-config.xml,
        /WEB-INF/test3-faces-config.xml
      </param-value>
    </context-param>
    <servlet>
      <servlet-name>Faces Servlet</servlet-name>
      <servlet-class>javax.faces.webapp.FacesServlet</servlet-class>
      <load-on-startup>1</load-on-startup>
    </servlet>
    <servlet-mapping>
      <servlet-name>Faces Servlet</servlet-name>
      <url-pattern>*.faces</url-pattern>
    </servlet-mapping>
</web-app>
```

Note that the JSF Configuration files listed in the **param-value** element can be located anywhere in the Web application; they are not required to be underneath the **WEB-INF** directory. It is just a useful convention to put such things in the **WEB-INF** directory. Also, the files can be named anything you choose; they need not be named **faces-config.xml**.

- Check for the existence of a **/WEB-INF/faces-config.xml** file and load it if it exists.

Ordering of faces-config.xml Files

One unfortunate side-effect of the practice of scanning all jar files in **WEB-INF/lib** for configuration files is the unpredictability of the ordering in which these files are processed. The Sun JavaVM will process the files according to the alphabetical order of the filename, but this is not guaranteed by the Java Language Specification and is therefore not reliable. In most cases, the order in which the **faces-config.xml** files within jar files are processed by the runtime is not important, but in some cases it is *very* important. As shown in Chapter 13, much of the core JSF runtime can be replaced or decorated, and frequently this decoration is done using a "chain of responsibility" pattern. In such cases, it is possible for multiple jar files to conflict with each other, for example, if both jar files contain a **FacesContextFactory** decorator that wants to be at the front of the chain. JSF 2.0 introduces a facility to declare the relative and absolute ordering of **faces-config.xml** files to solve these kinds of problems.

Following is a description of the new **absolute-ordering** and **ordering** features as of JavaServer Faces 2.0. An example of these elements in action is provided later in the chapter.

- The optional **name** element can be used to declare the name of a JSF XML configuration file in case it needs to be loaded as part of an **absolute-ordering** or relative **ordering** scheme. An example will be shown in the section titled **The absolute-ordering Element**.
- If the **/WEB-INF/faces-config.xml** file specifies the optional **absolute-ordering** element, then the order in which JSF XML configuration files are loaded is dictated by the order in which child **name** elements appear. Settings found in named XML configuration files that occur later in the order will override settings in those found earlier in the order. If the **absolute-ordering** element contains an **others** child element, then any other XML configuration files that are not specified with **name**

elements will be loaded according to any relative **ordering** schemes (described in the section titled **The ordering Element**). If the **others** child element is not specified, then the other XML configuration files will not be loaded.

- Any **/META-INF/faces-config.xml** files found in jars, or those specified in **javax.faces.CONFIG_FILES**, may specify an optional **ordering** element that can be used to specify ordering relative to other named JSF XML configuration files. If the **ordering** element is specified, then it must have a **before** child element and/or an **after** child element.

How the JSF Runtime Scans Classes for Configuration Annotations

Following is a description of the new Java EE 5 annotation scanning features in JavaServer Faces 2.0.

- If a value of "true" is specified for the **metadata-complete** attribute of **/WEB-INF/faces-config.xml**, then annotation scanning will not be performed.
- Otherwise, all classes found in **/WEB-INF/classes** will be scanned for JSF-related annotations, as well as all jar files in the **/WEB-INF/lib** directory, providing that the jar contains a **/META-INF/faces-config.xml** file or a file that ends with **faces-config.xml**. For example, if the jar contained the file **/META-INF/my-special-faces-config.xml**, it would be found.
- Note that if there is a conflict between an entry within the XML configuration and a discovered annotation, then the XML configuration will take precedence.

PART III

The Faces Configuration Elements

Table 15-1 lists and describes each of the elements used to configure the JSF runtime. Additionally, the table specifies the cardinality (or number of times an element must be nested inside its parent element) for each element and the versions of JSF configuration files the elements apply to.

Element	Description	Cardinality	JSF Versions
absolute-ordering	Encapsulates the set of elements that specify the absolute order by which named JSF XML configuration files are to be loaded.	Zero or once	2.0
action-listener	Specifies the fully qualified class name of a **javax.faces.event.ActionListener** implementation class that will replace the JSF implementation's default action listener implementation.	Zero to unlimited	1.0, 1.1, 1.2, 2.0
after	Specifies that the containing JSF XML configuration file is to be loaded as part of the relative **ordering** scheme **after** the JSF XML configuration file(s) specified in the nested child elements are loaded.	Zero or once	2.0

Table 15-1 The Complete List of Elements of the JSF Configuration File *(continued)*

Element	Description	Cardinality	JSF Versions
application	Encapsulates the set of elements that specify application configuration details. All of the subelements of this element are used for replacing or decorating per-application singleton classes, such as the **ViewHandler** or the **NavigationHandler**.	Zero to unlimited	1.0, 1.1, 1.2, 2.0
application-extension	Encapsulates any elements specific to a JSF implementation for the **application** element. See the section "Extension Elements."	Zero to unlimited	1.2, 2.0
application-factory	Specifies the fully qualified class name of a **javax.faces.application.ApplicationFactory** implementation class that will replace the JSF implementation's default application factory implementation.	Zero to unlimited	1.0, 1.1, 1.2, 2.0
attribute	Encapsulates the set of elements used to specify the details for an attribute.	Zero to unlimited	1.0, 1.1, 1.2, 2.0
attribute-class	Specifies the fully qualified class name for an attribute's value.	Once	1.0, 1.1, 1.2, 2.0
attribute-extension	Encapsulates any elements specific to a JSF implementation for a given **attribute** element. See the section "Extension Elements."	Zero to unlimited	1.0, 1.1, 1.2, 2.0
attribute-name	Specifies the logical name for an attribute under which the attribute's value will be stored.	Once	1.0, 1.1, 1.2, 2.0
base-name	Specifies the fully qualified class name of a **javax.util.ResourceBundle** instance that will be registered with the JSF application with a logical name specified by an associated **var** element.	Once	1.2, 2.0
before	Specifies that the containing JSF XML configuration file is to be loaded as part of the relative **ordering** scheme **before** the JSF XML configuration file(s) specified in the nested child elements are loaded.	Zero or once	2.0
behavior	Encapsulates the set of elements that specify a behavior, which can be attached to a UI Component in order to provide additional functionality to the component.	Zero to unlimited	2.0
behavior-class	Specifies the fully qualified class name of a **javax.faces.component.behavior.Behavior** implementation class.	Once	2.0
behavior-extension	Encapsulates any elements specific to the JSF implementation for a given **behavior** element. See the section "Extension Elements."	Once	2.0

TABLE 15-1 The Complete List of Elements of the JSF Configuration File *(continued)*

Element	Description	Cardinality	JSF Versions
behavior-id	Specifies the logical name for the behavior.	Once	2.0
client-behavior-renderer	Encapsulates the set of elements that specify a client behavior renderer, which manifests itself in the form of script content on the client.	Zero to unlimited	2.0
client-behavior-renderer-class	Specifies the fully qualified class name of a **javax.faces.render.ClientBehaviorRenderer** implementation for a given **client-behavior-renderer** element.	Once	2.0
client-behavior-renderer-type	Specifies the logical name of a **client-behavior-renderer**.	Once	2.0
component	Encapsulates the set of elements used to specify the details for a UI component.	Zero to unlimited	1.0, 1.1, 1.2, 2.0
component-class	Specifies the fully qualified class name for a UI component.	Once	1.0, 1.1, 1.2, 2.0
component-extension	Encapsulates any elements specific to a JSF implementation for a given **component** element. See the section "Extension Elements."	Zero to unlimited	1.0, 1.1, 1.2, 2.0
component-family	Specifies the component family to which a renderer will be linked.	Once	1.0, 1.1, 1.2, 2.0
component-type	Specifies the logical name for a UI component.	Once	1.0, 1.1, 1.2, 2.0
converter	Encapsulates the set of elements used to specify the details for a converter.	Zero to unlimited	1.0, 1.1, 1.2, 2.0
converter-class	Specifies the fully qualified class name for a converter implementation.	Once	1.0, 1.1, 1.2, 2.0
converter-extension	Encapsulates any elements specific to a JSF implementation for a given converter element. See the section "Extension Elements."	Zero to unlimited	1.2, 2.0
converter-for-class	Specifies the fully qualified class name with which a converter will be associated.	Once	1.0, 1.1, 1.2, 2.0
converter-id	Specifies the logical name for a converter.	Once	1.0, 1.1, 1.2, 2.0
default-locale	Specifies the default locale for the JSF application.	Zero or once	1.0, 1.1, 1.2, 2.0
default-render-kit-id	Specifies the logical name of a render kit that will replace the JSF implementation's default render kit.	Zero to unlimited	1.0, 1.1, 1.2, 2.0

TABLE 15-1 The Complete List of Elements of the JSF Configuration File *(continued)*

Element	Description	Cardinality	JSF Versions
default-validators	Encapsulates the set of validator-id elements that specify the validators that will be attached to every **EditableValueHolder** in every view of the application.	Zero or once	2.0
default-value	Specifies the default value for an attribute or a property.	Zero or once	1.0, 1.1, 1.2, 2.0
description	See the section "Metadata Elements."	Zero to unlimited	1.0, 1.1, 1.2, 2.0
display-name	See the section "Metadata Elements."	Zero to unlimited	1.0, 1.1, 1.2, 2.0
el-resolver	Specifies the fully qualified class name of a **javax.el.ELResolver** implementation class that will replace the JSF implementation's default expression language resolver implementation.	Zero to unlimited	1.2, 2.0
exception-handler-factory	Specifies the fully qualified class name of a **javax.faces.context.ExceptionHandlerFactory** implementation class that will replace or decorate the JSF implementation's default exception handler factory implementation.	Zero or once	2.0
external-context-factory	Specifies the fully qualified class name of a **javax.faces.context.ExternalContextFactory** implementation class that will replace or decorate the JSF implementation's default external context handler factory implementation.	Zero or once	2.0
faces-config	Is the root element for the JSF configuration file and thus encapsulates all other elements in the file.	Once	1.0, 1.1, 1.2, 2.0
faces-config-extension	Encapsulates any elements specific to a JSF implementation for the **faces-config** element. See the section "Extension Elements." *Note: This element was created to host application metadata that is global in scope.*	Zero to unlimited	1.2, 2.0
faces-context-factory	Specifies the fully qualified class name of a **javax .faces.context.ApplicationFactory** implementation class that will replace the JSF implementation's default faces context factory implementation.	Zero to unlimited	1.0, 1.1, 1.2, 2.0
facet	Encapsulates the set of elements used to specify the details for a facet.	Zero to unlimited	1.1, 1.2, 2.0
facet-extension	Encapsulates any elements specific to a JSF implementation for the **facet** element. See the section "Extension Elements."	Zero to unlimited	1.1, 1.2, 2.0

Table 15-1 The Complete List of Elements of the JSF Configuration File *(continued)*

Element	Description	Cardinality	JSF Versions
facet-name	Specifies the logical name for a facet.	Once	1.1, 1.2, 2.0
factory	Encapsulates the set of elements that specify factory configuration details.	Zero to unlimited	1.0, 1.1, 1.2, 2.0
factory-extension	Encapsulates any elements specific to the JSF implementation for the **factory** element. See the section "Extension Elements."	Zero to unlimited	1.2, 2.0
from-action	Specifies an action reference expression that must have been executed in order to have the associated navigation case selected.	Zero or once	1.0, 1.1, 1.2, 2.0
from-outcome	Specifies the logical outcome value that an action method must generate in order to have the associated navigation case selected.	Zero or once	1.0, 1.1, 1.2, 2.0
from-view-id	Specifies the view ID that a navigation rule applies to.	Zero or once	1.0, 1.1, 1.2, 2.0
icon	See the section "Metadata Elements."	Zero to unlimited	1.0, 1.1, 1.2, 2.0
if	Specifies an EL expression that must evaluate to a boolean value (true or false). If the value is true, then it will cause the parent **navigation-rule** to fire. It is valid to have EL here instead of a literal String.	Zero or once	2.0
key	Specifies the key for a map entry defined by the **map-entry** element.	Once	1.0, 1.1, 1.2, 2.0
key-class	Specifies the fully qualified class name of an object type that all keys will be converted to before being added to a map defined by a **map-entries** element.	Zero or once	1.0, 1.1, 1.2, 2.0
large-icon	See the section "Metadata Elements."	Zero or once	1.0, 1.1, 1.2, 2.0
lifecycle	Encapsulates the set of elements that specify lifecycle configuration details.	Zero to unlimited	1.0, 1.1, 1.2, 2.0
lifecycle-extension	Encapsulates any elements specific to a JSF implementation for the **lifecycle** element. See the section "Extension Elements."	Zero to unlimited	1.2, 2.0
lifecycle-factory	Specifies the fully qualified class name of a **javax.faces.lifecycle.ApplicationFactory** implementation class that will replace the JSF implementation's default lifecycle factory implementation.	Zero to unlimited	1.0, 1.1, 1.2, 2.0

Table 15-1 The Complete List of Elements of the JSF Configuration File *(continued)*

Element	Description	Cardinality	JSF Versions
list-entries	Encapsulates a list of values that will be used to populate a **java.util.List** instance or an array that will serve as the value for a managed property or to populate a managed bean that is itself an instance of **java.util.List**.	Once	1.0, 1.1, 1.2, 2.0
locale-config	Encapsulates the set of elements that specify the application's locale configuration details.	Zero to unlimited	1.0, 1.1, 1.2, 2.0
managed-bean	Encapsulates the set of elements used to specify the details for a managed bean.	Zero to unlimited	1.0, 1.1, 1.2, 2.0
managed-bean-class	Specifies the fully qualified class name for a managed bean.	Once	1.0, 1.1, 1.2, 2.0
managed-bean-extension	Encapsulates any elements specific to the JSF implementation for a given **managed-bean** element. See the section "Extension Elements."	Zero to unlimited	1.2, 2.0
managed-bean-name	Specifies the logical name for a managed bean.	Once	1.0, 1.1, 1.2, 2.0
managed-bean-scope	Specifies the Web application scope in which the managed bean will be stored when it is instantiated.	Once	1.0, 1.1, 1.2, 2.0
managed-property	Encapsulates the set of elements used to specify the details for a managed bean's property.	Zero to unlimited	1.0, 1.1, 1.2, 2.0
map-entries	Encapsulates a set of key-value pairs that will be used to populate a **java.util.Map** instance that will serve as the value for a managed property or to populate a managed bean that is itself an instance of **java.util.Map**.	Once	1.0, 1.1, 1.2, 2.0
map-entry	Encapsulates a key-value pair that makes up an entry for a map defined by a **map-entries** element.	Zero to unlimited	1.0, 1.1, 1.2, 2.0
message-bundle	Specifies the fully qualified base name of a resource bundle that will be used for the JSF application.	Zero to unlimited	1.0, 1.1, 1.2, 2.0
name	Specifies the name of a JSF XML configuration file in case it needs to be loaded as part of an **absolute-ordering** or relative **ordering** scheme. Can also be used to specify the name of a **view-param**.	Zero or once	2.0
navigation-case	Encapsulates the set of elements that specify navigation case configuration details.	Zero to unlimited	1.0, 1.1, 1.2, 2.0

TABLE 15-1 The Complete List of Elements of the JSF Configuration File *(continued)*

Element	Description	Cardinality	JSF Versions
navigation-handler	Specifies the fully qualified class name of a **javax.faces.application.NavigationHandler** implementation class that will replace the JSF implementation's default navigation handler implementation.	Zero to unlimited	1.0, 1.1, 1.2, 2.0
navigation-rule	Encapsulates the set of elements that specify navigation rule configuration details.	Zero to unlimited	1.0, 1.1, 1.2, 2.0
navigation-rule-extension	Encapsulates any elements specific to the JSF implementation for a given **navigation-rule** element. See the section "Extension Elements."	Zero to unlimited	1.2, 2.0
null-value	Indicates that the property defined by the enclosing element must be initialized to **null**.	Once	1.0, 1.1, 1.2, 2.0
ordering	Encapsulates the set of elements that specify the relative order by which named JSF XML configuration files are to be loaded.	Zero or once	2.0
others	Specifies that all other JSF XML configuration files are to be loaded as part of the parent **absolute-ordering** or relative **ordering** scheme.	Zero or once	2.0
partial-view-context-factory	Specifies the fully qualified class name of a **javax.faces.context.PartialViewContextFactory** implementation class that will replace or decorate the JSF implementation's default partial view context factory implementation.	Zero or once	2.0
phase-listener	Specifies the fully qualified class name of a **javax.faces.event.PhaseListener** implementation class that will be notified of all phase changes during the JSF request processing lifecycle.	Zero to unlimited	1.0, 1.1, 1.2, 2.0
property	Encapsulates the set of elements used to specify the details for a property.	Zero to unlimited	1.0, 1.1, 1.2, 2.0
property-class	Specifies the fully qualified class name for a property's value.	Zero or once	1.0, 1.1, 1.2, 2.0
property-extension	Encapsulates any elements specific to a JSF implementation for a given **property** element. See the section "Extension Elements."	Zero to unlimited	1.0, 1.1, 1.2, 2.0
property-name	Specifies the logical name for a property.	Once	1.0, 1.1, 1.2, 2.0
property-resolver	Specifies the fully qualified class name of a **javax.faces.el.PropertyResolver** implementation class that will replace the JSF implementation's default property resolver implementation.	Zero to unlimited	1.0, 1.1, 1.2, 2.0

TABLE 15-1 The Complete List of Elements of the JSF Configuration File *(continued)*

Element	Description	Cardinality	JSF Versions
redirect	Indicates that the associated navigation case to view ID URL should be navigated to using an HTTP redirect instead of the standard View Handler processing.	Zero or once	1.0, 1.1, 1.2, 2.0
referenced-bean	Encapsulates the set of elements used to specify the details for a referenced bean.	Zero to unlimited	1.0, 1.1, 1.2, 2.0
referenced-bean-class	Specifies the fully qualified class name of an external bean that is supposed to be available to the JSF application at runtime by existing in one of the Web application scopes (request, session, or application).	Once	1.0, 1.1, 1.2, 2.0
referenced-bean-name	Specifies the logical name for a referenced bean.	Once	1.0, 1.1, 1.2, 2.0
render-kit	Encapsulates the set of elements used to specify the details for a render kit.	Zero to unlimited	1.0, 1.1, 1.2, 2.0
render-kit-class	Specifies the fully qualified class name for a render kit implementation.	Zero or once	1.0, 1.1, 1.2, 2.0
render-kit-extension	Encapsulates any elements specific to a JSF implementation for the **render-kit** element. See the section "Extension Elements." *Note: This element was created to host metadata that applies to the entire render kit, not to just one renderer.*	Zero to unlimited	1.2, 2.0
render-kit-factory	Specifies the fully qualified class name of a **javax.faces.render.RenderKitFactory** implementation class that will replace the JSF implementation's default render kit factory implementation.	Zero to unlimited	1.0, 1.1, 1.2, 2.0
render-kit-id	Specifies the logical name for a render kit.	Zero or once	1.0, 1.1, 1.2, 2.0
renderer	Encapsulates the set of elements used to specify the details for a renderer.	Zero to unlimited	1.0, 1.1, 1.2, 2.0
renderer-class	Specifies the fully qualified class name for a renderer implementation.	Once	1.0, 1.1, 1.2, 2.0
renderer-extension	Encapsulates any elements specific to a JSF implementation for a given renderer element. See the section "Extension Elements."	Zero to unlimited	1.0, 1.1, 1.2, 2.0
renderer-type	Specifies the logical name for a renderer.	Once	1.0, 1.1, 1.2, 2.0
resource-bundle	Encapsulates the set of elements that specify resource bundle configuration details.	Zero to unlimited	1.2, 2.0

Table 15-1 The Complete List of Elements of the JSF Configuration File *(continued)*

Element	Description	Cardinality	JSF Versions
resource-handler	Specifies the fully qualified class name of a **javax.faces.application.ResourceHandler** implementation class that will replace the JSF implementation's default resource handler implementation.	Zero or once	2.0
source-class	Specifies the fully qualified class name of a **java.lang.Object** extended class of the instance that causes **system-event-class** to be fired.	Zero or once	2.0
small-icon	See the section "Metadata Elements."	Zero or once	1.0, 1.1, 1.2, 2.0
state-manager	Specifies the fully qualified class name of a **javax.faces.application.StateManager** implementation class that will replace the JSF implementation's default state manager implementation.	Zero or once	1.0, 1.1, 1.2, 2.0
suggested-value	Specifies the suggested value for an attribute or a property.	Zero or once	1.0, 1.1, 1.2, 2.0
supported-locale	Specifies a locale supported by the JSF application.	Zero to unlimited	1.0, 1.1, 1.2, 2.0
system-event-class	Specifies the fully qualified class name of a **javax.faces.event.SystemEvent** implementation class.	Once	2.0
system-event-listener	Encapsulates the set of elements used to specify the details for a listener that will be notified of application-scoped system events during the JSF request processing lifecycle.	Zero to unlimited	2.0
system-event-listener-class	Specifies the fully qualified class name of a **javax.faces.event.SystemEventListener** implementation class that will be notified of application-scoped system events.	Once	2.0
tag-handler-delegate-factory	Specifies the fully qualified class name of a **javax.faces.view.facelets.TagHandlerDelegateFactory** implementation class that will replace or decorate the JSF implementation's default tag handler delegate factory implementation.	Zero or once	2.0
to-view-id	Specifies the view ID for a view that will be displayed if the navigation case associated with that view ID is selected. In JSF 2.0, it is valid to have EL here, instead of a literal string value.	Once	1.0, 1.1, 1.2, 2.0
validator	Encapsulates the set of elements used to specify the details for a validator.	Zero to unlimited	1.0, 1.1, 1.2, 2.0
validator-class	Specifies the fully qualified class name for a validator.	Once	1.0, 1.1, 1.2, 2.0

Table 15-1 The Complete List of Elements of the JSF Configuration File *(continued)*

Element	Description	Cardinality	JSF Versions
validator-extension	Encapsulates any elements specific to a JSF implementation for a given validator element. See the section "Extension Elements."	Zero to unlimited	1.2, 2.0
validator-id	Specifies the logical name for a validator.	Once	1.0, 1.1, 1.2, 2.0
value	Specifies the literal value or value binding expression that generates a value for a list entry, managed property, or map entry.	Once	1.0, 1.1, 1.2, 2.0
value-class	Specifies the fully qualified class name of an object type that all values will be converted to before being added to a list defined by a **list-entries** element or a map defined by a **map-entries** element.	Zero or once	1.0, 1.1, 1.2, 2.0
var	Specifies the logical name for a resource bundle instance that will be registered with the JSF application.	Once	1.2, 2.0
variable-resolver	Specifies the fully qualified class name of a **javax.faces.el.VariableResolver** implementation class that will replace the JSF implementation's default variable resolver implementation.	Zero to unlimited	1.0, 1.1, 1.2, 2.0
view-declaration-language-factory	Specifies the fully qualified class name of a **javax.faces.view.ViewDeclarationLanguageFactory** implementation class that will replace or decorate the JSF implementation's view declaration language factory implementation.	Zero or once	2.0
view-handler	Specifies the fully qualified class name of a **javax.faces.application.ViewHandler** implementation class that will replace the JSF implementation's default view handler implementation.	Zero to unlimited	1.0, 1.1, 1.2, 2.0
view-param	Encapsulates the set of elements used to specify the details of a view parameter when using the **redirect** element to redirect to a different view.	Zero to unlimited	2.0
visit-context-factory	Specifies the fully qualified class name of a **javax.faces.component.visit.VisitContextFactory** implementation class that will replace or decorate the JSF implementation's visit context factory implementation.	Zero or once	2.0

TABLE 15-1 The Complete List of Elements of the JSF Configuration File *(continued)*

EXPERT GROUP INSIGHT *The *-extension elements may contain any well-formed XML, but JCP JSR 276 is currently in process at the time of this writing. This JSR, called "Design Time Metadata for JSF Components," will specify an XML schema for the contents of the *-extension elements that will provide a richer vocabulary for components to describe themselves to IDEs.*

The remainder of this chapter discusses each element in detail, including a complete description of the element, a table that lists the element's usage rules, a usage example for the element, and if applicable, a usage example of associated annotations. In the tables that describe each element's usage rules, pay special attention to the JSF Versions rule, which specifies the JSF versions to which the given element is applicable.

The absolute-ordering Element

The **absolute-ordering** element encapsulates the set of elements that specify the absolute order by which named JSF XML configuration files are to be loaded. This element may only be used in the application's **/WEB-INF/faces-config.xml** file. It may not be used in any **/META-INF/faces-config.xml** file found in a jar or in any file listed in **javax.faces.CONFIG_FILES** key in **web.xml**. This element has no other use than to denote the beginning and end of absolute ordering details.

Usage Rules

Rule	Value
JSF Versions	2.0
Parent Elements	faces-config
Child Elements	name (2.0), others (2.0) *Note: The parenthetical numbers represent the JSF versions that the corresponding child element applies to if the child element does not apply to all JSF versions.*
Annotation(s)	None
Uniqueness Constraints	None

Example Usage

The following example illustrates the usage of the **absolute-ordering** element:

```
<faces-config>
  <absolute-ordering>
    <name>A</name>
    <name>B</name>
    <name>C</name>
    <others />
  </absolute-ordering>
</faces-config>
```

The action-listener Element

The **action-listener** element is used to specify the fully qualified class name of a **javax.faces.event.ActionListener** implementation class that will replace the JSF implementation's default action listener implementation. The action listener is called during the Invoke Application phase of the JSF request processing lifecycle and is responsible for processing **javax.faces.event.ActionEvent** events. The **action-listener** element provides the ability to override the default JSF event processing by plugging in a custom **ActionListener**.

More detail on the application of this element can be found in Chapter 11. An example **ActionListener** is shown in Chapter 14.

Usage Rules

Rule	Value
JSF Versions	1.0, 1.1, 1.2, 2.0
Parent Elements	application
Child Elements	None
Annotation(s)	None
Uniqueness Constraints	None

Example Usage

The following example illustrates the usage of the **action-listener** element:

```
<faces-config>
  <application>
    <action-listener>
      com.example.jsf.TestActionListener
    </action-listener>
  </application>
</faces-config>
```

The after Element

The **after** element specifies that the containing JSF XML configuration file is to be loaded as part of the relative **ordering** scheme **after** the JSF XML configuration file(s) specified in the child elements are loaded.

Usage Rules

Rule	Value
JSF Versions	2.0
Parent Elements	ordering
Child Elements	name (2.0), others (2.0) *Note: The parenthetical numbers represent the JSF versions that the corresponding child element applies to if the child element does not apply to all JSF versions.*
Annotation(s)	None
Uniqueness Constraints	None

Example Usage

The following example illustrates the way in which the **after** element can be nested:

```
<faces-config>
  <ordering>
    <after>
      <name>B</name>
    </after>
    <before>
      <others />
    </before>
  </ordering>
</faces-config>
```

The application Element

The **application** element is used to encapsulate the set of elements that specify application singleton classes, such as overriding or decorating the default **ViewHandler** or **ActionListener**. This element has no other use than to denote the beginning and end of the application configuration details.

Usage Rules

Rule	Value
JSF Versions	1.0, 1.1, 1.2, 2.0
Parent Elements	faces-config
Child Elements	action-listener, application-extension, default-render-kit-id, default-validators (2.0), el-resolver, locale-config, message-bundle, navigation-handler, property-resolver, resource-bundle, resource-handler (2.0), state-manager, system-event-listener (2.0), variable-resolver, view-handler *Note: The parenthetical numbers represent the JSF versions that the corresponding child element applies to if the child element does not apply to all JSF versions.*
Annotation(s)	None
Uniqueness Constraints	None

Example Usage

The following example illustrates the usage of the **application** element:

```
<faces-config>
  <application>
    <action-listener>
      com.example.jsf.TestActionListener
    </action-listener>
```

```
    <state-manager>
      com.example.jsf.TestStateManager
    </state-manager>
  </application>
</faces-config>
```

The application-factory Element

The **application-factory** element is used to specify the fully qualified class name of a **javax.faces.application.ApplicationFactory** implementation class that will replace or decorate the JSF implementation's default application factory implementation. The application factory is used to retrieve and store a **javax.faces.application.Application** instance for the current Web application. See Chapter 11 for more details.

Usage Rules

Rule	Value
JSF Versions	1.0, 1.1, 1.2, 2.0
Parent Elements	factory
Child Elements	None
Annotation(s)	None
Uniqueness Constraints	None

Example Usage

The following example illustrates the usage of the **application-factory** element:

```
<faces-config>
  <factory>
    <application-factory>
      com.example.jsf.TestApplicationFactory
    </application-factory>
  </factory>
</faces-config>
```

The attribute Element

The **attribute** element is used to encapsulate the set of elements specifying the details for an attribute. This element has no other use than to denote the beginning and end of an attribute's configuration details.

There are four ways that the **attribute** element can be used, as listed here and shown later, in the section "Example Usage."

- An attribute can be defined for a UI component by nesting **attribute** elements inside the **component** element.
- An attribute can be defined for a converter by nesting **attribute** elements inside the **converter** element.

- An attribute can be defined for a renderer by nesting **attribute** elements inside the **renderer** element.
- An attribute can be defined for a validator by nesting **attribute** elements inside the **validator** element.

Expert Group Insight *All of these usages convey information intended for use at design time, such as by a tool. For example, it is useful to know that the* ***UIOutput*** *component has a* ***value*** *attribute, and that the* ***javax.faces.Messages*** *renderer has a* ***layout*** *attribute. A tool would use this information to populate a palette of options. The content of these elements has no runtime meaning; however, any XML errors will prevent the application from deploying at runtime.*

Usage Rules

Rule	Value
JSF Versions	1.0, 1.1, 1.2, 2.0
Parent Elements	component, converter, renderer, validator
Child Elements	attribute-class, attribute-extension, attribute-name, default-value, description (1.0, 1.1), descriptionGroup (1.2), display-name (1.0, 1.1), icon (1.0, 1.1), suggested-value *Note: The parenthetical numbers represent the JSF versions that the corresponding child element applies to if the child element does not apply to all JSF versions.*
Annotation(s)	None
Uniqueness Constraints	None

Example Usage

As mentioned, there are four ways that the **attribute** element can be used. The first way, shown here, defines an attribute for a UI component:

```
<faces-config>
  <component>
    <component-type>
      com.example.jsf.TestComponent
    </component-type>
    <component-class>
      com.example.jsf.UITestComponent
    </component-class>
    <attribute>
      <attribute-name>testAttribute</attribute-name>
      <attribute-class>java.lang.String</attribute-class>
    </attribute>
  </component>
</faces-config>
```

The following is the second way to use the **attribute** element:

```
<faces-config>
  <converter>
    <component-for-class>
      java.lang.Long
    </component-for-class>
    <component-class>
      com.example.jsf.LongConverter
    </component-class>
    <attribute>
      <attribute-name>testAttribute</attribute-name>
      <attribute-class>java.lang.String</attribute-class>
    </attribute>
  </converter>
</faces-config>
```

The third way to use the **attribute** element is shown here:

```
<faces-config>
  <render-kit>
    <renderer>
      <component-family>
        javax.faces.Data
      </component-family>
      <renderer-type>
        javax.faces.Table
      </renderer-type>
      <renderer-class>
        com.sun.faces.renderkit.html_basic.TableRenderer
      </renderer-class>
      <attribute>
        <attribute-name>testAttribute</attribute-name>
        <attribute-class>java.lang.String</attribute-class>
      </attribute>
    </renderer>
  </render-kit>
</faces-config>
```

The fourth and final way to use the **attribute** element is shown here:

```
<faces-config>
  <validator>
    <validator-id>
      javax.faces.Length
    </validator-id>
    <validator-class>
      javax.faces.validator.LengthValidator
    </validator-class>
    <attribute>
      <attribute-name>testAttribute</attribute-name>
      <attribute-class>java.lang.String</attribute-class>
    </attribute>
  </validator>
</faces-config>
```

The attribute-class Element

The **attribute-class** element is used to specify the fully qualified class name for an attribute's value—for example, **java.lang.String** for string values and **java.lang.Integer** for an integer value.

Usage Rules

Rule	Value
JSF Versions	1.0, 1.1, 1.2, 2.0
Parent Elements	attribute
Child Elements	None
Annotation(s)	None
Uniqueness Constraints	None

Example Usage

The following example illustrates the usage of the **attribute-class** element:

```
<faces-config>
  <validator>
    <validator-id>
      javax.faces.Length
    </validator-id>
    <validator-class>
      javax.faces.validator.LengthValidator
    </validator-class>
    <attribute>
      <attribute-name>testAttribute</attribute-name>
      <attribute-class> java.lang.String</attribute-class>
    </attribute>
  </validator>
</faces-config>
```

The attribute-name Element

The **attribute-name** element is used to specify the logical name for an attribute under which the attribute's value will be stored.

Usage Rules

Rule	Value
JSF Versions	1.0, 1.1, 1.2, 2.0
Parent Elements	attribute
Child Elements	None
Annotation(s)	None
Uniqueness Constraints	None

Example Usage

The following example illustrates the usage of the **attribute-name** element:

```
<faces-config>
  <validator>
    <validator-id>
      javax.faces.Length
    </validator-id>
    <validator-class>
      javax.faces.validator.LengthValidator
    </validator-class>
    <attribute>
      <attribute-name>testAttribute</attribute-name>
      <attribute-class>java.lang.String</attribute-class>
    </attribute>
  </validator>
</faces-config>
```

The base-name Element

The **base-name** element is used to specify the fully qualified class name of a **javax.util .ResourceBundle** instance that will be registered with the JSF application with a logical name specified by an associated **var** element.

Expert Group Insight *This element was added in JSF 1.2 to provide application-scoped localization exposed via the EL. Prior to this feature it was only possible to define* ***ResourceBundles*** *on a per-view basis using the* ***f:setBundle*** *element.*

Usage Rules

Rule	Value
JSF Versions	1.2, 2.0
Parent Elements	resource-bundle
Child Elements	None
Annotation(s)	None
Uniqueness Constraints	None

Example Usage

The following example illustrates the usage of the **base-name** element:

```
<faces-config>
  <application>
    <resource-bundle>
      <base-name>
        com.example.jsf.TestResources
      </base-name>
```

```
      <var>testResources</var>
    </resource-bundle>
  </application>
</faces-config>
```

The before Element

The **before** element specifies that the containing JSF XML configuration file is to be loaded as part of the relative **ordering** scheme **before** the JSF XML configuration file(s) specified in the child elements are loaded.

Usage Rules

Rule	Value
JSF Versions	2.0
Parent Elements	ordering
Child Elements	name (2.0), others (2.0) *Note: The parenthetical numbers represent the JSF versions that the corresponding child element applies to if the child element does not apply to all JSF versions.*
Annotation(s)	None
Uniqueness Constraints	None

Example Usage

The following example illustrates the way in which the **before** element can be nested:

```
<faces-config>
  <ordering>
    <after>
      <name>B</name>
    </after>
    <before>
      <others />
    </before>
  </ordering>
</faces-config>
```

The behavior Element

The **behavior** element is used to encapsulate the set of elements that specify a behavior, which can be attached to a UI Component in order to provide additional functionality to the component.

Usage Rules

Rule	Value
JSF Versions	2.0
Parent Elements	faces-config
Child Elements	attribute, behavior-class (2.0), behavior-extension (2.0), behavior-id (2.0), description (1.0, 1.1), descriptionGroup (1.2), display-name (1.0, 1.1), icon (1.0, 1.1), property *Note: The parenthetical numbers represent the JSF versions that the corresponding child element applies to if the child element does not apply to all JSF versions.*
Annotation(s)	@FacesBehavior
Uniqueness Constraints	None

Example Usage

The following example illustrates the usage of the **behavior** element:

```
<faces-config>
  <behavior>
    <behavior-id>
      test.behavior
    </behavior-id>
    <behavior-class>
      com.example.jsf.TestBehavior
    </behavior-class>
  </behavior>
</faces-config>
```

The following example illustrates equivalent configuration via the **@FacesBehavior** annotation:

```
@FacesBehavior(value="test.behavior")
public class TestBehavior extends BehaviorBase {
  ...
}
```

The behavior-class Element

The **behavior-class** element specifies the fully qualified class name of a **javax.faces.component.behavior.Behavior** implementation class.

Usage Rules

Rule	Value
JSF Versions	2.0
Parent Elements	behavior
Child Elements	None
Annotation(s)	None
Uniqueness Constraints	None

Example Usage

The following example illustrates the usage of the **behavior-class** element:

```
<faces-config>
  <behavior>
    <behavior-id>
      test.behavior
    </behavior-id>
    <behavior-class>
      com.example.jsf.TestBehavior
    </behavior-class>
  </behavior>
</faces-config>
```


The behavior-id Element

The **behavior-id** element specifies the logical name of a behavior.

Usage Rules

Rule	Value
JSF Versions	2.0
Parent Elements	behavior
Child Elements	None
Annotation(s)	None
Uniqueness Constraints	None

Example Usage

The following example illustrates the usage of the **behavior-id** element:

```
<faces-config>
  <behavior>
    <behavior-id>
      test.behavior
    </behavior-id>
```

```
    <behavior-class>
      com.example.jsf.TestBehavior
    </behavior-class>
  </behavior>
</faces-config>
```

The client-behavior-renderer Element

The **client-behavior-renderer** element encapsulates the set of elements that specify a client behavior renderer, which manifests itself in the form of script content on the client.

Usage Rules

Rule	Value
JSF Versions	2.0
Parent Elements	faces-config
Child Elements	client-behavior-renderer-type (2.0), client-behavior-renderer-class (2.0) *Note: The parenthetical numbers represent the JSF versions that the corresponding child element applies to if the child element does not apply to all JSF versions.*
Annotation(s)	@FacesBehaviorRenderer
Uniqueness Constraints	None

Example Usage

The following example illustrates the usage of the **client-behavior-renderer** element:

```
<faces-config>
  <client-behavior-renderer>
      <client-behavior-renderer-type>
        test.clientBehaviorRenderer
      </client-behavior-renderer-type>
      <client-behavior-renderer-class>
        com.example.jsf.TestClientBehaviorRenderer
      </client-behavior-renderer-class>
  </client-behavior-renderer>
</faces-config>
```

The following example illustrates equivalent configuration via the **@FacesBehaviorRenderer** annotation:

```
@FacesBehaviorRenderer(
  rendererType="test.clientBehaviorRenderer",
  renderKitId="test")
public class TestClientBehaviorRenderer
  extends ClientBehaviorRenderer {
  ...
}
```

The client-behavior-renderer-class Element

The **client-behavior-renderer-class** element specifies the fully qualified class name of a **javax.faces.render.ClientBehaviorRenderer** implementation for a given **client-behavior-renderer** element.

Usage Rules

Rule	Value
JSF Versions	2.0
Parent Elements	client-behavior-renderer
Child Elements	None
Annotation(s)	None
Uniqueness Constraints	None

Example Usage

The following example illustrates the usage of the **client-behavior-renderer-class** element:

```
<faces-config>
  <client-behavior-renderer>
      <client-behavior-renderer-type>
        test.clientBehaviorRenderer
      </client-behavior-renderer-type>
      <client-behavior-renderer-class>
        com.example.jsf.TestClientBehaviorRenderer
      </client-behavior-renderer-class>
  </client-behavior-renderer>
</faces-config>
```

The client-behavior-renderer-type Element

The client-behavior-renderer-type element specifies the logical name of a client-behavior-renderer.

Usage Rules

Rule	Value
JSF Versions	2.0
Parent Elements	client-behavior-renderer
Child Elements	None
Annotation(s)	None
Uniqueness Constraints	None

Example Usage

The following example illustrates the usage of the **client-behavior-renderer-type** element:

```
<faces-config>
  <client-behavior-renderer>
      <client-behavior-renderer-type>
        test.clientBehaviorRenderer
      </client-behavior-renderer-type>
      <client-behavior-renderer-class>
        com.example.jsf.TestClientBehaviorRenderer
      </client-behavior-renderer-class>
  </client-behavior-renderer>
</faces-config>
```

The component Element

The **component** element is used to encapsulate the set of elements specifying the details for a UI component. This element has no other use than to denote the beginning and end of the UI component details.

Usage Rules

Rule	Value
JSF Versions	1.0, 1.1, 1.2, 2.0
Parent Elements	faces-config
Child Elements	attribute, component-class, component-extension, component-type, description (1.0, 1.1), descriptionGroup (1.2), display-name (1.0, 1.1), facet, icon (1.0, 1.1), property *Note: The parenthetical numbers represent the JSF versions that the corresponding child element applies to if the child element does not apply to all JSF versions.*
Annotation(s)	@FacesComponent
Uniqueness Constraints	None

Example Usage

The following example illustrates the usage of the **component** element:

```
<faces-config>
  <component>
    <component-type>
      javax.faces.Input
    </component-type>
    <component-class>
      javax.faces.component.UIInput
    </component-class>
  </component>
</faces-config>
```

The following example illustrates equivalent configuration via the **@FacesComponent** annotation:

```
@FacesComponent(value="test.component")
public class TestComponent extends UIComponentBase {
  ...
}
```

The component-class Element

The **component-class** element is used to specify the fully qualified class name for a UI component implementation. The implementation must extend from the **javax.faces.component.UIComponent** abstract base class.

Usage Rules

Rule	Value
JSF Versions	1.0, 1.1, 1.2, 2.0
Parent Elements	component
Child Elements	None
Annotation(s)	None
Uniqueness Constraints	None

Example Usage

The following example illustrates the usage of the **component-class** element:

```
<faces-config>
  <component>
    <component-type>
      javax.faces.Input
    </component-type>
    <component-class>
      javax.faces.component.UIInput
    </component-class>
  </component>
</faces-config>
```

The component-family Element

The **component-family** element is used to specify the component family that a renderer will be linked to. Component families are used to group families of components together and are used along with renderer types to uniquely identify a specific rendering.

Usage Rules

Rule	Value
JSF Versions	1.0, 1.1, 1.2, 2.0
Parent Elements	renderer
Child Elements	None
Annotation(s)	None
Uniqueness Constraints	None

Example Usage

The following example illustrates the usage of the **component-family** element:

```
<faces-config>
  <render-kit>
    <renderer>
      <component-family>
        javax.faces.Command
      </component-family>
      <renderer-type>
        javax.faces.Button
      </renderer-type>
      <renderer-class>
        com.sun.faces.renderkit.html_basic.ButtonRenderer
      </renderer-class>
    </renderer>
  </render-kit>
</faces-config>
```

The component-type Element

The **component-type** element is used to specify the logical name for a UI component. The logical name is used to register the UI component with JSF so that it can later be accessed by the same logical name.

Usage Rules

Rule	Value
JSF Versions	1.0, 1.1, 1.2, 2.0
Parent Elements	component
Child Elements	None
Annotation(s)	None
Uniqueness Constraints	None

Example Usage

The following example illustrates the usage of the **component-type** element:

```
<faces-config>
  <component>
    <component-type>
      javax.faces.Input
    </component-type>
    <component-class>
      javax.faces.component.UIInput
    </component-class>
  </component>
</faces-config>
```

The converter Element

The **converter** element is used to encapsulate the set of elements specifying the details for a converter. This element has no other use than to denote the beginning and end of the converter details.

Usage Rules

Rule	Value
JSF Versions	1.0, 1.1, 1.2, 2.0
Parent Elements	faces-config
Child Elements	attribute, converter-class, converter-extension (1.2), converterfor-class, converter-id, description (1.0, 1.1), descriptionGroup (1.2), display-name (1.0, 1.1), icon (1.0, 1.1), property *Note: The parenthetical numbers represent the JSF versions that the corresponding child element applies to if the child element does not apply to all JSF versions.*
Annotation(s)	@FacesConverter
Uniqueness Constraints	None

Example Usage

The following example illustrates the usage of the **converter** element:

```
<faces-config>
  <converter>
    <converter-for-class>
      java.lang.Double
    </converter-for-class>
    <converter-class>
      javax.faces.convert.DoubleConverter
    </converter-class>
  </converter>
</faces-config>
```

The following example illustrates the usage of the **@FacesConverter** annotation to handle the same class as the **<converter-for-class>** element:

```
@FacesConverter(forClass=" java.lang.Double")
public class DoubleConverter implements Converter {
  ...
}
```

To use the annotation to declare a converter by **<converter-id>**, the following syntax is used:

```
@FacesConverter(value=" my-converter")
public class MyConverter implements Converter {
  ...
}
```

The converter-class Element

The **converter-class** element is used to specify the fully qualified class name for a converter implementation. The implementation must implement the **javax.faces.convert.Converter** interface.

Usage Rules

Rule	Value
JSF Versions	1.0, 1.1, 1.2, 2.0
Parent Elements	converter
Child Elements	None
Annotation(s)	None
Uniqueness Constraints	None

Example Usage

The following example illustrates the usage of the **converter-class** element:

```
<faces-config>
  <converter>
    <converter-for-class>
      java.lang.Double
    </converter-for-class>
    <converter-class>
      javax.faces.convert.DoubleConverter
    </converter-class>
  </converter>
</faces-config>
```

The converter-for-class Element

The **converter-for-class** element is used to specify the fully qualified class name for which a converter will be associated. JSF uses two mechanisms for associating converters:

by ID (logical name) with the **converter-id** element, or by registering the converter to a corresponding class with the **converter-for-class** element.

Usage Rules

Rule	Value
JSF Versions	1.0, 1.1, 1.2, 2.0
Parent Elements	converter
Child Elements	None
Annotation(s)	None
Uniqueness Constraints	Values for this element must be unique within the configuration file.

Example Usage

The following example illustrates the usage of the **converter-for-class** element:

```
<faces-config>
  <converter>
    <converter-for-class>
      java.lang.Double
    </converter-for-class>
    <converter-class>
      javax.faces.convert.DoubleConverter
    </converter-class>
  </converter>
</faces-config>
```

PART III

The converter-id Element

The **converter-id** element is used to specify the logical name for a converter. The logical name is used to register the converter with JSF so that it can later be accessed by the same logical name. JSF uses two mechanisms for associating converters: by ID (logical name) with the **converter-id** element, or by registering the converter to a corresponding class with the **converter-for-class** element.

Usage Rules

Rule	Value
JSF Versions	1.0, 1.1, 1.2, 2.0
Parent Elements	converter
Child Elements	None
Annotation(s)	None
Uniqueness Constraints	Values for this element must be unique within the configuration file.

Example Usage

The following example illustrates the usage of the **converter-id** element:

```
<faces-config>
  <converter>
    <converter-id>
      javax.faces.Boolean
    </converter-id>
    <converter-class>
      javax.faces.convert.BooleanConverter
    </converter-class>
  </converter>
</faces-config>
```

The default-locale Element

The **default-locale** element is used to specify the default locale for the JSF application. JSF uses locale information to retrieve all localized resources for the application. JSF uses the default locale setting if another locale is not specified (e.g., via the browser). The locale value specified with the **default-locale** element must be in the following format:

language_country_variant

The *language, country,* and *variant* arguments of the locale definition must be separated by either an underscore (_) or a hyphen (-). The *country* and *variant* arguments are optional. The *language* argument must be specified using a valid two-letter ISO-639 language code (e.g., "en" for English or "es" for Spanish). The *country* argument must be specified using a valid uppercase two-letter ISO-3166 country code (e.g., "US" for United States or "CA" for Canada). The *variant* argument is for a vendor- or browser-specific code (e.g., "WIN" for Windows or "MAC" for Macintosh). For a listing of each of the ISO language and country codes, visit their respective specification Web sites listed here:

www.unicode.org/unicode/onlinedat/languages.html
www.unicode.org/unicode/onlinedat/countries.html

To illustrate the rules of locales, consider the following example locale definitions:

- **en** English
- **en_US** United States English
- **en_US_WIN** United States English on Windows
- **es** Spanish
- **es_MX** Mexican Spanish
- **es_MX_MAC** Mexican Spanish on Macintosh

Usage Rules

Rule	Value
JSF Versions	1.0, 1.1, 1.2, 2.0
Parent Elements	locale-config
Child Elements	None
Annotation(s)	None
Uniqueness Constraints	None

Example Usage

The following example illustrates the usage of the **default-locale** element:

```
<faces-config>
  <application>
    <locale-config>
      <default-locale>en</default-locale>
      <supported-locale>es</supported-locale>
      <supported-locale>fr_FR</supported-locale>
    </locale-config>
  </application>
</faces-config>
```


The default-render-kit-id Element

The **default-render-kit-id** element is used to specify the logical name of a render kit that will replace the JSF implementation's default render kit. The default render kit is responsible for rendering views via the view handler. The **default-render-kit-id** element provides the ability to override the default JSF view rendering by plugging in a custom render kit.

Usage Rules

Rule	Value
JSF Versions	1.0, 1.1, 1.2, 2.0
Parent Elements	application
Child Elements	None
Annotation(s)	None
Uniqueness Constraints	None

Example Usage

The following example illustrates the usage of the **default-render-kit-id** element:

```
<faces-config>
  <application>
    <default-render-kit-id>
      testRenderKit
    </default-render-kit-id>
  </application>
</faces-config>
```

The default-validators Element

The **default-validators** element encapsulates the set of validator-id elements that specify the validators that will be attached to every UIComponent (that implements EditableValueHolder) in every view of the application.

Usage Rules

Rule	Value
JSF Versions	2.0
Parent Elements	application
Child Elements	validator-id
Annotation(s)	@FacesValidator
Uniqueness Constraints	None

Example Usage

The following example illustrates the way in which the **default-validators** element can be used:

```
<faces-config>
  <application>
    <default-validators>
      <validator-id>
        com.example.jsf.TestDefaultValidator
      </validator-id>
    </default-validators>
  </application>
</faces-config>
```

The following example illustrates equivalent configuration via the **@FacesValidator** annotation:

```
@FacesValidator(isDefault=true, value="test.Validator")
public class TestDefaultValidator implements Validator {
  ...
}
```

The default-value Element

The **default-value** element is used to specify the default value for an attribute or a property. Default values differ from suggested values in that default values will be assigned to an attribute or property whereas suggested values are only suggestions and may or may not be applied to an attribute or property.

Usage Rules

Rule	Value
JSF Versions	1.0, 1.1, 1.2, 2.0
Parent Elements	attribute, property
Child Elements	None
Annotation(s)	None
Uniqueness Constraints	None

Example Usage

There are two ways that the **default-value** element can be used. The first way, shown here, defines a default value for an attribute:

```
<faces-config>
  <component>
    <component-type>
      com.example.jsf.TestComponent
    </component-type>
    <component-class>
      com.example.jsf.UITestComponent
    </component-class>
    <attribute>
      <attribute-name>testAttribute</attribute-name>
      <attribute-class>java.lang.String</attribute-class>
      <default-value>testDefaultValue</default-value>
    </attribute>
  </component>
</faces-config>
```

The following is the second way to use the **default-value** element to define a default value for a property:

```
<faces-config>
  <converter>
    <component-for-class>
      java.lang.Long
    </component-for-class>
    <component-class>
      com.example.jsf.LongConverter
    </component-class>
```

```
    <property>
      <property-name>testAttribute</property-name>
      <property-class>java.lang.String</property-class>
      <default-value>testDefaultValue</default-value>
    </property>
  </converter>
</faces-config>
```

The el-resolver Element

The **el-resolver** element is used to specify the fully qualified class name of a **javax.el.ELResolver** implementation class that will replace the JSF implementation's default expression language resolver implementation. The expression language resolver is called each time an expression must be resolved. The **el-resolver** element provides the ability to override the default JSF expression language resolving by plugging in a custom **ELResolver**. For more on this topic, see Chapter 11.

Usage Rules

Rule	Value
JSF Versions	1.2, 2.0
Parent Elements	application
Child Elements	None
Annotation(s)	None
Uniqueness Constraints	None

Example Usage

The following example illustrates the usage of the **el-resolver** element:

```
<faces-config>
  <application>
    <el-resolver>
      com.example.jsf.TestELResolver
    </el-resolver>
  </application>
</faces-config>
```

The exception-handler-factory Element

The **exception-handler-factory** element is used to specify the fully qualified class name of a **javax.faces.context.ExceptionHandlerFactory** implementation class that will replace or decorate the JSF implementation's default exception handler factory implementation. The exception handler factory is used to retrieve and store a **javax.faces.context.ExceptionHandler** instance for the current Web application. See Chapter 6 for more details.

Usage Rules

Rule	Value
JSF Versions	2.0
Parent Elements	factory
Child Elements	None
Annotation(s)	None
Uniqueness Constraints	None

Example Usage

The following example illustrates the usage of the **exception-handler-factory** element:

```
<faces-config>
  <factory>
    <exception-handler-factory>
      com.example.jsf.TestExceptionHandlerFactory
    </exception-handler-factory>
  </factory>
</faces-config>
```


The external-context-factory Element

The **external-context-factory** element is used to specify the fully qualified class name of a **javax.faces.context.ExternalContextFactory** implementation class that will replace or decorate the JSF implementation's default external context factory implementation. The external context factory is used to retrieve and store a **javax.faces.context.ExternalContext** instance for the current Web application. See Chapter 13 for more details.

Usage Rules

Rule	Value
JSF Versions	2.0
Parent Elements	factory
Child Elements	None
Annotation(s)	None
Uniqueness Constraints	None

Example Usage

The following example illustrates the usage of the **external-context-factory** element:

```
<faces-config>
  <factory>
    <external-context-factory>
```

```
      com.example.jsf.TestExternalContextFactory
    </external-context-factory>
  </factory>
</faces-config>
```

The faces-config Element

The **faces-config** element is the root element for the JSF configuration file and thus encapsulates all other elements in the file. This element has no other use than to denote the beginning and end of the configuration data. Note that JSF 2.0 adds the new **metadata-complete** attribute to the **faces-config** element, which may only be used in the /WEB-INF/ faces-config.xml file. If true, then annotation scanning will not be performed.

Attributes

Attribute	Description	Required
version	Specifies the JSF implementation version that the configuration file is for. *Note: This attribute was introduced in JSF 1.2 and does not apply to previous versions.*	*Yes*

Usage Rules

Rule	Value
JSF Versions	1.0, 1.1, 1.2, 2.0
Parent Elements	None
Child Elements	absolute-ordering (2.0), application, behavior (2.0), component, converter, faces-config-extension (1.2), factory, lifecycle, managed-bean, name (2.0), ordering (2.0), navigation-rule, referenced-bean, render-kit, validator *Note: The parenthetical numbers represent the JSF versions that the corresponding child element applies to if the child element does not apply to all JSF versions.*
Annotation(s)	None
Uniqueness Constraints	Because this element is the root element for the JSF configuration file, it must occur only once.

Example Usage

The following example illustrates the usage of the **faces-config** element:

```
<faces-config>
  <application>
    <action-listener>
```

```
      com.example.jsf.TestActionListener
    </action-listener>
  </application>
</faces-config>
```

The faces-context-factory Element

The **faces-context-factory** element is used to specify the fully qualified class name of a **javax.faces.context.ApplicationFactory** implementation class that will replace the JSF implementation's default faces context factory implementation. The faces context factory is used to retrieve a **javax.faces.context.FacesContext** instance for the current Web application.

Usage Rules

Rule	Value
JSF Versions	1.0, 1.1, 1.2, 2.0
Parent Elements	factory
Child Elements	None
Annotation(s)	None
Uniqueness Constraints	None

Example Usage

The following example illustrates the usage of the **faces-context-factory** element:

```
<faces-config>
  <factory>
    <faces-context-factory>
      com.example.jsf.TestFacesContextFactory
    </faces-context-factory>
  </factory>
</faces-config>
```

The facet Element

The **facet** element is used to encapsulate the set of elements specifying the details for a facet. This element has no other use than to denote the beginning and end of the facet details.

There are two ways that the **facet** element can be used, as listed here and shown later, in the section "Example Usage."

- A facet can be defined for a UI component by nesting **facet** elements inside the **component** element.
- A facet can be defined for a renderer by nesting **facet** elements inside the **renderer** element.

Usage Rules

Rule	Value
JSF Versions	1.1, 1.2, 2.0
Parent Elements	component, renderer
Child Elements	description (1.0, 1.1), descriptionGroup (1.2), display-name (1.0, 1.1), facet-extension, facet-name, icon (1.0, 1.1) *Note: The parenthetical numbers represent the JSF versions that the corresponding child element applies to if the child element does not apply to all JSF versions.*
Annotation(s)	None
Uniqueness Constraints	None

Example Usage

As mentioned, there are two ways that the **facet** element can be used. The first way, shown here, defines a facet for a UI component:

```
<faces-config>
  <component>
    <component-type>
      com.example.jsf.TestComponent
    </component-type>
    <component-class>
      com.example.jsf.UITestComponent
    </component-class>
    <facet>
      <facet-name>header</facet-name>
    </facet>
  </component>
</faces-config>
```

The following is the second way to use the **facet** element:

```
<faces-config>
  <render-kit>
    <renderer>
      <component-family>
        javax.faces.Output
      </component-family>
      <renderer-type>
        javax.faces.Text
      </renderer-type>
      <renderer-class>
        com.sun.faces.renderkit.html_basic.TextRenderer
      </renderer-class>
```

```
      <facet>
        <facet-name>header</facet-name>
      </facet>
    </renderer>
  </render-kit>
</faces-config>
```

The facet-name Element

The **facet-name** element is used to specify the logical name for a facet. The logical name is used to register the facet with JSF so that it can later be accessed by the same logical name.

Usage Rules

Rule	Value
JSF Versions	1.1, 1.2, 2.0
Parent Elements	facet
Child Elements	None
Annotation(s)	None
Uniqueness Constraints	None

Example Usage

The following example illustrates the usage of the **facet-name** element:

```
<faces-config>
  <component>
    <component-type>
      com.example.jsf.TestComponent
    </component-type>
    <component-class>
      com.example.jsf.UITestComponent
    </component-class>
    <facet>
      <facet-name>header</facet-name>
    </facet>
  </component>
</faces-config>
```

The factory Element

The **factory** element is used to encapsulate the set of elements that specify factory configuration details. This element has no other use than to denote the beginning and end of the factory configuration details.

Usage Rules

Rule	Value
JSF Versions	1.0, 1.1, 1.2, 2.0
Parent Elements	faces-config
Child Elements	application-factory, exception-handler-factory (2.0), external-context-factory (2.0), faces-context-factory, lifecycle-factory, partial-view-context-factory (2.0), render-kit-factory, tag-handler-factory (2.0), view-declaration-language-factory (2.0), visit-context-factory (2.0) *Note: The parenthetical numbers represent the JSF versions that the corresponding child element applies to if the child element does not apply to all JSF versions.*
Annotation(s)	None
Uniqueness Constraints	None

Example Usage

The following example illustrates the usage of the **factory** element:

```
<faces-config>
  <factory>
    <application-factory>
      com.example.jsf.TestApplicationFactory
    </application-factory>
    <lifecycle-factory>
      com.example.jsf.TestLifeCycleFactory
    </lifecycle-factory>
  </factory>
</faces-config>
```

The from-action Element

The **from-action** element is used to specify an action reference expression that must have been executed in order to have the associated navigation case selected.

Usage Rules

Rule	Value
JSF Versions	1.0, 1.1, 1.2, 2.0
Parent Elements	navigation-case
Child Elements	None
Annotation(s)	None
Uniqueness Constraints	None

Example Usage

The following example illustrates the usage of the **from-action** element:

```
<faces-config>
  <navigation-rule>
    <from-view-id>/main.jsp</from-view-id>
    <navigation-case>
      <from-action>#{loginForm.execute}</from-action>
      <from-outcome>success</from-outcome>
      <to-view-id>/details.jsp</to-view-id>
    </navigation-case>
  </navigation-rule>
</faces-config>
```

The from-outcome Element

The **from-outcome** element is used to specify the logical outcome value that an action method must generate in order to have the associated navigation case selected.

Usage Rules

Rule	Value
JSF Versions	1.0, 1.1, 1.2, 2.0
Parent Elements	navigation-case
Child Elements	None
Annotation(s)	None
Uniqueness Constraints	None

Example Usage

The following example illustrates the usage of the **from-outcome** element:

```
<faces-config>
  <navigation-rule>
    <from-view-id>/main.jsp</from-view-id>
    <navigation-case>
      <from-outcome>details</from-outcome>
      <to-view-id>/details.jsp</to-view-id>
    </navigation-case>
  </navigation-rule>
</faces-config>
```

The from-view-id Element

The **from-view-id** element is used to specify the view ID that a navigation rule applies to. If a navigation rule does not specify a from view ID with this element, the navigation rule will apply to all view IDs. Similarly, an asterisk (*) can be used to signify a global navigation case.

Usage Rules

Rule	Value
JSF Versions	1.0, 1.1, 1.2, 2.0
Parent Elements	navigation-rule
Child Elements	None
Annotation(s)	None
Uniqueness Constraints	None

Example Usage

The following example illustrates the usage of the **from-view-id** element:

```
<faces-config>
  <navigation-rule>
    <from-view-id>/main.jsp</from-view-id>
    <navigation-case>
      <from-outcome>details</from-outcome>
      <to-view-id>/details.jsp</to-view-id>
    </navigation-case>
  </navigation-rule>
</faces-config>
```

The if Element

The **if** element is used to specify an EL expression that must evaluate to a boolean value (true or false). If the value is true, then it will cause the containing **navigation-rule** to fire.

Usage Rules

Rule	Value
JSF Versions	2.0
Parent Elements	navigation-case
Child Elements	None
Annotation(s)	None
Uniqueness Constraints	None

Example Usage

The following example illustrates the usage of the **if** element:

```
<faces-config>
  <navigation-rule>
    <from-view-id>/main.jsp</from-view-id>
    <navigation-case>
      <if>#{testManagedBean.approved}</if>
      <to-view-id>/details.jsp</to-view-id>
```

```
    </navigation-case>
  </navigation-rule>
</faces-config>
```

The key Element

The **key** element is used to specify the key for a map entry defined by the **map-entry** element. Keys specified by the **key** element will be converted to the object type specified by an associated **key-class** element if present. If the **key-class** element is not present for the encompassing **map-entries** element, all keys for the map will be converted to **java.lang.String**.

Usage Rules

Rule	Value
JSF Versions	1.0, 1.1, 1.2, 2.0
Parent Elements	map-entry
Child Elements	None
Annotation(s)	None
Uniqueness Constraints	None

Example Usage

The following example illustrates the usage of the **key** element:

```
<faces-config>
  <managed-bean>
    <managed-bean-name>
      testManagedBean
    </managed-bean-name>
    <managed-bean-class>
      com.example.jsf.TestManagedBean
    </managed-bean-class>
    <managed-bean-scope>
      session
    </managed-bean-scope>
    <managed-property>
      <property-name>testProperty</property-name>
      <map-entries>
        <key-class>java.lang.Integer</key-class>
        <map-entry>
          <key>1000</key>
          <value>testValue1</value>
        </map-entry>
        <map-entry>
          <key>2000</key>
          <null-value/>
        </map-entry>
      <map-entries>
    </managed-property>
  </managed-bean>
</faces-config>
```

PART III

The key-class Element

The **key-class** element is used to specify the fully qualified class name of an object type that all keys will convert to before being added to a map defined by a **map-entries** element. If this element is not nested inside a **map-entries** element, all map entry keys will default to **java.lang.String** as their object type.

Usage Rules

Rule	Value
JSF Versions	1.0, 1.1, 1.2, 2.0
Parent Elements	map-entries
Child Elements	None
Annotation(s)	None
Uniqueness Constraints	None

Example Usage

The following example illustrates the usage of the **key-class** element:

```
<faces-config>
  <managed-bean>
    <managed-bean-name>
      testManagedBean
    </managed-bean-name>
    <managed-bean-class>
      com.example.jsf.TestManagedBean
    </managed-bean-class>
    <managed-bean-scope>
      session
    </managed-bean-scope>
    <managed-property>
      <property-name>testProperty</property-name>
      <map-entries>
        <key-class>java.lang.Integer</key-class>
        <map-entry>
          <key>1000</key>
          <value>testValue1</value>
        </map-entry>
        <map-entry>
          <key>2000</key>
          <null-value/>
        </map-entry>
      <map-entries>
    </managed-property>
  </managed-bean>
</faces-config>
```

The lifecycle Element

The **lifecycle** element is used to encapsulate the set of elements that specify lifecycle configuration details. This element has no other use than to denote the beginning and end of the lifecycle configuration details.

Usage Rules

Rule	Value
JSF Versions	1.0, 1.1, 1.2, 2.0
Parent Elements	faces-config
Child Elements	phase-listener
Annotation(s)	None
Uniqueness Constraints	None

Example Usage

The following example illustrates the usage of the **lifecycle** element:

```
<faces-config>
  <lifecycle>
    <phase-listener>
      com.example.jsf.TestPhaseListener
    </phase-listener>
  </lifecycle>
</faces-config>
```


The lifecycle-factory Element

The **lifecycle-factory** element is used to specify the fully qualified class name of a **javax.faces .lifecycle.LifecycleFactory** implementation class that will replace the JSF implementation's default lifecycle factory implementation. The lifecycle factory is used to store and retrieve **javax.faces.lifecycle.Lifecycle** instances for the current Web application as well as to retrieve a list of the IDs for lifecycles supported by the factory.

Usage Rules

Rule	Value
JSF Versions	1.0, 1.1, 1.2, 2.0
Parent Elements	factory
Child Elements	None
Annotation(s)	None
Uniqueness Constraints	None

Example Usage

The following example illustrates the usage of the **lifecycle-factory** element:

```
<faces-config>
  <factory>
    <lifecycle-factory>
      com.example.jsf.TestLifecycleFactory
    </lifecycle-factory>
  </factory>
</faces-config>
```

The list-entries Element

The **list-entries** element is used to encapsulate a list of values that will be used to populate a **java.util.List** instance or an array that will serve as the value for a managed property or to populate a managed bean that is itself an instance of **java.util.List**.

Usage Rules

Rule	Value
JSF Versions	1.0, 1.1, 1.2, 2.0
Parent Elements	managed-bean, managed-property
Child Elements	null-value, value, value-class
Annotation(s)	None
Uniqueness Constraints	None

Example Usage

The following example illustrates the usage of the **list-entries** element to populate a managed property's value with a **java.util.List** instance:

```
<faces-config>
  <managed-bean>
    <managed-bean-name>
      testManagedBean
    </managed-bean-name>
    <managed-bean-class>
      com.example.jsf.TestManagedBean
    </managed-bean-class>
    <managed-bean-scope>
      session
    </managed-bean-scope>
    <managed-property>
      <property-name>testProperty</property-name>
      <list-entries>
        <value>1000</value>
        <value>2000</value>
      <list-entries>
    </managed-property>
  </managed-bean>
</faces-config>
```

The second way to use the **list-entries** element is shown here:

```
<faces-config>
  <managed-bean>
    <managed-bean-name>
      testManagedBean
    </managed-bean-name>
    <managed-bean-class>
      com.example.jsf.TestManagedBean
    </managed-bean-class>
    <managed-bean-scope>
      session
    </managed-bean-scope>
    <list-entries>
      <value>1000</value>
      <value>2000</value>
    <list-entries>
  </managed-bean>
</faces-config>
```

This example populates a managed bean that is itself an instance of **java.util.List**.

The locale-config Element

The **locale-config** element is used to encapsulate the set of elements that specify the application's locale configuration details. This element has no other use than to denote the beginning and end of the locale configuration details.

Usage Rules

Rule	Value
JSF Versions	1.0, 1.1, 1.2, 2.0
Parent Elements	application
Child Elements	default-locale, supported-locale
Annotation(s)	None
Uniqueness Constraints	None

Example Usage

The following example illustrates the usage of the **locale-config** element:

```
<faces-config>
  <application>
    <locale-config>
      <default-locale>en</default-locale>
      <supported-locale>es</supported-locale>
      <supported-locale>fr_FR</supported-locale>
    </locale-config>
  </application>
</faces-config>
```

The managed-bean Element

The **managed-bean** element is used to encapsulate the set of elements specifying the details for a managed bean. Managed beans are beans that JSF manages for an application by providing lifecycle services. Managed beans are instantiated and populated by JSF at runtime as needed. For detailed information on managed beans, see Chapter 4.

Usage Rules

Rule	Value
JSF Versions	1.0, 1.1, 1.2, 2.0
Parent Elements	faces-config
Child Elements	description (1.0, 1.1), descriptionGroup (1.2), display-name (1.0, 1.1), icon (1.0, 1.1), list-entries, managed-bean-class, managed-bean-extension, managed-bean-name, managed-bean-scope, managed-property, map-entries *Note: The parenthetical numbers represent the JSF versions that the corresponding child element applies to if the child element does not apply to all JSF versions.*
Annotation(s)	@ManagedBean
Uniqueness Constraints	None

Example Usage

The following example illustrates the usage of the **managed-bean** element:

```
<faces-config>
  <managed-bean>
    <managed-bean-name>
      testManagedBean
    </managed-bean-name>
    <managed-bean-class>
      com.example.jsf.TestManagedBean
    </managed-bean-class>
    <managed-bean-scope>
      session
    </managed-bean-scope>
    <managed-property>
      <property-name>testProperty</property-name>
      <value>testValue</value>
    </managed-property>
  </managed-bean>
</faces-config>
```

The following example illustrates the usage of the **@ManagedBean** annotation:

```
@ManagedBean(name="testManagedBean")
@SessionScoped
```

```
public class TestManagedBean {
  ...
}
```

The managed-bean-class Element

The **managed-bean-class** element is used to specify the fully qualified class name of a managed bean.

Usage Rules

Rule	Value
JSF Versions	1.0, 1.1, 1.2, 2.0
Parent Elements	managed-bean
Child Elements	None
Annotation(s)	None
Uniqueness Constraints	None

Example Usage

The following example illustrates the usage of the **managed-bean-class** element:

```
<faces-config>
  <managed-bean>
    <managed-bean-name>
      testManagedBean
    </managed-bean-name>
    <managed-bean-class>
      com.example.jsf.TestManagedBean
    </managed-bean-class>
    <managed-bean-scope>
      session
    </managed-bean-scope>
    <managed-property>
      <property-name>testProperty</property-name>
      <value>testValue</value>
    </managed-property>
  </managed-bean>
</faces-config>
```

The managed-bean-name Element

The **managed-bean-name** element is used to specify the logical name for a managed bean. The logical name is used to register the managed bean with JSF so that it can later be accessed by the same logical name.

Usage Rules

Rule	Value
JSF Versions	1.0, 1.1, 1.2, 2.0
Parent Elements	managed-bean
Child Elements	None
Annotation(s)	None
Uniqueness Constraints	Values for this element must be unique within the configuration file.

Example Usage

The following example illustrates the usage of the **managed-bean-name** element:

```
<faces-config>
  <managed-bean>
    <managed-bean-name>
      testManagedBean
    </managed-bean-name>
    <managed-bean-class>
      com.example.jsf.TestManagedBean
    </managed-bean-class>
    <managed-bean-scope>
      session
    </managed-bean-scope>
    <managed-property>
      <property-name>testProperty</property-name>
      <value>testValue</value>
    </managed-property>
  </managed-bean>
</faces-config>
```

The managed-bean-scope Element

The **managed-bean-scope** element is used to specify the Web application scope that the managed bean will be stored in when it is instantiated. The values this element accepts are **request**, **session**, **application**, or **none**. JSF 2.0 adds the **custom** and **view** scope as well. A value of **none** indicates that the managed bean should be instantiated, but not be stored in a Web application scope. Using **none** is helpful in the scenario of dynamically creating trees of related objects.

JSF 2.0 also introduces the **flash** scope feature, which allows developers to pass objects between views. However use-case for flash scope does not lend itself to beans that are managed by the JSF managed bean facility; neither does it lend itself to annotation-based discovery at startup time. Instead, developers must get the **javax.faces.context.Flash** object by calling **ExternalContext.getFlash( )** and call the **get, keep, put, and putNow** methods programmatically. The flash is covered in detail in Chapter 6.

Usage Rules

Rule	Value
JSF Versions	1.0, 1.1, 1.2, 2.0
Parent Elements	managed-bean-scope
Child Elements	None
Annotation(s)	@ApplicationScoped, @CustomScoped, @NoneScoped, @RequestScoped. @SessionScoped, @ViewScoped
Uniqueness Constraints	None

Example Usage

The following example illustrates the usage of the **managed-bean-scope** element:

```
<faces-config>
  <managed-bean>
    <managed-bean-name>
      testManagedBean
    </managed-bean-name>
    <managed-bean-class>
      com.example.jsf.TestManagedBean
    </managed-bean-class>
    <managed-bean-scope>
      session
    </managed-bean-scope>
    <managed-property>
      <property-name>testProperty</property-name>
      <value>testValue</value>
    </managed-property>
  </managed-bean>
</faces-config>
```

The following example illustrates the usage of the **@SessionScoped** annotation:

```
@ManagedBean(name="testManagedBean")
@SessionScoped
public class TestManagedBean {
  ...
}
```

The managed-property Element

The **managed-property** element is used to encapsulate the set of elements specifying the details for a managed bean's property. This element has no other use than to denote the beginning and end of a managed property's configuration details.

PART III

Usage Rules

Rule	Value
JSF Versions	1.0, 1.1, 1.2, 2.0
Parent Elements	managed-bean
Child Elements	description (1.0, 1.1), descriptionGroup (1.2), display-name (1.0, 1.1), icon (1.0, 1.1), list-entries, map-entries, null-value, property-class, property-name, value *Note: The parenthetical numbers represent the JSF versions that the corresponding child element applies to if the child element does not apply to all JSF versions.*
Annotation(s)	@ManagedProperty
Uniqueness Constraints	None

Example Usage

The following example illustrates the usage of the **managed-property** element:

```
<faces-config>
  <managed-bean>
    <managed-bean-name>
      testManagedBean
    </managed-bean-name>
    <managed-bean-class>
      com.example.jsf.TestManagedBean
    </managed-bean-class>
    <managed-bean-scope>
      session
    </managed-bean-scope>
    <managed-property>
      <property-name>testProperty</property-name>
      <value>testValue</value>
    </managed-property>
  </managed-bean>
</faces-config>
```

The following example illustrates the usage of the **@ManagedProperty** annotation:

```
@ManagedBean(name="testManagedBean")
@SessionScoped
public class TestManagedBean {
  @ManagedProperty(value="#{shoppingCart}")
  private ShoppingCart shoppingCart;

  public ShoppingCart getShoppingCart() {
    return shoppingCart;
  }
```

```
  public void setShoppingCart(ShoppingCart shoppingCart) {
    this.shoppingCart = shoppingCart;
  }
```

The map-entries Element

The **map-entries** element is used to encapsulate a set of key-value pairs that will be used to populate a **java.util.Map** instance that will serve as the value for a managed property or to populate a managed bean that is itself an instance of **java.util.Map**.

Usage Rules

Rule	Value
JSF Versions	1.0, 1.1, 1.2, 2.0
Parent Elements	managed-bean, managed-property
Child Elements	key-class, map-entry, value-class
Annotation(s)	None
Uniqueness Constraints	None

Example Usage

The following example illustrates the usage of the **map-entries** element to populate a managed property's value with a **java.util.Map** instance:

```
<faces-config>
  <managed-bean>
    <managed-bean-name>
      testManagedBean
    </managed-bean-name>
    <managed-bean-class>
      com.example.jsf.TestManagedBean
    </managed-bean-class>
    <managed-bean-scope>
      session
    </managed-bean-scope>
    <managed-property>
      <property-name>testProperty</property-name>
      <map-entries>
        <map-entry>
          <key>testKey1</key>
          <value>1000</value>
        </map-entry>
        <map-entry>
          <key>testKey2</key>
          <null-value/>
        </map-entry>
      <map-entries>
    </managed-property>
  </managed-bean>
</faces-config>
```

The second way to use the **map-entries** element is shown here:

```
<faces-config>
  <managed-bean>
    <managed-bean-name>
      testManagedBean
    </managed-bean-name>
    <managed-bean-class>
      com.example.jsf.TestManagedBean
    </managed-bean-class>
    <managed-bean-scope>
      session
    </managed-bean-scope>
    <map-entries>
      <map-entry>
        <key>testKey1</key>
        <value>1000</value>
      </map-entry>
      <map-entry>
        <key>testKey2</key>
        <null-value/>
      </map-entry>
    <map-entries>
  </managed-bean>
</faces-config>
```

This example populates a managed bean that is itself an instance of **java.util.Map**.

The map-entry Element

The **map-entry** element is used to encapsulate a key-value pair that makes up an entry for a map defined by a **map-entries** element.

Usage Rules

Rule	Value
JSF Versions	1.0, 1.1, 1.2, 2.0
Parent Elements	map-entries
Child Elements	key, null-value, value
Annotation(s)	None
Uniqueness Constraints	None

Example Usage

The following example illustrates the usage of the **map-entry** element:

```
<faces-config>
  <managed-bean>
    <managed-bean-name>
      testManagedBean
    </managed-bean-name>
```

```
    <managed-bean-class>
      com.example.jsf.TestManagedBean
    </managed-bean-class>
    <managed-bean-scope>
      session
    </managed-bean-scope>
    <managed-property>
      <property-name>testProperty</property-name>
      <map-entries>
        <map-entry>
          <key>testKey1</key>
          <value>testValue1</value>
        </map-entry>
        <map-entry>
          <key>testKey2</key>
          <null-value/>
        </map-entry>
      <map-entries>
    </managed-property>
  </managed-bean>
</faces-config>
```


The message-bundle Element

The **message-bundle** element is used to specify the fully qualified base name of a resource bundle that will be used for the JSF application. The value specified with this element must use Java's dot (.) package notation to separate directories and the resource bundle file name. Here is an example:

```
dir1.dir2.dir3.ResourceBundleFileName
```

Note that the **.properties** extension of the resource bundle file name should not be included in the value specified with the **message-bundle** element. JSF automatically appends that to the file name at runtime along with any locale information that might be necessary.

Usage Rules

Rule	Value
JSF Versions	1.0, 1.1, 1.2, 2.0
Parent Elements	application
Child Elements	None
Annotation(s)	None
Uniqueness Constraints	None

Example Usage

The following example illustrates the usage of the **message-bundle** element:

```
<faces-config>
  <application>
```

```
    <message-bundle>
      com.example.jsf.TestResources
    </message-bundle>
  </application>
</faces-config>
```

The name Element

The **name** element is used to declare the name of a JSF XML configuration file in case it needs to be loaded as part of an **absolute-ordering** or relative **ordering** scheme.

There are four ways that the **name** element can be used, as listed here and shown later, in the section "Example Usage."

- The **name** element can be nested inside a **faces-config** element, which will declare the name of the JSF XML configuration file.
- The **name** element can be nested one or more times inside an **absolute-ordering** element, which will specify an absolute ordering scheme by which named JSF XML configuration files are to be loaded.
- The **name** element can be nested one or more times inside an **ordering** element, which will specify a relative ordering scheme by which named JSF XML configuration files are to be loaded.
- Unrelated to any **absolute-ordering** or relative ordering scheme, the **name** element can be nested within a **view-param** element in order to specify the name of a view parameter.

Usage Rules

Rule	Value
JSF Versions	2.0
Parent Elements	faces-config, absolute-ordering, ordering, view-param
Child Elements	None
Annotation(s)	None
Uniqueness Constraints	Each JSF XML Configuration file within an application must have a unique value for the name element.

Example Usage

The following example illustrates the first way in which the **name** element can be nested:

```
<faces-config>
  <name>A</name>
</faces-config>
```

The following example illustrates the second way in which the **name** element can be nested:

```
<faces-config>
  <absolute-ordering>
    <name>A</name>
    <name>B</name>
    <name>C</name>
    <others />
  </absolute-ordering>
</faces-config>
```

The following example illustrates the third way in which the **name** element can be nested:

```
<faces-config>
  <ordering>
    <after>
      <name>B</name>
    </after>
    <before>
      <others/>
    </before>
  </ordering>
</faces-config>
```

The following example illustrates the fourth way in which the **name** element can be nested:

```
<faces-config>
  <navigation-rule>
    <from-view-id>/main.jsp</from-view-id>
    <navigation-case>
      <from-outcome>details</from-outcome>
      <to-view-id>/details.jsp</to-view-id>
      <redirect include-view-params="true">
        <view-param>
          <name>testViewParam</name>
          <value>testValue</value>
        </view-param>
      </redirect>
    </navigation-case>
  </navigation-rule>
</faces-config>
```

The navigation-case Element

The **navigation-case** element is used to encapsulate the set of elements that specify navigation case configuration details. This element has no other use than to denote the beginning and end of the navigation case configuration details.

Usage Rules

Rule	Value
JSF Versions	1.0, 1.1, 1.2, 2.0
Parent Elements	navigation-rule
Child Elements	description (1.0, 1.1), descriptionGroup (1.2), display-name (1.0, 1.1), from-action, from-outcome, icon (1.0, 1.1), if (2.0), redirect, to-view-id *Note: The parenthetical numbers represent the JSF versions that the corresponding child element applies to if the child element does not apply to all JSF versions.*
Annotation(s)	None
Uniqueness Constraints	None

Example Usage

The following example illustrates the usage of the **navigation-case** element:

```
<faces-config>
  <navigation-rule>
    <from-view-id>/main.jsp</from-view-id>
    <navigation-case>
      <from-outcome>details</from-outcome>
      <to-view-id>/details.jsp</to-view-id>
    </navigation-case>
  </navigation-rule>
</faces-config>
```

The navigation-handler Element

The **navigation-handler** element is used to specify the fully qualified class name of a **javax.faces.application.NavigationHandler** implementation class that will replace the JSF implementation's default navigation handler implementation. The navigation handler is called during the Invoke Application phase of the JSF request processing lifecycle and is responsible for managing the navigation between views in a JSF application. The **navigation-handler** element provides the ability to override the default JSF navigation handling by plugging in a custom **NavigationHandler**.

Usage Rules

Rule	Value
JSF Versions	1.0, 1.1, 1.2, 2.0
Parent Elements	application
Child Elements	None
Annotation(s)	None
Uniqueness Constraints	None

Example Usage

The following example illustrates the usage of the **navigation-handler** element:

```
<faces-config>
  <application>
    <navigation-handler>
      com.example.jsf.TestNavigationHandler
    </navigation-handler>
  </application>
</faces-config>
```

The navigation-rule Element

The **navigation-rule** element is used to encapsulate the set of elements that specify navigation rule configuration details. This element has no other use than to denote the beginning and end of the navigation rule configuration details.

Usage Rules

Rule	Value
JSF Versions	1.0, 1.1, 1.2, 2.0
Parent Elements	faces-config
Child Elements	description (1.0, 1.1), descriptionGroup (1.2), display-name (1.0, 1.1), from-view-id, icon (1.0, 1.1), navigation-case *Note: The parenthetical numbers represent the JSF versions that the corresponding child element applies to if the child element does not apply to all JSF versions.*
Annotation(s)	None
Uniqueness Constraints	None

Example Usage

The following example illustrates the usage of the **navigation-rule** element:

```
<faces-config>
  <navigation-rule>
    <from-view-id>/main.jsp</from-view-id>
    <navigation-case>
      <from-outcome>details</from-outcome>
      <to-view-id>/details.jsp</to-view-id>
    </navigation-case>
  </navigation-rule>
</faces-config>
```

The null-value Element

The **null-value** element is used to indicate that the property defined by the enclosing element must be initialized to null. Note that the **null-value** element does not accept any values and is to be used as an empty element, as shown here:

```
</null-value>
```

There are three ways that the **null-value** element can be used, as listed here and shown later, in the section "Example Usage."

- A list entry can be initialized to null by nesting a **null-value** element inside the **list-entries** element.
- A managed property of a managed bean can be initialized to null by nesting a **null-value** element inside the **managed-property** element.
- A map entry can be initialized to null by nesting a **null-value** element inside the **map-entry** element.

Usage Rules

Rule	Value
JSF Versions	1.0, 1.1, 1.2, 2.0
Parent Elements	list-entries, managed-property, map-entry
Child Elements	None
Annotation(s)	None
Uniqueness Constraints	None

Example Usage

As mentioned, there are three ways that the **null-value** element can be used. The first way, shown here, defines a null entry for a list:

```
<faces-config>
  <managed-bean>
    <managed-bean-name>
      testManagedBean
    </managed-bean-name>
    <managed-bean-class>
      com.example.jsf.TestManagedBean
    </managed-bean-class>
    <managed-bean-scope>
      session
    </managed-bean-scope>
    <managed-property>
      <property-name>testProperty</property-name>
      <list-entries>
        <value>testValue1</value>
        <null-value/>
        <value>testValue3</value>
      <list-entries>
```

```
    </managed-property>
  </managed-bean>
</faces-config>
```

The following is the second way to use the **null-value** element for instantiating a managed property to null:

```
<faces-config>
  <managed-bean>
    <managed-bean-name>
      testManagedBean
    </managed-bean-name>
    <managed-bean-class>
      com.example.jsf.TestManagedBean
    </managed-bean-class>
    <managed-bean-scope>
      session
    </managed-bean-scope>
    <managed-property>
      <property-name>testProperty</property-name>
      <null-value/>
    </managed-property>
  </managed-bean>
</faces-config>
```

The third and final way to use the **null-value** element is shown here:

```
<faces-config>
  <managed-bean>
    <managed-bean-name>
      testManagedBean
    </managed-bean-name>
    <managed-bean-class>
      com.example.jsf.TestManagedBean
    </managed-bean-class>
    <managed-bean-scope>
      session
    </managed-bean-scope>
    <managed-property>
      <property-name>testProperty</property-name>
      <map-entries>
        <map-entry>
          <key>testKey1</key>
          <value>testValue1</value>
        </map-entry>
        <map-entry>
          <key>testKey2</key>
          <null-value/>
        </map-entry>
      <map-entries>
    </managed-property>
  </managed-bean>
</faces-config>
```

This example shows how to initialize a map entry to null.

The ordering Element

The **ordering** element encapsulates the set of elements that specify the relative order by which named JSF XML configuration files are to be loaded. This element may used in any **/META-INF/faces-config.xml** file found in a jar, or in any file listed in the javax.faces.CONFIG_FILES key in **web.xml**. However, it may not be used in the application's **/WEB-INF/faces-config.xml** file. This element has no other use than to denote the beginning and end of relative ordering details.

Usage Rules

Rule	Value
JSF Versions	2.0
Parent Elements	faces-config
Child Elements	after (2.0), before (2.0) *Note: The parenthetical numbers represent the JSF versions that the corresponding child element applies to if the child element does not apply to all JSF versions.*
Annotation(s)	None
Uniqueness Constraints	None

Example Usage

The following example illustrates the usage of the **ordering** element:

```
<faces-config>
  <ordering>
    <after>
      <name>B</name>
    </after>
    <before>
      <others />
    </before>
  </ordering>
</faces-config>
```

The others Element

The **others** element specifies that all other JSF XML configuration files are to be loaded as part of the **absolute-ordering** or relative **ordering** scheme.

There are two ways in which the **others** element can be used:

- The **others** element can be nested inside an **absolute-ordering** element, which will specify that all other JSF XML configuration files are to be loaded as part of the absolute ordering scheme.

- The **others** element can be nested inside an **after** or **before** element, which will specify that all other JSF XML configuration files are to be loaded as part of the relative ordering scheme.

Usage Rules

Rule	Value
JSF Versions	2.0
Parent Elements	absolute-ordering, after, before
Child Elements	None
Annotation(s)	None
Uniqueness Constraints	None

Example Usage

The following example illustrates the first way in which the **others** element can be nested:

```
<faces-config>
  <absolute-ordering>
    <name>A</name>
    <name>B</name>
    <name>C</name>
    <others />
  </absolute-ordering>
</faces-config>
```

The following example illustrates the second way in which the **others** element can be nested:

```
<faces-config>
  <ordering>
    <after>
      <name>B</name>
    </after>
    <before>
      <others />
    </before>
  </ordering>
</faces-config>
```

The partial-view-context-factory Element

The **partial-view-context-factory** element is used to specify the fully qualified class name of a **javax.faces.context.PartialViewContextFactory** implementation class that will replace or decorate the JSF implementation's default partial view context factory implementation. The partial view context factory is used to retrieve and store a **javax.faces.context.PartialViewContext** instance for the current Web application. See Chapter 12 for more details.

PART III

Usage Rules

Rule	Value
JSF Versions	2.0
Parent Elements	factory
Child Elements	None
Annotation(s)	None
Uniqueness Constraints	None

Example Usage

The following example illustrates the usage of the **partial-view-context-factory** element:

```
<faces-config>
  <factory>
    <partial-view-context-factory>
      com.example.jsf.TestPartialViewContextFactory
    </partial-view-context-factory>
  </factory>
</faces-config>
```

The phase-listener Element

The **phase-listener** element is used to specify the fully qualified class name of a **javax.faces .event.PhaseListener** implementation class that will be notified of all phase changes during the JSF request processing lifecycle.

Usage Rules

Rule	Value
JSF Versions	1.0, 1.1, 1.2, 2.0
Parent Elements	lifecycle
Child Elements	None
Annotation(s)	None
Uniqueness Constraints	None

Example Usage

The following example illustrates the usage of the **phase-listener** element:

```
<faces-config>
  <lifecycle>
    <phase-listener>
      com.example.jsf.TestPhaseListener
    </phase-listener>
  </lifecycle>
</faces-config>
```

The property Element

The **property** element is used to encapsulate the set of elements specifying the details for a property. This element has no other use than to denote the beginning and end of a property's configuration details.

There are three ways that the **property** element can be used, as listed here and shown later, in the section "Example Usage."

- A property can be defined for a UI component by nesting **property** elements inside the **component** element.
- A property can be defined for a converter by nesting **property** elements inside the **converter** element.
- A property can be defined for a validator by nesting **property** elements inside the **validator** element.

Usage Rules

Rule	Value
JSF Versions	1.0, 1.1, 1.2, 2.0
Parent Elements	component, converter, validator
Child Elements	default-value, description (1.0, 1.1), descriptionGroup (1.2), display-name (1.0, 1.1), icon (1.0, 1.1), property-class, property-extension, property-name, suggested-value *Note: The parenthetical numbers represent the JSF versions that the corresponding child element applies to if the child element does not apply to all JSF versions.*
Annotation(s)	None
Uniqueness Constraints	None

Example Usage

As mentioned, there are three ways that the **property** element can be used. The first way, shown here, defines a property for a UI component:

```
<faces-config>
  <component>
    <component-type>
      com.example.jsf.TestComponent
    </component-type>
    <component-class>
      com.example.jsf.UITestComponent
    </component-class>
    <property>
      <property-name>testProperty</property-name>
      <property-class>java.lang.String</property-class>
    </property>
  </component>
</faces-config>
```

PART III

The following is the second way to use the **property** element:

```
<faces-config>
  <converter>
    <component-for-class>
      java.lang.Long
    </component-for-class>
    <component-class>
      com.example.jsf.LongConverter
    </component-class>
    <property>
      <property-name>testProperty</property-name>
      <property-class>java.lang.String</property-class>
    </property>
  </converter>
</faces-config>
```

The third and final way to use the **property** element is shown here:

```
<faces-config>
  <validator>
    <validator-id>
      javax.faces.Length
    </validator-id>
    <validator-class>
      javax.faces.validator.LengthValidator
    </validator-class>
    <property>
      <property-name>testProperty</property-name>
      <property-class>java.lang.String</property-class>
    </property>
  </validator>
</faces-config>
```

The property-class Element

The **property-class** element is used to specify the fully qualified class name for a property's value—for example, **java.lang.String** for string values and **java.lang.Integer** for an integer value.

Usage Rules

Rule	Value
JSF Versions	1.0, 1.1, 1.2, 2.0
Parent Elements	property
Child Elements	None
Annotation(s)	None
Uniqueness Constraints	None

Example Usage

The following example illustrates the usage of the **property-class** element:

```
<faces-config>
  <validator>
    <validator-id>
      javax.faces.Length
    </validator-id>
    <validator-class>
      javax.faces.validator.LengthValidator
    </validator-class>
    <property>
      <property-name>testProperty</property-name>
      <property-class> java.lang.String</property-class>
    </property>
  </validator>
</faces-config>
```

The property-name Element

The **property-name** element is used to specify the logical name for a property under which the property's value will be stored.

Usage Rules

Rule	Value
JSF Versions	1.0, 1.1, 1.2, 2.0
Parent Elements	property
Child Elements	None
Annotation(s)	None
Uniqueness Constraints	None

Example Usage

The following example illustrates the usage of the **property-name** element:

```
<faces-config>
  <validator>
    <validator-id>
      javax.faces.Length
    </validator-id>
    <validator-class>
      javax.faces.validator.LengthValidator
    </validator-class>
    <property>
      <property-name>testProperty</property-name>
      <property-class>java.lang.String</property-class>
    </property>
  </validator>
</faces-config>
```

The property-resolver Element

The **property-resolver** element is used to specify the fully qualified class name of a **javax .faces.el.PropertyResolver** implementation class that will replace the JSF implementation's default property resolver implementation. The property resolver is used to process value binding expressions and is called each time a value binding expression must be resolved. The **property-resolver** element provides the ability to override the default JSF property resolving by plugging in a custom **PropertyResolver**.

Usage Rules

Rule	Value
JSF Versions	1.0, 1.1, 1.2, 2.0
Parent Elements	application
Child Elements	None
Annotation(s)	None
Uniqueness Constraints	None

Example Usage

The following example illustrates the usage of the **property-resolver** element:

```
<faces-config>
  <application>
    <property-resolver>
      com.example.jsf.TestPropertyResolver
    </property-resolver>
  </application>
</faces-config>
```

The redirect Element

The **redirect** element is used to indicate that the associated navigation case's to-view-id URL should be navigated to using an HTTP redirect instead of the standard View Handler processing. Note that JSF 2.0 has introduced the optional **include-view-params** attribute, the value of which must be a boolean (true or false). If true, then any view parameters specified with **f:viewParam** will be included in the generated URL.

Usage Rules

Rule	Value
JSF Versions	1.0, 1.1, 1.2, 2.0
Parent Elements	navigation-case
Child Elements	view-param (2.0) *Note: The parenthetical numbers represent the JSF versions that the corresponding child element applies to if the child element does not apply to all JSF versions.*
Annotation(s)	None
Uniqueness Constraints	None

Example Usage

The following example illustrates the usage of the **redirect** element:

```
<faces-config>
  <navigation-rule>
    <from-view-id>/main.jsp</from-view-id>
    <navigation-case>
      <from-outcome>details</from-outcome>
      <to-view-id>/details.jsp</to-view-id>
      <redirect include-view-params="true" />
    </navigation-case>
  </navigation-rule>
</faces-config>
```


The referenced-bean Element

The **referenced-bean** element is used to encapsulate the set of elements specifying the details for a referenced bean. Referenced beans are external beans that are supposed to be available to a JSF application at runtime by existing in one of the Web application scopes (request, session, or application). This element has no other use than to denote the beginning and end of the referenced bean details.

Usage Rules

Rule	Value
JSF Versions	1.0, 1.1, 1.2, 2.0
Parent Elements	faces-config
Child Elements	description (1.0, 1.1), descriptionGroup (1.2), display-name (1.0, 1.1), icon (1.0, 1.1), referenced-bean-class, referenced-bean-name *Note: The parenthetical numbers represent the JSF versions that the corresponding child element applies to if the child element does not apply to all JSF versions.*
Annotation(s)	@ReferencedBean
Uniqueness Constraints	None

Example Usage

The following example illustrates the usage of the **referenced-bean** element:

```
<faces-config>
  <referenced-bean>
    <referenced-bean-name>
      testReferencedBean
    </referenced-bean-name>
    <referenced-bean-class>
      com.example.jsf.TestReferencedBean
    </referenced-bean-class>
  </referenced-bean>
</faces-config>
```

The following example illustrates the usage of the **@ReferencedBean** annotation:

```
@ReferencedBean(name="testReferencedBean")
public class TestReferencedBean {
    ...
}
```

The referenced-bean-class Element

The **referenced-bean-class** element is used to specify the fully qualified class name of an external bean that is supposed to be available to the JSF application at runtime by existing in one of the Web application scopes (request, session, or application).

Usage Rules

Rule	Value
JSF Versions	1.0, 1.1, 1.2, 2.0
Parent Elements	referenced-bean
Child Elements	None
Annotation(s)	None
Uniqueness Constraints	None

Example Usage

The following example illustrates the usage of the **referenced-bean-class** element:

```
<faces-config>
  <referenced-bean>
    <referenced-bean-name>
      TestReferencedBean
    </referenced-bean-name>
    <referenced-bean-class>
      com.example.jsf.TestReferencedBean
    </referenced-bean-class>
  </referenced-bean>
</faces-config>
```


The referenced-bean-name Element

The **referenced-bean-name** element is used to specify the logical name for a referenced bean. The logical name is used to register the referenced bean with JSF so that it can later be accessed by the same logical name.

Usage Rules

Rule	Value
JSF Versions	1.0, 1.1, 1.2, 2.0
Parent Elements	referenced-bean
Child Elements	None
Annotation(s)	None
Uniqueness Constraints	None

Example Usage

The following example illustrates the usage of the **referenced-bean-name** element:

```
<faces-config>
  <referenced-bean>
    <referenced-bean-name>
      TestReferencedBean
    </referenced-bean-name>
```

```
    <referenced-bean-class>
      com.example.jsf.TestReferencedBean
    </referenced-bean-class>
  </referenced-bean>
</faces-config>
```

The render-kit Element

The **render-kit** element is used to encapsulate the set of elements specifying the details for a render kit. This element has no other use than to denote the beginning and end of the render kit details.

Usage Rules

Rule	Value
JSF Versions	1.0, 1.1, 1.2, 2.0
Parent Elements	faces-config
Child Elements	client-behavior-renderer (2.0), description (1.0, 1.1), descriptionGroup (1.2), display-name (1.0, 1.1), icon (1.0, 1.1), render-kit-class, render-kit-extension (1.2), render-kit-id, renderer *Note: The parenthetical numbers represent the JSF versions that the corresponding child element applies to if the child element does not apply to all JSF versions.*
Annotation(s)	None
Uniqueness Constraints	None

Example Usage

The following example illustrates the usage of the **render-kit** element:

```
<faces-config>
  <render-kit>
    <render-kit-id>test</render-kit-id>
    <render-kit-class>
      com.example.jsf.TestRenderKit
    </render-kit-class>
    <renderer>
      <component-family>
        javax.faces.Data
      </component-family>
      <renderer-type>
        javax.faces.Table
      </renderer-type>
      <renderer-class>
        com.sun.faces.renderkit.html_basic.TableRenderer
      </renderer-class>
    </renderer>
  </render-kit>
</faces-config>
```

The render-kit-class Element

The **render-kit-class** element is used to specify the fully qualified class name for a render kit implementation. The implementation must extend the **javax.faces.render.RenderKit** abstract base class.

Usage Rules

Rule	Value
JSF Versions	1.0, 1.1, 1.2, 2.0
Parent Elements	render-kit
Child Elements	None
Annotation(s)	None
Uniqueness Constraints	None

Example Usage

The following example illustrates the usage of the **render-kit-class** element:

```
<faces-config>
  <render-kit>
    <render-kit-id>test<render-kit-id>
    <render-kit-class>
      com.example.jsf.TestRenderKit
    </render-kit-class>
    <renderer>
      <component-family>
        javax.faces.Data
      </component-family>
      <renderer-type>
        javax.faces.Table
      </renderer-type>
      <renderer-class>
        com.sun.faces.renderkit.html_basic.TableRenderer
      </renderer-class>
    </renderer>
  </render-kit>
</faces-config>
```


The render-kit-factory Element

The **render-kit-factory** element is used to specify the fully qualified class name of a **javax.faces .render.RenderKitFactory** implementation class that will replace the JSF implementation's default render kit factory implementation. The render kit factory is used to store and retrieve **javax.faces.render.RenderKit** instances for the current Web application as well as to retrieve a list of the IDs for render kits supported by the factory.

Usage Rules

Rule	Value
JSF Versions	1.0, 1.1, 1.2, 2.0
Parent Elements	factory
Child Elements	None
Annotation(s)	None
Uniqueness Constraints	None

Example Usage

The following example illustrates the usage of the **render-kit-factory** element:

```
<faces-config>
  <factory>
    <render-kit-factory>
      com.example.jsf.TestRenderKitFactory
    </render-kit-factory>
  </factory>
</faces-config>
```

The render-kit-id Element

The **render-kit-id** element is used to specify the logical name for a render kit. The logical name is used to register the render kit with JSF so that it can later be accessed by the same logical name.

Usage Rules

Rule	Value
JSF Versions	1.0, 1.1, 1.2, 2.0
Parent Elements	render-kit
Child Elements	None
Annotation(s)	None
Uniqueness Constraints	None

Example Usage

The following example illustrates the usage of the **render-kit-id** element:

```
<faces-config>
  <render-kit>
    <render-kit-id>test<render-kit-id>
    <render-kit-class>
      com.example.jsf.TestRenderKit
    </render-kit-class>
```

```
    <renderer>
      <component-family>
        javax.faces.Data
      </component-family>
      <renderer-type>
        javax.faces.Table
      </renderer-type>
      <renderer-class>
        com.sun.faces.renderkit.html_basic.TableRenderer
      </renderer-class>
    </renderer>
  </render-kit>
</faces-config>
```

The renderer Element

The **renderer** element is used to encapsulate the set of elements specifying the details for a renderer. This element has no other use than to denote the beginning and end of the renderer details.

Usage Rules

Rule	Value
JSF Versions	1.0, 1.1, 1.2, 2.0
Parent Elements	render-kit
Child Elements	attribute, component-family, description (1.0, 1.1), descriptionGroup (1.2), display-name (1.0, 1.1), facet, icon (1.0, 1.1), renderer-class, renderer-extension, renderer-type *Note: The parenthetical numbers represent the JSF versions that the corresponding child element applies to if the child element does not apply to all JSF versions.*
Annotation(s)	@FacesRenderer
Uniqueness Constraints	None

Example Usage

The following example illustrates the usage of the **renderer** element:

```
<faces-config>
  <render-kit>
    <renderer>
      <component-family>
        javax.faces.Data
      </component-family>
      <renderer-type>
        javax.faces.Table
      </renderer-type>
```

```
        <renderer-class>
          com.sun.faces.renderkit.html_basic.TableRenderer
        </renderer-class>
      </renderer>
    </render-kit>
</faces-config>
```

The following example illustrates the usage of the **@FacesRenderer** annotation:

```
@FacesRenderer(
  componentFamily="javax.faces.Data",
  rendererType="javax.faces.Table",
  renderKitId="HTML_BASIC")
public class TableRenderer extends Renderer {
  ...
}
```

The renderer-class Element

The **renderer-class** element is used to specify the fully qualified class name for a renderer implementation. The implementation must extend from the **javax.faces.render.Renderer** abstract base class.

Usage Rules

Rule	Value
JSF Versions	1.0, 1.1, 1.2, 2.0
Parent Elements	renderer
Child Elements	None
Annotation(s)	None
Uniqueness Constraints	None

Example Usage

The following example illustrates the usage of the **renderer-class** element:

```
<faces-config>
  <render-kit>
    <renderer>
      <component-family>
        javax.faces.Data
      </component-family>
      <renderer-type>
        javax.faces.Table
      </renderer-type>
      <renderer-class>
        com.sun.faces.renderkit.html_basic.TableRenderer
      </renderer-class>
    </renderer>
  </render-kit>
</faces-config>
```

The renderer-type Element

The **renderer-type** element is used to specify the logical name for a renderer. The logical name is used to register the renderer with JSF so that it can later be accessed by the same logical name.

Usage Rules

Rule	Value
JSF Versions	1.0, 1.1, 1.2, 2.0
Parent Elements	renderer
Child Elements	None
Annotation(s)	None
Uniqueness Constraints	None

Example Usage

The following example illustrates the usage of the **renderer-type** element:

```
<faces-config>
  <render-kit>
    <renderer>
      <component-family>
        javax.faces.Data
      </component-family>
      <renderer-type>
        javax.faces.Table
      </renderer-type>
      <renderer-class>
        com.sun.faces.renderkit.html_basic.TableRenderer
      </renderer-class>
    </renderer>
  </render-kit>
</faces-config>
```


The resource-bundle Element

The **resource-bundle** element is used to encapsulate the set of elements that specify resource bundle configuration details. This element has no other use than to denote the beginning and end of the resource bundle configuration details.

Usage Rules

Rule	Value
JSF Versions	1.2, 2.0
Parent Elements	application
Child Elements	base-name, descriptionGroup, var
Annotation(s)	None
Uniqueness Constraints	None

Example Usage

The following example illustrates the usage of the **resource-bundle** element:

```
<faces-config>
  <application>
    <resource-bundle>
      <base-name>
        com.example.jsf.TestResources
      </base-name>
      <var>testResources</var>
    </resource-bundle>
  </application>
</faces-config>
```

The resource-handler Element

The **resource-handler** element is used to specify the fully qualified class name of a **javax.faces.application.ResourceHandler** implementation class that will replace the JSF implementation's default resource handler implementation. The resource handler is called when resource requests rendered and decoded. The **resource-handler** element provides the ability to override the default JSF resource handler by plugging in a custom **ResourceHandler**.

Usage Rules

Rule	Value
JSF Versions	2.0
Parent Elements	application
Child Elements	None
Annotation(s)	None
Uniqueness Constraints	None

Example Usage

The following example illustrates the usage of the **resource-handler** element:

```
<faces-config>
  <application>
    <resource-handler>
      com.example.jsf.TestResourceHandler
    </resource-handler>
  </application>
</faces-config>
```

The source-class Element

The **source-class** element is used to specify the fully qualified class name of a **java.lang.Object** extended class of the instance that causes **system-event-class** to be fired.

Usage Rules

Rule	Value
JSF Versions	2.0
Parent Elements	system-event-listener
Child Elements	None
Annotation(s)	None
Uniqueness Constraints	None

Example Usage

The following example illustrates the usage of the **source-class** element:

```
<faces-config>
  <application>
    <system-event-listener>
      <system-event-listener-class>
        com.example.jsf.TestSystemEventListener
      </system-event-listener-class>
      <system-event-class>
        javax.faces.event.PostConstructApplicationEvent
      </system-event-class>
      <source-class>
        com.example.jsf.TestSource
      </source-class>
    </system-event-listener>
  </application>
</faces-config>
```

The state-manager Element

The **state-manager** element is used to specify the fully qualified class name of a **javax.faces .application.StateManager** implementation class that will replace the JSF implementation's default state manager implementation. The state manager is called during the Restore View and Render Response phases of the JSF request processing lifecycle and is responsible for storing and retrieving the state of current view between HTTP requests. The **state-manager** element provides the ability to override the default JSF state management by plugging in a custom **StateManager**.

Usage Rules

Rule	Value
JSF Versions	1.0, 1.1, 1.2, 2.0
Parent Elements	application
Child Elements	None
Annotation(s)	None
Uniqueness Constraints	None

Example Usage

The following example illustrates the usage of the **state-manager** element:

```
<faces-config>
  <application>
    <state-manager>
      com.example.jsf.TestStateManager
    </state-manager>
  </application>
</faces-config>
```

The suggested-value Element

The **suggested-value** element is used to specify the suggested value for an attribute or a property. Suggested values differ from default values in that suggested values may or may not be assigned to an attribute or property whereas default values will be assigned to an attribute or property.

Usage Rules

Rule	Value
JSF Versions	1.0, 1.1, 1.2, 2.0
Parent Elements	attribute, property
Child Elements	None
Annotation(s)	None
Uniqueness Constraints	None

Example Usage

There are two ways that the **suggested-value** element can be used. The first way, shown here, defines a suggested value for an attribute:

```
<faces-config>
  <component>
    <component-type>
      com.example.jsf.TestComponent
    </component-type>
    <component-class>
      com.example.jsf.UITestComponent
    </component-class>
    <attribute>
      <attribute-name>testAttribute</attribute-name>
      <attribute-class>java.lang.String</attribute-class>
      <suggested-value>testSuggestedValue</suggested-value>
    </attribute>
  </component>
</faces-config>
```

The following is the second way to use the **suggested-value** element to define a suggested value for a property:

```
<faces-config>
  <converter>
    <component-for-class>
      java.lang.Long
    </component-for-class>
    <component-class>
      com.example.jsf.LongConverter
    </component-class>
    <property>
      <property-name>testAttribute</property-name>
      <property-class>java.lang.String</property-class>
      <suggested-value>testDefaultValue</suggested-value>
    </property>
  </converter>
</faces-config>
```


The supported-locale Element

The **supported-locale** element is used to specify a locale supported by the JSF application. JSF uses locale information to retrieve all localized resources for the application. JSF uses the default locale setting if another locale is not specified (e.g., via the browser). The locale value specified with the **supported-locale** element must be in the following format:

language_country_variant

The *language, country,* and *variant* arguments of the locale definition must be separated by either an underscore (_) or a hyphen (-). The *country* and *variant* arguments are optional. The *language* argument must be specified using a valid two-letter ISO-639 language code (e.g., "en" for English or "es" for Spanish). The *country* argument must be specified using a valid uppercase two-letter ISO-3166 country code (e.g., "US" for United States or "CA" for Canada). The *variant* argument is for a vendor- or browser-specific code (e.g., "WIN" for Windows or "MAC" for Macintosh). For a listing of each of the ISO language and country codes, visit their respective specification Web sites listed here:

www.unicode.org/unicode/onlinedat/languages.html
www.unicode.org/unicode/onlinedat/countries.html

To illustrate the rules of locales, consider some of the following example locale definitions.

- **en** English
- **en_US** United States English
- **en_US_WIN** United States English on Windows
- **es** Spanish
- **es_MX** Mexican Spanish
- **es_MX_MAC** Mexican Spanish on Macintosh

Usage Rules

Rule	Value
JSF Versions	1.0, 1.1, 1.2, 2.0
Parent Elements	locale-config
Child Elements	None
Annotation(s)	None
Uniqueness Constraints	None

Example Usage

The following example illustrates the usage of the **supported-locale** element:

```
<faces-config>
  <application>
    <locale-config>
      <default-locale>en</default-locale>
      <supported-locale>es</supported-locale>
      <supported-locale>fr_FR</supported-locale>
    </locale-config>
  </application>
</faces-config>
```

The system-event-class Element

The **system-event-class** element is used to specify the fully qualified class name of a **javax .faces.event.SystemEvent** extended class.

Usage Rules

Rule	Value
JSF Versions	2.0
Parent Elements	system-event-listener
Child Elements	None
Annotation(s)	None
Uniqueness Constraints	None

Example Usage

The following example illustrates the usage of the **system-event-class** element:

```
<faces-config>
  <application>
    <system-event-listener>
      <system-event-listener-class>
        com.example.jsf.TestSystemEventListener
      </system-event-listener-class>
      <system-event-class>
```

```
        javax.faces.event.PostConstructApplicationEvent
      </system-event-class>
    </system-event-listener>
  </application>
</faces-config>
```

The system-event-listener Element

The **system-event-listener** element is used to encapsulate the set of elements that specify the details for a listener that will be notified of application scoped system events during the JSF request processing lifecycle. This element has no other use than to denote the beginning and end of the system event listener details.

Usage Rules

Rule	Value
JSF Versions	2.0
Parent Elements	application
Child Elements	system-event-listener-class (2.0), system-event-class, source-class (2.0) *Note: The parenthetical numbers represent the JSF versions that the corresponding child element applies to if the child element does not apply to all JSF versions.*
Annotation(s)	@ListenerFor
Uniqueness Constraints	None

Example Usage

The following example illustrates the usage of the **system-event-listener** element:

```
<faces-config>
  <application>
    <system-event-listener>
      <system-event-listener-class>
        com.example.jsf.TestSystemEventListener
      </system-event-listener-class>
      <system-event-class>
        javax.faces.event.PostConstructApplicationEvent
      </system-event-class>
    </system-event-listener>
  </application>
</faces-config>
```

The following example illustrates equivalent configuration via the **@ListenerFor** annotation:

```
@ListenerFor(systemEventClass = javax.faces.event.PostConstructApplicationEvent.class)
public class TestSystemEventListener implements SystemEventListener {
  ...
}
```

PART III

The system-event-listener-class Element

The **system-event-listener-class** element is used to specify the fully qualified class name of a **javax.faces.event.SystemEventListener** implementation class that will be notified of application scoped system events.

Usage Rules

Rule	Value
JSF Versions	2.0
Parent Elements	system-event-listener
Child Elements	None
Annotation(s)	None
Uniqueness Constraints	None

Example Usage

The following example illustrates the usage of the **system-event-listener-class** element:

```
<faces-config>
  <application>
    <system-event-listener>
      <system-event-listener-class>
        com.example.jsf.TestSystemEventListener
      </system-event-listener-class>
      <system-event-class>
        javax.faces.event.PostConstructApplicationEvent
      </system-event-class>
    </system-event-listener>
  </application>
</faces-config>
```

The tag-handler-delegate-factory Element

The **tag-handler-delegate-factory** element is used to specify the fully qualified class name of a **javax.faces.view.facelets.TagHandlerDelegateFactory** implementation class that will replace or decorate the JSF implementation's default tag handler delegate factory implementation. The tag handler delegate factory is used to retrieve and store a **javax.faces.view.facelets .TagHandlerDelegate** instance for the current Web application.

Usage Rules

Rule	Value
JSF Versions	2.0
Parent Elements	factory
Child Elements	None
Annotation(s)	None
Uniqueness Constraints	None

Example Usage

The following example illustrates the usage of the **tag-handler-delegate-factory** element:

```
<faces-config>
  <factory>
    <tag-handler-delegate-factory>
      com.example.jsf.TestTagHandlerDelegateFactory
    </tag-handler-delegate-factory>
  </factory>
</faces-config>
```

The to-view-id Element

The **to-view-id** element is used to specify the view ID for a view that will be displayed if the navigation case that the view ID is associated with is selected.

Usage Rules

Rule	Value
JSF Versions	1.0, 1.1, 1.2, 2.0
Parent Elements	navigation-case
Child Elements	None
Annotation(s)	None
Uniqueness Constraints	None

Example Usage

The following example illustrates the usage of the **to-view-id** element:

```
<faces-config>
  <navigation-rule>
    <from-view-id>/main.jsp</from-view-id>
    <navigation-case>
      <from-outcome>details</from-outcome>
      <to-view-id>/details.jsp</to-view-id>
    </navigation-case>
  </navigation-rule>
</faces-config>
```

The validator Element

The **validator** element is used to encapsulate the set of elements specifying the details for a validator. This element has no other use than to denote the beginning and end of the validator details.

Usage Rules

Rule	Value
JSF Versions	1.0, 1.1, 1.2, 2.0
Parent Elements	faces-config
Child Elements	attribute, description (1.0, 1.1), descriptionGroup (1.2), display-name (1.0, 1.1), icon (1.0, 1.1), property, validator-class, validator-extension (1.2), validator-id *Note: The parenthetical numbers represent the JSF versions that the corresponding child element applies to if the child element does not apply to all JSF versions.*
Annotation(s)	@FacesValidator
Uniqueness Constraints	None

Example Usage

The following example illustrates the usage of the **validator** element:

```
<faces-config>
  <validator>
    <validator-id>
      javax.faces.Length
    </validator-id>
    <validator-class>
      javax.faces.validator.LengthValidator
    </validator-class>
  </validator>
</faces-config>
```

The following example illustrates the usage of the **@FacesValidator** annotation:

```
@FacesValidator(value="javax.faces.Length")
public class LengthValidator implements Validator {
  ...
}
```

The validator-class Element

The **validator-class** element is used to specify the fully qualified class name for a validator implementation. The implementation must implement the **javax.faces.validator.Validator** interface.

Usage Rules

Rule	Value
JSF Versions	1.0, 1.1, 1.2, 2.0
Parent Elements	validator
Child Elements	None
Annotation(s)	None
Uniqueness Constraints	None

Example Usage

The following example illustrates the usage of the **validator-class** element:

```
<faces-config>
  <validator>
    <validator-id>
      javax.faces.Length
    </validator-id>
    <validator-class>
      javax.faces.validator.LengthValidator
    </validator-class>
  </validator>
</faces-config>
```


The validator-id Element

The **validator-id** element is used to specify the logical name for a validator. The logical name is used to register the validator with JSF so that it can later be accessed by the same logical name.

Usage Rules

Rule	Value
JSF Versions	1.0, 1.1, 1.2, 2.0
Parent Elements	validator
Child Elements	None
Annotation(s)	None
Uniqueness Constraints	Values for this element must be unique within the configuration file.

Example Usage

The following example illustrates the usage of the **validator-id** element:

```
<faces-config>
  <validator>
    <validator-id>
      javax.faces.Length
```

```
    </validator-id>
    <validator-class>
      javax.faces.validator.LengthValidator
    </validator-class>
  </validator>
</faces-config>
```

The value Element

The **value** element is used to specify the literal value or value binding expression that generates a value for a list entry, managed property, or map entry.

Usage Rules

Rule	Value
JSF Versions	1.0, 1.1, 1.2, 2.0
Parent Elements	list-entries, managed-property, map-entry, view-param (2.0) *Note: The parenthetical numbers represent the JSF versions that the corresponding child element applies to if the child element does not apply to all JSF versions.*
Child Elements	None
Annotation(s)	None
Uniqueness Constraints	None

Example Usage

There are three ways that the **value** element can be used. The first way, shown here, uses the **value** element to specify list entry values:

```
<faces-config>
  <managed-bean>
    <managed-bean-name>
      testManagedBean
    </managed-bean-name>
    <managed-bean-class>
      com.example.jsf.TestManagedBean
    </managed-bean-class>
    <managed-bean-scope>
      session
    </managed-bean-scope>
    <managed-property>
      <property-name>testProperty</property-name>
      <list-entries>
        <value>1000</value>
        <value>#{myBean.myProperty}</value>
      <list-entries>
    </managed-property>
  </managed-bean>
</faces-config>
```

The second way to use the **value** element is for a managed property and is shown here:

```
<faces-config>
  <managed-bean>
    <managed-bean-name>
      testManagedBean
    </managed-bean-name>
    <managed-bean-class>
      com.example.jsf.TestManagedBean
    </managed-bean-class>
    <managed-bean-scope>
      session
    </managed-bean-scope>
    <managed-property>
      <property-name>testProperty</property-name>
      <value>testValue</value>
    </managed-property>
  </managed-bean>
</faces-config>
```

Following is the third way to use the **value** element:

```
<faces-config>
  <managed-bean>
    <managed-bean-name>
      testManagedBean
    </managed-bean-name>
    <managed-bean-class>
      com.example.jsf.TestManagedBean
    </managed-bean-class>
    <managed-bean-scope>
      session
    </managed-bean-scope>
    <managed-property>
      <property-name>testProperty</property-name>
      <map-entries>
        <map-entry>
          <key>testKey1</key>
          <value>1000</value>
        </map-entry>
        <map-entry>
          <key>testKey2</key>
          <null-value/>
        </map-entry>
      <map-entries>
    </managed-property>
  </managed-bean>
</faces-config>
```

The value-class Element

The **value-class** element is used to specify the fully qualified class name of an object type that all values will be converted to before being added to a list defined by a **list-entries** element or a map defined by a **map-entries** element. If this element is not nested inside a **list-entries** or **map-entries** element, all list or map entry values will default to **java.lang .String** as their object type.

There are two ways that the **value-class** element can be used, as listed here and shown later, in the section "Example Usage."

- To specify the fully qualified class name of an object type for list entry values by nesting **value-class** elements inside the **list-entries** element.
- To specify the fully qualified class name of an object type for map entry values by nesting **value-class** elements inside the **map-entries** element.

Usage Rules

Rule	Value
JSF Versions	1.0, 1.1, 1.2, 2.0
Parent Elements	list-entries, map-entries
Child Elements	None
Annotation(s)	None
Uniqueness Constraints	None

Example Usage

As mentioned, there are two ways that the **value-class** element can be used. The first way, shown here, defines the value class for a list:

```
<faces-config>
  <managed-bean>
    <managed-bean-name>
      testManagedBean
    </managed-bean-name>
    <managed-bean-class>
      com.example.jsf.TestManagedBean
    </managed-bean-class>
    <managed-bean-scope>
      session
    </managed-bean-scope>
    <managed-property>
      <property-name>testProperty</property-name>
      <list-entries>
        <value-class>java.lang.Integer</value-class>
        <value>1000</value>
        <value>2000</value>
      <list-entries>
    </managed-property>
  </managed-bean>
</faces-config>
```

The following is the second way to use the **value-class** element for defining the value class for a map:

```
<faces-config>
  <managed-bean>
    <managed-bean-name>
      testManagedBean
    </managed-bean-name>
    <managed-bean-class>
      com.example.jsf.TestManagedBean
    </managed-bean-class>
    <managed-bean-scope>
      session
    </managed-bean-scope>
    <managed-property>
      <property-name>testProperty</property-name>
      <map-entries>
        <value-class>java.lang.Integer</value-class>
        <map-entry>
          <key>testKey1</key>
          <value>1000</value>
        </map-entry>
        <map-entry>
          <key>testKey2</key>
          <null-value/>
        </map-entry>
      <map-entries>
    </managed-property>
  </managed-bean>
</faces-config>
```


The var Element

The **var** element is used to specify the logical name for a resource bundle instance that will be registered with the JSF application. The resource bundle instance can then be later accessed by a call to the **javax.faces.application.Application.getResourceBundle( )** method passing in the value specified by the **var** element.

Usage Rules

Rule	Value
JSF Versions	1.2, 2.0
Parent Elements	resource-bundle
Child Elements	None
Annotation(s)	None
Uniqueness Constraints	None

Example Usage

The following example illustrates the usage of the **var** element:

```
<faces-config>
  <application>
    <resource-bundle>
      <base-name>
        com.example.jsf.TestResources
      </base-name>
      <var>testResources</var>
    </resource-bundle>
  </application>
</faces-config>
```

The variable-resolver Element

The **variable-resolver** element is used to specify the fully qualified class name of a **javax.faces.el.VariableResolver** implementation class that will replace the JSF implementation's default variable resolver implementation. The variable resolver is used to process value binding expressions and is called each time a value binding expression must be resolved. The **variable-resolver** element provides the ability to override the default JSF variable resolving by plugging in a custom **VariableResolver**.

Usage Rules

Rule	Value
JSF Versions	1.0, 1.1, 1.2, 2.0
Parent Elements	application
Child Elements	None
Annotation(s)	None
Uniqueness Constraints	None

Example Usage

The following example illustrates the usage of the **variable-resolver** element:

```
<faces-config>
  <application>
    <variable-resolver>
      com.example.jsf.TestVariableResolver
    </variable-resolver>
  </application>
</faces-config>
```

The view-declaration-language-factory Element

The **view-declaration-language-factory** element is used to specify the fully qualified class name of a **javax.faces.view.ViewDeclarationLanguageFactory** implementation class that will replace or decorate the JSF implementation's default view declaration language factory implementation. The view declaration language factory is used to retrieve and store a **javax.faces.view.ViewDeclarationLanguage** instance for the current Web application.

Usage Rules

Rule	Value
JSF Versions	2.0
Parent Elements	factory
Child Elements	None
Annotation(s)	None
Uniqueness Constraints	None

Example Usage

The following example illustrates the usage of the **view-declaration-language-factory** element:

```
<faces-config>
  <factory>
    <view-declaration-language-factory>
      com.example.jsf.TestViewDeclarationLanguageFactory
    </view-declaration-language-factory>
  </factory>
</faces-config>
```


The view-handler Element

The **view-handler** element is used to specify the fully qualified class name of a **javax.faces.application.ViewHandler** implementation class that will replace the JSF implementation's default view handler implementation. The view handler is called during the Restore View and Render Response phases of the JSF request processing lifecycle and is responsible for managing response generation and saving and restoring the state for each view. The **view-handler** element provides the ability to override the default JSF view handling by plugging in a custom **ViewHandler**.

Usage Rules

Rule	Value
JSF Versions	1.0, 1.1, 1.2, 2.0
Parent Elements	application
Child Elements	None
Annotation(s)	None
Uniqueness Constraints	None

Example Usage

The following example illustrates the usage of the **view-handler** element:

```
<faces-config>
  <application>
    <view-handler>
      com.example.jsf.TestViewHandler
    </view-handler>
  </application>
</faces-config>
```

The view-param Element

The **view-param** element encapsulates the set of elements used to specify the details of a view parameter when using the **redirect** element to redirect to a different view. The view parameter **name** and **value** will be added to the generated URL as parameters.

Usage Rules

Rule	Value
JSF Versions	2.0
Parent Elements	redirect
Child Elements	name (2.0), value
Annotation(s)	None
Uniqueness Constraints	None

Example Usage

The following example illustrates the usage of the **view-param** element:

```
<faces-config>
  <navigation-rule>
    <from-view-id>/main.jsp</from-view-id>
    <navigation-case>
      <from-outcome>details</from-outcome>
      <to-view-id>/details.jsp</to-view-id>
      <redirect include-view-params="true">
        <view-param>
          <name>testViewParam</name>
          <value>testValue</value>
        </view-param>
      </redirect>
    </navigation-case>
  </navigation-rule>
</faces-config>
```

The visit-context-factory Element

The **visit-context-factory** element is used to specify the fully qualified class name of a **javax.faces.component.visit.VisitContextFactory** implementation class that will replace or decorate the JSF implementation's default visit context factory implementation. The visit context factory is used to retrieve and store a **javax.faces.component.visit.VisitContext** instance for the current Web application.

Usage Rules

Rule	Value
JSF Versions	2.0
Parent Elements	factory
Child Elements	None
Annotation(s)	None
Uniqueness Constraints	None

Example Usage

The following example illustrates the usage of the **visit-context-factory** element:

```
<faces-config>
  <factory>
    <visit-context-factory>
      com.example.jsf.TestVisitContextFactory
    </visit-context-factory>
  </factory>
</faces-config>
```

Extension Elements

Many of the Web application frameworks preceding JSF fell short from a configuration perspective because they made it cumbersome, or in some cases impossible, to extend their configuration files. The limited extensibility of these files is due to the files being governed by rigid DTD or XML schema specifications. JSF configuration files, conversely, were designed from the beginning to be extensible.

JSF solved the extensibility problem by adding extension points throughout the configuration file that allow proprietary XML elements to be inserted. These extension points allow individual JSF implementations to make use of proprietary configuration data without requiring a separate configuration file. More important, the extension points prevent the various implementations that utilize proprietary elements from impacting other implementations that might not recognize the proprietary elements. An implementation that does not recognize the proprietary elements will simply ignore any elements nested inside the extension elements. The extension points also provide a mechanism for you to extend the configuration data for your own applications if you wish.

The following table lists each of the extension points in the JSF configuration file. The Parent Element column specifies the parent element that acts as an extension point, and the Extension Element column specifies the name of the child element in which proprietary elements can be nested.

Parent Element	Extension Element
Application	application-extension
Attribute	attribute-extension
Behavior	behavior-extension
Component	component-extension
Converter	converter-extension
faces-config	faces-config-extension
Facet	facet-extension
Factory	factory-extension
Lifecycle	lifecycle-extension
managed-bean	managed-bean-extension
navigation-rule	navigation-rule-extension
Property	property-extension
render-kit	render-kit-extension
Renderer	renderer-extension
Validator	validator-extension

The following example illustrates how extension elements are used to add proprietary configuration data to a JSF configuration file.

```
<faces-config>
  <application>
    <application-extension>
      <proprietary-tag-a>value a</proprietary-tag-a>
      <proprietary-tag-b>value b</proprietary-tag-b>
      <proprietary-tag-c>value c</proprietary-tag-c>
    </application-extension>
  </application>
</faces-config>
```

A particular JSF implementation or application that does not recognize the **proprietary-tag-a**, **proprietary-tag-b**, and **proprietary-tag-c** elements will simply ignore them altogether.

Metadata Elements

Several of the elements for the JSF configuration file give you the option to nest metadata elements. The metadata elements exist solely for adding extra information to the configuration file that will be displayed in GUI tools and the like; JSF implementations themselves ignore the metadata elements. The following list mentions the elements that support nesting of metadata elements.

Attribute
Component
Converter
Facet
managed-bean
managed-property
navigation-case
navigation-rule
Property
referenced-bean
render-kit
Renderer
resource-bundle
Validator

Most of the metadata elements do not have any attributes; thus you simply add text between their opening and closing elements to specify their value, as shown here:

```
<validator>
  <description>Validator that validates credit card numbers.</description>
  <display-name>Credit Card Validator</display-name>
  <icon>
    <small-icon>small.gif</small-icon>
    <large-icon>large.gif</large-icon>
  </icon>
  <validator-id>CreditCardValidator</validator-id>
  <validator-class>com.example.jsf.CreditCardValidator</validator-class>
</validator>
```

The **display-name** and **description** elements are the only metadata elements that have attributes. These elements both have a single attribute: **xml:lang**. The **xml:lang** attribute is used to specify the language of the element's value. The following snippet illustrates this use for Spanish:

```
<display-name xml:lang="es">Nombre de la Exhibición</display-name>
<description xml:lang="es">Descripción</description>
```

The language specified with the **xml:lang** attribute is a lowercase two-letter code for a language as defined by the ISO-639 standard. A listing of these codes can be found online at **www.unicode.org/unicode/onlinedat/languages.html**.

The following table lists and describes each of the metadata elements:

Element	Description
description	Defines descriptive text for the enclosing element.
display-name	Defines a short description (or name) for the enclosing element.
icon	Encapsulates an instance of the **large-icon** and the **small-icon** elements.
large-icon	Defines the location for a large (32 × 32 pixel) icon to associate to the enclosing element. The icon may be in either GIF, JPG, or PNG format. (Note that the PNG format is not supported for versions prior to JSF 1.2.)
small-icon	Defines the location for a small (16 × 16 pixel) icon to associate to the enclosing element. The icon may be in either GIF, JPG, or PNG format. (Note that the PNG format is not supported for versions prior to JSF 1.2)

16

CHAPTER

The Standard JSF Component Library

This chapter serves as a reference to the *standard* JSF component library. This library must be provided by any implementation that adheres to the JSF specification. The standard JSF library consists of four parts: the core library, the HTML library, the Facelet Templating tag library, and the Composite Component tag library.

NOTE *Because JSP is included in JSF 2.0 mainly for backward compatibility, only the core and HTML libraries are available for JSP applications.*

The core library is associated with the **f:** namespace and provides common application development utilities in the areas of validation, conversion, internationalization, and overall application development. It is important to note that the core library is not specific to HTML clients and that none of the components in the core library have any visual representation for the end user. The HTML library is associated with the **h:** namespace and is specifically for HTML clients and provides a set of widgets rendered in HTML that are common in most Web applications, such as text fields, buttons, checkboxes, and so on. JSF 2.0 introduced the Facelet Templating library, which is associated with the **ui:** namespace and adds template/layout functionality. JSF 2.0 also introduced the Composite Component tag library, which is associated with the **cc:** namespace and adds the ability to define a usage contract for Facelet Composite Components.

A Brief Review of JSF, Facelets, and JSP Tag Nomenclature

The following is a quick review of the various terms associated with the Facelets and JSP View Declaration Languages (VDLs), upon which JSF relies. Understanding these terms will be helpful, since the remaining reference chapters dealing with custom JSF component libraries use them extensively.

Term	Description
Facelet Tag	Similar in concept to a JSP Tag, a Facelet Tag is an XML element used in a Facelet document that typically corresponds to a JSF UIComponent or Facelet Composite Component.
Facelet Tag Library	Refers to a file that defines a collection of tags that are associated with a namespace and can be used in a Facelet document by page authors.
Facelet Composite Component	Refers to a JSF UIComponent that is composed of one or more other components using markup.
JSP Action	JSP actions are elements that can create and access programming language objects and affect the output stream. The JSP 2.1 specification defines a set of approximately 16 standard actions that must be provided by any compliant JSP implementation. These include **<jsp:useBean>**, **<jsp:setProperty>**, and so on.
JSP Tag	JSP tags are responsible for invoking the underlying JSP actions. JSP actions are invoked by JSP tags in a JSP page. The terms "JSP tag" and "JSP action" are often used synonymously.
Custom JSP Action	Custom JSP actions can be developed in addition to the standard actions provided in the JSP specification. Development of custom actions has been supported since JSP version 1.1.
Custom JSP Tag	Similar to standard JSP tags and actions, a custom JSP tag allows for the invocation of a custom JSP action.
Custom JSP Tag Library	A collection of custom actions and custom tags, along with a tag library descriptor (tld) file. To use JSF within JSP, custom JSP tag libraries are used.
JSF UIComponent	An underlying Java class (**UIComponent**) that defines the behavior of a JSF user interface element. A **UIComponent** can have code that renders itself embedded in them, or it can use a separate **Renderer** class.
JSF Renderer	An optional Java class (**Renderer**) that is used to **render** a user interface element. It works in concert with an associated **UIComponent** class. It is optional because **UIComponent** classes can include code to render themselves.
JSF JSP Tag	A custom JSP tag that extends **UIComponentTag** and provides a JSP-based method of invocation of an associated **UIComponent** and (optionally) a JSF **Renderer**. (For more details on custom JSF UI component development, see Chapter 10.)

Acquiring and Installing the Standard Libraries

The standard JSF component libraries are part of the specification and also come with any standard JSF implementation such as Sun's reference implementation or the MyFaces implementation. Chapter 2 provides detailed instructions on how to download Sun's JSF implementation, known as Mojarra, along with how to install and integrate it into your Web applications.

What You Get (Binary)

The jar files you get when downloading Mojarra are **jsf-api.jar** and **jsf-impl.jar**, available at the Mojarra Web site: **https://javaserverfaces.dev.java.net**.

TIP *As of JSF 1.2, the JSF binaries are bundled with Java EE–compliant containers such as Glassfish.*

What You Get (Source)

The source for the standard components is available but is not provided in the reference implementation. Instead, the reference implementation source code is available as a separate download from the Mojarra Web site.

The Tag Library Reference

This next section serves as a comprehensive reference for the Standard Core library, the HTML component library, the Standard Facelets Templating Library, and the Standard Facelets Composite Component Library.

The Standard Core Library

The standard core library is accessible in Facelets and JSP as a tag library with a URI of **http://java.sun.com/jsf/core** and default prefix of **f**. A quick reference of the standard core library is provided in Table 16-1.

Tag Name	Description	View Declaration Language	JSF Version(s)
f:actionListener	Enables a page author to declaratively register an **ActionListener** instance on a **UIComponent**.	Facelets, JSP	1.0, 1.1, 1.2, 2.0
f:ajax	Enables a page author to declaratively add Ajax behavior to the **UIComponent** associated with the parent tag, or adds Ajax behavior to the **UIComponent**(s) associated with any child tags.	Facelets	2.0
f:attribute	Enables a page author to declaratively set an attribute value on a **UIComponent**.	Facelets, JSP	1.0, 1.1, 1.2, 2.0
f:convertDateTime	Enables a page author to declaratively register a **DateTimeConverter** instance on a **UIComponent**.	Facelets, JSP	1.0, 1.1, 1.2, 2.0

TABLE 16-1 The Standard Core Library Quick Reference *(continued)*

PART III

Tag Name	Description	View Declaration Language	JSF Version(s)
f:convertNumber	Enables a page author to declaratively register a NumberConverter instance on a **UIComponent**.	Facelets, JSP	1.0, 1.1, 1.2, 2.0
f:converter	Enables a page author to declaratively register a named **Converter** instance on a **UIComponent**.	Facelets, JSP	1.0, 1.1, 1.2, 2.0
f:event	Enables a page author to declaratively register a **ComponentSystemEventListener** on a **UIComponent**.	Facelets	2.0
f:facet	Associates a named facet with a **UIComponent**.	Facelets, JSP	1.0, 1.1, 1.2, 2.0
f:loadBundle	Inserts a resource bundle localized for the locale of the current view, and exposes it (as a **Map**) in the request attributes for the current request. This makes the contents of the **ResourceBundle** available via the expression language.	Facelets, JSP	1.0, 1.1, 1.2, 2.0
f:metadata	Encapsulates the set of elements used to specify the metadata for a Facelet **view**.	Facelets	2.0
f:param	Enables a page author to declaratively add a child **UIParameter** to a **UIComponent**. Some components, such as **commandLink**, convert nested param tags into URL query parameters.	Facelets, JSP	1.0, 1.1, 1.2, 2.0
f:phaseListener	Enables a page author to declaratively register a **PhaseListener** instance to the **UIViewRoot**.	Facelets, JSP	1.2, 2.0
f:selectItem	Enables a page author to declaratively add a child **UISelectItem** to a parent **UIComponent**.	Facelets, JSP	1.0, 1.1, 1.2, 2.0
f:selectItems	Enables a page author to declaratively add a child **UISelectItems** to a parent **UIComponent**.	Facelets, JSP	1.0, 1.1, 1.2, 2.0
f:setPropertyActionListener	Enables a page author to declaratively register an **ActionListener** on **UIComponent**. This **actionListener** will cause the value given by the **value** attribute to be set into the **ValueExpression** given by the **target** attribute.	Facelets, JSP	1.2, 2.0

TABLE 16-1 The Standard Core Library Quick Reference

Tag Name	Description	View Declaration Language	JSF Version(s)
f:subview	Container action for all JSF core and component custom actions used on a nested page included via **<jsp:include>** or any custom action that dynamically includes another page from the same Web application, such as JSTL's **<c:import>**. Note: In JSF 1.2, a subview is not required for includes, and although Facelets supports this tag for the sake of completeness, there is no reason to use it within a Facelets **view**.	JSP	1.0, 1.1, 1.2, 2.0
f:validateBean	Enables a page author to declaratively register one or more JSR 303 validator groups within a single **UIComponent** or encapsulating a set of UIComponents.	Facelets, JSP	2.0
f:validateDoubleRange	Enables a page author to declaratively register a **DoubleRangeValidator** instance on a **UIComponent**.	Facelets, JSP	1.0, 1.1, 1.2, 2.0
f:validateLength	Enables a page author to declaratively register a **LengthValidator** instance on a **UIComponent**.	Facelets, JSP	1.0, 1.1, 1.2, 2.0
f:validateLongRange	Enables a page author to declaratively register a **LongRangeValidator** instance on a **UIComponent**.	Facelets, JSP	1.0, 1.1, 1.2, 2.0
f:validateRegex	Enables a page author to declaratively register a **RegexValidator** instance on a **UIComponent**.	Facelets, JSP	2.0
f:validateRequired	Enables a page author to declaratively register a **RequiredValidator** instance on a **UIComponent**.	Facelets, JSP	2.0
f:validator	Enables a page author to declaratively register a named **Validator** instance on a **UIComponent**.	Facelets, JSP	1.0, 1.1, 1.2, 2.0
f:valueChangeListener	Enables a page author to declaratively register a **ValueChangeListener** instance on a **UIComponent**.	Facelets, JSP	1.0, 1.1, 1.2, 2.0

Table 16-1 The Standard Core Library Quick Reference *(continued)*

Tag Name	Description	View Declaration Language	JSF Version(s)
f:verbatim	Enables a page author to declaratively register a child **UIOutput** instance on the **UIComponent** associated with the closest parent **UIComponent** custom action that renders nested (HTML/XML/Markup) content. Note: Although Facelets supports this tag for the sake of completeness, there is no reason to use it within a Facelets view.	JSP	1.0, 1.1, 1.2, 2.0
f:view	Specifies a **UIViewRoot** for all JSF core and custom components used on a page. Note: This tag is required to declare a view with JSP, but this tag is optional with Facelets.	Facelets, JSP	1.0, 1.1, 1.2, 2.0
f:viewParam	Enables a page author to declaratively register a **UIViewParameter** as **metadata** associated with the parent **view**.	Facelets	2.0
* For some tags, there is actually no underlying **UIComponent** and the tag operates on its own.			

Table 16-1 The Standard Core Library Quick Reference *(continued)*

A detailed reference for the tags/components referenced in Table 16-1 follows next.

The f:actionListener Tag

Enables a page author to declaratively register an **ActionListener** instance on a **UIComponent**.

Attributes

Attribute	Type	Description	Required
type	String	A fully qualified Java class name of an **ActionListener** to be created and registered.	Yes (1.1) No(1.2, 2.0)*
binding (1.2, 2.0)	ValueExpression	A **ValueExpression** expression that evaluates to an object that implements **javax.faces.event.ActionListener**.	No*
for (2.0)	String	Usage of the **for** attribute with the **f:actionListener** tag only has significance when the tag is nested as a child of a Composite Component. If specified, then the value must be equal to the value of an **id** attribute associated with an exposed object.	Yes (if nested as a child tag of a Composite Component), otherwise, No.
* In JSF 1.2 /2.0, either a type or a binding must be provided.			

Example Usage

```
<f:actionListener type="fully-qualified-classname"
  binding="valueExpression"/>
```

TIP *If type and binding are both specified, the type is used to instantiate the class and the binding is employed as the target of a "set" operation where the value will be the created* ***ActionListener*** *instance. This is useful if you want to manage your listener instances manually yet still allow them to be created from code referenced from the markup page.*

The f:ajax Tag (2.0)

Enables a page author to declaratively add Ajax behavior to the **UIComponent** associated with the parent tag, or adds Ajax behavior to the **UIComponent**(s) associated with any child tags.

Attributes

Attribute	Type	Description	Required
disabled	Boolean	If a boolean value of "true" is specified, then the underlying **AjaxBehavior** will not be rendered. The default value is false, so that the **AjaxBehavior** will indeed be rendered.	false
event	String	The value must be a String that indicates the type of user interface event that will trigger the **AjaxBehavior**. Valid values for components that manifest themselves as HTML would be DOM event names such as **blur**, **valueChanged**, and so on, rather than the JavaScript event names such as ***on*blur**, ***on*change**, and so on. The complete list of supported DOM event names depends entirely on the browser because JSF will simply pass the event registration on to the browser, which either will support the event or simply ignore it.	false

(continued)

PART III

Attribute	Type	Description	Required
execute	String or ValueExpression	If specified, the value must be a String literal or a **Collection** of one or more String elements that indicate the set of components in the view that are to process events during the **Execute portion** of the JSF lifecycle. If elements are values of **id** attributes elsewhere in the view, then the elements must be delimited by spaces in the String literal. Note that an **id** attribute on an element in the rendered HTML is equivalent to a JSF **clientId** for a JSF Component in the server-side view hierarchy. As an alternative to the list of **id** literals, any one of the following predefined keywords: **@this**, **@form**, **@all**, **@none**. For more on the meaning of these keywords, please see Chapter 12.	false
immediate	Boolean	If a boolean value of "true" is specified then the events that are generated by the underlying **AjaxBehavior** are handled during the APPLY_REQUEST_VALUES phase of the JSF lifecycle. Otherwise, the events are handled during the INVOKE_APPLICATION phase. The default value is "false".	false
listener	MethodExpression	If specified, then the value must be a **MethodExpression** that refers to a method that has the same signature as the **processAjaxBehavior** method in the **AjaxBehaviorListener** interface.	false
onevent	String	If specified, then the value must indicate the name of the JavaScript function that will handle user interface events, rather than the default function that is provided by the JSF implementation.	false

Attribute	Type	Description	Required
onerror	String	If specified, then the value must indicate the name of the JavaScript function that will handle errors, rather than the default function that is provided by the JSF implementation.	false
render	String or ValueExpression	The meaning of this attribute is exactly the same as the **execute** attribute except that it applies to the **Render portion** of the JSF lifecycle.	false

Example Usage

```
<f:ajax execute="blur" render="@this idOfOtherComponent" />
```


The f:attribute Tag

The **f:attribute** tag adds an attribute with a specified name and string value to the component whose tag it is nested inside, if the component does not already contain an attribute with the same name. This tag creates no output to the page currently being created. Attributes are stored in the **Map** returned by **UIComponent.getAttributes( )**. Note that values stored in this map are persisted as a part of the component's state when the view is saved and restored across postbacks.

TIP *EL expressions are not stored in the Map returned by* ***UIComponent.getAttributes( )****; instead, they are stored via* ***setValueExpression( )****.*

Attributes

Attribute	Type	Description	Required
name	String	The name of the component attribute to be set.	Yes (1.1) No (1.2, 2.0)
value	Object	The value of the component attribute to be set.	Yes (1.1) No (1.2, 2.0)

Example Usage

```
<f:attribute name="employeeNo" value="#{bean.empno}" />
```

The f:convertDateTime Tag

The **f:convertDateTime** tag creates and configures an instance of the converter registered with the ID **javax.faces.DateTime** and associates it with the closest parent **UIComponent**. In general, it's used to convert between **String** and **java.util.Date** values.

Attributes

Attribute	Type	Description	Required
dateStyle	String	Formatting style that determines how the date component of a date string is to be formatted and parsed. Applied only if type is "date" or "both". Valid values are "default" (default), "short", "medium", "long", and "full".	No
for (2.0)	String	Usage of the **for** attribute with the **f:convertDateTime** tag only has significance when the tag is nested as a child of a Composite Component. If specified, then the value must be equal to the value of an **id** attribute associated with an exposed object.	Yes (if nested as a child tag of a Composite Component), otherwise, No.
locale	String	Locale with specific styles for dates and times used during formatting or parsing. If not specified, the Locale returned by **FacesContext .getViewRoot( ).getLocale( )** will be used. Value must be either a **ValueExpression** that evaluates to a **java.util.Locale** instance, or a string that is valid to pass as the first argument to the constructor **java.util .Locale(String language, String country)**. The empty string is passed as the second argument.	No
pattern	String	A custom formatting pattern that determines how the date/time string should be formatted and parsed.	No
timeStyle	String	A predefined formatting style that determines how the time component of a date string is to be formatted and parsed. Applied only if type is "time" or "both". Valid values are "default" (default), "short", "medium", "long", and "full".	No
timeZone	String	A time zone used to interpret any time information in the date string. Value must be either a **ValueExpression** that evaluates to a **java.util.TimeZone** instance, or a string that is a timezone ID as described in the Javadocs for **java.util.TimeZone.getTimeZone( )**.	No

Attribute	Type	Description	Required
type	String	Specifies whether the string value will contain a date, time, or both.	No
binding (1.2, 2.0)	ValueExpression	A **ValueExpression** expression that evaluates to an object that implements **javax.faces.convert.Converter**.	No

Example Usage

```
<h:inputText id="hiredate" value="#{employee.hireDate}">
  <f:convertDateTime dateStyle="full"/>
</h:inputText>
```

Pattern Formats

A pattern of symbols determines what the formatted date and time looks like. Examples of locale-sensitive date and time pattern formats are "EEE, MMM d, yyyy" and "h:mm a", which generate the output "Thu, Apr 9, 1998" and "6:15 PM" if the U.S. locale is specified. See the Java class **java.text.SimpleDateFormat** for more information about date and time patterns and symbols.

PART III

The f:convertNumber Tag

The **convertNumber** tag creates and configures an instance of the converter registered with the ID **javax.faces.Number**. Associates it with the closest parent **UIComponent**. In general, it's used to convert between **String** and **java.lang.Number** values.

Attributes

Attribute	Type	Description	Required
currencyCode	String	ISO-4217 currency code (e.g., US Dollar = "USD").	No
currencySymbol	String	String to use as currency symbol (e.g.,'$' for USD).	No
for (2.0)	String	Usage of the **for** attribute with the **f:convertNumber** tag only has significance when the tag is nested as a child of a Composite Component. If specified, then the value must be equal to the value of an **id** attribute associated with an exposed object.	Yes (if nested as a child tag of a Composite Component), otherwise, No.
groupingUsed	boolean	If true (default), grouping separators are included in the result.	No

(continued)

Attribute	Type	Description	Required
integerOnly	boolean	If true, only the integer portion is parsed. The default is false.	No
locale	String or java.util.Locale	The locale to use instead of the default determined by **FacesContext.getViewRoot( ) .getLocale( )**.	No
maxFractionDigits	int	The maximum number of fraction digits to be formatted (in the output).	No
maxIntegerDigits	int	The maximum number of integer digits to be formatted (in the output).	No
minFractionDigits	int	The minimum number of fraction digits to be formatted (in the output).	No
minIntegerDigits	int	The minimum number of integer digits to be formatted (in the output).	No
pattern	String	The symbols forming a number pattern that is defined in **java .text.DecimalFormat**.	No
type	String	One of the accepted type values: Valid values are "number", "currency", and "percentage". The default value is "number".	No
binding (1.2, 2.0)	ValueExpression	The **ValueExpression** expression that evaluates to an object that implements **javax.faces.convert .Converter**.	No

Example Usage

```
<h:inputText id="sal" value="#{employee.salary}">
  <f:convertNumber integerOnly="true"/>
</h:inputText>
```

Pattern Formats

A pattern of symbols determines what a formatted number looks like. For example, the locale-sensitive pattern ###,###.### generates the formatted number 123,456.789 if the locale is en_US. See the Java class **java.text.DecimalFormat** for more information about number patterns and symbols.

The f:converter Tag

The **f:converter** tag creates an instance of the class registered with the specified converter ID, which must implement the **javax.faces.convert.Converter** interface, and associates it with the component represented by the closest parent **UIComponent**.

Attributes

Attribute	Type	Description	Required
converterId	String	The ID (shown next) used to register a class implementing the **Converter** interface.	Yes (1.1) No (1.2, 2.0)
for (2.0)	String	Usage of the **for** attribute with the **f:converter** tag only has significance when the tag is nested as a child of a Composite Component. If specified, then the value must be equal to the value of an **id** attribute associated with an exposed object.	Yes (if nested as a child tag of a Composite Component), otherwise, No.
binding (1.2, 2.0)	ValueExpression	A **ValueExpression** expression that evaluates to an object that implements **javax.faces.convert.Converter**.	No

Example Usage

```
<h:inputText>
  <f:converter converterId="Converter ID"/>
</h:inputText>
```

Converter ID List

- javax.faces.BigDecimal
- javax.faces.BigInteger
- javax.faces.Boolean
- javax.faces.Byte
- javax.faces.Character
- javax.faces.DateTime
- javax.faces.Double
- javax.faces.Float
- javax.faces.Integer
- javax.faces.Long
- javax.faces.Number
- javax.faces.Short

PART III

TIP *If type and binding are both specified, the type is used to instantiate the class and the binding is used as the target of a "set" operation where the value will be the created* **Converter** *instance. This is useful if you want to manage your converter instances manually yet still allow them to be created from code referenced from the JSP page.*

The f:event Tag (2.0)

The **f:event** tag enables a page author to declaratively register a **ComponentSystemEventListener** on a **UIComponent**.

Attributes

Attribute	Type	Description	Required
listener (2.0)	MethodExpression	If specified, then the value must be a **MethodExpression** that refers to a method that has the same signature as the **processEvent** method in the **ComponentSystemEventListener** interface.	true
type (2.0)	String	Specifies the event name, which can be one of: **preRenderComponent**, **preRenderView**, **postAddToView**, **preValidate**, **postValidate**. Additionally, any fully qualified class name that extends **ComponentSystemEvent** may be specified.	true

Example Usage

```
<f:event type="preRenderComponent"
listener="#{testManagedBean.beforeRenderListener}" />
<f:event type="javax.faces.event.PreRenderComponentEvent"
listener="#{testManagedBean.beforeRenderListener}" />
```

The f:facet Tag

The **f:facet** tag signifies a nested component that has a special relationship to its enclosing tag. For example, stating that the "header" of a table is to be provided by a JSF component. This element adds the component represented by the JSF action in its body as a facet with the specified name to the component represented by the closest JSF component parent action element. This tag only allows one component to be nested within itself. To use multiple components as a facet, create them as children of a simple container component. For example, nest the corresponding HTML library component actions within the body of a **panelGroup** component.

Attributes

Attribute	Type	Description	Required
name	String	The name of the facet to be created.	Yes (1.1) No (1.2, 2.0)

Example Usage

```
<h:dataTable>
  <h:column>
    <f:facet name="header">
      <h:panelGroup>
        <h:outputText value="header name" />
      </h:panelGroup>
    </f:facet>
    <h:outputText value="column value"/>
  </h:column>
</h:dataTable>
```

The f:loadBundle Tag

The **f:loadBundle** tag is a localization tag that specifies a resource bundle localized for the **locale** of the current view and exposes it as a **Map**. The action creates an instance of the class implementing the **java.util.Map** interface with a **get( )** method that returns the value of the corresponding resource in the specified resource bundle and saves the instance as a variable in the request scope. Localized resources from the bundle can then be accessed through the **Map** with regular JSF EL expressions.

Attributes

Attribute	Type	Description	Required
basename	String	The base name of the resource bundle to be used.	Yes (1.1) No (1.2, 2.0)
var	String	The name of a usable (request-scoped) variable under which the resource bundle will be exposed as a **Map**.	Yes

Example Usage

Let's assume there is a **ResourceBundle** answering to the fully qualified Java class name of **com.foo.ResourceBundle** in the Web application's classpath and that the **ResourceBundle** has a key called **UserNameLabel**. A variable named **resources** is also assigned to this resource bundle. The following JSP code loads the bundle into the request scope and then references a value from that bundle.

```
<f:loadBundle
  basename="com.foo.ResourceBundle"
  var="resources"/>
<h:outputText value="#{resources.UserNameLabel}" />
```

Recall that the scoped name space searching rules described in Chapter 4 will automatically cause the request scope to be searched.

TIP *Use of this tag is discouraged. Users are encouraged to use the* **<resource-bundle>** *element in the* ***faces-config.xml*** *file, as shown in Chapter 10.*

PART III

Using Resource Bundles in JSF

Load the resource bundle specified by the **basename** attribute, localized for the locale of the **UIViewRoot** component of the current view, and expose its key-values pairs as a **Map** under the attribute key specified by the **var** attribute. In this way, value binding expressions may be used to conveniently retrieve localized values. If the named bundle is not found, a **JspException** is thrown. Note: This tag must be nested inside the **<f:view>** component/action.

The f:metadata Tag (2.0)

The **f:metadata** tag encapsulates the set of elements used to specify the metadata for a Facelet **view**, and therefore must be a child of the **f:view** tag and may not appear in a template.As of JSF 2.0, the only purpose of this tag is to encapsulate **f:viewParam** tags.

Attributes

None

Example Usage

```
<f:metadata>
  <f:viewParam
    name="customerId" value="#{customer.customerId}">
      <f:validateLongRange />
  </f:viewParam>
</f:metadata>
```

The f:param Tag

UIComponent class: **javax.faces.component.UIParameter**

Component type: **javax.faces.Parameter**

The **param** component adds a child **UIParameter** component to the **UIComponent** associated with the closest parent **UIComponent**. It can be used to substitute message parameters when used inside an **<h:outputFormat>** or to add query string name-value pairs to a request when used inside of **<h:commandLink>** or **<h:outputLink>**.

Attributes

Attribute	Type	Description	Required
name	String	The base name of the resource bundle to be loaded.	No
value	String	The name of a request scope attribute under which the resource bundle will be exposed as a **Map**.	Yes
binding	ValueBinding (1.0, 1.1) or ValueExpression (1.2, 2.0)	A **ValueBinding** or **ValueExpression** expression to a backing bean property bound to the component instance for the **UIComponent** created by this custom action.	No
id	String	The component identifier of the component.	No

Example Usage

The following is a simple way to test **f:param** inside a **commandLink**:

```
<h:commandLink >
  <h:outputText value="Click Here" />
  <f:param name="empid" value="123456" />
</h:commandLink>
<h:outputText value=" Employee Id is: #{param.empid}" />
```

Usage of **f:param** inside of an **outputFormat** is shown in the following:

```
<h:outputFormat value="Welcome back, {0}" >
  <f:param value="#{Employees.firstName}" />
</h:outputFormat>
```

The f:phaseListener Tag (1.2, 2.0)

UIComponent class: **n/a**

Component type: **n/a**

The **phaseListener** tag registers a **PhaseListener** instance on the **UIViewRoot** in which this tag is nested.

Attributes

Attribute	Type	Description	Required
type	String	A fully qualified Java class name of a **PhaseListener** to be created and registered.	No
binding	ValueExpression	**A ValueExpression** that evaluates to an object that implements **javax.faces.event .PhaseListener**.	No

The f:selectItem Tag

UIComponent class: **javax.faces.component.UISelectItem**

Component type: **javax.faces.SelectItem**

The **selectItem** component adds a child **UISelectItem** component to the closest parent **UIComponent**.

Attributes

Attribute	Type	Description	Required
binding	ValueBinding (1.0, 1.1) or ValueExpression (1.2, 2.0)	A **ValueBinding** or **ValueExpression** expression to a backing bean property bound to the component instance for the **UIComponent** created by this custom action.	No
id	String	The component identifier of the component.	No
itemDescription	String	A description of the item.	No
itemDisabled	String	The boolean flag used to display the item as disabled. The default value is false.	No
itemLabel	String	The displayed label of the item.	No
itemValue	String	The actual (nondisplayed) value of the item.	No
noSelectionOption	Boolean	The boolean flag that indicates that the **itemValue** of this tag is to be regarded as a nonselection by the user, which will cause required-validation of the parent selection component to fail. The default value is "false".	
value	String	The value of the component.	No

Example Usage

Several **f:selectItem** components providing select options for an **h:selectOneMenu** are shown in the following.

```
 <h:selectOneMenu id="colorId" required="true"
value="#{testManagedBean.colorId}">
    <f:selectItem itemLabel="-- Select --" itemValue="0"
noSelectionOption="true" />
    <f:selectItem itemLabel="Red" itemValue="1" />
    <f:selectItem itemLabel="Green" itemValue="2" />
    <f:selectItem itemLabel="Blue" itemValue="3" />
</h:selectOneMenu>
```

The f:selectItems Tag

UIComponent class: **javax.faces.component.UISelectItems**

Component type: **javax.faces.SelectItems**

The **f:selectItems** tag locates the closest parent **UIComponent**, creates a new **UISelectItems** component, and attaches it as a child of the associated **UIComponent**. The implementation class for this action must meet the requirements shown in the following table.

Attributes

Attribute	Type	Description	Required
binding	ValueBinding (1.0, 1.1) or ValueExpression (1.2, 2.0)	**A ValueBinding** or **ValueExpression** expression to a backing bean property bound to the component instance for the **UIComponent** created by this custom action.	No
id	String	The component identifier of the component.	No
itemDescription (2.0)	String	A string value that specifies the description of the item.	No
itemDisabled (2.0)	boolean	A boolean value that specifies whether or not the value is disabled.	No
itemLabel (2.0)	String	A string value that specifies the label for the item.	No
itemLabelEscaped (2.0)	Boolean	A boolean value that specifies whether or not the label that is rendered should be escaped, meaning special HTML and XML characters ("<", ">", etc.) as character entity codes ("<", ">", respectively). If true, generated markup is escaped in a manner appropriate for the markup language being rendered. The default value is false.	No
itemValue (2.0)	ValueExpression	A string or any primitive wrapper such as Long or Integer that can be implicitly converted to a String. Otherwise, if an instance of a custom class is specified, then a converter will need to be specified as a sibling tag.	No
noSelectionValue (2.0)	String	A string value that is to be regarded as a nonselection by the user, which will cause required-validation of the parent selection component to fail.	No
value	ValueExpression	A value binding expression of source of items. May resolve to a Java language **Collection**, **javax.faces.model.DataModel**, or array, containing any type of object. See the following value description.	Yes
var (2.0)		An iterator variable name that gets introduced into the EL and represents the current item in the iteration over the **value** attribute.	No

Example Usage

The following is an example with the **f:selectItems** value bound to a **CountriesMap Map**. This will display a list of countries.

```
<h:selectOneMenu
  <f:selectItems value="#{CountriesMap}"/>
</h:selectOneMenu>
```

The following is an example with the **f:selectItems** value bound to a **Collection** of Color objects. It shows how to use the new attributes introduced in JSF 2.0.

```
<h:selectOneMenu id="colorId" required="true"
    value="#{testManagedBean.colorId}">
    <f:selectItems
        value="#{testManagedBean.colors}" var="color"
        itemValue="#{color.colorId}"
        itemLabel="#{color.name}"
        itemDescription="#{color.description}"
        itemDisabled="#{color.disabled}"
        itemLabelEscaped="true"
        noSelectionValue="#{testManagedBean.colors[0]}">
    </f:selectItems>
</h:selectOneMenu>
```

The Value Attribute Description

Prior to JSF 2.0, the **ValueBinding** expression for the **value** attribute was required be one of the following instances:

- An individual **javax.faces.model.SelectItem**
- A Java language array of **javax.faces.model.SelectItem**
- A java.util.Collection of **javax.faces.model.SelectItem**
- A java.util.Map where the keys are converted to Strings and used as labels, and the corresponding values are converted to Strings and used as values for newly created **javax.faces.model.SelectItem** instances. The instances are created in the order determined by the iterator over the keys provided by the **Map**.

As of JSF 2.0, the ValueBinding expression for the value attribute is no longer exclusively tied to **javax.faces.model.SelectItem** but can be any **Collection**, **array**, or instance of **javax.faces.model.DataModel**.

The f:setPropertyActionListener Tag (1.2, 2.0 Only)

The **setPropertyActionListener** tag registers an **ActionListener** instance on the **UIComponent** associated with the closest parent **UIComponent** custom action. This **actionListener** will cause the value given by the **value** attribute to be set into the **ValueExpression** given by the **target** attribute. This is useful for easily placing objects into managed beans or other objects accessible via EL.

Attributes

Attribute	Type	Description	Required
for (2.0)	String	Usage of the **for** attribute with the **f:setPropertyActionListener** tag only has significance when the tag is nested as a child of a Composite Component. If specified, then the value must be equal to the value of an **id** attribute associated with an exposed object.	Yes (if nested as a child tag of a Composite Component), otherwise, No.
value	ValueExpression	**A ValueExpression** to be stored as the value of the **target** attribute.	Yes
target	ValueExpression	**A ValueExpression** that is the destination of the **value** attribute.	Yes

Example Usage

```
<h:commandButton action="#{backingBean.registerUser}" value="Register">
  <f:setPropertyActionListener
    target="#{sessionScope.User}" value="#{User}"/>
</h:commandButton>
```


The f:subview Tag

UIComponent class: **javax.faces.component.UINamingContainer**

Component type: **javax.faces.NamingContainer**

The **subview** component is useful with JSP but serves no purpose with JSF 2.0 Facelets. It serves as a container component for all **UIComponents** used on a nested page included via **<jsp:include>** or any custom action that dynamically includes another page from the same Web application, such as JSTL's **<c:import>**. Note: In JSF 1.2 and 2.0, its use is optional around JSP includes. And in 1.1, 1.2, and 2.0 it can be used if you want a **NamingContainer** added to the component hierarchy for ID disambiguation.

Attributes

Attribute	Type	Description	Required
binding	ValueBinding (1.0, 1.1) or ValueExpression (1.2, 2.0)	**A ValueExpression** expression to a backing bean property bound to the component instance for the UIComponent created by this custom action.	No
id	String	The component identifier of the component.	Yes
rendered	boolean	A boolean flag indicating whether or not this component is to be rendered during the RENDER_RESPONSE phase of the JSF lifecycle. The default value is "true".	No

Example Usage

Locates the closest parent **UIComponent** and creates a new **UINamingContainer** component, afterward attaching it as a child of the associated **UIComponent**. Such a component provides a scope within which child component identifiers must be unique, but allows child components to have the same simple identifier as child components nested in some other naming container. This is useful in the following scenarios:

main.jsp

```
<f:view>
  <c:import url="foo.jsp"/>
  <c:import url="bar.jsp"/>
</f:view>
```

foo.jsp

```
<f:subview id="aaa">
.. components and other content ...
</f:subview>
```

bar.jsp

```
<f:subview id="bbb">
  components and other content ...
</f:subview>
```

In this scenario, **<f:subview>** custom actions in imported pages establish a naming scope for components within those pages. Identifiers for **<f:subview>** custom actions nested in a single **<f:view>** custom action must be unique, but it is difficult for the page author (and impossible for the JSP page compiler) to enforce this restriction.

The following is an example showing a parent JSP page **main.jsp**:

```
<f:view>
  <f:subview id="aaa">
    <c:import url="foo.jsp"/>
  </f:subview>
  <f:subview id="bbb">
    <c:import url="bar.jsp"/>
  </f:subview>
</f:view>
```

Contents of **foo.jsp**:

```
JSF components and other content...
```

Contents of **bar.jsp**

```
JSF components and other content...
```

In this scenario, the **<f:subview>** custom actions are in the including page, rather than in the included page. As in the previous scenario, the **id** values of the two subviews must be unique; but this fact is much easier to verify using this style. It is also possible to use this approach to include the same page more than once but maintain unique identifiers:

Contents of **main.jsp**:

```
<f:view>
  <f:subview id="aaa">
    <c:import url="foo.jsp"/>
  </f:subview>
  <f:subview id="bbb">
    <c:import url="foo.jsp"/>
  </f:subview>
</f:view>
```

Contents of **foo.jsp**:

```
JSF components and other content...
```

In all of the preceding examples, note that **foo.jsp** and **bar.jsp** may not contain **<f:view>**.

The f:validateBean Tag (2.0)

The **f:validateBean** tag provides integration with the JSR 303 Bean Validation API. Using this tag causes a **javax.faces.validator.BeanValidator** instance to be registered on the parent **UIComponent** that implements **EditableValueHolder**, such as **HtmlInputText**. When used in conjunction with a Composite Component, it causes a BeanValidator instance to be registered on the EditableValueHolder whose **id** equals the value of the **for** attribute. It can also be used to encapsulate one or more child tags that correspond to UIComponents that implement EditableValueHolder, thus causing bean validation to take place on a set of components.

PART III

Attributes

Attribute	Type	Description	Required
binding (2.0)	ValueExpression	A **ValueExpression** to a backing bean property of type **javax.faces.validator.BeanValidator**.	false
disabled (2.0)	Boolean	A boolean value that specifies whether or not the validation will take place. If the **f:validateBean** tag is specified as a child of a tag that corresponds to an EditableValueHolder, and if disabled is "true", then validation will not take place on that parent EditableValueHolder. If the **f:validateBean** tag is used to encapsulate one or more child tags that correspond to EditableValueHolders, and if disabled is "true", then validation will not take place on each child EditableValueHolder. The default value is false.	false

(continued)

Attribute	Type	Description	Required
for (2.0)	String	Usage of the **for** attribute with the **f:validateBean** tag only has significance when the tag is nested as a child of a Composite Component. If specified, then the value must be equal to the value of an **id** attribute associated with an exposed object.	Yes (if nested as a child tag of a Composite Component), otherwise, No.
validationGroups (2.0)	String	One or more fully qualified class names separated by commas. Each item corresponds to a JSR 303 validation group. The default value is **javax.validation.groups .Default**, which is the default JSR 303 validation group.	false

Example Usage

The following example causes JSR 303 validation to take place on a single **HtmlInputText** component.

```
<h:inputText value="#{testManagedBean.firstName}">
  <f:validateBean>
</h:inputText>
```

The following example causes JSR 303 validation to take place on all **HtmlInputText** components except for the "middleName".

```
<f:validateBean>
  <h:inputText value="#{testManagedBean.firstName}" />
  <h:inputText disabled="true"
    value="#{testManagedBean.middleName}" />
  <h:inputText value="#{testManagedBean.lastName}" />
</f:validateBean>
```

The following example causes validation to take place according to a custom JSR 303 validation group.

```
<f:validateBean
  validationGroups="com.example.jsf.TestValidationGroup">
    <h:inputText value="#{testManagedBean.firstName}" />
    <h:inputText value="#{testManagedBean.middleName}" />
    <h:inputText value="#{testManagedBean.lastName}" />
</f:validateBean>
```

The f:validateDoubleRange Tag

The **f:validateDoubleRange** tag creates and configures an instance of the **validator** registered with the ID **javax.faces.DoubleRange** and associates this instance with the closest parent **UIComponent**. It's used to validate a component's **double** value within a specified range.

Attributes

Attribute	Type	Description	Required
binding (1.2, 2.0)	ValueExpression	A **ValueExpression** to a backing bean property of type **javax.faces.validator .DoubleRangeValidator**.	No
disabled (2.0)	Boolean	A boolean flag that specifies whether or not the validator is enabled. The default value is "false", meaning that the validator is enabled.	No
for (2.0)	String	Usage of the **for** attribute with the **f:validateDoubleRange** tag only has significance when the tag is nested as a child of a Composite Component. If specified, then the value must be equal to the value of an **id** attribute associated with an exposed object.	Yes (if nested as a child tag of a Composite Component), otherwise, No.
maximum	double	The maximum value allowed for this component.	No
minimum	double	The minimum value allowed for this component.	No

Example Usage

The following is an example of **f:validateDoubleRange** used in an **inputText** component.

```
<h:inputText id="price" value="#{basket.price}">
  <f:validateDoubleRange minimum="0.0"/>
</h:inputText>
```

Either of the **maximum** or **minimum** attributes can be specified individually, or they can be specified together, as shown in the preceding example.

Constraints

- Must be nested inside an **EditableValueHolder** custom action whose value is (or is convertible to) a **double**.
- Must specify either the **maximum** attribute, the **minimum** attribute, or both.
- If both limits are specified, the maximum limit must be greater than the minimum limit. If this tag is not nested inside a **UIComponent** custom action, or the **UIComponent** implementation class does not correctly implement **EditableValueHolder**, then a **JspException** is thrown.

The f:validateLength Tag

The **validateLength** tag creates and configures an instance of the **validator** registered with the ID **javax.faces.Length** and associates it with the closest parent **UIComponent**. It is used to validate the String length of a component's value's within a specified range.

Attributes

Attribute	Type	Description	Required
binding (1.2, 2.0)	ValueExpression	A **ValueExpression** to a backing bean property of type **javax.faces.validator .LengthValidator**.	No
disabled (2.0)	Boolean	A boolean flag that specifies whether or not the validator is enabled. The default value is "false", meaning that the validator is enabled.	false
for (2.0)	String	Usage of the **for** attribute with the **f:validateLength** tag only has significance when the tag is nested as a child of a Composite Component. If specified, then the value must be equal to the value of an **id** attribute associated with an exposed object.	Yes (if nested as a child tag of a Composite Component), otherwise, No.
maximum	int	The maximum String length allowed for this component's value.	No
minimum	int	The minimum String length allowed for this component's value.	No

Example Usage

```
<h:inputText id="zip" value="#{employee.zipCode}">
  <f:validateLength minimum="5" maximum="9"/>
</h:inputText>
```

Either of the **maximum** or **minimum** attributes can be specified individually, or they can be specified together, as shown in the preceding example.

Constraints

- Must be nested inside an **EditableValueHolder** custom action whose value is a **String**.
- Must specify either the **maximum** attribute, the **minimum** attribute, or both.
- If both limits are specified, the maximum limit must be greater than the minimum limit. If this tag is not nested inside a **UIComponent** custom action, or the **UIComponent** implementation class does not correctly implement **EditableValueHolder**, then a **JspException** is thrown.

The f:validateLongRange Tag

The **validateLongRange** tag creates and configures an instance of the **validator** registered with the ID **javax.faces.LongRange** and associates it with the closest parent **UIComponent**.

Attributes

Attribute	Type	Description	Required
binding (1.2, 2.0)	ValueExpression	A **ValueExpression** to a backing bean property of type **javax.faces.validator .LongRangeValidator**.	No
disabled (2.0)	Boolean	A boolean flag that specifies whether or not the validator is enabled. The default value is "false", meaning that the validator is enabled.	No
for (2.0)	String	Usage of the **for** attribute with the **f:validateLongRange** tag only has significance when the tag is nested as a child of a Composite Component. If specified, then the value must be equal to the value of an **id** attribute associated with an exposed object.	Yes (if nested as a child tag of a Composite Component), otherwise, No.
maximum	long	The maximum value allowed for this component.	No
minimum	long	The minimum value allowed for this component.	No

Example Usage

```
<h:inputText id="sal" value="#{employee.salary}">
  <f:validateLongRange minimum="28000" maximum="100000"/>
</h:inputText>
```

Either of the **maximum** or **minimum** attributes can be specified individually, or they can be specified together, as shown in the preceding example.

Constraints

- Must be nested inside an **EditableValueHolder** custom action whose value is a **long**, which is convertible to a **Long**.
- Must specify either the **maximum** attribute, the **minimum** attribute, or both.
- If both limits are specified, the maximum limit must be greater than the minimum limit. If this tag is not nested inside a **UIComponent** custom action, or the **UIComponent** implementation class does not correctly implement **EditableValueHolder**, then a **JspException** is thrown.

PART III

The f:validateRegex Tag (2.0)

The **f:validateRegex** tag creates and configures an instance of the **validator** registered with the ID **javax.faces.RegularExpression** and associates it with the closest parent **UIComponent**.

Attributes

Attribute	Type	Description	Required
binding (2.0)	ValueExpression	A **ValueExpression** to a backing bean property of type **javax.faces.validator .RegexValidator**.	No
disabled (2.0)	Boolean	A boolean flag that specifies whether or not the validator is enabled. The default value is "false", meaning that the validator is enabled.	No
for (2.0)	String	Usage of the **for** attribute with the **f:validateRegex** tag only has significance when the tag is nested as a child of a Composite Component. If specified, then the value must be equal to the value of an **id** attribute associated with an exposed object.	Yes (if nested as a child tag of a Composite Component), otherwise, No.
pattern (2.0)	String	A regular expression that has syntax that would be acceptable to pass as an argument to the **javax.util.regex .Pattern.compile(regex)** method.	Yes

Example Usage

```
<h:inputText value="#{testManagedBean.emailAddress}">
  <f:validateRegex pattern=" .+[@].+[.].+"/>
</h:inputText>
```

The f:validateRequired Tag (2.0)

The **f:validateRequired** tag creates and configures an instance of the **validator** registered with the ID **javax.faces.Required** and associates it with the closest parent **UIComponent**. This tag is essentially the same as setting the required attribute of an EditableValueHolder to "true" but was necessary to include in JSF 2.0 so that it would be easy for page authors to declaratively specify that an exposed EditableValueHolder in a Composite Component requires a value.

Attributes

Attribute	Type	Description	Required
binding (2.0)	ValueExpression	A **ValueExpression** to a backing bean property of type **javax.faces.validator .RequiredValidator**.	No
disabled (2.0)	Boolean	A boolean flag that specifies whether or not the validator is enabled. The default value is "false", meaning that the validator is enabled.	No
for (2.0)	String	Usage of the **for** attribute with the **f:validateRequired** tag only has significance when the tag is nested as a child of a Composite Component. If specified, then the value must be equal to the value of an **id** attribute associated with an exposed object.	No

Example Usage

```
<h:inputText value="#{testManagedBean.firstName}">
  <f:validateRequired />
</h:inputText>
```

The f:validator Tag

The **validator** tag creates and registers a named **Validator** instance on the closest parent **EditableValueHolder**. In JSF 2.0, new functionality was added such that the validator will be added to all child components, regardless of whether or not the parent tag is an EditableValueHolder.

Attributes

Attribute	Type	Description	Required
binding (1.2, 2.0)	ValueExpression	A **ValueExpression** that evaluates to an object of type **javax.faces.validator .Validator**.	No*
disabled (2.0)	Boolean	A boolean flag that specifies whether or not the validator is enabled. The default value is "false", meaning that the validator is enabled.	No

(continued)

PART III

Attribute	Type	Description	Required
for (2.0)	String	Usage of the **for** attribute with the **f:validator** tag only has significance when the tag is nested as a child of a Composite Component. If specified, then the value must be equal to the value of an **id** attribute associated with an exposed object.	Yes (if nested as a child tag of a Composite Component), otherwise, No.
validatorId	String	The validator identifier of the **Validator** to be created.	Yes (1.1) No (1.2, 2.0)*
* See constraints.			

Example Usage

The following is an example using the **javax.faces.Length** validator.

```
<h:inputText value="#{UserBean.bio}" >
  <f:validator validatorId="javax.faces.Length"/>
</h:inputText>
```

Constraints

- Must be nested inside a **UIComponent** that implements **EditableValueHolder**.
- **validatorId** and/or **binding** must be specified. If this tag is not nested inside a **UIComponent**, or the **UIComponent** implementation class does not correctly implement **EditableValueHolder**, a **JspException** is thrown.

The f:valueChangeListener Tag

The **valueChangeListener** tag registers a **ValueChangeListener** instance on the **UIComponent** associated with the closest parent **UIComponent** custom action.

Attributes

Attribute	Type	Description	Required
binding (1.2, 2.0)	ValueExpression	The **ValueExpression** expression that evaluates to an object that implements **javax.faces.event .ValueChangeListener**.	No*
type	String	The fully qualified Java class name of a **ValueChangeListener** to be created and registered.	Yes (1.1) No (1.2, 2.0)*
* See constraints.			

Example Usage

The following shows an example where a custom **ValueChangeListener** instance (**jsf.MyValChangeListener**) is associated with an **inputText**.

```
<h:inputText id="inputText1">
  <f:valueChangeListener type="jsf.MyValChangeListener"/>
</h:inputText>
```

Constraints

- Must be nested inside a **UIComponent**.
- The corresponding **UIComponent** implementation class must implement **EditableValueHolder** and therefore define a public **addValueChangeListener( )** method that accepts a **ValueChangeListener** parameter.
- The specified listener class must implement **javax.faces.event.ValueChangeListener**.
- **type** and/or **binding** must be specified.

The f:verbatim Tag

UIComponent class: **javax.faces.component.UIOutput**

Component type: **javax.faces.Output**

The **verbatim** component is useful with JSP but serves no purpose with JSF 2.0 Facelets. It creates and registers a child **UIOutput** instance on the **UIComponent** associated with the closest parent **UIComponent** custom action that renders nested XML, HTML, or other markup body content.

Attributes

Attribute	Type	Description	Required
escape	boolean	The boolean value indicating whether or not to render special HTML and XML characters ("<", ">", etc.) as character entity codes ("<", ">", respectively). If true, generated markup is escaped in a manner appropriate for the markup language being rendered. The default value is false.	No
rendered (1.2, 2.0)	boolean	A boolean flag indicating whether or not this component is to be rendered during the RENDER_RESPONSE phase of the JSF lifecycle. The default value is "true".	No

Example Usage

The following is a generic example.

```
<f:verbatim escape="true">
  ...(HTML/XML Markup/Template text)
</f:verbatim>
```

Constraints

- The body may be either markup or JSP content. However, no **UIComponent** custom actions, or custom actions from the JSF core tag library, may be nested inside.

The f:view Tag

UIComponent class: **javax.faces.component.UIViewRoot**

Component type: **javax.faces.ViewRoot**

The **view** component serves as the container for all JSF core and component custom actions used on a page.

Attributes

Attribute	Type	Description	Required
locale	String or Locale	The name of a locale to use for localizing this page (such as en_uk), or a value binding expression that returns a **Locale** instance	No
renderKitId (1.2, 2.0)	String	The identifier for the render-kit to use for rendering this page	No
beforePhase (1.2, 2.0)	String	The **MethodExpression** expression that points to a method whose signature takes a single **PhaseEvent** parameter	No
afterPhase (1.2, 2.0)	String	The **MethodExpression** expression that points to a method whose signature takes a single **PhaseEvent** parameter	No

Example Usage

The following is an example with custom before and after **PhaseListeners**:

```
<f:view beforePhaseListener="#{bean.MyBeforePhaseListener}"
  afterPhaseListener="#{bean.MyAfterPhaseListener}">
  ...(Nested template text and custom actions)
</f:view>
```

Constraints

- Any JSP-created response using actions from the JSF core tag library, as well as actions extending **javax.faces.webapp.UIComponentTag or javax.faces.webapp .UIComponentELTag** from other tag libraries, must be nested inside an occurrence of the **<f:view>** action.
- JSP page fragments included via the standard **<%@ include %>** directive need not have their JSF actions embedded in a **<f:view>** action, because the included template text and custom actions will be processed as part of the outer page as it is compiled, and the **<f:view>** action on the outer page will meet the nesting requirement.

- For JSF 1.1 only, JSP pages included via **<jsp:include>** or any custom action that dynamically includes another page from the same Web application, such as JSTL's **<c:import>**, must use an **<f:subview>** (either inside the included page itself, or surrounding the **<jsp:include>** or custom action that is including the page).
- If the **renderKitId** attribute is present, its value is stored in **UIViewRoot**. If the **renderKitId** attribute is not present, then the default render-kit identifier as returned by **Application.getDefaultRenderKitId( )** is stored in **UIViewRoot** if it is not null. Otherwise, the render-kit identifier as specified by the constant **RenderKitFactory .HTML_BASIC_RENDER_KIT** is stored in **UIViewRoot**.
- If the **locale** attribute is present, its value overrides the **Locale** stored in **UIViewRoot**, normally set by the **ViewHandler**, and the **doStartTag( )** method must store it by calling **UIViewRoot.setLocale( )**.

The f:viewParam Tag (2.0)

The **f:viewParam** tag enables a page author to declaratively register a **UIViewParameter** as metadata associated with the parent **view**, and must be a child of the **f:metadata** tag. The main purpose of view parameters is to support "bookmarkable" Facelet views that are invoked via the HTTP GET operation. Since **UIViewParameter** extends **UIInput**, view parameters can be fortified with converters and validators. Validators can be especially helpful, since they can be used to validate that only valid data is specified as a request parameter value within the bookmarkable URL.

PART III

Attributes

Attribute	Type	Description	Required
binding (2.0)	ValueExpression	A **ValueExpression** that evaluates to an object of type **javax.faces .component.UIViewParameter**	false
converter (2.0)	ValueExpression	The fully qualified name of a class that implements the **javax.faces .convert.Converter** interface.	false
converterMessage (2.0)	String	When present, this overrides the default **Converter** validation message. The message can be a **ValueExpression**.	false
id (2.0)	String	The identifier for the component.	false
maxlength (2.0)	int	Indicates the maximum length of the value specified in the value attribute. If not specified, then the value can be of any length.	false

(continued)

Attribute	Type	Description	Required
name (2.0)	String	Specifies the name of the view parameter, which defines the query parameter name in the URL rendered by the **h:link** tag.	true
required (2.0)	Boolean	A boolean flag that indicates whether or not a value is required for this view parameter.	false
requiredMessage (2.0)	String	When present, this overrides the default required validation message. The message can be a **ValueExpression**.	false
validator (2.0)	MethodExpression	If specified, then the value must be a **MethodExpression** that refers to a method that has the same signature as the **validate** method in the **javax.faces .validator.Validator** interface.	false
validatorMessage (2.0)	String	When present, this overrides the default **Validator** validation message. The message can be a **ValueExpression**.	false
value (2.0)	Object	The value of the component.	false
valueChangeListener (2.0)	MethodExpression	A **MethodExpression** that refers to a method that returns void and accepts a single **ValueChangeEvent** argument. (1.0, 1.1, 1.2, 2.0) A **MethodExpression** that refers to a method that takes zero parameters and has a return type of void. Bear in mind that with this type of method signature, there is no way to determine the “old” and “new” values of the component. (2.0)	false

Example Usage

```
<f:metadata>
  <f:viewParam
    name="customerId" value="#{customer.customerId}">
      <f:validateLongRange />
  </f:viewParam>
</f:metadata>
```

The Standard HTML Library

The Standard HTML Library is accessible in Facelets and JSP as a tag library with a URI of **http://java.sun.com/jsf/html** and default prefix of **h**. A quick reference of the standard HTML library is provided in Table 16-2.

Tag	Description	JSF Version(s)
h:body	Renders the HTML **<body>** element. This element is required when using resource relocation, such as rendering references to JavaScript or CSS files.	2.0
h:button	Renders an HTML button that, when clicked, submits an HTTP GET (not post) to the JSF server. The destination of the button comes from a JSF navigation rule (implicit or explicit).	2.0
h:column	The child container component for a **dataTable** component. The element can be equipped with **header** and **footer** facets for a column header and footer. Its children are used to display/process the column's data.	1.0, 1.1, 1.2, 2.0
h:commandButton	Renders as an HTML **<input>** element with the **type** attribute set to "submit", "reset", or "image", depending on the value of this action element's type and **image** attribute values, the **name** attribute set to the component's client ID, and the **value** attribute set to the component's value.	1.0, 1.1, 1.2, 2.0
h:commandLink	Renders as an HTML **<a>** element with an **href** attribute containing "#", and an **onclick** attribute.	1.0, 1.1, 1.2, 2.0
h:dataTable	Renders an HTML **<table>**element where **UIColumn** child components are responsible for rendering the table columns. The columns can hold any type of component, including input and command. The **value** attribute value can be of any type, but the primary model type is the **javax.faces.model.DataModel** class. Both the **dataTable** component and its column children components may be equipped with **header** and **footer** facets. The table rows are rendered within a **<tbody>** element with a **<tr>** element for each row and a **<td>** element for each column child. The first row to render and how many rows to render can be specified by the first and rows attributes.	1.0, 1.1, 1.2, 2.0

TABLE 16-2 The Standard HTML Library Quick Reference *(continued)*

PART III

Tag	Description	JSF Version(s)
h:form	Renders as an HTML input form. The inner tags of the form receive the data that will be submitted with the form. Displays an HTML **<input>** element with an **action** attribute set to the URL that defines the view containing the form, and a **method** attribute set to "post". When the form is submitted, only components that are children of the submitted form are processed.	1.0, 1.1, 1.2, 2.0
h:graphicImage	Displays an image. The component is rendered as an HTML **<input>** element with the **src** attribute holding the component's value or the **url** attribute, adjusted to a context-relative path.	1.0, 1.1, 1.2, 2.0
h:head	Renders the HTML **<head>** element. This element is required when using resource relocation, such as rendering references to JavaScript or CSS files.	2.0
h:inputHidden	Renders as an invisible field, which is an HTML **<input>** element with the **type** attribute set to "hidden", a **name** attribute set to the component's client ID, and a **value** attribute set to the component's value.	1.0, 1.1, 1.2, 2.0
h:inputSecret	Renders as an HTML **<input>** element with the **type** attribute set to "password", a **name** attribute set to the component's client ID, and a **value** attribute set to the component's value only if the action's redisplay attribute is set to "true".	1.0, 1.1, 1.2, 2.0
h:inputText	Renders as an HTML **<input>** element with the **type** attribute set to "text", a **name** attribute set to the component's client ID, and a **value** attribute set to the component's value.	1.0, 1.1, 1.2, 2.0
h:inputTextarea	Renders as an input text area for multiple lines of text. Displays an HTML **<textarea>** element with a **name** attribute set to the component's client ID and a body holding the component's value.	1.0, 1.1, 1.2, 2.0
h:message	Displays the first **Faces** message queued for the component and identified by its **for** attribute.	1.0, 1.1, 1.2, 2.0
h:messages	Displays all queued **Faces** messages or only those queued without a component identifier if the **globalOnly** attribute is set to "true".	1.0, 1.1, 1.2, 2.0
h:link	Renders an HTML anchor that, when clicked, submits an HTTP GET to the JSF server. The destination of the link comes from a JSF navigation rule (implicit or explicit).	2.0
h:outputFormat	Can display parameterized and/or localized messages.	1.0, 1.1, 1.2, 2.0

TABLE 16-2 The Standard HTML Library Quick Reference

Tag	Description	JSF Version(s)
h:outputLabel	Renders as an HTML **<label>** element with a **value** as content. Has an optional **for** attribute that can be set to the client ID for the component identified by the action element's **for** attribute value.	1.0, 1.1, 1.2, 2.0
h:outputLink	Renders as an HTML **<a>** element with an **href** attribute set to the component's value.	1.0, 1.1, 1.2, 2.0
h:outputScript	Render a reference to an external script file, usually JavaScript.	2.0
h:outputStyleSheet	Render a reference to an external CSS stylesheet file.	2.0
h:outputText	Renders as text within an HTML **<span>** element if any of the HTML attributes or the **id** attribute is set.	1.0, 1.1, 1.2, 2.0
h:panelGrid	Renders an HTML table that serves as a container for other components.	1.0, 1.1, 1.2, 2.0
h:panelGroup	Creates a panel container to group a set of components under one parent. It renders its children within an HTML **<span>** element if any of the HTML attributes or the **id** attribute is set.	1.0, 1.1, 1.2, 2.0
h:selectBooleanCheckbox	Renders as a **boolean** checkbox. Displays an HTML **<input>** element with the **type** attribute set to "checkbox" and a **name** attribute set to the client ID.	1.0, 1.1, 1.2, 2.0
h:selectManyCheckbox	Renders as a set of checkboxes from which the user can select multiple values.	1.0, 1.1, 1.2, 2.0
h:selectManyListbox	Renders as a **<select>** element where multiple items can be selected.	1.0, 1.1, 1.2, 2.0
h:selectManyMenu	Renders as a **<select>** element with a **name** attribute set to the component's client ID, a **multiple** attribute, and a **size** attribute set to "1" as the value.	1.0, 1.1, 1.2, 2.0
h:selectOneListBox	Renders as a **<select>** element with a **name** attribute set to the component's client ID, a **multiple** attribute, and a **size** attribute set to "1" as the value.	1.0, 1.1, 1.2, 2.0
h:selectOneMenu	Renders as a **<select>** element with a **name** attribute set to the component's client ID, a **multiple** attribute, and a size attribute set to "1" as the value.	1.0, 1.1, 1.2, 2.0
h:selectOneRadio	Renders as a set of radio buttons from which the user can select one value.	1.0, 1.1, 1.2, 2.0

Table 16-2 The Standard HTML Library Quick Reference *(continued)*

A detailed description for the components referenced in Table 16-2 follows.

The h:body Tag (2.0)

UIComponent class: **javax.faces.component.html.HtmlBody**

Component type: **javax.faces.OutputBody**

The **h:body** tag is responsible for rendering the begin **<body>** and end **</body>** tags in a view. Although JSF 2.0 Facelets permits the page author to put HTML tags directly in the view markup, this tag was introduced into JSF 2.0 in order to provide a way for tags such as **h:outputScript** and **h:outputStylesheet** to specify "body" as the value of their target attribute. In such cases, the **h:body** tag is responsible for rendering such resources just before the end **</body>** tag. In the case of scripts, placing them at the bottom of an HTML page can often times cause the page to load faster in the end user's Web browser.

Note that in a portlet environment, the JSR 329 JSF Portlet Bridge implementation is required to override the renderer for the **h:body** tag, in order to delegate responsibility for rendering resources within an HTML **<body>** tag to the portlet container.

Core Attributes

Attribute	Type	Description	Required
binding (2.0)	ValueExpression	A **ValueExpression** that evaluates to an object of type **javax.faces.component.html .HtmlBody**.	No
title (2.0)	String	The title of the component. This is passed through to the rendered HTML **title** attribute.	No

Internationalization Attributes

Attribute	Type	Description	Required
dir (2.0)	String	The reading direction of the generated HTML component: RTL (right to left) or LTR (left to right).	No
lang (2.0)	String	The applied **lang** attribute to the generated HTML output. For more information on the HTML **lang** attribute, visit **www.w3.org/TR/ REC-html40/struct/dirlang.html**.	No

Style Attributes (2.0)

Attributes for CSS styles that are applied to the generated HTML output of the component are shown next.

style	styleclass

JavaScript Attributes (2.0)

Attributes for the common JavaScript events are shown next.

onclick	ondblclick	onkeydown	onkeypress	onkeyup
onload	onmousedown	onmousemove	onmouseout	onmouseover
onmouseup	onunload			

All JavaScript attributes accept arguments of type **String**, and none are specifically required.

Example Usage

```
<h:head />
<h:body>
  <h:form>
    <h:outputLabel for="firstName" value="First Name" />
    <h:inputText value="#{testManagedBean.firstName}" />
    <h:commandButton value="Submit" />
  </h:form>
</h:body>
```

PART III

The h:button Tag (2.0)

UIComponent class: **javax.faces.component.html.HtmlOutcomeTargetButton**

Component type: **javax.faces.OutcomeTarget**

Similar to the **h:link** tag, the **h:button** tag was introduced in JSF 2.0 in order to enable full support of "bookmarkable" Facelet views that are invoked via the HTTP GET operation. The rendered markup is an HTML **<input />** tag with the **onclick** attribute rendered as "window .location.href=", with the target URL being determined by the value of the **outcome** attribute. If there are any child **f:param** tags, then the corresponding name=value pairs will be appended as query parameters for the target URL. This approach is sometimes referred to as "preemptive navigation" because the navigation cases are processed before the user has clicked the button. This is made possible by having the navigation-handler processes the **outcome** attribute and produce the target URL during the RENDER_RESPONSE phase of the JSF lifecycle.

Note that usage of the **h:button** tag *requires JavaScript to be enabled* in the end user's Web browser. If it is not possible for JavaScript to be enabled, then the **h:link** tag should be used instead.

Ungrouped Attributes

Attribute	Type	Description	Required
accesskey (2.0)	char	The mnemonic character used to establish focus to this component.	No
alt (2.0)	String	The alternate textual description of the element rendered by this component.	No

(continued)

Attribute	Type	Description	Required
fragment (2.0)	String	Refers to the named anchor of the target page that is to be rendered in the browser. If specified, then a pound/hash (#) character followed by the value of this attribute will be appended to the URL in the rendered **onclick** attribute.	No
image (2.0)	String	The absolute or relative URL of the image to be displayed for this button. If specified, this "input" element will be of type "image".	No
includeViewParams (2.0)	Boolean	If this boolean flag is "true", then the name/value pairs of any **f:viewParam** tags specified in the **f:metadata** section of the target view will be appended as query parameters in the target URL in the rendered **onclick** attribute.	No
outcome (2.0)	String	The logical outcome that is passed to the NavigationHandler that is used to generate the target URL that is rendered in the onclick attribute. If a viewId is specified, then implicit navigation will take place, and the target URL will point to the specified viewId.	Yes
rendered (2.0)	Boolean	A boolean flag indicating whether or not this component is to be rendered during the RENDER_RESPONSE phase of the JSF lifecycle. The default value is "true".	No
tabindex (2.0)	int	Determines the tabbing order position of the component. The value must be an integer between 0 and 32767.	No
value (2.0)	String	The value of this component, which is passed through to the rendered HTML as the text of the button label.	No

Core Attributes

Attribute	Type	Description	Required
binding (2.0)	ValueExpression	A **ValueExpression** that evaluates to an object of type **javax.faces.component.html.HtmlOutcomeTargetButton**.	No
id (2.0)	String	The identifier for the component.	No
title (2.0)	String	The title of the component. This is passed through to the rendered HTML **title** attribute.	No

Internationalization Attributes

Attribute	Type	Description	Required
dir (2.0)	String	The reading direction of the generated HTML component: RTL (right to left) or LTR (left to right).	No
lang (2.0)	String	The applied **lang** attribute to the generated HTML output. For more information on the HTML **lang** attribute, visit **www.w3.org/TR/REC-html40/struct/dirlang.html**.	No

Style Attributes (2.0)

Attributes for CSS styles that are applied to the generated HTML output of the component are shown next.

style	styleclass

JavaScript Attributes (2.0)

Attributes for the common JavaScript events are shown next.

onblur	onclick	ondblclick	onfocus	onkeydown
onkeypress	onkeyup	onmousedown	onmousemove	onmouseout
onmouseover	onmouseup			

Example Usage

The following example markup would appear in a Facelet view document named **page2 .xhtml** so that the user could navigate back to **page1.xhtml** with the **f:viewParam** name=value pairs from **page1.xhtml** appended as query parameters to the target URL in the onclick attribute. Additionally, the **companyId** would be appended as a query parameter, since it is specified as a child tag of **h:button**.

```
<h:button
  includeViewParams="true"
  outcome="page1" value="Apply Again">
  <f:param
    name="companyId"
    value="#{testManagedBean.companyId}" />
</h:button>
```

The h:column Tag

UIComponent class: **javax.faces.component.UIColumn, (1.2, 2.0) javax.faces.component .html.HtmlColumn**

Component type: **javax.faces.Column**

PART III

The **h:column** tag serves as an immediate child of an **<h:dataTable>** tag. The element can be equipped with **header** and **footer** facets for a column header and footer. Its children are used to process the column's data.

Attributes

Attribute	Type	Description	Required
binding	ValueBinding (1.0, 1.1) or ValueExpression (1.2, 2.0)	The binding reference to a like **UIComponent** instance.	No
id	String	The identifier for the component.	No
rendered	boolean	A boolean flag indicating whether or not this component is to be rendered during the RENDER_RESPONSE phase of the JSF lifecycle. The default value is "true".	No
footerClass (1.2, 2.0)	String	The space-separated list of CSS style class(es) that is applied to any column footer generated for this table.	No
headerClass (1.2, 2.0)	String	The space-separated list of CSS style class(es) that is applied to any column header generated for this table.	No

Example Usage

Use the "header" facet on a **column** to create the column header. The following example creates a two-column table with the column headers "Firstname" and "Lastname":

```
<h:dataTable>
  <h:column>
    <f:facet name="header">
      <h:outputText value="Firstname"/>
    </f:facet>
    ...
  </h:column>
  <h:column>
    <f:facet name="header">
      <h:outputText value="Lastname"/>
    </f:facet>
    ...
  </h:column>
</h:dataTable>
```

The child components of each **column** display the data for each row in that column. The **column** does not create child components per row; instead, each child is repeatedly rendered (stamped) once per row. Because of this stamping behavior, only certain types of components are supported as children inside a **column**.

The h:commandButton Tag

UIComponent class: **javax.faces.component.html.HtmlCommandButton**

Component type: **javax.faces.HtmlCommandButton**

The **commandButton** component is rendered as an HTML **<input>** element with the **type** attribute set to "submit", "reset", or "image", depending on the value of this action element's **type** and **image** attribute values, the **name** attribute set to the component's client ID, and the **value** attribute set to the component's value.

Ungrouped Attributes

Attribute	Type	Description	Required
accesskey	char	The mnemonic character used to establish focus to this component.	No
action	javax.faces.el.MethodBinding (1.0, 1.1) javax.el.MethodExpression (1.2, 2.0)	The reference to an action method sent by the command component, or the static outcome of an action.	No
actionListener	javax.faces.el.MethodBinding (1.0, 1.1) javax.el.MethodExpression (1.2, 2.0)	A **MethodExpression** that refers to a method that takes a single parameter of type **ActionEvent** and has a return type of void. (1.0, 1.1, 1.2, 2.0) A **MethodExpression** that refers to a method that takes zero parameters and has a return type of void. Bear in mind that if this method signature is used, then there is no way to determine the source of the event. (2.0)	No
alt	String	The alternate textual description of the element rendered by this component.	No
disabled	boolean	When **true**, renders the component in a disabled state.	No
image	String	The absolute or relative URL of the image to be displayed for this button. If specified, this "input" element will be of type "image". (1.0, 1.1, 1.2, 2.0)	No

(continued)

Attribute	Type	Description	Required
		If the value starts with the forward slash character, then the rendered URL will be prepended with the Web application context root folder name. (2.0)	
immediate	boolean	Determines whether or not data validation should occur when events are generated by this component. When **true**, any action or **ActionListener** should be executed during the Apply Request Values phase instead of the Invoke Application phase.	No
readonly	boolean	The boolean flag that specifies whether the component is read only.	No
rendered	boolean	A boolean flag indicating whether or not this component is to be rendered during the RENDER_RESPONSE phase of the JSF lifecycle. The default value is "true".	No
tabindex	int	Determines the tabbing order position of the component. The value must be an integer between 0 and 32767.	No
type	String	Must be submitted or reset.	No

Core Attributes

Attribute	Type	Description	Required
binding	ValueBinding (1.0, 1.1) or ValueExpression (1.2, 2.0)	The binding reference to a like **UIComponent** instance.	No
id	String	The identifier for the component.	No
value	String	The value of the component.	No

Internationalization Attributes

Attribute	Type	Description	Required
dir	String	The reading direction of the generated HTML component: RTL (right to left) or LTR (left to right).	No
lang	String	The applied **lang** attribute to the generated HTML output. For more information on the HTML **lang** attribute, visit **www.w3.org/TR/REC-html40/struct/dirlang.html**.	No

Style Attributes

Attributes for CSS styles that are applied to the generated HTML output of the component are shown next.

style	styleclass

These style attributes accept arguments of type **String** and are not specifically required.

JavaScript Attributes

Attributes for the common JavaScript events are shown next.

onblur	onchange	onclick	ondblclick	onfocus
onkeydown	onkeypress	onkeyup	onmousedown	onmousemove
onmouseout	onmouseover	onmouseup	onselect	

All JavaScript attributes accept arguments of type **String**, and none are specifically required.

Example Usage

The following is an example of a button rendered with "Register" text that submits the form and invokes the **action** method specified by "#{Register_Backing.register}".

```
<f:form>
  <h:inputText id="firstName" value="Jake"
     binding="{Register_Backing.firstNameInputText}" />
  <h:commandButton value="Register" action="#{Register_Backing.register}"/>
</f:form>
```

The following is an additional **commandButton Cancel** button that submits the form but without performing any validation.

```
<f:form>
  <h:inputText id="firstName" value="Jake"
     binding="{Register_Backing.firstNameInputText}" />
  <h:commandButton value="Register" action="#{Register_Backing.register}"/>
  <h:commandButton value="Cancel" immediate="true" action="cancel"/>
</f:form>
```

PART III

The h:commandLink Tag

UIComponent class: **javax.faces.component.html.HtmlCommandLink**

Component type: **javax.faces.HtmlCommandLink**

The **commandLink** component renders an HTML hyperlink using an **<a>** anchor element but also executes a form submit when clicked.

Ungrouped Attributes

Attribute	Type	Description	Required
accesskey	char	The mnemonic character used to establish focus to this component.	No
action	javax.faces.el.MethodBinding (1.0, 1.1) javax.el.MethodExpression (1.2, 2.0)	The reference to an action method sent by the command component, or the static outcome of an action.	No
actionListener	javax.faces.el.MethodBinding (1.0, 1.1) javax.el.MethodExpression (1.2, 2.0)	A **MethodExpression** that refers to a method that takes a single parameter of type ActionEvent and returns void. (1.0, 1.1, 1.2, 2.0) A **MethodExpression** that refers to a method that takes zero parameters and has a return type of void. Bear in mind that if this method signature is used, then there is no way to determine the source of the event. (2.0)	No
charset	String	The character encoding of the resource referred by this hyperlink.	No
coords	String	This attribute is used in conjunction with client-side image maps, and indicates the position and shape of the hotspot that the end user can click.	No
hreflang	String	The language code of the resource designated by this hyperlink.	No

Attribute	Type	Description	Required
immediate	boolean	Determines whether or not data validation should occur when events are generated by this component. When **true**, any action or **ActionListener** should be executed during the Apply Request Values phase instead of the Invoke Application phase.	No
rel	String	A comma-separated list of relationships described by this link.	No
rendered	boolean	A boolean flag indicating whether or not this component is to be rendered during the RENDER_RESPONSE phase of the JSF lifecycle. The default value is "true".	No
rev	String	The reverse link from the anchor specified by this hyperlink to the current document. The value of this attribute is a space-separated list of link types.	No
shape	String	The shape of the hotspot in client-side image maps. Valid values are **default**, **circle**, **rect**, and **poly**.	No
tabindex	int	The tabbing order position of the component. The value must be an integer between 0 and 32767.	No
target	String	The name of a frame where the resource retrieved via this hyperlink is to be displayed.	No
type	String	Specifies the content type of the resource found at the URL specified in the href attribute.	No

(continued)

Core Attributes

Attribute	Type	Description	Required
binding	ValueBinding (1.0, 1.1) or ValueExpression (1.2, 2.0)	The binding reference to a like **UIComponent** instance.	No
id	String	The identifier for the component.	No
title	String	The title of the component. This is passed through to the rendered HTML **title** attribute.	No
value	String	The value of the component.	No

Internationalization Attributes

Attribute	Type	Description	Required
dir	String	The reading direction of the generated HTML component: RTL (right to left) or LTR (left to right).	No
lang	String	The applied **lang** attribute to the generated HTML output. For more information on the HTML **lang** attribute, visit **www.w3.org/TR/REC-html40/struct/dirlang.html**.	No

Style Attributes

Attributes for CSS styles that are applied to the generated HTML output of the component are shown next.

style	styleclass

These style attributes accept arguments of type **String** and are not specifically required.

JavaScript Attributes

Attributes for the common JavaScript events are shown next.

onblur	onchange	onclick	ondblclick	onfocus
onkeydown	onkeypress	onkeyup	onmousedown	onmousemove
onmouseout	onmouseover	onmouseup	onselect	

All JavaScript attributes accept arguments of type **String**, and none are specifically required.

Example Usage

The following is a simple **commandLink** example of a button that submits an input field.

```
<h:commandLink action="an action"
    binding="#{backing_newhello.commandLink2}"
    id="commandLink2">
  <h:outputText value="This text will appear as a link"
```

```
    binding="#{backing_newhello.outputText1}"
    id="outputText1"/>
</h:commandLink>
```

The preceding creates an input form. The inner tags of the form receive the data that will be submitted with the form. It displays an HTML **<input>** element with an action attribute set to the URL that defines the view containing the form and a method attribute set to "post". When the form is submitted, only components that are children of the submitted form are processed.

The h:dataTable Tag

UIComponent class: **javax.faces.component.html.HtmlDataTable**

Component type: **javax.faces.HtmlDataTable**

The **dataTable** component is a tabular container component for other child components that is rendered as an HTML **<table>** with a number of attributes, such as **border**, **width**, and so on, which are directly passed to the rendered HTML table. The component's children are rendered in the table cells, with new rows added when the number of columns is reached.

For further information on the attributes that are passed on to the rendered HTML table, visit **www.w3.org/TR/REC-html40/struct/tables.html**.

Ungrouped Attributes

Attribute	Type	Description	Required
bgcolor	String	The background color of the rendered HTML table representing the **dataTable**.	No
border	int	The border size in pixels of the rendered HTML table.	No
cellpadding	int	The **cellpadding** attribute of the rendered HTML table.	No
cellspacing	int	The **cellspacing** attribute of the rendered HTML table.	No
first	int	The first row to display (starting with 0).	No
frame	String	A **frame** that is passed on to the rendered HTML table. This attribute specifies which sides of the frame surrounding the table will be visible. Valid values are **none**, **above**, **below**, **hsides**, **vsides**, **lhs**, **rhs**, **box**, and **border**.	No
rendered	boolean	A boolean flag indicating whether or not this component is to be rendered during the RENDER_RESPONSE phase of the JSF lifecycle. The default value is "true".	No
rows	int	Determines how many rows are displayed in the rendered table.	No
rules	String	A **rules** attribute that is passed on to the rendered HTML table. Valid values are **none**, **groups**, **rows**, **cols**, and **all**.	No

(continued)

Attribute	Type	Description	Required
summary	String	A **summary** attribute that is passed on to the rendered HTML table.	No
var	String	An iterator variable name that gets introduced into the EL and represents the current item in the iteration over the **value** attribute.	No
width	String	A **width** attribute that is passed on to the rendered HTML table. For pixel width, enter a nonzero integer. For percentage width, append '%' to the value. For example: "80%".	No

Core Attributes

Attribute	Type	Description	Required
binding	ValueBinding (1.0, 1.1) or ValueExpression (1.2, 2.0)	The binding reference to a like **UIComponent** instance.	No
id	String	The identifier for the component.	No
title	String	The title of the component. This is passed through to the rendered HTML **title** attribute.	No
value	String	The value of the component.	No

Style Attributes

Attribute	Type	Description	Required
columnclasses	String	The comma-separated list of CSS classes to be associated with the rendered columns. The classes will be applied in a repeating fashion to all columns in the **panelGrid** component.	No
footerclass	String	The CSS class to be associated with the rendered HTML table footer (bottom row).	No
headerclass	String	The CSS class to be associated with the rendered HTML table header (top row).	No
rowclasses	String	A comma-separated list of CSS classes to be associated with the rendered rows. The classes will be applied in a repeating fashion to all rows in the **panelGrid** component.	No
style	String	Inline style(s) that are applied to the **panelGrid** component.	No
styleclass	String	The CSS style class that is applied to the **panelGrid** component.	No

Internationalization Attributes

Attribute	Type	Description	Required
dir	String	The reading direction of the generated HTML component: RTL (right to left) or LTR (left to right).	No
lang	String	The applied **lang** attribute to the generated HTML output. For more information on the HTML **lang** attribute, visit **www.w3.org/TR/REC-html40/struct/dirlang.html**.	No

JavaScript Attributes

Attributes for the common JavaScript events are shown next.

onclick	ondblclick	onkeydown	onkeypress	onkeyup
onmousedown	onmousemove	onmouseout	onmouseover	onmouseup

All JavaScript attributes accept arguments of type **String**, and none are specifically required.

Example Usage

The following is a simple **dataTable** example containing two child **column**s with nested **outputText** components.

```
<h:dataTable >
  <h:column>
    <h:outputText value="outputText1"/>
  </h:column>
  <h:column>
    <h:outputText value="outputText2"/>
  </h:column>
</h:dataTable>
```

Consider a managed bean **EmpList** of type **java.util.ArrayList** with list items defined in **faces-config** as **list-entries**. The following **dataTable** example will render the **Emplist** in an HTML table.

```
<h:dataTable border="1" value="#{EmpList}" var="row">
  <h:column>
    <f:facet name="header">
      <h:outputText value="Emplist"/>
    </f:facet>
    <h:outputText value="#{row}"/>
  </h:column>
</h:dataTable>
```

The following is a more advanced usage example from the Virtual Trainer application in Chapter 9. It displays all of the training events for a particular user in the application.

```
<h:dataTable id="eventsTable" rows="5"
    value="#{Main_Backing.trainingEventsForUser}"
    var="te" rowClasses="list-row-odd, list-row-even"
    width="100%" binding="#{Main_Backing.data}">
  <h:column rendered="#{UserBean.trainer}">
```

PART III

```
    <f:facet name="header">
      <h:outputText value="User Account"/>
    </f:facet>
    <h:outputText value="#{te.userAcctId}"/>
  </h:column>
  <h:column>
    <f:facet name="header">
      <h:outputText value="Event Name"/>
    </f:facet>
    <h:outputText value="#{te.ename}"/>
  </h:column>
  <h:column>
    <f:facet name="header">
      <h:outputText value="Completion Date"/>
    </f:facet>
    <h:outputText value="#{te.completionDate}">
      <f:convertDateTime pattern="MM-dd-yy"/>
    </h:outputText>
  </h:column>
...
</h:dataTable>
```

The h:form Tag

UIComponent class: **javax.faces.component.html.HtmlForm**

Component type: **javax.faces.HtmlForm**

The **form** component renders as an input form. The inner tags of the form receive the data that will be submitted with the form. It displays an HTML **<input>** element with an action attribute set to the URL that defines the view containing the form and a method attribute set to "post". When the form is submitted, only components that are children of the submitted form are processed.

Ungrouped Attributes

Attribute	Type	Description	Required
accept	String	The list of content types that a server processing this form will handle correctly.	No
acceptcharset	String	The list of character encodings for input data that are accepted by the server processing this form.	No
enctype	String	The content type used to submit the form to the server. If not specified, the default value is "application/x-www-form-urlencoded".	No
rendered	boolean	A boolean flag indicating whether or not this component is to be rendered during the RENDER_RESPONSE phase of the JSF lifecycle. The default value is "true".	No
target	String	The name of a frame where the response retrieved after the form submit is to be displayed.	No

Core Attributes

Attribute	Type	Description	Required
binding	ValueBinding (1.0, 1.1) or ValueExpression (1.2, 2.0)	A binding reference to a like **UIComponent** instance.	No
id	String	The identifier for the component.	No
prependId (1.2, 2.0)	boolean	A boolean value indicating whether or not this form should prepend its **id** to its descendant's **id** during the **clientId** generation process. The default is true.	No
title	String	The title of the component. This is passed through to the rendered HTML **title** element.	No
value	String	The value of the component.	No

Internationalization Attributes

Attribute	Type	Description	Required
dir	String	The reading direction of the generated HTML component: RTL (right to left) or LTR (left to right).	No
lang	String	The applied **lang** attribute to the generated HTML output. For more information on the HTML **lang** attribute, visit **www.w3.org/TR/REC-html40/struct/dirlang.html**.	No

Style Attributes

Attributes for CSS styles that are applied to the generated HTML output of the component are shown next.

style	styleclass

These style attributes accept arguments of type **String** and are not specifically required.

JavaScript Attributes

Attributes for the common JavaScript events are shown next.

onclick	ondblclick	onkeydown	onkeypress	onkeyup
onmousedown	onmousemove	onmouseout	onmouseover	onmouseup

All JavaScript attributes accept arguments of type **String**, and none are specifically required.

Example Usage

```
<h:form id="formid" >
  ...(form input components)
</h:form>
```

The h:graphicImage Tag

UIComponent class: **javax.faces.component.html.HtmlGraphicImage**

Component type: **javax.faces.HtmlGraphicImage**

The **graphicImage** component displays an image. It is rendered as an HTML **<img>** element with the **src** attribute holding the component's **value** or the **URL** attribute, adjusted to a context-relative path. (If the URL is preceded by a slash ("/"), then it uses a context-relative path, otherwise it uses a relative path.)

As of JSF 2.0, the new **library** and **name** attributes have been added in order to support rendering of images from a resource library. The JSF 2.0 spec requires that Web application resources be located in the **/resources** folder under the Web application root. Alternatively, resources can be located in the **META-INF/resources** folder of any JAR file in the classpath. Each resource must adhere to the following naming convention:

```
[localePrefix/][libraryName/][libraryVersion/]resourceName[/resourceVersion]
```

Ungrouped Attributes

Attribute	Type	Description	Required
alt	String	An alternate textual description of the element rendered by this component.	No
height	String	The override for the height of this image.	No
ismap	boolean	The boolean flag indicating that this image is to be used as a server-side image map. Such an image must be enclosed within a hyperlink ("a").	No
longdesc	String	The URI to a long description of the image represented by this element.	No
library (2.0)	String	The name of the library that contains the script resource.	No
name (2.0)	String	The name of the image resource.	No
rendered	boolean	A boolean flag indicating whether or not this component is to be rendered during the RENDER_ RESPONSE phase of the JSF lifecycle. The default value is "true".	No
usemap	String	The name of a client-side image map (an HTML map element) for which this element provides the image.	No
url	String	The context-relative URL indicating the location of the image resource.	No
width	String	The override for the width of this image.	No

Core Attributes

Attribute	Type	Description	Required
binding	ValueBinding (1.0, 1.1) or ValueExpression (1.2, 2.0)	A binding reference to a like **UIComponent** instance.	No
id	String	The identifier for the component.	No
title	String	The title of the component. This is passed through to the rendered HTML **title** attribute.	No
value	String	The value of the component.	No

Internationalization Attributes

Attribute	Type	Description	Required
dir	String	The reading direction of the generated HTML component: RTL (right to left) or LTR (left to right).	No
lang	String	The applied **lang** attribute to the generated HTML output. For more information on the HTML **lang** attribute, visit **www.w3.org/TR/REC-html40/struct/dirlang.html**.	No

Style Attributes

Attributes for CSS styles that are applied to the generated HTML output of the component are shown next.

style	styleclass

These style attributes accept arguments of type **String** and are not specifically required.

JavaScript Attributes

Attributes for the common JavaScript events are shown next.

onclick	ondblclick	onkeydown	onkeypress	onkeyup
onmousedown	onmousemove	onmouseout	onmouseover	onmouseup

All JavaScript attributes accept arguments of type **String**, and none are specifically required.

Example Usage

The following example usage shows how to render a graphic image according to a URL:

```
<h:graphicImage id="graphicImage1"
url="/myimage.jpg" height="143" width="143"
  binding="#{backing.graphicImage1}" />
```

The following example usage shows how to render a graphic image from a resource library.

```
<h:graphicImage library="testlibrary" name="myimage.jpg" />
```

The h:head Tag (2.0)

UIComponent class: **javax.faces.component.html.HtmlHead**

Component type: **javax.faces.OutputHead**

The **h:head** tag is responsible for rendering the begin **<head>** and end **</head>** tags in a view. Although JSF 2.0 Facelets permits the page author to put HTML tags directly in the view markup, this tag was introduced into JSF 2.0 in order to provide a way for tags such as **h:outputScript** and **h:outputStylesheet** to specify "head" as the value of their target attribute. In such cases, the **h:head** tag is responsible for rendering such resources just before the end **</head>** tag.

Note that in a portlet environment, the JSR 329 JSF Portlet Bridge implementation is required to override the renderer for the **h:head** tag, in order to delegate responsibility for rendering resources within an HTML **<head>** tag to the portlet container.

Core Attributes

Attribute	Type	Description	Required
binding (2.0)	ValueExpression	A **ValueExpression** that evaluates to an object of type **javax.faces.component.html.HtmlHead**	No

Internationalization Attributes

Attribute	Type	Description	Required
dir (2.0)	String	The reading direction of the generated HTML component: RTL (right to left) or LTR (left to right).	No
lang (2.0)	String	The applied **lang** attribute to the generated HTML output. For more information on the HTML **lang** attribute, visit **www.w3.org/TR/REC-html40/struct/dirlang.html**.	No

Example Usage

```
<h:head />
<h:body>
  <h:form>
    <h:outputLabel for="firstName" value="First Name" />
    <h:inputText value="#{testManagedBean.firstName}" />
    <h:commandButton value="Submit" />
  </h:form>
</h:body>
```

The h:inputHidden Tag

UIComponent class: **javax.faces.component.html.HtmlInputHidden**

Component type: **javax.faces.HtmlInputHidden**

The **inputHidden** component renders a field that is invisible to the user, which is typically used to pass variables from page to page. Displays an HTML **<input>** element with the **type** attribute set to "hidden", a **name** attribute set to the component's client ID, and a **value** attribute set to the component's value.

Attributes

Attribute	Type	Description	Required
binding	ValueBinding (1.0, 1.1) or ValueExpression (1.2, 2.0)	A binding reference to a like **UIComponent** instance.	No
converter	String	Converter instance registered with this component.	No
converterMessage (1.2, 2.0)	String	When present, this overrides the default **Converter** validation message. The message can be a **ValueExpression**.	No
id	String	The identifier for the component.	No
immediate	boolean	When **true**, the component's value must be converted and validated immediately during the Apply Request Values phase rather than waiting until the Process Validations phase.	No
rendered	boolean	A boolean flag indicating whether or not this component is to be rendered during the RENDER_RESPONSE phase of the JSF lifecycle. The default value is "true".	No
required	boolean	The boolean flag specifying whether this component is required to have a value.	No
requiredMessage (1.2, 2.0)	String	When present, this overrides the default **required** validation message. The message can be a **ValueExpression**.	No

(continued)

Attribute	Type	Description	Required
validator	String	If specified, then the value must be a **MethodExpression** that refers to a method that has the same signature as the **validate** method in the javax.faces. validator.Validator interface.	No
validatorMessage (1.2, 2.0)	String	When present, this overrides the default **Validator** validation message. The message can be a **ValueExpression**.	No
value	String	The value of the component.	No
valueChangeListener	MethodBinding (1.0, 1.1) or MethodExpression (1.2, 2.0)	**MethodExpression** that refers to a method that returns void and accepts a single **ValueChangeEvent** argument. (1.0, 1.1, 1.2, 2.0) A **MethodExpression** that refers to a method that takes zero parameters and has a return type of void. Bear in mind that with this type of method signature, there is no way to determine the "old" and "new" values of the component. (2.0)	No

Example Usage

The following shows a simple usage of **InputHidden**.

```
<h:inputHidden id="inputHidden1"
binding="#{backing_bean.inputHidden1}"
    value="A hidden value"/>
```

The h:inputSecret Tag

UIComponent class: **javax.faces.component.html.HtmlInputSecret**

Component type: **javax.faces.HtmlInputSecret**

The **inputSecret** component renders as a password input field. It displays an HTML **<input>** element with the **type** attribute set to **password**, a **name** attribute set to the component's client ID, and a **value** attribute set to the component's **value** only if the action's redisplay attribute is set to **true**.

Ungrouped Attributes

Attribute	Type	Description	Required
accesskey	char	The mnemonic character used to establish focus to this component.	No
alt	int	The alternate textual description of the element rendered by this component.	No
converter	String	The fully qualified name of a class that implements the **javax.faces .convert.Converter** interface.	No
converterMessage (1.2, 2.0)	String	When present, this overrides the default **Converter** validation message. The message can be a **ValueExpression**.	No
disabled	boolean	When **true**, this renders the component in a disabled state.	No
immediate	boolean	When **true**, the component's value must be converted and validated immediately during the Apply Request Values phase rather than waiting until the Process Validations phase.	No
maxlength	int	The integer value specifying the maximum length of the rendered HTML input element.	No
readonly	boolean	When **true**, this renders the component in a read-only state.	No
redisplay	boolean	The boolean flag indicating that any existing value in this field should be rendered when the form is created. Because this is a potential security risk, password values are not displayed by default.	No
rendered	boolean	A boolean flag indicating whether or not this component is to be rendered during the RENDER_ RESPONSE phase of the JSF lifecycle. The default value is "true".	No
required	boolean	The boolean flag specifying whether text area is required to have a value.	No

(continued)

PART III

Attribute	Type	Description	Required
requiredMessage (1.2, 2.0)	String	When present, this overrides the default **required** validation message. The message can be a **ValueExpression**.	No
size	int	The size (in characters) of the input component.	No
tabindex	int	The tabbing order position of the component. The value must be an integer between 0 and 32767.	No
validator	String	If specified, then the value must be a **MethodExpression** that refers to a method that has the same signature as the **validate** method in the **javax.faces .validator.Validator interface**.	No
validatorMessage (1.2, 2.0)	String	When present, this overrides the default **Validator** validation message. The message can be a **ValueExpression**.	No
valueChangeListener	MethodBinding (1.0, 1.1) or MethodExpression (1.2, 2.0)	A **MethodExpression** that refers to a method that returns void and accepts a single **ValueChangeEvent** argument. (1.0, 1.1, 1.2, 2.0) A **MethodExpression** that refers to a method that takes zero parameters and has a return type of void. Bear in mind that with this type of method signature, there is no way to determine the "old" and "new" values of the component. (2.0)	No

Core Attributes

Attribute	Type	Description	Required
binding	ValueBinding (1.0, 1.1) or ValueExpression (1.2, 2.0)	A binding reference to a like **UIComponent** instance.	No
id	String	The identifier for the component.	No
title	String	The title of the component. This is passed through to the rendered HTML **title** attribute.	No
value	String	The value of the component.	No

Internationalization Attributes

Attribute	Type	Description	Required
dir	String	The reading direction of the generated HTML component: RTL (right to left) or LTR (left to right).	No
lang	String	The applied **lang** attribute to the generated HTML output. For more information on the HTML **lang** attribute, visit **www.w3.org/TR/REC-html40/struct/dirlang.html**.	No

Style Attributes

Attributes for CSS styles that are applied to the generated HTML output of the component are shown next.

style	styleclass

These style attributes accept arguments of type **String** and are not specifically required.

JavaScript Attributes

Attributes for the common JavaScript events are shown here:

onblur	onchange	onclick	ondblclick	onfocus
onkeydown	onkeypress	onkeyup	onmousedown	onmousemove
onmouseout	onmouseover	onmouseup	onselect	

All JavaScript attributes accept arguments of type **String**, and none are specifically required.

Example Usage

An example showing a simple usage of **inputSecret**.

```
<h:inputSecret id="password"
value="#{UserBean.password}" />
```

The h:inputText Tag

UIComponent class: **javax.faces.component.html.HtmlInputText**

Component type: **javax.faces.HtmlInputText**

The **inputText** component renders as a user input text field. It displays an HTML **<input>** element with the **type** attribute set to "text", a **name** attribute set to the component's client ID, and a **value** attribute set to the component's value.

PART III

Ungrouped Attributes

Attribute	Type	Description	Required
accesskey	char	The mnemonic character used to establish focus to this component.	No
alt	int	The number of columns or width of the rendered text area.	No
converter	String	The fully qualified name of a class that implements the **javax.faces.convert.Converter** interface.	No
converterMessage (1.2, 2.0)	String	When present, this overrides the default **Converter** validation message. The message can be a **ValueExpression**.	No
disabled	boolean	When **true**, this renders the component in a disabled state.	No
immediate	boolean	When **true**, the component's value must be converted and validated immediately during the Apply Request Values phase rather than waiting until the Process Validations phase.	No
maxlength	int	The integer value specifying the maximum length of the rendered HTML input element.	No
readonly	boolean	When **true**, this renders the component in a read-only state.	No
rendered	boolean	A boolean flag indicating whether or not this component is to be rendered during the RENDER_RESPONSE phase of the JSF lifecycle. The default value is "true".	No
required	boolean	The boolean flag specifying whether the text area is required to have a value.	No
requiredMessage (1.2, 2.0)	String	When present, this overrides the default **required** validation message. The message can be a **ValueExpression**.	No
size	int	The size (in characters) of the input component.	No

Attribute	Type	Description	Required
tabindex	int	The tabbing order position of the component. The value must be an integer between 0 and 32767.	No
validator	String	If specified, then the value must be a **MethodExpression** that refers to a method that has the same signature as the validate method in the **javax.faces .validator.Validator** interface.	No
validatorMessage (1.2, 2.0)	String	When present, this overrides the default **Validator** validation message. The message can be a **ValueExpression**.	No
valueChangeListener	MethodBinding (1.0, 1.1) or MethodExpression (1.2, 2.0)	A **MethodExpression** that refers to a method that returns void and accepts a single **ValueChangeEvent** argument. (1.0, 1.1, 1.2, 2.0) A **MethodExpression** that refers to a method that takes zero parameters and has a return type of void. Bear in mind that with this type of method signature, there is no way to determine the "old" and "new" values of the component. (2.0)	No

Core Attributes

Attribute	Type	Description	Required
binding	ValueBinding (1.0, 1.1) or ValueExpression (1.2, 2.0)	A binding reference to a like **UIComponent** instance.	No
id	String	The identifier for the component.	No
title	String	The title of the component. This is passed through to the rendered HTML **title** attribute.	No
value	String	The value of the component.	No

Internationalization Attributes

Attribute	Type	Description	Required
Dir	String	The reading direction of the generated HTML component: RTL (right to left) or LTR (left to right).	No
Lang	String	The applied **lang** attribute to the generated HTML output. For more information on the HTML **lang** attribute, visit **www.w3.org/TR/REC-html40/struct/dirlang.html**.	No

Style Attributes

Attributes for CSS styles that are applied to the generated HTML output of the component are shown next.

style	styleclass

These style attributes accept arguments of type **String** and are not specifically required.

JavaScript Attributes

Attributes for the common JavaScript events are shown next.

onblur	onchange	onclick	ondblclick	onfocus
onkeydown	onkeypress	onkeyup	onmousedown	onmousemove
onmouseout	onmouseover	onmouseup	onselect	

All JavaScript attributes accept arguments of type **String**, and none are specifically required.

Example Usage

An example showing the simple usage of **InputText**.

```
<h:inputText id="userid"/>
```

The h:inputTextarea Tag

UIComponent class: **javax.faces.component.html.HtmlInputTextarea**

Component type: **javax.faces.HtmlInputTextarea**

The **inputTextarea** component renders as a user HTML input text area with multiple lines of text. The rendered HTML **<textarea>** element's name attribute is set to the component's client ID and a body holding the component's **value**.

Ungrouped Attributes

Attribute	Type	Description	Required
accesskey	char	The mnemonic character used to establish focus to this component.	No
cols	int	The number of columns or width of the rendered text area.	No
converter	String	The fully qualified name of a class that implements the **javax.faces.convert.Converter** interface.	No
converterMessage (1.2, 2.0)	String	When present, this overrides the default **Converter** validation message. The message can be a **ValueExpression**.	No
disabled	boolean	When **true**, this renders the component in a disabled state.	No
immediate	boolean	When **true**, the component's value must be converted and validated immediately during the Apply Request Values phase rather than waiting until the Process Validations phase.	No
readonly	boolean	When **true**, this renders the component in a read-only state.	No
rendered	boolean	A boolean flag indicating whether or not this component is to be rendered during the RENDER_ RESPONSE phase of the JSF lifecycle. The default value is "true".	No
required	boolean	The boolean flag specifying whether text area is required to have a value.	No
requiredMessage (1.2, 2.0)	String	When present, this overrides the default **required** validation message. The message can be a **ValueExpression**.	No
rows	int	The number of rows of the rendered text area.	No
tabindex	int	The tabbing order position of the component. The value must be an integer between 0 and 32767.	No

(continued)

Attribute	Type	Description	Required
validator	String	If specified, then the value must be a **MethodExpression** that refers to a method that has the same signature as the **validate** method in the **javax.faces .validator.Validator** interface.	No
validatorMessage (1.2, 2.0)	String	When present, this overrides the default **Validator** validation message. The message can be a **ValueExpression**.	No
valueChangeListener	MethodBinding (1.0, 1.1) or MethodExpression (1.2, 2.0)	A **MethodExpression** that refers to a method that returns void and accepts a single **ValueChangeEvent** argument. (1.0, 1.1, 1.2, 2.0) A **MethodExpression** that refers to a method that takes zero parameters and has a return type of void. Bear in mind that with this type of method signature, there is no way to determine the "old" and "new" values of the component. (2.0)	No

Core Attributes

Attribute	Type	Description	Required
binding	ValueBinding (1.0, 1.1) or ValueExpression (1.2, 2.0)	A binding reference to a like **UIComponent** instance.	No
id	String	The identifier for the component.	No
title	String	The title of the component. This is passed through to the rendered HTML **title** attribute.	No
value	String	The value of the component.	No

Internationalization Attributes

Attribute	Type	Description	Required
dir	String	The reading direction of the generated HTML component: RTL (right to left) or LTR (left to right).	No
lang	String	The applied **lang** attribute to generated HTML output. For more information on the HTML **lang** attribute, visit **www.w3.org/TR/REC-html40/struct/dirlang.html**.	No

Style Attributes
Attributes for CSS styles that are applied to the generated HTML output of the component are shown next.

style	styleclass

These style attributes accept arguments of type **String** and are not specifically required.

JavaScript Attributes
Attributes for the common JavaScript events are shown next.

onblur	onchange	onclick	ondblclick	onfocus
onkeydown	onkeypress	onkeyup	onmousedown	onmousemove
onmouseout	onmouseover	onmouseup	onselect	

All JavaScript attributes accept arguments of type **String**, and none are specifically required.

Example Usage
An example showing a simple usage of **InputTextarea**.

```
<h:inputTextarea id="inputTextarea1"
  binding="#{backing_bean.inputTextarea1}"
  value="this is some text in a text area"/>
```

The h:link Tag (2.0)

UIComponent class: **javax.faces.component.html.HtmlOutcomeTargetLink**

Component type: **javax.faces.OutcomeTarget**

Similar to the h:button tag, the **h:link** tag was introduced in JSF 2.0 in order to enable full support of "bookmarkable" Facelet views that are invoked via the HTTP GET operation. The rendered markup is an HTML **<a />** (anchor) tag with the **href** attribute rendered with the target URL being determined by the value of the **outcome** attribute. If there are any child **f:param** tags, then the corresponding name=value pairs will be appended as query parameters for the target URL. This approach is sometimes referred to as "preemptive navigation" because the navigation cases are processed before the user has clicked on the button. This is made possible by having the navigation handler process the **outcome** attribute and produce the target URL during the RENDER_RESPONSE phase of the JSF lifecycle.

Ungrouped Attributes

Attribute	Type	Description	Required
accesskey (2.0)	char	The mnemonic character used to establish focus to this component.	No
alt (2.0)	String	The alternate textual description of the element rendered by this component.	No
charset (2.0)	String	The character encoding of the resource referred by this hyperlink.	No
cords (2.0)	String	This attribute is used in conjunction with client-side image maps and indicates the position and shape of the hotspot that the end user can click.	No
disabled (2.0)	Boolean	When **true**, the component is not usable and is rendered in a disabled state.	No
fragment (2.0)	String	Refers to the named anchor of the target page that is to be rendered in the browser. If specified, then a pound/hash (#) character followed by the value of this attribute will be appended to the URL in the rendered **href** attribute.	No
includeViewParams (2.0)	Boolean	If this boolean flag is "true" then the name/value pairs of any **f:viewParam** tags specified in the **f:metadata** section of the target view will be appended as query parameters in the target URL in the rendered **href** attribute.	No
outcome (2.0)	String	The logical outcome that is passed to the NavigationHandler that is used to generate the target URL that is rendered in the onclick attribute. If a viewId is specified, then implicit navigation will take place, and the target URL will point to the specified viewId.	Yes
rel (2.0)	String	A comma-separated list of relationships described by this link.	No
rendered (2.0)	Boolean	A boolean flag indicating whether or not this component is to be rendered during the RENDER_RESPONSE phase of the JSF lifecycle. The default value is "true".	No
tabindex (2.0)	int	Determines the tabbing order position of the component. The value must be an integer between 0 and 32767.	No
rev (2.0)	String	A space-separated list of link types that describes a reverse link from the one that is specified by the href attribute.	No

Attribute	Type	Description	Required
shape (2.0)	String	The shape of the hotspot in client-side image maps. Valid values are **default**, **circle**, **rect**, and **poly**.	No
target (2.0)	String	Specifies the name of the HTML **<frame>** that should display the contents of the URL specified in the **href** attribute.	No
type (2.0)	String	Specifies the content type of the resource found at the URL specified in the **href** attribute.	No
value (2.0)	String	The value of this component, which is passed through to the rendered HTML as the text in between the rendered begin **<a>** tag and the end **</a>** tag.	No

Core Attributes

Attribute	Type	Description	Required
binding (2.0)	ValueExpression	A **ValueExpression** that evaluates to an object of type **javax.faces.component.html.HtmlOutcomeTargetLink**	No
id (2.0)	String	The identifier for the component.	No
title (2.0)	String	The title of the component. This is passed through to the rendered HTML **title** attribute.	No

Internationalization Attributes

Attribute	Type	Description	Required
dir (2.0)	String	The reading direction of the generated HTML component: RTL (right to left) or LTR (left to right).	No
hreflang (2.0)	String	This attribute is passed on to the rendered HTML hyperlink and is the language code of the resource designated by this hyperlink.	No
lang (2.0)	String	The applied **lang** attribute to the generated HTML output. For more information on the HTML **lang** attribute, visit **www.w3.org/TR/REC-html40/struct/dirlang.html**.	No

Style Attributes (2.0)

Attributes for CSS styles that are applied to the generated HTML output of the component are shown next.

style	styleclass

JavaScript Attributes (2.0)

Attributes for the common JavaScript events are shown next.

onblur	onclick	ondblclick	onfocus	onkeydown
onkeypress	onkeyup	onmousedown	onmousemove	onmouseout
onmouseover	onmouseup			

Example Usage

The following example markup would appear in a Facelet view document named **page2.xhtml** so that the user could navigate back to **page1.xhtml** with the **f:viewParam** name=value pairs from **page1.xhtml** appended as query parameters to the target URL in the onclick attribute. Additionally, the companyId would be appended as a query parameter, since it is specified as a child tag of h:link.

```
<h:link
  includeViewParams="true"
  outcome="page1" value="Apply Again">
  <f:param
    name="companyId"
    value="#{testManagedBean.companyId}" />
</h:link>
```

The h:message Tag

UIComponent class: **javax.faces.component.html.HtmlMessage**

Component type: **javax.faces.HtmlMessage**

The **message** component renders a Faces message for the component identified by the **for** attribute. The message properties identified by the **showdetail** and **showsummary** attributes for this message are rendered as text, within an HTML **<span>** element if any of the CSS style attributes apply or the **id** attribute is set. If the **tooltip** attribute is set to **true** and both the summary and the detailed text are rendered, the message summary is rendered as the value of the **<span>** element's **title** attribute.

Ungrouped Attributes

Attribute	Type	Description	Required
for	String	The ID of the UI component with which to be associated.	Yes
rendered	boolean	A boolean flag indicating whether or not this component is to be rendered during the RENDER_RESPONSE phase of the JSF lifecycle. The default value is "true".	No
showDetail	boolean	When **true**, this displays the detail portion of message. The default is **false**.	No

Attribute	Type	Description	Required
showSummary	boolean	When **true**, this displays the summary portion of the message. The default is **true**.	No
tooltip	boolean	A boolean flag indicating whether the detail portion of the message should be displayed as a tooltip.	No

Core Attributes

Attribute	Type	Description	Required
binding	ValueBinding (1.0, 1.1) or ValueExpression (1.2, 2.0)	A binding reference to a like **UIComponent** instance.	No
id	String	The identifier for the component.	No
title	String	The title of the component. This is passed through to the rendered HTML **title** attribute.	No

Style Attributes

Attribute	Type	Description	Required
errorclass	String	The CSS style class to apply to any message with a severity class of "ERROR".	No
errorstyle	String	The CSS style(s) to apply to any message with a severity class of "ERROR".	No
fatalclass	String	The CSS style class to apply to any message with a severity class of "FATAL".	No
fatalstyle	String	The CSS style(s) to apply to any message with a severity class of "FATAL".	No
infoclass	String	The CSS style class to apply to any message with a severity class of "INFO".	No
infostyle	String	The CSS style(s) to apply to any message with a severity class of "INFO".	No
style	String	The CSS style(s) to be applied when this component is rendered.	No
styleClass	String	The space-separated list of CSS style class(es) to be applied when this element is rendered.	No
warnclass	String	The CSS style class to apply to any message with a severity class of "WARN".	No
warnstyle	String	The CSS style(s) to apply to any message with a severity class of "WARN".	No

Example Usage

The following displays any Faces messages for the **inputTextarea1** field.

```
<h:inputTextarea id="inputTextarea1" &hellips; />
<h:message for="inputTextarea1"/>
```

The messages Component

UIComponent class: **javax.faces.component.html.HtmlMessages**

Component type: **javax.faces.HtmlMessages**

The **messages** component renders all queued messages, or only those queued without a component identifier if the **globalOnly** attribute is set to **true**. The message properties identified by the **showDetail** and **showSummary** attributes for this message are rendered as cells in an HTML table if the layout attribute is set to **table** or an HTML list if set to **list**.

Ungrouped Attributes

Attribute	Type	Description	Required
globalOnly	boolean	The boolean flag indicating that only global messages (not associated with any client ID) are to be displayed.	No
layout	String	The type of HTML layout used when rendering error messages. Valid values are **list** (default) or **table**.	No
rendered	boolean	A boolean flag indicating whether or not this component is to be rendered during the RENDER_ RESPONSE phase of the JSF lifecycle. The default value is "true".	No
showDetail	boolean	When **true**, this displays the detail portion of the message. The default is **false**.	No
showSummary	boolean	When **true**, this displays the summary portion of the message. The default is **true**.	No
tooltip	boolean	The boolean flag indicating whether the detail portion of the message should be displayed as a tooltip.	No

Core Attributes

Attribute	Type	Description	Required
binding	ValueBinding (1.0, 1.1) or ValueExpression (1.2, 2.0)	A binding reference to a like **UIComponent** instance.	No
id	String	The identifier for the component.	No
title	String	The title of the component. This is passed through to the rendered HTML **title** attribute.	No

Style Attributes

Attribute	Type	Description	Required
errorclass	String	The CSS style class to apply to any message with a severity class of "ERROR".	No
errorstyle	String	The CSS style(s) to apply to any message with a severity class of "ERROR".	No
fatalclass	String	The CSS style class to apply to any message with a severity class of "FATAL".	No
fatalstyle	String	The CSS style(s) to apply to any message with a severity class of "FATAL".	No
infoclass	String	The CSS style class to apply to any message with a severity class of "INFO".	No
infostyle	String	The CSS style(s) to apply to any message with a severity class of "INFO".	No
style	String	The CSS style(s) to be applied when this component is rendered.	No
styleClass	String	The space-separated list of CSS style class(es) to be applied when this element is rendered.	No
warnclass	String	The CSS style class to apply to any message with a severity class of "WARN".	No
warnstyle	String	The CSS style(s) to apply to any message with a severity class of "WARN".	No

Example Usage

The following example displays global Faces messages with details.

```
<h:messages layout="list" globalOnly="true"
  showDetail="true"/>
```

The h:outputFormat Tag

UIComponent class: **javax.faces.component.html.HtmlOutputFormat**

Component type: **javax.faces.HtmlOutputFormat**

The **outputFormat** component renders parameterized text. Text is rendered within an HTML **<span>** element if any of the CSS style attributes are set or the **id** attribute is set.

Accrues the values of any child **UIParameter** components, converts the list of parameter values to an **Object** array, and calls **MessageFormat.format( )**, passing the value of this component as the first argument, and the array of parameter values as the second argument. It then renders the result. If no arguments are provided, it just renders the **value** of the component unmodified.

PART III

Attributes

Attribute	Type	Description	Required
binding	ValueBinding (1.0, 1.1) or ValueExpression (1.2, 2.0)	A binding reference to a like **UIComponent** instance.	No
converter	String	The fully qualified name of a class that implements the **javax.faces.convert .Converter** interface.	No
escape	boolean	The boolean flag indicating whether or not to *escape* HTML or XML characters in the value of the component. For example, when **true**, the character "<" is escaped to "<". It is **true** by default.	No
id	String	The identifier for the component.	No
rendered	boolean	The boolean attribute that defines whether the component is rendered. The default value is "true".	No
style	String	The inline style(s) that is applied to the **panelGrid** component.	No
styleClass	String	The CSS style class that is applied to the **panelGrid** component.	No
title	String	The title of the component. This is passed through to the rendered HTML **title** attribute.	No
value	String	The value of the component.	No

Example Usage

The following is an example of the formatted output with a parameter.

```
<h:outputFormat id="outputFormat1" binding="#{backing.outputFormat1}">
  <f:param name="parname" value="parval" />
</h:outputFormat>
```

The h:outputLabel Tag

UIComponent class: **javax.faces.component.html.HtmlOutputLabel**

Component type: **javax.faces.HtmlOutputLabel**

The **outputLabel** component renders as a text label using the HTML **<label>** element and can optionally be specified for an input field. The client ID for the associated component is set using the component's **for** attribute value. The generated **<label>** element body is provided by the **h:outputLabel** body and/or its **value** attribute.

Ungrouped Attributes

Attribute	Type	Description	Required
accesskey	char	The mnemonic character used to establish focus to this component.	No
converter	String	The fully qualified name of a class that implements the **javax.faces.convert.Converter** interface.	No
for	String	The ID of the UI component with which to be associated.	No
rendered	boolean	The boolean attribute that defines whether the component is rendered. The default value is "true".	No
tabindex	int	The tabbing order position of the component. The value must be an integer between 0 and 32767.	No

Core Attributes

Attribute	Type	Description	Required
binding	ValueBinding (1.0, 1.1) or ValueExpression (1.2, 2.0)	A binding reference to a like **UIComponent** instance.	No
id	String	The identifier for the component.	No
title	String	The title of the component. This is passed through to the rendered HTML **title** attribute.	No
value	String	The value of the component.	No

Internationalization Attributes

Attribute	Type	Description	Required
dir	String	The reading direction of the generated HTML component: RTL (right to left) or LTR (left to right).	No
lang	String	The applied **lang** attribute to the generated HTML output. For more information on the HTML **lang** attribute, visit **www.w3.org/TR/REC-html40/struct/dirlang.html**.	No

Style Attributes

Attributes for CSS styles that are applied to the generated HTML output of the component are shown next.

style	styleclass

These style attributes accept arguments of type **String** and are not specifically required.

JavaScript Attributes

Attributes for the common JavaScript events are shown next.

onblur	onclick	ondblclick	onfocus
onkeydown	onkeypress	onkeyup	onmousedown
onmousemove	onmouseout	onmouseover	onmouseup

All JavaScript attributes accept arguments of type **String**, and none are specifically required.

Example Usage

The following is an example of the simple usage of an **outputLabel** associated with an **inputTextarea**:

```
<h:outputLabel for="inputTextarea1"
  value="Text Input Label" />
<h:inputTextarea id="inputTextarea1" />
```

The h:outputLink Tag

UIComponent class: **javax.faces.component.html.HtmlOutputLink**

Component type: **javax.faces.HtmlOutputLink**

The **outputLink** component is rendered as an HTML hyperlink, **<a>**, element with an **href** attribute set to the component's value. If the component has **UIParameter** component children, their name and value properties are added as query string parameters to the **href** attribute value, with both the name and value URL encoded. If the component's children are not **UIParameter** components, they are rendered as the content of the **<a>** element, such as the link text or image.

Ungrouped Attributes

Attribute	Type	Description	Required
accesskey	char	The mnemonic character used to establish focus to this component.	No
charset	String	The character encoding of the resource referred by this hyperlink.	No
converter	String	The fully qualified name of a class that implements the **javax.faces.convert.Converter** interface.	No
coords	String	This attribute is used in conjunction with client-side image maps, and indicates the position and shape of the hotspot that the end user can click.	No

Attribute	Type	Description	Required
rel	String	A comma-separated list of relationships described by this link.	No
rendered	boolean	A boolean flag indicating whether or not this component is to be rendered during the RENDER_RESPONSE phase of the JSF lifecycle. The default value is "true".	No
rev	String	A space-separated list of link types that describes a reverse link from the one that is specified by the **href** attribute.	No
shape	String	The shape of the hotspot in client-side image maps. Valid values are **default**, **circle**, **rect**, and **poly**.	No
tabindex	int	The tabbing order position of the component. The value must be an integer between 0 and 32767.	No
target	String	Specifies the name of the HTML **<frame>** that should display the contents of the URL specified in the **href** attribute.	No
type	String	Specifies the content type of the resource found at the URL specified in the **href** attribute.	No

Core Attributes

Attribute	Type	Description	Required
binding	ValueBinding (1.0, 1.1) or ValueExpression (1.2, 2.0)	A binding reference to a like **UIComponent** instance.	No
id	String	The identifier for the component.	No
title	String	The title of the component. This is passed through to the rendered HTML **title** attribute.	No
value	String	The value of the component.	No

Internationalization Attributes

Attribute	Type	Description	Required
dir	String	The reading direction of the generated HTML component: RTL (right to left) or LTR (left to right).	No
lang	String	The applied **lang** attribute to the generated HTML output. For more information on the HTML **lang** attribute, visit **www.w3.org/TR/REC-html40/struct/dirlang.html**.	No
hreflang	String	This attribute is passed on to the rendered HTML hyperlink and is the language code of the resource designated by this hyperlink.	No

Style Attributes

Attributes for CSS styles that are applied to the generated HTML output of the component are shown next.

style	styleclass

These style attributes accept arguments of type **String** and are not specifically required.

JavaScript Attributes

Attributes for the common JavaScript events are shown next.

onblur	onclick	ondblclick	onfocus	onkeydown
onkeypress	onkeyup	onmousedown	onmousemove	onmouseout
onmouseover	onmouseup			

All JavaScript attributes accept arguments of type **String**, and none are specifically required.

Example Usage

The following is an example of a simple **outputLink** usage that links to the Google Web site.

```
<h:outputLink value="http://google.com" >
  <f:verbatim >This will appear as a Link to Google.</f:verbatim>
</h:outputLink>
```

The h:outputScript Tag (2.0)

UIComponent class: **javax.faces.component.UIOutput**

Component type: **javax.faces.Output**

The **h:outputScript** tag is responsible for rendering an HTML **<script>** tag with a **src** attribute whose value is determined by the optional **name** and **library** attributes of the **h:outputScript** tag. If the value of the **target** attribute is "**head**", then there must also be an **h:head** tag in the same view as **h:outputScript** tag. The **h:head** tag would then be responsible for invoking the renderer of the **h:outputScript** tag such that the HTML **<script>** tag would be rendered before the closing **</head>** tag. If the value of the **target** attribute is "**body**", then there must also be an **h:body** tag in the same view as **h:outputScript** tag. The h:body tag would then be responsible for invoking the renderer of the **h:outputScript** tag such that the HTML **<script>** tag would be rendered before the closing **</body>** tag. If the value of the **target** attribute is "**form**", then there must also be an **h:form** tag in the same view as **h:outputScript** tag. The **h:form** tag would then be responsible for invoking the renderer of the **h:outputScript** tag such that the HTML **<script>** tag would be rendered before the closing **</form>** tag.

The JSF 2.0 spec requires that Web application resources be located in the **/resources** folder under the Web application root. Alternatively, resources can be located in the **META-INF/resources** folder of any JAR file in the classpath. Each resource must adhere to the following naming convention:

```
[localePrefix/][libraryName/][libraryVersion/]resourceName[/resourceVersion]
```

Ungrouped Attributes

Attribute	Type	Description	Required
converter (2.0)	N/A	Because the UIOutput class implements the ValueHolder interface, the converter attribute is valid for the **h:outputScript** tag. However, since the **value** attribute has no meaning to the **h:outputScript** renderer, the converter attribute is consequently ignored.	No
library (2.0)	String	The name of the library that contains the script resource.	No
name (2.0)	String	The name of the script resource.	Yes
rendered (2.0)	Boolean	The boolean attribute that defines whether the component is rendered. The default value is "true".	No
target (2.0)	String	Valid values are "head", "body", and "form". If no value is specified, then the renderer will render the HTML **<script>** tag inline according to its placement in the component tree.	No
value (2.0)	N/A	Because the **UIOutput** class implements the ValueHolder interface, the value attribute is valid for the **h:outputScript** tag. However, since the value attribute has no meaning to the **h:outputScript** renderer, the value attribute is consequently ignored.	No

Core Attributes

Attribute	Type	Description	Required
binding (2.0)	ValueExpression	A **ValueExpression** that evaluates to an object of type **javax.faces.component.UIOutput**.	No
id (2.0)	String	The identifier for the component.	No

Example Usage

```
<h:outputScript
  library="testlibrary"
  name="testscript.js" target="head" />
```

The h:outputStylesheet Tag (2.0)

UIComponent class: **javax.faces.component.UIOutput**

Component type: **javax.faces.Output**

The **h:outputStylesheet** tag is responsible for rendering an HTML **<link>** tag with an **href** attribute whose value is determined by the optional **name** and **library** attributes of the **h:outputStylesheet** tag. Additionally, it is responsible for rendering a **rel** attribute with a value of "stylesheet" and a **type** attribute of "text/css". Unlike the the **h:outputScript** tag, the **h:outputStylesheet** tag does not have a **target** attribute, since HTML **<link>** tags should always be placed inside the **<head>** tag of an HTML page. Consequently, there must be an **h:head** tag in the same view as **h:outputStylesheet** tag.

The JSF 2.0 spec requires that Web application resources be located in the **/resources** folder under the Web application root. Alternatively, resources can be located in the **META-INF/resources** folder of any JAR file in the classpath. Each resource must adhere to the following naming convention:

```
[localePrefix/][libraryName/][libraryVersion/]resourceName[/resourceVersion]
```

Ungrouped Attributes

Attribute	Type	Description	Required
converter (2.0)	N/A	Because the UIOutput class implements the ValueHolder interface, the converter attribute is valid for the **h:outputStylesheet** tag. However, since the **value** attribute has no meaning to the **h:outputStylesheet** renderer, the converter attribute is consequently ignored.	No
library (2.0)	String	The name of the library that contains the script resource.	No
name (2.0)	String	The name of the script resource.	Yes
rendered (2.0)	Boolean	The boolean attribute that defines whether the component is rendered. The default value is "true".	No
value (2.0)	N/A	Because the **UIOutput** class implements the ValueHolder interface, the value attribute is valid for the **h:outputStylesheet** tag. However, since the value attribute has no meaning to the **h:outputStylesheet** renderer, the value attribute is consequently ignored.	No

Core Attributes

Attribute	Type	Description	Required
binding (2.0)	ValueExpression	A **ValueExpression** that evaluates to an object of type **javax.faces.component.UIOutput**.	No
id (2.0)	String	The identifier for the component.	No

Example Usage

```
<h:outputStylesheet
  library="testlibrary" name="test.css" />
```

The h:outputText Tag

UIComponent class: **javax.faces.component.html.HtmlOutputText**

Component type: **javax.faces.HtmlOutputText**

The **outputText** component renders the component's **value** as text within the page.

Ungrouped Attributes

Attribute	Type	Description	Required
converter	String	The fully qualified name of a class that implements the **javax.faces.convert.Converter** interface.	No
escape	boolean	The boolean flag indicating whether or not to escape HTML or XML characters in the value of the component. For example, when **true**, the character "<" is escaped to "<". It is **true** by default.	No
rendered	boolean	A boolean flag indicating whether or not this component is to be rendered during the RENDER_RESPONSE phase of the JSF lifecycle. The default value is "true".	No

Core Attributes

Attribute	Type	Description	Required
binding	ValueBinding (1.0, 1.1) or ValueExpression (1.2, 2.0)	A binding reference to a like **UIComponent** instance.	No
id	String	The identifier for the component.	No
title	String	The title of the component. This is passed through to the rendered HTML **title** attribute.	No
value	String	The value of the component.	No

Style Attributes

Attributes for CSS styles that are applied to the generated HTML output of the component are shown next.

style	styleclass

These style attributes accept arguments of type **String** and are not specifically required.

Internationalization Attributes

Attribute	Type	Description	Required
dir (1.2, 2.0)	String	The reading direction of the generated HTML component: RTL (right to left) or LTR (left to right).	No
lang (1.2, 2.0)	String	The applied **lang** attribute to the generated HTML output. For more information on the HTML **lang** attribute, visit **www.w3.org/TR/REC-html40/struct/dirlang.html**.	No

Example Usage

The following is an example of a simple usage of **outputText**.

```
<h:outputText value="This is an outputText component" />
```

The h:panelGrid Tag

UIComponent class: **javax.faces.component.html.HtmlPanelGrid**

Component type: **javax.faces.HtmlPanelGrid**

The **panelGrid** component is a tabular container for other child components and is rendered as an HTML **<table>** with a number of attributes that are directly passed on to the rendered HTML table, such as border, width, and so on. The component's children are rendered in the table cells, with new rows as the number of columns is reached.

For further information on the attributes that are passed on to the rendered HTML table, visit **www.w3.org/TR/REC-html40/struct/tables.html**.

Ungrouped Attributes

Attribute	Type	Description	Required
bgcolor	String	The background color of the rendered HTML table representing the **panelGrid**.	No
border	int	The border size in pixels of the rendered HTML table.	No
cellpadding	int	The **cellpadding** attribute of the rendered HTML table.	No
cellspacing	int	The **cellspacing** attribute of the rendered HTML table.	No
columns	int	The number of columns to be rendered in the HTML table.	No
frame	String	A **frame** that is passed on to the rendered HTML table. This attribute specifies which sides of the frame surrounding the table will be visible. Valid values are **none**, **above**, **below**, **hsides**, **vsides**, **lhs**, **rhs**, **box**, and border.	No

Attribute	Type	Description	Required
rendered	boolean	A boolean flag indicating whether or not this component is to be rendered during the RENDER_RESPONSE phase of the JSF lifecycle. The default value is "true".	No
rules	String	A **rules** attribute that is passed on to the rendered HTML table. Valid values are **none**, **groups**, **rows**, **cols**, and **all**.	No
summary	String	A **summary** attribute that is passed on to the rendered HTML table.	No
width	int or String	A **width** attribute that is passed on to the rendered HTML table. For pixel width, enter a nonzero integer. For percentage width, append "%" to the value (e.g., "80%").	No

Core Attributes

Attribute	Type	Description	Required
binding	ValueBinding (1.0, 1.1) or ValueExpression (1.2, 2.0)	A binding reference to a like **UIComponent** instance.	No
id	String	The identifier for the component.	No
title	String	The title of the component. This is passed through to the rendered HTML **title** attribute.	No

Style Attributes

Attribute	Type	Description	Required
columnclasses	String	A comma-separated list of CSS classes to be associated with the rendered columns. The classes will be applied in a repeating fashion to all columns in the **panelGrid** component.	No
footerclass	String	The CSS class to be associated with the rendered HTML table footer (bottom row).	No
headerclass	String	The CSS class to be associated with the rendered HTML table header (top row).	No
rowclasses	String	A comma-separated list of CSS classes to be associated with the rendered rows. The classes will be applied in a repeating fashion to all rows in the **panelGrid** component.	No
style	String	Inline style(s) that are applied to the **panelGrid** component.	No
styleClass	String	The CSS style class that is applied to the **panelGrid** component.	No

Internationalization Attributes

Attribute	Type	Description	Required
dir	String	The reading direction of the generated HTML component: RTL (right to left) or LTR (left to right).	No
lang	String	The applied **lang** attribute to generated HTML output. For more information on the HTML **lang** attribute, visit **www.w3.org/TR/REC-html40/struct/dirlang.html**.	No

JavaScript Attributes

Attributes for the common JavaScript events are shown next.

onclick	ondblclick	onkeydown	onkeypress	onkeyup
onmousedown	onmousemove	onmouseout	onmouseover	onmouseup

All JavaScript attributes accept arguments of type **String**, and none are specifically required.

Example Usage

A **panelgrid** containing an **outputText** and an **inputText**. The code that follows will render a two-column HTML table with border 2 and a silver background. The contents of the table will contain the rendered UI components.

```
<h:panelGrid border="2" bgcolor="Silver" columns="2" >
  <h:outputText value="Name: "/>
  <h:inputText value="enter name here" />
</h:panelGrid>
```

The h:panelGroup Tag

UIComponent class: **javax.faces.component.html.HtmlPanelGroup**

Component type: **javax.faces.HtmlPanelGroup**

The **panelGroup** component creates a container to group a set of components under one parent. It renders its children, within an HTML **<span>** element, and can be used to conditionally render groups of UI components by employing its **rendered** attribute.

Attributes

Attribute	Type	Description	Required
binding	ValueBinding (1.0, 1.1) or ValueExpression (1.2, 2.0)	A binding reference to a like **UIComponent** instance.	No
id	String	The identifier for the component.	No

Attribute	Type	Description	Required
layout (1.2, 2.0)	String	The type of layout to use when rendering this group. If the value is "block", the renderer produces an HTML "div" element; otherwise, the HTML "span" element is produced.	No
rendered	boolean	The boolean attribute that defines whether the component is rendered. The default value is "true".	No
style	String	The inline style for the component.	No
styleClass	String	The referenced style class to be applied to the component.	No

Example Usage

The following example displays some UI components inside a **panelGroup**. It will only render if **Bean.renderOption** is **true**.

```
<h:panelGroup id="panelGroup1" rendered="#{Bean.renderOption}">
  <f:verbatim>This is <cTypeface:Italic>HTML</i>
  inside of a panelGroup</f:verbatim>
  <h:selectManyCheckbox id="pizzaToppings" value="#{PizzaBean.toppings}">
    <f:selectItems value="#{PizzaBean.toppingsList}"/>
</h:selectManyCheckbox>
  ...
</h:panelGroup>
```

PART III

The h:selectBooleanCheckbox Tag

UIComponent class: **javax.faces.component.html.HtmlSelectBooleanCheckbox**

Component type: **javax.faces.HtmlSelectBooleanCheckbox**

The selectBooleanCheckbox component renders as a single HTML **<input>** element of type "checkbox". The name attribute is set to the client ID.

Ungrouped Attributes

Attribute	Type	Description	Required
accesskey	char	A mnemonic character used to establish focus to this button.	No
converter	String	A full classpath reference to **Converter** to associate with this component.	No
converterMessage (1.2, 2.0)	String	When present, this overrides the default **Converter** validation message. The message can be a **ValueExpression**.	No

(continued)

Attribute	Type	Description	Required
disabled	boolean	When **true**, the component is not usable and is rendered in a disabled state.	No
immediate	boolean	When **true**, the component's value must be converted and validated immediately during the Apply Request Values phase rather than waiting until the Process Validations phase.	No
readonly	boolean	Displays the component as read-only when **true**.	No
rendered	boolean	The boolean attribute that defines whether the component is rendered. The default value is "true".	No
required	boolean	When **true**, this will cause a validation error when no value is supplied.	No
requiredMessage (1.2, 2.0)	String	When present, this overrides the default **required** validation message. The message can be a **ValueExpression**.	No
tabindex	int	The tabbing order position of the component. The value must be an integer between 0 and 32767.	No
validator	String	If specified, then the value must be a **MethodExpression** that refers to a method that has the same signature as the validate method in the **javax.faces.validator.Validator** interface.	No
validatorMessage (1.2, 2.0)	String	When present, this overrides the default **Validator** validation message. The message can be a **ValueExpression**.	No
valueChangeListener	MethodBinding (1.0, 1.1) or MethodExpression (1.2, 2.0)	A **MethodExpression** that refers to a method that returns void and accepts a single **ValueChangeEvent** argument. (1.0, 1.1, 1.2, 2.0) A **MethodExpression** that refers to a method that takes zero parameters and has a return type of void. Bear in mind that with this type of method signature, there is no way to determine the "old" and "new" values of the component. (2.0)	No

Core Attributes

Attribute	Type	Description	Required
binding	ValueBinding (1.0, 1.1) or ValueExpression (1.2, 2.0)	A binding reference to a like **UIComponent** instance.	No
id	String	The identifier for the component.	No
title	String	The title of the component. This is passed through to the rendered HTML **title** attribute.	No
value	String	The value of the component.	No

Internationalization Attributes

Attribute	Type	Description	Required
dir	String	The reading direction of the generated HTML component: RTL (right to left) or LTR (left to right).	No
lang	String	The applied **lang** attribute to the generated HTML output. For more information on the HTML **lang** attribute, visit **www.w3.org/TR/REC-html40/struct/dirlang.html**.	No

Style Attributes
Attributes for CSS styles that are applied to the generated HTML output of the component are shown next.

style	styleclass

These style attributes accept arguments of type **String** and are not specifically required.

JavaScript Attributes
Attributes for the common JavaScript events are shown in the following.

onblur	onchange	onclick	ondblclick	onfocus
onkeydown	onkeypress	onkeyup	onmousedown	onmousemove
onmouseout	onmouseover	onmouseup	onselect	

All JavaScript attributes accept arguments of type **String**, and none are specifically required.

Example Usage
Consider a managed bean (**UserBean**) with a **boolean** property of **smoker**. This can then be value-bound to the **SelectBooleanCheckbox** component, as shown in the following.

```
<h:outputLabel value="Do you smoke?:" for="smokercheck"/>
<h:selectBooleanCheckbox id="smokercheck" value="#{UserBean.smoker}"/>
```

The h:selectManyCheckbox Tag

UIComponent class: **javax.faces.component.html.HtmlSelectManyCheckbox**

Component type: **javax.faces.HtmlSelectManyCheckbox**

The **selectManyCheckbox** component renders as an HTML table with a set of checkboxes. The **<input>** checkboxes are represented by the child components **UISelectItem** and/or **UISelectItems** and are rendered with a **type** attribute set to "checkbox" and a **name** attribute set to the component's client ID. Each **<input>** checkbox is also nested within a **<label>** element with a **for** attribute set to the component's client ID.

Ungrouped Attributes

Attribute	Type	Description	Required
accesskey	char	The mnemonic character used to establish focus to this button.	No
border	int	The border width in pixels of the generated table around the options list.	No
collectionType (2.0)	String or ValueExpression	Can be a String literal that is the fully qualified Collection class or a **ValueExpression** that evaluates to the class itself.	No
converter	String	The fully qualified name of a class that implements the **javax.faces .convert.Converter** interface.	No
converterMessage (1.2, 2.0)	String	When present, this overrides the default **Converter** validation message. The message can be a **ValueExpression**.	No
disabled	boolean	When **true**, the component is not usable and rendered in a disabled state.	No
immediate	boolean	When **true**, the component's value must be converted and validated immediately during the Apply Request Values phase rather than waiting until the Process Validations phase.	No
layout	String	The option list orientation. This can be either **pageDirection** (vertical) or **lineDirection** (horizontal). When not specified, **lineDirection** is the default.	No

Attribute	Type	Description	Required
hideNoSelectionOption (2.0)	String	A boolean flag that indicates whether or not a child **f:selectItem** whose **noSelectionOption** attribute is "true" should be hidden.	No
readonly	boolean	Displays the component as read-only when **true**.	No
rendered	boolean	The boolean attribute that defines whether the component is rendered. The default value is "true".	No
required	boolean	When **true**, this will cause a validation error when no value is supplied.	No
requiredMessage (1.2, 2.0)	String	When present, this overrides the default **required** validation message. The message can be a **ValueExpression**.	No
tabindex	int	The tabbing order position of the component. The value must be an integer between 0 and 32767.	No
validator	String	If specified, then the value must be a **MethodExpression** that refers to a method that has the same signature as the validate method in the **javax**.faces. **validator.Validator** interface.	No
validatorMessage (1.2, 2.0)	String	When present, this overrides the default **Validator** validation message. The message can be a **ValueExpression**.	No
valueChangeListener	MethodBinding (1.0, 1.1) or MethodExpression (1.2, 2.0)	**MethodExpression** that refers to a method that returns void and accepts a single **ValueChangeEvent** argument. (1.0, 1.1, 1.2, 2.0) **MethodExpression** that refers to a method that takes zero parameters and has a return type of void. Bear in mind that with this type of method signature, there is no way to determine the "old" and "new" values of the component. (2.0)	No

Core Attributes

Attribute	Type	Description	Required
binding	ValueBinding (1.0, 1.1) or ValueExpression (1.2, 2.0)	A binding reference to a like **UIComponent** instance.	No
id	String	The identifier for the component.	No
title	String	The title of the component. This is passed through to the rendered HTML **title** attribute.	No
value	String	The value of the component.	No

Internationalization Attributes

Attribute	Type	Description	Required
dir	String	The reading direction of the generated HTML component: RTL (right to left) or LTR (left to right).	No
lang	String	The applied **lang** attribute to the generated HTML output. For more information on the HTML **lang** attribute, visit **www.w3.org/TR/REC-html40/struct/dirlang.html**.	No

Style Attributes

Attributes for CSS styles that are applied to the generated HTML output of the component are shown next.

disabledclass	enabledclass	Style	styleclass

These style attributes accept arguments of type **String** and are not specifically required.

JavaScript Attributes

Attributes for the common JavaScript events are shown here.

onblur	onchange	onclick	ondblclick	onfocus
onkeydown	onkeypress	onkeyup	onmousedown	onmousemove
onmouseout	onmouseover	onmouseup	onselect	

All JavaScript attributes accept arguments of type **String**, and none are specifically required.

Example Usage

Consider a managed bean (**PizzaBean**) with a **List** property of **toppingsList**. This can be value-bound to the **SelectManyCheckbox** component, as shown in the following:

```
<h:selectManyCheckbox id="pizzaToppings" value="#{PizzaBean.toppings}">
  <f:selectItems value="#{PizzaBean.toppingsList}"/>
</h:selectManyCheckbox>
```

Next is an example with hard-coded select items:

```
<h:selectManyCheckbox id ="pizzaToppings" value="#{PizzaBean.toppings}">
  <f:selectItem itemLabel="cheese" itemValue="ch"/>
  <f:selectItem itemLabel="pepperoni" itemValue="pep"/>
  <f:selectItem itemLabel="sausage" itemValue="saus"/>
  <f:selectItem itemLabel="mushrooms" itemValue="msh"/>
</h:selectManyCheckbox >
```

The h:selectManyListbox Tag

UIComponent class: **javax.faces.component.html.HtmlSelectManyListbox**

Component type: **javax.faces.HtmlSelectManyListbox**

The **selectManyListbox** component renders an HTML **<select>** with its **name** attribute set to the component's client ID, its **size** attribute set to the number of **selectItem** children, and its **multiple** attribute set to "multiple". Each menu choice is rendered by either **UISelectItem** and/or **UISelectItems** components and is rendered as an **<option>** element. If a choice is marked as disabled, the **disabled** attribute is also added to the option element.

Ungrouped Attributes

Attribute	Type	Description	Required
accesskey	char	The mnemonic character used to establish focus to this button.	No
collectionType (2.0)	String or ValueExpression	Can be a String literal that is the fully qualified Collection class or a **ValueExpression** that evaluates to the class itself.	No
converter	String	The fully qualified name of a class that implements the **javax.faces.convert.Converter** interface.	No
converterMessage (1.2, 2.0)	String	When present, this overrides the default **Converter** validation message. The message can be a **ValueExpression**.	No
disabled	boolean	When **true**, the component is not usable and rendered in a disabled state.	No
hideNoSelectionOption (2.0)	boolean	A boolean flag that indicates whether or not a child **f:selectItem** whose **noSelectionOption** attribute is "true" should be hidden.	No

(continued)

Attribute	Type	Description	Required
immediate	boolean	When **true**, the component's value must be converted and validated immediately during the Apply Request Values phase rather than waiting until the Process Validations phase.	No
readonly	boolean	Displays the component as read-only when **true**.	No
rendered	boolean	The boolean attribute that defines whether the component is rendered. The default value is "true".	No
required	boolean	When **true**, this will cause a validation error when no value is supplied.	No
requiredMessage (1.2, 2.0)	String	When present, this overrides the default **required** validation message. The message can be a **ValueExpression**.	No
tabindex	int	The tabbing order position of the component. The value must be an integer between 0 and 32767.	No
validator	String	If specified, then the value must be a **MethodExpression** that refers to a method that has the same signature as the validate method in the **javax.faces .validator.Validator** interface.	No
validatorMessage (1.2, 2.0)	String	When present, this overrides the default **Validator** validation message. The message can be a **ValueExpression**.	No
valueChangeListener	MethodBinding (1.0, 1.1) or MethodExpression (1.2, 2.0)	A **MethodExpression** that refers to a method that returns void and accepts a single **ValueChangeEvent** argument. (1.0, 1.1, 1.2, 2.0) A **MethodExpression** that refers to a method that takes zero parameters and has a return type of void. Bear in mind that with this type of method signature, there is no way to determine the "old" and "new" values of the component. (2.0)	No

Core Attributes

Attribute	Type	Description	Required
binding	ValueBinding (1.0, 1.1) or ValueExpression (1.2, 2.0)	A binding reference to a like **UIComponent** instance.	No
id	String	The identifier for the component.	No
title	String	The title of the component. This is passed through to the rendered HTML **title** attribute.	No
value	String	The value of the component.	No

Internationalization Attributes

Attribute	Type	Description	Required
dir	String	The reading direction of the generated HTML component: RTL (right to left) or LTR (left to right).	No
lang	String	The applied **lang** attribute to the generated HTML output. For more information on the HTML **lang** attribute, visit **www.w3.org/TR/REC-html40/struct/dirlang.html**.	No

Style Attributes

Attributes for CSS styles that are applied to the generated HTML output of the component are shown next.

disabledclass	enabledclass	style	styleclass

These style attributes accept arguments of type **String** and are not specifically required.

JavaScript Attributes

Attributes for the common JavaScript events are shown next.

onblur	onchange	onclick	ondblclick	onfocus
onkeydown	onkeypress	onkeyup	onmousedown	onmousemove
onmouseout	onmouseover	onmouseup	onselect	

All JavaScript attributes accept arguments of type **String**, and none are specifically required.

Example Usage

Consider a managed bean (**PizzaBean**) with a **List** property of **toppingsList**. This can then be value-bound to the **selectManyListbox** component, as in the following:

```
<h:selectManyListbox id="pizzaToppings" value="#{PizzaBean.toppings}">
  <f:selectItems value="#{PizzaBean.toppingsList}"/>
</h:selectManyListbox>
```

PART III

An example with hard-coded select items is shown next:

```
<h:selectManyListbox id ="pizzaToppings" value="#{PizzaBean.toppings}">
  <f:selectItem itemLabel="cheese" itemValue="ch"/>
  <f:selectItem itemLabel="pepperoni" itemValue="pep"/>
  <f:selectItem itemLabel="sausage" itemValue="saus"/>
  <f:selectItem itemLabel="mushrooms" itemValue="msh"/>
</h:selectManyListbox >
```

The h:selectManyMenu Tag

UIComponent class: **javax.faces.component.html.HtmlSelectManyMenu**

Component type: **javax.faces.HtmlSelectManyMenu**

The **selectManyMenu** component renders an HTML **<select>** with its **name** attribute set to the component's client ID, its **size** attribute set with a value of "1", and its **multiple** attribute set to "multiple". Each menu choice is rendered by either **UISelectItem** and/or **UISelectItems** components, and is rendered as an **<option>** element. If a choice is marked as disabled, the **disabled** attribute is also added to the option element.

Ungrouped Attributes

Attribute	Type	Description	Required
accesskey	char	The mnemonic character used to establish focus to this button.	No
collectionType	String or ValueExpression	Can be a String literal that is the fully qualified Collection class or a **ValueExpression** that evaluates to the class itself.	No
converter	String	The fully qualified name of a class that implements the **javax.faces.convert.Converter** interface.	No
converterMessage (1.2, 2.0)	String	When present, this overrides the default **Converter** validation message. The message can be a **ValueExpression**.	No
disabled	boolean	When true, the component is not usable and is rendered in a disabled state.	No
hideNoSelectionOption (2.0)	boolean	A boolean flag that indicates whether or not a child **f:selectItem** whose **noSelectionOption** attribute is "true" should be hidden.	No

Attribute	Type	Description	Required
immediate	boolean	When **true**, the component's value must be converted and validated immediately during the Apply Request Values phase rather than waiting until the Process Validations phase.	No
readonly	boolean	Displays the component as read-only when **true**.	No
rendered	boolean	A boolean flag indicating whether or not this component is to be rendered during the RENDER_RESPONSE phase of the JSF lifecycle. The default value is "true".	No
required	boolean	When **true**, this will cause a validation error when no value is supplied.	No
requiredMessage (1.2, 2.0)	String	When present, this overrides the default **required** validation message. The message can be a ValueExpression.	No
tabindex	int	The tabbing order position of the component. The value must be an integer between 0 and 32767.	No
validator	String	If specified, then the value must be a **MethodExpression** that refers to a method that has the same signature as the **validate** method in the **javax.faces.validator.Validator** interface.	No
validatorMessage (1.2, 2.0)	String	When present, this overrides the default **Validator** validation message. The message can be a **ValueExpression**.	No

(continued)

Attribute	Type	Description	Required
valueChangeListener	MethodBinding (1.0, 1.1) or MethodExpression (1.2, 2.0)	A **MethodExpression** that refers to a method that returns void and accepts a single **ValueChangeEvent** argument. (1.0, 1.1, 1.2, 2.0) A **MethodExpression** that refers to a method that takes zero parameters and has a return type of void. Bear in mind that with this type of method signature, there is no way to determine the "old" and "new" values of the component. (2.0)	No

Core Attributes

Attribute	Type	Description	Required
binding	ValueBinding (1.0, 1.1) or ValueExpression (1.2, 2.0)	A binding reference to a like **UIComponent** instance.	No
id	String	The identifier for the component.	No
title	String	The title of the component. This is passed through to the rendered HTML **title** attribute.	No
value	String	The value of the component.	No

Internationalization Attributes

Attribute	Type	Description	Required
dir	String	The reading direction of the generated HTML component: RTL (right to left) or LTR (left to right).	No
lang	String	The applied **lang** attribute to the generated HTML output. For more information on the HTML **lang** attribute, visit **www.w3.org/TR/REC-html40/struct/dirlang.html**.	No

Style Attributes

Attributes for CSS styles that are applied to the generated HTML output of the component are shown next.

disabledclass	enabledclass	style	styleclass

These style attributes accept arguments of type **String** and are not specifically required.

JavaScript Attributes

Attributes for the common JavaScript events are shown here.

onblur	onchange	onclick	ondblclick	onfocus
onkeydown	onkeypress	onkeyup	onmousedown	onmousemove
onmouseout	onmouseover	onmouseup	onselect	

All JavaScript attributes accept arguments of type **String**, and none are specifically required.

Example Usage

Consider a managed bean (**PizzaBean**) with a **List** property of **toppingsList**. This can then be value-bound to the **selectManyMenu** component, as in the following:

```
<h:selectManyMenu id="pizzaToppings" value="#{PizzaBean.toppings}">
  <f:selectItems value="#{PizzaBean.toppingsList}"/>
</h:selectManyMenu>
```

An example with hard-coded select items is shown next:

```
<h:selectManyMenu id ="pizzaToppings" value="#{PizzaBean.toppings}">
  <f:selectItem itemLabel="cheese" itemValue="ch"/>
  <f:selectItem itemLabel="pepperoni" itemValue="pep"/>
  <f:selectItem itemLabel="sausage" itemValue="saus"/>
  <f:selectItem itemLabel="mushrooms" itemValue="msh"/>
</h:selectManyMenu >
```

PART III

The h:selectOneListbox Tag

UIComponent class: **javax.faces.component.html.HtmlSelectOneListbox**

Component type: **javax.faces.HtmlSelectOneListbox**

The **selectOneListbox** component renders an HTML **<select>** with its **name** attribute set to the component's client ID, and its **size** attribute set to the number of **<option>** element choices rendered by either **UISelectItem** and/or **UISelectItems** components. If the **size** attribute is specified, it will override the number of **SelectItems** and pass through the size value to the rendered **<select>**. If a choice is marked as disabled, the **disabled** attribute is also added to the option element.

Ungrouped Attributes

Attribute	Type	Description	Required
accesskey	char	The mnemonic character used to establish focus to this button.	No

(continued)

Attribute	Type	Description	Required
converter	String	The fully qualified name of a class that implements the **javax.faces.convert.Converter** interface.	No
converterMessage (1.2, 2.0)	String	When present, this overrides the default **Converter** validation message. The message can be a **ValueExpression**.	No
disabled	boolean	When **true**, the component is not usable and is rendered in a disabled state.	No
hideNoSelectionOption (2.0)	boolean	A boolean flag that indicates whether or not a child **f:selectItem** whose **noSelectionOption** attribute is "true" should be hidden.	No
immediate	boolean	When **true**, the component's value must be converted and validated immediately during the Apply Request Values phase rather than waiting until the Process Validations phase.	No
readonly	boolean	Displays the component as read-only when **true**.	No
rendered	boolean	The boolean attribute that defines whether the component is rendered. The default value is "true".	No
required	boolean	When **true**, this will cause a validation error when no value is supplied.	No
requiredMessage (1.2, 2.0)	String	When present, this overrides the default **required** validation message. The message can be a **ValueExpression**.	No
size	int	Overrides the size attribute of the generated HTML select that is otherwise set to the number of **SelectItems**.	No
tabindex	int	The tabbing order position of the component. The value must be an integer between 0 and 32767.	No

Attribute	Type	Description	Required
validator	String	If specified, then the value must be a **MethodExpression** that refers to a method that has the same signature as the **validate** method in the **javax.faces.validator.Validator** interface.	No
validatorMessage (1.2, 2.0)	String	When present, this overrides the default **Validator** validation message. The message can be a **ValueExpression**.	No
valueChangeListener	MethodBinding (1.0, 1.1) or MethodExpression (1.2, 2.0)	A **MethodExpression** that refers to a method that returns void and accepts a single **ValueChangeEvent** argument. (1.0, 1.1, 1.2, 2.0) A **MethodExpression** that refers to a method that takes zero parameters and has a return type of void. Bear in mind that with this type of method signature, there is no way to determine the "old" and "new" values of the component. (2.0)	No

Core Attributes

Attribute	Type	Description	Required
binding	ValueBinding (1.0, 1.1) or ValueExpression (1.2, 2.0)	A binding reference to a like **UIComponent** instance.	No
id	String	The identifier for the component.	No
title	String	The title of the component. This is passed through to the rendered HTML **title** attribute.	No
value	String	The value of the component.	No

Internationalization Attributes

Attribute	Type	Description	Required
dir	String	The reading direction of the generated HTML component: RTL (right to left) or LTR (left to right).	No
lang	String	The applied **lang** attribute to the generated HTML output. For more information on the HTML lang attribute, visit **www.w3.org/TR/REC-html40/struct/dirlang.html**.	No

Style Attributes

Attributes for CSS styles that are applied to the generated HTML output of the component are shown next.

disabledclass	enabledclass	style	styleclass

These style attributes accept arguments of type **String** and are not specifically required.

JavaScript Attributes

Attributes for the common JavaScript events are shown next.

onblur	onchange	onclick	ondblclick	onfocus
onkeydown	onkeypress	onkeyup	onmousedown	onmousemove
onmouseout	onmouseover	onmouseup	onselect	

All JavaScript attributes accept arguments of type **String**, and none are specifically required.

Example Usage

Consider a managed bean **shirt** with a **List** property of **sizeList**. This can then be value-bound to the **SelectOneListBox** component, as shown in the following:

```
<h:selectOneListBox id="size" value="#{shirt.size }">
  <f:selectItems value="#{shirt.sizeList}"/>
</h:selectOneListBox>
```

An example with hard-coded select items is shown next:

```
<h:selectOneListBox id ="size" value="#{shirt.size}">
  <f:selectItem itemLabel="Small" itemValue="s"/>
  <f:selectItem itemLabel="Medium" itemValue="m"/>
  <f:selectItem itemLabel="Large" itemValue="l"/>
  <f:selectItem itemLabel="Extra-Large" itemValue="xl"/>
</h:selectOneListBox >
```

The h:selectOneMenu Tag

UIComponent class: **javax.faces.component.html.HtmlSelectOneMenu**

Component type: **javax.faces.HtmlSelectOneMenu**

The **selectOneMenu** component renders an HTML **<select>** with its **name** attribute set to the component's client ID and its **size** attribute set with a value of "1". Each menu choice is rendered by either **UISelectItem** and/or **UISelectItems** components and is rendered as an **<option>** element. If a choice is marked as disabled, the **disabled** attribute is also added to the option element.

Ungrouped Attributes

Attribute	Type	Description	Required
accesskey	char	The mnemonic character used to establish focus to this button.	No
converter	String	The fully qualified name of a class that implements the **javax.faces.convert.Converter** interface.	No
converterMessage (1.2, 2.0)	String	When present, this overrides the default **Converter** validation message. The message can be a **ValueExpression**.	No
disabled	boolean	When **true**, the component is not usable and is rendered in a disabled state.	No
hideNoSelectionOption (2.0)	boolean	A boolean flag that indicates whether or not a child **f:selectItem** whose **noSelectionOption** attribute is "true" should be hidden.	No
immediate	boolean	When **true**, the component's value must be converted and validated immediately during the Apply Request Values phase rather than waiting until the Process Validations phase.	No
readonly	boolean	Displays the component as read-only when **true**.	No
rendered	boolean	The boolean attribute that defines whether the component is rendered. The default value is "true".	No
required	boolean	When **true**, this will cause a validation error when no value is supplied.	No
requiredMessage (1.2, 2.0)	String	When present, this overrides the default required validation message. The message can be a **ValueExpression**.	No

(continued)

Attribute	Type	Description	Required
tabindex	int	The tabbing order position of the component. The value must be an integer between 0 and 32767.	No
validator	String	If specified, then the value must be a **MethodExpression** that refers to a method that has the same signature as the **validate** method in the **javax.faces .validator.Validator** interface.	No
validatorMessage (1.2, 2.0)	String	When present, this overrides the default **Validator** validation message. The message can be a **ValueExpression**.	No
valueChangeListener	MethodBinding (1.0, 1.1) or MethodExpression (1.2, 2.0)	A **MethodExpression** that refers to a method that returns void and accepts a single **ValueChangeEvent** argument. (1.0, 1.1, 1.2, 2.0) A **MethodExpression** that refers to a method that takes zero parameters and has a return type of void. Bear in mind that with this type of method signature, there is no way to determine the "old" and "new" values of the component. (2.0)	No

Core Attributes

Attribute	Type	Description	Required
binding	ValueBinding (1.0, 1.1) or ValueExpression (1.2, 2.0)	A binding reference to a like **UIComponent** instance.	No
id	String	The identifier for the component.	No
title	String	The title of the component. This is passed through to the rendered HTML **title** attribute.	No
value	String	The value of the component.	No

Internationalization Attributes

Attribute	Type	Description	Required
dir	String	The reading direction of the generated HTML component: RTL (right to left) or LTR (left to right).	No
lang	String	The applied **lang** attribute to the generated HTML output. For more information on the HTML **lang** attribute, visit **www.w3.org/TR/REC-html40/struct/dirlang.html**.	No

Style Attributes

Attributes for CSS styles that are applied to the generated HTML output of the component are shown next.

disabledclass	enabledclass	style	styleclass

These style attributes accept arguments of type **String** and are not specifically required.

JavaScript Attributes

Attributes for the common JavaScript events are shown next.

onblur	onchange	onclick	ondblclick	onfocus
onkeydown	onkeypress	onkeyup	onmousedown	onmousemove
onmouseout	onmouseover	onmouseup	onselect	

All JavaScript attributes accept arguments of type **String**, and none are specifically required.

Example Usage

Consider a managed bean **shirt** with a **List** property of **sizeList**. This can then be value-bound to the **SelectOneMenu** component, as shown in the following:

```
<h:selectOneMenu id="size" value="#{shirt.size}">
  <f:selectItems value="#{shirt.sizeList}"/>
</h:selectOneMenu>
```

An example with hard-coded select items is shown next:

```
<h:selectOneMenu id ="size" value="#{shirt.size}">
  <f:selectItem itemLabel="Small" itemValue="s"/>
  <f:selectItem itemLabel="Medium" itemValue="m"/>
  <f:selectItem itemLabel="Large" itemValue="l"/>
  <f:selectItem itemLabel="Extra-Large" itemValue="xl"/>
</h:selectOneMenu>
```

The h:selectOneRadio Tag

UIComponent class: **javax.faces.component.html.HtmlSelectOneRadio**

Component type: **javax.faces.HtmlSelectOneRadio**

The **selectOneRadio** component renders as an HTML table with a set of radio buttons from which the user can select. The **<input>** elements are represented by the children components **UISelectItem** and/or **UISelectItems** components and are rendered with a **type** attribute set to "radio" and a **name** attribute set to the component's client ID. Each **<input>** element is nested also within a **<label>** element with a **for** attribute set to the component's client ID.

Ungrouped Attributes

Attribute	Type	Description	Required
accesskey	char	The mnemonic character used to establish focus to this button.	No
border	int	The border width in pixels of the generated table around the options list.	No
converterMessage (1.2, 2.0)	String	When present, this overrides the default **Converter** validation message. The message can be a **ValueExpression**.	No
converter	String	The fully qualified name of a class that implements the **javax.faces.convert .Converter** interface.	No
disabled	boolean	When **true**, this component is not usable and is rendered in a disabled state.	No
hideNoSelectionOption (2.0)	boolean	A boolean flag that indicates whether or not a child **f:selectItem** whose noSelectionOption attribute is "true" should be hidden.	No
immediate	boolean	When **true**, this component's value must be converted and validated immediately during the Apply Request Values phase rather than waiting until the Process Validations phase.	No
layout	String	Option list orientation. Can be either **pageDirection** (vertical) or **lineDirection** (horizontal). When not specified, **lineDirection** is the default.	No

Attribute	Type	Description	Required
readonly	boolean	Displays the component as read-only when **true**.	No
rendered	boolean	The boolean attribute that defines whether the component is rendered. The default value is "true".	No
required	boolean	When **true**, this will cause a validation error when no value is supplied.	No
requiredMessage (1.2, 2.0)	String	When present, this overrides the default **required** validation message. The message can be a **ValueExpression**.	No
tabindex	int	The tabbing order position of the component. The value must be an integer between 0 and 32767.	No
validator	String	If specified, then the value must be a **MethodExpression** that refers to a method that has the same signature as the **validate** method in the **javax.faces.validator .Validator** interface.	No
validatorMessage (1.2, 2.0)	String	When present, this overrides the default Validator validation message. The message can be a **ValueExpression**.	No
valueChangeListener	MethodBinding (1.0, 1.1) or MethodExpression (1.2, 2.0)	A **MethodExpression** that refers to a method that returns void and accepts a single **ValueChangeEvent** argument. (1.0, 1.1, 1.2, 2.0) A **MethodExpression** that refers to a method that takes zero parameters and has a return type of void. Bear in mind that with this type of method signature, there is no way to determine the "old" and "new" values of the component. (2.0)	No

PART III

Core Attributes

Attribute	Type	Description	Required
binding	ValueBinding (1.0, 1.1) or ValueExpression (1.2, 2.0)	A binding reference to a like **UIComponent** instance.	No
id	String	The identifier for the component.	No
title	String	The title of the component. This is passed through to the rendered HTML **title** attribute.	No
value	String	The value of the component.	No

Internationalization Attributes

Attribute	Type	Description	Required
dir	String	The reading direction of the generated HTML component: RTL (right to left) or LTR (left to right).	No
lang	String	The applied **lang** attribute to the generated HTML output. For more information on the HTML lang attribute, visit **www.w3.org/TR/REC-html40/struct/dirlang.html**.	No

Style Attributes

Attributes for CSS styles that are applied to the generated HTML output of the component are shown next.

disabledclass	enabledclass	style	styleclass

These style attributes accept arguments of type **String** and are not specifically required.

JavaScript Attributes

Attributes for the common JavaScript events are shown next.

onblur	onchange	onclick	ondblclick	onfocus
onkeydown	onkeypress	onkeyup	onmousedown	onmousemove
onmouseout	onmouseover	onmouseup	onselect	

All JavaScript attributes accept arguments of type **String**, and none are specifically required.

Example Usage

Consider a managed bean **shirt** with a **List** property of *sizeList*. This can then be value-bound to the **selectOneRadio** component, as shown in the following:

```
<h:selectOneRadio id="size" value="#{shirt.size }">
  <f:selectItems value="#{shirt.sizeList}"/>
</h:selectOneRadio>
```

An example with hard-coded select items is shown next:

```
<h:selectOneRadio id ="size" value="#{shirt.size}">
  <f:selectItem itemLabel="Small" itemValue="s"/>
  <f:selectItem itemLabel="Medium" itemValue="m"/>
  <f:selectItem itemLabel="Large" itemValue="l"/>
  <f:selectItem itemLabel="Extra-Large" itemValue="xl"/>
</h:selectOneRadio>
```

The Standard Facelets Templating Library (2.0)

The Standard Facelets Templating Library is accessible in Facelets (but not JSP) as a tag library with a URI of **http://java.sun.com/jsf/facelets** and default prefix of **ui**. A quick reference of the Standard Facelets Templating Library is provided in Table 16-3.

Tag	Description	JSF Version(s)
ui:component	Similar to the **ui:composition** tag in that it encapsulates a reusable piece of markup, but unlike **ui:composition** it cannot specify a template for defining layout. Instead, this tag is to be used to encapsulate the definition of a facelet component. This tag is included for compatibility with applications that used Facelets prior to JSF 2.0. JSF 2.0 applications should use the composite component feature. If markup were to be placed outside of **ui:component**, it would be ignored by the Facelets view handler.	2.0
ui:composition	Encapsulates a reusable piece of markup and can optionally specify a template for defining layout. A typical use case for compositions is to use the **ui:include** tag to include them in Facelet views or other compositions. If markup were to be placed outside of **ui:composition**, it would be ignored by the Facelets view handler.	2.0
ui:debug	Provides developers with a way of obtaining detailed information regarding the state of a Facelet view.	2.0
ui:decorate	Functionally the same as the **ui:composition** tag in that it encapsulates a reusable piece of markup but also provides the ability to place markup before the begin **ui:decorate** tag and after the end **ui:decorate** tag.	2.0

TABLE 16-3 The Standard Facelets Templating Library Quick Reference *(continued)*

Tag	Description	JSF Version(s)
ui:define	Encapsulates a piece of markup that is intended to be inserted into a Facelet template via the **ui:insert** tag.	2.0
ui:fragment	Functionally the same as the **ui:component** tag in that it encapsulates the definition of a composite component but also provides the ability to place markup before the begin **ui:fragment** tag and after the end **ui:fragment** tag.	2.0
ui:include	The Facelets equivalent of the **jsp:include** tag. It provides the ability to include/insert markup into a Facelet view or composition that is contained in a separate XHTML file.	2.0
ui:insert	Inserts content into a Facelet template that is defined by a **ui:define** tag in a Facelet template client.	2.0
ui:param	Provides the ability to pass parameters as a name+value pair to an included file or template.	2.0
ui:remove	Removes markup at compile time. Consequently, the removed markup does not appear in the component tree and will not appear in the rendered page.	2.0
ui:repeat	Iterates over a collection and includes a copy of its child elements in the component tree for each iteration. It is similar to **h:dataTable** except that it does not render an HTML table by default.	2.0

TABLE 16-3 The Standard Facelets Templating Library Quick Reference *(continued)*

Example Website Project

The following XHTML markup files collectively form an example Web site project that demonstrates the templating functionality of the tags in the Standard Facelets Templating Library. To see an example project that shows how to use the **ui:component** tag, please refer to the section titled "The Standard Facelets Composite Component Library." Figure 16-1 shows a screen shot of the home page when viewed with a Web browser.

Template Source Markup

The following Facelet view markup would exist in a file named **template.xhtml** and would be placed in a subfolder named **WEB-INF/includes**. Its purpose is to be a template that would contain the basic layout of a Web site with sections such as header, navigation, main, and footer.

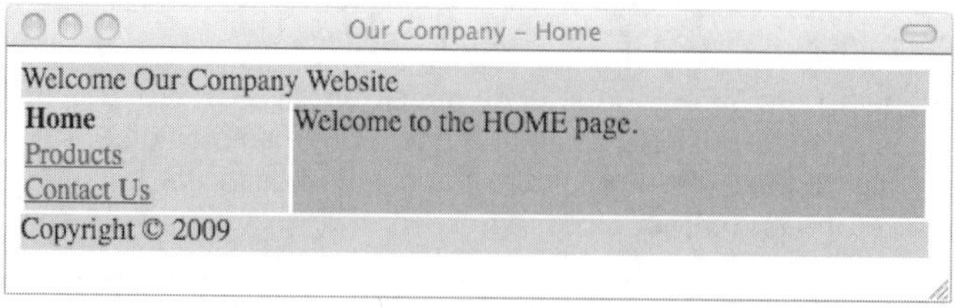

FIGURE 16-1 A rendering of a Facelet page

```
<?xml version="1.0" encoding="UTF-8"?>
<!DOCTYPE html PUBLIC "-//W3C//DTD XHTML 1.0 Transitional//EN"
"http://www.w3.org/TR/xhtml1/DTD/xhtml1-transitional.dtd">

<f:view xmlns="http://www.w3.org/1999/xhtml"
  xmlns:f="http://java.sun.com/jsf/core"
  xmlns:h="http://java.sun.com/jsf/html"
  xmlns:ui="http://java.sun.com/jsf/facelets">

  <!--
  Enables CTRL+SHIFT+D for activating Facelets debug window
  -->
  <ui:debug />

  <html>
    <h:head>
      <ui:insert name="htmlHead" />
      <link rel="stylesheet" type="text/css"
        href="css/template.css" />
    </h:head>
    <h:body>
      <h:panelGroup layout="block" styleClass="header">
        <ui:include src="/WEB-INF/includes/header.xhtml" />
      </h:panelGroup>
      <h:panelGrid columns="2"
        columnClasses="nav-col, main-col"
        styleClass="middle-table">
        <h:panelGroup layout="block">
          <h:form>
            <ui:insert name="navigation" />
          </h:form>
        </h:panelGroup>
        <h:panelGroup layout="block">
          <ui:insert name="main" />
        </h:panelGroup>
      </h:panelGrid>
      <h:panelGroup layout="block" styleClass="footer">
        <ui:include src="/WEB-INF/includes/footer.xhtml" />
      </h:panelGroup>
    </h:body>
  </html>
</f:view>
```

Header Source Markup

The following Facelet composition markup would exist in a file named **header.xhtml** and would be placed in a subfolder named **WEB-INF/includes**. Its purpose would be to contain typical header markup such as the company name and logo.

```
<?xml version="1.0" encoding="UTF-8"?>
<!DOCTYPE html PUBLIC "-//W3C//DTD XHTML 1.0 Transitional//EN"
"http://www.w3.org/TR/xhtml1/DTD/xhtml1-transitional.dtd">
<ui:composition xmlns:f="http://java.sun.com/jsf/core"
```

```
  xmlns:h="http://java.sun.com/jsf/html"
  xmlns:ui="http://java.sun.com/jsf/facelets">

  <h:outputText value="Welcome Our Company Website" />

</ui:composition>
```

Footer Source Markup

The following Facelet composition markup would exist in a file named **footer.xhtml** and would be placed in a subfolder named **WEB-INF/includes**. Its purpose would be to contain typical footer markup such as copyright, privacy, and legal notices.

```
<?xml version="1.0" encoding="UTF-8"?>
<!DOCTYPE html PUBLIC "-//W3C//DTD XHTML 1.0 Transitional//EN"
"http://www.w3.org/TR/xhtml1/DTD/xhtml1-transitional.dtd">
<ui:composition xmlns:f="http://java.sun.com/jsf/core"
  xmlns:h="http://java.sun.com/jsf/html"
  xmlns:ui="http://java.sun.com/jsf/facelets">

  <h:outputText escape="false"
    value="Copyright &amp;copy; 2009" />

</ui:composition>
```

Home Page Source Markup

The following Facelet composition markup would exist in a file named **home.xhtml** and would be placed in the document root. Its purpose is to be a company home page that would contain Facelet **ui:define** regions that get inserted into the template.

```
<ui:composition xmlns="http://www.w3.org/1999/xhtml"
  xmlns:h="http://java.sun.com/jsf/html"
  xmlns:f="http://java.sun.com/jsf/core"
  xmlns:ui="http://java.sun.com/jsf/facelets"
  template="/WEB-INF/includes/template.xhtml">

  <ui:define name="htmlHead">
    <meta name="description" content="Our Company Home Page" />
    <title>Our Company - Home</title>
  </ui:define>

  <ui:define name="navigation">
    <h:outputText styleClass="selected" value="Home" />
    <h:commandLink action="products" value="Products" />
    <h:commandLink action="contact-us" value="Contact Us" />
  </ui:define>

  <ui:define name="main">
    <h:outputText value="Welcome to the HOME page." />
  </ui:define>

</ui:composition>
```

Products Page Source Markup

The following Facelet composition markup would exist in a file named **products.xhtml** and would be placed in the document root. Its purpose is to be a company products page that would contain Facelet **ui:define** regions that get inserted into the template.

```
<ui:composition xmlns="http://www.w3.org/1999/xhtml"
  xmlns:h="http://java.sun.com/jsf/html"
  xmlns:f="http://java.sun.com/jsf/core"
  xmlns:ui="http://java.sun.com/jsf/facelets"
  template="/WEB-INF/includes/template.xhtml">

  <ui:define name="htmlHead">
    <meta name="description"
      content="Our Company Products Page" />
    <title>Our Company - Products</title>
  </ui:define>

  <ui:define name="navigation">
    <h:commandLink action="home" value="Home" />
    <h:outputText styleClass="selected" value="Products" />
    <h:commandLink action="contact-us" value="Contact Us" />
  </ui:define>

  <ui:define name="main">
    <h:outputText value="Welcome to the PRODUCTS page." />
  </ui:define>

</ui:composition>
```


Contact-Us Page Source Markup

The following Facelet composition markup would exist in a file named **contact-us.xhtml** and would be placed in the document root. Its purpose is to be a company contact page that would contain Facelet **ui:define** regions that get inserted into the template.

```
<ui:composition xmlns="http://www.w3.org/1999/xhtml"
  xmlns:h="http://java.sun.com/jsf/html"
  xmlns:f="http://java.sun.com/jsf/core"
  xmlns:ui="http://java.sun.com/jsf/facelets"
  template="/WEB-INF/includes/template.xhtml">

  <ui:define name="htmlHead">
    <meta name="description" content="Contact Our Company" />
    <title>Our Company - Contact Us</title>
  </ui:define>

  <ui:define name="navigation">
    <h:commandLink action="home" value="Home" />
    <h:commandLink action="products" value="Products" />
    <h:outputText styleClass="selected" value="Contact Us" />
  </ui:define>
```

```
    <ui:define name="main">
      <h:outputText value="Welcome to the CONTACT US page." />
    </ui:define>

</ui:composition>
```

CSS Source Markup

The following Facelet composition markup would exist in a file named **template.css** and would live in a subfolder named **css** relative to the document root. Its purpose is to provide styling to the various elements in the template.

```
.header,.footer {
  background-color: #cfcfcf;
  width: 800px;
}
.main {
  display: inline;
}
.middle-table {
  border-width: 0px;
  width: 800px;
}
.middle-table td {
  padding: 0px;
  vertical-align: top;
}
.nav-col {
  background-color: #ccccff;
  width: 30%;
}
.main-col {
  background-color: #aaaaaa;
  width: 70%;
}
.nav-col a {
  display: list-item;
  list-style: none;
}
.nav-col form {
  display: inline;
}
.nav-col .selected {
  font-weight: bold;
}
```

The ui:component Tag (2.0)

The **ui:component** tag is similar to the **ui:composition** tag in that it encapsulates a reusable piece of markup, but unlike **ui:composition** it cannot specify a template for defining layout. This tag is included for compatibility with applications that used Facelets prior to JSF 2.0.

JSF 2.0 applications should use the composite component feature. If markup were to be placed outside of **ui:component**, it would be ignored by the Facelets view-handler.

Attributes

Attribute	Type	Description	Required
id (2.0)	String	The identifier for the component.	No
binding (2.0)	ValueExpression	A **ValueExpression** expression that evaluates to an object that implements **javax.faces .component.UIComponent**.	No

The ui:composition Tag (2.0)

The **ui:composition** tag encapsulates a reusable piece of markup and can optionally specify a template for defining layout. A typical use case for compositions is to use the **ui:include** tag to include them in Facelet views or other compositions. If markup were to be placed outside of **ui:composition**, it would be ignored by the Facelets view handler.

Attributes

Attribute	Type	Description	Required
template (2.0)	String	The filename of the Facelets XHTML template.	No

Example Usage

```
<ui:composition xmlns="http://www.w3.org/1999/xhtml"
  xmlns:h="http://java.sun.com/jsf/html"
  xmlns:f="http://java.sun.com/jsf/core"
  xmlns:ui="http://java.sun.com/jsf/facelets"
  template="/WEB-INF/includes/template.xhtml">
  ...
</ui:composition>
```

The ui:debug Tag (2.0)

The **ui:debug** tag provides developers with a way of obtaining detailed information regarding the state of a Facelet view. After the view is rendered in a Web browser, the developer can press SHIFT-CTRL-D in order to pop up the Facelets debug window that includes a detailed hierarchical dump of the component tree. It also includes the names and values of request parameters, view attributes, request attributes, flash attributes, session attributes, and application attributes.

Attributes

Attribute	Type	Description	Required
hotkey (2.0)	String	The single character developers can press along with ctrl-shift in order to pop up the Facelets debug window. The default value is "D".	No
rendered (2.0)	boolean	A boolean flag indicating whether or not this component is to be rendered during the RENDER_RESPONSE phase of the JSF lifecycle. The default value is "true".	No

Example Usage

```
<f:view xmlns="http://www.w3.org/1999/xhtml"
  xmlns:f="http://java.sun.com/jsf/core"
  xmlns:ui="http://java.sun.com/jsf/facelets">

  <ui:debug />

</f:view>
```

The ui:decorate Tag (2.0)

The **ui:decorate** tag is functionally the same as the **ui:composition** tag in that it encapsulates a reusable piece of markup but also provides the ability to place markup before the begin **ui:decorate** tag and after the end **ui:decorate** tag.

Attributes

Attribute	Type	Description	Required
template (2.0)	String	The filename of the Facelets XHTML template.	No

Example Usage

```
<div xmlns="http://www.w3.org/1999/xhtml"
  xmlns:ui="http://java.sun.com/jsf/facelets">

  <span>Some markup before</span>
  <ui:decorate>
    ...
  </ui:decorate>
  <span>Some markup after</span>

</div>
```

The ui:define Tag (2.0)

The **ui:define** tag encapsulates a piece of markup that is intended to be inserted into a Facelet template via the **ui:insert** tag.

Attributes

Attribute	Type	Description	Required
name (2.0)	String	Defines the name of the content embedded within the begin **<ui:define>** and end **</ui:define>** tags so that the **ui:insert** tag can insert the named content into a template.	Yes

Example Usage

```
<ui:composition xmlns="http://www.w3.org/1999/xhtml"
  xmlns:h="http://java.sun.com/jsf/html"
  xmlns:ui="http://java.sun.com/jsf/facelets"
  template="/WEB-INF/includes/template.xhtml">

  ...
  <ui:define name="main">
    <h:outputText value="Welcome to the HOME page." />
  </ui:define>
  ...

</ui:composition>
```

The ui:fragment Tag (2.0)

The **ui:fragment** tag is functionally the same as the **ui:component** tag in that it encapsulates the definition of a composite component but also provides the ability to place markup before the begin **ui:fragment** tag and after the end **ui:fragment** tag.

Attributes

Attribute	Type	Description	Required
id (2.0)	String	The identifier for the fragment/component.	No
binding (2.0)	ValueExpression	A **ValueExpression** expression that evaluates to an object that implements **javax.faces.component.UIComponent**.	No

Example Usage

```
<div xmlns="http://www.w3.org/1999/xhtml"
  xmlns:ui="http://java.sun.com/jsf/facelets">
```

PART III

```
  <span>Some markup before</span>
  <ui:fragment>
    ...
  </ui:fragment>
  <span>Some markup after</span>

</div>
```

The ui:include Tag (2.0)

The **ui:include** tag is the Facelets equivalent of the **jsp:include** tag. It provides the ability to include/insert markup into a Facelet view or composition that is contained in a separate XHTML file.

Attributes

Attribute	Type	Description	Required
src (2.0)	String	The filename of the XHTML file that is to be included. The path of the file is relative to the location of the Facelet view.	Yes

Example Usage

```
<f:view xmlns="http://www.w3.org/1999/xhtml"
  xmlns:f="http://java.sun.com/jsf/core"
  xmlns:h="http://java.sun.com/jsf/html"
  xmlns:ui="http://java.sun.com/jsf/facelets">

  ...
  <h:panelGroup layout="block" styleClass="header">
    <ui:include src="/WEB-INF/includes/header.xhtml" />
  </h:panelGroup>
  ...

</f:view>
```

The ui:insert Tag (2.0)

The **ui:insert** tag inserts content into a Facelet template that is defined by a ui:define tag in a Facelet template client.

Attributes

Attribute	Type	Description	Required
The **ui:insert** tag has no attributes.			

Example Usage

```
<f:view xmlns="http://www.w3.org/1999/xhtml"
  xmlns:f="http://java.sun.com/jsf/core"
```

```
  xmlns:h="http://java.sun.com/jsf/html"
  xmlns:ui="http://java.sun.com/jsf/facelets">

  <h:panelGroup layout="block">
    <ui:insert name="main" />
  </h:panelGroup>

</f:view>
```

The ui:param Tag (2.0)

The **ui:param** tag provides the ability to pass parameters as a name+value pair to an included file or template. The value of the parameter can be retrieved by simply referencing the parameter name within an EL **ValueExpression**.

Attributes

Attribute	Type	Description	Required
name (2.0)	String	The name of the parameter that is to be passed.	No
value (2.0)	String	The value of the parameter that is to be passed.	No

Example Usage

```
<f:view xmlns="http://www.w3.org/1999/xhtml"
  xmlns:f="http://java.sun.com/jsf/core"
  xmlns:h="http://java.sun.com/jsf/html"
  xmlns:ui="http://java.sun.com/jsf/facelets">

  ...
  <h:panelGroup layout="block" styleClass="header">
    <ui:include src="/WEB-INF/includes/header.xhtml">
      <ui:param name="companyName" value="Our Company" />
    </ui:include>
  </h:panelGroup>
  ...

</f:view>
```

The ui:remove Tag (2.0)

The **ui:remove** tag removes markup at compile time. Consequently, the removed markup does not appear in the component tree and will not appear in the rendered page.

Attributes

Attribute	Type	Description	Required
The **ui:remove** tag has no attributes.			

PART III

Example Usage

```
<ui:remove>
  <span>This span will not be rendered</span>
</ui:remove>
```

The ui:repeat Tag (2.0)

The **ui:repeat** tag iterates over a collection and includes a copy of its child elements in the component tree for each iteration. It is similar to **h:dataTable** except that it does not render an HTML table by default.

Attributes

Attribute	Type	Description	Required
offset (2.0)	int	Indicates the number of item(s) in the start of the collection that are to be skipped before beginning the iteration. If not specified, then the iteration will take place over the entire collection.	No
size (2.0)	int	The size of the collection over which to iterate.	No
step (2.0)	int	The number of item(s) that are to be skipped for each iteration. If not specified then the iteration will take place over the entire collection.	No
value (2.0)	Object	The collection over which to iterate, which can be an individual object instance, an array, an instance of a **java.util.List**, or an instance of **java.sql.ResultSet**.	Yes
var (2.0)	String	An iterator variable name that gets introduced into the EL and represents the current item in the iteration over the **value** attribute.	Yes
varStatus (2.0)	String	An iterator variable name that gets introduced into the EL and represents the status of the current item in the iteration. The following properties will be available via EL during the iteration: Property Name: begin, Type: Integer Property Name: end, Type: Integer Property Name: even, Type: boolean Property Name: first, Type: boolean Property Name: index, Type: int Property Name: last, Type: boolean Property Name: odd, Type: boolean Property Name: step, Type: Integer	No

Example Usage

```
<ui:repeat value="#{testManagedBean.users}" var="user">
  <h:panelGroup layout="block">
    <h:outputLabel value="First Name:" />
```

```
    <h:outputText value="#{user.firstName}" />
  </h:panelGroup>
</ui:repeat>
```

The Standard Facelets Composite Component Library (2.0)

The Standard Facelets Composite Component Library is accessible in Facelets (but not JSP) as a tag library with a URI of **http://java.sun.com/jsf/composite** and a default prefix of **composite**. This library is only intended for use within a page that declares and defines a JSF composite component. Composite components are described in detail in Chapter 11. The reference material on the composite component library uses the following terms frequently, so it is important to understand them from the outset.

Composite Component Author The individual or role creating the composite component.

Composite Component Tag The tag in the *using page* that references a *composite component* declared and defined in a *defining page*.

Defining Page The Facelet page that contains the **cc:interface** and **cc:implementation** sections that declare and define the composite component.

Page Author The individual or role that creates pages that use the composite component.

Top-Level Component The **UIComponent** instance in the tree that is the parent of all **UIComponent** instances within the *defining page* and any pages used by that *defining page*.

Using Page The Facelet page in which the *composite component tag* is used.

A quick reference of the Standard Facelets Composite Component Library is provided in Table 16-4.

Tag	Description	JSF Version(s)
cc:actionSource	Can be used by a *composite component author* by nesting it within the **cc:interface** tag in order to declare that one or more target components in the **cc:implementation** section can have an **f:actionListener** attached.	2.0
cc:attribute	Can be used by a *composite component author* by nesting it within the **cc:interface** tag in order to declare that an attribute value may be set with the *composite component tag* in the *using page*.	2.0

TABLE 16-4 The Standard Facelets Composite Component Library Quick Reference *(continued)*

PART III

Tag	Description	JSF Version(s)
cc:editableValueHolder	Can be used by a *composite component author* by nesting it within the **cc:interface** tag in order to declare that one or more target components in the **cc:implementation** section can have a converter tag or **f:valueChangeListener** attached.	2.0
cc:extension	Can be used by a *composite component author* by nesting it within the **cc:interface** tag in order to encapsulate XML elements that are needed to support JSR 276 design-time metadata, or any other metadata not covered by the composite library.	2.0
cc:facet	Can be used by a *composite component author* by nesting it within the **cc:interface** tag in order to declare that a named facet exists in the **cc:implementation** section. The *page author* can supply the **f:facet** tag in the *using page* in order to insert content within the named facet of the composite component.	2.0
cc:implementation	Used by a *composite component author* in order to encapsulate the inner workings of the composite component that implements the contract defined by the **cc:interface** section.	2.0
cc:insertChildren	Can be used by a *composite component author* in order to have component tags (nested as children of the *composite component tag* by the *page author* in the *using page*) inserted at a specific point in the **cc:implementation** section.	2.0
cc:insertFacet	Can be used to insert a named facet at a specific location inside the **cc:implementation** section. The facet must be supplied to the top-level component by the composite component tag.	2.0
cc:interface	Used by a *composite component author* in order to encapsulate the contract that is implemented by the **cc:implementation** section that is to be adhered to by the *composite component tag* in the *using page*.	2.0
cc:renderFacet	Can be used to insert a named facet at a specific location inside the **cc:implementation** section. The facet must be supplied to the top-level component by the composite component tag.	2.0
cc:valueHolder	Can be used by a *composite component author* by nesting it within the **cc:interface** tag in order to declare that one or more target components in the **cc:implementation** section can have a converter tag attached.	2.0

TABLE 16-4 The Standard Facelets Composite Component Library Quick Reference *(continued)*

FIGURE 16-2 A rendering of a composite component

Example Project

The following XHTML markup and Java source code is an example project that demonstrates how to build a Facelet composite component that uses most of the tags in the Standard Facelets Composite Component Library. Figure 16-2 shows a screen shot of the composite component when viewed with a Web browser.

Composite Component Source Markup

The following Facelet composite component source markup would exist in a file named **inputColor.xhtml** and would be placed in a subfolder named **resources/testcc** relative to the Web application docroot. Its purpose is to be an Ajax-enhanced reusable component for selecting a color. Page authors would create instances of this component with the **<testcc:inputColor />** tag in a using page. The **cc:interface** section describes the usage contract for the component. The **cc:implementation** section contains the inner workings of the component that implements the contract.

```
<!DOCTYPE html PUBLIC "-//W3C//DTD XHTML 1.0 Transitional//EN"
"http://www.w3.org/TR/xhtml1/DTD/xhtml1-transitional.dtd">
<ui:component xmlns="http://www.w3.org/1999/xhtml"
  xmlns:c="http://java.sun.com/jsp/jstl/core"
  xmlns:f="http://java.sun.com/jsf/core"
  xmlns:h="http://java.sun.com/jsf/html"
  xmlns:ui="http://java.sun.com/jsf/facelets"
  xmlns:cc="http://java.sun.com/jsf/composite">

  <cc:interface>
    <cc:attribute name="value" required="true"
      type="com.example.jsf.Color">
      <cc:attribute name="red" required="true" />
      <cc:attribute name="green" required="true" />
      <cc:attribute name="blue" required="true" />
    </cc:attribute>
    <cc:actionSource name="colorPalette"
      targets="redSelector greenSelector blueSelector" />
```

```
    <cc:editableValueHolder name="colorFields"
      targets="redInputText greenInputText blueInputText" />
    <cc:extension>
      <some-jsr-276-meta-data />
    </cc:extension>
    <cc:facet name="header" required="true" />
  </cc:interface>

  <cc:implementation>
    <cc:renderFacet name="header" />
    <f:ajax render="preview kids">
      <h:panelGrid columns="2">
        <h:outputLabel value="R:" />
        <h:inputText id="redInputText"
          value="#{cc.attrs.value.red}">
          <f:validateLongRange minimum="0" maximum="255" />
        </h:inputText>
        <h:outputLabel value="G:" />
        <h:inputText id="greenInputText"
          value="#{cc.attrs.value.green}">
          <f:validateLongRange minimum="0" maximum="255" />
        </h:inputText>
        <h:outputLabel value="B:" />
        <h:inputText id="blueInputText"
          value="#{cc.attrs.value.blue}">
          <f:validateLongRange minimum="0" maximum="255" />
        </h:inputText>
      </h:panelGrid>
    </f:ajax>
    <h:outputText value="Color Preview: " />
    <c:set value="#{cc.attrs.value.red}" var="red" />
    <c:set value="#{cc.attrs.value.green}" var="green" />
    <c:set value="#{cc.attrs.value.blue}" var="blue" />
    <c:set value="#{red},#{green},#{blue}" var="rgb" />
    <h:outputText id="preview" value=" "
      style="border: 1px solid; padding: 1px 10px; background-color:
rgb(#{rgb});" />
    <f:ajax
      render="redInputText greenInputText blueInputText preview kids">
      <h:panelGrid border="1" columns="3">
        <f:facet name="header">
          <h:outputText value="Color Palette" />
        </f:facet>
        <h:commandLink id="redSelector" value="Red">
          <f:setPropertyActionListener
            target="#{cc.attrs.value.red}" value="255" />
          <f:setPropertyActionListener
            target="#{cc.attrs.value.green}" value="0" />
          <f:setPropertyActionListener
            target="#{cc.attrs.value.blue}" value="0" />
        </h:commandLink>
        <h:commandLink id="greenSelector" value="Green">
          <f:setPropertyActionListener
            target="#{cc.attrs.value.red}" value="0" />
```

```
          <f:setPropertyActionListener
            target="#{cc.attrs.value.green}" value="255" />
          <f:setPropertyActionListener
            target="#{cc.attrs.value.blue}" value="0" />
        </h:commandLink>
        <h:commandLink id="blueSelector" value="Blue">
          <f:setPropertyActionListener
            target="#{cc.attrs.value.red}" value="0" />
          <f:setPropertyActionListener
            target="#{cc.attrs.value.green}" value="0" />
          <f:setPropertyActionListener
            target="#{cc.attrs.value.blue}" value="255" />
        </h:commandLink>
      </h:panelGrid>
    </f:ajax>
    <br />
    <h:panelGroup id="kids">
      <cc:insertChildren />
    </h:panelGroup>
  </cc:implementation>
</ui:component>
```


Using Page Source Markup

The following Facelet view markup would exist in a file named **usingPage.xhtml** and would be placed in the Web application docroot folder. It shows how to create an instance of the **testcc:inputColor** composite component. It also shows how to connect it to a JSF model managed bean that is kept in JSF 2.0 View scope, which is necessary in order to keep model managed bean properties in memory for successive Ajax requests.

```
<?xml version="1.0" encoding="UTF-8"?>
<!DOCTYPE html PUBLIC "-//W3C//DTD XHTML 1.0 Transitional//EN"
"http://www.w3.org/TR/xhtml1/DTD/xhtml1-transitional.dtd">
<f:view xmlns="http://www.w3.org/1999/xhtml"
  xmlns:f="http://java.sun.com/jsf/core"
  xmlns:h="http://java.sun.com/jsf/html"
  xmlns:testcc="http://java.sun.com/jsf/composite/testcc"
  xmlns:ui="http://java.sun.com/jsf/facelets">
  <h:head />
  <h:body>
    <h:form>
      <h:messages />
      <testcc:inputColor value="#{testManagedBean.color}">

        <f:facet name="header">
          <h:outputText value="Please choose a color" />
        </f:facet>

        <f:actionListener for="colorPalette"
          type="com.example.jsf.ColorActionListener" />

        <f:valueChangeListener for="colorFields"
          type="com.example.jsf.ColorValueChangeListener" />
```

```
        <!--
        The following h:panelGrid will be used by
        the cc:insertChildren tag in the
        cc:implementation section of the
        testcc:inputColor composite component. -->
        <h:panelGrid columns="2">
          <f:facet name="header">
            <h:outputText value="You Selected: " />
          </f:facet>
          <h:outputLabel value="Red:" />
          <h:outputText
            value="#{testManagedBean.color.red}" />
          <h:outputLabel value="Green:" />
          <h:outputText
            value="#{testManagedBean.color.green}" />
          <h:outputLabel value="Blue:" />
          <h:outputText
            value="#{testManagedBean.color.blue}" />
        </h:panelGrid>
      </testcc:inputColor>
      <br />
      <h:commandButton value="Submit" />
    </h:form>
  </h:body>
</f:view>
```

Color Class Source Code

The following Java source code would be a class named **Color.java** and provides a way to specify a color using a Red, Green, Blue (RGB) definition.

```
package com.example.jsf;

public class Color {

  private int red;
  private int green;
  private int blue;

  public int getRed() {
    return red;
  }

  public void setRed(int red) {
    this.red = red;
  }

  public int getGreen() {
    return green;
  }

  public void setGreen(int green) {
    this.green = green;
  }
```

```
  public int getBlue() {
    return blue;
  }

  public void setBlue(int blue) {
    this.blue = blue;
  }
}
```

Model Managed Bean Source Code

The following Java source code would be a model managed bean class named **TestManagedBean.java** that is kept in JSF 2.0 View scope, which is necessary in order to keep model managed bean properties in memory for successive Ajax requests.

```
package com.example.jsf;

import javax.faces.bean.ManagedBean;
import javax.faces.bean.ViewScoped;

@ManagedBean(name = "testManagedBean")
@ViewScoped
public class TestManagedBean {

  private Color color = new Color();

  public Color getColor() {
    return color;
  }

  public void setColor(Color color) {
    this.color = color;
  }
}
```

Action Listener Source Code

The following Java source code serves as a JSF Action Listener that would be named **ColorActionListener.java** and listens to when the user clicks a link from the color palette.

```
package com.example.jsf;

import javax.faces.event.AbortProcessingException;
import javax.faces.event.ActionEvent;
import javax.faces.event.ActionListener;

public class ColorActionListener implements ActionListener {
  public void processAction(ActionEvent event) throws AbortProcessingException {
    String id = event.getComponent().getId();
    System.out.println("Selected palette link: " + id);
  }
}
```

Value Change Listener Source Code

The following Java source code serves as a JSF Value Change Listener that would be named **ColorValueChangeListener.java** and listens to when the Red, Green, and Blue field values are changed by the user.

```
package com.example.jsf;

import javax.faces.event.AbortProcessingException;
import javax.faces.event.ValueChangeEvent;
import javax.faces.event.ValueChangeListener;

public class ColorValueChangeListener
  implements ValueChangeListener {

  public void processValueChange(ValueChangeEvent event)
      throws AbortProcessingException {
    String color = event.getComponent().getId();
    System.out.println(color + " value changed: " +
      event.getNewValue());
  }
}
```

The cc:actionSource Tag (2.0)

The **cc:actionSource** tag can be used by a *composite component author* by nesting it within the **cc:interface** tag in order to declare that one or more target components in the **cc:implementation** section implement the **ActionSource2** behavioral interface and can therefore have an **f:actionListener** attached, as well as perform any other behaviors performed by **ActionSource2** components.

Attributes

Attribute	Type	Description	Required
name (2.0)	String	The name of the action source, which can be specified in the **for** attribute of an attached **f:actionListener** in a using page.	Yes
targets (2.0)	String	A space delimited list of id attribute values to which the **f:actionListener** in the using page will be attached. If no value is specified, then the value of the name attribute is used as the default value.	No

Example Usage

```
<cc:interface>
    ...
    <cc:actionSource name="redSelector" />
    <cc:actionSource name="greenSelector" />
    <cc:actionSource name="blueSelector" />
    ...
</cc:interface>
```

The cc:attribute Tag (2.0)

The **cc:attribute** tag can be used by a *composite component author* by nesting it within the **cc:interface** tag in order to declare that an attribute value may be set with the *composite component tag* in the *using page*. Note that **cc:attribute** tags can be nested within other **cc:attribute** tags.

Attributes

Attribute	Type	Description	Required
default (2.0)	String	The value that is to be used for the attribute if it is not required and a value has not been supplied by the *using page author*.	No
displayName (2.0)	String	Related to the **displayName** property of the **javax.beans.FeatureDescriptor** class, this indicates the localized display name of the attribute.	No
expert (2.0)	boolean	Related to the **expert** property of the **javax .beans.FeatureDescriptor** class, this boolean flag indicates whether or not the attribute is intended for an expert user or a typical user. The default value is "false" (typical user).	No
method-signature (2.0)	String	If specified, then the *page author* must specify an attribute value that is a **MethodExpression** matching the format specified by the method-signature attribute in the *composite component definition*. The following is an example method-signature: `java.lang.String methodName( int, java.lang.String )`	No
name (2.0)	String	The name of the attribute given by the composite component author, which the *using page author* can use to specify a value in the *component component tag* in the *using page*.	Yes
preferred (2.0)	boolean	Related to the **preferred** property of the **javax .beans.FeatureDescriptor** class, this boolean flag indicates whether or not the attribute has a high degree of importance to humans. The default value is "false".	No
required (2.0)	boolean	A boolean flag that indicates whether or not the page author must supply a value in the *composite component tag* in the *using page*.	No

(continued)

Attribute	Type	Description	Required
shortDescription (2.0)	String	Related to the **shortDescription** property of the **javax.beans.FeatureDescriptor** class, this indicates the short description of the attribute.	No
targets (2.0)	String	If the *composite component author* specifies a method-signature in the *composite component definition*, then the *composite component author* can also set the value of targets to a space-delimited list of names, each one corresponding to the id of an *inner component*. If the *composite component author* does not specify a value for the targets attribute, then the value of the name attribute is used.	Yes
type (2.0)	String	The fully qualified name of a class that defines the type of value that the *using page author* must specify in the value attribute of the *composite component tag*. The default value is "java.lang.Object".	No

Example Usage

```
<cc:interface>
  ...
    <cc:attribute name="value" required="true"
      type="com.example.jsf.Color">
      <cc:attribute name="red" required="true" />
      <cc:attribute name="green" required="true" />
      <cc:attribute name="blue" required="true" />
    </cc:attribute>
  ...
</cc:interface>
```

The cc:editableValueHolder Tag (2.0)

The **cc:editableValueHolder** tag can be used by a *composite component author* by nesting it within the **cc:interface** tag in order to declare that one or more target components in the **cc:implementation** section implement the **EditableValueHolder** behavioral interface; it can therefore have a converter tag or **f:valueChangeListener** attached, as well as perform any other behaviors performed by **EditableValueHolder** components.

Attributes

Attribute	Type	Description	Required
name (2.0)	String	The name of the editable value holder, which can be specified in the for attribute of an attached object. For the sake of writing less markup, if there is no value specified for the targets attribute, then the value of this name attribute is automatically assumed to be the id of the target component inside the **cc:implementation** section.	Yes
targets (2.0)	String	A space delimited list of id attribute values to which the converter tag or f:valueChangeListener in the using page will be attached. If no value is specified, then the value of the name attribute is used as the default value.	No

Example Usage

```
<cc:interface>
  ...
  <cc:editableValueHolder name="colorFields"
    targets="redInputText greenInputText blueInputText" />
  ...
</cc:interface>
```


The cc:extension Tag (2.0)

The **cc:extension** tag can be used by a *composite component author* by nesting it within the **cc:interface** tag in order to encapsulate XML elements that are needed to support JSR 276 design-time metadata, or any other kind of metadata not covered by the composite library.

Attributes

Attribute	Type	Description	Required
The **cc:extension** tag has no attributes.			

Example Usage

```
<cc:interface>
  ...
  <cc:extension>
    <some-jsr-276-meta-data />
  </cc:extension>
  ...
</cc:interface>
```

The cc:facet Tag (2.0)

The **cc:facet** tag can be used by a *composite component author* by nesting it within the **cc:interface** tag in order to declare that a named facet exists in the **cc:implementation** section. The *page author* can use the **f:facet** tag in the *using page* in order to insert content within the named facet of the composite component.

Attributes

Attribute	Type	Description	Required
displayName (2.0)	String	Related to the **displayName** property of the **javax.beans.FeatureDescriptor** class, this indicates the localized display name of the facet.	No
expert (2.0)	boolean	Related to the **expert** property of the **javax.beans .FeatureDescriptor** class, this boolean flag indicates whether or not the facet is intended for an expert user or a typical user. The default value is "false" (typical user).	No
name (2.0)	String	Related to the **name** property of the **javax.beans .FeatureDescriptor** class, this indicates the name of the facet.	Yes
preferred (2.0)	boolean	Related to the **preferred** property of the **javax .beans.FeatureDescriptor** class, this boolean flag indicates whether or not the facet has a high degree of importance to humans. The default value is "false".	No
required (2.0)	boolean	The boolean flag that indicates whether or not the using page must supply an **f:facet** tag with the associated name. The default value is false.	No
shortDescription (2.0)	String	Related to the **shortDescription** property of the **javax.beans.FeatureDescriptor** class, this indicates the short description of the facet.	No

Example Usage

```
<cc:interface>
  ...
  <cc:facet name="header" required="true" />
  ...
</cc:interface>
```

The cc:implementation Tag (2.0)

The **cc:implementation** tag is used by a *composite component author* in order to encapsulate the inner workings of the composite component that implements the contract defined by the **cc:interface** section. It is perfectly feasible to use other composite components within the **cc:implementation** section, with the important exception that a composite component may not nest itself within its **cc:implementation** section.

Attributes

Attribute	Type	Description	Required
The cc:implementation tag has no attributes.			

Example Usage

```
<cc:implementation>
  ...
</cc:implementation>
```

The cc:insertChildren Tag (2.0)

The **cc:insertChildren** tag can be used by a *composite component author* in order to have component tags (nested as children of the *composite component tag* by the *page author* in the *using page*) inserted at a specific point in the composite:cc:implementation section.

Attributes

Attribute	Type	Description	Required
The cc:insertChildren tag has no attributes.			

Example Usage

```
<cc:implementation>
  ...
  <cc:insertChildren />
  ...
</cc:implementation>
```

The cc:insertFacet Tag (2.0)

The **cc:insertFacet** tag can be used to insert a named facet at a specific location inside the **cc:implementation** section. The facet must be supplied to the top-level component by the composite component tag.

Attributes

Attribute	Type	Description	Required
name (2.0)	String	The name of the facet.	Yes
required (2.0)	boolean	The boolean flag that indicates whether or not the using page must supply an **f:facet** tag with the associated name. The default value is false. Note that this attribute potentially redundant with the required attribute of the **cc:facet** tag. The best practice would be to supply the same value for both required attributes.	No

Example Usage

```
<cc:implementation>
  ...
  <cc:insertFacet name="footer" />
  ...
</cc:implementation>
```

The cc:interface Tag (2.0)

The **cc:interface** tag is used by a *composite component author* in order to encapsulate the contract that is implemented by the **cc:interface** section and is to be adhered to by the *composite component tag* in the *using page*.

Attributes

Attribute	Type	Description	Required

componentType (2.0)	String	Specifies the component type for the composite component that associates it with a *composite component top-level component*. The default value is "javax.faces.NamingContainer". The following example shows how to create a Java class that has a component type value of "com.example.jsf.Command" that could be used to connect the composite component to a different *composite component top-level component*.
		`package com.example.jsf.component;`
		
		`import javax.faces.component.FacesComponent;`
		`import javax.faces.component.UICommand;`
		
		`@FacesComponent("com.example.jsf.Command")`
		`public class MyComponent extends UICommand {`
		`  ...`
		`}`
		Note that whatever actual **UIComponent** instance ends up being the *top-level component*, this instance must return "javax.faces.NamingContainer" from its **getFamily( )** method.
			No

displayName (2.0)	String	Related to the **displayName** property of the **javax.beans.FeatureDescriptor** class, this indicates the localized display name of the composite component.	No

Attribute	Type	Description	Required
expert (2.0)	boolean	Related to the **expert** property of the **javax.beans .FeatureDescriptor** class, this boolean flag indicates whether or not the composite component is intended for an expert user or a typical user. The default value is "false" (typical user).	No
name (2.0)	String	Related to the **name** property of the **javax.beans .FeatureDescriptor** class, this indicates the name of the composite component. The value specified by this attribute is advisory information for the JSF implementation. Instead, the name is determined from the filename of the composite component.	No
preferred (2.0)	boolean	Related to the **preferred** property of the **javax .beans.FeatureDescriptor** class, this boolean flag indicates whether or not the composite component has a high degree of importance to humans. The default value is "false".	No
shortDescription (2.0)	String	Related to the **shortDescription** property of the **javax.beans.FeatureDescriptor** class, this indicates the short description of the composite component.	No

Example Usage

```
<cc:interface>
  ...
</cc:interface>
```

The cc:renderFacet Tag (2.0)

The **cc:renderFacet** tag can be used to insert a named facet at a specific location inside the **cc:implementation** section. The facet must be supplied to the top-level component by the composite component tag.

Attributes

Attribute	Type	Description	Required
name (2.0)	String	The name of the facet. It corresponds to the name specified in the **cc:facet** tag in the **cc:interface** section.	Yes
required (2.0)	boolean	The boolean flag that indicates whether or not the using page must supply an **f:facet** tag with the associated name. The default value is false. Note that this attribute is potentially redundant with the required attribute of the **cc:facet** tag. The best practice would be to supply the same value for both required attributes.	No

Example Usage

```
<cc:implementation>
  ...
  <cc:renderFacet name="header" />
  ...
</cc:implementation>
```

The cc:valueHolder Tag (2.0)

The **cc:valueHolder** tag can be used by a *composite component author* by nesting it within the **cc:interface** tag in order to declare that one or more target components in the **cc:implementation** section implements **ValueHolder** and can therefore have a converter tag attached, as well as perform any other behaviors performed by **ActionSource2** components.

Attributes

Attribute	Type	Description	Required
name (2.0)	String	The name of the value holder, which can be specified in the **for** attribute of an attached object. For the sake of writing less markup, if there is no value specified for the target attribute, then the value of this name attribute is automatically assumed to be the id of the target component inside the **cc:implementation** section.	Yes
targets (2.0)	String	A space-delimited list of id attribute values to which the converter tag in the using page will be attached. If no value is specified, then the value of the name attribute is used as the default value.	No

Example Usage

```
<cc:interface>
  ...
  <cc:valueHolder name="dates"
    targets="dateOfBirth dateOfHire" />
  ...
</cc:interface>
```

APPENDIX

JSF Portlets

This appendix provides some practical reference material for developing JSF portlets. It explains the terminology used in discussing portlets, serves as a guide to selecting a JSF Portlet Bridge, and explains how to integrate JSF portlets with the main features provided by the JSR 168 (Portlet 1.0) and JSR 286 (Portlet 2.0) standards. Special attention is focused on ICEfaces portlets, and the benefits provided by ICEfaces Partial Submit and ICEfaces Ajax Push. Finally, this appendix shows how to use several of the features provided by PortletFaces, an open source project that provides close integration between JSF and Liferay Portal.

Overview of Portlet 1.0 and 2.0

Portlets are Web applications that are designed to run inside a *portlet container* that implements either the Portlet 1.0 or Portlet 2.0 standards from JCP. Portlet containers provide a layer of abstraction over the Java EE Servlet API and consequently require a servlet container, such as Apache Tomcat, to function. The reference implementation for Portlet 1.0 and 2.0 is the Apache Pluto project: **http://portals.apache.org/pluto/**.

Portals are standalone systems that use a portlet container as the runtime engine for executing portlets. When a portal is asked to deliver a portal page to the end user's Web browser, each portlet is asked to render itself as a fragment of HTML. It is the job of the portal to aggregate these HTML fragments into a complete HTML document.

Portlet Lifecycle

The Portlet 1.0 standard defines two lifecycle phases for the execution of a portlet that a compliant portlet container must support: The first is the **javax.portlet.PortletRequest .RENDER_PHASE**, in which the portlet container asks each portlet to render itself as a fragment of HTML. The second is the **javax.portlet.PortletRequest.ACTION_PHASE**, in which the portlet container invokes actions related to HTML form submission.

Expert Group Insight *It's no accident that the* ***RENDER_PHASE*** *and the* ***ACTION_PHASE*** *correspond nicely to* ***Lifecycle.render( )*** *and* ***Lifecycle.execute ( )*** *in JSF. JSF 1.0 was being developed simultaneously with Portlet 1.0, so there was ample opportunity for the teams to collaborate. In fact, the entire concept of* ***ExternalContext*** *was brought to JSF by IBM EG member Brendan Murray as a way to allow JSF to run well in a portlet environment.*

When the portal receives an HTTP GET request for a portal page, the portlet container executes the portlet lifecycle and each of the portlets on the page undergoes the RENDER_PHASE. When the portal receives an HTTP POST request, the portlet container executes the portlet lifecycle and the portlet associated with the HTML form submission will first undergo the ACTION_PHASE before the RENDER_PHASE is invoked for all of the portlets on the page.

The Portlet 2.0 standard adds two more lifecycle phases that define the execution of a portlet. The first is the **javax.portlet.PortletRequest.EVENT_PHASE**, in which the portlet container broadcasts events that are the result of an HTML form submission. During this phase, the portlet container asks each portlet to process events that it is interested in. The typical use case for the EVENT_PHASE is to achieve inter-portlet communication (IPC), whereby two or more portlets on a portal page share data in some way. The other new phase added by the Portlet 2.0 standard is the **javax.portlet.PortletRequest.RESOURCE_PHASE**, in which the portlet container asks a specific portlet to perform resource-related processing. One typical use case for the RESOURCE_PHASE is for an individual portlet to process Ajax requests. Another typical use case for the RESOURCE_PHASE is for an individual portlet to generate non-HTML content (for download purposes) such as a PDF or spreadsheet document.

Portlet Modes

The Portlet 1.0 and 2.0 standards define three portlet modes that a compliant portlet container must support: **javax.portlet.PortletMode.VIEW**, **javax.portlet.PortletMode.EDIT**, and **javax.portlet.PortletMode.HELP**. Portal vendors and portlet developers may supply custom modes as well. VIEW mode refers to the rendered portlet markup that is encountered by the user under normal circumstances. Perhaps a clearer name would be *normal* mode or *typical* mode, because the word *view* is also used by developers to review to the *view concern* of the MVC design pattern. EDIT mode refers to the rendered portlet markup that is encountered by the user when selecting custom values for portlet preferences. Perhaps a clearer name would be *preferences* mode. Finally, HELP mode refers to the rendered portlet markup that is encountered by the user when seeking help regarding the usage and/or functionality of the portlet. Screenshots of a portlet in VIEW, EDIT, and HELP modes are shown in Figures A-1, A-2, and A-3, respectively.

FIGURE A-1 Portlet in VIEW mode

FIGURE A-2 Portlet in EDIT mode

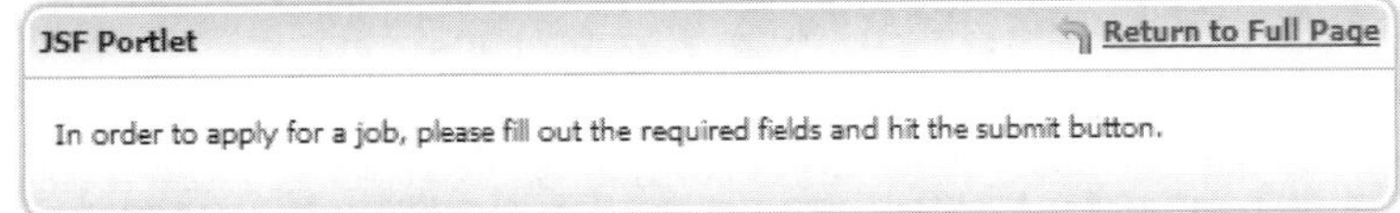

Figure A-3 Portlet in HELP mode

Portlet Window States

Portals typically manifest the rendered markup of a portlet in a rectangular section of the browser known as a *portlet window.* The Portlet 1.0 and 2.0 standards define three window states that a compliant portlet container must support: **javax.portlet.WindowState.NORMAL**, **javax.portlet.WindowState.MAXIMIZED**, and **javax.portlet.WindowState.MINIMIZED**. The NORMAL window state refers to the way in which the portlet container displays the rendered markup of a portlet when it can appear on the same portal page as other portlets. The MAXIMIZED window state refers to the way in which the portlet container displays the rendered markup of a portlet when it is the only portlet on a page, or when the portlet is to be rendered more prominently than other portlets on a page. Finally, the MINIMIZED window state refers to the way in which the portlet container displays a portlet when the markup is not to be rendered.

Portlet Preferences

Developers often have the requirement to provide the end user with the ability to personalize the portlet behavior in some way. To meet this requirement, the Portlet 1.0 and 2.0 standards provide the ability to define preferences for each portlet. Preference names and default values can be defined in the **WEB-INF/portlet.xml** configuration file. Portal end users start out interacting with the portlet user interface in portlet VIEW mode but can switch to portlet EDIT mode in order to select custom preference values.

Example Usage

The following example shows how to specify portlet preference names and associated default values in the **WEB-INF/portlet.xml** configuration file:

```
<portlet-app>
  <portlet>
    ...
    <portlet-preferences>
      <preference>
        <name>datePattern</name>
        <value>MM/dd/yyyy</value>
      </preference>
      <preference>
        <name>unitedStatesPhoneFormat</name>
        <value>###-###-####</value>
      </preference>
    </portlet-preferences>
    ...
  </portlet>
</portlet-app>
```

Inter-Portlet Communication

Inter-portlet communication (IPC) is a technique whereby two or more portlets on a portal page share data in some way. In a typical IPC use case, user interactions with one portlet affect the rendered markup of another portlet. The Portlet 2.0 standard provides two techniques to achieve IPC: Public Render Parameters and Server-Side Events.

The *Public Render Parameters* technique provides a way for portlets to share data by setting public/shared parameter names in a URL controlled by the portal. While this approach is relatively easy to implement, one drawback is that only small amounts of data can be shared. Typically, the kind of data that is shared is simply the value of a database primary key.

The *Server-Side Events* technique provides a way for portlets to share data using an event-listener design. When using this form of IPC, the portlet container acts as broker and distributes events and payload (data) to portlets. One requirement of this approach is that the payload must implement the **java.io.Serializable** interface, since it might be sent to a portlet in another WAR running in a different classloader.

It could be argued that the Portlet 2.0 approaches for IPC have a common drawback in that they can lead to a potentially disruptive end-user experience. This is because they cause either an HTTP GET or an HTTP POST, which results in a full-page refresh. Technologies such as ICEfaces Ajax Push can be used to solve this problem. See the later section in this appendix "ICEfaces Ajax Push and Inter-Portlet Communication" for more details. Figure A-4 shows a high-level overview of inter-portlet communication.

Liferay Portal is the most popular and widely downloaded open source portal available. The product supports the Portlet 2.0 standard and includes a built-in Content Management System (CMS). It also ships with over 60 out-of-the-box portlets, including social networking portlets such as Friends, Message Forums, Shared Calendar, Wiki, and Blogs. The project home page can be found at **www.liferay.com**.

Liferay, Inc., was of the first portal vendors to provide support for JSF portlets back in May 2005. Since then Liferay has provided support for JSF portlets running technologies including Mojarra, MyFaces, Facelets, and ICEfaces. A listing of sample JSF portlets can be found by searching for "JSF" at **www.liferay.com/web/guest/downloads/community_plugins**.

Figure A-5 shows the Liferay portal in action.

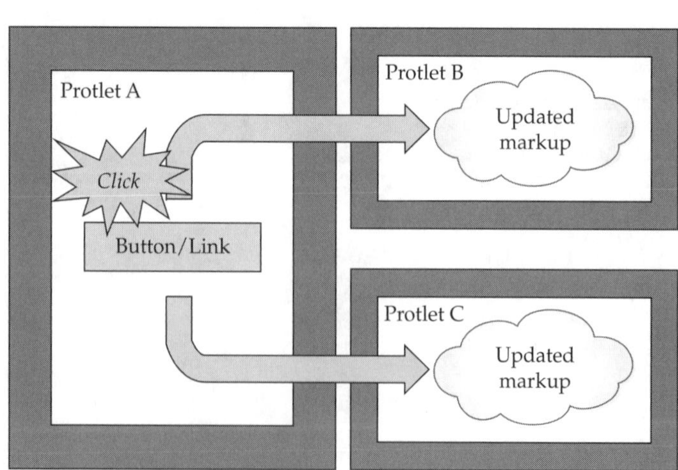

FIGURE A-4 Inter-portlet communication

FIGURE A-5 A Liferay Portal page

JSF Portlet Development

Strictly speaking, Portlet 1.0 and 2.0 only provide the ability for developers to write a Java class that writes HTML markup to the response that is delivered to the Web browser. Although it is possible to introduce a markup-based view technology like JSP, portlet developers often choose the JSF framework in order to leverage the MVC design pattern and robust UI component features.

JSF Portlet Bridges

As mentioned previously, the Portlet 1.0 and JSF 1.0 specifications were formulated during roughly the same time frame. Consequently, the JSF expert group was able to design a framework with portlet compatibility in mind. This is evidenced by methods like **ExternalContext.getRequest( )**, which returns a value of type **Object**, rather than a value of type **javax.servlet.http.HttpServletRequest**. When running inside a portlet container, the same method would return a value of type **javax.portlet.PortletRequest**. Although the JSF API provides a degree of portlet compatibility, in order to use JSF in a portlet, developers must specify a JSF *portlet bridge* in the **<portlet-class>** element of the **WEB-INF/portlet.xml** configuration file. JSF portlet bridges provide an abstraction layer such that developers can (in most cases) develop JSF portlets in the same way in which they would develop JSF Web applications. Bridge implementations are either based on the JSR 301 standard or the JSR 329 standard, or else they were developed as innovative open source projects prior to the formulation of the standards. The JSR 301 standard defines a bridge API for Portlet 1.0 + JSF 1.2, whereas the JSR 329 standard defines a bridge API for Portlet 2.0 + JSF 1.2. The reference implementations for JSR 301 and JSR 329 can be downloaded from the Apache MyFaces Portlet Bridge project: **http://myfaces.apache.org/portlet-bridge**.

Expert Group Insight *At the time of this writing, the Subversion repository for the JSR 329 MyFaces Portlet Bridge reference implementation provides a branch with prototype support for Portlet 2.0 + JSF 2.0: **http://svn.apache.org/repos/asf/myfaces/portlet-bridge/core/branches**.*

Also at the time of this writing, it has not yet been determined whether or not JSF 2.0 support will continue under JSR 329, under a new JSR, or without the structure of a JSR. With the advent of the Portlet 2.0 RESOURCE_PHASE for Ajax, bridges that support the Ajax features of JSF 2.0 will require a Portlet 2.0–compliant portlet container in which to run.

JSF portlet bridges are responsible for providing a "bridge" between the portlet lifecycle and the JSF lifecycle. For example, when a portal page that contains a JSF portlet is requested via HTTP GET, then the RENDER_PHASE of the portlet lifecycle should in turn execute the RESTORE_VIEW and RENDER_RESPONSE phases of the JSF lifecycle. Similarly, when the user submits a form contained within a JSF portlet via HTTP POST, then the ACTION_PHASE of the portlet lifecycle should execute the complete JSF lifecycle of RESTORE_VIEW, APPLY_REQUEST_VALUES, PROCESS_VALIDATIONS, UPDATE_MODEL_VALUES, INVOKE_APPLICATION, and RENDER_RESPONSE.

Since the portal is in full control of managing URLs, JSF portlet bridges are also responsible for asking the portal to generate URLs that are compatible with actions that invoke JSF navigation rules. Consequently, JSF portlets may not perform a redirect. If a different JSF view is to be rendered as a result of a JSF navigation rule, then the JSF portlet bridge simply displays the new JSF view in the same portlet window.

A quick reference of several JSF portlet bridges is provided in Table A-1.

Example Usage

The following example shows how to specify the **JSR 301** or **JSR 329 JSF Portlet Bridge** in the **WEB-INF/portlet.xml** configuration file, as well as default Facelet views that are to be rendered for VIEW mode, EDIT mode, and HELP mode:

```
<portlet-app>
  <portlet>
    <portlet-name>my_portlet</portlet-name>
    <display-name>My Portlet</display-name>
    <portlet-class>
      javax.portlet.faces.GenericFacesPortlet
    </portlet-class>
    <init-param>
      <name>javax.portlet.faces.defaultViewId.view</name>
      <value>/xhtml/applicantForm.xhtml</value>
    </init-param>
    <init-param>
```

```
      <name>javax.portlet.faces.defaultViewId.edit</name>
      <value>/xhtml/edit.xhtml</value>
    </init-param>
    <init-param>
      <name>javax.portlet.faces.defaultViewId.help</name>
      <value>/xhtml/help.xhtml</value>
    </init-param>
    <supports>
      <mime-type>text/html</mime-type>
      <portlet-mode>view</portlet-mode>
      <portlet-mode>edit</portlet-mode>
      <portlet-mode>help</portlet-mode>
    </supports>

    ...

  </portlet>
</portlet-app>
```

Example Usage

The following example shows how to specify the **Sun OpenPortal JSF Portlet Bridge** in the **WEB-INF/portlet.xml** configuration file, as well as default JSF views that are to be rendered for VIEW mode, EDIT mode, and HELP mode:

```
<portlet-app>
  <portlet>
    <portlet-name>my_portlet</portlet-name>
    <display-name>My Portlet</display-name>
    <portlet-class>
      com.sun.faces.portlet.FacesPortlet
    </portlet-class>
    <init-param>
      <name>com.sun.faces.portlet.INIT_VIEW</name>
      <value>/xhtml/applicantForm.xhtml</value>
    </init-param>
    <init-param>
      <name>com.sun.faces.portlet.INIT_EDIT</name>
      <value>/xhtml/edit.xhtml</value>
    </init-param>
    <init-param>
      <name>com.sun.faces.portlet.INIT_HELP</name>
      <value>/xhtml/help.xhtml</value>
    </init-param>
    <supports>
      <mime-type>text/html</mime-type>
      <portlet-mode>view</portlet-mode>
      <portlet-mode>edit</portlet-mode>
      <portlet-mode>help</portlet-mode>
    </supports>

    ...

  </portlet>
</portlet-app>
```

Bridge Name	Description
MyFaces Portlet Bridge JSR 301 Reference Implementation	**Project Web site**: http://myfaces.apache.org/portlet-bridge/1.0 **Portlet API:** Portlet 1.0 **Portlet Class**: javax.portlet.faces.GenericFacesPortlet **JSF Compatibility**: Mojarra 1.2, MyFaces 1.2 **View Handler**: JSP, unofficially works with FaceletPortletViewHandler **Component Compatibility**: Standard (f:, h:)
MyFaces Portlet Bridge JSR 329 Reference Implementation	**Project Web site**: http://myfaces.apache.org/portlet-bridge/2.0 **Portlet API:** Portlet 2.0 **Portlet Class**: javax.portlet.faces.GenericFacesPortlet **JSF Compatibility**: Mojarra 1.2, MyFaces 1.2 **View Handler**: JSP, unofficially works with FaceletPortletViewHandler **Component Compatibility**: Standard (f:, h:)
Sun OpenPortal JSF Portlet Bridge	**Project Web site**: https://jsfportletbridge.dev.java.net **Portlet API:** Portlet 1.0 and 2.0 **Portlet Class**: com.sun.faces.portlet.FacesPortlet **JSF Compatibility**: Mojarra 1.1, 1.2 **View Handler**: JSP, FaceletPortletViewHandler **Component Compatibility**: Standard (f:, h:), Woodstock (retired)
ICEfaces 1.x Portlet Bridge	**Project Web site**: www.icefaces.org **Portlet API:** Portlet 1.0 **Portlet Class**: com.icesoft.faces.webapp.http.portlet.MainPortlet **JSF Compatibility**: Mojarra 1.1, 1.2 **View Handler**: JSP, D2DFaceletViewHandler **Component Compatibility**: Standard (f:, h:), ICEfaces (ice:)
Apache Portals-Bridges JSF Portlet Bridge	**Project Web site**: http://portals.apache.org/bridges/multiproject/portals-bridges-jsf **Portlet API:** Portlet 1.0 **Portlet Class**: org.apache.portals.bridges.jsf.FacesPortlet **JSF Compatibility**: MyFaces 1.1 **View Handler**: JSP Only **Component Compatibility**: Standard (f:, h:)
MyFacesGenericPortlet	**Project Web site**: http://myfaces.apache.org/core11 **Portlet API:** Portlet 1.0 **Portlet Class**: org.apache.myfaces.portlet.MyFacesGenericPortlet **JSF Compatibility**: MyFaces 1.1, 1.2 **View Handler**: JSP, FaceletPortletViewHandler **Component Compatibility**: Standard (f:, h:), Tomahawk (t:)

TABLE A-1 JSF Portlet Bridge Quick Reference

Bridge Name	Description
JBoss Portlet Bridge JSR 301 Implementation	**Project Web site**: www.jboss.org/portletbridge **Portlet API:** Portlet 1.0 **Portlet Class**: javax.portlet.faces.GenericFacesPortlet **JSF Compatibility**: Mojarra 1.2, MyFaces 1.2 **View Handler**: JSP, JBoss FaceletPortletViewHandler **Component Compatibility**: Standard (f:, h:), RichFaces (rich:), Seam (s:)
JBoss Portlet Bridge JSR 329 Implementation	**Project Web site**: www.jboss.org/portletbridge/ **Portlet API:** Portlet 2.0 **Portlet Class**: javax.portlet.faces.GenericFacesPortlet **JSF Compatibility**: Mojarra 1.2, MyFaces 1.2 **View Handler**: JSP, JBoss FaceletPortletViewHandler **Component Compatibility**: Standard (f:, h:), RichFaces (rich:), Seam (s:)

TABLE A-1 JSF Portlet Bridge Quick Reference *(continued)*

JSF Portlet View Handlers

The default view handler for JSF 1.*x* is designed for JSP technology. With the advent of the Facelets view handler, JSF developers were able to migrate away from JSP-based views to XHTML-based views and take advantage innovative features such as Composite Components and Page Templates. The Facelets project can be found at: **https://facelets.dev.java.net**.

Although the **com.sun.facelets.FaceletViewHandler** class is not compatible with JSF portlets, the Facelets project supplies the **com.sun.facelets.FaceletPortletViewHandler** class in the "demo/portlet" folder of its source code distribution. Although this class is not contained in the jsf-facelets.jar binary distribution, the **FaceletPortletViewHandler.java** file can be coped into the Java source code folder of the portlet so that the Facelets view handler can be used instead of JSP.

Example Usage

The following example shows how to specify the portlet-compatible version of the Facelets view handler in the **WEB-INF/faces-config.xml** configuration file:

```
<faces-config>
  <application>
    <view-handler>
      com.sun.facelets.FaceletPortletViewHandler
    </view-handler>
  </application>
</faces-config>
```

The JSR 301 and JSR 329 standards only officially support JSP-based views with the default JSP view-handler provided by the JSF implementation. However, it is possible to use the FaceletPortletViewHandler in an unofficial manner.

EXPERT GROUP INSIGHT *Facelets is the premiere view technology for JSF 2.0 and the Mojarra MultiViewHandler automatically detects if JSF views are designed for Facelets or JSP. When portlet bridges officially support JSF 2.0, there will be no more need to include the FaceletPortlet ViewHandler source in the Java source code folder of the portlet when using Mojarra.*

JSF ExternalContext and the Portlet API

Just as JSF Web application developers rely on **ExternalContext** in order to get access to the Servlet API, JSF portlet developers also rely on **ExternalContext** in order to get access to the Portlet API. The two most common tasks that JSF portlet developers need to perform are to obtain an instance of the **javax.portlet.PortletRequest** object or to obtain one of the **javax.portlet.PortletResponse** object.

Example Usage

The following example shows how to get the **PortletRequest** and **PortletResponse** objects from within a JSF backing managed bean action method:

```
public class BackingBean {

  public String submit() {
    FacesContext facesContext =
      FacesContext.getCurrentInstance();

    ExternalContext externalContext =
      facesContext.getExternalContext();

    PortletRequest portletRequest =
      (PortletRequest) externalContext.getRequest();

    PortletResponse portletResponse =
      (PortletResponse) externalContext.getResponse();

    return "success";
  }
}
```

Note that developers using Liferay Portal can take advantage of the convenience methods of the **PortletFacesContext** class in order to perform ordinary JSF portlet tasks like the ones shown in the preceding example. See the later section "PortletFaces" for more information.

JSF and Portlet Preferences

Facelet views that are designed to be used in portlet EDIT mode are typically forms that enable the portlet end user to select custom preference values that override the default values specified in the **WEB-INF/portlet.xml** configuration file. JSR 301/329 bridge implementations are required to provide an EL resolver that introduces the **portletPreferences** variable into the EL, which is a mutable **java.util.Map** that provides read/write access to each portlet preference.

By utilizing the JSR 301/329 **portletPreferences** variable within an EL **ValueExpression**, portlet developers can declaratively bind the Facelet view to the portlet preference model data. In order to save the preferences, a backing bean must call the **javax.portlet.PortletPreferences.store( )** method.

Example Usage

The following example shows how to develop a Facelet view and associated backing managed bean to support portlet EDIT mode with a JSR 301/329 Portlet Bridge:

```
<!--
This is a file named edit.xhtml that can be used
for portlet EDIT mode. It utilizes the JSR 301/329
portletPreferences EL variable for gaining read/write
access to javax.portlet.PortletPreferences.
-->
<?xml version="1.0" encoding="UTF-8"?>
<!DOCTYPE html PUBLIC "-//W3C//DTD XHTML 1.0 Transitional//EN"
"http://www.w3.org/TR/xhtml1/DTD/xhtml1-transitional.dtd">
<f:view xmlns:f="http://java.sun.com/jsf/core"
  xmlns:h="http://java.sun.com/jsf/html">
  <h:form>
    <h:messages globalOnly="true" />
    <h:outputLabel for="datePattern" />
    <h:inputText id="datePattern"
      required="true"
      value="#{portletPreferences['datePattern'].value}" />
    <h:message for="datePattern" />
    <h:commandButton
      actionListener="#{backingBean.savePreferences}"
      value="Save Preferences" />
  </h:form>
</f:view>
/**
 * This is a JSF backing managed-bean that has a
 * savePreferences action-listener.
 */
public class BackingBean {

  public void savePreferences(ActionEvent actionEvent) {
    FacesContext facesContext =
      FacesContext.getCurrentInstance();

    ExternalContext externalContext =
      facesContext.getExternalContext();
    PortletRequest portletRequest =
      (PortletRequest) externalContext.getRequest();

    PortletPreferences portletPreferences =
      portletRequest.getPreferences();

    portletPreferences.store();
  }
}
```

PART III

JSF and Inter-Portlet Communication

The only JSF portlet bridges that can technically support Portlet 2.0 style IPC are those that subclass the Portlet 2.0 version of **javax.portlet.GenericPortlet** class. At the time of this writing, version 1.2.3 of the Sun OpenPortal JSF Portlet Bridge supports Public Render Parameters, and Server-Side Events will be supported in a subsequent version. Also at the time of this writing, the JSR 329 standard supports both Public Render Parameters and Server-Side Events. As the JSR 329 specification is currently only at Early Draft Review 2 (EDR2) status, please refer to the following sections of the specification for the latest details on how to leverage Portlet 2.0 IPC with JSF:

- Section 2.6.1, titled "Events"
- Section 2.6.3, titled "Public Render Parameters"
- Section 3.2, titled "Initializing the Bridge"
- Section 5.2.5, titled "Executing a Portlet Event Request"
- Section 5.3, titled "Processing Public Render Parameters"

Perhaps the most natural approach for a JSF developer to try for IPC is to specify *session* scope on a JSF managed bean. Surprisingly, this approach doesn't work. To understand why, it is necessary to discuss the fact that the Portlet 1.0 and 2.0 standards make a distinction between two kinds of session scopes: **javax.portlet.PortletSession.APPLICATION_SCOPE** and **javax.portlet.PortletSession.PORTLET_SCOPE**. The former can be used for sharing data between portlets packaged in the same WAR, but the latter cannot. The reason JSF session scope can't be used to share data between portlets is that all JSF portlet bridges use **PortletSession.PORTLET_SCOPE**.

In order to share data with **PortletSession.APPLICATION_SCOPE**, the JSF portlet developer can place a JSF model managed bean in request scope and use the getter/setter as a layer of abstraction.

Example Usage

The following example shows how to develop a request-scoped JSF managed bean that has a getter and setter that provides a layer of abstraction over **PortletSession.APPLICATION_SCOPE**:

```
public class ModelManagedBean {

  public static final String
    SHARED_STRING_KEY = "sharedStringKey";

  public String getSharedString() {
    return PortletSessionUtil.getSharedSessionAttribute(
      SHARED_STRING_KEY);
  }

  public void setSharedString(String value) {
    PortletSessionUtil.setSharedSessionAttribute(
```

```
      SHARED_STRING_KEY, value);
  }
}

public class PortletSessionUtil {

  public static Object getSharedSessionAttribute(
    String key) {

    FacesContext facesContext =
      FacesContext.getCurrentInstance();

    ExternalContext externalContext =
      facesContext.getExternalContext();

    PortletSession portletSession =
      (PortletSession) externalContext().getSession(false);

    return portletSession.getAttribute(
      key, PortletSession.APPLICATION_SCOPE);
  }

  public static void setSharedSessionAttribute(
    String key, Object value) {

    FacesContext facesContext =
      FacesContext.getCurrentInstance();

    ExternalContext externalContext =
      facesContext.getExternalContext();

    PortletSession portletSession =
      (PortletSession)externalContext().getSession(false);

    portletSession.setAttribute(
      key, value, PortletSession.APPLICATION_SCOPE);
  }
}
```

Alternatively, if using the Spring Framework to replace or augment the JSF Managed Bean Facility, then developers can store data in **PortletSession.APPLICATION_SCOPE** using the **globalSession** scope keyword.

Example Usage

The following example shows how to specify a Spring bean that is to be stored in **PortletSession.APPLICATION_SCOPE** by registering it in the **WEB-INF/applicationContext.xml** configuration file:

```
<bean
  id="sharedManagedBean"
  class="com.sample.jsf.SharedManagedBean"
  scope="globalSession"/>
```

PART III

ICEfaces Portlet Development

ICEfaces is an open source extension to JSF that enables developers with Java EE application skills to build Ajax-powered Rich Internet Applications (RIA) without writing any JavaScript code. The product contains a robust suite of Ajax-enabled JSF UI components, and also supports a broad array of Java application servers, IDEs, third-party components, and JavaScript effect libraries. The project home page can be found at **www.icefaces.org**.

Because of its integrated Ajax framework, ICEfaces is a particularly good choice for developing RIA portlets. Consider a portal page that contains two portlets: Portlet A and Portlet B. When submitting a form in Portlet A, an HTTP POST takes place and the entire portal page is refreshed. This can result in a disruptive end-user experience if the user had entered data in Portlet B prior to submitting Portlet A. ICEfaces allows you to combat this disruptive experience with RIA features in your portlets.

ICEfaces can be used in a variety of portal products, including Liferay Portal. Since July 2007, Liferay, Inc., and ICEsoft Technologies, Inc., have had a technology partnership in place to support customers that want to develop and deploy ICEfaces portlets within Liferay Portal.

ICEfaces Ajax with Partial Submit

When a portal page is requested for the first time via HTTP GET, portlets built with ICEfaces undergo the RENDER_PHASE of the portlet lifecycle just like any other portlet. From that point on, ICEfaces circumvents normal interaction through the portlet container. When doing a form submission from an ICEfaces portlet, an HTTP POST will not be performed; instead, form submission takes place via Ajax.

There are two techniques that developers can use in order to enable Ajax in a JSF view built with ICEfaces component tags:

1. Specify paritalSubmit="true" on the **ice:form** tag.
2. Specify partialSubmit="true" on each ICEfaces component tag.

Note that if the first technique is used, then ICEfaces component tags that are used to perform full form submissions (such as **ice:commandButton**) must specify partialSubmit="false".

Example Usage

The following example shows how to enable Ajax in a Facelet view built with ICEfaces component tags:

```
<?xml version="1.0" encoding="UTF-8"?>
<f:view xmlns="http://www.w3.org/1999/xhtml"
  xmlns:f="http://java.sun.com/jsf/core"
  xmlns:ice="http://www.icesoft.com/icefaces/component"
  xmlns:xsi="http://www.w3.org/2001/XMLSchema-instance"
  xsi:schemaLocation="http://www.w3.org/1999/xhtml
    http://www.w3.org/2002/08/xhtml/xhtml1-transitional.xsd">
  <ice:portlet>
    <ice:form partialSubmit="true">
      <ice:panelGrid columns="2">
        <ice:outputLabel
```

```
          for="firstName" value="First Name" />
        <ice:inputText
          value="#{modelManagedBean.firstName}" />
        <ice:message for="firstName" />
        <ice:outputLabel
          for="lastName" value="Last Name" />
        <ice:inputText
          value="#{modelManagedBean.lastName}" />
        <ice:message for="lastName" />
        <ice:commandButton
          action="#{backingManagedBean.submit}"
          partialSubmit="false" />
      </ice:panelGrid>
    </ice:form>
  </ice:portlet>
</f:view>
```

ICEfaces Direct-to-DOM RenderKit

Rather than writing markup directly to the response, ICEfaces components render themselves into a server-side Document Object Model (DOM) via the ICEfaces Direct-to-DOM (D2D) RenderKit. When a JSF view is requested for the first time, the markup inside the server-side DOM is delivered to the browser as part of the response. As the user interacts with the UI of the portlet, ICEfaces transparently submits user actions via Ajax and executes the JSF lifecycle. When the RENDER_RESPONSE phase of the JSF lifecycle completes, ICEfaces will compare the previous server-side DOM with the latest server-side DOM and send the incremental page updates back to the browser via the ICEfaces Ajax Bridge. In order to improve the application experience of the end user, ICEfaces will only permit fields that have been visited by the user to undergo validation during the PROCESS_VALIDATIONS phase of the JSF lifecycle.

This approach is sometimes referred to as "dom-diffing" and provides the following benefits for portlets:

- The end user is immediately presented with form validation failures for visited fields when pressing the TAB key.
- When a navigation rule fires and a new JSF view is to be rendered, ICEfaces will render the new JSF view by performing a complete update of the markup contained in the affected portlet, rather than causing the entire browser page to reload.
- ICEfaces portlets will not disturb other portlets on the same portal page.

The ice:portlet Tag

ICEfaces provides the ice:portlet component tag that developers should use to wrap the entire content of each portlet. It implements the **javax.faces.component.NamingContainer** interface so that it can apply the portlet namespace as the top level of the JSF ID hierarchy. Doing this makes the ID hierarchy more efficient and helps the ICEfaces framework uniquely identify components on the page, which is important when more than one ICEfaces portlet is placed on the same portal page.

ICEfaces 1.x Portlet Bridge

ICEfaces 1.*x* ships with a Portlet 1.0–compliant portlet bridge for deployment of ICEfaces portlets. Note that ICEfaces 2.*x* will use a Portlet 2.0–compliant bridge that will include the ability to channel the ICEfaces Ajax requests through the Portlet 2.0 **RESOURCE_PHASE** of the portlet lifecycle.

Example Usage

The following example shows how to specify the **ICEfaces 1.*x* Portlet Bridge** in the **WEB-INF/portlet.xml** configuration file, as well as default JSF views that are to be rendered for VIEW mode, EDIT mode, and HELP mode:

```
<portlet-app>
  <portlet>
    <portlet-name>my_portlet</portlet-name>
    <display-name>My Portlet</display-name>
    <portlet-class>
      com.icesoft.faces.webapp.http.portlet.MainPortlet
    </portlet-class>
    <init-param>
      <name>com.icesoft.faces.portlet.viewPageURL</name>
      <value>/xhtml/applicantForm.xhtml</value>
    </init-param>
    <init-param>
      <name>com.icesoft.faces.portlet.editPageURL</name>
      <value>/xhtml/edit.xhtml</value>
    </init-param>
    <init-param>
      <name>com.icesoft.faces.portlet.helpPageURL</name>
      <value>/xhtml/help.xhtml</value>
    </init-param>
    <supports>
      <mime-type>text/html</mime-type>
      <portlet-mode>view</portlet-mode>
      <portlet-mode>edit</portlet-mode>
      <portlet-mode>help</portlet-mode>
    </supports>

    ...

  </portlet>
</portlet-app>
```

ICEfaces 1.x D2DFaceletViewHandler

In order to use Facelets with the ICEfaces 1.*x* Portlet Bridge, it is necessary to use the ICEfaces **com.icesoft.faces.facelets.D2DFaceletViewHandler** class, which is designed to provide support for Facelet views and the D2D RenderKit.

Example Usage

The following example shows how to specify the ICEfaces D2D view handler in the **WEB-INF/faces-config.xml** configuration file:

```
<faces-config>
  <application>
    <view-handler>
      com.icesoft.faces.facelets.D2DFaceletViewHandler
    </view-handler>
  </application>
</faces-config>
```

ICEfaces 1.x and Portlet Window States

Since ICEfaces 1.*x* portlets never perform an HTTP post, they do not participate in the ACTION_PHASE of the portlet lifecycle. It is therefore not possible for ICEfaces 1.*x* portlets to programmatically change the portlet window state. However, ICEfaces portlets can respond accordingly when the user clicks links provided by the portal that control portlet window states.

ICEfaces Portlets and Concurrent DOM Views

ICEfaces provides a feature called Concurrent DOM Views that controls whether or not the ICEfaces framework supports multiple views of a single application from the same browser. When running in a portlet container, ICEfaces needs to treat the separate portlets on a single portal page as distinct views, so it is almost always necessary (and therefore safest) to have this parameter set to true.

Example Usage

The following example shows how to enable the ICEfaces Concurrent DOM Views feature in the **WEB-INF/web.xml** configuration file so that separate portlets on the same portal page are treated as distinct views:

```
<context-param>
  <param-name>
    com.icesoft.faces.concurrentDOMViews
  </param-name>
  <param-value>true</param-value>
</context-param>
```

ICEfaces 1.x Extended Request Scope

When developers specify a value of *request* for the scope a JSF managed bean, the scope is understood to be very short-lived, as it lasts for the duration of a request. When a developer specifies a value of *request* when using ICEfaces, then the ICEfaces Extended Request scope is applied by default. As an added benefit, the ICEfaces Extended Request scope lends itself quite well to portlets.

Expert Group Insight *The ICEfaces 1.x Extended Request scope was one of the inspirations for a new feature in JSF 2.0 called View scope. ICEfaces 2.x applications will use the new JSF 2.0 View scope in place of ICEfaces Extended Request scope.*

The ICEfaces Ajax Bridge is responsible for dispatching Ajax requests as a result of user-initiated actions and monitoring the status of each Ajax request. Developers can specify the

com.icesoft.faces.connectionTimeout context parameter in the **WEB-INF/web.xml** configuration file to change the length of time (in milliseconds) that the ICEfaces Ajax Bridge will wait before declaring the connection lost. The default value is 60000 (60 seconds).

Example Usage

The following example shows how to specify the length of time in the **WEB-INF/web.xml** configuration file that the ICEfaces Ajax Bridge will wait before declaring the connection lost:

```
<context-param>
  <param-name>
    com.icesoft.faces.connectionTimeout
  </param-name>
  <param-value>80000</param-value>
</context-param>
```

The duration of the ICEfaces Extended Request scope begins when the view is first requested, and stays active until one of the following conditions occurs:

- The user navigates to a different JSF view.
- The user navigates to a different portal page.
- The ICEfaces connection timeout occurs.
- The PortletSession expires.
- The user terminates the Web browser.

To disable the ICEfaces Extended Request scope, developers can specify the **com.icesoft .faces.standardRequestScope** context parameter in the **WEB-INF/web.xml** configuration file and set it to false.

Example Usage

The following example shows how to disable ICEfaces Extended Request scope and restore standard request scope in the **WEB-INF/web.xml** configuration file:

```
<context-param>
  <param-name>
    com.icesoft.faces.standardRequestScope
  </param-name>
  <param-value>true</param-value>
</context-param>
```

ICEfaces Ajax Push and Inter-Portlet Communication

While the Portlet 2.0 standard defines techniques for performing inter-portlet communication (IPC), they cause either an HTTP GET or HTTP POST, which results in a full-page reload and a disruptive end-user experience. ICEfaces provides a natural way for portlets to perform IPC via ICEfaces *Ajax Push*.

ICEfaces pioneered Ajax Push, which is sometimes referred to as *Reverse Ajax* or *Comet*. The technology provides the ability for server-initiated events to cause incremental page updates to be sent to the browser. With ICEfaces Ajax Push, developers can create collaborative and dynamic enterprise applications like never before.

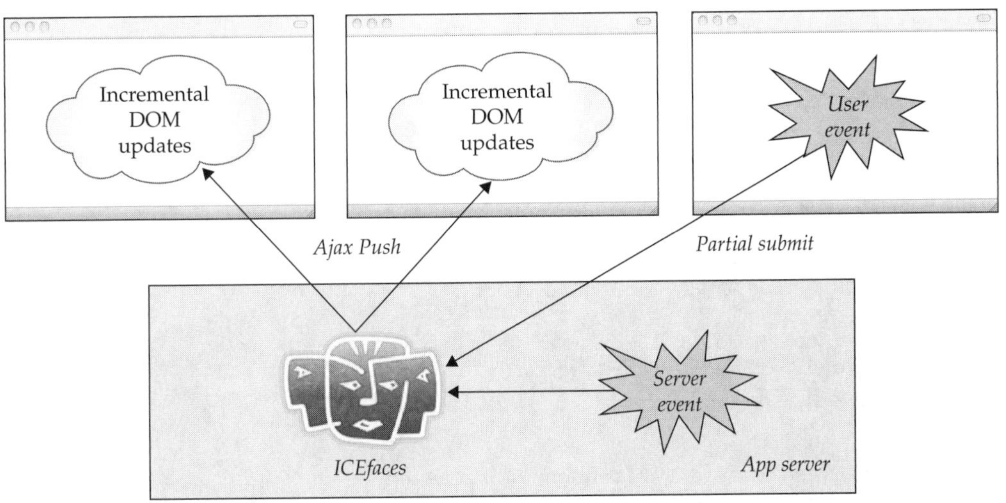

FIGURE A-6 Inter-portlet communication with Ajax Push

Because the mechanism facilitates asynchronous updates from the server to the client, interaction with one ICEfaces portlet can trigger communication with other ICEfaces portlets by changing values in JSF backing and model managed beans. This mechanism is not restricted to IPC among portlets on the same portal page in a single browser but can include updating other browsers that are interacting with the same portal page. The result is not just inter-portlet communication, but inter-portlet, inter-browser communication, as shown in Figure A-6. Additionally, ICEfaces Ajax Push solves the potentially disruptive end-user experience associated with the Portlet 2.0 standard IPC techniques.

The following is a list of guidelines for achieving IPC with ICEfaces Ajax Push:

- Package the portlets that need to communicate in the same WAR.
- In order to share data between portlets, use application-scoped beans or request-scoped beans that store data in **PortletSession.APPLICATION_SCOPE**.
- Use the ICEfaces Ajax Push **SessionRenderer** to trigger client updates when the shared data changes.

Example Usage

The following example shows how to develop a JSF managed bean in application scope that maintains a chat log that participates in ICEfaces Ajax Push using the **SessionRenderer**. This class does not address concurrency.

```
/*
 * This is a file named ChatRoomManagedBean.java
 * that is registered as a JSF managed-bean in
 * application scope.
 */
import com.icesoft.faces.async.render.SessionRenderer;
import java.util.ArrayList;
```

```
import java.util.List;
import javax.faces.event.ActionEvent;

public class ChatRoomManagedBean {

  private String messageText;

  private List<String> messages = new ArrayList<String>();

  private static final String
    AJAX_PUSH_GROUP_NAME = "chatRoom";

  public ChatRoomsModel() {
    SessionRenderer.addCurrentSession(
      AJAX_PUSH_GROUP_NAME);
  }

  public void addMessage(ActionEvent actionEvent) {
    messages.add(messageText);
    SessionRenderer.render(AJAX_PUSH_GROUP_NAME);
  }

  public List<String> getMessages() {
    return messages;
  }

  public String getMessageText() {
    return messageText;
  }

  public void setMessageText(String messageText) {
    this.messageText = messageText;
  }
}

<!-- This is a Facelet view named chatRoom.xhtml -->
<?xml version="1.0" encoding="UTF-8"?>
<f:view xmlns="http://www.w3.org/1999/xhtml"
  xmlns:f="http://java.sun.com/jsf/core"
  xmlns:ice="http://www.icesoft.com/icefaces/component"
  xmlns:xsi="http://www.w3.org/2001/XMLSchema-instance"
  xsi:schemaLocation="http://www.w3.org/1999/xhtml
    http://www.w3.org/2002/08/xhtml/xhtml1-transitional.xsd">
  <ice:portlet>
    <ice:form>
      <ice:dataTable
        value="#{chatRoomManagedBean.messages}"
        var="message">
        <ice:column>
          <ice:outputText value="#{message}" />
        </ice:column>
      </ice:dataTable>
      <ice:inputText
        value="#{chatRoomManagedBean.messageText}" />
      <ice:commandButton
```

```
        actionListener="#{chatRoomManagedBean.addMessage}" />
    </ice:form>
  </ice:portlet>
</f:view>
```

Note that the TritonSource project contains open source demonstration portlets that focus on ICEfaces portlets for Liferay Portal. Specifically, TritonSource has a demonstration portlet featuring an ICEfaces chat room that integrates with Liferay Portal's "Friends" Social Networking services. When friends sign in to Liferay Portal, a server-initiated event triggers ICEfaces Ajax Push so that other friends that are online become aware of their friend's online presence. Additionally, when the user clicks a "Chat" icon, ICEfaces Ajax Push is used for IPC to begin a new chat room in a Chat Portlet. The TritonSource project Web site can be found at: **www.tritonsource.org**.

ICEfaces Themes and Portal Themes

The ICEfaces Component Suite fully supports consistent component styling via a set of predefined CSS style classes and associated images. Changing the component styles for a Web application developed with the ICEfaces Component Suite is as simple as changing the style sheet used. ICEfaces ships with a set of predefined style sheets are available to be used as-is, or customized to meet the specific requirements of the application. There are five predefined ICEfaces style sheets included, two of which are designed to be used inside a portlet container:

- rime.css
- rime-portlet.css
- xp.css
- xp-portlet.css
- royale.css

Example Usage

The following example shows how to specify the portlet-compatible version of the ICEfaces "XP" theme:

```
<?xml version="1.0" encoding="UTF-8"?>
<f:view xmlns="http://www.w3.org/1999/xhtml"
  xmlns:f="http://java.sun.com/jsf/core"
  xmlns:ice="http://www.icesoft.com/icefaces/component"
  xmlns:xsi="http://www.w3.org/2001/XMLSchema-instance"
  xsi:schemaLocation="http://www.w3.org/1999/xhtml
    http://www.w3.org/2002/08/xhtml/xhtml1-transitional.xsd">
  <ice:portlet>
    <ice:outputStyle
      href="/xmlhttp/css/xp/xp-portlet.css" />
    <ice:form>
      ...
    </ice:form>
  </ice:portlet>
</f:view>
```

PART III

The Portlet 1.0 and 2.0 standards document a set of common CSS class names that should be applied to specific page elements in order to integrate with the portlet container's theme mechanism. When running in a portlet container, ICEfaces components will automatically render the following subset of Portlet 1.0 CSS class names where appropriate:

- portlet-form-button
- portlet-form-field
- portlet-form-input-field
- portlet-form-label
- portlet-menu
- portlet-menu-cascade-item
- portlet-menu-item
- portlet-menu-item-hover
- portlet-section-alternate
- portlet-section-body
- portlet-section-footer
- portlet-section-header
- portlet-msg-alert
- portlet-msg-error
- portlet-msg-info

To disable this feature, developers can specify the **com.icesoft.faces.portlet.renderStyles** context parameter in the **WEB-INF/web.xml** configuration file and set its value to false.

Example Usage

The following example shows how to disable automatic rendering of Portlet 1.0 / 2.0 standard CSS class names in the **WEB-INF/web.xml** configuration file:

```
<context-param>
  <param-name>
    com.icesoft.faces.portlet.renderStyles
  </param-name>
  <param-value>false</param-value>
</context-param>
```

ICEfaces Themes and Liferay Themes

Liferay Portal supports styling for Portlet 1.0 and 2.0 standard CSS class names as well as a set of vendor-specific CSS class names within the context of a Liferay *theme*. However, since Liferay themes do not contain styling for the ICEfaces Component Suite, it is necessary to select an ICEfaces style sheet that is visually compatible with the Liferay theme.

On some occasions, it becomes necessary to override some of the styling in a Liferay theme in order to make it more visually compatible with an ICEfaces portlet. For example, Liferay themes typically render spans of class **portlet-msg-error** with a margin that has too much space to be placed alongside a rendered **ice:inputText** component tag.

Example Usage

The following example shows how to override styling in a Liferay theme from within a Facelet view so that rendered output from **ice:messages** and **ice:message** have a more narrow margin:

```
<!--
This is a file named my-portlet-view.xhtml
-->
<?xml version="1.0" encoding="UTF-8"?>
<f:view xmlns="http://www.w3.org/1999/xhtml"
  xmlns:f="http://java.sun.com/jsf/core"
  xmlns:ice="http://www.icesoft.com/icefaces/component"
  xmlns:xsi="http://www.w3.org/2001/XMLSchema-instance"
  xsi:schemaLocation="http://www.w3.org/1999/xhtml
    http://www.w3.org/2002/08/xhtml/xhtml1-transitional.xsd">
  <ice:portlet>
    <ice:outputStyle
      href="/xmlhttp/css/xp/xp-portlet.css" />
    <ice:outputStyle
      href="liferay-theme-override.css" />
    <ice:form styleClass="my-portlet-view">
      <ice:messages globalOnly="true" />
      ...
    </ice:form>
  </ice:portlet>
</f:view>

/*
This is a separate file named liferay-theme-override.css
*/
.my-portlet-view .portlet-msg-error {
  margin: 1px 0px 0px 0px;
  padding: 1px 5px 1px 24px;
}
```

ICEfaces Ajax Bridge and Liferay Portal

Liferay Portal uses JavaScript to enhance both the developer and end-user experience. Portlet users can drag and drop portlets on the page without requiring a full page refresh. For the developer, Liferay makes it easy to hot-deploy and load portlets dynamically, which can be a big advantage in speeding up the development cycle. However, deploying ICEfaces portlets in this manner can be problematic because the JavaScript that ICEfaces relies on may not get executed properly. When an ICEfaces portlet is added to a portal page at runtime by the end user, the ICEfaces Ajax Bridge's **window.onload( )** logic will not be executed unless there is a full-page refresh.

As a workaround, Liferay Portal provides configuration parameters that allow the developer to specify that a full-page refresh is required. Doing this ensures that the ICEfaces bridge is properly initiated. The required parameters, render-weight and ajaxable, are specified in the **WEB-INF/liferay-portlet.xml** configuration file.

Example Usage

The following example shows how to specify that a full-page refresh should take place after the ICEfaces portlet is first added to the portal page:

```
<liferay-portlet-app>
  <portlet>
    <portlet-name>my_portlet</portlet-name>
      <instanceable>false</instanceable>
      <render-weight>1</render-weight>
      <ajaxable>false</ajaxable>
  </portlet>
</liferay-portlet-app>
```

ICEfaces Portlets and Liferay Request Attributes

In order to ensure compatibility with the Portlet 2.0 Technology Compatibility Kit (TCK), Liferay's implementation of the **javax.portlet.PortletRequest.getAttributeNames( )** method does not return a complete list of attribute names that are truly present in the PortletRequest object. Although certain attribute names are hidden, if they are known by the portlet developer, their respective values can be retrieved by calling Liferay's implementation of the **javax.portlet.PortletRequest.getAttribute(String name)** method.

In order for the ICEfaces 1.*x* portlet bridge to maintain compatibility with the ICEfaces Extended Request scope, it needs to make a copy of all of the request attributes. In order to ensure that ICEfaces copies the necessary hidden attributes, developers must specify the **com.icesoft.faces.portlet.hiddenAttributes** context parameter in the **WEB-INF/web.xml** configuration file.

Example Usage

The following example shows how to specify a space-delimited list of hidden request attributes in the **WEB-INF/web.xml** configuration file:

```
<context-param>
  <param-name>
    com.icesoft.faces.portlet.hiddenAttributes
  </param-name>
  <param-value>COMPANY_ID LAYOUT RENDER_PORTLET THEME_DISPLAY</param-value>
</context-param>
```

PortletFaces

The purpose of the PortletFaces project is to make it easier to develop JSF portlets that run within Liferay Portal. The project was founded by Joel Kozikowski and Neil Griffin and was originally sponsored by Liferay, Inc., under incubation. Since then, PortletFaces has been adopted by Mimacom AG and is a subproject of the edoras framework. PortletFaces contains a wealth of features that expose the standard features of the Portlet 2.0 API and vendor-specific features of Liferay in a way that is natural to JSF development. Open source demonstration portlets are available for download at the PortletFaces project home page: **www.portletfaces.org**.

The following is a high-level list of features provided by PortletFaces:

- PortletFacesContext
- EL additions
- UI component Tags
- Facelet composite component Tags
- File upload
- PortletPreferences integration
- Liferay theme integration
- Liferay language portlet integration
- Improved integration between Liferay Portal and ICEfaces 1.x

Downloading PortletFaces

You can obtain the PortletFaces JAR (and runtime dependencies) by downloading it from the project Web site, or if using Maven 2, include the PortletFaces dependency in your **pom.xml** file.

Example Usage

The following example shows how to specify PortletFaces as a dependency in a project's Maven 2 **pom.xml** configuration file:

```
<dependencies>
  <dependency>
    <groupId>org.edorasframework</groupId>
    <artifactId>
      org.edorasframework.portletfaces
    </artifactId>
    <version>1.3.0</version>
  </dependency>
</dependencies>
<repositories>
  <repository>
    <id>edorasframework-releases</id>
    <name>edorasframework.org releases</name>
    <releases>
      <enabled>true</enabled>
    </releases>
    <snapshots>
      <enabled>false</enabled>
    </snapshots>
    <url>http://repo.edorasframework.org/mvn/maven2/</url>
  </repository>
  <repository>
    <id>edorasframework-snapshots</id>
    <name>edorasframework.org snapshots</name>
    <releases>
      <enabled>false</enabled>
    </releases>
```

PART III

```
    <snapshots>
      <enabled>true</enabled>
    </snapshots>
    <url>http://repo.edorasframework.org/mvn/maven2-snapshots/</url>
  </repository>
</repositories>
```

PortletFacesContext

JSF Web application developers typically call **FacesContext.getCurrentInstance( )** in order to obtain the **ThreadLocal** singleton instance associated with the current request. While JSF portlet developers can certainly do the same, it's easier to call **PortletFacesContext .getInstance( )**, which returns an application-scoped singleton instance.

PortletFacesContext is an abstract class that extends the edoras framework's **ExtFacesContext** abstract class, which in turn extends the JSF **FacesContext** abstract class. Since **PortletFacesContext** ultimately extends **FacesContext**, it supplies all the same method signatures and can therefore do anything that **FacesContext** can do. Both **PortletFacesContext** and **ExtFacesContext** implement the delegation design pattern for methods defined by **FacesContext** by first calling **FacesContext.getCurrentInstance( )** and then delegating to corresponding methods. The benefit of using this technique is that JSF portlet developers only have to call **PortletFacesContext.getInstance( )** once and can save the singleton object reference for future use.

The **PortletFacesContext** class has a large set of methods that complement the **FacesContext** class and make it convenient for accessing the Portlet API as well as Liferay vendor-specific features. The Javadoc pages for **PortletFacesContext** documents the complete list of convenience methods and is available at the PortletFaces project Web site.

Example Usage

The following example shows how to obtain the **PortletFacesContext** singleton instance and easily add a standard Liferay error as a **FacesMessage** should an exception occur:

```
public class SessionScopedManagedBean {

  private PortletFacesContext portletFacesContext =
    PortletFacesContext.getInstance();

  public List<DlFileEntry> getDocuments(long folderId) {

    List<DLFileEntry> documents;
    try {
      documents =
        DLFileEntryLocalServiceUtil.getFileEntries(
          folderId);
    }
    catch (Exception e) {
      LOG.error(e.getMessage(), e);
      // Don't have to call
      // PortletFacesContext.getInstance() first
      // since a reference to it was obtained when
      // the bean was created.
```

EL Variable	Description
pf:inputFile	Renders an HTML **<input type="file" />** tag, which provides file upload capability.
pf:inputRichText	Renders a text area that provides the ability to enter rich text such as bold, italic, and underline.
pf:permissionsLink	Renders an HTML anchor tag (hyperlink) that the user can click in order to see the Liferay Permissions screen for the associated resource.

TABLE A-2 PortletFaces UI Component Tags

```
            portletFacesContext.
              addGlobalUnexpectedErrorMessage();
          }
          return documents;
        }
      }
```


PortletFaces Tags

PortletFaces includes several JSF UI Component tags and Facelet Composite Component tags that are helpful when developing JSF portlets for Liferay Portal.

A quick reference of the PortletFaces UI Component tags is found in Table A-2. The documentation at PortletFaces project Web site contains a complete description of each UI component tag.

A quick reference of the PortletFaces Composite Component tags is found in Table A-3. The documentation at PortletFaces project Web site contains a complete description of each composite component tag.

EL Variable	Description
pf:iceInfoDataPaginator	Encapsulates an ICEfaces **ice:dataPaginator** tag that renders pagination information for an associated **ice:dataTable**. The navigation information will match the internationalized Liferay "showing-x-x-of-x-results" message.
pf:iceInfoDataPaginator	Encapsulates an ICEfaces **ice:dataPaginator** tag that renders navigation controls for an associated **ice:dataTable**. The icons will match the current Liferay theme.
pf:icon	Encapsulates an HTML **img** tag whose **src** attribute contains a fully qualified URL to an icon in the Liferay theme.
pf:messages	Encapsulates the **h:messages** tag and automatically applies the JSR 286 standard class names.
pf:message	Encapsulates the **h:message** tag and automatically applies the JSR 286 standard class names.

TABLE A-3 PortletFaces Composite Component Tags

PortletFaces and Portlet Preferences

Similar to the JSR 301/329 **portletPreferences** EL variable, PortletFaces introduces an EL variable named **portletPreference** (singlular, not plural). Although the EL usage is similar in syntax, the implementation is different such that it is compatible with ICEfaces paritalSubmit (Ajax). One drawback of JSR 301/329 portletPreferences EL variable is that when used with ICEfaces **partialSubmit**, user preference selections from the EDIT mode view will be directly set inside the underlying **PortletPreferences** object. Even though the user might not click a "Save Preferences" button to store the preferences permanently, the preference values could potentially be active for the remainder of the PortletSession. The PortletFaces **portletPreference** EL variable does not store submitted values directly inside of the underlying **PortletPreferences** object. Instead, the submitted values are stored in a temporary copy, which solves the problem related to ICEfaces partialSubmit. Additionally, PortletFaces provides a convenience backing managed bean named PortletPreferencesForm that has an action-listener named **PortletPreferencesForm.submit( )** that will permanently store the portlet preferences.

Example Usage

The following example shows how to develop a Facelet view that uses the PortletFaces **portletPreference** EL variable to support portlet EDIT mode:

```
<!--
This is a file named edit.xhtml that can be used
for portlet EDIT mode. It utilizes the PortletFaces
portletPreference EL variable for gaining read/write
access to javax.portlet.PortletPreferences. Unlike the
JSR 301/329 approach, there is no need to write a backing
managed-bean because PortletFaces already provides one
named portletPreferencesForm.
-->
<?xml version="1.0" encoding="UTF-8"?>
<!DOCTYPE html PUBLIC "-//W3C//DTD XHTML 1.0 Transitional//EN"
"http://www.w3.org/TR/xhtml1/DTD/xhtml1-transitional.dtd">
<f:view xmlns:f="http://java.sun.com/jsf/core"
  xmlns:ice="http://www.icesoft.com/icefaces/component">

  <ice:messages globalOnly="true" />

  <ice:form partialSubmit="true">

    <ice:outputLabel for="datePattern" />
    <ice:inputText id="datePattern" required="true"
      value="#{portletPreference['datePattern']}" />
    <ice:message for="datePattern" />

    <ice:commandButton
      actionListener="#{portletPreferencesForm.submit}"
        partialSubmit="false" value="Save Preferences" />

  </ice:form>

</f:view>
```

PortletFaces Expression Language Additions

PortletFaces introduces a variety of Portlet API and Liferay vendor-specific features into the EL.

A quick reference of the PortletFaces EL Additions is found in Table A-4. The documentation at PortletFaces project Web site contains a complete description of each EL variable.

EL Variable	Description
i18n	As an abbreviation for the word "internationalization," the **i18n** EL variable enables page authors to declaratively specify message keys that hook into Liferay's Language Utility. Type: String
liferay	A utility managed bean that is designed to be kept in JSF request scope. Its purpose is to introduce some Liferay-specific variables into the JSF EL. Type: org.edorasframework.portletfaces.bean.util.Liferay
liferay.companyId	The Liferay companyId primary key value associated with the community/organization portal page that the current portlet is placed upon. Type: Long
liferay.documentLibraryURL	The absolute URL for the Liferay Document Library Struts action path. Type: String
liferay.imageGalleryURL	The absolute URL for the Liferay Image Gallery Struts action path. Type: String
liferay.imageURL	The absolute URL for the Liferay Image Servlet. Type: String
liferay.groupUser	The Liferay User that owns the Liferay community/organization portal page that the current portlet is placed upon. Type: com.liferay.portal.model.User
liferay.layout	The Liferay Layout associated with the community/organization portal page that the current portlet is placed upon. Type: com.liferay.portal.model.Layout
liferay.permissionChecker	The Liferay PermissionChecker associated with the current request and Liferay User. Type: com.liferay.portal.security.permission.PermissionChecker

TABLE A-4 PortletFaces EL Additions *(continued)*

EL Variable	Description
liferay.portalURL	The absolute URL for the portal. Type: String
liferay.portlet	The containing Liferay Portlet associated with the PortletRequest. Type: com.liferay.portal.model.Portlet
liferay.portraitURL	Designed to be called from the EL by passing a Liferay User or userId as an array index, returns the absolute URL to the user's portrait. Type: String
liferay.service	Designed to be called from the EL by passing a Liferay service name String (bean id) as an array index, returns the instance of the service class. Type: Object
liferay.theme	The Liferay Theme associated with the Liferay Layout. Type: com.liferay.portal.model.Theme
liferay.themeDisplay	The Liferay ThemeDisplay associated with the PortletRequest. Type: com.liferay.portal.theme.ThemeDisplay
liferay.themeImageURL	Designed to be called from the EL by passing a relative path to a theme image as an array index, returns the absolute URL to the theme image. Type: String
liferay.themeImagesURL	The absolute URL for the image path associated with the current Liferay Theme. Type: String
liferay.user	The Liferay User associated with the PortletRequest. Type: com.liferay.portal.model.User
liferay. userHasPortletPermission	Designed to be called from the EL by passing an action-key as an array index, returns a boolean indicating whether or not the Liferay User associated with the PortletRequest has permission to execute the specified action-key on the current portlet. Type: Boolean

Table A-4 PortletFaces EL Additions *(continued)*

PortletFaces and Localization

As an abbreviation for the word "internationalization," the **i18n** EL variable enables page authors to declaratively specify message keys that are provided by one of the following:

- Liferay's Language Utility
- Portlet WAR additions to Liferay's Language Utility
- The JSF standard message keys

The Liferay Language Utility is typically accessed by portlet developers by calling static Java methods found in the **com.liferay.portal.kernel.language.LanguageUtil** class. The utility operates by reading the locale-specific version of the portal's Language.properties file, which contains thousands of keys and internationalized messages.

Portlet developers can extend the Liferay Language Utility by creating a file within the portlet WAR named **WEB-INF/liferay-hook.xml** that points to locale-specific resource bundles that are in the runtime classpath of the portlet.

Example Usage

The following example shows how to register Liferay language extensions with a **WEB-INF/liferay-hook.xml** configuration file:

```
<?xml version="1.0" encoding="UTF-8"?>
<!DOCTYPE hook PUBLIC "-//Liferay//DTD Hook 5.2.0//EN"
"http://www.liferay.com/dtd/liferay-hook_5_2_0.dtd">
<hook>
  <language-properties>Language_en_US.properties</language-properties>
</hook>
```

Example Usage

The following example shows the contents of a file named **Language_en_US.properties**:

```
add-new-entry=Add New Entry
save-entry=Save Entry
```

Example Usage

The following example shows the syntax for using the **i18n** EL variable in a Facelet view:

```
<h:outputLabel value="#{i18n['first-name']}" />
<h:commandButton value="#{i18n['save-entry']}" />
```

Example Usage

The following example shows that when using JBoss EL, page authors can take advantage of the **i18n.replace( )** method in order to substitute values into the text of the message.

```
<!--
Note: The US English translation of the
x-has-x-friends key would look like the following:
```

PART III

```
x-has-x-friends={0} has {1} friends.
-->
<h:outputText
  value="#{i18n.replace('x-has-x-friends', liferay.groupUser.fullName,
friendsModel.dataModel.rowCount)}" />
```

Liferay Language Portlet Integration

In a normal JSF Web application, the Locale that is used to display internationalized values is dictated by the locale specified in the end user's Web browser. However, Liferay Portal permits the user to select a different locale (language) using the Language Portlet. The user's choice is ultimately saved as a **languageId** in the Liferay User object and is persisted to the database.

In order to provide seamless integration between JSF portlets and the language selected by the user, PortletFaces provides the **LiferayLocalePhaseListener**. The listener monitors the RESTORE_VIEW phase of the JSF lifecycle and will automatically set the locale inside the **UIViewRoot** according to the value specified by Liferay's **User.getLocale( )** method, which is aware of the selected languageId. This in turn causes internationalization techniques such as the **f:loadBundle** tag and the **i18n** EL keyword to automatically translate message keys into the language selected by the user with the Liferay Language Portlet, which is shown in Figure A-7.

Improved Integration Between Liferay and ICEfaces 1.x

As discussed in the sections within this appendix titled "ICEfaces Ajax with Partial Submit" and "ICEfaces Direct-to-DOM RenderKit," when an ICEfaces portlet is rendered on a portal page, the ICEfaces 1.*x* Portlet Bridge will participate in the Portlet RENDER_PHASE phase just like any other portlet. However, from that time on the ICEfaces 1.*x* bridge will bypass the portlet lifecycle and perform all subsequent interactions with the server via Ajax by hitting the ICEfaces PersistentFacesServlet. The ICEfaces 1.*x* Portlet Bridge is based on the JSR 168 (Portlet 1.0) API and therefore cannot take advantage of the new RESOURCE_PHASE of the Portlet 2.0 standard. The benefit of hitting the PersistentFacesServlet directly is that ICEfaces partial submits will execute faster than if they went through the the Portlet 2.0 RESOURCE_PHASE. The drawback is that certain Liferay objects are unusable after the initial RENDER_PHASE. Specifically, the Liferay PermissionChecker and ThemeDisplay objects get "recycled" at the end of the RenderRequest phase by Liferay's ServicePostAction.

PortletFaces works around this problem by making copies of Liferay's PermissionChecker and ThemeDisplay objects and keeping them in "request" scope, which will default to the ICEfaces Extended Request scope when ICEfaces is used in a portlet. These objects are available to JSF portlet developers via the PortletFacesContext.

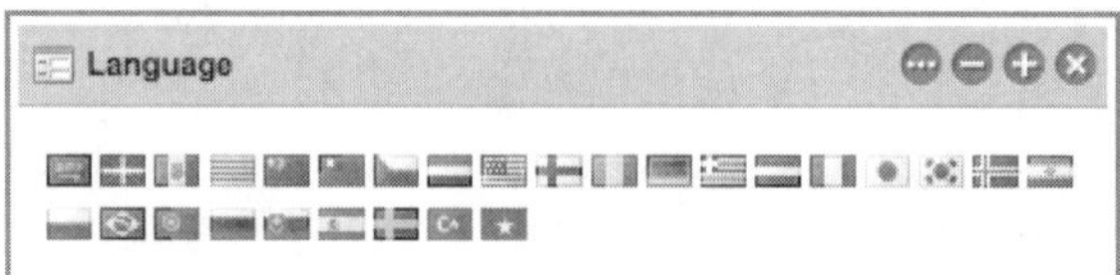

FIGURE A-7 A Language selection portlet

Example Usage

The following example shows how to get the Liferay PermissionChecker and ThemeDisplay objects from the PortletFacesContext:

```
import com.liferay.portal.security.permission.PermissionChecker;
import com.liferay.portal.theme.ThemeDisplay;

public class BackingManagedBean {

  PortletFacesContext portletFacesContext =
    PortletFacesContext.getInstance();

  public String submit() {
    PermissionChecker permissionChecker =
      PortletFacesContext.getPermissionChecker();

    ThemeDisplay themeDisplay =
      PortletFacesContext.getThemeDisplay();
  }
}
```

Index

D

F

G

I

J

K

L

Q

R

S

T

U